The Wiley World Handbook of Existential Therapy

Edited by

Emmy van Deurzen (editor in chief)
Erik Craig
Alfried Längle
Kirk J. Schneider
Digby Tantam
Simon du Plock

WILEY Blackwell

This edition first published 2019

Registered Office(s)
John Wiley & Sons, Inc., 111 River Street, Hoboken, NJ 07030, USA
John Wiley & Sons Ltd, The Atrium, Southern Gate, Chichester, West Sussex, PO19 8SQ, UK

Editorial Office
111 River Street, Hoboken, NJ 07030, USA
For details of our global editorial offices, customer services, and more information about Wiley products visit us at www.wiley.com.

Wiley also publishes its books in a variety of electronic formats and by print-on-demand. Some content that appears in standard print versions of this book may not be available in other formats.

Library of Congress Cataloging-in-Publication data is available
9781119167150 (paperback), 9781119167181 (epdf), 9781119167174 (epub)

Cover design by Wiley
Cover image: © Metropolitan Museum of Art / Wikimedia Commons

Printed and bound by CPI Group (UK) Ltd, Croydon, CR0 4YY

Set in 10/12.5pt ITC Galliard by SPi Global, Pondicherry, India

To all existential therapists worldwide, past, present, and future.

In celebration of what it is to be human,
In appreciation of the thinkers who came before us,
and with gratitude to those who will take up the challenges after us.

Contents

About the Editors

Editor in Chief

Emmy van Deurzen is a philosopher, psychologist, and psychotherapist who has worked as an existential therapist since 1973, both in France and the United Kingdom and has lectured on existential therapy around the world since the 1980s. She has been a professor with five universities and has contributed 17 books and hundreds of papers and chapters to the literature with her work being translated into many languages. She founded the Society for Existential Analysis, the School of Psychology and Psychotherapy at Regent's and also the New School of Psychotherapy and Counselling at the Existential Academy in London, where she is Principal. Her best sellers include *Everyday Mysteries* (Routledge), *Paradox and Passion in Psychotherapy* (Wiley), and *Existential Counselling and Psychotherapy in Practice* (Sage).

Editors

Erik Craig is an existential psychologist, author, and independent scholar and practitioner. He has published over 60 articles and edited two ground-breaking journal issues on Daseinsanalysis and existential depth psychotherapy. Having practiced for years in New England he now lives and works in Santa Fe, New Mexico. He is most interested in the intricacies of therapeutic relating, the analysis of dreams, and human affect and attachment. Having served on the full-time faculties of several graduate psychology programs, he now lectures and trains internationally. A past president of several psychological societies, he is currently president of the New Mexico Psychoanalytic Society.

Alfried Längle, born in 1951 in Austria, has a private practice in psychotherapy, general medicine and clinical psychology in Vienna (since 1982). He had a close collaboration with Viktor Frankl from 1981 to 1991. Alfied was a founder (1983) of the International Society for Logotherapy and Existential Analysis (Vienna). He is also a faculty member and professor of Applied Psychology at the Moscow's HSE-university (since 2004), at Vienna's Sigmund Freud university (2011), and Docent at the psychological department of the university of Klagenfurt, Austria. He is a founder of the state-approved training school of Existential-Analytical Psychotherapy, Vice President of the International Federation of Psychotherapy (2002–2010), and was, until 2017, President of the International Society for Logotherapy and Existential Analysis.

Kirk J. Schneider is a psychologist and leading spokesperson forcontemporary existential-humanistic psychology. A protégé of Rollo May and James Bugental, Kirk is past president of the Society for Humanistic Psychology of the American Psychological Association, recent past editor of the *Journal of Humanistic Psychology*, president of the Existential-Humanistic Institute, and adjunct faculty at Saybrook University and Teachers College, Columbia University. Kirk is also a Fellow of the American Psychological Association and has authored or edited 12 books, including *Existential-Integrative Psychotherapy* and (with Orah Krug) *Existential-Humanistic Therapy*.

Digby Tantam is Emeritus Professor of Psychiatry at the University of Sheffield and Visiting Professor at Middlesex University and the New School of Psychotherapy and Counselling. He has trained in family therapy, group analysis, cognitive behavioral therapy, psychodynamic psychotherapy, and more recently in existential therapy. He has practiced and supervised other therapists in one or other of these modalities since 1977. He is a Consultant Psychotherapist and Psychiatrist, Dilemma Consultancy Ltd. He is the author ofseveral hundred scientific papers and a dozen books, most recently *The Interbrain* published in 2018, (Jessica Kingsley).

Simon du Plock is Head of the Faculty of Post-Qualification and Professional Doctorates at the Metanoia Institute, London, UK, where he leads joint PhD, DPsych, and DCPsych research programs with Middlesex University, with whom he is a professor. He lectures internationally and has authored over 80 texts and journal papers. He has edited *Existential Analysis*, the journal of the British Society for Existential Analysis, since 1993. In 2006 he became the first Western therapist to be made an Honorary Member of the East European Association for Existential Therapy in recognition of his contribution to the development of collaboration between East and West European existential psychotherapy.

Notes on Contributors

Contributors to the Introduction

Editors

Erik Craig and Emmy van Deurzen

Contributor

Mick Cooper is Professor of Counselling Psychology at the University of Roehampton, where he is Director of the Centre for Research in Social and Psychological Transformation (CREST). A chartered psychologist, a UKCP-registered psychotherapist, and a Fellow of the British Association for Counselling and Psychotherapy (BACP), he is the author and editor of a range of texts on existential and relational approaches to therapy, including *Existential Therapies* (2e, Sage, 2017), *Existential Counselling and Psychotherapy: Contributions to a Pluralistic Practice* (Sage, 2015), *Existential Counselling Primer* (PCCS, 2012), and *Working at Relational Depth in Counselling and Psychotherapy* (2e, Sage, 2018, with Dave Mearns).

Contributors to Part I

Section Editor

Erik Craig, EdD is an existential psychologist, author, and independent scholar and practitioner. Erik has studied and collaborated intensively with the Daseinsanalysts Medard Boss and Paul Stern and currently practices in Santa Fe, NM.

Contributors

Loray Daws, PhD, is a clinical psychologist and psychoanalytic psychotherapist in British Columbia, Canada. She is a senior faculty member at the International Masterson Institute, NY and editor and author of various books and articles in psychoanalytic psychotherapy.

Thanasis Georgas, MD, is a psychiatrist, Daseinsanalyst, President of The Greek Society of Daseinsanalysis and IFDA board member. He has published and translated a number of important Daseinsanalytic texts and is co-editor of the Greek journal, *Εποχή/Epoché: Phenomenology-Psychotherapy-Hermeneutics.*

Alice Holzhey-Kunz, PhD, is a Swiss Daseinsanalyst, president of the Society for Hermeneutic Anthropology and Daseinsanalysis and co-president of the Daseinsanalytic Seminar in Zurich. She has published three books and numerous articles on a new approach to Daseinsanalytic thought and practice.

Perikles Kastrinidis, MD, is a Swiss psychiatrist and psychotherapist in private practice, teaching and supervising Daseinsanalysts. He was trained in Daseinsanalysis under Medard Boss and also studied short-term dynamic psychotherapy with Habib Davanloo and integrates aspects of these approaches.

Robert D. Stolorow, PhD, is a psychoanalyst, philosopher, and author of *World, Affectivity, Trauma: Heidegger and Post-Cartesian Psychoanalysis* (2011) and *Trauma and Human Existence* (2007). Has been absorbed for a half-century rethinking psychoanalysis as a form of phenomenological inquiry.

Contributors to Part II

Section Editor

Emmy van Deurzen, PhD, MPsych, MPhil, CPsychol, Fellow of BPS, UKCP, and BACP, is an existential therapist with Dilemma Consultancy Ltd, a Visiting Professor at Middlesex University, and Principal at the Existential Academy, London.

Contributors

Martin Adams, BSc, MA, ADEP, BACP (reg.), and UKCP (reg.) is an existential psychotherapist, supervisor, and writer whose most recent book is *An Existential Approach to Human Development.* He is a lecturer at the New School for Psychotherapy and Counselling and is also a sculptor.

Claire Arnold-Baker, BSc(Hons), MA, DCPsych, UKCP, and HCPC (reg.) is DCPsych Course Leader at NSPC, where she is also a lecturer, and a clinical and research supervisor. Claire is a counselling psychologist and existential psychotherapist who specialises in perinatal therapy in her private practice.

Laura Barnett, MA(Oxon), MA, MBACP (Sen. Accred.), UKCP (reg.), is an existential psychotherapist; for almost 20 years, she has two specialist services that she set up in the National Health Service (UK). She is editor of two books for Routledge on the dialogue between existential thought and therapeutic practice.

Chris Blackmore, BSc, MA, DipCoun, PhD, is a Senior University Teacher at the University of Sheffield. He has developed online psychotherapy training resources and has a special interest in the role of emotions in e-learning.

Edgar Correia, PhD, AdvD, Post-MA, MA, PgD, is a clinical psychologist and psychotherapist, a founding member of Portuguese Society for Existential Psychotherapy, and researcher at the Applied Psychology Research Center.

Helen Hayes, MA, UKCP Reg., BACP (Sen. Accred.), is an existential psychotherapist, lecturer, and clinical supervisor at the NSPC. She works in several voluntary sector and National Health Service (UK) services, and in private practice.

Ann Lagerström is a senior leadership consultant, certified existential coach, and writer. She studied existential philosophy and psychology at Södertörn University and at the Society for Existential Psychotherapy at an advanced level. She introduced existential coaching in Sweden.

Neil Lamont, DCPsych, CPsychol, BA (Hons), is a chartered psychologist and existential psychotherapist based in London, UK. Neil is a practitioner, tutor, and doctoral research supervisor at the Existential Academy.

Sasha van Deurzen-Smith, MA, is an existential coach specializing in creativity, self-esteem, and autism spectrum disorders. She is program leader of the MA in Existential Coaching at the New School of Psychotherapy and Counselling.

Simon du Plock, FRSM, AFBPsS, CPsychol, CSci, is Head of the Faculty of Post-Qualification and Professional Doctorates at the Metanoia Institute, London, UK, where he leads joint DPsych, DCPsych, and PhD research programs with Middlesex University with whom he is a professor.

Alison Strasser, DProf (Psychotherapy & Counselling) UKCP, PACFA, AAOS, is a psychotherapist, supervisor, coach, and Educator. She is also the Director of the Centre for Existential Practice in Sydney, Australia.

Digby Tantam, MA, MPH, PhD, FRCPsych, FBPsS, FBACP, UKCPF, FHEA, is Deputy Principal of the New School of Psychotherapy and Counselling at the Existential Academy in London and Consultant Psychotherapist and Psychiatrist at Dilemma Consultancy Ltd., Visiting Professor, Middlesex University, and Emeritus Professor of Psychiatry, University of Sheffield

Joel Vos, PhD, is psychologist and philosopher, program leader for the professional Doctorate in Existential Psychotherapy and Counselling at New School of Psychotherapy and Counselling, researcher at Metanoia, and chair of IMEC Meaning Conferences.

Contributors to Part III

Section Editor

Kirk J. Schneider, PhD, is a leading spokesperson for existential-humanistic psychology. A protégé of James Bugental and Rollo May, Kirk is president of the Existential-Humanistic Institute and has authored 12 books.

Contributors

Ken Bradford, PhD, is a Contemplative-Existential Psychologist. Publications include: *The I of the Other: Mindfulness-Based Diagnosis & the Question of Sanity*; and *Listening from the Heart of Silence.*

Nathaniel Granger, Jr., PsyD is the President-elect of the Society for Humanistic Psychology (American Psychological Association, Division 32) and is an Adjunct Faculty member at Saybrook University.

Louis Hoffman, PhD, is a licensed psychologist practicing in Colorado Springs, CO. He teaches at Saybrook University and through the International Institute for Existential-Humanistic Psychology.

Theopia Jackson, PhD, is Professor of Psychology and Director of the clinical psychology program at Saybrook University.

Orah T. Krug, PhD, has a psychotherapy practice in Oakland, CA, is the author of texts on existential-humanistic therapy and supervision, and is the past Program Director of Clinical Training and Education at the Existential Humanistic Institute, current Director of Krug Counseling, and Adjunct Professor at Saybrook University.

Ed Mendelowitz is a clinician, essayist, and psychologist living and workingin Boston, MA. He received the Rollo May Award for "independent and outstanding pursuit of new frontiers in humanistic psychology."

Shawn Rubin, PsyD is in independent Private Practice with children, adolescents, adults, and families, Is LGBTQIA and kink-competent, and is the chief editor of the *Journal of Humanistic Psychology.*

Ilene A. Serlin, PhD., BC-DMT, is an existential-humanistic psychologist and dance therapist in San Francisco and Marin, Fellow of the American Psychological Association, past-President of the Society for Humanistic Psychology, and editor of *Whole Person Healthcare.*

Xuefu Wang, PhD, is founder and Director of the Zhi Mian Institute for Existential Therapy in Nanjing, China.

Irvin Yalom is Professor Emeritus of psychiatry at Stanford University and author of *Existential Psychotherapy* and *Staring At the Sun.*

Mark Yang is co-founder and Director of the International Institute of Existential-Humanistic Psychology.

Contributors to Part IV

Section Editor

Alfried Längle, MD, PhD, MSc, holds multiple honorary Doctorships, multiple honorary Professorships, Professor for Applied Psychology (HSE Moscow), guest professor for psychotherapy (SFU Vienna), and founder of GLE-International (Society of Logotherapy and Existential Analysis).

Contributors

Emmanuel J. Bauer, Mag. Dr. Phil., Mag. Theol., psychotherapist (Existential Analysis), Professor for Philosophy, and Director of the Department of Philosophy at the Catholic theological faculty of the University of Salzburg.

Barbara Gawel, is a Doctor of Public Health, Master of Educational Science, and a psychotherapist in Vienna.

Derrick Klaassen, PhD, R. Psych., is an Assistant Professor of Counselling Psychology, Trinity Western University, Langley, BC, Canada.

Janelle Kwee, PsyD, RPsych, is an Associate Professor, Trinity Western University, a registered psychologist in private practice, Langley, BC, Canada.

Silvia Längle, Ph.D., chief editor of *Existenzanalyse-Journal*, trainer, supervisor, psychotherapist in own practice. She has a special interest in phenomenological research.

Mihaela Launeanu, PhD, Assistant Professor at Trinity Western University, psychotherapist in private practice in Vancouver, Canada.

Bruce A. Muir, CD, BA, BSW, MA, RSW, is a family therapist, Comox Valley, British Columbia, Canada.

Claudia Reitinger, MA Biology, PhD Philosophy, is a psychotherapist in private practice in St Johann/Pongau.

Karin Steinert, MA Psychology, is a psychotherapist in private practice in Vienna.

Contributors to Part V

Section Editor

Digby Tantam, MA, MPH, PhD, FRCPsych, FBPsS, FBACP, UKCPF, FHEA, is: Deputy Principal of the New School of Psychotherapy and Counselling at the Existential Academy in London; Consultant Psychotherapist and Psychiatrist, Dilemma Consultancy Ltd.; Visiting Professor, Middlesex University; and Emeritus Professor of Psychiatry, University of Sheffield

Contributors

Lynda Ansell has been a member of Slough therapeutic community for three years and has completed training with the Royal College of Psychiatrists as a Community of Communities peer reviewer. She also a peer mentor with Hope Recovery College.

Catherine C. Classen, PhD, CPsych., works for the Women's College Hospital, Toronto.

Emmy van Deurzen, PhD, CPsychol, FBPsS, is an existential psychotherapist who has worked with groups since the early 1970s. She is the Principal of the School of Psychotherapy and Counselling at the Existential Academy in London.

Marie S. Dezelic, PhD, PsyD, MS, LMHC, CCTP, CFTP, CCFP, NCLC, CFRC, NCAIP, Diplomate in Logotherapy, is an author, educator, and has a private psychotherapy, coaching, and consulting practice. Her clinical research focuses on an integrative meaning approach in trauma, grief, spirituality, relationships, and psycho-oncology.

Rex Haigh, is an National Health Service Consult (UK) consultant psychiatrist in medical psychotherapy in Berkshire. He has been in therapeutic communities as a medical student, a junior doctor, and for the last 24 years as a consultant. He has particular interests in co-creation, "personality disorders," and critical psychiatry.

Sarah Hamilton studied with the Bridge Pastoral Foundation at Douai Abbey to qualify as an Integrative Psychotherapist, and came along to the greencare group for the day as a professional visitor.

Orah T. Krug, PhD, is in private practice and is also the author of texts on Existential-Humanistic therapy and supervision. She is the past Program Director of Clinical Training and Education at the Existential Humanistic Institute, Director of Krug Counseling, and Adjunct Professor at Saybrook University.

Simone Lee, Adep, UKCP (reg.), MBACP, works as an existential phenomenological therapist and supervisor in private practice in London. She also works as a supervisor, tutor, and group facilitator in London-based training colleges.

Fiona Lomas went through the non-residential therapeutic community in Buckinghamshire several years ago. She then worked with the national personality disorder program and local services as an expert by experience, and greencare coordinator.

Sharon Tizzard has been under Slough mental health services for seven years and feels she has now (nearly) "come out the other side." She is a buddy, a peer mentor, and a Community of Communities peer reviewer.

Hilary Welsh is an Integrative Psychotherapist registered with BACP who works as a volunteer with Growing Better Lives CIC. Hils has always worked with youth and communities, and now works in private practice.

Contributors to Part VI

Section Editor

Professor Simon du Plock is Head of the Faculty of Post-Qualification and Professional Doctorates at the Metanoia Institute, London, UK, where he leads joint DPsych, DCPsych, and PhD research programs with Middlesex University.

Contributors

Lennart Belfrage, PhD Psychology of Religion, MA Existential Psychology, is a certified psychologist and has a private practice in Helsingborg, Sweden.

Lodovico E. Berra, MD, psychiatrist, and existential psychotherapist, is a Director of the Institute of Philosophy, Psychology, Psychiatry (ISFiPP).

Edgar A. Correia, PhD, AdvDipExPsy, MA, PgD, is a clinical psychologist and psychotherapist, as well as a founding member of Social Psychiatry and Psychiatric Epidemiology (SPPE).

Anders Dræby Sørensen, DProf, is a philosopher and existential therapist and supervisor in private practice. He is a lecturer at the Universities of Copenhagen and Aarhus.

Evgenia T. Georganda, PsyD, ECP, is a clinical psychologist-psychotherapist and a founding member and chief administrator of the Hellenic Association for Existential Psychology.

Bo Jacobsen, DPhil, PhD, is a psychologist and existential therapist, Copenhagen, Denmark and a Professor at the University of Copenhagen.

Jak Icoz clinical psychologist and existential therapist is also a founder of the Existential Academy of Istanbul.

Rimantas Kočiūnas, PhD, is Professor of the University of Vilnius, Director of the Institute of Humanistic and Existential Psychology, Birstonas, Lithuania, and Secretary General of the East European Association for Existential Therapy.

Dmitry Leontiev, PhD, Dr. Science, Professor of Psychology, Moscow State University, and is President of the Institute of Existential Psychology and Life Enhancement, Moscow.

Gideon Menda, Dr. of existential psychotherapy, and co-founder and head of the postgraduate existential psychotherapy program at Kibbutzim College, Tel-Aviv, Israel.

Yaqui Andrés Martínez Robles, PhD in Psychotherapy, and Founder of the Círculo Existencial México.

Yali Sar Shalom, MA, is an existential psychotherapist, and co-founder and coordinator of the postgraduate existential psychotherapy program at Kibbutzim College, Tel-Aviv, Israel.

Susana Signorelli, is a psychologist and President of the Latin-American Association of Existential Psychotherapy.

Joel Vos, PhD, is a psychologist, philosopher, researcher, and lecturer at Metanoia Institute, London and New School of Psychotherapy and Counselling, London. He is also the Director of Meaning Online.

Semjon Yesselson, is Chair of the Board of the International Institute of Existential Consultancy (MIEK) – Russia, Ukraine, Kazakhstan and is also Editor-in-chief of the journal *Existential Tradition: Philosophy, Psychology, Psychotherapy.*

Xuefu Wang, PhD, is founder and leading psychotherapist of the Zhi Mian School of Counselling and Psychotherapy, which offers a Chinese existential approach to psychotherapy and cultural transformation.

Conclusions

Emmy van Deurzen, Kirk J. Schneider, Alfried Längle, Digby Tantam, Simon du Plock, and Erik Craig.

Acknowledgments

The editors would like to express their appreciation for the work that was put into this handbook by all the contributors to the various parts of the book. Without their expertise and dedication to existential therapy this book could not have been produced. We are particularly grateful to Mick Cooper for having worked so closely with us in writing the "Introduction." We are also grateful to the anonymous reviewers of the first draft of this book. Their feedback made us think about our writing in a new way and was helpful in improving the standard of the book. Any and all mistakes and failings of the book remain our own. We look forward to having further feedback after publication and to producing a much more complex, updated second edition of the book some time in the future.

Preface

This volume, which we can finally hold in our hands, is the joint achievement of a large group of people who have worked as existential psychotherapists, teachers, and researchers separately and independently in our own cultures for decades. Now, inspired by the First World Congress for Existential Therapy, we have found ourselves working together like members of a big family who are all inspired by the same desire to understand life and human existence better. We share the same goal of finding out how to gain and give greater access to the life knowledge and living wisdom that have been gathered over so many years, in order to pass these on to our clients and patients, our colleagues, our students, and indeed to ourselves, seeking to throw some much-needed light in the darkness.

Together we have worked on this amazing and unprecedented project for many months and we have savored the different textures, shapes, and flavors of existential therapy that it has brought out into the open. We hope that the rich international and multicultural vista that has unfolded will make the field both more accessible and more faithful to its founding vision.

We are all equally passionate about existential therapy and we have read many of the same original texts and have felt touched and inspired by them. Yet we each represent a different aspect of the many existential ways of working, in the same way in which individuals differ from each other.

In true phenomenological tradition, by bringing together these different facets of existential therapy we have been able to create a more accurate, in-depth picture of our field and have been able to cover a broader and wider area than any one of us might have done individually.

We have gained greater perspective by acknowledging our differences and we have found surer ground under our feet by recognizing our profound similarities. The entire project has been a fascinating adventure of discovery for all of us and we now offer you our varied views with the joy and pleasure of seeing them so closely bound together in one volume.

We hope that the clarity that this book brings will add focus and definition to your way of working. Yet we are adamant that the book, far from restricting or normalizing the existential method, will paradoxically provide greater freedom for each of us to practice in our own individual manner, which may vary with each of our cultures, each of our backgrounds, each of our clients, each of our moments of practice. Existential therapy is a therapy of continuous change and diversity.

Committing to an experience-near-philosophical understanding of the human troubles with which our clients struggle, we celebrate the condition we all have in common: that of being present on this earth for the briefest of time and of aiming to make the most of the challenges and possibilities we encounter.

We entrust this volume to you, reader, in the hope that it will throw light on your path in the same way it has done for us, who edited and wrote it.

Emmy van Deurzen, Erik Craig, Alfried Längle,
Kirk J. Schneider, Digby Tantam, Simon du Plock, January 2019

Introduction

What is Existential Therapy?

Mick Cooper, Erik Craig, and Emmy van Deurzen[1]

What should we do with these lives that we have? These existences? Borne out of nothingness, hurtling towards annihilation.... How can we make sense of these fragile, fleeting moments of existence that we have been given? More precisely, how can we do justice to the being that has been bestowed upon us? This incomprehensible, awesome gift that is so easy to lose sight of: buried beneath the detritus of everyday mundanity.

Different therapies focus – no doubt helpfully – on different things. The cognitive approaches, for instance, explore our thoughts and our misperceptions; the psychodynamic approaches turn to our pasts and our modes of relating. But it is only in the existential therapies where our being – as a complex, whole gestalt – is taken as the focus of the work. Existential therapies explore our lives, as an engagement with existence and the world: they explore what it means to ex-ist, to stand out in the world. They investigate what it means to be here, right now, as a living being. Faced with choices, dilemmas and limitations existential therapies ask what it means to be human and how to best tackle our challenges, obstacles and problems. They explore – with courage, openness, and humility – the very grounds of human being.

What is existential therapy?

So what, actually, is existential therapy? In 2014 and 2015, a group of leading international existential therapists facilitated by Stephen Diamond, under the auspices of the World Confederation for Existential Therapy, worked together to create a broad definition of the existential approach (see http://www.existentialpsychotherapy.net/definition-of-existential-psychotherapy/). After two years, and following numerous discussions, disagreements, and revisions, they reached a consensually agreed statement on

[1] With thanks to Simon du Plock, Alfried Längle, Kirk J. Schneider, Digby Tantam

The Wiley World Handbook of Existential Therapy, First Edition. Edited by Emmy van Deurzen, Erik Craig, Alfried Längle, Kirk J. Schneider, Digby Tantam, and Simon du Plock.

the nature of existential therapy. This remains the most collaborative and comprehensive description of the approach available to date, albeit one likely to continue developing over time. Due to its historical significance, we reproduce it here in its entirety. The statement begins:

> Existential therapy is a philosophically informed approach to counselling or psychotherapy. It comprises a richly diverse spectrum of theories and practices. Due partly to its evolving diversity, existential therapy is not easily defined. For instance, some existential therapists do not consider this approach to be a distinct and separate "school" of counselling or psychotherapy, but rather an attitude, orientation, or stance towards therapy in general. However, in recent years, existential therapy is increasingly considered by others to be a particular and specific approach unto itself. In either case, it can be said that though difficult to formalize and define, at its heart, existential therapy is a profoundly philosophical approach characterized in practice by an emphasis on relatedness, spontaneity, flexibility, and freedom from rigid doctrine or dogma. Indeed, due to these core qualities, to many existential therapists, the attempt to define it seems contradictory to its very nature.
>
> As with other therapeutic approaches, existential therapy primarily (but not exclusively) concerns itself with people who are suffering and in crisis. Some existential therapists intervene in ways intended to alleviate or mitigate such distress when possible and assist individuals to contend with life's inevitable challenges in a more meaningful, fulfilling, authentic, and constructive manner. Other existential therapists are less symptom-centered or problem-oriented and engage their clients in a wide-ranging exploration of existence without presupposing any particular therapeutic goals or outcomes geared toward correcting cognitions and behaviors, mitigating symptoms or remedying deficiencies. Nevertheless, despite their significant theoretical, ideological and practical differences, existential therapists share a particular philosophically-derived worldview which distinguishes them from most other contemporary practitioners.
>
> Existential therapy generally consists of a supportive and collaborative exploration of patients', or clients', lives and experiences. It places primary importance on the nature and quality of the here-and-now therapeutic relationship, as well as on an exploration of the relationships between clients and their contextual lived worlds beyond the consulting room. In keeping with its strong philosophical foundation, existential therapy takes the human condition itself – in all its myriad facets, from tragic to wondrous, horrific to beautiful, material to spiritual – as its central focus. Furthermore, it considers all human experience as intrinsically inseparable from the ground of existence, or "being-in-the-world," in which we each constantly and inescapably participate.
>
> Existential therapy aims to illuminate the way in which each unique person – within certain inevitable limits and constraining factors – comes to choose, create and perpetuate his or her own way of being in the world. In both its theoretical orientation and practical approach, existential therapy emphasizes and honors the perpetually emerging, unfolding, and paradoxical nature of human experience, and brings an unquenchable curiosity to what it truly means to be human. Ultimately, it can be said that existential therapy confronts some of the most fundamental and perennial questions regarding human existence: 'Who am I?' 'What is my purpose in life?' 'Am I free or determined?' 'How do I deal with my own mortality?' 'Does my existence have any meaning or significance?' 'How shall I live my life?'

The statement goes on to describe existential therapy in practice.

> Existential therapists see their practice as a mutual, collaborative, encouraging and explorative dialogue between two struggling human beings – one of whom is seeking assistance from the other who is professionally trained to provide it. Existential therapy places special emphasis on cultivating a caring, honest, supportive, empathic yet challenging relationship between therapist and client, recognizing the vital role of this relationship in the therapeutic process.
>
> In practice, existential therapy explores how clients' here-and-now feelings, thoughts and dynamic interactions within this relationship and with others might illuminate their wider world of past experiences, current events, and future expectations. This respectful, compassionate, supportive yet nonetheless very real encounter – coupled with a phenomenological stance – permits existential therapists to more accurately comprehend and descriptively address the person's way of being in the world. Taking great pains to avoid imposing their own worldview and value system upon clients or patients, existential therapists may seek to disclose and point out certain inconsistencies, contradictions or incongruence in someone's chosen but habitual ways of being.... [The] therapeutic aim is to illuminate, clarify, and place these problems into a broader perspective so as to promote clients' capacity to recognize, accept, and actively exercise their responsibility and freedom: to choose how to be or act differently, if such change is so desired; or, if not, to tolerate, affirm and embrace their chosen ways of being in the world.
>
> Existential therapy does not define itself predominantly on the basis of any particular predetermined technique(s). Indeed, some existential therapists eschew the use of any technical interventions altogether, concerned that such contrived methods may diminish the essential human quality, integrity, and honesty of the therapeutic relationship. However, the one therapeutic practice common to virtually all existential work is the phenomenological method. Here, the therapist endeavors to be as fully present, engaged, and free of expectations as possible during each and every therapeutic encounter by attempting to temporarily put aside all preconceptions regarding the process. The purpose is to gain a clearer contextual in-depth understanding and acceptance of what a certain experience might signify to this specific person at this particular time in his or her life.

The overall purpose of existential therapy, then, "is to allow clients to explore their lived experience honestly, openly and comprehensively." It provides clients with an opportunity to look at their lives in depth and detail, and to find ways forward that may be more satisfying, fulfilling and rewarding. Existential therapy does not provide easy answers. From an existential perspective, there are no quick solutions. But through persistence, courage, and a willingness to look into the darkness, clients can be helped to make the most of the lives that they have.

Historical Foundations

Most forms of contemporary existential psychotherapy owe their ancestry to the confluence of two distinguished streams of European thought and practice: first, to the *contemplative, wisdom traditions* of continental philosophy of nineteenth-century existential thought, hermeneutics, and phenomenology, and, second, to the *psychological healing traditions* of depth psychology.

The *philosophical* ground for the very possibility of existential psychotherapy, well before it appeared as such, was laid by the venerable wisdom traditions of ancient Greece and Rome, but also in Persia, India, China, and Japan, which continue to inspire many existential therapists today. These old philosophies each describe human existence in their own way in order to arrive at better ways of living by entering into dialogue. All these philosophers, including Socrates, Plato, Aristotle, Epicurus, and Zeno in the West and Zoroaster, Buddha, Confucius, Laozi, and many others in the East were committed to helping people live more thoughtfully and deliberately by having a clearer grasp of what life was about.

The *psychological healing* tradition of depth psychology also owes is origins to a synthesis of traditions, namely the religio-magical and medical-scientific healing traditions, both of which gradually developed through centuries of irregular but unrelenting progress going back to the Greeks and before (Ellenberger 1970). Over the centuries following the Asklepion healing temples of ancient Greece, pre-scientific mystical cures were performed both locally and regionally by various shamanistic, religious, and popular healers. It was not until Franz Mesmer (1734–1815) that a few notable physicians began developing more medical-scientific approaches to relieving psychological suffering. Although Mesmer's early medical efforts were initially abandoned they were picked up nearly a century later by the French physicians Jean-Martin Charcot (1825–1893) and Pierre Janet (1859–1947), the German Neurologist Hippolyte Bernheim (1840–1919), and, eventually, Sigmund Freud, the founder of modern depth psychotherapy.

Whether speaking of either the wisdom or healing dimensions of practice, for existential therapists the notion of depth manifests in fundamental questions about human existence. Who are we? Why do we suffer? How might we best live while knowing in our living that we "owe" life our death? Even partial answers to these questions remain largely hidden from view, inaccessible. Eugen Bleuler (1910) was the first to refer to the scientific concern with this hiddenness as "depth psychology" (*Tiefenpsychologie*, p. 623). However, for phenomenologically oriented existential psychotherapists, the term depth psychology is understood spiritually or metaphorically and not in any substantial or topographical sense. The hermeneutic significance of depth is in its reference to the ontologically given circumstance that human existence is both finite and mysterious. Heidegger called the human being's phenomenologically given worldedness a clearing (*Lichtung*) that is simultaneously disclosive and concealing. When existential thinkers raise foundational questions about human existence, they know from the beginning that they do so in the face of two inescapable ontological conditions: our inherent human finitude and the fact that, as Heraclitus asserted, "things keep their secrets" (2001, p. 9).

The more ancient grounds for existential psychotherapy mentioned above lay largely fallow over many centuries, only to be tilled anew by three auspicious nineteenth-century intellectual developments in Europe, namely, early existential thought and literature, hermeneutics, and phenomenology.

Existential thought and literature

Born on the heels of Romanticism and the Enlightenment, existential thinking first re-appeared in the philosophical and creative literatures of the nineteenth century. Philosophically speaking, the works of Arthur Schopenhauer (1788–1860), Sören Kierkegaard (1813–1855), and Friedrich Nietzsche (1844–1900) variedly but significantly influenced such twentieth century existential thinkers as Heidegger, Camus, Sartre, Jaspers, Buber, and Tillich. Schopenhauer, Kierkegaard, and Nietzsche issued an implicit invitation to philosophers, psychologists, and lay persons alike to pay more attention to the human condition in its everydayness and especially in its problematic and paradoxical nature. For Schopenhauer that meant an emphasis on will, destiny, desire, love, sexuality, and human suffering; for Kierkegaard the focus was on individuality, subjectivity, anxiety, choice, responsibility, despair, and spiritual commitment; and for Nietzsche the important issues were fate, tragedy, power, transcendence, individuality, morality, and will.

Concurrent with these philosophers, the great nineteenth Century philo-psychological novelists, poets, and playwrights like Johann Wolfgang von Goethe (1749–1832), Fyodor Dostoyevsky (1821–1881), and Hendrik Ibsen (1828–1906) embodied these same ideas in the characters they created. Faust, Werther, Raskolnikov, Prince Mishkin, the nameless protagonist of *Notes from the Underground*, Brand, Peer Gynt, Hedda Gabler, and The Master Builder, and Halvard Solness were all existential "heroes" who suffered human tragedies with which readers could resonate. They brought to life the new philosophical understanding and applied it to daily life, in the same way the ancient Greek philosophers were mirrored by the famous Greek tragedies. This combination of philosophers and writers helped prepare Western culture for what was to become, in the twentieth century, a concentrated gathering of philosophies concerned with the human condition, broadly referred to as existential philosophy.

Yet, in science and philosophy, ideas are not enough. Epistemology, new ways of investigating, knowing, and understanding are also necessary, and it was two new "sciences of understanding and knowing" that became most critical for the development of existential psychotherapy, namely hermeneutics and phenomenology.

Hermeneutics

Hermeneutics, as the art, science, and practice of interpretation precedes by millennia the practice of phenomenology, which itself is the predominant method of existential psychotherapy. The Greek verb *hermēneuein* means to interpret or to translate and refers to a process or method that aims to understand the implicit meaning of things, not only that which appears at first glance but also that which shows itself only gradually over time with a continuing, openly reflective gaze. To be hermeneutic is to be concerned with grasping, understanding, and translating meanings, especially those secreted meanings hibernating within the things themselves. The term is widely thought to be derived from the name of the Olympic god, Hermes, who was the emissary of the gods, passing and translating messages between gods as well as between gods and men. Palmer (1969) notes that "the Greek word, *hermeois* referred to the priest at the Delphic Oracle" (p. 13). Heidegger also noted the relation of the word hermeneutic to the name Hermes in his 1923 summer course on *Ontology – The Hermeneutics of Facticity* (1988/1999) while also acknowledging the ultimate obscurity of its etymology. In any case, it is not known whether the word was derived from the name of the god or the name of the god from the word. Thus, appropriately enough in this case, Hermes was also known as a trickster.

Hermeneutic practice today refers to the process by which we gain an understanding of the meaning of things, particularly the hidden or so-called deep meanings. It is a way of making explicit what is implicit and of putting text into its context, while also revealing its so-called subtext. By paying close attention to what is initially hermetically sealed, we read the hidden depths of messages in order to bring them into awareness and understanding. One might say hermeneutics is a process of enlarging our awareness, moving, from mystery to meaning, from silence to speech, or from the concealed to the unconcealed.

Early use of the term hermeneutics is most commonly traced back to Aristotle's *Peri hermēnaias* (*On Interpretation*). Although popularly associated with biblical exegesis, historically the use of the term also came to apply to interpretation in philology, jurisprudence, linguistics, and philosophy. The early-nineteenth-century German philosopher Friedrich Schleiermacher (1768–1834) established hermeneutics as a science in and of itself, independent of any particular discipline and coined the term "the hermeneutic circle" to designate the ongoing reciprocal contribution of the part and the whole, the word and the sentence, the phenomenon and its context in all human understanding. An admirer and biographer of Schleiermacher, Wilhelm Dilthey (1833–1911) made the practice more widely accessible. Dilthey is still most widely recognized and remembered for his distinction between the natural sciences (*Naturwissenschaften*) and the human sciences (*Geisteswissenschaften*) first made in his *Introduction to the Human Sciences* (1883/1989). The following year, in *Ideas for a Descriptive and Analytic Psychology*, he explicated his focus on Life as it is lived and proposed hermeneutics as the only appropriate approach to the study of human beings (*Geisteswissenschaften*), particularly with reference to his own descriptive approach to psychology called the psychology of understanding (*Verstehens-Psychologie*). Dilthey's work was devoted to an understanding of life, life itself, the meaning of our actually lived experience (*Erlebnis*) as such, particularly as it shows itself through the individual actually living that life in practice. For Dilthey objectifying measures and categories extrinsic to life were subservient to the spirited reality of life itself. Although his work influenced such twentieth-century philosophers as Hans-Georg Gadamer (1900–2002), Karl Jaspers (1883–1969), and Martin Buber (1878–1965), it was his influence on Martin Heidegger that was to have the greatest impact on philosophy and the human sciences in the next century. Out of this would eventually emerge the practice of Daseinsanalysis as a specific approach to psychiatric and psychotherapeutic practice and, from this in turn, the development of existential psychotherapy in general. Heidegger's revolutionary ontological hermeneutic understanding of Being and human being (*Dasein*) was directly responsible for what came to be called, in the twentieth century, the "hermeneutic turn" in philosophy and the human sciences, including psychology.

Phenomenology

As the quintessential philosophical method for existential psychology and psychotherapy, phenomenology is an approach to knowledge and understanding based on the description and clarification of the phenomena we encounter in everyday life. It is an approach that returns us to our immediate experience of the world. In its pursuit of a radical freedom from prejudice and presupposition, it seeks to avoid the errors of what Husserl called the natural attitude, with which we draw our knowledge from belief, dogma, personal habits and history, politics, cultural customs, ulterior motives, and so forth. The term phenomenology comes from the Greek words *phainómenon*, meaning that which appears, shows itself, or, literally, "shines forth" and *logos* meaning word, discourse, or study. Thus phenomenology may be said to be an approach to studying phenomena in philosophy, science, the arts, and humanities that minimizes the influence of unexamined assumptions, biases, beliefs, concepts, or theories in order to remain as faithful as possible to what shows itself directly in experience. As Moran (2000) put it: "the programme of phenomenology sought to reinvigorate philosophy by returning it to the life of the living subject … an appeal to return to concrete, lived human experience in all its richness" (p. 5). As with Schleiermacher and Dilthey in hermeneutics, two German philosophers stand out as phenomenological progenitors for existential psychotherapy and Daseinsanalysis: namely the philosopher and descriptive psychologist, Franz Brentano (1838–1917), and the pure or transcendental phenomenologist, Edmund Husserl (1859–1938).

A philosopher, psychologist, and, for some time, a priest, Franz Brentano served on the faculty of the University of Vienna where he taught, among many others, both Sigmund Freud and Edmund Husserl. During Brentano's first year on the faculty in Vienna, Sigmund Freud, a medical student at the time, attended the philosopher's classes with his friend, a future physiologist, Joseph Paneth. Brentano took a liking to both students and even invited them over to his home to discuss some of their objections to his philosophy. So influential was Brentano on the young Freud that the future founder of psychoanalysis considered taking his PhD in philosophy and, albeit only briefly, even struggled with considering theistic belief. Although Freud never acknowledged Brentano's influence on his development of psychoanalysis, indications of the latter's emphases on description and intentionality are implicitly represented in Freud's thought.

Regardless of the uncertain impact Brentano may have had on Freud and psychoanalysis, there is no doubt about his impact on philosophy and phenomenology, especially through his influence on Carl Stumpf, Alexius Meinong, Martin Buber, and, most especially, Edmund Husserl. In Brentano's *Psychology from an Empirical Standpoint* (1874/2015), he distinguished between genetic and descriptive psychology (psychognosis), an approach he much later referred to as phenomenological psychology. Although Brentano's descriptive psychology was a crucial forerunner of phenomenology, Spiegelberg (1972) considered it merely "phenomenology in the making" (p.5). Nevertheless, on his way to a science of mental phenomena, Brentano reintroduced the medieval scholastic concept of ***intentionality***, designating the circumstance that every act of human consciousness includes within itself an object. As Brentano famously put it: "Every mental phenomenon includes something as object within itself … In presentation something is presented, in judgment something is affirmed or denied, in love loved, in hate hated, in desire desired and so on" (Brentano 1874/1973, pp. 88–89). With the introduction of Brentano's concept of intentionality, the overcoming of the Cartesian duality between self and world was finally underway, a surpassing which found its penultimate consummation in Heidegger's understanding of the existing human as a unitary being-in-the-world, as *Da-sein*, literally, there-being. In fact, it was Heidegger's reading of Brentano's doctoral dissertation, while preparing for Jesuit priesthood in 1907, that sent the then 18-year-old Heidegger on his lifelong path of questioning the meaning of Being.

Building on Brentano's early contributions to the development of a phenomenological psychology, his student, Edmund Husserl, became most widely regarded as the father of "the phenomenological movement," which Spiegelberg (1972) considered to have been "initiated by Husserl around 1910" (p. xxxii). Studying with Brentano ten years after Freud, Husserl was explicitly indebted to Brentano's life-philosophy (*Lebensphilosophie*), especially his understanding of intentionality, descriptive psychology, and as the study of consciousness. It was on the foundation of Brentano's thought that Husserl went on to develop his own understanding of the life-world (*Lebenswelt*), that entire, dynamic, ontical horizon of phenomena that constitutes our lives as lived and can only be known as it appears to us in consciousness. In order to overcome Cartesian dualism, Husserl (1913/1931) bridged the gap between Descartes' subject and object, by speaking instead in terms of *noesis and noema* to describe the constitution of all acts of consciousness by the subjective cogito (*nous*). Using an example from the context of social life, including that form of social existence called psychotherapy, noesis refers to the process of perceiving-of-the-other whereas noema refers to the-other-as-perceived. Thus, any such act of social consciousness is constituted as the-perceiving-of-the-other-as-perceived. Uniting all acts of consciousness in this way brought the human being even closer to its world. Husserl's transcendental phenomenology sought to remain as close as possible to phenomena just as they show themselves directly, immanently in experience. With Husserl's transcendental reduction we seek to find a space in which the process of perception aims for essences rather than appearances. In order to achieve such an uncontaminated perception of the essence (*eidos*) or meaning of things, Husserl revived the Hellenist skeptic's principle of epoché (*epokhē*) – also called phenomenological reduction or, simply, bracketing – which means the suspension of belief or judgement.

For Husserl, phenomenological reduction was the necessary first step to return "to the things themselves" (1900/2001, p. 168), to let things speak for themselves in their living immediacy. This first step is about filtering, clarifying, even purifying the very process of our consciousness to the extent that this is possible in each case. This step then leads to the eidetic reduction, where we take awareness of the noema in its most essential manifestation, by using minute description, imaginative variation, and verification. Ultimately this will enable the transcendental reduction where we find that place of inter-subjectivity where our subjective consciousness connects to consciousness in general. Husserl's most famous student, Martin Heidegger, whose thought lies at the center of most twentieth-century philosophy, wrote that his own research "would not have been possible if the ground had not been prepared by Edmund Husserl" (Heidegger 1927/1962, p.62).

Phenomenological and Existential Psychiatry

In the liminal period between 1890 and 1910, the burgeoning "modern" fields of psychiatry and psychotherapy were dominated by the natural scientific approaches of Emil Kraepelin's purely descriptive classification of psychiatric syndromes, Wernicke's neurobiological brain-based determinism, and Sigmund Freud's more recent naturalistic psychoanalytic speculations.

As the century unfolded a number of European psychiatrists became restless and disenchanted with the positivistic, natural scientific approaches of the day and turned to philosophy to overcome their limitations. These psychiatrists hoped to establish a more cogent and comprehensive understanding of human beings and their various modes of mental suffering. Although Freud's psychoanalysis, with its focus on an analytical psychology and psychotherapy was, for many, somewhat less offensive, it was also compromised by its excessive reliance on theoretical speculation. The German psychiatrist, Karl Jaspers (1883–1969), having read Husserl's *Logical Investigations* in 1909, was among the first to challenge the reigning natural scientific views of the day and assert the possibilities of phenomenology in psychiatry with a 1912 article on the phenomenological trend in psychopathology. He followed this in 1913 with his monumental General Psychopathology, a major work he continued to improve on throughout his career, and which was an attempt to replace classical psychiatric definitions of mental illness, with a phenomenological study of the experience of each form of psychopathology. Even though Jaspers was ambivalent about phenomenology and refused to call himself a phenomenologist, the philosophical historian Herbert Spiegelberg considered the German psychiatrist's work as indispensable for the position phenomenology came to hold in the field (Spiegelberg 1972). Jaspers not only complained about the "pseudo illumination" of psychoanalysis (Jaspers 1913/1963, p. 363) but also challenged what he later called the "precarious foundation" and "reign of imagined insights," found in both brain and psychoanalytic "mythologies" (1941/1956, p.170).

Jaspers was not alone in his objections to exclusively natural scientific psychology but was joined, especially, by four other gifted lifelong contemporaries, all of whom were born between 1881 and 1891, and also died within ten years of one another (1966–1976). These were the Swiss psychiatrist Ludwig Binswanger (1881–1966), the German psychiatrist Viktor von Gebsattel (1883–1976), the French psychiatrist Eugene Minkowski (1885–1972), and the German (later American) neurologist Erwin Straus (1891–1975). These four comprised a powerful "quadrumvirate" (Spiegelberg, 1972, 251), an influential circle of four phenomenological psychopathologists, who together sought a more adequate foundation for understanding the human being, a philosophical anthropology (literally, account of the human), not based on biological or physiological substrates but on the grounds of a disciplined investigation of concrete lived experience. Although they came to phenomenology by various paths they were bound together by their own connections with one another and their common commitment to the study of the totality of the human being in relation to its world. Whereas Binswanger primarily came to phenomenology through Husserl and Heidegger, the others found their way, directly or indirectly, through their own studies of human experience or philosophers such as Paul Natorp (1854–1924), Theodore Lipps (1851–1914), Henri Bergson (1859–1941), and Max Scheler (1874–1928).

In their concern for establishing a science of the whole human being, the original phenomenological foursome also eventually found intellectual company in the works of other Europeans such as the biologist Frederick Buytendijk (1887–1974), the German neurologist and physiologist Viktor von Weizsäcker (1886–1957), and the Swiss psychiatrist Roland Kuhn (1912–2005), to name just a few.

Today, existential psychologists and psychotherapists from all over the world can trace their lineage to one or more of these European phenomenological existential thinkers and practitioners. Among the dozen or so original phenomenological philosophers on whose work contemporary existential psychotherapy relies (Spiegelberg, 1972), the first systematic phenomenologist, Edmund Husserl, and his once intimate student, Martin Heidegger, were undoubtedly two of the most prominent and paradigm shaping. However, with respect to existential psychiatry, psychology, and psychotherapy in particular, it was Martin Heidegger who eventually stood alone as the most influential philosopher for its thought and practice (Cohn 1997, 2002; Correia, Cooper, and Berdondini 2015). Before we go on to consider Heidegger's contributions we should consider the works of two nineteenth-century philosophers whose thought helped prepare the way for his own, namely, Søren Kierkegaard and Friedrich Nietzsche.

Søren Kierkegaard (1813–1855)

Kierkegaard's status as the "father of existentialism" was hard earned by his careful and personal observations of human existence, which brought a new and more subjective depth to philosophical thinking in the nineteenth century. Kierkegaard documented his personal struggle to become an individual and he showed how this was a historical, developmental, evolutionary process, in so doing providing us with a blueprint for existential psychotherapy. While continental philosophy often rejects scientism, because it refuses to accept that the exact sciences are the only authority on human existence, Kierkegaard's approach illustrates this better than anyone else's, though Schopenhauer comes a close second. It was Kierkegaard's work that showed the importance of historical understanding of our life story. His historical, developmental approach recognized that we had to pass through numerous stages, from aesthetical enjoyment, through ethical rectitude, towards a more subjective doubting and questioning and eventually a leap of faith that would help us find a foothold in the search of an eternal truth. Kierkegaard's patient tracing of his own steps in this respect has inspired many existential therapists. It was Kierkegaard's original idea that we must learn to flounder into the anxiety that we feel when faced with the abyss and come to realize that we are alone in our responsibility to make something of the challenges facing us. It was Kierkegaard who said: "*Whoever has learned to be anxious in the right way has learned the ultimate*" (Kierkegaard 1844/1980, p. 155).

It was also Kierkegaard who understood that life is profoundly paradoxical and full of tensions that we must learn to live with and face. And it was Kierkegaard who described despair in such a profound manner and who understood that we condemn ourselves to despair when we fail to become ourselves and when we betray our deepest inner values. Kierkegaard used descriptions of his own struggles in life, especially in terms of his belief that he was cursed because of his father's past bad behavior and that he would live a short life (something that, indeed, came to pass), and also in terms of his struggle with religion, culture, and the society he lived in, as well as in relation to the grief he felt over the love he gave up when he opted for his solitude and his philosophical work. His book *Works of Love* is testament to the lessons he drew from all this reflection on life and it shows how he came to believe that we can only ever truly come to be a full human being by loving the universal laws beyond us. Kierkegaard set a high standard for existential therapists, for he demanded that we check ourselves for self-deception and that we aim to face the abyss of the ultimate rather than live in the comfort of an easy temporal life, or with values that have been handed down to us by our parents. He demands a depth of self-reflection that all good existential therapists seek to apply to their work, which always remains deeply personal.

Friedrich Nietzsche (1844–1900)

Similarly to Kierkegaard, Nietzsche, too, broke with the established form of philosophizing that required one to create a rigid theory, and instead wrote about human existence in a lyrical and poetic fashion that was deeply felt and personally relevant. Nietzsche's impact on Heidegger (and on Freud) is well established and indeed Heidegger lectured and wrote on Nietzsche copiously. The passionate verve of Nietzsche's work is unique in philosophy and because of this he is also a highly controversial figure, who has been accused of misleading young people and who has variously been reproached with being an atheist or a forerunner of Nazism. These kinds of interpretations of Nietzsche's work (unlike the accusations of Heidegger, whose Nazi writings and activities are well documented) are based in a superficial and distorted reading of his words.

It is true that Nietzsche spoke in dramatic terms of the "Will to Power" and that he aspired for human beings to transcend their current predicaments by rising above their animal nature and become like Gods. But he described this process in terms of a spiritual enlightenment and a search for truth, not as a political attempt at domination or superiority.

For Nietzsche the awakening of humankind can only come through a process of coming to awareness which is hard earned through suffering. He wrote: "The discipline of suffering, of great suffering – do you not know that only this discipline has created all enhancements of man so far?" (Nietzsche 1886/1990, p. 225). For Nietzsche human beings are constantly going across boundaries, they are always wayfaring. Our task is to be like a bridge in life, between those animal origins and those divine possibilities. We learn to make ourselves into this kind of rope that can be slung across the abyss, by daring to take risks and also sometimes by fearlessly going into the abyss of our suffering. People learn about life the hard way, says Nietzsche, and so his inspiration to existential therapists is to not be too keen to mollycoddle or protect and support, but rather to stand shoulder to shoulder with our clients when they suffer, enabling them to discover their own capacity for endurance and courage.

Where Kierkegaard saw learning as a sequence of stages along the way, Nietzsche saw challenges and contradictions as inspirations to our own capacity for overcoming and transcending. Both created a new background music to the development of the movement of phenomenology. Philosophers like Heidegger and Sartre, who have been so foundational for existential therapists, were much inspired by both these existential philosophies. They have also influenced novelists like Camus, Hemingway, and Murdoch and playwrights like Becket, Anouilh, and Brecht. It is important to remember that many existential therapists find great inspiration in novels, plays, films, and the arts in general.

Martin Heidegger (1989–1976)

Born on September 26, 1889 to devout Catholic parents in the little southwestern German village of Messkirch, Martin Heidegger never really left that village where he also died 86 years later on May 26, 1976. Both as a man and as a philosopher he was indelibly shaped by the Swabian culture and landscape, the simple, faithful life of its peasant denizens, and the profound spiritual and philosophical influence of rural Catholicism. Although even from childhood he was ushered toward a vocation as a Jesuit priest, he was denied that destiny when he was 20 due to a heart condition that also spared him having to complete military service five years later.

His path toward the life of a philosopher was profoundly influenced by his reading, at the age of 17, of Franz Brentano's 1862 doctoral dissertation, *On the Several Senses of Being in Aristotle*, and, two years later, the Catholic dogmatist Carl Braig's 1896 treatise, *On Being: An Outline of Ontology*, a work which also included extended passages from Aristotle as well as St. Thomas Aquinas. Unbeknownst to Heidegger at the time, these works would introduce him to the question of Being (*Seinsfrage*) that would come to occupy him for the remainder of his life. Although he was aided in his search for the meaning of Being by early readings of Dilthey, Nietzsche, Kierkegaard, Hegel, and Schelling; the literature of Dostoevsky; and the poetry of Hölderlin, Trakl, and Rilke; it was his personal relationship with Edmund Husserl, beginning in the spring of 1916 while a Privatdocent at Freiburg University, that would change the course of his life. Under Husserl's tutelage, Heidegger found the essential epistemological complement for his search for the meaning of Being: phenomenology and a radical obedience "To the things themselves" (Heidegger 1927/1962, p. 30). Within just a few years the two men became the most influential voices in phenomenology, a circumstance Husserl often celebrated by declaring, "you and I are phenomenology" (Sheehan 2010, p. 7).

Initially enjoying a productive philosophical dialogue at Freiberg, things began to change when Heidegger took a position at Marburg in 1923. The younger man's conception of the human being and the task of phenomenology had begun to evolve and their contacts became less frequent. While at Marburg, Heidegger struggled toward the completion of his magnum opus *Being and Time* (1927/1962) in which he opened the question of Being and laid out his analysis of the human being, *Dasein*, that kind of being capable of understanding being including its own. His analysis of Dasein (*Daseinsanalytik*) was to provide a radically new philosophical foundation for understanding of the human being, uncovering and elucidating 20 or so invariant ontological characteristics of Dasein. Heidegger called these fundamental, ontological characteristics the *existentialia* (existentials).

Many of these ontological characteristics are variously named, even by Heidegger himself, but here are just a few examples: facticity or Being-at-all (*Faktizität*), Being-thrown or thrownness (*Geworfenheit*), Being-in-the-world (*In-der-Welt-Sein*), Understanding of Being (*Seinsverständnis*), care (*Sorge*), Being-in-a-mood (*Befindlichkeit*), Everydayness (*Alltäglichkeit*), Being-in-time (*Zeitlichkeit*), Being-in-space (*Räumlichkeit*), Being-from-Birth (*Geborensein*), Being-towards-death (*Sein zum Tode*), Being embodied (*Leiblichkeit*), and Being-with-others (*Mitsein*). All such existentials are fundamentally equiprimordial, always present and co-determinate in the everyday being of Dasein. Taken as a whole, these fundamental, ontological characteristics constituted the philosophical bedrock not only for Daseinsanalytic psychology and psychotherapy but for much of existential psychotherapy as a whole. Spiegelberg (1972) summarized the importance of Heidegger's thought for psychology and psychiatry as a whole in the following passage:

> By introducing such themes as Being, Dasein, world, time, and death, Heidegger placed man and his psyche before a vast cosmic background that psychology had never before considered in this manner. What now emerged was that a real understanding of man, normal or abnormal, was possible only by seeing him in relation to this most comprehensive setting. How does man relate himself to Being? What is his world and his place in it? How does he experience time? Heidegger's phenomenological hermeneutics provides the horizon against which man's psyche stands out in depth. In its light, man is a being who is ultimately defined by his relation not only to other beings but to Being itself and its fundamental characteristics. It is thus Heidegger's new ontology which has ultimately revolutionized psychology and psychiatry. (pp. 20–21)

It is important to emphasize that Heidegger's fundamental ontology of Dasein was not simply one more speculative, abstract theory of human nature. Rather it was phenomenologically discovered from the ground up based on human beings' ordinary, everyday experience. Perhaps the most radical contribution of the interpretation of the human being as Dasein, as there-being, as ex-isting, was to overcome at last the Cartesian division of being into mind and body, self and world, subject and object. It was a culminating philosophical insight that built on and completed the earlier efforts of Brentano and Husserl. With the term Dasein, the human being is no longer understood as a being located in a physical space called the world but, rather, Dasein is itself a world, is itself worlded and worlding.

Although *Being and Time* is almost universally considered Heidegger's most prodigious and influential work he continued to develop his thought on the relationship between being and Dasein throughout his life. In the early 1930's and extending through the 40's, especially, Heidegger experienced what came to be known as "the turn" (Die Kehre) from phenomenology to thought, that is, a shift from Dasein's relation to Being, to Being's relation to Dasein and, with this, the event of their mutually dependent co-arising known as Ereignis or the re-owning of being. It was this so-called "second Heidegger" with whom Medard Boss studied and collaborated in person from 1949 to 1972. Meanwhile, however, another philosopher, the Frenchman Jean-Paul Sartre, also became greatly interested in the work of Husserl and Heidegger and developed an existential philosophy of his own, which reverberated independently with the philosophies of his colleagues Maurice Merleau-Ponty and Simone de Beauvoir.

Jean-Paul Sartre (1905–1980), Merleau-Ponty (1908–1961), and Simone de Beauvoir (1908–1986)

Together these French philosophers created an immensely popular movement that became known worldwide as "existentialism." This is sometimes mistakenly confused with the whole of existential philosophy, which is wider in range, and means that some people also wrongly refer to "existential therapy" as "existentialist therapy." It is important to note that neither the phenomenologists, nor the philosophers of freedom such as Kierkegaard or Nietzsche, nor indeed classical Greek or Roman philosophers, would have accepted the terms "existentialist" or "existentialism." Existentialism is exclusively reserved for that French philosophy created by Sartre and his colleagues, including his lifelong partner Simone De Beauvoir and his friend Maurice Merleau-Ponty, but also others like Albert Camus (1913–1960) and Gabriel Marcel (1889–1973). But it does not include other French philosophers influential for existential therapy such as Emmanuel Levinas (1905–1995) or Paul Ricoeur (1913–2005). Existentialism is also an existential philosophy (a philosophy about human existence) but it takes a very specific view of the world that is not generally accepted by existential therapists, most particularly not by many who practice in Eastern or South American areas, as it can be an intensely individualistic and self-assertive philosophy.

Existentialism was inspired by both Heidegger's and Husserl's phenomenological theories. It also drew on Kierkegaard, Nietzsche, and others like Jaspers and Scheler. Existentialism itself became widely influential in its own right and inspired the structuralists, the post-structuralists, the deconstructionists, as well as the humanistic psychologies in the United States.

Sartre's ideas were expressed in many forms, including in his philosophical treaties, his novels, his plays, and his political manifestos. His magnum opus *Being and Nothingness* (Sartre 1943/1956) is the most well-known of his works and in it he argues that, at heart, human beings are pure freedom, pure nothingness, so that we are doomed to find ways of making ourselves more concrete, more solid, more like an object. That subjective consciousness that we are capable of makes us inclined to live in "bad faith," that is, by deceiving ourselves into believing that we are solid or determined, when in actual fact we are always in flux and never just one thing or another. Sartre's famous illustration of this is his description of the waiter in the café who gingerly maneuvers his towel and tray in order to play act at being a waiter, when in fact he is a man struggling with an empty life and with many contradictions and possibilities. Sartre was very preoccupied with *l'homme serieux*, the person who takes himself too seriously and becomes frozen in this role play. This idea is very often at the foreground of existential therapists' minds when they listen to their clients, hearing the many ways in which people have chained themselves to false situations or to ideas about themselves that were never true but that have become mineralized and made solid, written in stone, so that they now cannot get rid of this way of defining their lives.

Sartre explored the many ways in which people are hindered by this mistaken way of living with bad faith. Initially he saw this as key to people's capacity for freedom and he is famous for having said that people are pure freedom and that the only choice we have not got is not to choose. Novice existential therapists, who are too enthusiastic about existentialism, may make the mistake of taking this to the letter and applying it in simplistic ways. But more mature existential therapists are generally acutely aware of the complex, problematic, and paradoxical nature of life. In the same way, Sartre in his later work (e.g., Sartre 1960/1976) was much more realistically aware of the many constrictions and restrictions that human existence entails, particularly the conditions of scarcity and lack that we all have to deal with. His vision of the intersection between our personal lives, our political lives, and our ethical decision making became more and more sophisticated and his later works can be very helpful in this sense.

Simone De Beauvoir, following a similar existentialist path, focused her work more on the detailed observation of individual experiences of the constrictions of life. She is well known for her work on the particular condition of women, which she elaborated in great detail in her magnum opus *The Second Sex* (Beauvoir 1948/1997). She, like Sartre, argued for the importance of political awakening to overcome societal oppression and alienation. She emphasized the difficulty in dealing with other people that Sartre also spoke about. Society restricts our capacity for being true to our own principles at times. "You can't draw a straight line in a curved space," she said in her autobiographic novel *The Mandarins* (1954/2005), "You can't lead a proper life in a society which isn't proper, in which every way you turn you are always caught" (p. 625).

She exposed the contradictions and ambiguity of human existence in a very clear manner in her book *The Ethics of Ambiguity* (1948) and in her philosophical papers (2004).

This same theme of ambiguity was also shared with friend and colleague Maurice Merleau-Ponty, whose application of phenomenology was directly inspired by his careful work on Husserl's papers, which he studied at the archive in Louvain. In his major book the *Phenomenology of Perception* (1945/1962) he elaborated a much more psychological and phenomenological theory of human embodiment, showing how the world is always disclosed to us through the ambiguity of our corporeal existence, where we are always doing something to the world while the world is doing something to us at the same time. Merleau-Ponty grasped the importance of intertwining between human beings and the world and used Husserl's concept of intersubjectivity to make sense of the relational and therefore always ambiguous relationship we have to it. This led Merleau-Ponty to question the nature of truth and time and many other aspects of human experience. Many existential therapists find his work very grounding as it always refers us back to our experience of the world through our senses. In a world where my perception is creative and changes things it is good to remember that my experience is nevertheless always sensed through a body that is beholden to a very concrete reality.

Martin Buber (1878–1965), Karl Jaspers (1883–1969), Max Scheler (1874–1928), Paul Tillich (1886–1965), Paul Ricoeur (1913–2005), and Emmanuel Levinas (1906–1995)

There are many other existential philosophers who are relevant to working existentially. Some of these we want to introduce a bit more specifically though we have previously referred to them in passing. Buber, Jaspers, Tillich, Scheler, Ricoeur, and

Levinas, have all made significant contributions to our thinking about human relationships in ways that neither Heidegger nor Sartre did. They are by no means the only existential philosophers we should be reading. There are many others, including Gabriel Marcel and Hannah Arendt, who are as relevant today as they were when they wrote. There are also less well-known philosophers in currently less existentially vocal regions of the world, whose works will undoubtedly become better known as existential therapists build their own work on these other philosophical ideas. Some examples of such philosophies may be found in Part VI of the book. The field is very wide and deep and people training in existential therapy have much to learn about human existence from a variety of human cultures and perspectives. However these are some of the ideas that are generally considered foundational in this field.

Max Scheler (1874–1928) was a less well-known phenomenologist because his work was suppressed by the Nazis. His unique contribution was to emphasize the importance of emotional understanding in pinpointing human existence. Scheler followed Husserl's idea that experience is what knowledge starts from and thus we should always end with experience again in a loop of verification. This led to Scheler's understanding that human relationships are a form of participation in another person's world and in their being. This is an important aspect of practical training as it is not the same to allow ourselves to participate in other people's experience as to feel or show empathy. Scheler indeed spoke of sympathy rather than of empathy and this is about deeply joining with the other in their experience. Instead of disengaging in order to see the other objectively, we become subjectively connected. This is not dissimilar to Kierkegaard's injunction that we should learn to be subjective about others and objective about ourselves and it links directly with Husserl's notion of inter-subjectivity, which is the idea that we are always in relationship rather than separate.

Martin Buber (1878–1965) also elaborated this idea of our interconnectivity and he is well known for his recognition that human beings are always in the in-between. Relationships are not about you or I, but they are about the connection between us. They are about what we created together in the space that separates us. Buber made the distinction between I–Thou and I–It relationships, recognizing that we can relate to the other either as an object, an It, or as a subject, a Thou. We ourselves become an object when we relate in an I–It way and we become whole and connected when we relate in I–Thou mode. Among the existential authors, Buber's preferencing of relatedness, his favoring of the other over the self, was the most radical. For Buber (1963), in seeking one's own way one must strive, "to begin with oneself, but not to end with oneself; to start from oneself, but not to aim at oneself; to comprehend oneself, but not to be preoccupied with oneself" (pp. 31–32). For Buber, all life was relation.

Karl Jaspers (1883–1969), as we have seen earlier, contributed his work on psychopathology, aiming for a phenomenological model of human mental health struggles, but he also contributed his very personal existential philosophy. His ideas about limit situations and the way in which human beings have a tendency to avoid or negate them was very influential. His own life story, being scorned by Heidegger and others because he was married to a Jewish wife, is very interesting in existential terms, and it allowed him to speak with feeling about limits, but also about the importance of loyalty to love. He understood something that is vital for existential therapists: that we need to remember that people come to us because they want to recover their passion for life, their enthusiasm for existence, and their capacity to love. Jaspers (1938/1971) put it very succinctly:

> Contrary to a life either without solid substance or a life in which this substance is never affected, only the enthusiastic attitude means a life awake, a life in totality and authenticity. Enthusiasm is becoming oneself in the act of devoting oneself. (p. 119)

Paul Tillich (1886–1965) was similarly inspired by phenomenological ideas to consider how human beings face up to the ultimate concerns that determine the limits of human experience. He was a German theologian and philosopher who moved to the United States in the Second World War and he was extremely influential in terms of the birth of humanistic psychology. Tillich found a way to speak about god in a manner that went beyond the atheism of existentialism and that allowed people to rediscover a spiritual aspect to their lives. His book *The Courage to Be* (1952) was a response to his doctoral student Rollo May's dissertation on the *Meaning of Anxiety* (1950), which was written after May contracted tuberculosis and struggled with his own anxiety and sense of meaning. Both their contributions are inspirational to existential therapists who have to work with suicidal or demotivated people who are overwhelmed by a sense of absurdity.

Emmanuel Levinas (1906–1995) was a Jewish philosopher who turned our understanding of human relationships inside-out by making the claim that the existence of the Other comes before our own existence, and is always more important (Levinas 1961/1969). He was trained by Husserl and Heidegger but established his very own ontology, which was profoundly rooted in ethics and the question of how we should act morally in relation to the world and in particular in relation to others. This moral question reverberates to some extent with Sartre's project of reconsidering ethics, but where Sartre continued to favor individual responsibility in responding in a moral way, Levinas addressed the matter in a more spiritual and theological manner. This is because Levinas took the view that the other, as foreign to us, is always treated as standing in the place of infinity. He was much inspired and influenced by his study of the Talmud. This illustrates the way in which different existential thinkers had different religious backgrounds and were by no means all atheists, as people sometimes wrongly assume.

Paul Ricoeur (1913–2005) was a French philosopher whose work on interpretation and discourse is directly relevant to existential therapists as it looks very closely at the sort of conversation that therapists have with their clients. Ricoeur challenged the kind of interpretation that therapists have long been used to in terms of applying a specific theoretical framework to somebody's words and experiences, in order to analyze them. His critical distinction between a "hermeneutics of suspicion" (e.g., Freudian) and a "hermeneutics of faith" (e.g., Rogerian), is critical for existentialists who must always linger between the two in the liminal space between what is manifest and hidden. Ricoeur reminded us of the importance of hermeneutic interpretation where there is room for the freedom of interaction between the partners of a conversation to determine the meanings they are gleaning. Ricoeur's work on dialogue is crucial for existential therapists, especially when he argues that we can never find any true meaning other than in dialogue. Indeed, we need to approach meanings from various perspectives and take the time to talk through our ideas with another in order to be able to make sense. Understanding the role that narrative plays in our existential therapeutic work is paramount to us remaining true to the other person's experiences. Narratives can be expressed in many different ways, with words, with gestures, and with tone of voice as well as with feelings, or other expressions like music, or pictures.

The schools of existential therapy

Most schools of existential therapy would use some of the philosophical ideas described above, but as this handbook will demonstrate and illustrate they do so in very different ways. From this early start in Daseinsanalysis – and with the inspiration of an ever greater number of contemporary existential philosophers – existential psychotherapy evolved into a number of different schools, methods, and approaches. These form the structure for the present handbook and can be introduced as follows.

Daseinsanalysis

Daseinsanalysis, the first of the systematic approach to existential psychology and psychotherapy, was developed by two Swiss psychiatrists, Ludwig Binswanger and Medard Boss. They combined the psychoanalytic practice of Sigmund Feud with the fundamental ontology of Martin Heidegger. Whereas Binswanger's primary aspiration was to develop a phenomenological approach to psychiatric science and psychopathology, Boss's aim was to provide a more philosophically sound foundation for psychotherapeutic thought and practice. Although he thought Freud's approach to therapeutic practice was unparalleled, Binswanger's focus was on replacing the prevailing natural scientific view of the human being (*homo natura*) with a human scientific understanding of the whole human being as an historically existing whole (*homo existentialis*). In contrast, as a traditionally trained psychoanalyst, Boss attempted to uncover and articulate a phenomenological approach to Freud's psychoanalytic practice.

For example, the use of the couch and free association were seen by Boss (1963, 1979) as an opportunity for an individual, not unlike that of being asleep and dreaming, to relax into openness and give oneself up to oneself, allowing the totality of one's own existence to show itself freely in its own time. Boss was particularly critical of Freud's notion of the "unconscious," declaring that it was nothing other than an unnecessary objective reification of the mystery of Being and being human: the fundamental ontological hiddenness or concealment of being that lies inherently everywhere within and around us. Boss also challenged Freud's notion of the transference and, in particular, the idea that the feelings arising between therapist and client were not real but merely false and misleading mechanical replications of early childhood relational scenarios. Rather, Boss considered the therapeutic relationship as a fully real encounter between two human beings, one built not on transference and countertransference but on an authentic encounter of two human individuals characterized by an individual's genuine love for a therapist and that therapist's reciprocally genuine "therapeutic eros" toward the individual. Finally, Boss took issue with the psychoanalyst's technical habit of explaining the past by asking the question, "why," when what was most at stake was the future and the individuals' freedom to carry out the full range of their own existential possibilities for being-in-the-world, especially those which have been blocked or forsaken in the past. Thus, instead of asking why, Boss would ask "why not?" Why not let go of your fears? Why not behave more freely?

Central to Boss's theoretical critique of psychoanalysis was his repudiation of any such idea of inner psychic entities like ego, id, and superego and even the notion of an isolated inner mind like the psyche as such. For Boss, the human being exists as a singular, inseparable whole, always unfolding with and as a whole realm of world relational possibilities. Our essence is not in our heads but in our ex-istence, our literally standing out in the world and as worlded or worlding.

Boss's Daseinsanalysis was built, not only on his study of and relationship with, Heidegger and the most prominent psychoanalysts of his day, but also on the spiritual inspiration of an intense period of discipleship, in the Kashmir valley, with a Hindu wise man and master, Swami Govinda Kaul.

Existential-phenomenological therapy

The emergence of existential-phenomenological therapy was quite different from Daseinsanalysis and happened to a large extent in the United Kingdom with the work of R.D. Laing and his colleagues. R.D. Laing was a much loved, though controversial and somewhat maverick Scottish psychiatrist, who drew on a range of existential and phenomenological teachings to critique the psychiatric assumptions of his – and to a large extent, our – day. He was much more influenced by the later existential philosophies of Sartre, Camus, and Merleau-Ponty than by the Heideggerian ideas underpinning Daseinsanalysis. In contrast to an "objective," detached psychiatric standpoint, Laing (1965) argued that psychiatrists needed to enter the lived–world of their patients, and that there they would find a far greater understanding of the client's 'madness' than they had ever imagined. In his best-known book, *The Divided Self* (1965), Laing attempted to show how a condition as seemingly unintelligible as schizophrenia could become intelligible and meaningful if one attempts to understand it from the patient's standpoint. For instance, he argued that a "paranoid" person may have experienced messages in childhood that were so confusing and conflicting that they have learnt their survival depends on not trusting anything that people around them say or do.

Laing rejected therapeutic systems and techniques, and in this respect he made no attempt to codify a "Laingian" approach to therapy (though clients' reports suggest that he was a highly attentive, focused, and challenging listener, Resnick 1997). In the mid-1980s, however, a British School of Existential Analysis began to emerge, now considered part of a wider "existential-phenomenological" approach (Cooper 2017; van Deurzen and Adams 2016), that drew on many of Laing's writings and ideas. The principal driving force behind this development was Emmy van Deurzen (2010, 2012, 2015), a clinical psychologist, philosopher. and existential psychotherapist, born in the Netherlands. Van Deurzen's approach draws on a range of philosophical insights – including those beyond the bounds of existentialism and phenomenology – to help clients address the basic existential question: "How can I live a better life?"

Van Deurzen's starting point is that life is an "endless struggle where moments of ease and happiness are the exception rather than the rule" (van Deurzen 1998, p. 132); and that problems in living arise when people are reluctant to face the realities of their imperfect, dilemma-ridden, and challenging existences. Hence, the aim of existential therapy, for van Deurzen (1997), is to help clients wake up from "self-deception" or "alienation," to face the challenge of living head on, and to discover their talents and possibilities.

Like Laing and van Deurzen, most therapists within the existential-phenomenological school adopt a primarily descriptive, phenomenologically based approach to therapy, in which clients' difficulties are seen as *problems in living* rather than mental illnesses (see du Plock 1997). The British school, however, can only be considered a school in the loosest sense of the word. As van Deurzen writes: "The movement has its own history of splitting and fighting and there is a healthy disagreement about what existential work should be" (2012, p. xi). In particular, in contrast to van Deurzen's "philosophical existential-phenomenological therapy," Spinelli (2005, 2006, 2015) has advocated a more exploratory, "relational existential-phenomenological" approach to practice, in which therapists are encouraged to bracket their beliefs and assumptions and to engage their clients from a stance of "un-knowing."

Existential-humanistic and Existential-integrative therapy

In the United States, an *existential-humanistic* approach to therapy emerged under the leadership of Rollo May. May originally trained as a minister and was strongly influenced by the teachings of his mentor, the existential theologian Paul Tillich. In 1958, May co-edited the landmark handbook on existential psychotherapy *Existence*, which introduced the writings and practices of European existential and phenomenological psychiatrists to America for the first time. Other key figures in the development of the existential-humanistic approach include James Bugental, Irvin Yalom, and Kirk J. Schneider – all of whom worked in close collaboration with May.

Unlike Daseinsanalysis and the existential-phenomenological approaches, existential-humanistic therapy adopted several of psychoanalysis's core theoretical assumptions. In particular it assumes that people experience psychological difficulties when they try to defend themselves against unconscious feelings of anxiety. For the existential-humanists, however, what creates our most basic fears is not our relationships with our parents or conflicts between different instinctual drives, but our knowledge of the unavoidable *givens* of life: in particular, our mortality, freedom, aloneness, and meaninglessness (Yalom 1980). This can also be understood as our relations with the groundlessness of existence (Schneider and Krug 2017). Accordingly we try to push an awareness of these existential realities down into our unconscious – for instance, by trying to convince ourselves that we are invulnerable and can live forever – but then these defensive strategies end up doing more harm than good. Hence, the aim of existential-humanistic therapy is to try to help clients overcome problematic defenses (or "protections"), and to meet the anxieties of existence with an attitude of openness yet decisiveness and resolve: To "stand naked in the storm of life" (Becker 1973, p. 86). Therapeutic strategies range from the gently exploratory to the highly confrontational and are often orientated around an exploration of the dynamics of the therapeutic relationship within a "here-now" experiential context. In more recent years, existential-humanistic therapy has expanded into an integrative therapy (Schneider 2008; Shahar and Schiller 2016). This existential-integrative trend has been increasingly influential on a variety of mainstream and cross-cultural therapeutic modes (Wolfe 2016). It has also more explicitly embraced spiritual dimensions of practice, including those that bear on the well-being of communities and not only individuals (Schneider and Krug 2017).

Logotherapy and existential analysis

Logotherapy is a form of existential therapy that specifically aims to help clients discover purpose and meaning in their lives – *Logos* being the Greek term for meaning (Frankl 1984) – and to overcome feelings of meaninglessness and despair. It was developed by the Viennese psychiatrist, Viktor Frankl, around 1929 – and 'tested out' during his time in the Nazi concentration camps, where he found that those prisoners who had some sense of meaning and hope survived better than those who succumbed to a sense of meaninglessness and futility (Frankl 1984).

According to Frankl, human beings' primary motivation (deeper than the strivings for pleasure or power) is to find meaning in their lives (Frankl 1984, 1967/1985, 1986). Without this, human beings will experience deep feelings of frustration, emptiness, and depression, which can develop into more serious existential neuroses and suicidality (Frankl 1986). Here, individuals may turn to such self-destructive patterns as addictions, compulsions, or phobias in an attempt to fill their existential vacuum. In terms of actual practice, logotherapists use a range of relatively didactic techniques to help clients find meaning and purpose: from Socratic dialogue, which vigorously challenges them to find out their life's meaning, to a gentler exploration of what they find satisfying and rewarding.

Originally descended from Logotherapy, Längle started in 1983 with trainings in Existential Analysis, a broader and phenomenologically based attempt to develop a fully-fledged psychotherapy with specific treatments for clinical disorders (Längle 2015). The practical aim of Existential Analysis is to help clients to live with *inner consent* to what they do. This personally felt consent ("yes") is complex and the result of a fourfold "yes" to all the layers or fundamental dimensions of existence. They are called the four "fundamental existential motivations" – accepting the given, turning towards the values, respecting the own and other person, and getting into accordance with the actual meaning in life – which, when frustrated or disturbed, may lead to specific psychopathological difficulties.

Recent years have also seen the emergence of meaning-centered therapies for people with physical illnesses. Like other forms of logotherapy and existential analysis, these tend to be relatively focused, directive, and inclusive of a wide range of therapeutic techniques. Usually, however, they are delivered in a group – rather than an individual – format, though this is not always the case (e.g., Henry et al. 2010). In recent years, this structured meaning-centered approach has also been extended to other groups of clients, such as palliative care nurses (Fillion et al. 2009), bereaved individuals (MacKinnon et al. 2014), and psycho-oncology (Breitbart et al., 2016). Of all the existential approaches to therapy, these show the best evidence of effectiveness (Vos, Craig, and Cooper 2014).

Existential group therapy

Existential psychotherapy, as an approach that is concerned with our human relationship to the world around us, has indeed been a prime candidate for the development of group therapeutic approaches. Yalom's work with groups, which initially began as a form of interpersonal work, found its most eminent expression in his work with terminal cancer patients. Yalom discovered that the existential aspects of the group work were highly relevant and that people considered that existential discussions in the group work enhanced their ability to deal with their problems greatly. Yalom's work stands out as an example of a form of existential group therapy. Logotherapy and meaning-centered therapies have also been successfully applied to groups of terminally ill patients, with a particular focus on the exploration of limit situations. Group analysis, though not deliberately existential, has translated a range of existential ideas into group practice, in particular the work of Foulkes and Elias. Hans Cohn, originally trained as a group analyst, developed an explicitly existential description of group work, and he joined with the existential-phenomenological school to connect his work further to this tradition. Others, like van Deurzen, have shown how working in a group is an essentially phenomenological practice, where people, by drawing on each other's perceptions of reality, find a way to get a better perspective on their own concerns.

Dimensions of existential practice

As can be seen, considerable variety exists across the existential approaches to therapy. To help conceptualize this, Cooper (2017) has proposed nine basic dimensions of existential practice. Existential approaches and therapists do not neatly sit at one or other end of these dimensions, and there is a great deal of diversity across practitioners and at different times with different clients. But these nine dimensions can be useful ways of thinking about how the different forms of existential therapy vary, and also of seeing how widely diverse practices can all come within the same existential umbrella.

- *Knowing versus Not knowing.* Does the existential therapist encounter the client holding a range of assumptions and beliefs (interpreting), or do they encounter clients from a (phenomenological) stance of openness and "not-knowing"?
- *Directive versus Non-directive.* Does the existential therapist take charge of the therapeutic process, or do they allow the client to take more of a lead?
- *Explanatory versus Descriptive.* Does the existential therapist help the client to "unpack" their experiences as experienced, or do they try to identify underlying contents/meanings?

- *Pathologizing versus De-pathologizing.* Does the existential therapist understand the client's difficulties in terms of maladaptations and dysfunctional (fixed) ways of being, or do they focus on the intelligibility and purposefulness of the client's symptoms?
- *Techniques versus Not techniques.* Does the existential therapist engage in a relatively unstructured, informal dialogue, or do they orientate their work around specific therapeutic methods?
- *Immediacy versus Non-immediacy.* Does the existential therapist encourage the client to explore their here-and-now relationships with the therapist, or not?
- *Psychological versus Philosophical.* Does the existential therapist focus on emotional, cognitive, and behavioral process, or do they discuss with the client wider issues of life and its meaning? That is, is the focus of the work on "healing" or on "wisdom"?
- *Individualizing versus Universalizing.* Does the existential therapist understand the client's difficulties in terms of the client's *particular* psychological processes, or in terms of more universal challenges for *all* human beings?
- *Subjective versus Inter-worldly.* Does the existential therapist focus on psychological processes "inside" the client's psyche, or on their relationship to their world?

Reducing these dimensions further, it is possible to conceptualize the existential approaches as lying roughly along a *hard–soft* axis (Cooper 2017): with the more directive, pathologizing, interpretative, and technique-based ways of working at the former end; and the more phenomenological, descriptive, relational practices at the latter. So a harder existential approach challenges clients to face up to particular existential givens; while a softer existential approach supports them to explore and understand the ways in which they experience their world. And, to a great extent, this hard–soft axis is representative of a wider tension within the existential-phenomenological field: from a *harder* existential philosophy, which holds that there are certain truths about the human condition that people need to face up to; to a softer existential position, which holds that all truths, including existential ones, are ultimately only particular perspectives or viewpoints on how the world is.

About the handbook

This handbook aims to bring together the entire field of existential therapy as we currently know it. This will include looking at how the different strands of existential therapy have developed worldwide over the past century. It is the first time that this project has been attempted since Rollo May and his colleagues edited their landmark book *Existence* in the 1950s (May, Angel, and Ellenberger 1958) and much has changed and evolved since then.

It became possible and desirable to edit this present volume when the representatives of existential therapy came together to share their different ways of working at the First World Congress for Existential Therapy in London in 2015. It became immediately obvious that it was necessary to put in writing what was so vividly and enthusiastically experienced by all as existential therapists from the four corners of the world came together in order to explore differences and similarities in our ways of working. For four days we enjoyed the richness of a field we had not previously realized had been so fertile. We took great joy in listening to each other, recognizing the way in which each of our different existential ways of working had evolved and had begun to blossom. We found we had much in common, as we had read the same philosophies and were familiar with the works of the same historical practitioners. But we were also amazed at how much we could learn from each other's unique interpretation of existential therapy. Our discussions were vibrant with excitement, and we felt eager to gather in the harvest of our years of isolated practice. We were gratified and joyful to realize that we had so many colleagues around the world who were like-minded and who had struggled with the same issues, but often in different ways and coming up with different ideas and solutions. It was enlightening, and we wanted to hold on to the richness we had discovered. Inevitably many colleagues who were not able to come to London asked for a record of that historical meeting and wished to have access to the range of existential approaches presented on that occasion. The idea of a Handbook was born, but we wanted it to be a fresh project, one that would build further on what was achieved at the congress. The papers of the congress were published earlier in the journal *Existential Analysis.*

In terms of readership, the book is therefore aimed at all existential therapists – as well as those who draw from an existential base – who are interested in reading about the many ways in which existential therapy can be understood and practiced. It is for trainees and experienced practitioners alike. Though there is some inevitable repetition in terms of the historical roots and philosophical themes that hold us all together, the detail of each approach will show many different ways of thinking and working existentially. This is entirely in line with the philosophy of existential work, which thrives on freedom and originality and which invites each practitioner to reinvent the approach with each client and with each session of existential therapy. Anyone reading this volume will find some new impulses and stimulation to think and reflect about the meaning of life, not just in terms of the predicaments of our clients, but in terms of our personal and most intimate way of being in the world ourselves. As always with existential work, the book is not a handbook of technical prescription, but an invitation to become immersed and engaged and to discover and explore new ways of understanding and living for yourself.

Structurally, the book is divided into six parts. The first four of these cover the principal forms of existential theory and therapeutic practice: Daseinsanalysis, existential-phenomenological therapy, existential-humanistic and existential-integrative therapy, and logotherapy and existential analysis. A fifth part then goes on to consider group forms of existential therapy. Each of these sections is divided into six chapters: 1) History, 2) Philosophy and theory, 3) Method and practice, 4) Therapy illustration, 5) Key texts, and 6) Challenges and new developments. The chapters are written by a range of authors, all of whom are leading experts in these areas. In a final section, the book covers newly evolving forms of existential therapy around the world, with chapters on Scandinavia, Russia and the Baltic States, Southern Europe, Latin and Central America, and Asia as well as a chapter on research.

Conclusion

Today, the existential approach is thriving, with training institutes in 42 countries around the globe (Correia, Cooper, and Berdondini 2014). Indeed, there are claims that the existential approach is growing (e.g., Barnett and Madison 2012; Shahar and Schiller 2016); and the proliferation of existential texts, societies and training courses would testify to this (Correia et al. 2014). Perhaps one reason for this is the somewhat anarchic and anti-conformist nature of the existential approach (Cooper 2015): its refusal to be categorized or defined. In an era dominated by evidence-based practices and manualized "treatments," existential therapy provides an opportunity for psychotherapists to express their creativity and independence – their unwillingness to conform to "best practice, as defined by "the One." Existential therapy provides the "clearing" in which being, in whatever form it takes, can truly come to light.

References

Barnett, L. and Madison, G. (eds.) (2012). *Existential Psychotherapy: Vibrancy, Legacy and Dialogue*. London: Routledge.

Beauvoir, S. de (1997). *The Second Sex* (trans. H.M. Parshley) London: Vintage. (Original work published 1949.)

Beauvoir, S. de (2004). Pyrrhus and Cinéas. In: *Philosophical Writings* (ed. M.A. Simons, M. Timmerman, and M.B. Mader), 77–150. Urbana: University of Illinois Press.

Beauvoir, S. de (2005). *The Mandarins*. London: Harper Perennial Modern Classics. (Original work published 1954.)

Becker, E. (1973). *The Denial of Death*. New York: Free Press Paperbacks.

Bleuler, E. (1910). Die Psychanalyse Freud's: Verteidigung und kritische Bemerkungen. *Jahrbuch fur Psychoanalytische und Psychopathologische Forschungen II*, 623–730.

Brentano, F. (1973). *Psychology from an Empirical Standpoint* (trans. L.L. McAlister). New York: Routledge. (Original work published 1874.)

Boss, M. (1963). *Psychoanalysis and Daseinsanalysis*. New York: Basic Books.

Boss, M. (1979). *Existential Foundations of Medicine and Psychology* (trans. S. Conway and A. Cleaves). Northvale, NJ: Jason Aronson Inc.

Breitbart, W., Rosenfeld, B., Gibson, C. et al. (2016). Meaning-centered group psychotherapy for patients with advanced cancer: A pilot randomized controlled trial. *Psycho-oncology 19* (1): 21–28.

Buber, M. (1963). *The Way of Man: According to the Teachings of Hasidism*. London: Vincent Stuart.

Cohn, H.W. (1997). *Existential Thought and Therapeutic Practice: An Introduction to Existential Psychotherapy*. London: Sage.

Cohn, H.W. (2002). *Heidegger and the Roots of Existential Therapy*. London: Continuum.

Cooper, M. (2015). *Existential Psychotherapy and Counselling: Contributions to a Pluralistic Practice*. London: Sage.

Cooper, M. (2017). *Existential Therapies*, 2e. London: Sage.

Correia, E., Cooper, M., and Berdondini, L. (2014). The worldwide distribution and characteristics of existential psychotherapists and counsellors. *Existential Analysis 25* (2): 321–337.

Correia, E., Cooper, M., and Berdondini, L. (2015). Existential psychotherapy: An international survey of the key authors and texts influencing practice. *Journal of Contemporary Psychotherapy 45* (1): 3–10.

Craig, E. (ed.). (1988). Psychotherapy for freedom: The Daseinsanalytic way in psychology and psychoanalysis. [Special issue] *The Humanistic Psychologist 16* (1).

Craig, E. (2015). The lost language of being: Ontology's perilous destiny in existential psychotherapy. *Philosophy, Psychiatry, and Psychology 20* (2): 79–92.

Deurzen, E. van (1998). *Paradox and Passion in Psychotherapy: An Existential Approach to Therapy and Counselling*. Chichester: John Wiley and Sons.

Deurzen, E. van (2010). *Everyday Mysteries*, 2e. London: Routledge.

Deurzen, E. van (2012). *Existential Counselling and Psychotherapy in Practice*, 3e. London: Sage.

Deurzen, E. van (2014). Structural Existential Analysis (SEA): A phenomenological research method for counselling psychology. *Counselling Psychology Review 29* (2): 70–83.

Deurzen, E. van (2015). *Paradox and Passion in Psychotherapy: An Existential Approach*, 2e. Chichester: John Wiley and Sons.

Deurzen, E. van and Adams, M. (2016). *Skills in Existential Counselling and Psychotherapy*, 2e. London: Sage.

Deurzen-Smith, E. van (1997). *Everyday Mysteries*. London: Routledge.

Dilthey, W. (1989). *Introduction to the Human Sciences: Selected Works*, vol. 1 (ed. R.A Makkreel and F. Rodi). Princeton, NJ: Princeton University Press. (Original work published 1883.)

Du Plock, S. (ed.) (1997). *Case Studies in Existential Psychotherapy and Counselling*. Chichester: John Wiley.

Ellenberger, H.F. (1970). *The Discovery of the Unconscious: The History and Evolution of Dynamic Psychiatry*. New York: Basic Books.

Fillion, L., Duval, S., Dumont, S. et al. (2009). Impact of a meaning-centered intervention on job satisfaction and on quality of life among palliative care nurses. *Psycho-Oncology, 18* (12): 1300–1310.

Frankl, V.E. (1984). *Man's Search for Meaning* (revised and updated ed.). New York: Washington Square Press.

Frankl, V. (1985). *Psychotherapy and Existentialism. Selected Papers on Logotherapy*. New York: Simon & Schuster. (Original work published 1967.)

Frankl, V.E. (1986). *The Doctor and the Soul: From Psychotherapy to Logotherapy*, 3e (trans. R. Winston and C. Winston). New York: Vintage Books.

Heidegger, M. (1962). *Being and Time* (trans. J. McQuarrie and E. Robinson). New York: Harper & Row. (Original work published 1927.)

Heidegger, M. (1999). *Ontology – The Hermeneutics of Facticity* (trans. J. van Buren). Bloomington: Indiana University Press. (Original work published 1988.)

Henry, M., Cohen, S.R., Lee, V. et al. (2010). The Meaning-Making intervention (MMi) appears to increase meaning in life in advanced ovarian cancer: A randomized controlled pilot study. *Psycho-Oncology 19* (12): 1340–1347.

Heraclitus. (2001). *Fragments: The Collected Wisdom of Heraclitus* (trans. B. Haxton). New York: Viking Penguin.

Husserl, E. (1931). *Ideas: General Introduction to Pure Phenomenology* (trans. W.R.B. Gibson). New York: Macmillan. (Original work published 1913.)

Husserl, E. (2001). *Logical Investigations*, vol. *1* (trans. J.N. Findlay). New York: Harper & Row. (Original work published 1900.)

Jaspers, K. (1956). *Existenzphilosophie* (trans. W. Kaufmann). In: *Existentialism from Dostoevsky to Sartre* (ed. W. Kaufmann), 138–252. London: Penguin Books (Original work published 1941.)

Jaspers, K. (1963). *General Psychopathology* (trans. J. Hoenig and M.W. Hamilton). Chicago: University of Chicago Press. (Original work published 1913.)

Jaspers, K. (1971). *Philosophy of Existence* (trans. R.F. Greban). Philadelphia: University of Pennsylvania Press. (Original work published 1938.)

Kierkegaard, S. (1980). *The Concept of Anxiety* (trans. R. Thomte). Princeton, NJ: Princeton University Press. (Original work published 1844.)

Laing, R.D. (1965). *The Divided Self: An Existential Study in Sanity and Madness.* Harmondsworth: Penguin.

Längle, A. (2015). The power of logotherapy and the need to develop existential analytic psychotherapy. *International Journal of Psychotherapy 19* (1): 73–80.

Levinas, E. (1969). *Totality and Infinity: An Essay on Exteriority* (trans. A. Lingis). Pittsburgh, PA: Duquesne University Press. (Original work published 1961.)

MacKinnon, C.J., Smith, N.G., Henry, M. et al. (2014). Meaning-based group counseling for bereavement: Bridging theory with emerging trends in intervention research. *Death Studies, 38* (3): 137–144.

May, R. (1950). *The Meaning of Anxiety.* New York: Roland Press.

May, R., Angel, E., and Ellenberger, H.F. (eds.) (1958). *Existence: A New Dimension in Psychiatry and Psychology.* New York: Basic Books.

Merleau-Ponty, M. (1962). *Phenomenology of Perception* (trans. C. Smith). London: Routledge and Kegan Paul. (Original work published 1945.)

Moran, D. (2000). *Introduction to Phenomenology.* New York: Routledge.

Nietzsche, F. (1990). *Beyond Good and Evil* (trans. R.J. Hollingdale). Harmondsworth: Penguin. (Original work published 1886.)

Palmer, R. (1969). *Hermeneutics: Interpretation Theory in Schleiermacher, Dilthey, Heidegger and Gadamer.* Evanston, IL: Northwestern University Press.

Resnick, J. (1997). Jan Resnick. In: *R.D. Laing: Creative Destroyer* (ed. B. Mullan), 377–395. London: Cassell.

Sartre, J.-P. (1956). *Being and Nothingness – An Essay on Phenomenological Ontology* (trans. H. Barnes). New York: Philosophical Library. (Original work published 1943.)

Sartre, J.-P. (1976). *The Critique of Dialectical Reason* (trans. A. Sheridan-Smith). London: New Left Books. (Original work published 1960.)

Schneider, K.J. (2008). *Existential–Integrative Psychotherapy: Guideposts to the Core of Practice.* New York: Routledge.

Schneider, K. and Krug, O. (2017). *Existential-Humanistic Therapy.* Washington, DC: American Psychological Association.

Shahar, G. and Schiller, M. (2016). A conqueror by stealth: Introduction to the special issue on humanism, existentialism, and psychotherapy integration. *Journal of Psychotherapy Integration, 26* (1): 1–4.

Sheehan, T. (ed.) (2010). *Heidegger: The Man and the Thinker.* London: Transaction Publishers.

Spiegelberg, H. (1972). *Phenomenology in Psychology and Psychiatry: A Historical Introduction.* The Hague: Martinus Nijhoff.

Spinelli, E. (2005). *The Interpreted World: An Introduction to Phenomenological Psychology*, 2e. London: Sage.

Spinelli, E. (2006). *Tales of Un-Knowing: Therapeutic Encounters from an Existential Perspective.* Ross-on-Wye, UK: PCCS.

Spinelli, E. (2015). *Practising Existential Psychotherapy: The Relational World*, 2e. London: Sage.

Tillich, P. (1952). *The Courage to Be.* New Haven, CT: Yale University Press.

Vos, J., Craig, M., and Cooper, M. (2014). Existential therapies: A meta-analysis of their effects on psychological outcomes. *Journal of Consulting and Clinical Psychology, 83* (1): 115–128.

Wolfe, B.E. (2016). Existential-humanistic therapy and psychotherapy integration: A commentary. *Journal of Psychotherapy Integration 26* (1): 56–60.

Yalom, I. D. (1980). *Existential Psychotherapy.* New York: Basic Books.

Part I
Daseinsanalysis

Edited by
Erik Craig

Introduction

We humans have always been an issue for ourselves. Whether looking up at the night sky or gazing at a landscape; hungry, cold, and in need of food or shelter; shopping, dancing, playing a game, or fighting traffic; watching other human beings or nature; interacting with friends or loved ones; witnessing a birth or death; waking from a dream; brushing our teeth or making love; or simply feeling or wanting something without knowing what or why; we are always concerned with ourselves, our world, and even being itself, especially the fact that we now are, once were not, and, sooner than we might wish, once again won't be.

What is this world? Who am I to it? What does it matter? Does anything matter? Freud, like Plato, would say such questions arise from the healthy redirection of our more primitive erotic urges to more sublime activities like science and philosophy. The American existential psychologist Rollo May might say they come from a search for a sense of one's own being, an "I am experience." I suspect the humanistic integrative existentialist, Kirk J. Schneider, might suggest our wonderings arise from a sheer sense of awe. Frankl would likely find the source in the human being's search for meaning. Neuroscientists claim such questions are a product of what they call the human brain's "seeking system." Daseinsanalysts might suggest it is from our shadowy awareness of what it means to be and our anxiety about not-being. But do not be misled, for existentialists as a whole, the primary concern is not to explain our everyday life but, first and foremost, to *live* it, to *be* oneself, to *be* human. Along with these most basic of questions, every day existential therapists also wonder and engage others in wondering what it means to flourish and to suffer, to be limited or free, false or true. These are just some of the fundamentally human concerns that preoccupy

The Wiley World Handbook of Existential Therapy, First Edition. Edited by Emmy van Deurzen, Erik Craig, Alfried Längle, Kirk J. Schneider, Digby Tantam, and Simon du Plock.

existential psychotherapists, albeit each with their own unique language, focus, and aim that are in turn grounded in their own particular assumptions, theories, practices, and, most important, life experiences.

While all forms of existential therapy require more than the usual amount of study, focus, and life experience, Daseinsanalysis is particularly daunting, especially for students and aspiring practitioners whose first and often only language is English. Every major original text central to Daseinsanalysis was originally written in German by three men, one philosopher and two psychiatrists, all of whom lived within less than 100 km of one another as the crow flies. The philosopher Martin Heidegger spent virtually his entire life in southeastern Germany. His one Swiss psychiatrist devotee, Ludwig Binswanger, was born and lived most of his life in Kreuzlingen, Switzerland on the shores of Lake Constance. The other Swiss psychiatrist, Medard Boss, spent all but two years of his life in Zurich. These three daseinsanalytic thinkers lived less than two hours away by today's standards, and enjoyed not only regular visits but a rich and long-lasting correspondence. Deprived of access to this relatively small central European world, the majority of anglophiles are left without an experience of the historical, geographical, cultural, and relational context from which Daseinsanalysis arose. Even more challenging is the fact that exclusively English-speaking readers are only able to access the most important original texts through inadequate English translations replete with already obscure Heideggerian German rendered in even more off-putting hyphenated English translations.

However, all is not lost. In spite of their characteristic impenetrability, the translations also include many brilliantly clarifying passages that can suddenly remove, as Binswanger once put it, "the cataracts" of habitual thought and light up what we have never once thought before or, perhaps, thought but had neither the words nor daring to say. Many of these illuminating passages stay with one for the rest of one's life, altering forever the way one sees, lives, practices, and thinks. The genuinely striking thing about daseinsanalytic thought is that it so often turns everything of which we have remained so confident completely on its head, opening our eyes to a cosmos we could never have anticipated like those chained individuals of Plato's Cave who dared to leave the confines of the familiar and stare the sun in the face.

Adding to this more promising view, we have made a conscientious effort, wherever possible, to minimize the use of typically bewildering terminology of Heideggerese and write in the language of concrete everyday life. Whenever the use of German daseinsanalytic terms was necessary, we have done our best to voice them in clear English with the idea that accessible communication takes precedence over philosophical purity, a position also firmly maintained by Gion Condrau, Boss's analysand and most productive student.

Finally, we have not only tried to present the essential concepts, principles and practices of daseinsanalytic therapy but, where possible, to tell the stories of the circumstances and individuals behind them, hoping the stories will make the ideas themselves come alive for the reader.

Chapter 1 presents a detailed account of the birth and development of Daseinsanalysis as the first systematic approach to existential psychotherapy along with many less well known stories and perspectives of its two extraordinary "sleep-waking" twentieth-century progenitors, the psychoanalyst Sigmund Freud and the philosopher Martin Heidegger, before turning to the lives and works of the psychiatric Daseinsanalyst, Ludwig Binswanger, and the psychotherapeutic Daseinsanalyst, Medard Boss. In Chapter 2, the hermeneutic Daseinsanalyst Alice Holzhey-Kunz presents her exceptional historical and philosophical grasp of the theory and philosophy of Daseinsanalysis, reviewing the perspectives of both Binswanger and Boss before going on to present her own new third approach grounded in a fresh hermeneutic understanding of the meaning of psychic suffering. In Chapter 3 the reader will find a critical review of the early history of training in daseinsanalytic psychotherapy and a brief summary of the contributions of three senior practicing Daseinsanalysts who worked with Medard Boss in person and who have made significant contributions to the English pedagogy and literature in the field. In Chapter 4, Perikles Kastrinidis presents two fascinating case studies with one individual presenting with serious psychiatric symptoms and the other with the quintessentially existential concern of his own mortality. Chapter 5 presents an annotated bibliography of selective daseinsanalytic works and an extensive list of references for readers wanting to continue study on their own. Finally, Chapter 6 reviews the historical daseinsanalytic events occurring over the last 20 years of Medard Boss's life and going on to offer brief biographies of five major contributors to English daseinsanalytic literature. This is followed with an extensive discussion of the International Federation of Daseinsanalysis (IFDA), standards of training and education for becoming a Daseinsanalyst and basic issues facing the field today. The chapter closes with a brief discussion of present and future challenges for the field.

One of the difficulties of producing this part has been finding experienced English-speaking daseinsanalytic therapists, especially those personally acquainted with the Zurich school of Daseinsanalysis and Medard Boss, to make cogent contributions. I am most grateful to the Zurich Daseinsanalysts Alice Holzhey-Kunz and Perikles Kastrinidis for their intrepid commitment from the beginning. I am also uniquely appreciative to the Canadian psychoanalyst, Loray Daws, who unexpectedly appeared and took on much of the work required for the last two chapters, and, finally, for the generous, critical contributions of Thanasis Georgas from Greece and Robert Stolorow from the United States.

To close, in today's impatient, ambitious, and goal-oriented therapeutic climate the long, deep listening of talk therapy is often frowned upon, most often by those espousing rigidly defined evidenced-based practice. Daseinsanalysts take issue with such a perspective recalling not only Heidegger's remark that "language is the house of being" but also Freud's admonition of his similarly critical interlocutor in *The Question of Lay Analysis* questioning the value of mere words:

> Do not let us despise the *word*; it is the means by which we convey our feelings to one another, our method of influencing other people. Words can do unspeakable good and cause terrible wounds. No doubt 'in the beginning was the deed' and the word came later; in some circumstances it meant an advance in civilization when deeds were softened into words. But originally the word was magic – a magical act; and it has retained much of its ancient power. (Freud, 1926/1959, pp. 187–188)

Daseinsanalysts thus remind us in two ways not to disparage "mere conversation" for where there are words there is feeling and meaning, a life waiting to be born, if only we have the patience to listen and wait.

Reference

Freud, S. (1959). *The Question of Lay Analysis.* New York: Norton. (Original work published 1926.)

1

The History of Daseinsanalysis

Erik Craig

Initially appearing in the early 1940s, Daseinsanalysis was the first systematic approach to existential psychotherapy and arguably remains the most comprehensive, decidedly ontological approach in today's community of existential thinkers and practitioners. The original architects of Daseinsanalysis were two Swiss psychiatrists, Ludwig Binswanger (1881–1966) and Medard Boss (1903–1990), both of whom who were personally acquainted with the psychoanalyst Sigmund Freud (1856–1939) and the philosopher Martin Heidegger (1889–1976), to whom the approach unquestionably owes its very existence. Binswanger and Boss, each in their own way, fashioned their versions of Daseinsanalysis as an existential-ontological revisioning of Freud's psychoanalysis, drawing on Heidegger's phenomenological, hermeneutic analysis of the human being called *Daseinsanalytik*.

A Preliminary Overview

The term Daseinsanalysis refers to the analysis of human being, of what it is to *be* human. Heidegger used the term *Dasein* from the everyday German term meaning presence, existence, or being to designate human being. Heidegger interpreted *Dasein*, literally "there-being," as that distinctive kind of being who is capable of understanding being, including its own being, and who exists as being-in-the-world and inseparable from it. Though an uninviting term for many English speakers, the word *Da-sein* has the potential advantage of stripping away hidden, sedimented biases and assumptions that might come with the English words "human being." As for the second part of the compound, "*analysis*" is not carried out, as is commonly imagined, in the interest of dissecting or reducing things to smaller or separate units as it is in the natural sciences but, rather, for the purpose of loosening up or unraveling (from the Greek, *analyein*) the original-most meaning of things, emancipating wider, more

The Wiley World Handbook of Existential Therapy, First Edition. Edited by Emmy van Deurzen, Erik Craig, Alfried Längle, Kirk J. Schneider, Digby Tantam, and Simon du Plock.

authentic possibilities of human existence. As Heidegger (1987/2001, p. 115) pointed out, it was first used to describe Penelope's unraveling of her weaving and was also used, most aptly for psychotherapy, to describe the untying of the ropes of a prisoner or slave when being freed. Such an understanding of analysis discloses the fundamental nature and purpose of Daseinsanalysis as an essentially emancipatory, hermeneutic process releasing human beings to take up their right to be and to embrace their own possibilities for fuller, freer, more authentic ways of being in the world.

The earliest formulation of Daseinsanalysis belongs to Binswanger, who sought to develop a more adequate *scientific foundation for psychiatry and psychopathology*. A colleague, friend, and admirer of Sigmund Freud since first meeting him in 1907, Binswanger turned to phenomenology to provide a philosophical foundation for understanding the human being in psychology and psychoanalysis. Initially influenced by Edmund Husserl, Binswanger later turned to Martin Heidegger's analysis of human being, called *Daseinsanalytik*, to formulate "a phenomenological hermeneutic exegesis on an ontic-anthropological level" (Binswanger 1958a, pp. 269–270) before returning to Husserl once again late in life.

Unlike Binswanger, whose primary interest was scientific, Medard Boss was concerned with developing a *Daseinsanalytic foundation for therapeutic practice*. Originally an aspiring but disappointed artist, Boss turned to medicine and became a classically trained psychoanalyst, beginning with some preliminary analytic sessions with Sigmund Freud in Vienna and going on to include supervision with Eugen Bleuler in Zurich, orthodox supervision and study at the psychoanalytic institutes of London and Berlin, and ten years of study with Jung. In the late 1930s, the senior Binswanger introduced Boss to phenomenology and the works of Heidegger, but, after contacting Heidegger in the summer of 1947 and meeting him in person in 1949, Boss adopted the philosopher as his only authoritative teacher, although adding to this the deeply compatible influence of Eastern wise men with whom he apprenticed in the 1950s.

The brief historical accounts given below draw from the experiences, perspectives, and, to use a quintessentially daseinsanalytical term, the "thrownness" of the author who, thereby, assumes full responsibility for its unavoidable biases and omissions.

Ancestry of Existential Psychotherapy

Although the term psychotherapy only appeared in the final decades of the nineteenth century (Shamdasani 2005), its etymology comes from the ancient Greek *psyche*, meaning soul, and *therapeuein*, meaning to attend, serve, or wait upon. Ancient precursors of what we today call psychotherapy appeared in the Asclepian temples in Greece in 400–500 BCE where the connections between illness, dream, and cure were firmly established. Over the ensuing centuries, many fields of human endeavor have tried to alleviate human suffering though their respective methods, whether they be religious, superstitious, philosophical, or scientific (Ellenberger 1970).

From the fourteenth to the nineteenth centuries the Renaissance, the Enlightenment, and Romanticism steadily progressed from belief and suspicion to science and reason. The end of the Renaissance produced two extraordinary intellects and humanitarians:

William Shakespeare (1564–1616) and Rene Descartes (1596–1650). Whereas Shakespeare exposed the might of our human passions, their triumphs, tragedies, and comedies, moving and inspiring human beings to this day, Descartes clung to a supreme faith in the human intellect, laying a ground for the entire future of Western science and philosophy. As valuable as the latter's thought was for human progress, the dualism upon which it rested only rent the human being into two incompatible substances, a thinking thing (*res cogitans*) and a bodily, material thing (*res extensa*), but also tore human individuals from their fellow humans and their world by separating them into isolated minds, whole emotional worlds of experience entirely split off from one another. Contrary to the more unitive philosophies of the East, Western philosophy and science was plagued with this pernicious dualism.

Following in the footsteps of Descartes, the Enlightenment prioritized objective science, reason, the intellect, and cultural achievement over passion, the appetites, and the individual. It was not until early in the nineteenth century that Romanticism balanced the Enlightenment's partiality to science, certainty, and the definable, by emphasizing creativity and the arts, passions and the irrational, mystery and the ephemeral. The Romantics embraced a deep feeling for nature and mankind's relation to it and craved an understanding of the secrets of the human soul, including its most mysterious and enigmatic manifestations such as dreams, paranormal phenomena, madness, creativity, and genius.

Born in the wake of the Enlightenment and Romanticism, the nineteenth century brought the work of such writers and thinkers as Goethe, Kierkegaard, Dostoyevsky, Ibsen, Nietzsche, Schleiermacher, Dilthey, and Brentano, all contributing to the emergence of the three auspicious nineteenth-century intellectual developments, namely, existential thought, hermeneutics, and phenomenology, which are discussed in some detail in the introductory chapter of this volume.

1900: A Milestone Year

The end of the nineteenth century found philosophy and psychiatry in a crisis with respect to the study and understanding of human nature. The above mentioned philosophers, disgruntled with purely material, biological views of human nature, were hungry for a more essential view of the human as human, one that lay closer to *the experience of being human*, to what it really means to be human. Meanwhile, Sigmund Freud, a psychiatrist still in his mid-forties, was at the same time seeking to overcome the limitations of both neurobiological analysis and technical behavioral analysis with his new "science of the life of the soul" (*Wissenschaft vom Seelenleben*), called psychoanalysis, which sought the hidden meaningfulness of human suffering and shortcoming.

Then came the year 1900, the year of Nietzsche's death and a year that was to hold momentous promise for the future development of existential psychology. This one year alone saw the publication of Sigmund Freud's *The Interpretation of Dreams* (1900/1953), Edmund Husserl's, phenomenological *Logical Investigations* (1900/2001), and Wilhelm Dilthey's *The Rise of Hermeneutics* (1900/1996). With these publications in psychoanalysis, phenomenology, and hermeneutics, the three most essential foundations for Daseinsanalysis had been laid. Without a doubt, however, without Sigmund Freud there would be no such thing as Daseinsanalysis at all. His work is where Binswanger and Boss each began their own daseinsanalytic journeys.

Sigmund Freud: Reluctant Doctor, Unhappy Philosopher

In spite of Freud's indispensable contribution to modern psychotherapy, readers may puzzle over the fact that the phenomenological psychiatrists Ludwig Binswanger and Medard Boss would feel so indebted to a thinker who held appearances with such suspicion and invented a whole underworld of imagined psychological entities. Yet, in many ways Sigmund Freud was a quintessential existential man: anxious, willful, committed, self-conscious, meaning-driven, despairing and despondent, aware of the impermanence and transience of all living things, yet terrified of death.

As a child of the Enlightenment, with its emphasis on science and reason, and Romanticism, with its fascination with mystery and the irrational, even as a youth, Freud was greedy for knowledge of the world, especially of the human world. As deeply as he wanted to be a philosopher, his financial difficulties and political circumstances at the time pressed him to the unhappy choice of medicine. Thus, as the hermeneutic psychoanalyst Paul Ricoeur put it, Freud always found himself torn between "two universes of discourse: the discourse of meaning and the discourse of force" (1970, p. 92).

Freud's pre-ontological understanding of human being

Although Binswanger and Boss both recognized how hobbled Freud was by his natural scientific training and assumptions, they were steadfastly impressed by the underlying intuitive insights upon which his often absurd theories rested, what we might call Freud's *pre-ontological understanding* regarding the *meaningfulness*, the *hiddenness*, and the historical and relational *situatedness* of human existence.

On meaningfulness In spite of his naturalistic theories about human nature, when Freud declared that all dreams have "a meaning which can be inserted at an assignable point in the mental activities of waking life" (Freud 1953/1900, p. 1) and followed this with equal conviction regarding symptoms, jokes, everyday errors, and more, he was essentially designating his "science of the life of the soul" as a human science (*Geisteswissenschaft*), a science of meaning. As Boss put it, Sigmund Freud "was the first to have the audacity to claim that … meaningfulness was all-pervasive" (1963, p. 85) and to show "the thorough-going meaningfulness of all mental phenomena" (1963, p. 86). Thus, without once using the word, *Freud essentially designated all psychoanalysis as hermeneutic, a quest for meaning.*

On hiddenness In his search for meaning, Freud soon realized that a vast portion of what it is to be human and ourselves remains veiled, hidden, inaccessible to immediate perception and awareness. This led him to postulate the existence of unconscious processes of which he admitted "we know nothing" but, nevertheless, "are obliged to assume" (1933/1964, p. 70). Thus Boss wrote "in his untiring search for the unconscious, Freud was on his way to the concealed, to concealment as such ... but was unable to let concealment be the secret it is" (1963, p. 101). Instead, according to Boss, Freud "found it necessary to make subjectivistic, psychologic objects out of concealment in order to be able to drag it into the light and make it usable" (1963, p. 101). While Binswanger and Boss both acknowledged this flaw in Freud's thinking, Binswanger accepted the notion of an unconscious, simply understanding it "in a different way," namely in terms of "the various phenomenologically demonstrable modes and structures of being-in-the-world" (Binswanger 1957, p. 64). Meanwhile, Boss stridently opposed it, considering Freud's assumption of unconscious mental life, and even the idea of consciousness itself, to be entirely unnecessary (1963, pp. 85–101). In spite of this difference they both recognized that Freud had *grasped the essential ontological opacity of human existence.*

On situatedness Freud's understanding of human development, his theory of drives, his explanations of the aetiology of neurosis, and his concept of transference, all situated the human being in its world and in time. His understanding of the meaning of the drives and of neurotic symptoms emphasized both their whence and their whither, both the significance of being shaped by the past while also striving on their way toward its future. Likewise, although Freud's understanding of the psyche or soul (*Seele*) was radically dualistic, he intuitively understood that the individual was inextricably tied to its world as his theory of drives required an "object," some other being, whether human or otherwise, to achieve its aim. In other words, Freud saw that *the human being could not exist without an intimate connection with its world.*

Summary

Given these underlying insights of Freud, Boss was convinced of Freud's "deep understanding of man" (1963, p. 78), his "deep though unarticulated awareness of man's basic condition" (1963, p. 62). With such comments, Boss was not endorsing his analyst's speculative, natural scientific explanations of human phenomena but, rather, his tacit, pre-ontological understanding of the kind of being called human.

A Philosophical Revolt: Tilling the Soil for Daseinsanalysis

In the first decades of the new century, a number of European psychiatrists were disenchanted and restless with the positivistic/natural scientific and speculative/theoretical views of the human being predominant at the time. The German psychiatrist Karl Jaspers was among the first to challenge the "precarious foundation" and "reign of imagined insights," found in both brain and psychoanalytic "mythologies" (Jaspers 1941/1956, p.170). He was soon joined by four other gifted European contemporaries – Ludwig Binswanger, Viktor von Gebsattel, Eugene Minkowski, and Erwin Straus – to form a sophisticated pioneering cadre of phenomenological psychopathologists seeking a more adequate understanding in philosophical anthropology and grounded in a disciplined investigation of lived experience. These four also found considerable early intellectual and scientific companionship among such early-twentieth-century philosophers as Paul Natorp, Theodore Lipps, Henri Bergson, Max Scheler, and Martin Buber.

Although contemporary existential psychologists and psychotherapists may trace their heritage to one or more of these thinkers and practitioners, *the road to Daseinsanalysis unquestionably went through the psychoanalyst Sigmund Freud and the philosopher Martin Heidegger*. Boss and Binswanger both understood that Freud and Heidegger, though coming from completely separate disciplines and for different reasons, shared a common commitment to uncover and understand the essence of what it is to be human, particularly in the ways those essential truths remain hidden from view. Both Daseinsanalysts also understood that Heidegger's hermeneutic phenomenology was ideally suited mode of research for "making what was previously concealed, covered up, available as unconcealed, as out in the open" (Heidegger 1988/1999, p. 8). What Freud described, from his speculative, natural-scientific thinking, as "where id was, ego shall be" (Freud 1933/1964, p. 80), Heidegger described hermeneutically as "the task of making the Dasein which is in each case our own accessible to this Dasein itself with regard to the character of its being… hunting down the alienation from itself with which it is smitten" (Heidegger 1988/1999b, p.11). For Heidegger, the "understanding which arises in interpretation" is nothing less than "the *wakefulness* of Dasein for itself" (p. 12).

Martin Heidegger: From Consciousness to Existence

Born on September 26, 1889 in the village of Messkirch, Germany, Martin Heidegger's whole life and thought was imbued with the influence of the pastoral landscapes and mountains of Swabia and the simple fidelity of its people. Included within this world was the ordering presence of rural Catholicism and his Jesuit education where he excelled in Greek, Latin, and German and "acquired everything of lasting value" (Heidegger 1957/2010, p. 21). Even as a teenager, Heidegger was deeply intrigued by the fundamental concerns of theology and philosophy and, in 1907 when he was just 17, reading Franz Brentano's doctoral dissertation, *On the Several Senses of Being in Aristotle*, became "*the* ceaseless impetus" for *Being and Time* and his lifelong absorption in the question of the meaning of Being (Heidegger 1957/2010, p. 21). A year later, in 1908, Heidegger had discovered Hölderlin, and, in another year still, he had begun reading Husserl's *Logical Investigations.*

Heidegger received his doctorate in philosophy in 1913 and returned in the summer of 1915 as a *Privatdozent*, lecturing on Parmenides, Aristotle, and Kant. When, in the spring of 1916, Edmund Husserl joined Freiburg's philosophy faculty, Heidegger became his assistant, an arrangement that led to an intensely collaborative friendship. Within a few years the two had become the most influential voices in phenomenology, a powerful new mode of inquiry based on the elder's maxim, "To the things themselves" (Heidegger 1927/1962, p. 30). Although phenomenology was, for Heidegger, the most appropriate way to approach the question of being, his understanding of phenomenology gradually evolved from Husserl's transcendental attitude to a hermeneutic one which Heidegger much later described as letting "that which shows itself be seen from itself in the very way in which it shows itself from itself" (Heidegger 1927/1962, p. 58).

By the time Heidegger took a position at Marburg in 1923, his conception of the human being and the task of phenomenology was already evolving. *Whereas for Husserl the wonder of wonders was embodied in the human being's transcendental consciousness, for Heidegger, the greatest wonder was Being as such, the wonder that "there are beings at all and… not rather nothing"* (Heidegger 1929/1977b, p. 112). *Thus, to Heidegger, phenomenology was no longer a study of the contents of consciousness but, rather, a study of Dasein's whole every day, fundamentally embodied engagement in and with its world.* Nevertheless, their differences did not keep Heidegger from acknowledging that his own research "would not have been possible if the ground had not been prepared by Edmund Husserl" (Heidegger 1927/1962, p.62) and dedicating *Being and Time* to Husserl "*in friendship and admiration.*" Sadly, Heidegger's behavior and attitude toward his old master in the ensuing years followed the sad and familiar story of an acolyte's betrayal of a once beloved teacher and dear friend, a betrayal that began long before the former disciple's affiliation with the National Socialist party but certainly made deeper and more painful because of it. We shall return to this matter briefly again in Chapter 6 of this section.

Already a mature and spellbinding lecturer, with *Being and Time*, the 38-year old Heidegger had established himself as the pre-eminent philosopher of Being, tracing his most essential lineage back to the Greeks and Aristotle. For Heidegger, the first question of philosophy was the question of being (*Seinsfrage*), namely what it means *to be* in the first place. Since such a question could only be considered by the human being, *Dasein*, that a kind of being capable of understanding being (verb) and beings (noun), his second question became "*What is the way of being of human Dasein?*" How is it that human beings are such that they are capable of and concerned with understanding being? Although Heidegger began *Being and Time* by raising the first question, nearly the entire rest of the book was dedicated to answering the second with his *fundamental ontology of Dasein*.

Heidegger's Daseinsanalytik eventually uncovered and elucidated 20 or so invariant, universal structures or ontological characteristics. These include, among many others 1) the fact that *we are* at all; 2) that we are *thrown* a into time and culture not of our own choosing; 3) that, as a result, we of necessity fall in with our culture and time and largely exist as an inauthentic "they-self" or "herd-self;" 4) that we exist from beginning to end as always social, as *with-others*; 5) that we exist not just as being, but being-in-the-world; 6) that we exist as *stretching out in time* between the two profoundly personal and inescapable moments of 7) *being from our birth* and 8) *towards our death*; 9) that we exist as unavoidably *embodied* and, therefore, destined to decay and die; 10) that we are born with the *capacity to understand being, including our own*; 11) that from this very same capacity for understanding we see our human frailty, finitude, and unavoidable death and anxiously flee in the face of these human conditions; and 12) that we cannot help but be concerned with our world, the others with us, and we ourselves.

Taken as a whole, these and the other equiprimordial fundamental, ontological characteristics provide the philosophical, ontological bedrock for Daseinsanalytic psychology and psychotherapy. Bringing us thus face to face with our own fundamental condition is something "psychology had never before considered in this manner" and, in doing so, Heidegger "ultimately revolutionized psychology and psychiatry" (Spiegelberg 1972, pp. 20–21). Paul Tillich wrote that "only in the light of an ontological understanding of human nature can the body of material provided by psychology… be organized into a consistent and comprehensive theory" (1952, p. 65). Rollo May thought such ontological analysis of the existing human could also "give us a structural base for our psychotherapy" (May 1961, p. 83). Taken as a whole, these and the other equiprimordial fundamental, ontological characteristics provide the philosophical, ontological bedrock for Daseinsanalytic psychology and psychotherapy (Craig 2015).

As English readers often find Heidegger's obtuse, iconoclastic language forbiddingly rarified, it is easy for them to overlook the circumstance that, in fact, his entire fundamental ontology grows out of a respectful phenomenological analysis of how things present themselves simply and concretely in everyday life. He began from the bottom up, that is, with a careful phenomenological-hermeneutic analysis of our ordinary quotidian (*ontical*) human existence, just at it is lived by each and every human being.

Although *Being and Time* is almost universally considered Heidegger's most prodigious and influential work, he continued to develop his thought on the relationship between Being and Dasein throughout his life. Especially significant were a number of his works between 1930 and 1941, including his second great work, *Contributions to Philosophy (From Enowning)* (Heidegger 1989/1999a). These works reveal what is often referred to as "the turn" (*Die Kehre*) from phenomenology to thought, or from Dasein's relation to Being to Being's relation to Dasein, and the event of their mutually inter dependent co-arising known as *Ereignis*. It was actually this so-called "second Heidegger" with whom Medard Boss studied and collaborated in person from 1949 to 1972.

Daseinsanalysis: The Birth of Existential Psychiatry, Psychology, and Psychotherapy

A major difficulty for English students of Daseinsanalysis is that both Binswanger and Boss referred to their approaches as Daseinsanalysis (*Daseinsanalyse*). Although this demonstrates their shared, albeit distinctive, allegiance to Heidegger's ontological understanding of human existence, their respective Daseinsanalytic works represent largely different projects, each with their own separate aims, aspirations, and ways of understanding Daseinsanalysis as such. Whereas Binswanger designed and understood his Daseinsanalysis as *a research method* aimed at providing a more adequate *scientific foundation for psychiatry*, Boss fashioned his Daseinsanalysis as a radical, phenomenological revisioning of psychoanalytic *psychotherapeutic practice*. Finding appropriate, consistent English nomenclature for their two approaches has been a confounding preoccupation for secondary source English authors such as May, Angel, and Ellenberger (1958), who unfortunately translated Binswanger's Daseinsanalyse as "existential analysis" and Spiegelberg (1972, p.333), who, equally unfortunately for English readers, used only Heidegger's German term Daseinsanalytik to designate Boss's approach. In this part of the Wiley World Handbook we shall retain the term Daseinsanalysis (*Daseinsanalyse*) to refer to the work of both Daseinsanalysts, trusting the context to distinguish which approach, Binswanger's psychiatric or Boss's psychotherapeutic is being addressed.

One of the distinguishing characteristics of Daseinsanalysis compared to other existential psychotherapies, is its stalwart appreciation for Freud. Although many existential therapists today appear reactive to such Freudian constructs as transference, resistance, and repetition, according to Boss and Binswanger these ideas all refer to actual concrete human phenomena, albeit inadequately explained in crudely reductive bio-mechanistic terms. Today, Daseinsanalysts still claim that it is just as erroneous to dismiss Freud out of hand as it is to embrace his thinking as doctrinal truth. What is needed, rather, is a thoughtful, open-minded phenomenological-hermeneutic reformulation of the psychoanalyst's remarkable insights, no longer trapped in the language of *homo natura* but liberated into an understanding of *homo existentialis*, of *the human being as human and as a whole*. Boss and Binswanger were not entirely alone among existential therapists in their critical appreciation for Freud. American existential analysts like Rollo May, James Bugental, Henry Elkin, and Paul Stern also embrace essential elements of Freud's thought and practice, albeit with varying phenomenological criticisms and reappraisals.

Ludwig Binswanger: Daseinsanalytic psychiatry and psychopathology

Ludwig Binswanger was born April 13, 1881 into a family of prominent Swiss psychiatrists. His grandfather, the senior Ludwig Binswanger, founded the famously humanitarian psychiatric center, the Bellevue Sanatorium in Kreuzlingen, and his uncle, Otto Binswanger, treated Friedrich Nietzsche at the Mental Asylum in Jena, Germany. Deciding as a youth to follow in his family's footsteps, Ludwig Binswanger undertook medical studies in Zurich, Lausanne, and Heidelberg, then returned to Zurich to complete his training and education with Eugen Bleuler and Carl Jung at the Burghölzli Hospital.

When Freud invited Jung and his wife to visit him in Vienna, Jung invited Binswanger to join them, arriving together on the evening March 2, 1907. At 10 am the next morning, Freud and Jung met for the first time, not interrupting their conversation for 13 hours. Both Jung and Binswanger attended their first meeting of the Vienna Psychoanalytic Society the following Wednesday evening, March 6. When the Jungs left Vienna for holidays a few days later, the captivated Binswanger remained alone for another week. Thus began a decades-long friendship that continued to the end of Freud's life. Though their admiration for one another was not always reciprocal, Binswanger always held Freud with unwavering "personal affection and reverence" (Binswanger 1957, p. 99), never failing to acknowledge his "greatness and the indomitable spiritual and moral force of his personality" (Fichtner 2003, p. 219), so much so that, after a visit in 1927, Binswanger wrote in his diary, "with nobody else does one feel so small" (Fichtner 2003, p. 238).

Binswanger's appreciation for Freud's friendship and his "monumental" psychoanalytic technique did not deter him from disagreement. Dissatisfied with Freud's natural scientific understanding of human nature and hungry for a more adequate philosophic foundation for psychology and psychoanalysis, Binswanger soon took up the project of developing a *phenomenological anthropology*, a view of the human being in its totality with "a psychiatric-phenomenological research method" adequate to its subject. Binswanger was not concerned "primarily with mentally *ill* man, but with *man as such*" (Binswanger 1956, p.144), not with Freud's *homo natura* (natural man) but, rather, *homo existentialis* (existential or historical man; Binswanger 1963a, p. 150).

Binswanger's scientific phenomenology took a radical turn in 1927 with the publication of Heidegger's *Being and Time*. Initially coming to Heidegger's works through Husserl, the psychiatrist finally met Heidegger in person in January 1929. Binswanger first used the term Dasein in his mytho-poetic 1930 study entitled *Dream and Existence* (Binswanger 1930/1963a). In 1936 Binswanger presented his paper for Freud's eightieth year Festschrift entitled *Freud's Conception of Man in the Light of Anthropologie* (Binswanger 1947/1963b, pp. 149–181), challenging his friend and mentor's understanding of human beings as *homo natura* with a human scientific anthropological critique. Binswanger had been particularly impressed by Heidegger's hermeneutic understanding of *Dasein* as *being-in-the-world* (*In-der-Welt-sein*) with world being understood not as a physical world but a horizon of meaningful relationships and possibilities. For Binswanger, such an understanding of the human being meant the final destruction of "*the cancerous evil of all psychology* ... namely the dogma of the subject-object-cleavage of the world," (Binswanger 1946/1958b, p. 193, translation of "*das Krebsübel aller Psychologie*, nämlich der Lehre von der Subjekt-Objekt *spaltung* der 'Welt'" in Binswanger 1946/1947, p. 193).

Heidegger's understanding of Dasein's worldedness also meant that one could understand human beings, independent of health or illness, as simply having different ways or modes of being-in-the-world, modes that Binswanger, following Heidegger, called "World Designs" or "World Projects" (*Welt-Entwurf*). Binswanger went on to suggest that Dasein's world as such was constituted by three different but interrelated everyday worlds. He called these the "around-world" or "one-world" (*Umwelt*), meaning the environment including the body; the "with-world" (*Mitwelt*), referring to the social or human relational world; and the "own-world" or "self-world" (*Eigenwelt*), referring to the "inner," reflexive, self-relational world without at all implying that this tri-dimensional perspective in any way betrayed the primordial unity of Dasein.

Just as Binswanger did not hesitate to differ from Freud, he also questioned Heidegger's starkly individualistic characterization of Dasein at the expense of the social existence, especially loving "bi-modal" interpersonal relations, or the we-hood character of human existence. Deeply influenced by the relational existential philosopher Martin Buber, whom he knew personally and with whom he shared a decades long correspondence, Binswanger unfolded a "phenomenology of love," specifically in reaction to human loving having been "left freezing in the cold outside of Heidegger's picture of existence" (see Spiegelberg 1972, p. 206). Binswanger's phenomenology of love was thoroughly in keeping with the affectionate family atmosphere of his Kreuzlingen family sanatorium roots, albeit at odds with Heidegger's fundamental ontology of Dasein wherein Care (*Sorge*) was understood to naturally include the ontical possibility of love as a way of carrying out one's ontological capacity for being-with-others (*Mitsein*). Although Heidegger praised Binswanger's work and encouraged him to continue his understanding of psychopathology through a fundamental ontology of Dasein, he also recognized how the psychiatrist had stepped beyond *Being and Time* and failed to grasp its full ontological import. Binswanger eventually acknowledged his failure and attributed it to what he called a productive misunderstanding. Nevertheless, Binswanger and Heidegger continued to enjoy a thoughtful correspondence well into the 1950s even though Medard Boss had become Heidegger's so-called authorized spokesman in psychiatry, psychology, and psychotherapy. Unlike Boss, Binswanger continued to follow his own inclinations as an independent thinker and eventually returned to his previous master, Edmund Husserl, and phenomenological research emphasizing the importance of experience which, at that point, replaced the previous use of the term world (Holzhey-Kunz 2006, p. 286).

Unfortunately, little is known of Binswanger's actual, everyday practice of psychotherapy. Even his most well-known case studies include no account of his own specific, concrete psychotherapeutic activity, a lacuna perhaps explained by his comment that "with Daseinsanalysis alone, we cannot do psychotherapy. What is needed is the colossal knowledge and craft that has been put at our disposal by psychoanalysis" (Binswanger 1960, p. 254, author's free translation). Binswanger's few comments on the actual practice of psychotherapy were primarily attitudinal, emphasizing, for instance, Daseinsanalysis as a loving encounter between existential partners (*Daseinspartner*), who, eschewing abstract, theoretical discourse, meet person to person, Dasein to Dasein, and converse in the language of the individual's own everyday life (Binswanger 1960, p. 253). Beyond these broad strokes of insight, it was left to Medard Boss to develop and articulate a systematic Daseinsanalytic approach to psychotherapy.

Medard Boss: Daseinsanalytic psychotherapy[1]

Medard Boss was born October 4, 1903 in St. Gallen, Switzerland. When he was two, his parents moved to Zurich, where he remained for the rest of his life. Unlike Binswanger, Boss's parents were not doctors and his path to medicine was not so straight. Originally aspiring to be an artist, Boss was discouraged by his father, who thought painting a "breadless profession." Scheming to cure his son of his artist dreams he took him to the Pinakothek Museum in Munich to see the work of European masters. Boss ruefully admitted he had overestimated his own talents, succumbing to his father's "cure," though continuing to paint for the rest of his life.

On the way to psychoanalysis Returning to more pragmatic aspirations, Boss enrolled in medical school at the University of Zurich. When he happened across and read Freud's *Introductory Lectures on Psychoanalysis* (Freud 1916–1917/1961), he decided to take his 1925 summer semester at the University of Vienna, hoping to meet with Freud in person. Although his father supported medical studies in Vienna he refused

[1] Biographical material drawn from an autobiographical article by Boss (1973) and an interview by Craig (1988).

to pay for such a thing as analytic sessions with Freud. Undeterred, Boss wrote to Freud to request an appointment and the 69-year-old psychoanalyst agreed to meet with him at a reduced fee. To pay these fees, Boss had to forego meals, using his father's food allowance for his appointments instead. The cost of this strategy was that Boss's free associations were often accompanied by stomach growls to which Freud sometimes responded by dropping some shillings in Boss's pocket as he left, saying only that he didn't want the 22-year-old student to go hungry. Boss was struck by the fact that this was hardly in keeping with Freud's technical recommendations for the conduct of therapy.

After returning to Zurich to complete medical studies Boss continued his own psychoanalysis with Hans Behn-Eschenburg, affiliated with the Swiss Society for Psychoanalysis, and, like Binswanger, assisted Eugen Bleuler at the Burghölzli. He then trained at the Berlin Psychoanalytic Institute where he was supervised by Karen Horney, whom he described as the most human of the faculty, Otto Fenichel, and Harald Schultz-Hencke. Boss also took Institute classes with Wilhelm Reich, Hanns Sachs, and Siegfried Bernfeld and, for a time, worked at the Brain Injury Research Institute as an assistant to Kurt Goldstein. Boss's education and training at the highly orthodox Berlin Institute indelibly shaped his future opinion of psychoanalysis as hopelessly rigid and unable to escape the assumptions of the nineteenth-century physical sciences. Boss also trained for six months at the London Psychoanalytic Institute and assisted Ernest Jones at the National Hospital for Nervous Diseases. Boss returned to Zurich and the Burghölzi before finally opening his private practice and becoming director of the Schlössli Psychiatric Clinic in 1936.

Two years later, in 1938, Carl Jung invited Boss to join semi-weekly seminars at his lakeside home in Küsnacht. Although impressed by Jung's more "phenomenological" approach to depth psychotherapy and his criticism of Freud's causal-genetic thinking, when Jung ended the seminars after ten years, Boss left him behind. Nevertheless, Jung's influence remained with respect to the interpretation of dreams resulting in some dream scholars continuing to consider Boss a Jungian.

On the way to phenomenology Boss continued to grow more dissatisfied with the speculative, reductionistic theories of psychoanalysis, especially the replacement of the everyday phenomena of dreaming or waking, with representational symbols for Freud's drives or Jung's archetypes. Such hypothesized entities were never things one can encounter or experience directly but, for Boss, "merely assumed abstractions" (Boss 1953/1958, p. 58). Boss especially came to resent the labyrinthine symbolic interpretations requiring therapists to perform theoretically "tedious acrobatics" (Boss 1963, p. 234) that, as he admitted, may well cure patients of their initial symptoms but at the cost of developing "a new neurosis best called 'psychoanalytis'" (Boss 1963, p. 236). Given his discontent with such natural scientific theories, it came as quite a relief, even before meeting Jung, to find the more respectful human approach to psychological science found in the work of Ludwig Binswanger. Binswanger introduced his younger colleague to systematic phenomenology in the late 1930s, and Boss's earliest publications regularly cited Binswanger and other phenomenological psychologists including Erwin Straus, Victor von Gebsattel, and Hans Kunz. Most significantly, Binswanger introduced Boss to Heidegger's *Being and Time.*

On the way to Daseinsanalysis Boss began his own personal study of Heidegger in earnest while confined to a military bunker in the Alps during the Second World War. His initial experience was both disappointing and unpleasant as he initially found it impossible to understand even a single sentence. Doggedly persisting by reading passages over and over, he gradually began, as his friend Paul Stern later put it, "seizing upon islets of meaning in a vast sea of incomprehension" (Stern 1979, p. xiii.). The most decisive of these islets appeared to Boss in Heidegger's interpretation of the two different ways human beings care for other humans, namely, *intervening care* and *anticipatory care* (Heidegger 1927/1962, pp. 158–159). There, Boss recognized that what Heidegger called anticipatory care was a consummate philosophical description of Freud's technical recommendations for a therapist's relation to patients. Intervening care involves helping others by "leaping in" on their behalf by, for example, giving advice, medication, material assistance, or the like, thus taking over responsibility for others where they are unable to do so for themselves. Such care, however, comes with the danger of making them dependent and possibly even dominated and demoralized. In contrast to this, anticipatory or "leaping ahead" care, involves opening up perception and awareness within which others can see clearly for themselves just how things stand for them and freeing them to be responsible for themselves. With such anticipatory care, the therapist waits, Boss later wrote, "ahead of the patient in his existential unfolding" (Boss 1963, p. 73). For Boss, this distinction was the most incisive description he had ever read for Freud's recommendations regarding what psychoanalysts should and should not do.

Seeing the possibility for a richer, philosophically grounded understanding of his own psychoanalytic practice, after the war Boss wrote to Heidegger to inquire about the possibility of meeting him in person for help with his own contemplative or "reflective thinking" (*Besinnliche Denken*). Heidegger wrote back on August 3, 1947 with an invitation to visit him at his mountain hut in Totnauberg and asking for some Swiss "chocolate to support his work and thought." Although Boss and Heidegger exchanged a handful of letters over the ensuing two years, due to the border situation after the war, Heidegger did not meet Boss in person (or receive his chocolate) until the midsummer of 1949. From that time on, their relationship unfolded with increasing complexity. By the early 1950s Boss had devoted himself almost exclusively to his apprenticeship with the philosopher and the implications of his *Daseinsanalytik* for psychology, psychotherapy, and psychoanalysis, a devotion that Heidegger repaid by authorizing Boss's and not Binswanger's version of Daseinsanalysis as most authoritatively faithful to the philosopher's thought. Over the ensuing years their relationship grew not only through a correspondence of some 256 letters but also from personal visits and family journeys to Italy, Greece, and Turkey. They frequently visited one another in Heidegger's homes in Freiburg and Totnauberg and Boss's in Zurich and Lenzerheide. However, the culminating event of their relationship and for psychology and psychotherapy was the establishment of a series of seminars arranged for Boss's students and colleagues in Zurich, held almost entirely in Boss's own home in Zollikon and suitably known as the *Zollikon Seminars* (Heidegger 1987/2001). Auspiciously, Daseinsanalysts now have a detailed, albeit far from complete, record of their friendship and collaboration.

What is most remarkable, however, is that such a friendly, intensely collaborative relationship between an eminent philosopher and a medically trained psychoanalyst could ever occur in the first place. According to Boss, from the beginning Heidegger "saw the possibility that his philosophical insights would not be confined merely to the philosopher's quarters but might also benefit many more people, especially suffering people" (Boss 1987/2001, p. xvii). Heidegger's interest in providing a sound philosophical understanding of human beings for the regional sciences of psychology and medicine was matched by Boss's own professional aspirations, which were to use Heidegger's fundamental ontology to provide a philosophically "solid theoretical foundation, the genuine foundational science of another, completely new psychology, psychopathology and psychotherapy" (Boss 2002–2003, p. 26).

Prior to meeting Heidegger, Boss had openly acknowledged his indebtedness to Binswanger's published works and personal guidance in order to bring a phenomenological perspective to the practice of psychotherapy. His first major work emphasizing the perspective was on sexual "deviation" and relied on Binswanger's understanding of "the dual mode of existential love" and of sexual deviation as "an existential illness," not a medical disease. However, by the time the book was translated and published in English as *Meaning and Content of Sexual Perversions* in 1949 he had already begun criticizing Binswanger and other phenomenologists based on his new mentor Heidegger's *Daseinsanalytik.* Boss's second significant German work, this one on dream interpretation, appeared in 1953, with the English translation following five years later as *The Analysis of Dreams* (1958). In it, Boss critiques psychoanalytic, neo-analytic, and non-analytic views of the dream and introduces a phenomenological approach emphasizing a return to the dream itself, the reality of which, Boss declared, is to be considered as valid as that of waking. His case of a fortyish engineer (pp. 113–117) who reported 823 dreams in a three-year analysis became an instant classic in the field of dream interpretation. In 1954 Boss published a still untranslated German introduction to psychosomatic medicine, moving from a strictly biological view to the individual's own concrete experience of being embodied.

Boss's first comprehensive, systematic exegesis of his own Daseinsanalytic psychology and psychotherapy, *Psychoanalysis and Daseinsanalysis* (1963), significantly expanded an earlier, much smaller 1957 German book of the same title. In it, the impact of his decade-and-a-half-long study and collaboration with Heidegger were finally systematically exposed. This first major work provided a detailed comparison of the philosophical systems and assumptions underlying psychoanalytic and Daseinsanalytic views of the human being and offered Daseinsanalytic alternatives for understanding such clinical phenomena as "transference," "resistance," the "unconscious," and dreams. Boss followed this two years later with an English translation of his own favorite book, *A Psychiatrist Discovers India* (1959/1965), which described two lengthy stays in India and Indonesia, where he apprenticed with spiritual masters, and compared their thought with that of Martin Heidegger. Boss returned to the topic of dreams with his especially practical *I dreamt last night…* (1975/1977) articulating his phenomenological approach to dream analysis, called *explication*, and sharply distinguishing it from Freud's association-based symbolic interpretations. In a discerning phenomenologically guided discussion of dreaming and waking he writes, "Waking and dreaming" are "but two different modes of carrying to fulfillment the one and same historical human existence" (1975/1977, p. 190). In his magnus opus, *Existential Foundations of Medicine and Psychology* (1971/1979), Boss relentlessly impugned the psychoanalytic and medical worlds' unexamined tendency to subscribe to an objectifying, natural scientific ideal. The alternative, grounded in Martin Heidegger's *Daseinsanaytik*, was a rigorous philosophical interrogation of the human being as a new and adequate phenomenological foundation for thinking and practice. Boss was both proud and grateful to have Heidegger's own "patient and painstaking care" (Boss 1978, p. 12). Perhaps Boss's most gratifying Daseinsanalytic project, one that he worked on over the last years of his life, was to edit Heidegger's letters and conversations with him as well as transcripts and notes taken from the *Zollikon Seminars* (Heidegger 1987/2001).

The following three chapters of this section deal more explicitly with the philosophy, theory, practice, and method of Daseinsanalytic psychotherapy. However, before moving on to these more contemporary perspectives in daseinsanalytic theory and therapy, this chapter will close with an overview of critical theoretical considerations with respect to Heidegger's fundamental ontology of Dasein, especially as Being and ontology are so essential for understanding Daseinsanalysis in particular and, to some extent, existential psychology and psychotherapy in general. What follows is based on what Boss himself taught the author in person and was then presented in one of Boss's last articles, entitled *Recent Considerations in Daseinsanalysis* (1988). This view of fundamental ontology is unquestionably molded by the Heidegger after the "turn" who was the only Heidegger Boss knew.

Fundamental Ontology: The Philosophical Foundation of Daseinsanalysis

Heidegger's phenomenological hermeneutic analysis of Dasein, called Fundamental Ontology (*Daseinsanalytik*), provided a philosophical foundation for psychotherapeutic Daseinsanalysis, challenging both the scientistic-biologic and the conjectural-psychoanalytic views of *homo natura* reigning at turn of the century. As noted earlier, such a hermeneutic ontology also provides existential psychology and psychotherapy in general with a radical epistemological alternative to the kinds of calculative (quantitative) and speculative (theoretical) psychologies that have ruled the field for decades (Craig 2015, p. 84).

The term ontology, combining the roots *ontos*-, from the Greek word *on* (*ον*) for being, and *logos*, from the Greek word *logia* (λογία) for discourse, reason, or science, has been commonly understood as the science of being (the verb *is*), a pre-eminent concept of Daseinsanalysis and one vital for many other forms of existential psychotherapy as well. As Rollo May once put it, "the distinctive character of existential analysis is … that it is concerned with ontology, the science of being" (May 1958, p. 37). The term *being* is so prominent in existential counseling and psychotherapy that Deurzen and Kenwood's (2005) dictionary for the field lists 13 different compounds beginning with the word being, in addition to the word Being itself. As central as being may be to the field, there is no broad consensus as to its meaning and significance, and some approaches to existential psychotherapy, such as that of Irvin Yalom, eschew ontology entirely.

This reluctance to consider ontology is easy to understand in view of Boss's own admission that it took a full dozen years after first contacting Heidegger to feel like even a genuine beginner in understanding the philosopher's thought (Boss 1987/2001, p. xviii). Another obstacle is that Heidegger's primary concern was philosophy, not psychology which primarily deals of our most familiar ways of being, the concrete ontical mode of everyday human existence which brings most people into psychotherapy in the first place. Although Heidegger began his *ontological* existential (*existentiale*) analysis from and with this quotidian mode of existence, called *ontical* or *existentiell*, his ultimate concern was with the meaning of the very being (verb) of beings (noun), what it means *to be*, namely, the *is*-ness of being that allows everything that *is* to be at all. Nevertheless, as Boss intuited, such an ontico-ontological analysis would prove essential for understanding what it means to be human. Without an understanding of the human as such, how could any therapist ever hope to understand the particular human beings who appear concretely in his or her office.

The Human Being, Dasein

Heidegger considered the human being's (Dasein's) capacity to understand being, including its own being (*Seinsverstandnis*), to be not only the reigning characteristic of human being but "the sole concern of *Being and Time*" (Heidegger 1987/2001, p.188). Thus he wrote that Dasein is "ontically distinguished by the fact that in it's very Being, that Being is an issue for itself" and that "Dasein is ontically distinctive in that it *is* ontological" (Heidegger 1927/1962, p. 32). In our everyday existence as Dasein we just live our lives completely absorbed in the hustle and bustle of the day without stopping to reflect on its meaning. However, even in this unreflective mode of our quotidian existence, we always maintain an unthought, unspoken *pre-ontological* awareness of what it means to be, only vaguely, albeit occasionally disturbingly, apprehending our ontological nature. We all exist, whether we like it or not, with at least a dim appreciation of our more fundamental humanity, a way of being from which there is no escape, a way of being that, as human, we have to be (*zu sein haben*; Heidegger 1927/1962, pp, 32–33, 173).

A second primary ontological characteristic making Daseinsanalysis even possible is Dasein's constitution as *Da*, there, being-in-the-world (*In-der-welt-sein*). Although this there-ness of Dasein is often the first of its ontological characteristics to be discussed, there is more to the *Da* than is commonly recognized. As Heidegger put it, "In *Being and Time*… the 'Da' [of Da-sein] is determined… as 'the open'" (*das Offene* 1987/2001, p. 225), which, in *Being and Time* itself, is more often referred to as "the clearing" (*Lichtung*) or "realm of *world openness* or *world-illumination*." All three interpretations of *Da* – "there," "being-in-the-world," and "the open" or "clearing" – denote, not some location in physical space, but, rather, the whole horizon of meaningful engagements, relationships, and possibilities as which *Dasein* primordially exists.

These ontological reflections on Dasein, as abstract and daunting as they may seem, are in no way irrelevant to psychotherapy. Having been cast into the world as a human being and no other kind of being, we *have to be* these ways, and our relation to these fundamental characteristics as which we exist is, for Daseinsanalysts, the ultimate existential source of our suffering. We are there in the midst of a confusing and unpredictable world, realizing what it is to be and to be fragile, finite, vulnerable, uncertain, transient, and always on our way to death. This is no less true of the therapist's existence than it is of the those who come for help.

To summarize, Daseinsanalysis rests on three particularly foundational ontological characteristics of Dasein: (1) its understanding of being including its own being, (2) its there-ness, worldedness, or open-ness of being, and (3) its ontico-ontologic essence and, with this, its everyday pre-ontological understanding of what it means to have to be a human being.

Three basic meanings of the word *being* in Daseinsanalysis

Heidegger used the word being (*sein*) in so many different ways in his collected works that readers and even serious scholars are often left completely baffled as to what actually is meant. The Heidegger scholar Tom Sheehan (2015) identified over 60 of these different uses, not including the many compound terms using the word to Dasein (pp. 5–8). In the face of such perplexity, Boss wrote to Heidegger to ask how best to translate the most basic of terms for the English edition of *Psychoanalysis and Daseinsanalysis*. Heidegger replied as follows:

> The suggestion to translate (a) *das Seiende* or *Seiendes* as "being" or "particular being," (b) *Seiendheit*, in the sense of the mode of being of a specific species of things or living beings, as "being-ness, 2 (lower case), and (c) *Seyn*, as such, as Being-ness (capitalized) seems best. To be sure, in the sufficient distinction between (b) and (c) the whole road of my thinking is concealed. (Boss 1963, 36ftn)

What follows is a discussion of this dense, illuminating, but widely overlooked passage.

Particular being The first and most familiar way as which Dasein finds itself is as a particular (ontic) human being, in its everyday (ontic) particular world. For instance, right now I exist as a particular man, writing a particular sentence, watching a particular cat outside, sitting under a particular tree. This concrete ontical way of being is how we live our concrete lives, how we usually find ourselves living, breathing, and having our being. Ironically, although we may feel "ontically 'closest'" to ourselves in this everyday world, we are simultaneously "ontologically farthest" (Heidegger 1927/1962, p. 37). In our everyday ontical worlds we are usually only dimly aware of *what* we are ontologically, namely, that kind of being called human with all its inescapable contingencies, limitations, and possibilities. Our absorption in the everydayness of existence leaves us strangers to our humanity, our distinctively human being-ness. And yet, without this concrete, particular way of being, we would not be at all. Although psychotherapeutic practice is carried out in this ontical mode of existing, this same everyday practice requires that we understand what it is to be human in the first place, the very human-ness or being-ness that we share with those who come to visit.

Being-ness The ontological concern with being-ness is the central concern of each of the regional sciences. Felinology, for instance, is concerned with the cat-ness of all particular cats and dendrology with the tree-ness of all particular trees. In the regional science of psychology and psychotherapy we are concerned with the being-ness, the human-ness of all particular humans, with what makes all human beings *human* in the first place. The quintessential question for Daseinsanalysts and, hopefully, for other existential psychotherapists is: *What universal, invariant, ontologically given characteristics constitute us as human and not some other kind of being?* To be ontological (note lower-case) a characteristic must obtain in every moment of every single human being's existing (Craig 2015, p. 84). Such a standard exacts the highest standards of discernment and delimits the number of possibilities for such claims in advance and, according to Churchill (2013, p. 220), Heidegger himself only identified some twenty-plus or so such invariant characteristics, called *existentials*, in the whole of *Being and Time*. Taken as a whole these characteristics are determinative of the human *as* human, the being-ness of Dasein (again, note lower-case being-ness). As noted earlier, Boss was convinced that these phenomenologically derived ontological characteristics could provide a "solid theoretical foundation, the genuine foundational science of another, completely new psychology" (Boss 2002–2003, p. 26). The existentials, taken as a whole, thus constitute the hermeneutic Daseinsanalytic understanding of the human, replacing the calculative, biological, and the speculative, theoretical epistemological grounds that otherwise dominate our field. *Concern with these fundamental ontological characteristics of the human being is what defines Daseinsanalytic science.*

Many of these two dozen or so characteristics such as facticity, understanding of being, being-in-the-world, being mooded, being social, being thrown, being finite, being free, being-towards-birth, and being-towards-death have been mentioned previously in this chapter as well as the introduction. However it is essential to note that although these characteristic are determinative of the human as human, they are not determinative of the way of being of our individual lives as lived. Rather, while given to us *a priori* simply by virtue of being human, it is left for each us to choose (or not) how we shall fulfill (or not) the possibilities of each universal human characteristic, that is, how we shall understand, how we shall be social, how we shall be free, how we shall live knowing we are on our way to death, and so on. In other words, the characteristics are given to us as fallow, open fields of existential potentiality for being that remain our responsibility to fulfill within the context of our everyday ontic existence. Indeed it is the essential task of the Daseinsanalytic psychotherapist to accompany and engage the other in the appropriation of this freedom to be.

Four advantages recommend such a phenomenological-hermeneutic fundamental ontology. First, such findings can be intuitively verified in our own immediate experience. Second, they provide an elegant and at the same time profound structural understanding of the meaning of *the human as human and as a whole*. Third, this meaningful structural understanding, this ontological scaffolding, is capable of organizing and holding the possibilities and results of our entire body of psychological research. Finally, these ontological characteristics provide the therapist with a vibrant perspective for understanding and engaging the individual, the possibilities of which will be discussed in detail in the following three chapters.

Beingness-as-such Heidegger closed his famous inaugural address at Freiburg with this question: "Why are there beings at all, and why not rather nothing?" (1929/1977b). In raising this question, he was not pointing to some kind of hopeless nihilism, as many may be tempted to read it, but, rather to that miracle that anything is, that we ourselves are. Heidegger's original being question (*Seinsfrage*) is not about particular being or being-ness but, rather, about the being (verb) of these beings (noun). What does it mean to be at all? What is this *event* we call being, *the shared is-ness that allows everything that is to be in the first place?* Heidegger designated this particular meaning of the term being as *Being-ness* (note upper-case) or Beingness-as-Such and called this distinction between beings (noun) and being (verb), the *Ontological difference.* After the so-called turn, Heidegger puzzled over how to highlight this difference, sometimes spelling the German *Sein* as *Seyn*, or *Sein* with an X through it, designating the fact that Beingness-as-Such was not really any kind of entity or being but rather nothing. Heidegger was clear that the question of Beingness-as-Such lay beyond the province of the regional sciences, including psychology, but rather was entirely the concern of philosophical ontology. Ironically, Heidegger ultimately had to admit that he himself had failed to answer this question for himself.

Nevertheless, it remains the case that as both simple human beings and psychotherapists we go on, usually unwittingly presupposing this wonder of Being-as-such. As Craig (2015) put it, "although the meaning of Being-as-such rests beyond the reach of the regional sciences, including psychology, Being itself lies trembling, undulating beneath them all, like the ocean beneath our mightiest scientific armadas which navigate across its surface entirely at its affordance" (p. 85). While the answer to the question of the meaning of that most simple and mighty of words, *is* and *to be*, lies beyond the reach of the practicing psychotherapist, the matter of sheer existence, *that* we are, what Heidegger called "facticity" (*Faktizität*), does prove opportunities for valuable therapeutic reflection. How would it be for you not to exist? What might it have been like if your particular mother, father, sister, brother, lover, or teacher had never existed at all? What if such and such a thing had never happened? Such questions of non-being often yield startling, never previously considered meanings of being.

Heidegger's "Turn" (*Kehre*): Fundamental Ontology to the Reciprocal Openness (*Offenheit*) of Being and Dasein

In the 1930s Heidegger shifted his focus from the phenomenology of Dasein to the reciprocal openness of Being and Dasein. According to the later Heidegger, the openness of Being as such afforded the possibility that such a being as the human being, Dasein, could be in the first place, and the perceiving, understanding openness of Dasein, in turn, is what affords Being the possibility to appear and to be understood as well. Boss put this as follows:

> A human openness is required for anything to become present, or to be, but also the openness of Dasein itself, in turn requires Being in order for it [Dasein] to be. The "light-of-human-existence" and "everything-else-that-is" require one another and "call on" one another in a unified inseparable "e-vent" [Ereignis]. Ereignis is the indivisible unity of the appeal of Being to Dasein and of Dasein's response to this appeal. (Boss 1988, p. 61, author's brackets)

Many psychoanalysts and even some Daseinsanalysts find this turn unfortunate as, with it, Heidegger not only abandoned fundamental ontology but his original, creative understanding of hermeneutic phenomenology as well. Although Heidegger himself denied that, with this turn or reversal, he had abandoned the fundamental question of *Being and Time*, question of Being and Time" with this turn or "reversal" (Heidegger 1963, p. xviii), the question is widely debated among Daseinsanalysts today.

Nevertheless, having been taught by the later Heidegger, for his own Daseinsanalytic psychotherapy Medard Boss wholeheartedly embraced Heidegger's understanding of Dasein as the being whose ontological calling is to serve as a "Shepherd of Being" (Heidegger (1947/1977a, p. 210), a role which Heidegger describes as follows:

> Man is ... "thrown" from being itself into the Truth of Being, so that ek-sisting in this fashion he might guard the truth of Being, in order that beings might appear in the light of their Being as the beings they are. (1947/1977a, p. 210)

Always the therapist and concerned with the philosophical foundation for therapeutic Daseinsanalysis, near the end of his life Boss drew Heidegger's later thinking into the practice of psychotherapy as follows: "the relationship between Being and Dasein not only makes psychotherapy possible in the first place, but also gives psychotherapy its most fundamental purpose, that is, for the therapist to respond to the appeal of the patient to be" (Boss 1988, p. 61).

References

Binswanger, L. (1947). *Uber die daseinsanalytische Forschungsrichtung in der Psychiatrie* [On the direction of daseinsanalytic research in psychiatry]. In: *Ausgewahlte Vortrage und Aufsatz:* vol. I, *Zur Phenomenologischen Anthropologie* (ed. L. Binswanger), 190–217. Bern: A Franke AG. Verlag. (Original work published 1946.)

Binswanger, L. (1956). Existential analysis and psychotherapy. In: *Progress in Psychotherapy* (ed. F. Fromm-Reichman and J.L. Moreno), 144–148. New York: Grune & Stratton. (Original work published 1954 as *Daseinsanalyse and Psychoanalyse* [Daseinsanalysis and psychoanalysis]).

Binswanger, L. (1957). *Sigmund Freud: Reminiscences of a Friendship* (trans. N. Guterman). New York: Grune & Stratton.

Binswanger, L. (1958a). The case of Ellen West (trans. E. Angel.). In: *Existence: A New Dimension in Psychiatry and Psychology* (ed. R. May, E. Angel, and H.F. Ellenberger), 237–364. New York: Basic Books. (Original work published 1946.)

Binswanger, L. (1958b). The existential analysis school of thought (trans. E. Angel). In: *Existence: A New Dimension in Psychiatry and Psychology* (ed. R. May, E. Angel, and H.F. Ellenberger), 191–213. New York: Basic Books. (Original work published 1946.)

Binswanger, L. (1960). Daseinsanalyse und Psychotherapie ll. *Acta Psychotherapeutica et Psychosomatica 8*: 251–260.

Binswanger, L. (1963a). Dream and existence. In: *Being-in-the-World: Selected Papers of Ludwig Binswanger* (ed. and trans. J. Needleman), 222–248. New York: Basic Books. (Original work published 1947.)

Binswanger, L. (1963b). Freud's conception of man in the light of anthropology. In: *Being-in-the-world: Selected papers of Ludwig Binswanger* (ed. and trans. J. Needleman), 149–181. New York: Basic Books. (Original work published 1947.)

Boss, M. (1949). *Meaning and Content of Sexual Perversions: A Daseinsanalytic Approach to Psychopathology and the Phenomenon of Love* (trans. L.L. Abell). New York: Grune & Stratton. (Original work published 1947.)

Boss, M. (1958). *The Analysis of Dreams* (trans. A.J. Pomerans). New York: Philosophical Library. (Original work published 1953.)

Boss, M. (1963). *Psychoanalysis and Daseinsanalysis* (trans. L.B. Lefebre). New York: Basic Books. (Original work published 1957.)

Boss, M. (1965). *A Psychiatrist Discovers India* (trans. H.A. Frey). London: Oswald Wolff. (Original work published 1959.)

Boss, M. (1973). Medard Boss. In: *Psychotherapie in Selbstdarstellungen* [Psychotherapy in autobiography] (ed. H.G. Pongratz), 75–106. Bern: Verlag Hans Huber.

Boss, M. (1977). *"I Dreamt Last Night...": A New Approach to the Revelations of Dreaming – and its Uses in Psychotherapy* (trans. S. Conway). New York: Gardner Press. (Original work published 1975.)

Boss, M. (1979). *Existential Foundations of Medicine and Psychology* (S. Conway and A. Cleaves, Trans.). New York: Jason Aronson.

Boss, M. (1988) Recent considerations in Daseinsanalysis. *The Humanistic Psychologist 16* (1): 58–74.

Boss, M. (2001). Preface to the first German edition of Martin Heidegger's Zollikon lectures. In: M. Heidegger, *Zollikon Seminars: Protocols – Conversations - Letters* (ed. M. Boss, trans. F. Mayer and R. Askay), xi–xxi. Evanston, IL: Northwestern University Press. (Original work published 1987.)

Boss, M. (2002–2003). Martin Heidegger applied to psychiatry and the modern world. *Review of Existential Psychology and Psychiatry 27* (1–3): 23–31.

Craig, E. (1988). An encounter with Medard Boss. *The Humanistic Psychologist 16* (1): 24–55.

Craig, E. (2015). The lost language of being: Ontology's perilous destiny in existential psychotherapy. *Philosophy, Psychiatry, and Psychology 22* (2): 79–92.

Churchill, S.D. (2013). Hemeneutic pathways through trauma and recovery: A "hermeneutics of facticity." *The Humanistic Psychologist 41* (3): 227–282.

Deurzen, E. van and Kenwood, R. (2005). *Dictionary of Existential Psychotherapy and Counseling*. London: Sage.

Dilthey, W. (1996). The rise of hermeneutics. In: *Hermeneutics and the Study of History: Selected Works*, vol. *IV* (ed. R.A Makkreel and F. Rodi), 235–260. Princeton, NJ: Princeton University Press. (Original work published 1900.)

Ellenberger, H.F. (1970). *The Discovery of the Unconscious: The History and Evolution of Dynamic Psychiatry*. New York: Basic Books.

Fichtner, G. (ed.) (2003). *The Sigmund Freud-Ludwig Binswanger Correspondence: 1908–1938* (trans. A.J. Pomerans). London: Open Gate Press.

Freud, S. (1953). The interpretation of dreams. In: *The Standard Edition of the Complete Psychological Works of Sigmund Freud*, vols. 4 and 5 (ed. and trans., J. Strachey), 1–625). London: Hogarth Press. (Original work published 1900.)

Freud, S. (1961). Introductory lectures on psycho-analysis. In: *The Standard Edition of the Complete Psychological Works of Sigmund Freud*, vols. 15 and 16, (ed. and trans. J. Strachey). London: Hogarth Press. (Original work published 1916–1917.)

Freud, S. (1964). New introductory lectures on psycho-analysis. In: *The Standard Edition of the Complete Psychological Works of Sigmund Freud*, vol. *22* (ed. and trans. J. Strachey), 1–182. London: Hogarth Press. (Original work published 1933.)

Heidegger, M. (1962). *Being and Time* (trans. J. McQuarrie and E. Robinson). New York: Harper and Row. (Original work published in 1927.)

Heidegger, M. (1963). Preface (a letter to Father Richardson). In: *Heidegger: Through Phenomenology to Thought* (ed. W.J. Richardson), viii–xxiv. The Hague: Martinus Nijhoff.

Heidegger, M. (1977a). Letter on humanism. In: *Basic Writings* (ed. D.F. Krell), 193–242. New York: Harper & Row. (Original work published 1947.)

Heidegger, M. (1977b). What is metaphysics? (trans. D.F. Krell). In: *Basic Writings* (ed. D.F. Krell), 91–112. New York: Harper & Row. (Original work published 1929.)

Heidegger, M. (1999a). *Contributions to Philosophy (from Enowning)* (trans. P. Emad and K. Maly). Bloomington: Indiana University Press. (Original work published 1989.)

Heidegger, M. (1999b). *Ontology – The Hermeneutics of Facticity* (trans. J. van Buren). Bloomington: Indiana University Press. (Original work published 1988.)

Heidegger, M. (2001). *Zollikon Seminars: Protocols – Conversations - Letters* (ed. M. Boss, trans. F. Mayer and R. Askay). Evanston, IL: Northwestern University Press. (Original work published 1987.)

Heidegger, M. (2010). A recollection (trans. H. Seigfried). In: *Heidegger, The Man and the Thinker* (ed. T. Sheehan), 21–22. New Brunswick, NJ: Transaction Publishers. (Original work published 1957.)

Holzhey-Kunz, A. (2006). Ludwig Binswanger: Psychiatry based on the foundation of philosophical anthropology. In: *Images in Psychiatry: German Speaking Countries* (ed. E.M. Wolpert, K. Maurer, A.H. Rifai et al.), 271–288. Heidelberg, Germany: Universitatsverlag Winter.

Husserl, E. (2001). *Logical Investigations*: Vol. *1* (trans. J.N. Findlay). New York: Harper & Row. (Original work published 1900.)

Jaspers, K. (1956). On my way to philosophy. In: W. Kaufmann (Ed.), *Existentialism from Dostoevsy to Sartre* (ed. W. Kaufmann), 158–185. New York: Plume, Penguin Group. (Original work published 1941.)

May, R. (1958). Contributions of existential psychotherapy. In: *Existence: A New Dimension in Psychiatry and Psychology* (ed. R. May, E. Angel, and H.F. Ellenberger), 37–91. New York: Basic Books.

May, R. (ed.) (1961). *Existential Psychology*. New York: Random House.

May, R., Angel, E., and Ellenberger, H.F. (eds.) (1958). *Existence: A New Dimension in Psychiatry and Psychology*. New York: Basic Books.

Ricoeur, P. (1970). *Freud and Philosophy: An Essay on Interpretation* (trans. D. Savage). New Haven, CT: Yale University Press.

Shamdasani, S. (2005). "Psychotherapy": The invention of a word. *History of the Human Sciences 18* (1): 1–22.

Sheehan, T. (2015). *Making Sense of Heidegger: A Paradigm Shift*. London: Rowman & Littlefield International.

Spiegelberg, H. (1972). *Phenomenology in Psychology and Psychiatry: A Historical Introduction*. The Hague: Martinus Nijhoff.

Stern, P.J. (1979). Introduction to the English translation. In M. Boss. *Existential Foundations of Medicine and Psychology* (trans. S. Conway and A. Cleaves), ix–xxii. New York: Jason Aronson.

Tillich, P. (1952). *The Courage to Be*. New Haven, CT: Yale University Press.

2

Philosophy and Theory

Daseinsanalysis – An Ontological Approach to Psychic Suffering Based on the Philosophy of Martin Heidegger

Alice Holzhey-Kunz

Introduction

The Role of Philosophy in Daseinsanalysis

Daseinsanalysis is unique in the central importance it accords to philosophy. Where other psychotherapeutic movements refer to philosophy, they do so purely to provide a philosophical basis to their psychological theories and therapeutic methods. Only Daseinsanalysis draws its conceptions and methods directly from philosophy – chiefly from Martin Heidegger's philosophy. Therefore, in Daseinsanalysis the usual distinction between psychology and philosophy is suspended. Whereas usually descriptions of specific phenomena of human existence are distinctively "psychological" because they are guided by a specific psychological theory, Daseinsanalytic descriptions of such phenomena are "philosophical" because they are guided by a philosophical understanding of the human being.

At first sight, this shared philosophical orientation seems to provide a solid common foundation for Daseinsanalytic thinking and Daseinsanalytic practice. But the opposite is the case. As we have seen in the previous chapter, Daseinsanalysis cannot even be traced back to one single origin, although Ludwig Binswanger was the first who started to refer to his work as "Daseinsanalytic" in 1946. As early as 1952, his former student Medard Boss put forward a radically different approach, which he also termed "Daseinsanalytic" (1952) and in 1957 he even claimed to be the sole representative of "Daseinsanalysis," arguing that Binswanger's work was based on a radical misinterpretation of Heidegger's philosophy and that therefore he was not entitled to use the Heideggerian term "Daseinsanalytic" as its label (Boss 1963).

Boss's claim is supported by the fact that he was philosophically guided by Heidegger himself thanks to a personal friendship and collaboration that had started shortly after

The Wiley World Handbook of Existential Therapy, First Edition. Edited by Emmy van Deurzen, Erik Craig, Alfried Längle, Kirk J. Schneider, Digby Tantam, and Simon du Plock.

the Second World War. But this is not the only or even the decisive reason for the unbridgeable gulf between the two versions of "Daseinsanalysis." The decisive reason is a fundamental change or "turn" in Heidegger's thinking that began in the 1930s. Whereas Binswanger relied exclusively on the early masterpiece *Being and Time* (published in 1927), Boss received philosophical instruction from the "late" Heidegger in the 1950s and 1960s, when the philosopher had long since abandoned his early position in *Being and Time*. Accordingly, the unbridgeable gulf between the two schools of Daseinsanalysis is primarily created by Binswanger's reliance on *Being and Time* and Boss's adherence to the late Heideggerian conception of being after the "turn" in his thinking.

However, Boss's criticism of Binswanger's interpretation of *Being and Time* was not unfounded, even if it did not identify the main problem. Binswanger did lack the genuinely existential approach that is central to Heidegger's understanding of human being as "Dasein." If you rely on "*Being and Time*" as an *existential* analysis of Dasein, it delivers the philosophical base for a third Daseinsanalytic approach to psychic suffering, which I have developed as an existential-hermeneutic alternative first to Boss's approach, but also to Binswanger's.

The Role of Psychopathology in Daseinsanalysis

There is a deep conviction in Daseinsanalysis that all psychotherapy must be grounded in an adequate understanding of the patient's suffering. This is a conviction that Daseinsanalysis shares with psychoanalysis and which distances it from psychotherapeutic movements that focus one-sidedly on what makes a life meaningful and fulfilled without requiring any developed understanding of psychic suffering. But whereas Freudian psychoanalysis approaches psychic suffering from a psychological perspective of early childhood development, Daseinsanalysis explores it from a philosophical perspective that is taken from Heidegger's ontological understanding of the human being. Because this is true of all three Daseinsanalytic schools of thought, I think it most informative to focus on the three alternative psychopathological conceptions and to explain their distinctive characteristics as the result of three diverging references to Heidegger's philosophy.

Ludwig Binswanger: Daseinsanalytic Psychiatric Research Guided by a Transcendental-ontological Perspective

It is important to realize that Binswanger conceptualized Daseinsanalysis as a form of psychiatric research and not as a kind of psychotherapeutic practice. Only with Boss did Daseinsanalysis become a therapeutic alternative to psychoanalysis and begin to be regarded as a special school of psychotherapy. Accordingly, Binswanger's method of research does not depend on any personal therapeutic relationship between the investigator and the patient. Binswanger is proud of having developed a thoroughly scientific method of research that is not contaminated by any of the researcher's personal prejudices because it does not even demand empathy for the patient to be investigated. In this he follows *Edmund Husserl*'s ideal of phenomenology as a "strict science."

"World-project" as the Key Term of Binswanger's Daseinsanalytic Research

However problematic Binswanger's reference to the philosophy of Heidegger may be judged to be, it was highly productive because it gave Binswanger the idea of a totally new and highly original understanding of mental illness. This understanding is guided by the term "world-project," which Binswanger has drawn from Heidegger's lecture "The essence of reasons" (Heidegger 1929/1995; see Binswanger 2004, 191ff.; Holzhey-Kunz 2006). I shall try to explain this term as concisely as possible. "World" is used to refer neither to the universe of things nor to a person's inner or external world but to the all-embracing "horizon of meaning" in which all a person's experiencing, thinking, and acting take place. Because this horizon is never identical for different individuals, it is exactly their own "world" or "world-project" that makes each person a unique individual. Binswanger introduces this term into psychiatry because he realizes that this term allows for a non-judgmental distinction between mentally healthy and mentally ill individuals. The logic runs as follows: if every man and woman lives in his or her own world-project, the same must be equally true for those who are mentally ill: they are distinguished from healthy individuals by living in a different world-project (see Binswanger 2004, p. 198, explanatory note 9).

The Concept of the Individual "World-project" as a Hermeneutic Tool

Daseinsanalytic research is therefore the investigation of the individual world-project of someone labelled with a psychiatric diagnosis. Two major advantages of exploring the underlying world-project in mental illness should be indicated. First, this allows for a view of the neurotic or psychotic individual in its *wholeness*. Second, it enables the Daseinsanalyst to look for a *hidden meaning* in the manifestly meaningless symptoms from which the patient is suffering. If it is true that everything any person feels, thinks, or does has its meaning as part of his own individual world-project, then the same holds true for the feelings, thoughts, and doings of a mentally ill person. Therefore, their hidden meaning can be discovered as soon as light is shed on the underlying world-project of someone suffering from a mental illness (Binswanger 2004, p. 202). Placing a *hermeneutic tool* in the hand of the Daseinsanalytic psychiatrist is a big advantage compared with traditional psychiatric descriptions, which usually do nothing other than look for the patient's mental deficiencies in comparison with mentally healthy people. It is noticeable that the interpretation of symptoms based on this concept is totally different from the psychoanalytic one. Whereas Freud and his followers look for an infantile or psychogenetic meaning by relating the symptoms to repressed childhood experiences, Binswanger looks for their "ontological" meaning by relating them to the specific world-project, which is, according to Binswanger, an ultimate given that even underlies the psychoanalytic "unconscious."

The "World-project" as an Individual A Priori

This brings us to the ontological status of the world-project, which generates an ontological instead of a psychological concept of psychic suffering. Binswanger underlines the uniqueness of his approach by calling the world-project an "a priori or transcendental form" (Binswanger 2004, p. 205). Taken as a transcendental *a priori*, the world-project can only be an inborn "predisposition," containing the constitutional conditions within the limits of which the patient lives his life from the beginning. This means that the individual world-project does not take shape in early childhood, but already determines the infant's experiences and even the Freudian unconscious (Binswanger 2004, p. 203).

Critical Perspectives

When Binswanger calls the world-project a "transcendental form," he reveals how he has read and adopted the ontology of Dasein given in *Being and Time*, namely not as an *existential* ontology, but as a *transcendental* one in the tradition of Kant and Husserl (see Binswanger 2004, p. 194). In other words: he has missed the *existential turn* that makes this work a masterpiece. I will explain the difference later when describing my own Daseinsanalytic approach to psychic suffering. Here I will just mention two highly problematic consequences of this misinterpretation: first, mental illness is given a deterministic aspect that gives psychotherapeutic treatment few prospects of success, although Binswanger himself seemed unaware of this consequence. Second, the world-project itself – as a transcendental *a priori* – is no longer hermeneutically explicable. The predominant question now concerns the specific *structure* of the world-project underlying mental illness. This means that the Daseinsanalytic investigation of the world-project starts as a hermeneutic one, but then returns to the traditional psychiatric discourse, looking for "deviations from the norm" and judging the mentally ill person's world-projects as "restricted," "impoverished," "simplified," and "depleted" Binswanger 2004, pp. 205, 209).

Medard Boss: Daseinsanalysis as the endeavor to overcome the possessive subjectivism of Descartes' philosophy in the field of medicine and psychology

As already mentioned, Boss – contrary to Binswanger – understood Daseinsanalysis from the outset as a psychotherapeutic practice. His claim, however, went far beyond this, as is already clear from the title of his major theoretical work *Grundriss der Medizin und Psychologie* (1971; published in translation in 1994 as *Existential Foundations of Medicine and Psychology*).

Boss's Claim of Daseinsanalysis as the First post-Cartesian School of Thought in Medicine and Psychology

This much broader aspiration is a result of Heidegger's direct participation in the development of Boss's Daseinsanalysis. Heidegger not only gave the "Zollikon Seminars" between 1959 and 1969, but he also gave Boss personal instruction. Heidegger had in fact nothing to contribute in the field of psychopathology and psychotherapy, but a great deal to contribute to the philosophical foundations of modern medicine as an applied natural science. Heidegger was interested in conducting the Zollikon Seminars because he wished to exert a direct influence on scientifically misguided medical doctors by informing them about the philosophy of subjectivity that underpins medical work, which is represented above all by the name of *René Descartes.* Heidegger wanted to demonstrate to the doctors gathered in these seminars that Descartes had instigated a "dictatorship of the mind" over the modern age to which the whole of medicine also bows (Heidegger 2001, p. 107). He wanted the doctors to realize how urgent it is to overcome the scientific paradigm that dominates in medicine and psychology, including Freudian psychoanalysis (Heidegger 2001, pp. 7, 207).

For Heidegger it was so important to speak about Descartes' philosophy of subjectivity because he was convinced that this philosophy was responsible for the modern devaluation of all phenomena – even the human being – into measurable and calculable objects ready for exploitation, and he predicted the "self-destruction of the human being" as the final consequence of this merely technical approach to the world (Heidegger 2001, p. 94). Therefore he expounded his "new view of the basic constitution of human existence," which overcomes Cartesianism, right at the beginning of the Zollikon Seminars (on September 1959; Heidegger 2001, p. 4) with the following drawing:

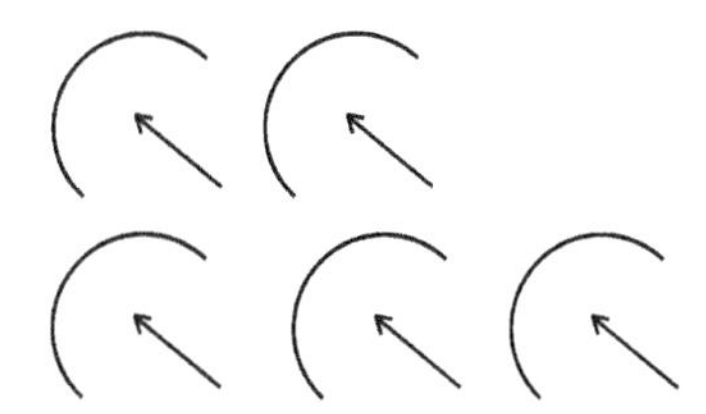

Heidegger explains his drawing as follows: "This drawing should only illustrate that human existing in its essential ground is never just … a self-contained object. Instead, this way of existing consists of 'pure,' invisible, intangible capacities for receiving-perceiving [*Vernehmen*] what it encounters and what addresses it" (1987/2001, pp. 3–4). How far this drawing goes against the traditional philosophical understanding of the human being does not become evident until you change the position of the adverb "only" in Heidegger's explanation: "This drawing should illustrate that human existing *only* consists of 'pure" invisible, intangible capacities for receiving-perceiving." This is why this drawing does not contain any center that is traditionally called "the self," and – much more importantly: the "Vernehmen" is only directed to what approaches from the world, not to oneself, to one's own being. This omission of any relationship to oneself goes more against Kierkegaard than against Descartes. Kierkegaard, the father of existential philosophy, defined the "self" as "a relation which relates to itself" (Kierkegaard 2004, p. 43).

Because Boss's Daseinsanalysis was the first to introduce this change in thinking into medicine and psychology, it represents the first attempt to establish a radically de-subjectivized approach to mental illness. And insofar as the "intersubjective turn" in psychoanalysis also claims to overcome the Cartesian world view (see Stolorow, Atwood, and Orange 2002), Boss's Daseinsanalysis can also be seen as a forerunner of this movement.

From Existence to Ek-sistence

Heidegger does not look for a new term to express the non-subjective nature of human Dasein, but de-subjectivizes the term "existence" by making recourse to the old Greek form ek-sistence. To ek-sist now means nothing other than "standing out into the open" and "sustaining a realm of openness" (Heidegger 1987/2001, p. 218). Even before considering Boss's concept of psychic illness it is easy to anticipate that there is only one question left that avoids any subjectivism and it is therefore permissible to ask: "*How* do mentally ill people ek-sist?"; "*how* are they receiving-perceiving what encounters them?"

Critical Perspectives on Boss's Ek-sistential Approach to Psychic Suffering

The key problem of any approach to neurotic or psychotic phenomena is that they are manifestly not understandable because they are evidently inapposite to the manifest reality to which they belong. Therefore, Boss's question of "how a mentally troubled person ek-sists" is necessarily transformed into the question of *how* and *how much* a mentally troubled person *has lost the capacity* for receiving-perceiving what encounters him or her? Boss speaks of "impairments" or "infringements." The Daseinsanalytic task consists in describing carefully whatever impairments are hindering someone from receiving-perceiving what encounters him or her in a truly open and free way.

Except for its use of an ontological terminology, this approach to psychic suffering is not new, but is identical to the leading approach of medical psychiatry. In a medical-psychiatric perspective, the mentally ill person is by definition someone who lacks certain capacities with which the mentally healthy person is equipped. Therefore, the Daseinsanalytic therapeutic aim coincides with the medical-psychiatric goal that seeks to remove deficiencies and re-establish normality or psychic health.

It is important to see how this differs from a psychoanalytic approach. Although Freud claimed for psychoanalysis the status of a natural science, he actually discovered and elaborated a hermeneutic approach to psychic suffering. Boss's philosophical approach to psychic suffering, by contrast, rejects any interpretations because all interpretation is regarded as forcing an artificial meaning on the phenomena, which makes a hermeneutic approach as detrimental as a natural scientific approach. Boss's Daseinsanalysis is therefore unable to provide a philosophically grounded alternative to the psychoanalytic hermeneutics of psychic suffering, and instead reverts to a mere description of "infringements" that is less developed than psychoanalysis.

However, there is yet another problem in this post-Cartesian approach to mental suffering. Because both Heidegger and Boss emphasize the need to overcome Cartesian body–mind dualism, Boss no longer differentiates between somatic and psychic illness (Boss 1994, pp. 100–106). In *Existential Foundations of Medicine and Psychology* (1994), he puts forward "a *general* Daseinsanalytic phenomenology of illness" regarding *every form* of illness, be it somatic or psychic, as an "infringement" of receiving-perceiving what encounters us. If for instance you have a broken leg, the Daseinsanalysts will ask which infringements of receiving-perceiving belong to suffering from a broken leg just as he would ask in relation for example to a case of depression. This suspension of any distinction between somatic and psychic illness is unhelpful and promotes a kind of description that is rather obtuse.

In sum, there are three objections to Boss's ontological approach to psychic suffering: first, it is not able to capture a view of the patient's individuality as a whole because it is only focused on "infringements"; second, the description of infringements gives a very bland impression of the suffering person because it has to be free of any subjectivism; third, the description of infringements becomes extremely normative and judgmental because it is guided by the ideal of an unconditional openness to whatever encounters us from the world. This idealistic norm is evidently not only inaccessible to finite human beings, but logically nonsensical.

Alice Holzhey: Daseinsanalysis as an Existential-Hermeneutic Approach to Psychic Suffering

My main *philosophical* divergence from the founding fathers of Daseinsanalysis, Binswanger and Boss, is my adherence to the keyword "existential" of "*Being and Time*." I therefore reject the "transcendental" reading of Binswanger as well as Boss's "ek-sistential" reading. This enables me to advance a *hermeneutic* approach to psychic suffering that accords with psychoanalysis without adopting its highly questionable metapsychological premises.

Three Key points that attract me to *Being and Time*

I would like to mention three key points of *Being and Time* that are fundamental to my understanding of psychic suffering. All three are taken over from Sören Kierkegaard (1813–1855), but only Heidegger was able to give them a precise ontological meaning and to show their relevance to a new approach to the human condition.

(1) An existential understanding of subjectivity It is most important to realize that in *Being and Time* Heidegger does not yet intend to supersede the modern definition of the human being as a "subject," but to conceptualize it in an existential way. In other words: he does not yet identify subjectivity with the will to exploit the world, but with "existing" in the sense of "***having to be***" one's own life instead of being naturally "hard-wired" like other living beings. The human subjectivity lies in nothing other than "having to be" and being ***disclosed to*** this basic endeavor. This is a weak but nevertheless radical notion of subjectivity.

(2) The philosophical (ontological) dimension of human self-disclosedness It is equally important that in *Being and Time* human self-disclosedness is twofold. We are not only disclosed to ourselves as these individual persons but also to our own condition of being human that we share with everybody else. Heidegger therefore carefully distinguishes between our "ontico-existentiell" and our "ontological-existential" relationship to ourselves. This means that an elementary form of philosophizing is part of human life itself.

(3) The pre-eminent role of the moods in disclosing our own being Similarly, important is the enormous philosophical revaluation of the moods. Heidegger insists that originally neither perceptions nor thoughts but only our moods can disclose our being.

Examples that Elucidate the Three Key Points

Examples of first key point This concerns Heidegger's existential understanding of subjectivity in *Being and Time*, which is deeply intertwined with Kierkegaard's term "existence." Traditionally the term "existence" was philosophically irrelevant because it was only used to indicate that something is "real" and not just a fantasy. Therefore it is totally against this tradition when Heidegger states in *Being and Time* that "*the essence of Dasein lies in its existence*" (Heidegger 1927/1962, p. 40). Now "existence" is a central philosophical term because it defines the essence of human beings. As such it is restricted to human beings: only we human beings "exist." And being a "subject" now means to "exist" in the sense of having to take over and lead one's own life as this individual person.

Example 1: Having to be our basic biological needs. We human beings are not simply hungry or tired or sexually aroused as animals are, but we have "to be" all our basic needs by finding ways to satisfy them. Of course, there are always socially accepted customs relating to how to cope with them, but customs do not determine us but must be adapted by each of us, which always includes the possibility to revolt openly or secretly against them.

Example 2: Having to be our social status. If I am wealthy whether by inheritance or by my own efforts, this social status does not just belong to me, but I have to be it. This means that I cannot do other than take a stance to it, being either proud or ashamed of it, finding reasons why I deserve it or donating to charity to assuage my guilt feelings and so on.

Example 3: Having to be our past and our future. It is important to see that "having to be" is not confined to the present but includes our past and future as well. Whatever we did or omitted to do in the past, we still "have to be," whether by trying to forget it, by whitewashing it, by constantly looking for explanations for it and so on. The same is true of our future. We also "exist" our future by expecting a change for the better or by fearing any change or by trying to foresee and control what is neither foreseeable nor controllable.

Examples of second key point This is concerned with an elementary form of philosophizing that is part of everyone's daily life. We will see later that psychic suffering has exactly to do with this factor. The following examples illustrate why ontological experiences are always present in everyday life.

Example 1: Feeling hungry. When I feel hungry I normally care about when and how I will satisfy this need. This means that I focus on the ontical concrete meaning of feeling hungry and ignore the ontological message in this same feeling, which tells me about my being deeply dependent on the external world and on others because my body needs food as long as I live.

Example 2: Taking a look at my watch. When I look at my watch I do not just get the specific ontical information about what time it is now, but also the ontological information about the basic truth that time is passing and that I am growing incessantly older. So every look at my watch includes the ontological message about my own being temporal and finite.

Example 3: Having to make a minor decision. When I have to decide whether to accept an invitation for a dinner or not, then I may again focus on the ontical concrete pros and cons, but there are two very uncanny ontological messages even in such an everyday decision: the first tells me that whenever I take a decision I have to sacrifice other possibilities, and the second tells me that every decision is a "leap" into uncertainty because the consequences a decision will have in the future are not foreseeable.

Examples of third key point This deals with *how* we are primarily confronted with our ontological conditions, namely not in "understanding," but in "*being in a mood*" (Heidegger 1927/1996, p. 126). This assumption goes totally against traditional philosophy, and it only becomes understandable when we draw on our starting point that "the essence of the human being lies in its existence." This means that the essence of our human being no longer lies in *what* we are, for instance rational or social-political or self-seeking, but in the pure fact *that we have to be* whatever we are. This pure "*that*" of our having to be cannot be grasped by any understanding, but only by being in a particular mood. Understanding is always related to *what* is or *how* or *why* something is. Only moods are able to disclose what Heidegger calls the "*naked*" or "*pure*" facticity of our being.

When we remember the given examples, we see that their ontological message is always only concerned with the naked *that* of our ontological conditions: *that* we are not self-sufficient, *that* we are temporal, *that* we cannot avoid sacrificing possibilities, and so on.

The Existential Understanding of Angst as an "Eminent Disclosedness of Da-sein"

You are in good Daseinsanalytic company when you refuse to concede special status to *Angst* (anxiety or dread). Binswanger and Boss agreed at least on this one point. They both saw Heidegger's interpretation of *Angst* in *Being and Time* as a basic flaw of this work. And both thought that Heidegger had misunderstood a neurotic and immature emotion as a fundamental ontological one. But as soon as you take the existential perspective on the human being, you will realize that this critique is not sustainable.

The existential concept of *Angst* that Heidegger takes over from Kierkegaard becomes accessible when we refer to how moods *usually* and *for the most time* disclose the "that" of our having to be: namely by *turning away* from it (see Heidegger 1927/1996, p. 128). Therefore all different moods with the exception of *Angst* can be seen as different kinds of disclosing the unfathomable "thatness" of our existence in the way of protecting us from really becoming exposed to it. This "turning away" is not only usual but makes sense because the unshielded exposure to our own being in its naked facticity is a deeply threatening experience (Heidegger 1927/1996, p. 177).

Let us try to understand why this ontological experience is so threatening. It is due to its being an experience beyond words. As such it cannot be shared with others and therefore leaves each of us utterly alone with ourselves and reveals a final solitude that seems unbearable (Heidegger 1927/1996, p. 176).

Kierkegaard never tired of admonishing his readers that *Angst* is an exclusive emotion "totally different from fear and similar concepts" (Kierkegaard 1980, p. 42). The main difference is that "fear" is an *ontical emotion* that has as its objects all sorts of concrete dangers, whereas *Angst* is an *ontological emotion* that has as its only object the facticity of our being thrown into the human condition. Therefore, fear is often irrational and deceptive, whereas *Angst* is never deceptive because it tells us nothing but the truth about the inalterable human condition.

Undisturbed Everydayness as a Constant Flight from Anxiety

You may now wonder whether you have ever experienced *Angst*. Heidegger makes two statements that seem hardly compatible. On the one hand he states that *Angst* "can arise in the most harmless situations"; on the other he states that "'real' Angst is rare" (Heidegger 1927/1996, p. 177). I am sure you too remember situations when you have been scared to death or have been deeply ashamed or felt enormously guilty just because of nothing that is worth being afraid of, ashamed of, or guilty about. Afterwards you may have shaken your head about your seemingly exaggerated reaction. But when we look at such incidents from an ontological perspective, the seemingly inadequate reactions become understandable as reactions to a sudden invasion of *Angst* in everyday life, which was evoked by the ontological message of an ontically harmless situation that came unexpectedly to the fore.

But the other statement that "real" *Angst* is rare is true as well. First, because what we call everydayness and average normality is the result of a successful flight from anxiety into the "common sense of the they" (Heidegger 1927/1996, pp. 288, 156); second, because when *Angst* arises it is normally misinterpreted as fear. Therefore, fear is often "Angst which ... is inauthentic and concealed from itself as such" (Heidegger 1927/1996, p. 177).

Authenticity and Inauthenticity as Strictly Ontological Terms

Anyone who is acquainted with *Being and Time* will wonder why I have avoided the two popular terms "authenticity" and "inauthenticity" until now. Their popularity explains why it is that these terms are mostly understood in a psychological sense, which is totally against Heidegger's intention. In *Being and Time*, living inauthentically means living mostly protected from *Angst* thanks to the participation in the common sense of the "they." "Inauthenticity" is therefore the average and normal way of living and not an immature psychic state that we should or could overcome. The same applies to authenticity. It has nothing to do with showing oneself to others as one really and truthfully is instead of hiding behind a mask, but with a readiness to turn towards the ontological truth about human existence and endure *Angst*. Equally important is that according to Heidegger this readiness is never lasting, but always leads to living again in inauthenticity (Heidegger 1927/1996, pp. 41, 204).

Psychic Suffering as "Suffering from One's Own Being"

I have mentioned the terms authenticity and inauthenticity because they give me the opportunity to ask where my own concept of psychic suffering is to be located in Heidegger's existential analysis of Da-sein. Other than in the works of Kierkegaard

(1949/2004 and Sartre(1943/2003), pathological phenomena do not play any role in *Being and Time*. This is why pathological phenomena cannot have any existential relevance as long as the relation to one's own being is seen as either authentic or inauthentic. Psychic suffering has to be understood existentially as *a third way* of being disclosed to one's own being that is neither inauthentic nor authentic.

To understand psychic suffering as a third way to attribute people who suffer from so-called mental disorders a *special sensitivity (Hellhörigkeit) for their own being*. Due to this special sensitivity, they are open to the ontological message of everyday issues. The word "sensitivity" has the advantage of expressing in positive terms what makes the suffering person suffer: namely hearing and seeing *more than the average* and therefore being nearer to the ontological truth. His particular sensitivity makes the mentally suffering person a "*reluctant philosopher.*" He exists philosophically even when he is not philosophizing in the usual sense of rationally reflecting about the human condition. He exists philosophically by experiencing the anxiety-laden truth of his ontological condition in its naked facticity. But the suffering person cannot use his sensitivity as a gift. That is why I call him a *reluctant* philosopher. He is *unwillingly* exposed to a philosophical experience which overburdens and even traumatizes him.

The Two Stages of an Existential-hermeneutic Approach to Psychic Suffering

In the first stage we ask *what the suffering person is suffering from*. This is a hermeneutic question and is identical to the question of *to what he is especially sensitive*. The general answer to this question is always the same: the person seemingly suffering from a mental disorder is *suffering from his own being*. This is true for neurotic, psychosomatic, and even psychotic suffering. But when we deal with an individual person with specific symptoms, we have to ask *to which ontological truth he or she is especially sensitive*.

In a second stage, we ask *how the suffering person responds to* what he or she is especially sensitive to. The general answer to this question is also always the same: because the ontological experience is threatening or even traumatizing, he responds by either trying to battle against it with the illusionary aim of overcoming its message, or by capitulating and retreating into a state of depression. For an illustration of both stages we can turn again to our examples:

Illustration 1 When someone suffers from anorexia or bulimia we can ask if he or she is especially sensitive to what it means ontologically to be subjected to the biological need to feed oneself day by day as long as one lives. We can guess that feeling hungry has become an ontological experience for this person, which reminds him of being inevitably dependent on bodily needs, which is not only experienced as threatening, but also as insulting because it goes against the ideal of self-sufficiency.

Illustration 2 When someone suffers from a severe disturbance of his time-management, we can guess that he or she is especially sensitive to what it means ontologically to be subjected to the law of time. And we can guess that the seemingly harmless look at the watch is enormously threatening to this person because it reminds him of his finitude.

Illustration 3 If someone feels paralyzed whenever he has to take a decision, we can guess that he or she is especially sensitive either to the ontological truth that to decide always means having to renounce other opportunities, or for the ontological truth that you can never know for certain if you do not take a wrong decision you will deeply regret later on. Both truths can have a paralyzing effect.

Illustration 4 If someone suffers from hypochondria, we can ask if he or she is especially sensitive to the ontological message in even minor bodily symptoms such as a mild headache, because even a mild headache ontologically indicates our bodily frailty and our being inevitably, as Heidegger put it, "towards death."

Our second question is concerned with the *hidden desire* in all psychic symptoms. There is something very special and even shocking about this desire because it is not compatible with the "normal" wish to be freed from the limiting pathological symptoms and regain mental health. If we assume that psychic suffering is a suffering from our own being, then the character of its inherent desire cannot be other than ontological. Someone who is oversensitive for the ontological conditions wants to evade them or to battle against them. But whereas we can at least in principle overcome ontical reasons for suffering, there is no way of getting rid of the human condition. Therefore the desire inherent in all psychic suffering is an illusory one.

More precisely, our second question is concerned with the concrete "*acting out*" of the ontological desire, which is realized in the manifest symptoms. Instead of taking these symptoms as mere deficiencies, we understand them now as ontical actions with an illusory ontological purpose.

Illustration 5 We can guess that a person suffering from anorexia seems to believe that she can free herself from being subjected to bodily laws if she avoids eating enough food.

Illustration 6 We can guess that a person suffering from severe time-problems seems to believe that he can free himself from being temporal by revolting against all specific timetables and ignoring all temporal arrangements.

Illustration 7 We can guess that a person suffering from an inability to take decisions seems to believe that he can save all his possibilities for the future or, more often, that he can avoid becoming guilty by refraining from taking any decisions.

Illustration 8 We can guess that a person who suffers from hypochondria seems to believe that he can gain total control over his body by constantly studying it and that he can overcome its fundamental vulnerability by his own ontical means.

Of course, all these examples constitute mere guesswork. More than this can only be achieved through an engaged dialogue with the patient and by listening carefully to what he tells us about his suffering.

There are two remaining questions that are connected to each other. Both are important but must stay unanswered here. The first concerns the origin of an ontological oversensitivity (see Holzhey-Kunz 2016, 16 – 27); the second concerns the role of childhood experiences in psychic suffering (see Holzhey-Kunz 2014).

A Final Remark about Daseinsanalytic Therapy and the Daseinsanalytic Therapist

It is evident that it cannot be the aim of a Daseinsanalytic therapy to cure our patients' special sensitivity because this is not seen as a deficiency but as a positive distinction of them. So the therapeutic work is mainly a hermeneutic one: to understand together with the patient what he is especially sensitive to and what is the illusionary purpose of the symptoms that he has to abandon.

Because Daseinsanalytic therapists do not only know rationally about the possibility to confront and accept the anxiety-laden ontological experiences that impose themselves on people of a special sensitivity, but also are – at least ideally – experienced in confronting and tolerating their own anxiety, they are *ontologically experienced companions* on the therapeutic way that they undergo together with the patient.

References

Binswanger, L. (2004). The existential analysis school of thought (trans. E. Angel). In: *Existence: A New Dimension in Psychiatry and Psychology* (ed. R. May, E. Angel, and H.F. Ellenberger) 191–213. Lanham, MD: Aronson Book/Rowman & Littlefield. (Original work published 1947.)

Boss, M. (1963). *Psychoanalysis and Daseinsanalysis* (trans. L.E. Lefebre). New York: Basic Books.

Boss, M. (1994). *Existential Foundations of Medicine and Psychology* (trans. S. Conway and A. Cleaves). New York and London, Aronson. (Original work published 1971.)

Heidegger M. (1995). *Vom Wesen des Grundes*, 8e. Frankfurt: Klostermann. (Original work published 1929.)

Heidegger, M. (1996). *Being and Time* (trans. J. Stambaugh). Albany: State University of New York Press. (Original work published 1927.)

Heidegger, M. (2001). *Zollikon Seminars. Protocols – Conversations – Letters* (ed. M. Boss, trans. F. Mayr and R. Askay). Evanston IL: Northwestern University Press. (Original work published 1987.)

Holzhey-Kunz, A. (2006). Ludwig Binswanger: Psychiatry based on the foundation of philosophical anthropology. In: *Images in Psychiatry: German Speaking Countries Austria-Germany-Switzerland* (ed. E.M. Wolpert, K. Maurer, A.H. Rifai et al.), 271–288. Heidelberg, Germany: Universitatsverlag Winter.

Holzhey-Kunz A. (2014). *Daseinsanalysis* (trans. S. Leighton). London: Free Association Books.

Holzhey-Kunz A. (2016). Why the distinction between ontic and ontological trauma matters for existential therapists. *Existential Analysis 27* (1): 16–27.

Kierkegaard, S. (1980). *The Concept of Anxiety* (ed. and trans. R. Thomte and A.B. Anderson). Princeton NJ: Princeton University Press. (Original work published 1844.)

Kierkegaard, S. (2004). *The Sickness unto Death. A Christian Psychological Exposition for Edification and Awakening by Anti-Climacus* (trans. A. Hannay). London: Penguin Books. (Original work published 1849.)

Sartre, J.-P. (2003). *Being and Nothingness. An Essay on Phenomenological Ontology* (trans. H.E. Barnes). London and New York: Routledge. (Original work published 1943.)

Stolorow, R., Atwood, G., and Orange, D. (2002). *Worlds of Experience: Interweaving Philosophical and Clinical Dimensions in Psychoanalysis.* New York: Basic Books.

3

Method and Practice

Daseinsanalytic Structure, Process, and Relationship

Erik Craig and Perikles Kastrinidis

Introduction

The founder and first practitioner of psychotherapeutic Daseinsanalysis, was the psychoanalytically trained Swiss psychiatrist, Medard Boss. Initially drawn to a more phenomenological perspective, first, through studies with Carl Jung and, then, through the tutelage and work of the psychiatric Daseinsanalyst, Ludwig Binswanger, in the late-1930s and early to mid-1940s, Boss was most deeply influenced by the thought and person of Martin Heidegger beginning with their first exchanges in the late-1940s. For some years, Boss was largely alone in his rethinking of classical psychoanalysis along the phenomenological-hermeneutic lines of Heidegger's *Being and Time* (1927/1962). However, at some point as his collaboration with Heidegger progressed, especially with the initiation of the Zollikon Seminars, he began falling in with Heidegger's so-called "turn" in thinking which reversed the relationship between Being and Dasein, revolutionizing Boss's understanding of the practice of psychotherapy. Having largely left hermeneutics behind, Heidegger focused on the reciprocal openness of Being and Dasein which emphasized Dasein's "calling" as the "Shepherd of Being" (Heidegger 1947/1977, p. 210). Thus, nearing the end of his life, Boss wrote that "the relationship between Being and Dasein not only makes psychotherapy possible in the first place, but also gives psychotherapy its most fundamental purpose, that is, for the therapist to respond to the appeal of the patient to be" (Boss 1988, p. 61).

The Early Years of Daseinsanalytic Psychotherapy and Training

The first systematic training in Daseinsanalytic psychotherapy granting an accredited Diploma as a Daseinsanalytic Psychotherapist to successful candidates was formed in 1971, with the organizational initiative of Gion Condrau, who was Boss's most

The Wiley World Handbook of Existential Therapy, First Edition. Edited by Emmy van Deurzen, Erik Craig, Alfried Längle, Kirk J. Schneider, Digby Tantam, and Simon du Plock.

well-known disciple and who attended the Zollikon Seminars from the very beginning. The training, the Daseinsanalytic Institute for Psychotherapy and Psychosomatics, included advanced coursework in psychology and philosophy, the completion of a personal analysis, and both group and individual supervision. Analysts in training, including two of this part's authors, Alice Holzhey-Kunz and Perikles Kastrinidis, were systematically exposed to a combination of Boss's daseinsanalytically interpreted Freudian clinical psychoanalysis and philosophical foundations for psychology and psychotherapy based on Martin Heidegger's *Daseinsanalytik.*

With respect to the former clinical subject matter, the Institute's publications, lectures, seminars, case conferences, and supervision, offered a distinctively daseinsanalytic re-reading of Freud's psychoanalytic theory and practice. This daseinsanalytic understanding was grounded in Boss's conviction that Freud had unwittingly "gained an immediate and primary understanding of man through his discovery and practice of psychoanalysis" but that "he had destroyed this primary understanding in a truly catastrophic fashion when he introduced his theoretical constructions" (Boss 1963, p. 78). For instance, Boss thought Freud's concepts of transference and resistance "testify to Freud's deep understanding of man" as they "indisputably refer to actual phenomena of interhuman relationships (although in a veiled way)" (Boss 1963, p. 79). For Boss, Freud's theory of the drives, which Freud himself called a mythology (Freud 1933/1964a, p. 95), only served to cover and vitiate the legitimacy of the actual relational phenomena themselves and to such a degree he (Boss) would often scornfully call it a pure "science fiction." Nevertheless, the clinical track of the Institute's training program addressed such therapeutic concerns as:

1 the therapeutic setting and framework, including the frequency of sessions, the use of the couch, and the role of each of the therapeutic partners, namely free association for the patient and evenly hovering attention for the therapist;
2 critical appraisals of psychoanalytic conceptions as transference and countertransference and their replacement with a corresponding daseinsanalytic understanding of therapeutic relationship, therapeutic eros and genuine love; and
3 a similar critical appraisal and corresponding daseinsanalytic understanding and handling of dreams, psychosomatic symptoms, and other therapeutic phenomena psychoanalysis "misleadingly" referred to as regression, repression, and repetition.

This Bossian daseinsanalytic understanding of psychoanalytic principles, concepts, and process may still be found today scattered throughout his own published English works as well as, most systematically, in Chapter 16 of his magnum opus, *Existential Foundations of Psychology and Medicine* (Boss 1971/1979). There in particular, one finds a consistently daseinsanalytic re-reading of the central tenants and processes of psychoanalytic practice.

With respect to philosophical subject matter, publications, lectures, and supervision followed the thought of the later Heidegger, especially as expressed in the Zollikon lectures, above all recommending the therapist's radical openness for the being of the patient. Although both Boss and Condrau had received analytic training and included this in their instruction of candidates at the Institute, in keeping with the influence of

Heidegger's emphasis on openness and presence, candidates were repeatedly encouraged to just "be there" for the patient, be open and receptive to the being of the patient. As Boss once put this in his writings, "In silent listening the analyst opens himself to, and belongs to, the patient's as yet concealed wholeness; and this silence alone can free the patient for his own world by providing him with the necessary interhuman openness" (Boss 1963, p. 64). It was presumed that by simply being open, the meanings of the patient's suffering and possibilities would reveal themselves in immediate, "intuitive" apprehension and show the way to newfound authenticity and freedom for the individual. Boss's complete faith in the power and efficacy of such simple, genuine human presence was such that students often heard him declare that the work of a therapist was like "a holiday."

When asked for concrete guidance about how to handle specific clinical situations Boss often replied with such startlingly simple advice as "you have to feel it in your fingertips" (Craig 1988a, p. 33). For Boss, the most basic aim and goal of therapy was, most simply put, to "to help other human beings to come into their being," their "own best fullness" (Craig 1988a, p. 27). This faith in the human being's capacity to unfold within the context of an open, caring, intuitively discerning therapeutic relationship led to the invention of a characteristically Bossian suggestion. Instead of the old psychoanalytic tendency to ask "why?" to explain present symptoms on the basis of the *past*, Boss recommended directing individuals toward their *future* possibilities by asking "Why not?," "Why in the world not" overcome their fears. Why in the world *not* behave more freely? Thus it was the accepted rule of the day that simply being there for the patient and asking "Why not?" would ultimately enable individuals to overcome their inhibitions and regain their lost freedom.

While such clinical recommendations are not entirely without merit and are certainly faithful to the post *Being and Time* Heidegger, a number of the early candidates at the Institute recognized there was more to psychotherapy than this.

In contrast with this emphasis on the later Heidegger, leading Daseinsanalysts, consistently asserted that "Daseinsanalysis is guided by a rigorous phenomenological-hermeneutic methodology" (Condrau 1998, p. 26). Unfortunately what was actually meant by the terms phenomenological and hermeneutic was, apparently, never exposed and examined in detail. In fact, in his two major systematic works Boss (1963, 1971/1977) never even mentions hermeneutics. With respect to phenomenology, following Heidegger, Boss notes that the word phenomena is "derived from the Greek *phainesthai*, that is, to shine forth, appear, unveil itself, come out of concealment or darkness themselves" (Boss 1963, p. 28). This may implicitly suggest a reference to Heidegger's hermeneutic understanding of phenomenon as that which "proximally and for the most part does *not* show itself" and "lies hidden" but at the same time "is something that belongs to what … shows itself, and belongs to it in such a way and … belongs to it so essentially as to constitute it's meaning and ground" (Heidegger 1927/1962), but it does not clarify any specific hermeneutic process for daseinsanalytic therapists to follow. Boss's understanding of phenomenology was similarly vague. Although in his 1963 Harvard lectures he stated that the "phenomenological approach is by no means only a passive attitude" (Boss 1964, p. 63) he never describes what an active phenomenology might be. In that same lecture, he describes his phenomenological approach by citing Husserl's plea "back to the things themselves" and, along with this, Goethe's aphorism, "do not search behind the things, they themselves do the teaching" (Boss 1964, p. 62). Beyond this, he offered only this advice:

> to allow the phenomena of our world to speak to us directly, to allow the world to reveal itself to us without any conceptual distortion; to keep ourselves from forcing everything that crosses our path to take the shape we want to impose on it, so that we may drain as much energy as possible from it" (Boss 1964, p. 62)

This lack of specificity about daseinsanalytic phenomenological-hermeneutic process is entirely understandable given the decades subsequent to the publication of *Being and Time* (1927/1962) when Heidegger rarely spoke of either phenomenology or hermeneutics. However, this does not help the practicing Daseinsanalyst with understanding how, exactly, to go about realizing a genuine phenomenological-hermeneutic process other than reverently receiving the message of Being within the clearing (*Lichtung*) of his or her own being as Dasein.

Along with the promised simplicity and ease Medard Boss claimed to have found in his daseinsanalytic therapeutic practice, one must also remember he was a deeply and thoroughly trained psychoanalyst and, even as the original Daseinsanalytic psychotherapist, this training was surely not lost on him when faced with challenging clinical situations. Indeed, many of Boss's own students and their students in turn, have noted that the practice of psychotherapy is far from a holiday, understandably imbued as it is with troubling questions, impasses, ruptures, and the demand for constant, conscientious attention and difficult therapeutic decisions and actions. Aspiring Daseinsanalysts are therefore well-advised to heed Binswanger's caution that "with Daseinsanalysis alone, we cannot do psychotherapy" (Binswanger 1960, p. 254). Indeed, as the remainder of this chapter shows, many serious Daseinsanalysts have turned to various other resources to supplement their work with other perspectives and practices. Such diversity testifies to the wisdom of Nietzsche's counsel that "One repays a teacher badly if one remains nothing but a pupil."

Nevertheless, Boss's indispensable intensive effort at bringing a phenomenological-hermeneutic perspective to an understanding of human suffering and psychotherapy, even if he did not have the time or inclination to move beyond this, provides his former students and others who follow with an important foundation to continue daseinsanalytic thought and practice work for themselves.

Contemporary Daseinsanalytic Psychotherapy

At this point, a full half century after the end of the Zollikon Seminars (Heidegger 1987/2001), it is no longer possible to present a single comprehensive view of daseinsanalytic psychotherapy. The defining voices of the founders of Daseinsanalysis, Ludwig Binswanger and Medard Boss, have long since fallen silent with their deaths. There are now teaching and/or training institutes in seven different countries and today's independent daseinsanalytically oriented practitioners are also spread across the globe. Sensitive to the contingencies of their particular professional and cultural contexts, these contemporary Daseinsanalysts are tailoring their practices to their own ongoing studies and respective individualities, the particular social and cultural climates in which they practice, and the unique needs and personalities of the individuals whom they serve. Legal, ethical, institutional, and governmental policies and regulations also obtrude on the practice of psychotherapy in general, requiring constant rethinking and adaptation. New scientific discoveries and trends in research theory, and practice, continue to shape psychotherapeutic approaches of all kinds and Daseinsanalysts are in no way immune to the impact of these vast social, scientific, institutional, and political changes. Some Daseinsanalysts have undertaken intensive study and training in other schools of practice such as relational and intersubjective psychoanalysis, intensive, short-term psychotherapies, Eastern meditational psychotherapies, cognitive and developmental psychology, attachment theory, affect regulation science, and neuroscience, integrating these studies into their own distinctive versions of daseinsanalytic thought and practice.

Given this diversity of contemporary approaches to daseinsanalytic psychotherapy it is unlikely any one single, cohesive, unified approach would be agreeable to the majority of practitioners today. In our opinion however, this is a natural and desirable development, as the history of psychoanalysis has shown, since disagreement is a vital element of any thriving philosophy or science and the enemy of dogmatism and hubris. Fortunately, as we have seen well illustrated in the previous chapter by one of Boss's most gifted second generation students, Alice Holzhey-Kunz, disagreement is alive and well in the field. In view of the lack of consensus about what daseinsanalytic psychotherapy is, its purposes and aims, and how it proceeds, we present three quite different, contemporary approaches to daseinsanalytic practice by daseinsanalytic therapists who have published significant works in English and who actually knew and worked intensively with Medard Boss himself. In order of the degree to which they collaborated, studied, and worked with Boss, they are Alice Holzhey-Kunz, Perikles Kastrinidis, and Erik Craig.

Three Contemporary Approaches to Daseinsanalytic Practice

Although their perspectives, backgrounds, and approaches to daseinsanalysis and daseinsanalytic therapy differ considerably, all three present day daseinsanalytically oriented therapists and authors happen to have five basic attitudes in common. First, in contrast to Boss, rather than categorically rejecting any notion of an unconscious, they have each sought to develop an existential understanding of that which "does not show itself at all" and "lies hidden," (Heidegger 1927/1962, p. 59), concealed, covered up, or forgotten (see Craig 2008; Holzhey-Kunz 2014, pp. 113–121). Second, also in contrast to Boss, rather than simply dismissing Freud's ideas and practices as "science fiction," they take seriously what Boss himself also acknowledged, namely, that Freud had a "deep, though unarticulated, awareness of man's basic condition" (Boss 1963, p. 62), perceiving and understanding various real, distinctly human phenomena albeit in a distorted way. Reluctant to throw the psychoanalytic baby out with its theoretically speculative bathwater by rejecting such ideas as transference, resistance, repetition, and the like, they have each, to one degree or another, sought to reinterpret such secret-bearing phenomena in a hermeneutic manner.

Third, they each varyingly embrace certain aspects of Freud's original concrete recommendations for therapeutic practice that Boss, again, had cast aside. Fourth, they have each returned to Heidegger's original fundamental ontology of *Being and Time* (1927/1962) emphasizing the significance of Dasein's ontological characteristics not only as a more adequate foundation for existential science (Craig 2015) but also for understanding human suffering (Holzhey-Kunz 2014, pp. 133–156). Fifth, and finally, all three individuals have returned to Heidegger's abandoned phenomenological hermeneutic analysis in contrast to Boss's more strictly phenomenological one. This brief overview of common concerns is neither complete nor meant to suggest an homogeneity of thought among these three contemporary Daseinsanalysts. Quite the contrary, they tend to disagree on a number of points in each of these five areas.

We begin with Holzhey-Kunz's hermeneutic approach, following this with Craig's humanistic, relational approach, before concluding with Kastrinidis's short-term approach to which we give considerably more attention since the follow Chapter 4 presents two of his actual cases.

Alice Holzhey-Kunz: Hermeneutic Daseinsanalysis

Alice Holzhey-Kunz earned her PhD in philosophy and history from the University of Zurich in 1971, was one of the first analytic candidates of the Daseinsanalytic Institute for Psychotherapy and Psychosomatics. She received her diploma in 1975 and has worked since that time as a psychotherapist, supervisor, lecturer, and author in Daseinsanalysis. Holzhey-Kunz was the first Daseinsanalyst to publish a critique of Medard Boss's *Existential Foundations of Psychology and Medicine* (1971/1979), challenging its reliance on Heidegger's late "thinking of Being," which reverses the relationship between Being and Dasein and, with this, losing sight of Dasein as a "self." According to Holzhey-Kunz, this means that, for Boss, Dasein is only related to the world, but never to him- or herself. She asserts that such a philosophical concept of the human being is incapable of providing an understanding of the meaning of a patient's suffering. She holds to Heidegger's original hermeneutic understanding of Dasein from his early work *Being and Time* (Heidegger 1927/1962) which interprets normal everydayness as the result of a constant flight of the Dasein from the anxiety which lies "in the ground of its being" and makes it possible to disclose the secret meanings of psychic suffering. Here we should note that Holzhey-Kunz's work is largely centered on a new hermeneutic concept of mental suffering that is existential to its core. We include her approach to psychotherapy here as well as it offers such a vivid understanding of hermeneutic process in psychotherapy.

Again, rather than follow Boss into the late Heideggerian understanding of Being and its relation to Dasein, Holzhey-Kunz returns to Heidegger's original thinking of *Being and Time* (1927/1962) with its phenomenological-*hermeneutic* approach, supplementing this with aspects of the thinking of Kierkegaard and Sartre. She also appreciates Sigmund Freud's original commitment to a hermeneutic understanding of human suffering, though in no way follows his particular hermeneutic approach, which was guided by his naturalistic view of the human being, his drive theory, and so on. Nevertheless, she does adopt Freud's most central technical recommendations for her practice of psychotherapy: namely, (1) free association and, at least in some situations, the use of the couch, (2) evenly hovering attention for the therapist, and (3) the principle of abstinence for both therapeutic partners, though giving an existential ontological interpretation of both this rule and of evenly hovering attention, which she calls listening with a philosophical ear.

Supporting these choices are Holzhey-Kunz's distinctions between different types of conversations (Holzhey-Kunz 2014, pp. 203–208) such as dialogical, friendly, professional, and scientistic, contrasting each of these with the distinctly analytic kind of conversation, the only one she deems appropriate for approaching both the emotional and ontological truths that lie hidden in seemingly senseless symptoms. No other kind of conversation is structured as both fully collaborative and asymmetrical in purpose and process, an essential requirement for the kind of freedom and safety, risk and protection necessary for both partners in the common therapeutic endeavor.

In contrast to Boss, who was deeply suspicious of interpretation of all kinds and who nowhere in his major English publications even mentions the term hermeneutic, for Holzhey-Kunz, daseinsanalytic therapy is hermeneutic through and through. As she herself puts it, "The daseinsanalytic process is in every respect a hermeneutic one: hermeneutic is its method, hermeneutic is its object, hermeneutic is its goal. To be radically hermeneutic is therefore the essence of the daseinsanalytic process" (Holzhey-Kunz 2012, p. 200). In fact, she asserts, "Daseinsanalysis is an analytic therapy only in being hermeneutic" (Holzhey-Kunz 2012, p. 200).

Considering the hermeneutic circle as a dialectic between the part and the whole, Holzhey-Kunz sees the challenge of disclosing the hidden meaning of manifestly nonsensical symptoms as tied to discovering those as yet unrevealed aspects of the whole that make intelligible what is otherwise nonsensical. Since Dasein is constituted as an ontico-ontological being, Holzhey-Kunz understands the hidden meanings of psychic suffering as arising not only from the individual's own ontical life history, what Freud called his or her "reminiscences," but also from a specific ontological sensitivity (*Hellhörigkeit*) for his or her own being, his or her inescapable human condition (Holzhey-Kunz 2014, pp. 203–204).

Given this "dual mode" of psychic suffering, one challenge in hermeneutic listening is uncovering of the individual's own personal (ontic) history. However since all psychic experience also contains a pre-ontological understanding of the own being as human, for Holzhey-Kunz the symptoms of psychic suffering also make sense in terms of the patient's relation to the fundamental ontological conditions of the own being as Dasein. Where Daseinsanalysis differs from psychoanalysis is in its going through an ontical (existentiell) understanding of the hidden meanings of suffering to an ontological (existential) one. This requires, according to Holzhey-Kunz, both free association and a philosophical grasp of the ontological (existential) conditions that are primordially experienced only by anxiety, ontological guilt-feelings, and ontological feelings of shame of being human. Holzhey-Kunz's whole way of thinking, including in her therapeutic practice, is guided by the difference between the ontical and the ontological and constantly questioning how the ontological manifests itself in the concrete, ontical phenomena.

For Holzhey-Kunz this entire daseinsanalytic process depends not only on the possibilities of a genuinely hermeneut analysis but also on the particular character of the two therapeutic partners. For Holzhey-Kunz what makes psychotherapy even possible in the first place is the extraordinary sensitivity (*Hellhörigkeit*) of the neurotic whose very "particular sensitivity makes the mentally suffering person a *reluctant philosopher*" (Holzhey-Kunz 2014, p. 146). In order to grasp this particular sensitivity of the person who bears such soul suffering, daseinsanalytic therapists must also possess such a sensitivity to the hidden nature of such suffering, not only from their own individual life experience and history but also from their own conflicts and anxiety over being cast into this world as inescapably human.

Erik Craig: Humanistic, Relational Daseinsanalysis

Unlike the other two daseinanalytical psychotherapists presented in this chapter Erik Craig did not meet Boss or any of his Swiss colleagues and students until the summer of 1986 when a brief, but fruitful three-year collaboration with Boss and other Zurich Daseinsanalysts, led to the first extensive English introduction to the "Zurich School of Daseinsanalysis" with the publication of *Psychotherapy for Freedom: The Daseinsanalytic Way in Psychology and Psychoanalysis* (Craig 1988b).

Craig's path to Daseinsanalysis, years before even hearing of it, began in 1968 with 12 years of study and collaboration the existential child psychotherapist, Clark Moustakas (1956 1966). Influenced by Otto Rank, Moustakas referred to his own approach as "relationship therapy," emphasizing experiencing over behaving, being over doing, feeling over thinking, and authentic immediate relating over exploring the past. In 1978, Craig happened to meet another humanistic psychologist, the existential psychoanalyst Paul Stern (1964, 1972, 1979) who had been a close friend of Boss's in Zurich for many years and, after emigrating to the United States, his chief American advocate. Stern was, in some ways, the existential opposite of Moustakas, more philosophical than experiential, more thoughtful than emotionally expressive, more measured than spontaneous. After Stern's untimely 1982 death at the age of 62, Craig contacted Boss directly in the spring of 1985 and met him in person at his Zollikon home in August of the following year (Craig 1988a).

Craig's first published article on practice, *Sanctuary and Presence* (Craig 1986/2000), appearing just months before first meeting Boss, focused on the existential therapist's contribution to psychotherapy and laid out basic therapeutic values, attitudes, perspectives, and practices that still guide him to this day. There, Craig characterized therapy (from the Greek root, *therapeúein* meaning to attend, wait upon, care for, or serve) as requiring a kind of radical self-transcendence on the part of the therapist, a temporary suspension of personal needs, interests, and ambitions liberating the therapist to use his or her own experience to attend more cogently to the other. With the term *sanctuary*, Craig was referring to the actual felt-sense for the patient of what Freud called the therapeutic pact, a clear and reliable "frame" (Milner 1952, p. 183) establishing a set of agreements about time, money, expectations, goals, and responsibilities within which the individual may palpably experience "the safety and freedom to know and be him/herself, to take up his/her own authentic possibilities for being-in-the-world" (Craig 1986/2000, p.271). Although the agreements defining the frame may vary, depending on the particular therapeutic circumstances and the therapeutic partners involved, it ensures a mutual, albeit asymmetrical conversation, that is, one primarily for the use and benefit of the patient. For Craig, what allows this unavoidably ambiguous situation to be both sustained and productive is the therapist's abiding, alert, clearheaded, and caring *presence*, what Boss called "therapeutic eros" (Boss 1963, pp. 259–260). Nevertheless, with the term presence, in contrast to Boss's "mere" presence, characterized by the advice to "just be there" for the patient, Craig emphasizes "disciplined original presence" (Craig 1986/2000, p. 272). For Craig, such presence is no substitute for thoroughgoing training, continued conscientious study and practice, critical self-reflection, and a deep understanding of human existence and the variety and meanings of human suffering. Only such disciplined study and practice frees the therapist to bring a fresh, unrehearsed, spontaneous original presence to each moment of each hour, just as practicing chords eight hours a day all week allowed Ray Charles the freedom and skill of hands to let the songs play themselves on concert night.

At the heart of Craig's approach is an immediately and mutually experienced person-to-person connection on the basis of which psychological growth and the most reliable understanding of the individual's existence and suffering can occur. Within the "playground" (Freud 1911–1915, 1958, p. 154; Boss 1963, p. 239) of such an immediately unfolding, relational encounter, the therapist can experience the patient's actual lived reality within the therapist's own existence. For Craig, the psychotherapeutic process begins with and is, throughout, entirely dependent on the quality of a mutually experienced felt connection, a co-regulation of affects beginning with implicit non-verbal, pre-verbal, or what Trevarthen (2005) and, later, Schore (2012, p. 331) called "proto-conversation." The therapist's most important task is attentively tracking the matches and repairing the mismatches in the connection. Daniel Stern (1985) first called this process affect attunement not unlike the meaning of the Daseinsanalytic term *Gestimmtsein*, from the German verb, *stimmen*, meaning to tune, incline, or dispose and the noun, *Stimmung*, meaning tuning, mood, disposition, or frame of mind. Once the connection is matched or attuned, it is possible to work toward and, hopefully develop, a mutually disclosive understanding of what is going on in the moment and how this relates to the patient's established ways of being and suffering. In Daseinsanalysis, this understanding is given through a thoughtful hermeneutic listening for ontico-ontological meanings that occurs simultaneously with the process of tracking and repairing the felt connections (matches) or disconnections (mismatches or ruptures). The psychoanalyst and attachment researcher and theorist, Peter Fonagy somewhat awkwardly describes this reflective process of understanding one's own and others' minds and behaviors as "mentalization" (Fonagy 2001, pp. 165–170; Fonagy et al. 2002).

In recent years, Craig has been increasingly influenced by the work of attachment theory, developmental psychology, and neuroscience which he sees as corroborating many of the analytic and philosophical perspectives of Daseinsanalysis. Of particular significance for the practice of psychotherapy is the research in developmental psychology and psychoanalysis that has consistently shown that affective self-regulation and understanding always begins as co-regulation with another, be it a parent, a therapist, or some other important attachment figure, before being taken over independently for oneself. What is distinctive about daseinsanalytic psychotherapy is that this regulation and understanding of self occurs both with respect to one's own unique everyday (ontic) experience and history and with respect to what it means, ontologically, to be a human being as such and like all others.

Perikles Kastrinidis: Short-term Daseinsanalytic Therapy

Perikles Kastrinidis, a Swiss psychiatrist who earned his degree from the University of Vienna, was another of the first Diplomates of the Daseinsanalytic Institute for Psychotherapy and Psychosomatics who left the Institute in the 1970s and later formed a new training program under the rubric of Swiss Society for Daseinsanalysis. In addition to his training as a Daseinsanalyst, Kastrinidis also trained in Balint group work and was supervised by a senior psychoanalyst from South America. A significant turning point in his own approach to Daseinsanalytic psychotherapy came with his studies of intensive short-term dynamic psychotherapy (ISTDP) with Habib Davanloo in the 1980s. Today, Kastrinidis maintains a psychotherapist private practice and is a teaching and supervising Daseinsanalyst in Zurich. In the next Chapter, Kastrinidis reports two cases, one occurring early in his training and the other roughly 30 years later, to illustrate his search for his own way to remain daseinsanalytic even with some significant changes in the therapeutic method.

A pivotal point in Kastrinidis career came relatively early in his training at the Daseinsanalytic Institute when he found himself therapeutically constrained, not only by basic psychoanalytic ground rules that were imposed but also by the Institute's expectation of such lengthy, multi-year treatments. Within his very first few years as a candidate he began considering how to shorten the process by working in a more focused, intensive manner, especially given the emphasis on time in Daseinsanalysis and, with this, the knowledge that we are all on our way to death and thus that every hour of life is both priceless and irreplaceable to us. If our finitude is one of the ontological conditions with which we struggle most intensely, "Why," Kastrinidis wondered, "should anyone spend so much of this most precious resource in analysis?" These and other doubts led the young analyst to search for his own way to be and remain daseinsanalytic. The criteria used as standards for his search were neither philosophical nor theoretical but, rather, built on the evidence of his own actual lived experience with patients, namely, with respect to the felt-sense of fit with his own personality and the observed responses of patients to the their unique process and relationship.

It was not long before Kastrinidis along with other Institute colleagues, began to question Boss's apparently unquestioning, wholesale adoption of the "late" Heidegger's thinking and the circumstance that, "wherever he (Boss) could, he demarcated his Daseinsanalysis from Freud's psychoanalysis" (Kastrinidis 2005, pp. 95–96). Consequently, following his Swiss colleague Alice Holzhey-Kunz, who contributed the first major philosophical critique of Boss, Kastrinidis began to return to the Heidegger of *Being and Time* (1927/1962) and the kind of hermeneutic search for hidden meanings, which has so much in common with psychoanalysis as long as it is read in a "human scientific, that is a hermeneutic-narrative way" (Kastrinidis 2005, p. 96). He also experimented with various components of Freud's psychoanalytic technique seeking to decide which and which not to include in what eventually became short-term daseinsanalytic psychotherapy. Kastrinidis eschews the use of the couch and, with this, the requirement of free association and evenly hovering attention, and, in keeping with the basic practices of Davanloo's ISTDP, introduced the audiovisual recording of sessions. With this move, he came to construe the participation of the psychotherapist as one of highly focused *active hermeneutic listening*, contrasting this with purely *receptive phenomenal listening* in the fact that it steadily seeks and actively investigates hidden or unrecognized meanings both with respect to the individual's own unique developmental history and also with respect to the ontological or pre-ontological content of their experience. Paradoxically, even with this emphasis on active hermeneutic inquiry and listening, Kastrinidis held firmly to the psychoanalytic principle of abstinence on the part of both therapeutic partners, an abstinence by which he maintains a steady, intensive focus on the daseinsanalytic therapeutic process, never allowing this intensive interaction to slip over into the gratifications of everyday friendly conversation or intellectual discourse.

For Kastrinidis, the first requirement of his short-term daseinsanalytic psychotherapy, by which he means roughly anything from three months to three years usually on a once weekly basis, is the establishment of a mutually engaged *dynamic therapeutic relationship* and, consequently, *a dynamic therapeutic process.*

The therapeutic relationship In practicing this approach to daseinsanalytic psychotherapy, Kastrinidis focuses on two key elements: *the therapeutic alliance* and *abstinence.* In his view, every depth psychotherapeutic relationship is based on the *therapeutic alliance* between patient and therapist. Drawing from his later studies and practice of Davanloo's ISTDP Kastrinidis understands the therapeutic alliance as having both conscious and unconscious components, with the latter being, by far, the most crucial for therapeutic productivity and effectiveness (Abbass 2015; Davanloo 1980, 1990, 2000).

The *conscious therapeutic alliance* refers to the deliberate purposeful agreements, established between patient and therapist that Freud called the therapeutic "pact" (*Vertrag*, meaning agreement or covenant; 1940/1964b, pp. 173–179), which essentially "bands them ... together" and actually "constitutes the analytic situation" (Freud 1940/1964b, p. 173). Since such an alliance requires mutually experienced informed consent beginning with an individual's free choice to work with the particular therapist Kastrinidis begins the entire endeavor with a trial period of one to four sessions. Without this conscious working alliance no meaningful work is at all possible and the relationship is under the constant threat of collapse. Nonetheless this conscious alliance alone is not at all sufficient for a productive therapeutic relationship. Kastrinidis asserts that such a productive therapeutic experience also requires what Davanloo called an *unconscious therapeutic alliance*, which largely depends on the subtle, implicit dynamics of the relationship. One can track the development of such an alliance by observing bodily and facial gestures, vocal tones and rhythms, fresh spontaneous associations, unpredicted new insights, and the like. It is critical for the therapist to attend to the earliest appearance of these and other concrete evidences by noting and exploring their meanings as they occur.

The other essential component of the therapeutic relationship is *therapeutic abstinence,* as first asserted and qualified by Freud (Freud 1911–1915/1958, pp. 163–165).

Kastrinidis considers this an indispensable principle when navigating through the existential challenges of the dynamic process. This is no easy task for either of the therapeutic partners as patients often long to experience from the therapist the satisfactions denied them in life. Therapists, too, may be tempted by this, as one patient put it, "impossible possibility," but this is where they have the advantage of their own teaching analysis. Patients, on the other hand, have no such advantage which is all the more reason that long-buried emotions, longings, impulses, and fantasies begin to emerge, whether these be hostile or affectionate.

With the mutual commitment to abstinence, reinforced with concrete experience and behavior, patients are given the necessary protective assurance they will not be responded to in kind. Short-term Daseinsanalytic psychotherapy also often evokes intense feelings in therapists as well, severely challenging their own capacity to regulate their own affects.

Since therapists are not able to solve patients issues for them on a merely ontical level, they (the therapists) must learn to bear the anxiety evoked by the acute suffering of the other and be content with their primary analytic contribution of understanding the meaning of the individual's ontic and ontological conflicts.

The dynamic therapeutic process The therapeutic process usually begins when a person who is suffering from certain psychologic and/or psychosomatic symptoms first seeks help in alleviating these troubles by consulting a professional. At this point the individual often has only a vague and often misleading sense of how these difficulties might be related to current or prior life experiences but no idea at all about either the meaning or solution to these symptoms. The Daseinsanalyst's initial tasks are therefore to come to a clear common understanding, first, of what might actually be bringing the person to therapy and, second, of the specific initial goals of the together.

The daseinsanalytic therapeutic process is unique in that it involves dealing with not one kind of suffering but two: the ontical suffering that comes from one's everyday life and the ontological suffering that comes from one's very being *as* human with all the inescapable contingencies of being that kind of being and no other. In Kastrinidis's short-term Daseinsanalysis this dual focus requires both a *basic, general stance* on the part of the therapist as well as the deliberate implementation of *situation specific interventions.*

The *basic stance* (*Haltung*) is a definite, steady hermeneutic attunement towards the patient, one that demonstrates genuine but unbiased interest in and acceptance of the individual, an actively hermeneutic listening not only to everything the person says or "is" during the time together but also an equally active focusing to what lies "between the lines" of their manifest speech and being and bringing these thoughts and observations to the individual's attention. Usually such a welcoming hermeneutic presence is totally surprising and unfamiliar to the patient, fostering trust in and attachment to the therapist. This is typically when the first signs of unconscious therapeutic alliance begin to appear.

The *more situation specific interventions* aim at facilitating the individual's self-knowledge, particularly with respect to his or her conflicts. It is this aspect of the therapy that brings out both tactical and characterological defenses against knowing and being known as the tone of the conversation shifts quite radically from the familiar everyday covering-up kind of conversation to a serious, intimate, and sincere experience of deep emotions, new thoughts, and fantasies. According to Kastrinidis, usually it is here that intense longing, rage, mourning, and the like become activated and, with this, extreme measures of characterological and tactical self-protection, defense, or resistance appear. Ultimately, the therapist must side with the wanting against the not wanting tendencies of the patient by calmly and confidently pointing out the individual's attempts to evade or sideline painful issues along with the consequences of such efforts and gently inviting them to put such habits into question and have a thoughtful look at what it all means. Always only with the individual's consent, links between presence and past are brought out and explored along with new possibilities for understanding and changing the individual's self-limiting and even self-harming ways of being. For most patients this new way of relating often is the most important source of finding the courage to progressively risk new decisions and behaviors and eventually step more freely forward in their lives with confidence and satisfaction.

Daseinsanalytically understood, the consequences of this entire process may be described, as Heidegger put it in Being and Time, as the realization of one's "possibility of being a whole" (Heidegger 1927/1962, pp. 279f), one's "authentic potentiality-for-being" (Heidegger 1927/1962, pp. 312f) requiring, above all an existential attitude of "anticipatory resoluteness" (Heidegger 1927/1962, pp. 352–358). In short-term daseinsanalytic psychotherapy, such anticipatory resoluteness springs from the mutual understanding of what it is to be ontically one's particular self and ontologically simply human. As Heidegger put it, "Along with the sober anxiety (*nüchternen Angst*) which brings us face to face with our individualized potentiality-for-Being, there goes an unshakable joy (*gerüstete Freude*) in this possibility" (Heidegger 1927/1962, p. 358). Heidegger's comments here are particularly apt with respect to the affects that commonly appear in short-term Daseinsanalytic therapy, namely, on the one side, anxiety and sobriety, to which Kastrinidis also adds mourning that comes with deep self-examination and, on the other hand the profound sense of release and deep joy that comes with the long overdue freedom of understanding and becoming both truly oneself and deeply human.

Finally, while acknowledging that generalizations about something as complex and basically idiosyncratic as psychotherapy are misleading and can never capture the course of any one given psychotherapy, Kastrinidis finds it useful to differentiate four broad aspects of the therapeutic process: entering the process; the experience and exploration of deep feelings; hermeneutic understanding of ontical historical life and basic conflicts with the ontological; and dissolution of therapeutic process and relationship with parting, mourning, and acceptance. Clearly these aspects tend to occur in a roughly sequential order but in no way come in any fixed chronological sequence but, rather, often overlap, circle around one another and may even all occur in a single session. Nevertheless, Daseinsanalytic therapists hoping to intensify and shorten their work with individuals, sparing them both money and time, may find the reminder of the essential aspects useful to hold in mind.

References

Abbass, A. (2015). *Reaching through the Resistance*. Kansas City, MO: Seven Leaves Press.

Binswanger, L. (1960). Daseinsanalyse und Psychotherapie ll. *Acta Psychotherapeutica et Psychosomatica 8*: 251–260.

Boss, M. (1963). *Psychoanalysis and Daseinsanalysis* (trans. L.B. Lefebre). New York: Basic Books. (Original work published 1957.)

Boss, M. (1964). What makes us behave at all socially? *Review of Existential Psychology and Psychiatry 4* (1): 53–68.

Boss, M. (1979). *Existential Foundations of Medicine and Psychology* (trans. S. Conway and A. Cleaves). New York: Jason Aronson. (Original work published 1971.)

Boss, M. (1988) Recent considerations in Daseinsanalysis. *The Humanistic Psychologist 16* (1): 58–74.

Condrau, G. (1998). *Martin Heidegger's Impact on Psychotherapy*. New York: Edition MOSAIC.

Craig, E. (1986). Sanctuary and presence: An existential view of the therapist's contribution. *The Humanistic Psychologist 14* (1): 22–28. (Reprinted in Classics in humanistic psychology (2000) a special issue of *The Humanistic Psychologist* 28 (1–3): 267–274.)

Craig, E. (1988a). An encounter with Medard Boss. *The Humanistic Psychologist 16* (1): 24–55.

Craig, E. (ed.). (1988b). Psychotherapy for freedom: The daseinsanalytic way in psychology and psychoanalysis [Special issue]. *The Humanistic Psychologist 16* (1).

Craig, E. (2008). The human and the hidden: Existential wonderings about depth, soul, and the unconscious. *The Humanistic Psychologist 36* (3–4): 227–282.

Craig, E. (2012). Existential psychotherapy: Discipline and demarche. In: *Existential Psychotherapy: Legacy, Vibrancy and Dialogue* (ed. L. Barnett and G. Madison), 7–19. London: Routledge.

Craig, E. (2015). The lost language of being: Ontology's perilous destiny in existential psychotherapy. *Philosophy, Psychiatry, and Psychology 20* (2): 79–92.

Davanloo, H. (ed.) (1980). *Short-term Dynamic Psychotherapy*. Northvale, NJ: Jason Aronson.

Davanloo, H. (1990). *Unlocking the Unconscious: Selected Papers of Habib Davanloo, MD*. New York: John Wiley & Sons.

Davanloo, H. (2000). *Intensive Short-term Dynamic Psychotherapy: Selected Papers of Habib Davanloo, MD*. New York: John Wiley & Sons.

Fonagy, P. (2001). *Attachment Theory and Psychoanalysis*. New York: Other Press.

Fonagy, P., Gergely, G., Jurist, E. et al. (2002). *Affect Regulation, Mentalization, and the Development of the Self*. New York: Other Press.

Freud, S. (1958). Papers on technique. In: *The Standard Edition of the Complete Psychological Works of Sigmund Freud*, vol. *12* (ed. and trans. J. Strachey), 83–173. London: Hogarth Press. (Original works published 1911–1915.)

Freud, S. (1964a). New introductory lectures on psycho-analysis. In: *The Standard Edition of the Complete Psychological Works of Sigmund Freud*, vol. *22* (ed. and trans. J. Strachey), 1–182. London: Hogarth Press. (Original work published 1933.)

Freud, S. (1964b). An outline of psychoanalysis. In: *The Standard Edition of the Complete Psychological Works of Sigmund Freud*, vol. *23* (ed. and trans. J. Strachey), 138–207. London: Hogarth Press. (Original work published 1940.)

Heidegger, M. (1962). *Being and Time* (trans. J. McQuarrie and E. Robinson). New York: Harper and Row. (Original work published 1927.)

Heidegger, M. (1977). Letter on humanism. In: *Basic Writings* (ed. D. Krell), 193–242. New York: Harper & Row. (Original work published 1947.)

Heidegger, M. (2001). *Zollikon Seminars: Protocols – Conversations – Letters* (ed. M. Boss, trans. F. Mayr and R. Askay) Evanston, IL: Northwestern University Press. (Original work published 1987.)

Holzhey-Kunz, A. (2012). What defines the Daseinsanalytic process? *Existential Analysis 8* (1): 200–210.

Holzhey-Kunz, A. (2014). *Daseinsanalysis* (trans. S. Leighton). London: Free Association Books.

Kastrinidis, P. (2005). Between human illusion and inhuman reality: A Daseinsanalytic contribution to the understanding of masochism. In: *Daseinsanalysis: The Twenty-second Annual Symposium of the Simon Silverman Phenomenology Center* (ed. D.J Martino), 89–109. Pittsburgh: Simon Silverman Phenomenology.

Milner, M. (1952). Aspects of symbolism in comprehension of the non-self. *International Journal of Psychoanalysis 33* (2): 181–194.

Moustakas, C.E. (ed.) (1956). *The Self: Explorations in Personal Growth.* New York: Harper & Row.

Moustakas, C.E. (ed.) (1966). *Existential Child Therapy: The Child's Discovery of Himself.* New York: Basic Books.

Schore, A.N. (2012). *The Science of the Art of Psychotherapy.* New York: W.W. Norton.

Stern, D. (1985). *The Interpersonal World of the Infant.* New York: Basic Books.

Stern, P.J. (1964). *The Abnormal Person and His World: An Introduction to Psychopathology.* Princeton, NJ: D. Van Nostrand.

Stern, P.J. (1972). *In Praise of Madness: Realness Therapy – the Self Reclaimed.* New York: W.W. Norton & Company.

Stern, P.J. (1979). Introduction (to the English translation). In: *Existential Foundations of Medicine and Psychology* (ed. M. Boss, trans. S. Conway and A. Cleaves), ix–xxii. New York: Jason Aronson.

Trevarthen, C. (2005). First things first: Infants make good use of the sympathetic rhythm of imitation, without reason or language. *Journal of Child Psychotherapy 31* (1): 91–113.

4

Case Studies

A Therapist's Search for His Own Way of Being Daseinsanalytic

Perikles Kastrinidis

Introduction

This chapter presents two case studies revealing how a daseinsanalytic approach may appear concretely in therapeutic practice. The first case is from my earliest years as a therapist while just learning daseinsanalytic psychotherapy and being supervised by both a training analyst at the Daseinsanalytic Institute in Zürich and a senior South American psychoanalyst from the Swiss Psychoanalytic Society. The patient, whom I shall call Sylvia, was a young woman suffering with epilepsy and what was then called neurotic depression. Sylvia's psychotherapy employed the classic analytic setting, using the couch three times a week for almost three years. The second case, occurring only recently in my 60s, was with "Ernest," a man in his 70s suffering with depression and a severe death anxiety. Ernest and I sat face-to-face for weekly sessions with gradually diminishing frequency over the next three years.

In presenting these cases, I will focus on my own perceptions, reactions, and activity as the therapist so readers may follow how one classically trained daseinsanalytic therapist's practice evolved over 40 years of practical existential inquiry. Never wed to stereotypical daseinsanalytic technique, from the beginning I was determined to find my own way and still be daseinsanalytic with patients. What I learned, most essentially, was that the premises of a phenomenological, hermeneutic psychoanalysis can only be realized through a therapist's own lived humanity. For me, genuine daseinsanalytic therapy is an illusion if it is not carried out by therapists who sincerely seek their own daseinsanalytic understanding of *both* their life and their practice. Daseinsanalysis is a unique relationship between two uniquely searching human beings or it is not Daseinsanalysis at all.

The Wiley World Handbook of Existential Therapy, First Edition. Edited by Emmy van Deurzen, Erik Craig, Alfried Längle, Kirk J. Schneider, Digby Tantam, and Simon du Plock.

A Young Woman with Idiopathic Grand Mal Epilepsy

I was a 28-year-old psychiatrist just starting my psychotherapeutic training in Daseinsanalysis when "Sylvia," a 24-year-old woman was referred to me by an outpatient neurological clinic in Zurich. From the beginning, though obviously intelligent and thoughtful, she appeared to make some effort not to be noticed. Slightly heavy set and soft spoken, she dressed in plain, pale colors matching her introverted demeanor. She was the eldest of two daughters in a working-class family and, at the time of her referral, was in training to become a pedagogical therapist.

In her initial session Sylvia complained of an intense pain in her chest that felt like a single massive wound completely excavating and drying out her entire insides. She said this had been going on for the past year-and-a-half and, more recently, she had also begun experiencing abdominal cramps forcing her to the emergency room where they were unable to identify any physical cause. In addition, Sylvia experienced regular vertigo-attacks and dissociative episodes, the latter occurring in social situations, particularly when conflict was involved and usually found herself anxious or depressed for days after these symptoms first appeared. Finally, Sylvia said she began having epileptic grand mal seizures when she was 14. She was prescribed anti-convulsive medication at the time, discontinuing it four years prior to seeing me, and picking it up again a couple of years later when symptoms began to reappear. Sylvia told me that her neurologists had said that her symptoms were a combination of idiopathic epilepsy and unspecified psychological factors and that she should continue her medication.

Even with all this somatic disquiet, Sylvia struck me as quite a self-reflective young woman. Soon she spoke about some troublesome events in her recent professional life in a long-term residential setting where she was training and working as pedagogical therapist for children and adolescents with severe behavioral problems. Although she generally felt great empathy for these disturbed children, she was ashamed to say that there were a number of situations in which she felt intense anger, even hatred and rage, towards these same children, sometimes to the point of having dark intrusive fantasies and even impulses to beat them. On one occasion she actually slapped one of the children on the head. This suddenly reminded her of her mother who regularly flew into irrational rages and beat Sylvia as a child. She was horrified by the thought that she might also be capable of behaving toward the children as her mother had toward her, losing complete control and brutally beating one of the children in her care.

The Opening Phase of Sylvia's Psychotherapy

In the initial stages of her therapy Sylvia found it quite difficult to communicate in a direct, emotional manner. While not an unusual problem early in any psychotherapy, with Sylvia, the difficulty was striking. From the first, Sylvia found it almost impossible to make eye contact and her anxiety was so obvious I could see carotid arteries throbbing. Sylvia rarely uttered anything close to a normal voice tone and I had to strain even to hear her sighing. Often completely unable to finish her sentences, she raspily whispered words through her dry lips. The first year was thus not easy for either of us. Especially challenging for me was the contagion of her dissociative tendencies as found in my own difficulties to remain present, open, and alert. I often felt guilty about my difficulty maintaining a thoughtful attentiveness in the face of Sylvia's intense anxiety, inhibited speech, and tendency to dissociate.

Fortunately for us, Sylvia had an immediate active interest in her dreams. In her very first session she reported a dream of the night before in which she was standing on a tower, some 60 feet above a vast ocean. Although she knew she had to leap into the sea below, she dared not. Then, suddenly, her father appeared and immediately leapt into the sea, emboldening her to do so as well. We together understood the dream to relate to her anxiety about leaping into psychotherapy. It also occurred to me that her father might well have played a strong, supportive role in her waking life and, if so, it was likely she would need something similar from me. This was only the first of many instances in which we were together given illuminating access to the meaning of her unique world of dreams, her *idios kosmos.*

From the very beginning Sylvia relayed three to four dreams per week with their details often taking as long as 40 minutes to describe. I generally responded by simply listening and making cautious elaborative inquiries and, for quite some time, this dream inquiry soundly supported and maintained our therapeutic alliance. Nevertheless, I was struck by the contrast between her freedom in discussing dreams versus her difficulty in discussing waking life. Even as a novice I soon realized this pattern indicated her profound anxiety and ambivalence about intimacy in her relationships with others, both fearing and desiring the possibility of knowing and being known. When I finally commented on this circumstance and she acknowledged its veracity, I noticed the first slight signs of her relaxation in our conversations. Eventually I even came to understand that Sylvia needed to know we could acknowledge and discuss her anxiety without being disturbed by it. As with dream work, dealing early and directly with anxiety and ambivalence, is an essential feature of daseinsanalytic psychotherapy.

This opening phase of treatment lasted just a few months. As the novice daseinsanalytic candidate I was at the time, I followed quite closely the Daseinsanalytic recommendation to employ Freud's (1912/1958) psychoanalytic rules of free association and evenly hovering attention in order to be present and open for whatever the patient brought to the hour. It was not long, however, before I found myself disappointed by the admixture of Sylvia's reticent ambivalence to speak of her waking life and the daseinsanalytic demand for my strictly passive/receptive attitude. I therefore decided, again quite early, to cautiously diverge from the received daseinsanalytic opinion and experiment with a different therapeutic attitude and manner of attention.

The Second Phase of Therapy

The second phase of Sylvia's psychotherapy began when I started more actively participating in our conversations, gradually taking more initiative by inviting clarifications and asking more focused questions about her experiences and circumstances. This in turn required that I also listen beyond what she said and felt to what she was not saying or feeling. I soon observed how helpful it was for both of us to "read between the lines" for the unrecognized details of her ways of being in the world including especially her ways of being with me. This radical change from purely descriptive, *phenomenal listening* to the manifest content of the spoken word to an actively investigating, meaning seeking *hermeneutic listening* proved to be a significant shift in our relationship, as well as in my development as a psychotherapist.

In Sylvia's case, moving from an exclusively passive, receptive mode of listening to phenomenal content to an actively inquiring hermeneutic mode of listening for hidden dimensions of experience and meaning led, almost immediately, to some interesting discoveries. For instance, my more active participation in our dialogue increased her specific fears that I might misunderstand, judge, or even reject her, thus further deepening our understanding of her conflicts about genuine intimacy and how this influenced her relationships, including her relationship with me.

An example of how this co-constructed nature of the world of our therapeutic relationship unfolded occurred one day when Sylvia reported a dream in which a raging woman, dressed in bright red and waving a large knife appeared in front of her. At that time, I still tended to perceive her as a shy, relatively victimized young woman and interpreted her dream with respect to the threatening nature of her world relationships. To my surprise Sylvia shared that she felt completely misunderstood and abandoned by me because I did not link the appearance of this violent woman with her own emotional impulsivity and murderous rage. As soon as I too saw my failure to appreciate her own power and aggression, I acknowledged my error as well as her courage in confronting me. Dealing with this empathic rupture led to an eruption of memories of her mother's violent and sadistic behaviors toward her, including not only severe physical beatings but the shameful summoning of the parish priest to exorcise the devil from Sylvia, neither of which abuses the mother ever visited on Sylvia's younger sister. Fortunately, the priest in this instance refused to attempt such an exorcism on the innocent child but, instead, invited her to attend the church's youth programs where Sylvia found herself more relaxed and happy to be with others than she had ever felt previously.

With my confidence in being a more hermeneutically engaged psychotherapist growing, Sylvia felt free to begin considering some of the disappointing aspects of her relationship with her overly idealized father. As sympathetic and supportive as he may have been to her, Sylvia also began to see that he had never really protected her from her mother's abuse. Thus, by the end of the first year in therapy, my more focused here-and-now engagement began to bear fruit, yielding an open discussion of some of the more complex and contradictory realities in her life. At this point we were approaching the third, loosely defined phase of therapy. The two valuable early phases – the initial more exclusively receptive and the latter more engaged, hermeneutic manner of listening – had opened the way for a freer and unembarrassed therapeutic relating.

The Third Phase of Therapy

The above described transformations in our reciprocal ways of being-with-one-another, our *Miteinandersein*, paved the way for what became the third phase of her therapy, characterized by a felt sense of partnership or, as Binswanger would put it, a sense of being genuine "Daseinpartners" (Binswanger 1960, p. 253) that typified the third phase of the therapy.

For example, six months into this phase of our work she reported a dream of the death of her father in which I and her therapy also appeared for the first time. In the dream, she kept looking into his eyes to see if he was actually dead as he lay lifeless and still in a hard, cold, metallic coffin. Painfully grief stricken, she hurriedly cleaned and prepared the hearse while at the same time being aware of not wanting to miss our rapidly approaching analytic session. Discussing this dream the next day, we arrived at the mutual understanding that she was cleaning up her relation to the past and turning toward her current therapy and the promise it held for her future. Gone were her old anxieties and ambivalences that had given way to present hunger for and commitment to her future possibilities.

Our new therapeutic intimacy and freedom allowed us to focus more intently on Sylvia's professional aspirations for working with special needs children and, beyond this, her now open desire for a relationship with a man, a desire which became increasingly apparent at the time of her dream of her father's death. It was during this same period of remarkable growth that Sylvia stopped taking her antiepileptic medication as neurological tests had shown no signs of epileptic brain activity for almost two years. It was no mere coincidence that her chest-pains and abdominal cramps had also disappeared as she gained a thoughtful reflectiveness on what it meant for her to simply *be* herself, a woman with all her basic needs, desires, frailties, and vulnerabilities. But this thoughtfulness came with a new sort of "suffering" that was no longer strictly connected with the particular vicissitudes of her everyday ontical existence but now could be decidedly ontological as ontological, that is, concerned with what it is to be human and to be oneself.

For instance, Sylvia became increasingly aware that much of her earlier suffering was not only related to the disappointments and irritations of her everyday life but also to her own personal response to basic human moods, needs, and desires shared in one manner or another by all human beings. More specifically, she began to see that her own hyper-sensitivity and many of her private and professional social difficulties arose in response to her own unrealistic fantasies and wishes for unconflicted human connection as well as her longing to be seen, understood, accepted, and genuinely valued by others. Gradually, she saw that she had been confronted with these basic human challenges already as a child when she was utterly bereft of empathic support, the kind of concerned human understanding that would allow her to face and integrate her experiences into the development of her own personality. Finally realizing the extent and severity of maternal failure in her childhood and youth, she began having dreams in which her mother behaved in her old, familiar cruel and condescending fashion but, to her own surprise, Sylvia herself no longer reacted with terror and submission but, instead, with an increasingly confident sense of opposition and self-assertion. Although she was often left feeling utterly alone, especially as her father appeared in the dreams as weak and intimidated, at least Sylvia's own differentiation from her mother was reliably underway. Again, it was no mere coincidence that she found herself increasingly free to oppose her mother when similar conflicts arose in her waking life. At one point, when she realized that it would be impossible to change her mother's personality, she decided to accept that their relationship could be maintained only on the basis of casual, sadly superficial communication.

Fortunately, with these mature and realistic changes in her relationship with her mother, Sylvia also came to realize that her aggressive feelings, fantasies, and reactions towards the children with whom she was working could be understood as merely displaced expressions of rage toward her mother, especially when the children were dismissive, disrespectful, and abusive toward her in precisely the same ways her mother related to her. These insights enabled her to maintain the kind of healthy emotional distance from them she needed to perform in a caring but thoroughly professional manner with them.

Eventually Sylvia moved away from her hometown to a much larger city where she developed new relationships with both men and women. At this point she at last felt free to speak of her intense longing for greater intimacy in her life, especially for sexual intimacy with a man. As much as she longed for such intimacy, whenever a man showed the least interest, she would pull away to protect herself from what she took to be the inevitability of humiliating rejection, based on how poorly she thought of herself. As a part of these same conversations, it was no easy thing for Sylvia to also disclose and discuss her masturbatory practices and the guilt and isolation that followed. Although earlier she masturbated to reduce the tension of her destructive rage towards her mother, later on she would do so to release the tensions of her unsatisfied desires for intimate sexual gratification. It was not long before she realized these strategies also reduced her motivation to risk reaching out, further deepening her terrible loneliness and isolation.

Thinking back on these last months with Sylvia, I now realize how helpful and crucial it was for her to have experienced me as an actively engaged, inquiring, and accepting participant in our conversations. My early passive/receptive stance could only have left her feeling alone and objectified in discussing these most intimate aspects of her life. With the conclusion of these exceptionally tender and intimate conversations, Sylvia's therapy finally came to an end when she decided to leave Switzerland a little over three years after it began.

Nearly a decade later I was surprised to receive a call from Sylvia to request a single session during which I learned that she had married and was raising three children. The once shy, confused, and unassertive child-woman appeared now a conscious, confident adult one who had grown into her own way of being in the world with genuine purpose and self-determined direction.

Some Concluding Reflections

Before moving on to the second case I will very briefly reflect on two points in my work with Sylvia: a dynamic hermeneutic understanding of idiopathic epilepsy and the significance of the therapeutic alliance.

As we saw with Sylvia and has been asserted by at least one empirical investigation (Torda 1977), idiopathic grand mal epilepsy can be associated with unexamined, unintegrated, even murderous rage toward abusive early childhood attachment figures. Torda's study involving more than 60 individuals suffering from epilepsy showed that when such unacknowledged childhood rage threatens to break through into awareness and overwhelm individuals they can dissociate, lose consciousness, and become swept up in a grand mal seizure. Although this phenomenally manifest dynamic has been discussed in psychoanalytic literature what was so striking in the Torda study was the way that those individuals exhibited such an uncannily similar pattern to the one seen here in the therapy with Sylvia.

With respect to the therapeutic alliance with Sylvia, I must admit that much of what I now explicitly see and understand about the nature and quality of our relationship was, at the time of her treatment, only vaguely grasped on a purely intuitive level. As a relatively inexperienced daseinsanalytic training candidate when I began working with Sylvia I found myself more often informed by my felt sense of our actual working relationship than by any theoretical understanding, be it psychoanalytic, daseinsanalytic, or otherwise. Thus I only quite cautiously and tentatively explored her relationship and feelings toward me, always taking care not to exceed her capacity to bear the anxiety of immediately experienced closeness with me. The more I felt her connection with me increasing, the gradually bolder I became in investigating her most anxiety-laden issues. Especially when she dreamt of her father lying in his casket while feeling an urgent concern that she not miss our session, I finally experienced the soundness of our therapeutic connection. Although at the time that was all I could say about what was happening between us, today I have a much richer, explicitly analytic understanding. Since that time, I have been fortunate to have been exposed more fully to psychoanalytic thought and practice, including Greenson's 1967 classic on psychoanalytic technique of which I was only somewhat familiar at the time but, most importantly, the work of Habib Davanloo and his colleagues in the development of intensive short-term dynamic psychotherapy (ISTDP) which places what they refer to as the "unconscious therapeutic alliance" at the very center of analytic work. Looking back on Sylvia's therapy today, particularly on the change in my own attitude during the second phase, I realize I also was looking out for signs of a positive but hidden therapeutic relation with me, what I would now call, based on the theory and practice of ISTDP, the unconscious therapeutic alliance. Abbass (2015) has described such an alliance as not only crucial for the patient's collaboration in the painful aspects of the analytic process but also as a powerful psychodynamic counter force to the resistances. ISTDP makes a clear distinction between this hidden alliance and the conscious, working alliance and repeatedly demonstrates how, once recognized, understood, and embraced by the therapist, it profoundly enhances a mutual commitment to the therapeutic task in such a way that the most painful issues can be addressed and brought openly into the therapeutic dialogue.

After a Thirty-Year Interlude

Some 30 years of daseinsanalytic psychotherapeutic practice passed before undertaking this next case. By then, I was in my mid-60s and had changed quite considerably as a therapist and as a person. I had not only developed a more differentiated understanding of Daseinsanalysis as I experienced it in my own practice, but also of therapeutic Daseinsanalysis per se. I also had to come to terms with 30 years of my own human existing with all its unavoidable twists and turns and, through this too, become the therapist and person I am today.

With respect to the professional side of this equation, the three decades afforded me the opportunity to study and consider a variety of other psychotherapeutic systems, perspectives, and practices, each of which, shaped in one way or another, my own thinking, understanding, and practice of daseinsanalytic psychotherapy itself.

As I mentioned above, one of the most significant influences came from the study and practice of Habib Davanloo's ISTDP which I first undertook in the mid-1980s. Two specific aspects of ISTDP have been especially influential in helping shape my experience and understanding of the possibilities of a genuinely daseinsanalytic practice. I have already mentioned the first, namely, ISTDP's view of the therapeutic alliance, especially the hidden, unspoken, or "unconscious therapeutic alliance." The second influential aspect of ISTDP is how it construes and structures the therapeutic process in a very practical, concrete fashion, especially with reference to actively engaging the individual's affects, anxieties, and defenses, specifically by inviting intense affects, blocking defenses against such emotional experiences, and monitoring the different pathways of anxiety. But I have to stress that regardless of the value of over three decades of psychotherapeutic study and practice, the other significant change between these two cases came through the unfolding process of my very own human existence. So daseinsanalytic psychotherapy, as I see it, explicitly includes one's own most existential transformation as a person.

Purgatory, Hell, or Nothing

Some 30 years after meeting and working with Sylvia, I received a call from a man in his 70s, whom I shall call Ernest, and who had been referred by a hospital for depressive symptoms after having been admitted for a pulmonary embolism. Obviously any man in his 70s is faced with wholly different concerns than a young woman in her 20s, a difference that clearly affects the entire clinical context and situation, including its goals and manner of relating. Also, at that point in my mid-60s, I had, as already mentioned, long since abandoned the classical Daseinsanalytic use of the couch in favor of sitting face-to-face in full view of one another.

Even in my very first interview with Ernest, when I met him in the hospital, he spoke freely and openly of being obsessed by the single thought he would soon become Nothing, that nothing would be left of him after his death with the possible exception of a few ashes. As it turned out, Ernest had been absorbed with thoughts of aging and a potentially imminent death ever since turning 70 when he began frequently listening to his heartbeat or interrupting his breathing to see if his life force was sufficient for its renewal. He was particularly haunted by the knowledge that his own father had died at precisely his own present age and also from a pulmonary embolism. Two relatively recent experiences only increased the intensity of his anxieties. First, one of his closest friends had died some time ago and he recently visited the widow in the home they shared for many years. While there he noticed the urn containing his friend's remains still resting in the living room. The absurdity of the moment triggered his own intense anxiety and, nearly in a panic, he fled the house. Also, another of Ernest's friends had even more recently talked about wanting his ashes spread out on a lake after his death. Although this conversation was slightly more tolerable, he was still haunted by it and it only served to heighten the intensity of his unrelenting obsessive thoughts of his own in escapable extinction. As a Daseinsanalyst I could not avoid being reminded of Heidegger's description of the fundamental (ontological) uncanniness of human existence he calls *Unheimlichkeit* (not-at-home-ness). I said nothing about this, however, as Ernest's experience of anxiety at that point were not yet an expression of an ontological encounter with death but, rather, of his distinctive, everyday ontical phobic-obsessive symptoms.

The First Year

Working face-to-face, Ernest and I met for nearly three years, initially on a roughly weekly basis but with gradually decreasing frequency especially over the final year. Throughout the initial 35 sessions of his first year of therapy, Ernest continually reiterated his anxiety over dissolving into Nothing, the fact that whenever his death came to reclaim his existence it would dissolve into absolutely Nothing. He found it impossible to stop ruminating over the facts that only shapeless, meaningless dust would remain of his body and that any memories of him as a living person would last, at most, a mere generation or two. He found it intolerable to think that within mere decades nothing at all would be left to mark even the tiny raw fact of his existence. Such thoughts of his utter annihilation triggered immediate, palpable anxiety and phobic ideations. I responded to his dread by acknowledging the unavoidable reality of his mortality and finitude while also encouraging him to recall and reflect on *his life as a whole*, including his childhood, youth, and lengthy adulthood through to his maturity.

Ernest immediately dismissed my suggestions as he considered his more distant past to be irrelevant with respect to his present life and it's relentless, unbearable anxiety. Undeterred, I questioned his initial intellectualized resistance to reflecting on his life as a whole and not long after he found himself recalling his Catholic upbringing with its threats of eternal suffering if he did not religiously adhere to the creeds and cannons of the church. Recognizing there was something irrational behind his current dilemma, he one day admitted finding it quite strange that even after all these years he still feared that when he died he would be sent straight to hell, or purgatory at the very best in spite of the fact that he was no longer a practicing believer. For instance, he recalled feeling that he had committed the "mortal sin," one punishable by eternal damnation, of biting into the host of Holy Communion, the very body of Christ, instead of holding it in his mouth until it dissolved completely on its own. He found it odd that even as a "rational" and secular adult now in his 70s, he thought himself unworthy of a heaven, and terrified of either a hell or purgatory on one side or Nothing on the other. Still, intellectually understanding that his despair was somehow irrational did nothing to relieve it.

As I continued deliberately focusing our conversations on Ernest's intense death anxiety even more childhood memories began to surface. For instance one day he recalled the horse-drawn funeral processions that were the custom in the little Catholic village of his childhood. He especially remembered how terrified he was that, as the procession passed him, the corpse would suddenly rise from the coffin and come back to life. He also recalled once witnessing a cremation and seeing the corpse of the dead person rise up in the moment of being consumed by the flames. With these memories he began to doubt what he really believed, emotionally and fundamentally, with respect to life, death, and life after death.

As our therapeutic reconstruction of his life-history continued, Ernest began to see the larger conflicts and the complexities of his anxiety in relation to mortality.

He began to realize that, as he no longer accepted Catholic theology, his only alternative was to face that he would inescapably come to Nothing at all, the mere thought of which was an excruciating torment. Ernest's anamnestic reconstructions soon led to questioning how he had actually lived his life up to that point and he realized that as an adult he had only managed to avoid these old moral, religious, and philosophical questions by throwing himself into his everyday (ontic) life, focusing entirely on his immediate relationships and achievements. With this, he also began to acknowledge and appreciate his successful academic career, his two marriages and three children, and the fact that he had been able to maintain positive, supportive relationships with both of his exes and each of his fine adult children. He was grateful, too, that he had never suffered anything like a serious, life impairing or life-threatening illness until his recent episode of a pulmonary embolism. Ironically, none of these deeply positive affirmations mitigated in the least his extreme thanatophobia, his horror at the thought of becoming nothing at all.

Around this time, Ernest began reading popular esoteric books on being and nothingness and emptiness. Although not academics, the authors expressed their ideas quite eloquently, promising relief from the anxiety that had followed him everywhere. Nevertheless, Ernest remained disappointed as he found many their ideas difficult to follow. His personal research, however did have an important positive aspect in that he became *more emotionally engaged* in our relationship and in coming to terms with the mystery of nothingness. He also began wondering about the deeper meaning of being human in the first place and the kinds of emotions this meaning might bring up for him.

The Second Year

Toward the end of the first and throughout the second year of psychotherapy I began to join Ernest in the kind of mutual relationship already mentioned in the case of Sylvia that might, following Binswanger, be called "Daseinpartnership," wherein we reflected together on the emotions and thoughts stimulated by his reading. When he asked about my own experience and questions I answered him straightforwardly, disclosing aspects of my own ideas, knowledge, and philosophy along with aspects of my own personal emotions, experiences, and questions regarding what it is to be human, to have to grow old, and to die. Through these conversations, Ernest grew to realize that his fundamental anxiety about the Nothing and many of his related questions and anxieties would have to remain unresolved as they concerned what is humanly unfathomable and can only be realized and accepted as such.

In spite of these rather profound conversations with such clearly ontological implications, we consistently focused directly on his everyday experience as well. This was psychotherapy, not a seminar or tutorial: we were not there together to read and discuss great works and ideas but, rather, only to uncover and discuss Ernest's vital everyday experiences, questions, and concerns. Our therapeutic mission was to uncover and consider what our unavoidable human finitude might mean for him emotionally and for how he might consequentially choose to conduct his life both now and in the future. Thus, Ernest came to see that although he could learn to manage his everyday ontic anxieties regarding his practical concerns in the face of aging and death, he could not at all avoid his own personal anxiety in the face of The Nothing. His challenge, therefore, was to accept the painful circumstance that, like all of his fellow human beings, he could know nothing of *The Nothing* but only resolve to stand *in* his anxiety right in the face of such unfathomable Nothingness.

Although our steady focus was on Ernest's own experiences and questions, obviously I, too, was living through my own aging and oncoming death and I did not at all hide this fact from him. For instance, during one of our sessions, disclosing my own thoughts came out in a moment of humor. I mentioned that when Woody Allen was once asked about life after death Allen wisecracked in return, "The problem is not whether there is a Hereafter or not, the problem is how far it is from the city and how late it stays open." Such moments of our shared black humor became a unique dimension of our therapeutic conversations, reaffirming the reality that each of us has to find our own beliefs, not in books or the advice and wisdom of others but, rather, in our own personal inclinations, experiences, convictions, and choices. We alone are responsible for how we choose to stand in the face of such ultimate concerns.

At this point our therapeutic conversations were characterized by moods ranging from sober contemplation, to sadness, grief, and painful mourning, to mutually shared sardonic humor. We now focused not only on his everyday anxieties but also on his despair and helplessness in the face of his own inescapable human condition. It was now clear that my therapeutic effort was not to eliminate but support Ernest in understanding and accepting his anxiety, guilt, sorrow, and powerlessness. As his acceptance of his so-called symptoms gradually grew, they paradoxically began to fade and even disappear. As he lost these sources of everyday ontical misery Ernest began to experience and accept more fully his suffering, that is, his painful ontological suffering over his emotionally experienced understanding and coming to terms with *la condition humaine*.

The Third Year

By the third year of therapy, Ernest's mood had grown noticeably lighter and he was coming only once a month. As the year progressed, he became much more active in everyday life than he had been for some time and his depressive, phobic, and hypochondriac thoughts were practically never mentioned again. Ernest had even picked up painting, a pastime he had once enjoyed but had long forgotten. Soon after this Ernest decided to end his psychotherapy. In our final session, it was not only Ernest who expressed gratitude for our three years of working together but I, too, expressed my appreciation for having the opportunity to work with him. Having done so, we said goodbye to one another.

Discussion

I will now look back on these two cases to remark on what I see as just a few of the most significant changes I have experienced in my 30 year effort to find my own way of being daseinsanalytically therapeutic.

Some 35 years ago, I began employing the original Daseinsanalytic setting and arrangement, which were largely borrowed from Freud's papers on technique.

However, even as early as just a few months into my classical daseinsanalytic training and education I found myself questioning the universal advisability of these classical recommendations.

A few months after I started seeing Sylvia I stopped insisting that she practice free association exclusively. I also altered my way of being with her, moving from the recommended evenly hovering attention (*Gleichschwebende Aufmerksamkeit*) to a more deliberately focused attention (*Fokussierende Aufmerksamkeit*) with which I began to engage her in more active and mutual exploration of issues and meanings. Although I continued using the couch setting with Sylvia, it was not long before I experimented with abandoning this with future patients as the face-to-face setting consistently led to more lively, therapeutically engaged conversation and yielded more noticeable changes in the individual's attitude and behavior both in and out of therapy. Thus, by the time I was seeing Ernest, I had abandoned all three classical pillars of daseinsanalytic setting: the use of the couch, the frequency of sessions, and the use free association and evenly hovering attention. What I never abandoned was Daseinsanalysis's phenomenological attitude, hermeneutic understanding, and ontological perspective. Thus, what distinguishes Daseinsanalysis for me today are these three essential characteristics: First, being phenomenologically attentive to the ways each of us are relating with ourselves and one another; second, to understand what presents itself through thoughtful hermeneutic analysis; and, three, to nurture an ontological perspective, a steady attentiveness to ontological content. In short, the two human therapeutic partners commit themselves, on the one hand, to disclosing, understanding, and alleviating the patient's ontical everyday ways of suffering and, on the other hand, to unfolding, understanding, and accepting the individual's uniquely painful ways of being ontologically vulnerable as a consequence of having to live as finite, "homeless," and historical human beings, a kind of vulnerability every human being shares with every other. All this because, as Heidegger (1927/1962) tells us, we are Dasein, that kind of being who "is ontically distinguished by the fact that, in its very Being, that being is an issue for it" (p. 32).

References

Abbass, A. (2015). *Reaching through Resistance*. Kansas City, MO: Seven Leaves Press.

Binswanger, L. (1960). Daseinsanalyse und Psychotherapie ll. *Acta Psychotherapeutica et Psychosomatica 8* (4): 251–260.

Boss, M. (1977). *"I Dreamt Last Night...": A New Approach to the Revelations of Dreaming – and its Uses in Psychotherapy* (trans. P.J. Stern). New York: Gardner.

Freud, S. (1958). Recommendations to physicians practicing psycho-analysis. In: *The Standard Edition of the Complete Psychological Works of Sigmund Freud*, vol. 12 (ed. and trans. J. Strachey), 109–120. London: Hogarth Press. (Original work published 1912.)

Greenson, R. (1967). *The Technique and Practice of Psychoanalysis*, vol. I. New York: International Universities Press.

Heidegger, M. (1962). *Being and Time* (trans. J. McQuarrie and E. Robinson). New York: Harper & Row. (Original work published 1927.)

Torda, C. (1977). On idiopathic epilepsy. *Journal of American Academy of Psychoanalysis 5* (1): 107–124.

5

Key Texts in Daseinsanalysis

Loray Daws and Erik Craig

Introduction to Daseinsanalytic Literature in English

Daseinsanalysis and daseinsanalytic psychotherapy represent a unique and sophisticated clinical and philosophical approach in modern day psychoanalysis. Unfortunately, both geographical and language limitations have impeded the active dissemination of its core principles and unique praxis. As discussed in the previous chapters both the birth and development of Daseinsanalysis can be traced to the very beginning of the psychoanalytic movement and the various intellectual contributions of the pillars of Daseinsanalysis, Ludwig Binswanger and Medard Boss. Unfortunately for English readers, the various valiant attempts to anglicize central German daseinsanalytic texts have met with only limited success.

Heidegger's *Being and Time* (1927/1962) itself attests to the challenge of finding appropriate English to describe ontological strata that account for Being and being human within the context of our rich and varied cultural and linguistic heritage. Heidegger's dense, evocative German concepts and descriptions such as Dasein, *Lebenswelt* (lived world/world design), *Sorge* (care), *thrownness* (*non*-chosen world engagement), our established social orders (*Mitwelt* or fate-world), our autochthony-alterity dialectic, our fallenness in relationship to the physical world (*Umwelt*), social world (*Mitwelt*), and personal world of self-relatedness (*Eigenwelt*) refer to textured concerns, already challenging to convey in German and infinitely more so in English

Just four years prior to the release of the first English translation of *Being and Time* by Macquarrie and Robinson, the classical anthology by May, Angel, and Ellenberger (Eds.), *Existence: A New Dimension in Psychiatry and Psychology* (1958), gave English speaking readers the first glimpse into the world of Daseinsanalytic psychiatry, psychology, and psychotherapy. This anthology included three of Binswanger's own works, most significantly, "The Existential School of Thought" and "The Case

The Wiley World Handbook of Existential Therapy, First Edition. Edited by Emmy van Deurzen, Erik Craig, Alfried Längle, Kirk J. Schneider, Digby Tantam, and Simon du Plock.

of Ellen West" (1958). *Existence* was followed by Jacob Needleman's *Being-in-the-World: The Selected Papers of Ludwig Binswanger* in 1963. The two edited works including Binswanger's own papers provide a snapshot of Binswanger's existential concerns as well as his anthropological-clinical application of daseinsanalytic conceptualizations to various psychiatric difficulties. His vivid case studies provide detailed phenomenological descriptions of schizophrenia, a heel phobia, eating disorders (anorexia nervosa), manic depression, and psychosis, all poignantly illustrating his phenomenological concern with articulating the troubled individual's world design, independent of labels of health or pathology. Sadly, not one of Binswanger's full major texts has been translated into English.

Binswanger also provided the initial the impetus for Medard Boss's ultimate embrace of phenomenology and Heidegger's fundamental ontology as the philosophical foundation for his psychotherapeutic Daseinsanalysis. Originally a classically trained orthodox psychoanalyst, over the years Boss grew increasingly dissatisfied with Freudian metapsychology. Thus, Boss's heartfelt receptivity to Binswanger's work was well-earned. However, it was Boss's close relationship with Martin Heidegger that led to a more thoughtful reading and adherence to Heidegger's *Daseinsanalytik*. Boss's oeuvre and contributions are rich and varied. Initially relying on *Being and Time*, Boss set forth to lay out a phenomenological foundation for psychology and psychotherapy with the hope of "humanizing" the field of medicine and setting psychoanalytic interpretations of human phenomena on a new, radical phenomenological ground. His *Psychoanalysis and Daseinsanalysis* (1963) is the most systematic expression of Daseinsanalysis from this period and is also his most well-known and widely read book. As Boss drew ever closer to Heidegger, he grew more comfortably into the philosopher's second period thought of Being and Dasein as interdependent partners, wherein the miraculous openness of Being was required for Dasein to even be in the first place and the openness of Dasein was, in turn, required for Being and beings to be apprehended and disclosed as that which they themselves are. This later period of Heidegger's thought and its impact on Boss's Daseinsanalysis is most thoroughly revealed in his *Zollikon Seminars* (1987/2001). It was during this last phase of their relationship that Boss published his second major systematic work, *Existential Foundations of Medicine and Psychology* (1971/1979) for which Boss enjoyed the support of Heidegger's, "patient and painstaking care" (Boss 1971/1979, p. 12). Unlike the circumstance with Binswanger's major, book-length works, five of Boss's six major works have been translated into English and are presented below.

Without question, the works of Binswanger, Boss, and their philosophical "master," Martin Heidegger, constitute the most significant body of Daseinsanalytic works available to the English-speaking world. Subsequently, a number of daseinsanalytically oriented authors have contributed to English articles in various publications. Four authors have also made volume-length contributions, reviewed below, in addition to their many articles. In chronological order, in 1988 Erik Craig edited an almost 300-page special edition of *The Humanistic Psychologist* entitled "Psychotherapy for Freedom: The Daseinsanalytic Way in Psychology and Psychoanalysis." This special edition was the first extensive English introduction to the work of Medard Boss and his students and colleagues in Zürich. The volume includes not only two verbatim interviews with Medard Boss by the editor but also original works by Boss himself and his fellow Swiss Daseinsanalysts, translated for the first time into English. This work was followed ten years later by the publication of Gion Condrau's *Martin Heidegger's Impact on Psychotherapy* (1998), which makes a valiant effort to present Heidegger and Daseinsanalysis in a more accessible vernacular, with several detailed case studies to support this effort. A third significant contribution to major English literature was made by the English Daseinsanalyst, Hans Cohn, whose 2002 *Heidegger and the Roots of Existential Therapy* offered a cogent yet approachable overview of Heidegger's challenging fundamental ontology and its relevance for psychotherapy. Finally, the philosopher and Daseinsanalyst, Alice Holzhey-Kunz published her own English work entitled *Daseinsanalysis* in 2014, offering a third alternative to the approaches of Binswanger and Boss, which she designates as "hermeneutic anthropology." In addition to the four above mentioned authors, the Swiss Daseinsanalyst Perikles Kastrinidis, the Hungarian Tamàs Fazekas, the English Anthony Stadlen, and the North Americans, Todd DuBose, Roger Frie, and Miles Groth have each contributed English language articles to the body of Bossian daseinsanalytic literature. Finally, a special mention is due Paul J. Stern, a close friend of Boss, who arranged for Boss's lectures at Harvard University in 1963 and who, the following year, published *The Abnormal Person and His World* comparing phenomenological and psychoanalytic views of abnormal psychological syndromes. Stern also wrote lucid introductions to Boss's *I dreamt last night...* (1975/1977) and *Existential Foundations* (1971/1979).

Annotated Bibliography

Boss, M. (1958). *The Analysis of Dreams* (trans. A.J. Pomerans). New York: Philosophical Library. (Original work published 1953.)

In the analysis of dreams Boss provides the reader with a thorough re-evaluation of the importance of dreams, both culturally and psychoanalytically. Boss also critically discusses Freudian dream theory as compared to that of the Zurich school, as well as to the neo-analytical dreams theories of H. Schultz-Hencke and the neo-Freudian dream theory of Erich Fromm. The exploration is deepened by the inclusion of the phenomenological works of R. Bossard and L Klages. These foundational explorations enable Boss to approach a dream ("strange dream of an urn"), in part two, from psychoanalytic and phenomenological vertices. Part three explores the dreamer's *possibilities of existing* as seen in shock dreams, reflective behavior in dreams, conscious thought in dreams, the telling lies in dreams, moral evaluations in dreams, and much more, as well as the dreamer's relationship to the divine in dreams, the experiencing of dreams within dreams, and the experience of non-sensical and paradoxical dreams.

Boss, M. (1963). *Psychoanalysis and Daseinsanalysis* (trans. L.B. Lefebre). New York: Basic Books. (Original work published 1957.)

A central text in Bossian Daseinsanalysis, Medard Boss's book sets forth a critical daseinsanalytic re-evaluation of psychoanalytic theory and praxis. Boss commences his daseinsanalytic approach with a thorough and personalized account of a Daseinsanalytic view of man, followed by both an outline of an analysis of Dasein and the frequent misunderstandings about the analysis of Dasein. This is followed by a re-evaluation of psychoanalysis as it pertains to Daseinsanalysis and its practice. The daseinsanalytic re-evaluation sees a thorough discussion of the neurosis (conversion hysteria, organ neurosis, psychosomatic disturbances, anxiety hysteria, obsessional neurosis, perversion) as well as the narcissistic neurosis (melancholia and the schizophrenias). Boss ends his work with a critical discussion concerning the impact of Daseinsanalysis on traditional psychoanalytic techniques. In this section Boss discusses the daseinsanalytic way in which to view transference and counter-transference, acting out, permissiveness and frustration in the relationship, dream interpretations, modifications of the frame, the goals of therapy, daseinsanalytic corrections in therapy, as well as the psychoanalytic "why" vs. the Daseinsanalytic "why not."

Boss, M. (1965). *A Psychiatrist Discovers India* (trans. H. Frey). London: Oswald Wolf. (Original work published 1959.) Review by Charles McArthur, with permission.

In the 1950s, Medard Boss made two trips to India and Southeast Asia. There he sought out and entered into long dialogues with several wise men; these conversations are the main thrust of this book. After some travelogue and a smattering of anthropological observations, aided by Boss being in the unusual position of taking Indian patients and his position as a visiting faculty at an Indian university, the book climaxes with the first of two series of exchanges with Hindu "masters." In the first of these exchanges, the sage ably and at length spells out the position of Brahman ontology. That doctrine emphasizes our existence in a world that is process, not objects. Its basis of being is the Brahman, the arising of something out of nothing. This miracle of being is understood as "a primarily 'contentless' lighting-up." Everything and everybody is a part of the Brahman. It is therefore our nature to illuminate things and especially people around us and our emergent illumination "is a 'free' and 'redemptive' opening-up." In opening ourselves to our possibility of entering into this activity, we also enter the much-misunderstood Hindu state of "bliss." When he heard this doctrine propounded, Boss tells us, "I could hardly believe my ears for I heard him (the Hindu wise man) say things which often corresponded, word for word, with phrases I had heard in the West from the lips of the philosopher – Martin Heidegger" (p. 128). Though he scrupulously listened for the differences between sage and philosopher, Boss found himself moved to wonder, "could it be that in quite another part of our earth, in the Black Forest of Germany, the same deepest insight into that which is trying to well forth" (p. 129). (Boss does not seem to have considered that this apparent multiple invention could well be an instance of cultural diffusion. One result of diffusion is that if you are looking for the very oldest form of a culture trait, you should look as far as possible from its center of origin.) Parallels to Heidegger kept emerging as Boss went on to visit sage after sage. In the homilies he heard from these men and in their answers to his cross-examinations (answers patiently spelled out, despite their containing almost every time the warning that he should talk less and let wisdom grow in silence) the reader can hear one by one the striking ideas of Daseinsanalyse anticipated one to four millennia ago. The Hindu sages, however, used simpler language. Indeed, Boss's explication of Brahman ontology will serve well as a skeleton key to the quiddities of the Germanic ontological system.

Boss, M. (1977) "*I Dreamt Last Night...*" (trans. S. Conway). New York: Gardner Press. (Original work published 1975.)

In his second book on dreaming Boss returns to various themes articulated earlier, that is, psychology and modern medicine's tendency to follow various fixed algorhythms and stratagems of dream interpretation, whether making extensive use of symbolism (Freudian or Jungian), relying on statistical dream research (C.S. Hall and L. Van de Castle), or detailed neurological and EEG studies, none of which is truly able to re-awaken the analysand toward a sense of his own potentialities. Boss sets out the difficulties encountered in Freudian and Jungian interpretations, as well as other approaches just cited. For Boss it remains best to simply ask the awakened dreamer "whether he can sense existential possibilities of his own that correspond to the meaningfulness of the features of dreamed phenomena, [as] the proper insight will reveal itself out of the patient's heart and be embraced" (p. 26).

Boss, M. (1979). *Existential Foundations of Psychology and Medicine* (trans. S. Conway and A. Cleares). New York: Jason Aronson. (Original work: *Grundriss der Medizxn*. Bern: Hans Iluber, 1971.) Review by Frederick Burrage, with permission.

Be it neurosis, psychosis, a bacterial infection, congenital defect, or broken bone, all "illnesses" have the common denominator of a constricted mode of being-in-the-world or shrinkage of one's freedom to carry out one's innate possibilities for relating to what one encounters. So Medard Boss cogently argues in this, his culminating systematic text.

Boss offers a stunning critique of psychology's and medicine's most cherished assumptions about human existence. Using Heidegger's ontology of Dasein and staying only with the phenomena as presented in experience, he renders useless or reformulates such pivotal ideas as the unconscious, motivation, defenses, drives, memory, the "psyche," the "soma," consciousness, stress, and cybernetics. He does away with all inferred, interpolated, and unprovable psychic entities and replaces them with the person's different modes of relating or being-in-the-world. Throughout his text, Boss instructively intersperses his theorizing with a "test case," a detailed account of a person who suffered from so-called psychosomatic and psychotic symptoms.

Key to understanding Boss's stance toward the phenomenon of illness is his contention that human existence is fundamentally a perceptive, responsive, world-spanning openness from the very beginning. Openness is not a characteristic or property of existence; it is existence. All psychologies miss the point that existence does not lie within a "psyche" but in the immediate presence of what it encounters, as relatedness. This is a difficult "leap" for many of us, for Boss is asking us to put in abeyance (as a good phenomenologist should) all theories and beliefs spawned by the genetic-causal, Cartesian thinking so prevalent in our professional training and language. However, this leap brings forth an understanding and clarity of certain phenomena that are inaccessible and incomprehensible by other modes of exploration. For example, Boss wonders how modern medicine can force together two heterogeneous categories like "psyche" and "soma" and say they interact; he proposes instead an approach which does away with such dualistic thinking in order to reflect the holistic behavior that human existence continually presents.

Illness, for Boss, is understandable only in terms of states of healthiness, and these can be determined only through detailing the ways in which existential "traits" can be carried out. These "traits" of existence include its spatio-temporal character, its attunement, its bodyhood, its being together with other people in a shared world, its historicity, its mortality, and its unfolding of inherent potentialities. Illness involves the "domination" or "withdrawal" (but not elimination) of some trait or traits with respect to others. Whether a person is a physician or a psychotherapist, Boss believes there are certain essential, and relatively simple, questions that need to be asked, above all, "How is one's freedom impaired?"

Boss's strength lies in his "returning to the things themselves" (Husserl) and stressing the uniqueness of each person's existence. As his title suggests, Boss does present a new foundation that has extraordinary implications for both medicine and psychology.

Cohn, H.W. (2002). *Heidegger and the Roots of Existential Therapy.* London: Continuum Books.

Cohn's *Heidegger and the Roots of Existential Therapy* reads deeply personal, that is, a thinking yet heartfelt engagement with Heidegger as person, philosopher, and intellectual elder. Cohn's clear and concise discussions remain close to the various contributions of Heidegger's oeuvre and his unique philosophy, its differences as compared to the work of his mentor Edmund Husserl, the subject/object split and Westerns civilization's Cartesian malaise, Heidegger's importance and relationship to the work of Binswanger, Boss, and Daseinsanalysis, as well as existential areas such as (a) two forms of solicitude, (b) language as being-with, (c) existence as body-mind, (d) existence' "attunement," (e) existence as temporality, (f) the priority of the phenomena, (g) Being and beings, (h) thrownness and choice, (i) the special position of human beings, and (j) "towards" an existential therapy. Cohn ends his work with a personal postscript that reflects an important existential attitude, a reminder to us all; "That beings are given to us, Heidegger sees as 'the wonder of all wonder', a 'gift', so to speak, that cannot be taken for granted, that asks us for engagement and response" (p. 127).

Condrau, G. (1998). *Martin Heidegger's Impact on Psychotherapy.* Vienna: MOSAIC.

As Boss's most senior student the work of Dr. Gion Condrau has been immensely influential in daseinsanalytic circles. It is truly unfortunate that many of his works have not been translated into English. In his book *Heidegger's Impact on Psychotherapy*, Condrau both theoretically and clinically sets out to (a) describe Daseinsanalysis as a holistic approach to human science and psychotherapy, (b) provide a daseinsanalytic approach to psychopathology, (c) discuss Daseinsanalysis as psychotherapy, and (d) explore Heidegger's immense impact on Swiss Psychiatry. Dr. Condrau also discusses Binswanger's *Psychiatric Daseinsanalysis*, Medard Boss's *Psychotherapeutic Daseinsanalysis*, the need for a phenomenological approach to the analysand, the significance of language, the treatment of psychopathology (with case studies), the psychotherapeutic situation, the role of dream analysis, the management of death and dying, and finally, various concerns surrounding contemporary daseinsanalytic training (i.e., training analysis, didactic analysis, difficulties in training, self-analysis).

Craig, E. (1988). Psychotherapy for freedom: the daseinsanalytical way in psychology and psychoanalysis, a special issue of *The Humanistic Psychologist*, 16 (1–3).

This anthology by Erik Craig, was brought together to introduce English speaking readers to Medard Boss's psychotherapeutic Daseinsanalysis as embodied here in articles by Boss and a number of senior Daseinsanalytic followers in Zurich. Two brief chapters, taken from the as yet untranslated Zollikon Seminars are also included. The volume, dedicated to Boss himself, stands as a varied explication of and testament to Boss's resolute 40-year effort to create the first comprehensive, systematic approach to existential psychotherapy. A state of the art publication at the time, the book is divided into four parts. Part one, entitled "Historical and Philosophical Inquiries" provides the reader with a rare opportunity to meet with Medard Boss at his home through verbatim transcripts of conversations with the editor in the summer of 1986. This is followed by an article by Boss himself as he explicates his latest thoughts and perspectives with respect to Heidegger's fundamental ontology and its implications for the practice of psychotherapy. Boss's article is followed by one of Heidegger's, mentioned above. Part two of the volume focuses on "Psychotherapeutic Inquiries" and consists of articles by such leading Daseinsanalysts such as Gion Condrau, Alois Hicklin, and Perikles Kastrinidis. Part three, "Analytic Inquiries," contains three examples of Daseinsanalytic research with phenomenological-hermeneutic expositions of narcissistic neurosis by Perikles Kastrinidis, the meaning of desire by Alice Holzhey-Kunz, and the analysis of dreams by the editor Craig. Part four, called "Continuing Inquiries," further clarifies key concepts discussed in part one of this volume, provides an annotated bibliography of seminal daseinsanalytic works, two special reports discussing formal daseinsanalytic training (for medical and non-medical clinicians), and ends with a discussion of the two Zurich-based daseinsanalytic training programs: The Daseinsanalytic Institute for Psychotherapy and Psychosomatics and the Swiss Society for Daseinsanalysis on the practice of Daseinsanalysis.

Fichtner, G. (1992/2003). *The Sigmund Freud-Ludwig Binswanger Correspondence* (trans. A. J. Pomerans). New York/London: The Other Press.

Gerhard Fichtner's book contains the correspondence between S. Freud and L. Binswanger from January 1908 to Freud's death in 1939. Also included are the letters of condolences between Binswanger, Martha and Anna Freud (dated January 11, 1940). The reader is allowed a unique glimpse into the close, if not warm relationship between two extraordinary men that spanned over three decades. It is well known that Freud referred many patients to Binswanger's Bellevue Sanatorium, and these referrals served as basis for many exchanges of ideas. Although Binswanger's theoretical interest and ideas differed from Freud's in many fundamental ways, both Freud and Binswanger found a respectful way to remain supportive and connected to each other's work, family life, political and institutional strife, and even personal losses and professional disappointments. As Freud himself remarked: "Unlike so many other people, you have not allowed your own intellectual development, which you have increasingly removed from my influence, to destroy our personal relationship, and you have no idea how much good such refinement does for a person."

Heidegger, M. (1962). *Being and Time* (trans. J. Macquarrie and E. Robinson). New York: Harper & Row. (Original work published 1927.) Review by Joseph J. Kockelmans, with permission.

According to many, *Being and Time* may very well be the most important contribution to philosophy written in the twentieth century. The book was supposed to have had two major parts, both subdivided into three major subdivisions. Yet in 1927 the book was published in an incomplete form. In its present form the book contains only the first two major subdivisions of the first part.

In *Being and Time* Heidegger attempts to apply "hermeneutic phenomenology" to an analytic of man's mode of Being, and carefully explains the sense in which hermeneutic phenomenology is to be understood. In Heidegger's opinion, philosophy's main concern is to be found in the question concerning the meaning of Being. This question is to be dealt with in ontology; yet such an ontology is to be prepared by a fundamental ontology which must take the form of an existential analytic of man's mode of Being, to be understood as Being-in-the-world. It is particularly in this fundamental ontology that the hermeneutic phenomenological method is to be employed. At the outset Heidegger makes it quite clear in *Being and Time* that what is to be understood by hermeneutic phenomenology is not identical with Husserl's transcendental phenomenology, although it is clear also that Heidegger sees the indispensable foundation for such a further development in Husserl's phenomenology.

In the first division, Heidegger takes as his guiding clue the fact that the essence of man consists in his ek-sistence; that toward which man stands out is the world; thus one can also say that the essence of man is Being-in-the-world. The main task of this first division now is to unveil the precise meaning of this compound expression; but in so doing the final goal remains the preparation of an answer for the question concerning the meaning of Being. The very asking of this question is one of man's modes of Being; and as such it receives its essential character from what is inquired about, namely Being itself. "This entity which each of us is himself and which includes inquiring as one of the possibilities of its Being we shall denote by the term '*Dasein*'." Thus the technical term *Dasein*, which usually is left untranslated, refers to man precisely insofar as he essentially relates to Being. The preparatory analysis of Dasein's mode of Being can only serve to describe the essence of this being; it cannot interpret its meaning ontologically.

The preparatory analysis merely tries to lay bare the horizon for the most primordial way of interpreting Being. Once this horizon has been reached, the preparatory analysis is to be replaced by a genuinely ontological interpretation. The horizon referred to here is temporality which thus determines the meaning of the Being of Dasein. This is the reason why all the structures of man's Being exhibited in the first division are to be re-interpreted in the second as modes of temporality.

Characteristic for Dasein thus is its comprehension of Being and this is the process by which Dasein transcends beings in the direction of Being, and comprehends all beings, itself included, in their Being. This explains why the essence of Dasein can also be defined as transcendence. It should be stressed here however, that the process of transcendence *is* inherently finite. For, first of all, Dasein is not master over its own origin; it simply finds itself thrown among beings (thrownness). Secondly, thrown among beings, Dasein must concern itself with these beings and, thus, has the tendency to lose itself among them (fallenness), and to forget its ontological "destination." Finally, transcendence is a process which inherently is unto Dasein's end, death. The ground of the negativity which manifests itself in these modalities is what Heidegger calls "guilt" which is here thus not to be understood in a moral sense.

The basic structure of finite transcendence consists of comprehension (*Verstehen*), that is, the component in and through which Dasein projects the world; ontological disposition or mood (*Befindlichkeit*), that is, the component through which Dasein's thrownness, fallenness, and the world's non-Being are disclosed; and logos (*Rede*), that is, the component through which Dasein can unfold and articulate "in language" what comprehension and original mood disclose. These components constitute a unity insofar as transcendence essentially is care (*Sorge*): ahead of itself Being already in the world as Being alongside beings encountered within the world. When this unity is considered as a totality, it is understood as coming to its end, that is, death. Finally, that which gives Dasein to understand its transcendence as well as its finitude and "guilt" and thus calls it to achieve its own self is what Heidegger calls the voice of conscience. To achieve itself Dasein must let itself be called toward its genuine self, that is, the process of finite transcendence. The act in and through which Dasein achieves authenticity is called resolve (*Entschlossenheit*).

Heidegger finally shows how care itself is founded in time insofar as the basic components of care, namely ek-sistence, thrownness, and fallenness, inherently refer to the three ek-stases of time, future, past, and present. By transcending beings toward Being, Dasein comes to its true self (*Zukunft*, future), but this self is always already as having been thrown forth (past), and concerning itself with beings, thus making them manifest and present (present). Interpreted from the perspective of temporality, resolve manifests itself as retrieve (*Wiederholung*); it lets the process of finite transcendence become manifest as historical. By fetching itself back time and again, Dasein lets its own self be in terms of its authentic past; in addition, it also is as constantly coming toward its authentic self (future). It is thus in this complex process that Dasein hands over to itself its own heritage and thus "finds" its true self.

Heidegger, M. (1977). *Basic Writings.* (ed. D.F. Krell). New York: Harper & Row. Review by Albert Pacheco, with permission.

The *Basic Writings* of Martin Heidegger, edited by David Krell present us with ten selections of Heidegger's work, spanning the 37 years from 1927 to 1964. This collection represents the path of thinking that began with his major work, *Being and Time.* Included in this collection is the introduction to *Being and Time* where Heidegger outlines the task that he will undertake answering his guiding question, the question of the meaning of being. Pro-paedeutic to this task is the laying out of a fundamental ontology of being for whom "understanding of Being is a determination of that being itself." And that being for Heidegger is human Dasein. The elucidation of the nature of Dasein is significant for Heidegger and laying out an adequate conception of "science." For Heidegger conceives of the sciences as nothing but concrete possible ways of being for Dasein by way of which it speaks out about the world in which it exists and about itself. Significantly, Heidegger culminates this opening with an exposition of his understanding of "the phenomenological method of investigation."

Heidegger's concern with the human being's relationship to science continues to occupy him even more so after his famous "turning" in the 1930s, a turning which he announces in the essay entitled "Letter on Humanism," the fifth among the works featured in the *Basic Writings*. In his "Letter," Heidegger reports that his thinking has undergone a "reversal" characterized by a turning away from a thinking about the nature of things that is still metaphysical, scientific in nature to a non-metaphysical, reflective way of thinking about the essence of things. As a result of this "turning," Heidegger begins to focus more closely at what science is especially as he sees it standing in distinction to "philosophy."

Heidegger believes that this reflective or meditative way of thinking is best exemplified in the thinking and the language of the poets. For the poet by way of the poem allows for the revelation of the essential nature of things for the truth of Being, to come to presence. And thus the essential nature of the human being as mortal and as being in relation to all things in either heaven or earth comes to disclose itself as well.

In the essays, "The Question Concerning Technology;" "Building, Dwelling, Thinking;" and "What Calls for Thinking;" which are included in this collection, Heidegger continually contrasts this more "poetic" way of thinking with the technological scientific way of thinking, which has come to singularly characterize the age in which we live. The author also lays out the "danger" inherent in this technological-scientific way of thinking on the nature of things and especially on the nature of the human being. This "danger" is clearly revealed in the works of Menard Boss which demonstrate how the natural scientific way of thinking restricts medical sciences understanding of the human being.

Heidegger, M. (2001). *Zollikon Seminars. Protocols – Conversations – Letters* (trans. R. Askay and F. Mayr). Northwestern University Press: Evanston, IL. (Original work published 1987.)

During compulsory medical service Boss came across *Being and Time* and made various attempts to study its content only to be left perplexed yet touched by its soulful content. The difficulties encountered in reading Heidegger "gave me no rest" (p. viii) and served as the main impetus for Boss contemplating further studies with Heidegger himself. Given various sentiments surrounding Heidegger post-Second World War, Boss was frequently dissuaded from contacting Heidegger personally although finally "As a doctor, I wrote a letter to the philosopher and asked for help in [reflective] thinking" (p. ix). This letter served as a basis for the two creative men to meet (in 1949), and a further 256 letters by the end of Heidegger's life. By 1959 Boss felt it important that Heidegger's thought should be shared with other doctors and as such 50–70 colleagues were invited to sit in on Heidegger's seminars, two to three times per semester. For Boss, during these seminars, Heidegger "exemplified selfless, loving solicitude which leaps ahead of the other [human being], returning to him with his own freedom" (p. xi). The Zollikon Seminars in essence reflect, through transcripts, the various areas addressed by Heidegger and the group of physicians between 1959 and 1969. It also includes personal conversations between Heidegger and Boss (1961–1972), as well as letters to Boss from 1947 to 1971. The Zollikon translators, Richard Askay and Franz Mayr, include two additional chapters discussing Heidegger's philosophy and its impact on psychology, Freud and existential psychoanalysis, as well as the question of Being, language, and translation.

Holzhey-Kunz, A. (2014). *Daseinsanalysis* (trans. S. Leighton). London: Free Association Books.

The analysand as *reluctant philosopher*, as understood through the hermeneutic anthropology and Daseinsanalysis of Alice Holzhey-Kunz, reveals the writings of both a seasoned philosopher and daseinsanalytic practitioner. Given the limited number of complete works available to English-speaking Daseinsanalysts or those interested in the practice of Daseinsanalysis or Daseins-psychotherapy, Holzhey-Kunz's textbook-like approach serves as a welcome contribution. The purpose of Holzhey-Kunz's work is to introduce her hermeneutic approach to Daseinsanalysis, based on a return to the Heidegger of *Being and Time* (1947/1962) as well as to Freud's discovery of the hidden meaning of human suffering. As both philosopher and clinician Holzhey-Kunz has built the foundation of her hermeneutic Daseinsanalysis on the psychoanalytic work of Sigmund Freud, the phenomenological, hermeneutic approach of the Martin Heidegger of *Being and Time*, the psychiatric Daseinsanalysis of Ludwig Binswanger and the psychotherapeutic Daseinsanalysis of Medard Boss supplementing this with critical aspects of the work of Kierkegaard, Sartre, and, to a lesser extent, the contextual phenomenologist, Robert Stolorow. The heart of her book is to present and explicate her new third approach to the daseinsanalytic understanding and treatment of psychic suffering. Holzhey-Kunz articulates the importance of early Heideggerian philosophy as a central way to understand human existence. For Holzhey-Kunz the philosophico–psychological aspects include embodiedness, temporality and historicity, human sociality, and the moods of anxiety, shame, and guilt. The latter is explored through various clinical realities – mood and anxiety disorders, character disorders, and psychosis, as well as a critical review on the psychoanalytic frame, daseinsanalytic hermeneutic listening to the meaningfulness of both the historically shaped ontic existence of the individual as well as the hidden ontological meanings contained therein. She advocates cultivating ontological sympathy, the attitude of abstinence as a relational offer, phenomenological-hermeneutic interpretation, and the impact of ontological truth in the life of the patients whose specific pre-ontological sensitivity (*Hellhörigkeit*) for their own being, their inescapable human condition (pp. 203–204) makes them reluctant philosophers.

May, R., Angel, E., and Ellenberger, H.F. (eds.) (1958). *Existence. A New Dimension in Psychiatry and Psychology.* New York: Basic Books.

As editors Rollo May and his colleagues bring together three important chapters on Binswanger's works. In chapter 7, "The Existential school of thought" (pp. 191–213) Binswanger gives special attention to the nature and goals of existential analysis and its phenomenological anthropology, the differentiation between human existence and that of the animal being, as well as the existential-analytical school-of-thought's contribution to a psychiatry that would focus on the patient's unique world-design rather than just general psychiatric descriptions. To explain the existential analytical approach Binswanger discussed various cases; a client with a heel phobia, a patient experiencing symptoms of schizophrenia, and the patient called Lola Voss. The case of Lola Voss is however discussed synoptically in this chapter. Part two of Needleman's book (1963) sees a more thorough discussion on Voss. In chapter 8 Binswanger introduces the reader to '*Insanity as life historical phenomenon and as mental disease: the case of Ilse*' (pp. 214–236). Ilse, a seemingly happily married patient of 39 of a protestant "angelic, self-effacing, touching kind mother," and an "extremely egotistical, hard and tyrannical father" developed a delusional system after watching Hamlet that she could influence her father to treat the mother better. In an act worthy of Shakespearian tragic Ilse forced her arm into a burning stove and thereafter held it out to her father saying; "Look, this is to show you how much I love you." The act, followed by a period of elation sees Ilse's lived world becoming increasingly self-referential, self-focused, and personalized (similar to Dr. Schreber), with an eventual stay at a health resort and later in Binswanger's care. The chapter follows a critical discussion of Ilse's illness and insanity as life-historical phenomena. "The case of Ellen West – An anthropological-clinical study" (chapter 9, pp. 237–364) is Binswanger's most well known and most often cited Daseinsanalytic case. Careful notation is made of a lifelong rift–connection duality between West's Eigenwelt (*idios kosmos*) and the Mit-and Umwelt (*fate-world*). Various existentials are explored, most notably, temporality of the ethereal world, death, the temporality of the tomb-world, and the temporality of the world of practical action.

Needleman, J. (ed. and trans.) (1963). *Being in the World: The Selected Papers of Ludwig Binswanger.* London: Souvenir.

In this finely edited work Needleman aids the reader in Daseinsanalysis on two fronts. Part one focusses on an overall characterization of the concept of the existential *a priori* as seen through various philosophers, mainly Kant, Heidegger, and Husserl. This is followed by the role of systematic explanation and science in psychoanalysis, the importance of the symbol in both classical psychoanalysis and Daseinsanalysis, the unconscious and thrownness, and what is meant by "psychopathology." Part one comes to a final discussion of great importance, that is, the relationship between Binswanger, Kant, Heidegger, and Sartre. In part two of *Being in the World* various selected papers of Binswanger reflect his main daseinsanalytic concerns; (i) Freud's idea of *homo natura*; (ii) the idea of *homo natura* in light of anthropology; (iii) Heidegger's analytic of existence and its importance to the domain of clinical psychiatry; (iv) the role of the dream; (v) a daseinsanalytic understanding of schizophrenia; and (vi) a detailed daseinsanalytic case study (of Lola Voss).

Stern, P. (1964). *The Abnormal Person and His World.* Princeton, NJ: D. Van Nostrand. Review by Charles McArthur, with permission.

Out of the richness of his reading in three languages and his university education on two continents, Paul Stern wrote a treatment of the abnormal person in his world that drew on both familiar and unfamiliar psychoanalytic and existential analytic literatures. The idea for the text was originally inspired by the possibility of providing Harvard Divinity School students with a substantive, though at the same time humanistic-existential, entrance to the study of psychopathology. True to his publisher's need for such a book to look like an "Abnormal Psych Text," Stern devoted one chapter to each of the well-known diagnostic categories. He preceded these obligatory topics with a seminal discussion of anxiety and followed them by a concluding essay on therapies for the classical disorders and for the twentieth-century problems of *ennui and angst*. For each diagnosis, he set psychoanalytic and existential formulations side by side. On occasion, he diverged to discuss the follies of biological therapies of mental disorders or detoured to develop some quintessentially Sternian position – as in his section on the Truth Value of Psychotic Delusions – and so to adumbrate the brilliance of *In Praise of Madness* (1972), his delightful book-length essay that was still to come.

Himself trained in philosophy, Stern relished thinkers like Binswanger and Merleau-Ponty. Boss is cited often; two of his cases get used. Beyond the major systems of clinical thought, psychoanalytic and existential, Stern found only a "paucity" of ideas.

Of existentialism, Stern wrote admiringly but not slavishly. He saw the "key to understanding" this philosophy, "in which psychoanalysis has found a contemporary extension," to be Binswanger and those influenced by him (Boss, Bally, Benedetti, Storch, and Wyrsch). Existentialism's contributions to therapy seemed to Stern to be: the abjuring of psychodynamic constructs; a new understanding of transference as something that goes on in the here and now and, to quote Binswanger, "with *precisely this* physician"; the resulting "shedding of the analytic incognito" and commitment by the therapist to the role of "an active caretaker"; the re-evaluation of dreams; and the redefining of therapy's goals, a climactic point on which he quoted Boss, who wanted the patient to learn to view himself as "a light emanating from the mystery of existence, in whose rays all things and fellow-beings are allowed to appear and unfold according to their nature." The result that Stern saw was that, "more radically than psychoanalysis ever did, existential analysis transcends the limits of a strictly medical behavior" and he anticipated that, in contrast to medicine existential analysis "is bound to come to grips with matters of ultimate concern." Stern nonetheless was able to put his finger on existentialism's danger: "the tendency to volatilize empirical psychology into a contourless mist of metaphysical speculation."

Bibliography of Key Daseinsanalytic Works in English

Binswanger, L. (1957). *Sigmund Freud: Reminiscences of a Friendship* (trans. N. Guterman). New York: Grune & Stratton.

Binswanger, L. (1958). The Case of Ellen West. In: *Existence: A New Dimension in Psychiatry and Psychology* (ed. R. May, E. Angel, and H. Ellenberger), 237–364. New York: Basic Books.

Binswanger, L. (1958/1959). Existential analysis and psychotherapy. *Psychoanalytic Review* *45* (C): 79–83.

Binswanger, L. (1963). Freud's conception of man in the light of anthropology. In: *Being-in-the World: The Selected Papers of Ludwig Binswanger* (ed. and trans. J. Needleman), 149–181. London: Souvenir.

Boss, M. (1949). *Meaning and Content of Sexual Perversions: A Daseinsanalytic Approach to Psychopathology and the Phenomenon of Love* (trans. L.L. Abell). New York: Grune & Stratton. (Original work published 1947.)

Boss, M. (1958). *The Analysis of Dreams* (trans. A.J. Pomerans). New York: Philosophical Library. (Original work published 1953.)

Boss, M. (1963). *Psychoanalysis and Daseinsanalysis* (trans. L.B. Lefebre). New York: Basic Books.

Boss, M. (1965). *A Psychiatrist Discovers India* (trans. H.A. Frey). London: Oswald Wolff. (Original work published, 1959.)

Boss, M. (1977). "*I Dreamt Last Night…*" (trans. S. Conway). New York: Gardner Press. (Original work published 1975.)

Boss, M. (1979). *Existential Foundations of Medicine and Psychology* (trans. S. Conway and A. Cleaves). New York: Jason Aronson. (Original work published 1971.)

Boss, M. (1988) Recent considerations in Daseinsanalysis. *The Humanistic Psychologist 16* (1): 58–74.

Cohn, H.W. (1997). *Existential Thought and Therapeutic Practice.* London: Sage.

Cohn, H.W. (2002). *Heidegger and the Roots of Existential Therapy.* London: Continuum Books.

Condrau, G. (1988). A seminar on daseinsanalytic psychotherapy. *The Humanistic Psychologist 16* (1): 99–129.

Condrau, G. (1993). Dream analysis: Do we need the unconscious? *Journal of the Society for Existential Analysis 4*: 1–18.

Condrau, G. (1998). *Martin Heidegger's Impact on Psychotherapy.* New York: Edition MOSAIC.

Craig, E. (ed.) (1988). Psychotherapy for freedom: The Daseinsanalytic way in psychology and psychoanalysis [Special issue]. *The Humanistic Psychologist, 16* (1).

Craig, E. (2002–2003). The opening of being and Dasein. *Review of Existential Psychology and Psychiatry 27*: 61–82.

Craig, E. (2008). The human and the hidden: Existential wonderings about depth, soul, and the unconscious. *The Humanistic Psychologist 36* (3–4): 227–282.

Craig, E. (2015). The lost language of being: Ontology's perilous destiny in existential psychotherapy. *Philosophy, Psychiatry, and Psychology 20* (2): 79–92.

Fichtner, G. (1992/2003). *The Sigmund Freud-Ludwig Binswanger Correspondence* (trans. A.J. Pomerans). New York/London: The Other Press.

Frie, R. (1999). Interpreting a misinterpretation: Ludwig Binswanger and Martin Heidegger. *Journal for the British Society for Phenomenology 30* (3): 244–257.

Groth, M. (1996). Existential therapy on Heideggerian principles. *Journal of the Society for Existential Analysis 8* (1): 57–75.

Groth, M. (2017). *After Psychotherapy: Essay and Thoughts on Existential Therapy.* New York: ENI Press.

Heidegger, M. (1962). *Being and Time* (trans. J. McQuarrie and E. Robinson). New York: Harper and Row. (Original work published in 1927.)

Heidegger, M. (1966). *Discourse on Thinking* (trans. J.M. Anderson and E.H. Freund). New York: Harper & Row. (Original work published 1959.)

Heidegger, M. (1977). *Basic Writings* (ed. D.F. Krell). New York: Harper & Row.

Heidegger, M. (1999a). *Contributions to Philosophy (from Enowning)* (trans. P. Emad and K. Maly). Bloomington: Indiana University Press. (Original work published 1989.)

Heidegger, M. (1999b). *Ontology – The Hermeneutics of Facticity* (trans. J. van Buren). Bloomington: Indiana University Press. (Original work published 1988.)

Heidegger, M. (2001). *Zollikon Seminars: Protocols – Conversations – Letters* (ed. M. Boss, trans. F. Mayr and R. Askay). Evanston, IL: Northwestern University Press. (Original work published 1987.)

Holzhey-Kunz, A. (1988). Emancipation and narcissism: On the meaning of desire. *The Humanistic Psychologist 16* (1): 186–202.
Holzhey-Kunz, A. (1996). What defines the Daseinsanalytic process? *Journal of the Society for Existential Analysis 8* (1): 93–104.
Holzhey-Kunz, A. (2014). *Daseinsanalysis*. London: Free Association Books.
Kastrinidis, P. (1988a). Daseinsanalytic psychotherapy with the elderly. *The Humanistic Psychologist 16* (1): 153–165.
Kastrinidis, P. (1988b). The phenomenology of narcissistic neurosis. *The Humanistic Psychologist 16* (1): 168–185.
Kastinidis, P. (2005). Between human illusion and inhuman reality: A Daseinsanalytic contribution to the understanding of masochism. In: *Daseinsanalysis* (ed. D.J. Martino), 89–109. Pittsburgh: Simon Silverman Phenomenology Center.
May, R., Angel, E., and Ellenberger, H.F. (eds.) (1958). *Existence. A New Dimension in Psychiatry and Psychology*. New York: Basic Books.
Needleman, J. (ed. and trans.) (1963). *Being-in-the-World: The Selected Papers of Ludwig Binswanger*. New York: Basic Books.
Stern, P.J. (1964). *The Abnormal Person and His World: An Introduction to Psychopathology*. Princeton, NJ: D. Van Nostrand.
Stern, P.J. (1972). *In Praise of Madness: Realness Therapy – The Self Reclaimed*. New York: W.W. Norton & Company.
Stern, P.J. (1979). Introduction to the English translation. In: M. Boss, *Existential Foundations of Medicine and Psychology* (trans. S. Conway and A. Cleaves), ix–xxii. New York: Jason Aronson.

6

Challenges and New Developments

Erik Craig, Loray Daws, Thanasis Georgas, and Robert D. Stolorow

With the death of Medard Boss on December 21, 1990 in Zürich, Switzerland, Daseinsanalysis entered a new and challenging phase of its existence. Binswanger had already died some years earlier, on February 5, 1966, and his family's famous Bellevue sanitarium in Kreuzlingen had closed in 1980.

When asked some years ago about the future of Daseinsanalysis, Boss replied, chuckling to himself, "I don't think about the future of Daseinsanalysis. It's completely stupid because you can't make such a future. If it's something worthwhile, it will grow and remain; or it may die. But it depends on the Daseinsanalysts and on the recipients. There may come a time when people will not be open to the meaning of what Daseinsanalysis [is] or of what Martin Heidegger has found, has seen, has discovered. Maybe their minds will be closed or maybe they will grow even more open. That doesn't depend on me. I did what I could to tell it, to hand on what I have received from Heidegger, but Daseinsanalysis has its own future now, its own fate." He then added, "Daseinsanalysis now has to make its own way. I have grown an old man and shall die, but there is the Daseinsanalytic Institute in Zürich and there is Condrau and Hicklin and Kastrinidis and these people. There is an association now in Sao Pablo, and Jerusalem and in India and so on" (cited in Craig 1988, p. 36).

This chapter explores what that future has come to be now, exactly 30 years after Boss spoke these words. We begin by summarizing developments over the last twenty years that Boss was alive.

Developments From 1971–1990

During the last twenty years of Boss's life there were a number of important institutional developments in Daseinsanalysis. Boss's foremost student and colleague, Gion Condrau, was instrumental in forming the Daseinsanalytic Institute for Psychotherapy

The Wiley World Handbook of Existential Therapy, First Edition. Edited by Emmy van Deurzen, Erik Craig, Alfried Längle, Kirk J. Schneider, Digby Tantam, and Simon du Plock.

and Psychosomatics (Medard Boss Foundation) in Zürich in 1971, the journal *Daseinsanalysis* in 1983, and the International Federation of Daseinsanalysis (IFDA) in 1990. Additionally, in 1970 a group of individuals who had studied and worked with Boss in Zürich reactivated the old Swiss Society for Daseinsanalysis holding *pro forma* meetings for the next 10 years. In 1981, the Society initiated a monthly program for discussing Daseinsanalytic questions and concerns called the Fora Daseinsanalyse, and, in 1983, established a training commission and a second formal training program for the practice of Daseinsanalytic psychotherapy in Zurich.

Beyond Zurich and the globally distributed official IFDA chapters, a number of independent daseinsanalytically oriented therapists kept in touch with Boss. Among these diverse individuals, of particular importance for English speaking existential therapists were Franz Mayer and Richard Askay, two philosophy professors from the University of Portland (Oregon), and Erik Craig, an American psychologist. Craig was the first to introduce Boss's Zurich school of Daseinsanalysis to the English speaking world with a 278 page special issue of *The Humanistic Psychology* entitled, *Psychotherapy for Freedom: The Daseinsanalytic Way in Psychology and Psychoanalysis* (Craig 1988). This issue contained English translations of articles by Martin Heidegger, Medard Boss, Gion Condrau, Alois Hicklin, Holzhey-Kunz, and Perikles Kastrinidis. Craig's anthology was the first compilation of daseinsanalytic authors since the publication, 30 years earlier, of *Existence* by May, Angel, and Ellenberger (1958) as well as the first dedicated exclusively to Boss's psychotherapeutic Daseinsanalysis. Meanwhile, Mayer and Askay worked closely with Boss from 1987 to 1990 on completing an adequate translation of Heidegger's 1987 *Zollikoner Seminare* (Heidegger 2001). Though Boss hoped to see the project to its full realization, his death in December 1990, prevented him even completing the preface. Mayer and Askay eventually published their English translation of the Heidegger's *Zollikon Seminars* (1987/2001) with the assistance of a number of eminent Heideggerian scholars a decade later.

Daseinsanalytic Voices beyond Binswanger and Boss

The deaths of both Binswanger and, especially, Boss left a potentially unfillable vacuum in the world of daseinsanalytic psychotherapy. Fortunately, several figures stepped in with their own continuing programs of research and practice. Although there are Daseinsanalysts now working and publishing all over the world, especially those connected with various national chapters that are a part of IFDA, we will focus here on those authors who have published daseinsanalytic articles or books in English. We will begin with five Daseinsanalysts who worked intensively with Boss himself.

Gion Condrau (1919–2006)

Certainly the most significant voice subsequent to the death of Boss was that of his fellow Daseinsanalyst, Gion Condrau. Born on January 9, 1919 in Disentis, deep in the mountains of the Romansch region of Graubünden, Switzerland, Condrau completed a medical degree in Bern and a PhD in philosophy in 1944, following this with his training in psychiatry at the Burghölzli Hospital under the supervision of Manfred

Bleuler, the son of Eugen Bleuler. He was a specialist in neurology, psychiatry, and psychotherapy, having completed independent training in psychoanalysis with Gregory Zilboorg at Butler Hospital in Providence, Rhode Island simultaneously with a Jungian analysis in the same city in (1951–1952). Back in Zurich he was also analyzed and trained by Medard Boss at what was then called that Institute for Medical Psychotherapy. Condrau thereafter became Boss's most significant and productive disciple, attending the Zollikon Seminars and, and later becoming the primary institutional organizer of Daseinsanalysis, founding the Daseinsanalytic Institute for Psychotherapy and Psychosomatics, the journal *Daseinsanalyse*, and the IFDA. Especially concerned with presenting Daseinsanalysis in a manner free of its typically obtuse Heideggerian jargon, he was a prolific writer, publishing a dozen books and well over 100 articles in philosophy, psychoanalysis, child development and family life, gynecology, and a number of existential themes. One of his favorite books was a beautifully illustrated book on the theme of death. From the beginning Condrau balked at the use of the linguistic intricacies of "Heideggerese," preferring instead to present daseinsanalytic thought and practice in a vernacular tongue. He was convinced that many talented therapists and psychoanalysts who were genuinely interested in Daseinsanalysis abandoned it prematurely because of what they themselves described as such "awful language." Although he published many articles, some of which were in English (Condrau 1988, 1993, 1996; Condrau and Boss 1967), and a number of books, his happiest achievement was his English book *Martin Heidegger's Impact on Psychotherapy* (1998). A robust, energetic skier, athlete, and politician, Condrau's health began to diminish in the early 2000s. When he died on November 21, 2006 in Zürich it was a blow to the dynamic, uninterrupted chain of powerful leadership that had held Daseinsanalysis for over half a century.

Paul J. Stern (1921–1982)[1]

Paul Stern, an American psychologist and one of the last graduates of Harvard University's famous PhD program in clinical psychology, was born into a German Reform Jewish family on June 6, 1921. His devastating Second World War experiences as a youth had a lifelong effect. He was captured by the Nazis in connection with the Kristallnacht at age 17 and briefly interned in Buchenwald before being ransomed by his family. Fleeing to Vichy France he was repeatedly caught and sent to French detention camps from which he just as repeatedly escaped. One of these escapes was effected with the help of a sympathetic SS officer who appreciated the gentle, intelligent spirit he observed when Stern presented and recited Western classics in the evening officer quarter "soirées" at the officer's "request." This act of kindness, led Stern, after the war to write an article, entitled "World War II as seen through the eyes of an SS Officer" for a famous Parisian publication.

Stern's early adulthood was indelibly shaped by the danger and uncertainty of the times, leaving him wary of strangers and passersby and, to the end of his life, harboring a dislike for anyone wearing sunglasses. Stern eventually managed to escape France altogether by stealing through mid-winter Alps with his uncle. From there, he

[1] The authors are grateful to Lillian Stern for her assistance in writing this review of her father's life.

gradually found his way to Zurich where he eventually met Medard Boss through his university studies. The two men developed an unusually tender relationship for Boss, one lasting until the unfortunately premature end of Stern's life from cancer in 1982. While in Switzerland, he supported himself by writing anonymous articles which were placed by a sympathetic stalwart woman press agent named Mrs. Dukas. After returning to France, Stern emigrated to the United States and continued his studies in psychology with J.F.T. Bugental at UCLA in the early 1950s. From there he enrolled in Harvard's PhD program in clinical psychology where he worked especially closely with Robert White and Gordon Allport. Throughout this time, he continued both a personal and professional relationship with Boss, not only arranging for Boss's 1963 lectures at Harvard but also, the following year, publishing a book for the Harvard Divinity School comparing existential (daseinsanalytic) and psychoanalytic approaches to human suffering and psychotherapy and entitled *The Abnormal Person and His World* (Stern 1964). His own short but scintillating masterpiece, *In Praise of Madness … The Self Reclaimed* (Stern 1972), introduces what he called "Realness Therapy" and contains evocative chapters on madness, dreams, and psychotherapy animated throughout with little gems like this: "The gentle therapist must be lucid and plain spoken. He need not be a simpleton" (Stern 1972, p. 116). He also wrote a revisionist biography of Carl Jung called "The Haunted Prophet" in 1976 while continuing to publish psychology articles for the European and American lay press. Stern's final contributions to the daseinsanalytic literature are found in his preface to Boss's second book on dreams (Stern 1977) and his introduction to Boss's *Existential Foundations of Medicine and Psychology* (Stern 1979).

Alice Holzhey-Kunz (1943–)

Alice Holzhey-Kunz, one of the first candidates of the Daseinsanalytic Institute, a student and collaborator with Medard Boss, and founder of hermeneutic Daseinsanalysis, was born near Zurich on March 20, 1943. Immediately following her graduation from gymnasium she taught in a Swiss village's "one-room schoolhouse" for a time before beginning her studies of history and philosophy at the University of Zurich in 1964. Writing her thesis on "Remembering and Forgetting," she received her PhD in 1971. Immediately thereafter she entered the newly founded Daseinsanalytic Institute for Psychotherapy and Psychosomatics in Zurich. Although she continued to collaborate with Boss himself, she left the Institute per se in 1975, the same year she published the first critique of Boss's main work, *Existential Foundations of Medicine and Psychology* (Boss 1971/1979). She and a number of other disaffected graduates of the Institute formed a new teaching and training program in Daseinsanalysis under the auspices of the old Swiss Society for Daseinsanalysis. In 2003 the society renamed itself as the Society for Hermeneutic Anthropology and Daseinsanalysis to reflect a return to the phenomenological-hermeneutic Heidegger of *Being and Time* (Heidegger 1927/1962). Holzhey-Kunz's own teaching and writing give the crucial discoveries of Sigmund Freud an ontological-existential meaning and, accordingly, approaches psychopathology by way of an existential hermeneutic that discloses human beings as a "suffering from our own being." Her proposal of an ontological interpretation of psychic suffering is based on Heidegger's distinction between ontic and ontological self-understanding and his discovery of Dasein's pre-ontological awareness of its own existence as being human.

In addition to her return to a genuinely hermeneutic Daseinsanalysis, Holzhey-Kunz continued to appreciate the breadth and depth of psychoanalysis and to dialogue it with existential philosophy. In 2012 she was awarded the Margrit-Egner Price by the University of Zürich for her work combining the psychoanalytic and existential-philosophical approaches to the human being and giving Daseinsanalysis a new turn mainly with respect to understanding individuals' suffering. Holzhey-Kunz's own conception of Daseinsanalysis issues two calls: first, to return to a phenomenological hermeneutic reconsideration of Sigmund Freud and his discovery that seemingly absurd and meaningless symptoms and phenomena always contain a hidden meaning and, second, to return to the early Heidegger and his masterpiece, *Being and Time* (1927/1962). Although Holzhey-Kunz is considered one of the foremost Binswanger scholars in the world (she is a co-editor of the 1994 second edition of his *Selected Works*), she sides neither Binswanger's nor Boss's understandings of Daseinsanalysis but, rather, offers her own third distinctive approach.

Holzhey-Kunz has published a large number of daseinsanalytic articles, including several in English (Holzhey-Kunz 1988, 2006, 2012; Holzhey-Kunz and Fazekas 2012), and three daseinsanalytic books, the last being also available in English. This major new work, *Daseinsanalysis: An Existential Perspective on Psychic Suffering and its Therapy* (Holzhey-Kunz 2014), unfolds a number of daseinsanalytic issues based on her ontological understanding of psychic suffering as a suffering from "one's own being." Today Holzhey-Kunz continues actively teaching and writing as well as seeing patients in her private practice in Zurich. Over the several years, she has also been teaching her new approach to psychopathological phenomena in Russia and Lithuania.

Perikles Kastrinidis (1946–)

Perikles Kastrinidis was born in Vienna, Austria on August 20, 1946 and, upon graduating from a Gymnasium in the city, he enrolled at the University of Vienna from which he received his medical diploma in 1970. From there he undertook specialization studies and training in psychiatry and psychotherapy, first in Austria and later in Switzerland. In 1975, he became a candidate for a Specialist in Psychiatry and Psychotherapy at the Daseinsanalytic Institute for Psychotherapy and Psychosomatics, receiving his Diploma in Daseinsanalytic Psychotherapy in 1979. He has maintained a practice in psychiatry and psychotherapy since then. In 1983, collaborating with Alice Holzhey-Kunz and other disaffected graduates of the Institute, he co-founded the training program in daseinsanalytic psychotherapy for the Swiss Daseinsanalytic Society, serving for several years as the president of the training commission. He received his Swiss Medical Diploma in Zurich in 1993 having previously practiced primarily in the Canton of Glarus, Switzerland. He has served as a teaching and supervisory psychiatrist and psychotherapist in several mental institutions in and around Zurich since 1981 and in recent years as a team supervisor for interdisciplinary medical teams in psychiatric institutions. He also is a Balint Group leader for physicians, clergy, lawyers, and educators. He has lectured and trained professionals in several European countries and, occasionally in the United States, most recently in 2004 at Duquesne University's Twenty-second Annual Simon Silverman Phenomenology Symposium.

A crucial turning point in his training and practice of daseinsanalytic psychotherapy came in 1984 when he first met Habib Davanloo, the founder ofintensive short-term dynamic psychotherapy (ISTDP) after which he undertook a series courses in Europe and the United States. Although his studies and practice of ISTDP significantly affected his own approach to psychotherapy, particularly with respect to effective ways to challenge defenses and monitor the ongoing level of anxiety throughout the session, it has never altered his commitment to finding his own particular way to be fundamentally daseinsanalytic. He has published one German book and several English articles on Daseinsanalytic related themes (Kastrinidis 1988a, 1988b, 2005, 2008).

Erik Craig (1944–)

Erik Craig is a psychologist, author, and independent scholar who currently lives, writes, and practices in Santa Fe, New Mexico while also lecturing, teaching, and training psychotherapist in Europe and Asia. Born on December 8, 1944, in Portland Maine, Craig grew up in a small village of 500 people at the edge of the Seacoast Region of New Hampshire. Initially educated in the Midwest, he returned to New England to teach at Assumption College in Worcester, Massachusetts and undertake doctoral studies at Boston University from which he received his degree in 1978. Craig had an unusual existential career having collaborated with and been mentored by Clark Moustakas, Paul Stern, Charles MacArthur, and Medard Boss for several years each. He has taught and practiced humanistic and existential psychotherapy for over 40 years, holding full-time graduate faculty positions at Assumption College, University of New Mexico, and Pacifica Graduate Institute.

His initial acquaintance with Daseinsanalysis came with his training in existential psychoanalysis with Paul Stern, a friend of Medard Boss's since the 1940s and, after emigrating to the United States, his American advocate. Two-and-a-half years after Stern's untimely death, Craig traveled to Switzerland to meet Medard Boss in person, which then led to several years of collaboration with Boss and his students in Zurich, culminating in the publication of *Psychotherapy for Freedom: The Daseinsanalytic Way in Psychology and Psychoanalysis* (Craig 1988). Since that time, Craig has published a series of articles unfolding existential-phenomenological interpretations of such classic psychoanalytic issues as the "soul" and the so-called "unconscious" (Craig 2008), dreams (Craig 1987, 2017), resistance (Craig 1995), transference and repetition (Craig 2005), and the role of fundamental ontology in existential psychology and psychotherapy (Craig 2015). Like Holzhey-Kunz, Craig especially values maintaining an active dialogue with psychoanalysis and is currently president of the New Mexico Society for Psychoanalysis. In 2004 began studying and collaborating with a former colleague and acquaintance of Boss, Prof. Dr. Rhee Dongshick (1921–2014), a South Korean Psychiatrist and founder of Tao Psychotherapy (Craig 2007). Craig serves on the boards of six scholarly journals and, in 2015, was given the Rollo May Heritage Award by APA's Society for Humanistic Psychology.

Other English Daseinsanalytic Authors

In addition to the contributions of the five major English-speaking daseinsanalytic authors above, there are several other individuals who have published worthwhile works in the field. In the United States, Todd DuBose (DuBose 2009, 2013), at the Illinois School for Professional Psychology in Chicago, is a frequent presenter of daseinsanalytic ideas in professional meetings and has developed a PhD specialty in existential psychology where Daseinsanalysis is a critical component. DuBose draws on his daseinsanalytic perspective to critique traditional norms and standards of care, including assessment, diagnosis, ethics, and the practice of psychotherapy, suggesting a new understanding of the psychologist as a "*Seelsorge*," one who practices "soul care." Many of these same themes are also articulated by Miles Groth (1987, 2008, 2017) who, like DuBose, consistently takes aim at various aspects of the field of therapy's "received" wisdom and language while developing an original daseinsanalytically oriented understanding of therapy he calls "Daseins-therapy."

The Canadian psychologist and Binswanger scholar, Roger Frie (1999, 2000, 2004) has also become a major, highly regarded contributor to the literature of post-modern psychology, particularly inter-subjective theory. Finally, also in Canada, Loray Daws (2015, 2018), a Masterson trained psychoanalyst, originally from South Africa, has focused on phenomenological-hermeneutic perspectives for psychoanalysis and daseinsanalysis, revisioning principles in such areas as mental health ethics and practice, cumulative trauma (Dasein-icide), and the experience of autochthony, to name just a few.

In the United Kingdom, the psychologist Anthony Stadlen (2003, 2005, 2007) has founded and continues to convene monthly "Inner Circle Seminars" that serve as a unique, "truth-seeking" venue for examining the often over-looked underbelly of history, theory, and practice in psychology. Today one of the most prolific presenters and authors in the field of Daseinsanalysis, Stadlen is a former Research Fellow of the Freud Museum, London. His articles focus on the life and works of Freud, Heidegger, Boss, Binswanger, and Laing, among many others. His intelligent, thoroughly researched, critical studies, and publications on Daseinsanalysis are an essential resource for Daseinsanalysts who appreciate incisive analysis of their approach's language, history, and practice.

The International Federation of Daseinsanalysis (IFDA)

Currently, the only international organization dedicated to the development, promotion, publication, and dissemination of daseinsanalytic thinking and practice is the IFDA. Today, the IFDA contains eight chapters located in Europe and South America. These national IFDA association members have each established training programs meeting the criteria for certification indicated below. They are currently located in the following countries: Austria, Belgium, Brazil, Czechoslovakia, Greece, Hungary, and, finally, Switzerland, which has 2 chapters. There were once groups in France, India, Japan, Canada, and Israel, but apparently these have long since faded away. According to IFDA chapter reports, the following countries currently have certificate candidates in training: Belgium, Brazil, Czechoslovakia, Greece, Hungary, and Switzerland. The entire Federation of eight chapters meets every four years for a two-day International Forum for Daseinsanalysis, at which time they share ideas, papers, and discussions as well as conduct the business of the Federation. Each of the chapters is expected to follow the By-laws of the Federation that contain specific standards for the training of daseinsanalytic candidates who aspire to receive a Diploma in Daseinsanalysis and become certified Daseinsanalysts. These training standards include the following:

1 Prequalification by the completion of a university degree or equivalent professional qualification in subjects relevant to psychotherapy.
2 Four years of basic daseinsanalytic training including at least 400 hours of theoretical study 250 hours of which must be specifically daseinsanalytic theory; 250 hours of individual psychotherapy, and 130 hours of clinical supervision; and 450 hours of supervised clinical work.
3 At least one scientific publication or presentation in the field of Daseinsanalysis.
4 The completion of a successful assessment by qualified, certified Daseinsanalysts.

All eight organizations belonging to IFDA remain dedicated to the teaching and disseminating daseinsanalytic perspectives and ideas. Six of those have active formal training programs conforming to IFDA rules and standards. Brazil has 15 members and one current candidate; Belgium has four training analysts and nine trainees; the society in Czechoslovakia, has approximately 50 certified Daseinsanalysts, as do the Hungarians, including five of whom are training analysts for the three current candidates. Thanasis Georgas, president of the Hellenic Society of Greece, reports having 36 members, including five training analysts, 14 candidates who have received training and full certification as daseinsanalytic therapists as well as 17 current trainees. The two societies in Zürich, Switzerland have a combined 60 or so trained and certified analysts, though no current candidates in training.

The fact that there are now two Swiss chapters of IFDA is worth clarifying. The former Daseinsanalytic Institute for Psychotherapy and Psychosomatics has been reorganized under the name the Association (*Fachverband*) for Daseinsanalytic Psychotherapy (SFDP) and the former Swiss Society for Daseinsanalysis now called, the "Daseinsanalytic Seminar" (DaS). In 2016 the DaS was accredited by the Swiss authorities to train psychologists as licensed daseinsanalytic therapists. The Daseinsanalysis taught at the DaS is based on Holzhey-Kunz's hermeneutic Daseinsanalysis which is grounded in Heidegger's ontological analysis of Dasein as found in *Being and Time* (Heidegger 1962). Since 2000, the DaS has been the only institution in Switzerland that trains daseinsanalytic psychotherapists, although the chapters are in talks to collaborate.

In addition to the roughly 200 certified Daseinsanalysts practicing the world, there are a number of independent daseinsanalytically oriented psychotherapists with private practices who also conduct lectures, seminars, and independent training. Unfortunately there is currently no certified English speaking chapter or training program in Daseinsanalysis or daseinsanalytic therapy, though Anthony Stadlen offers his Inner Circle seminars in England and Erik Craig offers independent trainings in the United States and abroad. In addition, a small association of phenomenological, daseinsanalytically oriented psychotherapists has formed in the states. This group, including Todd DuBose in Chicago, Erik Craig in Santa Fe, Miles Groth in New York, and

Ken Bradford in California, informally collaborate under the title American Association for Existential Analysis. Although this Association is not currently a member of IFDA, its four collaborators have attended and presented at a number of the International Daeseinsanalytic Fora and offer independent teaching, training, and supervision.

The ninth international Forum, held in Athens Greece and hosted by Thanasis Georgas, president of the Hellenic Society, focused on the question, "What does it mean to be a Daseinsanalyst?" According to Georgas, the question was taken up in round-table fashion with three basic themes, the format that set the tone for the weekend, Georgas pointed out the close relationship between the phenomenological-hermeneutical method of Daseinsanalysis and the Socratic method with both being grounded in a radical openness to "not knowing," especially as it is embodied in the Greek word, "*aporia*," referring to that which is obscure, mystifying, baffling, or confusing. Daseinsanalytic practice remains focused on allowing things "to speak for themselves." As Georgas noted, "In a culture more and more dominated by the 'positive thinking' of the scientific-technical method, we have lost touch with the inner meaning of silence" (Georgas 2016, p. 431). He goes on to point out that we have become accustomed to using words to assure ourselves of our knowledge of and communication with others, but raises this doubt: "What if the opposite is true? What if, in the silence of the '*not knowing*' and the '*aporia*' we establish true contact with our whole being and the being of the other?" (Georgas 2016, p. 431). Since, according to Heidegger, the phenomena of human existence always simultaneously hide and reveal at the same time, the full, ontological meaning of such phenomena are not initially obvious. Thus we have to continue to look, dwelling with "the things themselves," waiting for what is still hidden to show itself from itself. For this, Georgas asserts, the silence of "not knowing," of "*aporia*," is necessary. Thus, the first reply: Daseinsanalysis is a process of phenomenological-hermeneutic listening for the hidden meaning embodied in the things themselves.

This set the stage for the second round table focusing on the issue of what it is that distinguishes Daseinsanalysis from other forms of existential therapy. Here again, there was a concern with returning to phenomenological-hermeneutic analysis and, in particular, with the invariable ontological structures of the existing human. Distinguishing itself from other approaches to existential therapy depends entirely of the Daseinsanalyst's understanding of Dasein's enigmatic ontico-ontological way of being and constitution as that kind of being that is "ontically distinguished by the fact that, in its very Being, that Being is an issue for it" and that "understanding of Being (*Seinsverstandnis*) is a definite characteristic of Dasein's Being" (Heidegger 1927/1962, p. 32). With this basic understanding in common the round table went on, with various disagreements, controversies and convergences, to observe and consider the possibility of increased dialogue with psychoanalysis, the contrasts and convergences with humanistic existential therapies mainly supportive approaches, and the impact and relation to Eastern philosophies and the "fading of Selfhood (Selbstsein)" (Georgas 2016, p. 432). Each of these concerns represents major challenges for present and future Daseinsanalysts.

The third round table, moderated by Anthony Stadlen of the United Kingdom, focused on Heidegger's *Zollikon Seminars* (1987/2001) and its historic implications for Daseinsanalysis's self-understanding with reference to its past, present, and future.

It is clear that the modern Daseinsanalyst has to navigate the difficult clinical-theoretical dialectic between Heideggerian ontology and the burgeoning praxis of modern day psychoanalysis, and evidence-based practices. It was emphasized that considerable discipline and fortitude is required of contemporary Daseinsanalysts who must remain invested in a careful and thorough reading of Heidegger's ontology and phenomenology as it pertains to the theory and praxis of medicine, psychology, psychiatry, and psychotherapy.

Challenges for the Future of Daseinsanalysis

One of the challenges facing Daseinsanalysis today is simply being able to say precisely what Daseinsanalysis *is* given the variety of approaches currently being practiced. There are those who follow the concerns of Binswanger's psychiatric Daseinsanalysis; those who, like Craig, Holzhey-Kunz, and Kastrinidis, stick closely to the Heidegger of *Being and Time* (1927/1962); those who, like Konstantin Gemenetzis in Greece and Ado Huygens in Belgium are drawn, as Boss himself was, to the later Heidegger of *Ereignis* (event) and the reversal of the relationship between Being and Dasein as discussed elsewhere in this part; and, finally, those who entirely follow Holzhey-Kunz's new hermeneutic Daseinsanalysis. Considerable disagreement also exists in the degrees and ways contemporary Daseinsanalysts re-appropriate, or not, Sigmund Freud's psychoanalytic theory and practice. As challenging as it might be, such diversity can only serve to strengthen Daseinsanalysis as it ensures against the development of a single daseinsanalytic dogma and fosters self-reflection and criticism.

The Challenge of Language

Today Daseinsanalysis is challenged by language in two ways. First of all, the majority of daseinsanalytic literature is still in German and even current translations are far from adequate. Readers of both Binswanger and Boss are unhappy with the way in which their works have been rendered in English. Holzhey-Kunz's *Daseinsanalysis* (Holzhey-Kunz 2014) is a welcome exception. Nevertheless the ongoing English writers mentioned above continue to make contributions to the literature in their own language. Without question, however, there is clearly a paucity of excellent literature available to the English students and practitioners of Daseinsanalysis and daseinsanalytically oriented or influenced psychotherapy.

The other linguistic challenge lies in the obscurity of Heidegger's own language, which is already challenging in German and not only discouraging but often completely off putting for English readers. Although there is no doubt of the importance of his work, as it often turns Western philosophy and social science on its head and leads to a new kind of careful thoughtfulness about everything we do in the philosophical and social regional sciences, the language of Daseinsanalysis demands a level of thinking and philosophical familiarity for which most average psychotherapists simply do not have time or patience.

The Challenge of Cognitive Psychology and Evidence-based Treatment

Today, cognitive psychology is by far the predominant model for training in University psychology programs in the United States. The unquestioned alliance between this approach and the strictly scientistic emphasis on evidence-based treatments goes on largely unchallenged. What challenges are issued, and there are several significant ones, are brushed off by the positivists who consider most forms of humanistic and depth psychological psychotherapy to be without any scientific basis whatsoever. In fact, US students are often discouraged from considering clinical work entirely and are instead urged to pursue careers in research and university teaching.

Fortunately, a number of influential humanists like Bruce Wampold and psychoanalysts like Jonathan Schedler continue undaunted in their commitment to making the scientific foundations of depth and humanistic psychologies both more solid and well respected. Still, existential psychotherapy as a whole and Daseinsanalysis in particular have much more to do in this regard.

The Challenge of Heidegger, the Man

An especially crucial challenge for Daseinsanalysts in particular, not to mention existential therapists in general, is the almost unavoidable reliance on the thinking of Martin Heidegger whose *Being and Time* (1927/1962) continues to be considered by many philosophers and the social scientists the most significant philosophical work of the twentieth century. Since the late 1980s, however, a number of damning reports of the philosopher's affiliations with Germany's National Socialist Party and, especially, his subsequent silence and failure to explain or justify his affiliation and related actions, have shaken and disgusted many of his most ardent scholars. The character of Heidegger the man is now widely understood as a profoundly compromised one. He was neither honest with himself or others, including his daseinsanalytic psychotherapist disciple, Medard Boss. Daseinsanalytic scholars and practitioners are now left to question whether the philosopher's thinking and writing can be separated from his person and politics. Stolorow has reflected on the issue from the perspective of "Heidegger's personal world, including the theme of emotional Trauma" (Stolorow 2011, p. 81). Others have approached the problem philosophically, politically, and/or historically. Regretfully, it is impossible to address this matter in detail here, though there is a now a significant body of literature on the subject for those wishing to pursue it for themselves through the varied works of scholars as Cohn, Farias, Gendlin, Moehling, Ott, Rockmore and Margolis, Pöggeler, and Sheehan, to mention just a few. Daseinsanalysts today can no longer deny the evidence of this odious period in Heidegger's life and continue to idealize him as a man in the way Medard Boss did until the end of his own life. They must now study Heidegger's life and think anew omit with a sharp and discerning, yet open mind to find what remains significantly revelatory, meaningful, and authentic for themselves.

The Challenge and Promise of the Relational Turn in Psychoanalysis

Another challenge is with Daseinsanalysts relationship with Freud and psychoanalysis, another area in which there is considerable variation among practicing Daseinsanalysts. There is a growing awareness, for example, about subscribing to any rigid set of rules in the conduct of any given practice, whether those rules be humanistic, daseinsanalytic, or psychoanalytic in origin. A number of Daseinsanalysts, including for example Erik Craig and Alice Holzhey-Kunz has found considerable compatibility with the work of Robert Stolorow and his colleagues. We will close with some detailed remarks regarding this and the whole contemporary relational turn in psychoanalysis.

In many ways, the Daseinsanalysis anticipated the relational turn in psychoanalysis with its former's emphasis on a *sui generis* being-with-one-another (*Miteinandersein*) as opposed to the eruption of pre-determined transferential reactions from the present. Unfortunately, as David Smith remarks, Boss's genius was overridden by his failure "to grasp fully the revolutionary nature of Daseinsanalysis and the true magnitude of his own contribution to the revisioning of psychotherapy" (Smith 2010, p. 10). Ironically, while anticipated by Daseinsanalysis, contemporary relational psychoanalysis has in many ways surpassed Daseinsanalysis in its development of effective, uniquely human modes of therapeutic engagement.

Today there are actually two broad approaches to relational psychoanalysis that are continuing to revolutionize analytic practice. Both approaches exemplify what is broadly considered a "two-person psychology" and are grounded in the principle of Fairbairn's radical revisioning of the human being as "object-seeking" (i.e., oriented to relatedness with the other) not pleasure seeking (i.e., oriented to satisfying internal drives) (Fairbairn 1952, p. 210). One approach is the relational psychoanalysis of Stephen Mitchell, Jay Greenberg, Lewis Aron, Jeremy Safran, and others drawing not only on Sullivan's interpersonal theory but also on the early works of Ferenczi and his analysand and student Michael Balint. The other approach, originally known as intersubjective theory, grew out of Robert Stolorow and George Atwood's studies of phenomenology (Atwood and Stolorow 1984) and is now called phenomenological-contextual psychoanalysis, and includes the work of Stolorow and Atwood along with that of Bernard Brandchaft, Donna Orange, Roger Frie, and others. Although both approaches place their primary emphasis on the unfolding relationship as such, there are some significant differences in how to understand and approach the relationship.

Nevertheless, Atwood and Stolorow's approach is particularly relevant for Daseinsanalysts, since in 2000, Stolorow himself began turning to Heidegger's "ontological contextualism" for a more radical philosophical foundation for their psychoanalytic phenomenological contextualism. Stolorow has recently described the reason for this turn to Heidegger as follows:

> First was his [Heidegger's] crucial initial move in choosing the inquirer himself/herself as the entity to be interrogated as to its Being. Heidegger reasoned that, because an unarticulated, pre-philosophical understanding of our Being is constitutive of our kind of Being, we humans can investigate our own kind of Being by investigating our understanding of that Being. Accordingly, the investigative method in *Being and Time* is a *phenomenological* one, aimed at illuminating the fundamental structures of our understanding of our Being. Just as *Faces in a Cloud* begins (Atwood and Stolorow 1993) with our investigations of the personal phenomenologies of psychoanalytic theorists en route to a recasting of psychoanalysis as a form of phenomenological inquiry, *Being and Time* begins with the phenomenology of the inquirer en route to a claim that ontology is possible only as phenomenology.
>
> Second, Heidegger's ontological contextualism—his mending of the Cartesian subject/object split with the claim that our Being is always already a Being-in-the-world—immediately struck me as providing a solid philosophical grounding for our psychoanalytic contextualism, replacing the Cartesian isolated mind that undergirds Freudian theory.

> Third, and even more important for me, when I read the passages in *Being and Time* devoted to Heidegger's existential analysis of *Angst*, I nearly fell off my chair! Both his phenomenological description and ontological account of *Angst* bore a remarkable resemblance to what I had concluded about the phenomenology and meaning of emotional trauma some two years earlier (Stolorow 1999). In short, Heidegger's analysis of *Angst*, world-collapse, uncanniness, and thrownness into Being-toward-death provided me extraordinary philosophical tools for grasping the existential significance of emotional trauma. It was this discovery that motivated me to begin doctoral studies in philosophy and to write several articles, a dissertation, and two books (Stolorow 2007, 2011) on Heidegger and what Atwood and I had come to call *post-Cartesian psychoanalysis*. My dual aim in this work has been to show both how Heidegger's existential philosophy enriches post-Cartesian psychoanalysis and how post-Cartesian psychoanalysis enriches Heidegger's existential philosophy.
>
> Heidegger's existential analytic teaches that, contrary to the Freudian vision of a self-contained "mental apparatus," human existence is always already situated, intelligible only in terms of the world in which it is embedded. Context-dependence and death are two dimensions of human finitude that Heidegger has brought into bold relief, much to the benefit of clinical psychoanalytic work. Emotional trauma produces an affective state whose features bear a close similarity to the central elements in Heidegger's existential interpretation of anxiety, and it accomplishes this by plunging the traumatized person into a form of authentic (i.e., non-evasively owned) Being-toward-death. Post-Cartesian psychoanalysis gives an account of the relational contexts that make it possible for one to dwell in and bear the traumatizing emotional impact of human finitude, thereby illuminating the rich relationality of authentic existing. From the encounter between Heidegger's existential philosophy and post-Cartesian psychoanalysis, both emerge enriched (Stolorow 2016, NP13–NP15).

While it is clear from the above that Stolorow's phenomenological-contextual relational approach to psychoanalysis was enriched by what he describes as Heidegger's "ontological contextualism," particularly with its emphasis on Time, Finitude, Anxiety, and Death, what does his approach bring to the practice of Daseinsanalytic psychotherapy? We can suggest at least four points in this regard.

First, since Daseinsanalysis remains today one of many approaches to psychoanalysis, Stolorow's relational approach stands as one more challenge to the daseinsanalytic attachment to Sigmund Freud's classical psychoanalytic technique. Like Kastrinidis's eschewal of the use of the couch, free association, and silent, evenly hovering attention, Stolorow's approach emphasizes the face-to-face encounter and a thoughtful hermeneutic listening. Unlike Kastrinidis's approach, however, Stolorow rejects the possibility of anything like the classical understandings of neutrality and abstinence in the therapeutic relationship. For Stolorow, Gadamer's hermeneutic understanding of the inescapable nature of the human being's prejudice or prejudgment is telling with respect to the possibility of anything like neutrality, a term (*Neutralität*) that, incidentally, Freud himself never used even if his own German *Indifferenz* was translated as such in the *Standard Edition*. With respect to the therapist's abstinence and anonymity, Stolorow considers these aspects of so-called neutrality, not only impossible in the classical sense but potentially damaging to the therapeutic process and even individual him or herself.

Secondly, we suggest that these views are in keeping with Heidegger's understanding of human existence as inescapably thrown and, therefore, that as therapists we can never aspire to neutrality but always bring a perspective, in Heidegger's terms a definite "fore-structure" to our understanding of every living human situation, including the psychoanalytic one. Fortunately, although there is no escaping such fore-understanding, there is the promise in what Heidegger described as the hermeneutic circle and the possibility that we might "come into it in the right way" (Heidegger 1927/1962, p. 195), that is, making the scientific theme phenomenologically secure "by working out these fore-structures in terms of the things themselves" (Heidegger 1927/1962, p. 195).

Thirdly, in our mind, Stolorow's phenomenological-contextual approach to psychoanalysis offers promising, practical ways of stepping into the "hermeneutic circle of ontical relational therapeutic understanding." Though this occasion does not allow for a full explication of how Stolorow's therapeutic approach to historically (developmentally) constituted therapeutic relating may be employed, the intersubjective, phenomenological contextual psychoanalytic literature (e.g., Buirski and Haglund 2001; Stolorow and Atwood 1979, Stolorow, Atwood, and Orange 2002) is full of concrete case examples.

Finally, Stolorow's deep understanding of the historically and dynamically co-constructed character of intimate human relatedness might offer Daseinsanalysts a potentially more vital and palatable everyday English language for the often obtuse and off-putting Heideggerian German. Clinically speaking, Stolorow's therapeutic approach might actually be more in keeping with the deeply humanistic understanding of the human being as Dasein, than Boss's own more classically Freudian conduct of the analytic situation, thus potentially embracing what Smith called "the true magnitude of his own contribution to the revisioning of psychotherapy" (Smith 2010, p. 10). It is our conviction that of all the analytic approaches to psychotherapy, Daseinsanalysis ought to be truly and deeply relational, something we believe Stolorow's approach has the potential to achieve.

References

Atwood, G.E. and Stolorow, R.D. (1984). *Structures of Subjectivity: Explorations in Psychoanalytic Phenomenology.* Hillsdale, NJ: The Analytic Press.

Atwood, G.E. and Stolorow, R.D. (1993). *Faces in the Cloud: Intersubjectivity in Personality Theory.* Northvale, NJ: Jason Aronson.

Boss, M. (1979). *Existential Foundations of Medicine and Psychology* (trans. S. Conway and A. Cleaves). New York: Jason Aronson. (Original work published 1971.)

Buirski, P. and Hagland, P. (2001). *Making Sense Together: The Intersubjective Approach to Psychotherapy.* New York: Jason Aronson.

Condrau, G. (1988) A seminar on daseinsanalytic psychotherapy. *The Humanistic Psychologist 16* (1): 101–129.

Condrau, G. (1993). Dream analysis: Do we need an Unconscious? *Existential Analysis 4*: 1–12.

Condrau, G. (1996) Why Heidegger? *Existential Analysis 8* (1): 21–27.

Condrau, G. (1998). *Martin Heidegger's Impact on Psychotherapy.* New York: Edition MOSAIC.

Condrau, G. and Boss, M. (1967). Existential psychoanalysis. In: *Psychoanalytic Techniques: A Handbook for the Practicing Psychoanalyst* (ed. B.B. Wolman), 443–467. New York: Basic Books.

Craig, E. (1987). Dreaming, reality and allusion: An existential-phenomenological inquiry. In: *Advances in Qualitative Psychology: Themes and Variations* (ed. F.J. Van Zuuren, F.J. Wertz, and E. Mook), 115–136. Lisse, Netherlands: Swetts & Zeitlinger BV; Berwyn, PA: Swetts North America.

Craig, E. (ed.) (1988). Psychotherapy for freedom: The daseinsanalytic way in psychology and psychoanalysis [Special issue]. *The Humanistic Psychologist 16* (1).

Craig, E. (1995). Being contrary, being human: The pregnant, paradoxical openness of resistance. *The Humanistic Psychologist 23* (2): 161–186.

Craig, E. (2005). How is it with repetition and its offspring transference? A daseinsanalytic inquiry. In: *Daseinsanalysis: The Twenty-Second Annual Symposium of the Simon Silverman Phenomenology Center* (ed. D.J Martino), 27–62. Pittsburgh: Simon Silverman Phenomenology Center.

Craig, E. (2007). Tao psychotherapy: A new approach to humanistic practice. *The Humanistic Psychologist 34* (2): 109–133.

Craig, E. (2008). The human and the hidden: Existential wonderings about depth, soul, and the unconscious. *The Humanistic Psychologist 36* (3–4): 227–282.

Craig, E. (2015). The lost language of being: Ontology's perilous destiny in existential psychotherapy. *Philosophy, Psychiatry, and Psychology 20* (2): 79–92.

Craig, E. (2017). On the power of butterflies: Dreaming, waking, and the therapeutic potential of nocturnal beings. In: *Existential Psychology and the Way of the Tao: Meditations on the Writings of Zhuangzi* (ed. M. Yang), 73–89. New York: Routledge.

Daws, L. (2015). Autochthony versus the world-view of alterity (otherness): Possible implications for contemporary mental health practice and the mental health client as reluctant philosopher. *EPIS Journal 1*: 17–55.

Daws, L. (2018). The Wolf-Man: A daseinsanalytic reading of Sergei Pankejeff's ontological trauma. *EPIS Journal 1*: 31–51.

DuBose, T. (2009). *Daseinsanalysis.* In: *Encyclopedia of Psychology and Religion* (ed. D. Leeming, K. Madden, and S. Marlan), 209–211. Norwell, MA: Springer Science and Business Media.

DuBose, T. (2013). Where the crooked are made straight: "Being-with" the fated hope of escaping facticity. *Daseinsanalyse: Jahrbuch fur Phanomenologische Anthropology* [Daseinsanalysis: Journal for Phenomenological Anthropology and Psychotherapy] *27*: 43–50.

Fairbairn, W.R.D. (1952). *Psychoanalytic Studies of the Personality.* London: Tavistock.

Frie, R. (1999). Interpreting a misinterpretation: Ludwig Binswanger and Martin Heidegger. *Journal of the British Society for Phenomenology 30* (3): 244–257.

Frie, R. (2000). The existential and the interpersonal: Ludwig Binswanger and Harry Stack Sullivan. *Journal of Humanistic Psychology 40* (3): 108–129.

Frie, R. (2004). Formulating unconscious experience: From Freud to Binswanger and Sullivan. In: *Psychoanalysis at the Limit: Epistemology, Mind, and the Question of Science* (ed. J. Mills), 31–48. Albany, NY: SUNY Press.

Georgas, T. (2016). "What does it mean to be a Daseinsanalyst?" Report on the Ninth IFDA International Forum. *Horizon 5* (2): 428–439.

Groth, M. (1987). *Preparatory Thinking in Heidegger's Teaching.* New York: Philosophical Library.

Groth, M. (2008). Medard Boss and Martin Heidegger: "A Western Kind of Rishi." *Review of Existential Psychology and Psychiatry 27* (1–3): 43–59.

Groth, M. (2017). *Translating Heidegger*. Toronto, Canada: University of Toronto Press. (Original work published 2004.)

Heidegger, M. (1962). *Being and Time* (trans. J. McQuarrie and E. Robinson). New York: Harper & Row. (Original work published 1927.)

Heidegger, M. (2001). *Zollikon Seminars: Protocols – Conversations – Letters* (ed. M. Boss; trans. F. Mayr and R. Askay). Evanston, IL: Northwestern University Press. (Original work published 1987.)

Holzhey-Kunz, A. (1988). Emancipation and narcissism: On the meaning of desire. *The Humanistic Psychologist 16* (1): 186–202.

Holzhey-Kunz, A. (2006). Ludwig Binswanger: Psychiatry based on the foundation of philosophical anthropology. In: *Images in Psychiatry: German Speaking Countries* (ed. E.M. Wolpert, K. Maurer, A.H. Rifai et al.), 271–288. Heidelberg: Universitatsverlag Winter.

Holzhey-Kunz, A. (2012). What defines the Daseinsanalytic process? *Existential Analysis 8* (1), 200–210.

Holzhey-Kunz, A. (2014). *Daseinsanalysis* (trans. S. Leighton). London: Free Association Books.

Holzhey-Kunz, A. and Fazekas, T. (2012). Daseinsanalysis: A dialogue. In *Existential Psychotherapy: Legacy, Vibrancy and Dialogue* (ed. L. Barnett and G. Madison), 36–51. London: Routledge.

Kastrinidis, P. (1988a). Daseinsanalytic psychotherapy with the elderly. *The Humanistic Psychologist 16* (1): 153–165.

Kastrinidis, P. (1988b). The phenomenology of narcissistic neurosis. *The Humanistic Psychologist 16* (1), 168–185.

Kastrinidis, P. (2005). Between human illusion and inhuman reality: A Daseinsanalytic contribution to the understanding of masochism. In: *Daseinsanalysis* (ed. J. Martino), 89–109. Pittsburgh: Duquesne University.

Kastrinidis, P. (2008). Eros and abstinence in psychotherapy. *The Humanistic Psychologist 36* (3): 316–335.

May, R., Angel, E., and Ellenberger, H.F. (eds.) (1958). *Existence: A New Dimension in Psychiatry and Psychology*. New York: Basic Books.

Smith, D. (2010). From passive psyche to dynamic Dasein. *The Humanistic Psychologist 38* (3): 203–220.

Stadlen, A. (2003). Essay review: Martin Heidegger's impact on psychotherapy by Gion Condrau. *Existential Analysis 14* (1): 162–178.

Stadlen, A. (2005). Medical Daseinsanalysis. *Existential Analysis 16* (1): 169–177.

Stadlen, A. (2007). The madhouse of being. *Existential Analysis 18* (1): 117–154.

Stern, P.J. (1964). *The Abnormal Person and His World: An Introduction to Psychopathology*. Princeton, NJ: D. Van Nostrand.

Stern, P.J. (1972). *In Praise of Madness: Realness Therapy – The Self Reclaimed*. New York: W.W. Norton & Company.

Stern, P.J. (1976). *C.G. Jung: The Haunted Prophet*. New York: George Braziller

Stern, P.J. (1977). Forward. In: M. Boss, "*I Dreamt Last Night…": A New Approach to the Revelations of Dreaming – and its Uses in Psychotherapy* (trans. S. Conway), vii–xix. New York: Gardner Press.

Stern, P.J. (1979). Introduction to the English translation. In M. Boss, *Existential Foundations of Medicine and Psychology* (trans. S. Conway and A. Cleaves), ix–xxii. New York: Jason Aronson.

Stolorow, R.D. (1999). The phenomenology of trauma and the absolutisms of everyday life: A personal journey. *Psychoanalytic Psychology 16* (3): 464–468.

Stolorow, R.D. (2007). *Trauma and Human Existence: Autobiographical, Psychoanalytic, and Philosophical Reflections.* New York: Routledge.

Stolorow, R.D. (2011). *World, Affectivity, Trauma: Heidegger and Post-Cartesian Psychoanalysis.* New York: Routledge.

Stolorow, R.D. (2013). Heidegger and Post-Cartesian Psychoanalysis. In: *The Bloomsbury Companion to Heidegger* (ed. F. Raffoul and E. Nelson), 451–458. London: Bloomsbury Academic.

Stolorow, R.D. (2016). Using Heidegger (Letter to the Editor). *Journal of the American Psychoanalytic Association 66* (4): NP13–NP15.

Stolorow, R.D. and Atwood, G.E. (1979). *Faces in the Cloud: Intersubjectivity in Personality Theory.* New York: Jason Aronson.

Stolorow, R.D., Atwood, G.E., and Orange, D.M. (2002). *Worlds of Experience: Interweaving Philosophical and Clinical Dimensions in Psychoanalysis.* New York: Basic Books.

Part II
Existential-Phenomenological Therapy

Edited by
Emmy van Deurzen

Introduction

Existential-phenomenological therapy is a form of existential therapy that has grown from deep European roots and that has thrived spectacularly over the past decades. It found its origins on the European continent, rather like Daseinsanalysis, but flourished strongly in the United Kingdom, from where a diaspora of existential-phenomenological therapy then spread around the whole of Europe and then well beyond it. Existential-phenomenological therapy is now well established worldwide and for many practitioners is synonymous with Existential Therapy tout court. This particular modality of existential therapy, which this part of the book focuses on, was initially known as the "London School of Existential Psychotherapy" and later on as the "British School of Existential Psychotherapy."

If we were to continue using geographic terminology it would now be more correct to name it the "European School of Existential Therapy," but this would also be confusing and inaccurate, as there are many new streams of existential-phenomenological therapy around the world, well beyond Europe and there are other many other forms of existential therapy in Europe (see Part I and Part VI). Furthermore many of the contributing authors of existential-phenomenological therapy are neither British nor European. That is why we have now opted to call this form of existential therapyexistential-phenomenological therapy, EPTfor short to differentiate it from other forms of existential therapy (Cooper 2016; Deurzen and Adams 2016). Notwithstanding this, many authors continue to refer to this practice simply as existential therapy as this is much easier for clients and the wider public (Deurzen and Arnold-Baker 2018).

The deepest roots of EPT can be traced back to the development of philosophy in Athens two-and-a-half millennia ago (Deurzen 2012; Deurzen and Arnold-Baker 2018). It was the pre-Socratics, Socrates, Plato, and Aristotle who created the

The Wiley World Handbook of Existential Therapy, First Edition. Edited by Emmy van Deurzen, Erik Craig, Alfried Längle, Kirk J. Schneider, Digby Tantam, and Simon du Plock.

intellectual discipline of the love of wisdom (philo-sophia) that led us to explore human existence in a systematic way. In this sense classical Western philosophy is the first port of call for studies and training in existential-phenomenological therapy. Such training will always amply cover the important philosophical methods and ideas that underpin this way of working. There is for instance the practice of questioning assumptions and of using dialogical and interactive methods for the careful examination of views. There are also the well-established methods of dialectics and deductive thinking, first used by the Athenians. Then there is Socrates' art of maieutics: the method of giving birth to ideas already within a person by making explicit what was previously implicit. Socrates was a past master at getting his students to talk about a particular topic whilst prompting them with a series of astute and intelligent questions to clarify the terms of the debate and allow people to draw their own conclusions. This method is described in the Platonic dialogue, Meno, where Socrates is seen to extract wisdom from a young slave by interrogating him carefully, taking him from confusion and doubt to the discovery of knowledge and wisdom (Plato and Beresford 2005).

Existential therapists use other Socratic methods too, such as that of Socratic questioning, leading a person to *aporia*, that is, a sense of puzzlement that forces a person to learn to think in a more open and critical manner, starting from a position of wonder and not knowing. Existential phenomenological therapists are keen, like Socrates, to move away from superficial knowledge and especially to steer clear of the pretentious and spurious claims to knowledge so often demonstrated by rhetoricians or sophists (Plato 2003). The search for wisdom and the awareness of how little we know and how important it is to become more aware and learn to reflect more carefully is a crucial part of this way of working. This is embodied in Plato's idea of the allegory of the cave of ignorance, from which human beings have to escape by courageously throwing off the chains of security and by questioning the shadows they have taken for reality. To climb out of the cave is to climb from darkness back into the light. We do this by careful reflection and self-reflection in order to scrutinize what is hidden, lost, unknown, purloined, or forgotten (Plato 2007).

Investigating all that is and can be known, with great vigor and determination is therefore an essential part of existential practice for EPT. In this we follow the philosophers' habit of questioning definitions of concepts and of the assumptions that people carry with them. The existential phenomenological therapist enters into a dialogue, which is a genuine attempt at probing a worldview and meticulously examining it. We do this in order for a person to make room in their life and create a safe space in which to let things come to mind, elucidating and ordering things that were previously obscure and chaotic. We often do this with the dialectical method, first facilitated by Socrates and later developed by Hegel, who also first introduced the idea of phenomenology. This dialectical view of the world allows for things to be multiple, complex, and varied. It accepts that ideas are often paradoxical and come to us with contradictions, dilemmas, and conflicts. These tensions have to be taken seriously until they can be resolved by paying heed to both sides of the equation. We can then use the synergy released to achieve transcendence of the problems by taking them to a higher level, where their contradictions are integrated into a new formulation, whilst still retaining awareness and paying heed to the tensions of the original historical paradox. EPT emphasizes this generative, historical, genetic movement of human existence and seeks to honor the onto-dynamic process of change that guides human beings from birth to death. When we allow ourselves to be a fluid part of this process of change and learn to guide it and take charge of it, our lives come into their own. For we now flow with the river of life and can enjoy and relish that flow, instead of getting snagged up somewhere along the river bed, stagnating and ending up with sedimented views and repetitive actions that become mineralized and set in stone.

This idea of the importance of paradox was also one propounded by Kierkegaard, whose many publications are often seen as the grounding texts of existential therapy (Kierkegaard 1844, 1845, 1846). Kierkegaard's insistence that human beings need to dare to stand out of the crowd in order to claim their status as an individual gives us a blueprint for existential work. Kierkegaard's distinction between mineral, vegetative, aesthetic, ethical, thinking, and spiritual stages of human existence forms the basis of his understanding of human existence as evolutionary and dynamic (Adams 2018). He particularly emphasized the need for people to take a leap of faith into a more aware and devout way of life, surpassing contradictions and struggling with our own fate. The role of anxiety in bringing us to awareness is a stroke of genius, which was also adopted by Heidegger (1927). Thus Angst or anxiety for existential therapists is not something to fear, avoid, or cure. It is rather seen as a call to consciousness and responsibility as it wakes us up and faces us with our own capacity to act in the world in a moral way. Anxiety is an infusion of energy and awareness. If we focus it on a worthy purpose, it will be absorbed by our actions. Similarly shame and guilt hold an important function of bringing to awareness what we owe ourselves and what life is asking of us. All these feelings help us take more responsibility for our existence. This is all part of the human challenge to surpass our animal nature, to live with awareness in the tension between temporality and eternity.

The same notion of surpassing and holding of tensions can be found in Nietzsche's work (Nietzsche 1964, 1971, 1990) when he describes human beings as a rope and a bridge between animal and Superman. His idea of the will to power that drives us to evolve to a stronger state of mind and way of life is directly related to his nihilism. In his case this is based in the realization that human beings have killed God and now have to find their path alone, taking responsibility for everything we choose and do. He sees the challenge as one of wayfaring and overcoming our base instincts towards something greater, whilst being fully embodied in our animal nature at the same time. Human beings are a going across and a down going: our suffering is our greatest capacity, Nietzsche proposes. His idea that overcoming and laughter are the best way forward for humanity is always opposed by his recognition of the importance of adversity and martyrdom as well.

After these two inspirational existential philosophers of the nineteenth century the field was much in need of a strong existential methodology to bring clarity and this was the gift of phenomenology at the very start of the twentieth century (Husserl 1925, 1931, 2001). Phenomenology provides a range of other methods too, which were brought to us by the work of Brentano and Husserl in the nineteenth and early-twentieth centuries. Phenomenological methods were specifically developed to investigate human existence and human consciousness systematically, building a bridge between the social and the exact sciences. Interestingly, this coincided with the development of both scientific psychiatry and psychoanalysis. The history of existential-phenomenological therapy intersects with both of these at various points, but finds its own trajectory eventually, as we shall see in the first chapter of this part of the book. Over the years existential-phenomenological therapy has drawn on many other philosophers, such as Sartre (1939, 1943, 1946), de Beauvoir (1970, 2004) and Merleau-Ponty (1962) and continues to ground itself in the practice of philosophy, as this develops or brings us new perspectives on human existence from around the globe.

In this existential-phenomenological part of the book we shall consider this most philosophical of all existential approaches and cover the work of some of its main authors on the subject. This will show how even within this particular form of existential therapy there are important differences and distinctions between various ways of working. The history chapter will introduce and detail the complex heritage of existential-phenomenological therapy. The theory and practice chapters will provide pointers for the philosophy and method of this approach and these will be succinctly summarized in the key-texts chapter. There is a long case study in this part of the book, which represents the importance of the case study tradition for existential therapy and in particular for existential phenomenological therapy, which aims to show the dynamic changes and therapeutic interactions that enable a person to re-engage with their existence in a new way (Du Plock 2018). This is the longest case study in the book, which plumbs the reflective depth and breadth of existential work and which has a critical edge, to allow for a more thorough and direct exploration of the process between therapist and client. The final chapter on future challenges will show the wealth of developments already happening in this field. This very productive and popular approach is now very widespread across the continents. We shall finally be able to consider some of the future challenges to existential therapy, which are already waiting in the wings. Existential-phenomenological therapy will change as it spreads across the world and encounters many and varied challenges in an array of different cultures. But it will always emphasize its search for meaning (Deurzen 2008; Vos 2018) and for a deeper understanding of the mysteries of human existence (Deurzen 2010).

References

Adams, M. (2018). *An Existential Approach to Human Development: Philosophical and Therapeutic Perspectives.* London: Red Globe Press.

Beauvoir, S. de (1970). *The Ethics of Ambiguity* (trans. B. Frechtman). New York: Citadel Press.

Beauvoir, S. de (2004). Pyrrhus and Cinéas. In: *Philosophical Writings* (ed. M.A. Simons, M. Timmerman, and M.B. Mader), 77–150. Urbana: University of Illinois Press.

Cooper, M. (2016). *Existential Therapies*, 2e. London: Sage.

Deurzen, E. van (2008). *Psychotherapy and the Quest for Happiness.* London: Sage.

Deurzen, E. van (2010). *Everyday Mysteries: Handbook of Existential Therapy*, 2e. London: Routledge.

Deurzen, E. van (2012). *Existential Counselling and Psychotherapy in Practice*, 3e. London: Sage.

Deurzen, E. van and Adams, M. (2016). *Skills in Existential Counselling and Psychotherapy*, 2e. London: Sage.

Deurzen, E. van and Arnold-Baker, C. (2018). *Existential Therapy: Distinctive Features.* London: Routledge.

Du Plock, S. (2018). *Case Studies in Existential Therapy: Translating Theory into Practice.* London: PCCS Books.
Heidegger, M. (1927). *Being and Time* (trans. J. Macquarrie and E.S. Robinson). New York: Harper & Row.
Husserl, E. (1925). *Phenomenological Psychology* (trans. J. Scanlon). The Hague: Nijhoff.
Husserl, E. (1931). *Ideas: General Introduction to Pure Phenomenology* (trans. W.R.B. Gibson). New York: The Macmillan Company.
Husserl, E. (2001). *Logical Investigations*, vol. 1 (trans. J.N. Findlay). New York: Harper & Row.
Kierkegaard, S. (1844). *The Concept of Dread* (trans. W. Lowrie). Princeton, NJ: Princeton University Press.
Kierkegaard S. (1845). *The Point of View for my Work as an Author* (trans. W. Lowrie). New York: Oxford University Press.
Kierkegaard, S. (1846). *Concluding Unscientific Postscript* (trans. D.F. Swenson and W. Lowrie). Princeton, NJ: Princeton University Press.
Merleau-Ponty, M. (1962). *Phenomenology of Perception* (trans. C. Smith). London: Routledge and Kegan Paul.
Nietzsche, F. (1961). *Thus spoke Zarathustra* (trans. R.J. Hollingdale). Harmondsworth: Penguin.
Nietzsche, F. (1974). *The Gay Science* (trans. W. Kaufmann). New York: Random House.
Nietzsche, F. (1990). *Beyond Good and Evil* (trans. R.J. Hollingdale). Harmondsworth: Penguin.
Plato (2003). *The Last Days of Socrates* (trans. H. Tarrant and H. Tredennick) London: Penguin Classics.
Plato, (2007). *The Republic* (trans. M. Lane, H.D.P. Lee, and D. Lee). London: Penguin Classics.
Plato and Beresford, A. (2005). *Protagoras and Meno.* London: Penguin Classics.
Sartre, J.-P. (1939). *Sketch for a Theory of the Emotions.* London: Methuen.
Sartre, J.-P. (1943). *Being and Nothingness: An Essay on Phenomenological Ontology* (tr. H. Barnes). New York: Philosophical Library.
Sartre, J.-P. (1946). *Existentialism and Humanism* (trans. P. Mairet). London: Methuen.
Vos, J. (2018). *Meaning in Life: An Evidence-Based Practice Handbook for Practitioners*, London: Red Globe Press.

7

History of Existential-Phenomenological Therapy

Simon du Plock and Digby Tantam

Introduction

At the heart of existential therapy lies a supremely philosophical activity. Most existential therapists recognize that this philosophical search for a better and wiser life was initiated several millennia ago by Athenian and Roman philosophers like: Socrates, Plato, Aristotle, Epicurus, Cicero, Lucretius, Epictetus, Marcus Aurelius, and Plotinus; and that this search for existential wisdom was duplicated across the world by philosophers such as Confucius, Lao Tse, and Buddha. Some existential therapists draw more from this heritage than others. Existential philosophy focuses on human existence – a word derived from the Latin *existere* meaning "to stand out" – and existential therapists often use the phenomenological method, which provides existential thought with a practical way of investigating the world. Existential therapy (as it is known today) is a psychotherapeutic approach, which carefully considers the "phenomena" that the client brings, in order to describe and investigate what "shows" itself. It makes a concerted effort for the therapist to remain independent of presuppositions, explanations, and theories. As Cohn (1997, p. 22) has pointed out, when Freud, in his *Introductory Lectures*, states that, "*The phenomena perceived must yield in importance to the trends which are only hypothetical*," his aim is exactly the opposite to that of phenomenology.

Whether or not existential therapists use classical philosophy in their work, all existential therapists take inspiration from more recent existential philosophers as a way of grappling with everyday human dilemmas. The Danish philosopher, Søren Kierkegaard (1813–1855), is generally acknowledged as the earliest contributor to a formal modern school of existential philosophy. Truth, he argued, would ultimately emerge not from so-called scientific objectivity, but only from being; what was most lacking was people's courage to live with passion and commitment from the depth of existence.

The Wiley World Handbook of Existential Therapy, First Edition. Edited by Emmy van Deurzen, Erik Craig, Alfried Längle, Kirk J. Schneider, Digby Tantam, and Simon du Plock.

Friedrich Nietzsche (1844–1900) took this philosophy of life a stage further, stating that – since God was dead – it was incumbent upon individuals, in the absence of an ultimate law-giver, to decide how to live for themselves. He formulated a philosophy of freedom, which invited people to reject any rational or universal morality, and to discover their own will and power to live.

While much of the emotional impetus for existentialism is found in the work and lives of Kierkegaard and Nietzsche, it is the phenomenology of Edmund Husserl (1859–1938), with its methodology to describe and understand, rather than explain and analyze things, and to do this systematically, that provides its intellectual impetus. This potential bridge between the human and exact sciences emerged just as scientific psychiatry and psychoanalysis came to the fore.

Scientific psychiatry dates from the nineteenth century, and was, apparently, a triumph of mental health. General paralysis of the insane was discovered, and by the turn of the next century a treatment was found. The group at the University of Vienna that found this malarial treatment eclipsed the psychological work of the then senior lecturer in the department, Sigmund Freud, much to the latter's chagrin. For those who believed that there was more to psychiatry than just understanding the workings of the brain, hypnosis was a highly effective treatment in the hands of Bernheim and Charcot. Freud was interested in these methods and developed his ideas from there on, gaining considerable traction for the analysis of intrapersonal suppressed emotions and ideas that were seen to obstruct the person's freedom. Freud had attended Brentano's seminars on phenomenological ideas and intentionality, as had Husserl but they were each to take Brentano's ideas in very different directions. Freud looked to the inner person and elaborated Nietzsche's concept of the emotional unconscious, whereas Husserl developed the phenomenological method to address the entirety of consciousness, both in a subjective and an objective manner. Husserl sought to close the gap between contemplation and self-reflection on the one hand and the exact sciences on the other.

Meanwhile the First World War came along and changed the way people thought about psychiatry. The First World War, or the Great War as it was known then, turned the world upside down. Three emperors fell: the Kaiser in Germany, the Tsar in Russia, and the Emperor of Austria. Although Charles I continued to style himself Emperor, the empire itself was dismantled in 1918. The Ottoman Sultanate ended soon after, and the last Qing Emperor of China had been deposed in 1912. With the end of these empires came the end of their state religions, although initially only China and the then Union of Soviet Socialist Republics (USSR) became officially secular.

Some of the great figures of existential phenomenology were also deeply touched by the First World War. Martin Heidegger, serving as a young officer, lost his own personal religion in 1917 possibly as a result of working as a meteorologist, advising when and where gas attacks could be mounted. Karl Jaspers, a doctor who had first tried to get a permanent job in psychiatry, turned instead to teaching psychology. Edith Stein, a recent philosophy graduate, spent a year as a volunteer nurse looking after soldiers with typhoid and other infectious diseases. The experience may have propelled her back into religious faith, but this time the faith of St. Theresa and not of the Judaism of her upbringing. It may also have given her a practical experience of human community through empathy that inspired her doctoral thesis and influenced Edmund Husserl, her supervisor.

Husserl himself had moved substantially from the study of linear algebra to the adoption of phenomenology. The first volume of his intended trilogy, *Ideas*, was published in 1913 (Husserl 1913/1962) and was in the tradition of the idealism of Berkeley and the transcendentalism of Kant. The second volume, planned to deal with the apparent realities of the material and social world, never came together in his lifetime, despite the efforts of Edith Stein who wanted to make inter-subjectivity (or empathy as we might say now) the starting point for our grasp of the world, and not the consciousness that Husserl thought was primordial. Perhaps, Husserl found the eternal structures of mathematical logic more conducive to his conceptions of what cognition could, and should be, than the unseemly, chaotic destructiveness of social life during a brutal war.

The Second World War was equally significant to the development of existential phenomenological ideas and methods. The Nazis were sympathetic to transcendentalism, too, with their ideas about race and purity. Heidegger, originally Husserl's research assistant, then his successor, briefly saw himself as the philosopher of this new way of thinking, only to retreat in shame and silence a few years later; the Nazis were hostile to unbridled intellectual enquiry, especially if it was carried out, as much of it was, by Jews or communists. Many phenomenologists emigrated to the United States to escape Nazi persecution. Husserl, as is well-known, stifled by being denied access to his university, had nevertheless already passed his ideas on to a generation of French phenomenologists including Emmanuel Levinas and Maurice Merleau-Ponty, and indirectly to Jean-Paul Sartre and Simone de Beauvoir who were to develop a whole new perspective on applied phenomenology, calling it existentialism. Jaspers endured years of poverty and neglect but stayed, with his Jewish wife, in Heidelberg and was able to develop his own alternative phenomenological approach to psychiatry.

Psychoanalysis had risen on the coat tails of the nineteenth-century scientific revolution. Sigmund Freud had anticipated that he was founding a new science. Its growing pre-eminence and its popularity with the upper-middle class ensured its penetration into literature and culture. But it was rejected by the psychiatric establishment in Germany, Austria, and the United States. There were good reasons for this. It had little to say about major mental illness. It was limited in its formulation of interpersonal problems and, most importantly, it turned its back on everyday problems, worries, despair, and exploitation. Freud's defense of his friend Fliess in the face of the continuing nasal symptoms of their patient, Emma Eckstein, is symptomatic of this. Far from her symptoms being hysterical, they were due to inflammation around a pack that Fliess had inadvertently left in her nasal cavity (Masson 1984), but their psychological interpretations veiled this reality.

The interpersonal dimension was restored to psychoanalysis by subsequent generations of psychoanalysts, including Fairbairn, the object relationships school, interpersonal approaches like those of Erich Fromm and Harry Stack Sullivan, and most recently, the relational psychoanalysts. Some of their work does intersect with some forms of existential psychotherapy, particularly with Ernesto Spinelli's relational methods. Irvin Yalom, probably the best-known current existential therapist, was much influenced by Sullivan. Fromm emphasized the importance of human freedom in his work, and taxed Freud with failing to articulate clearly the preoccupation with death that entered his writing following the First World War (Fromm 1980). But none of these authors take the challenge of Husserl's phenomenology seriously until the existential-humanistic-integrative methods that were developed in the United States. They are discussed in full in Part III of this book.

Fromm, like Buber, was influenced by his study of the Talmud, and not by phenomenology. He was interested in applying his ideas to society in general, but not into psychiatry (there was little clinical psychology and no counselling psychology being practiced at this time, and psychiatric nurses were considered to be "attendants" rather than professionals).

There was more interest in the significance of psychotherapy to the practice of psychiatry in Switzerland where Bleuler, Binswanger, and Boss all became influenced by psychoanalysis. Bleuler collaborated on experiments with Jung, even before Jung became closely aligned with Freud. Binswanger was influenced by Jaspers and Heidegger. Boss invited Heidegger to teach his psychiatry trainees in Zollikon. Binswanger and Boss both developed psychological approaches that they claimed were grounded in Heidegger's fundamental ontology called *Daseinsanalytik* from *Being and Time* (1927/1962). Therefore, although they were describing entirely different projects, Binswanger and Boss also both named their approach Daseinsanalysis (*Daseinsanalyse*) based on Heidegger's term for the human being, *Dasein*, thus emphasizing the analysis of the whole world of human existence, not just an internal psyche as found in psychoanalysis. Nevertheless, whereas Binswanger's Daseinsanalysis referred to the *scientific project* of *Daseinsanalytic psychiatry* or psychopathology, Boss's Daseinsanalysis focused on the *clinical project* of *Daseinsanalytic psychotherapy*. Boss's psychotherapeutic Daseinsanalysis has been fully discussed in the Part I of this handbook. The history of these particular forms of existential theory and therapy is distinct from the development of existential-phenomenological therapy and yet also intersects with it at times.

It was the group aspects of psychoanalysis that connected most with the new ideas of continental phenomenologists and that led to the development of an existential-phenomenological form of therapy, especially in the United Kingdom. Psychoanalysis, despite the authoritarian structure that it established for its various schools and practitioners, also provided a home for unconventional figures like Lou Andreas-Salome and Eric Erikson. August Aichorn was one of the earliest of these figures, creating a therapeutic community for adolescent offenders and then a series of child guidance clinics in Vienna. Trigant Burrow in the United States created a therapeutic community, and changed roles with one of his analysands, as Ferenczi had done in Europe, who became the analyst whilst Burrow became the patient. Burrow, having been chair of the American Psychoanalytical Association, was expelled. This type of rebellious and radical psychiatry was to find its fertile ground in many other countries, including France with the institutional psychotherapy movement of François Tosquelles at Saint Alban, Jean Oury at la Borde, and Thomas Main in the United Kingdom. This in turn created a community psychiatry movement that was a stimulus to "deinstitutionalization" in the United Kingdom personified there by Maxwell Jones, Arie Querido in the Netherlands, and a decade later, Franco Basaglia, a student of phenomenology as well as a psychiatrist, in Italy.

The community as therapeutic movement, and group psychotherapy as a whole, received its biggest stimulus from that great upheaval in the twentieth century of the Second World War. There were precursors in existential therapy at an early stage, in Stein's monograph on the individual and the community (Stein 1922). Husserl's later work had it not been rejected by Horkheimer, would also have made a credible start to an existential-phenomenological therapy. Horkheimer was a co-founder of the Frankfurt school where "Michael" Foulkes, studied before moving to the United Kingdom, where he founded "group analysis," an approach that, according to some commentators, such as Hans Cohn, has many links with existential therapy in the United Kingdom. These existential group methods are discussed in Part V of this book.

If the First World War left devastation, its survivors could still believe that it was an honorable war. The Second World War left philosophy split between the empirical philosophies of the countries who fought but were never occupied, and the hermeneutic philosophies of the occupied countries. A new French movement sprang up out of disenchantment: nothingness was Sartre's starting point, "absurdity" that of Camus. The old order had to be subverted. It was, the psychiatrist Frankl argued, a problem of the failure of socially constructed meaning. Henceforth, we should not ask what the world can do for me, but what can I do for the world. And the first task was to find a meaning to live by. Frankl's ideas led to a whole other branch of existential therapies, called logotherapy and existential analysis, which are discussed in Part IV of this book. Applications of logotherapy and existential analysis to group therapy of these thinkers will also be discussed in Part V.

These French and Austrian ideas did not find much traction immediately in the United Kingdom that had not been directly (with the exception of the Channel Islands) affected by concentration camps, torture, or occupation by foreign troops. For pragmatic reasons, in the United Kingdom, psychiatric hospitals were becoming more open, their resident populations dropping, and safeguards were introduced in 1959 with the support of psychiatrists. Despite this, there was a crisis in the perception of psychiatry in the 1960s. Psychoanalysis once again provided R.D. Laing, the leader of the rebellion, with an approach to mental health, but it was the rediscovery of the French existentialists that inspired it, and not the work of Freud. The anti-psychiatrists (as David Cooper called them much to the irritation of his colleagues) extreme experiences were provided by drugs, and not by warfare. Laing and initially also David Cooper resonated to the same demand to overthrow of the old order that Sartre had used as his rallying call (Cooper and Laing 1964), but their dispossessed were not the proletariat but the mad, whose extreme experiences seemed to be akin to those of themselves and their friends whilst intoxicated with psychedelic medication. In the United States, Thomas Szasz, a psychoanalyst and psychiatrist of Hungarian origin was also taking issue with the overweening diagnostic claims of a psychiatric establishment that was dominated by psychoanalysts.

These US and UK movements were much inspired by Foucault's work on mental illness (Foucault 1961). Initially, in this UK movement, it was drugs and not phenomenology that provided new insights. When R.D. Laing and David Cooper created their anti-psychiatry movement, they saw it as experimental. They were the new Existentialists, the liberators who could engage with the nothingness and rebellion in people, rather than curing them of psychiatric disorders. They would encourage individuals struggling with human existence to have a break down, in order to break through to sanity. In a twist of perspective from "psychiatry" to "anti-psychiatry," Cooper suggested that he thought the mad might really be sane, and the psychiatrists and the families that they were allied with, might be the deluded ones. When Ronald David Laing and his colleagues founded the Philadelphia Association (PA) in London and created a radical therapeutic community at Kingsley Hall in the 1960s, they were seen as New Left activists and though Laing was a psychiatrist and had been trained at the Tavistock and was associated in various ways with John Bowlby, Donald Winnicott, and Charles Rycroft, his ideas and methods *were* radically new. They consisted mainly of inviting people to explore their craziness and to stop taking psychiatric medication and go on a therapeutic journey, with the use of various forms of intervention, including the use of LSD, of primal work, and of re-birthing.

After Kingsley Hall closed, a range of smaller therapeutic communities were created and many of these continue to this day, both in the PA and in the Arbours Association which had split off from the PA.

Laing's writings were highly popular for a time and his work attracted many young psychiatrists, psychologists, and therapists to London. One of these was Emmy van Deurzen, who had been trained as a philosopher, psychologist, and psychotherapist in France, where she had worked at the therapeutic communities of Saint Alban and later with François Tosquelles at the psychotherapeutic community of Agen. She joined the Arbours Association in London in 1977 and lived and worked in one of their communities and at their crisis center and she began teaching existential phenomenological therapy for the Arbours training program. This led to her establishing a much more therapeutically strategic and structured method of existential-phenomenological therapy than had been the case with R.D. Laing and his colleagues, who became more interested in French psychoanalysis. Van Deurzen's work also stood in direct opposition to Joe Berke's interpretation of existential therapy, which was based in a neo-Kleinian framework. Van Deurzen established her method through her many publications, by setting up a first existential master's degree for Antioch University in London in 1982 and then by creating a school of existential therapy at Regent's College, and later, in 1996, at the New School of Psychotherapy and Counselling, which was to move to the Existential Academy in 2014. She and many of her colleagues, but also with the collaboration of the PA and the Arbours, founded the Society for Existential Analysis in 1988 together with its journal *Existential Analysis.* It was through these vehicles that the new existential-phenomenological methods evolved and spread rapidly around many other European countries, initially particularly in Denmark through the efforts of Bo Jacobsen and his colleagues and in Sweden through the work of Dan Stiwne. These European developments are discussed in more detail in Part VI of the book. In the United Kingdom the existential-phenomenological school went through a series of splits and tensions as Ernesto Spinelli took over the School at Regent's and began publishing a very different form of existential-phenomenological therapy, which was less philosophical in nature and more influenced by person-centered therapy, humanistic, constructionist, and relational ideas. Many other authors also developed their own various interpretations of existential-phenomenological therapy, including Hans Cohn, who had a more analytical and group therapy approach. Others, including Simon du Plock, Mick Cooper, and Martin

Adams began to develop an amalgam of van Deurzen's and Spinelli's ways of working and made their own new contributions. Simon du Plock has edited *Existential Analysis* since 1993 and actively sought in his teaching and frequent international speaking (particularly in Portugal, Eastern Europe, and Russia) to promulgate what is distinctive about British existential-phenomenological therapy. He has made innovative contributions to a number of areas of therapeutic practice, including publications focusing on clinical supervision, working with issues of dependency and addiction, relationship therapy, and existential-phenomenological research. Martin Adams, who taught for both the Regent's and New School programs for decades, published his own work, with an emphasis on an original existential model of human development. Many other authors emerged around Europe to implement existential-phenomenological therapy further. Their contributions together with other international contributions are featured in Part VI.

We shall now consider the specific contributions of Laing, van Deurzen, Spinelli, and Cohn.

R.D. Laing's contribution

As we have seen the United Kingdom became a fertile ground for the development of the existential approach when R.D. Laing and David Cooper took Sartre's ideas as the impetus for a reconsideration of the notion of mental illness and its treatment (Laing 1960, 1961; Laing and Cooper 1964; Cooper 1967). Laing studied medicine at Glasgow University but also undertook a detailed philosophical education, acquainting himself with the main contemporary thinkers, particularly in the continental tradition of existentialism and phenomenology. While training as a psychiatrist he planned to study with Karl Jaspers in Basle but was prevented from doing so by being called up for National Service. He worked briefly in a research project begun by Thomas Freeman, a psychoanalyst and psychiatrist, one of the authors of two books about the psychology of psychosis. Laing began psychoanalytic training at the Tavistock Clinic in 1957 at the invitation of its director, Jock Sutherland, entering analysis with Charles Rycroft (a member of the independent group), and supervised by Marion Milner and Donald Winnicott.

Throughout his career Laing was engaged in an intricate balancing act with a number of disparate creeds and philosophies, among which may be counted Sartrean existentialism, Freudian psychoanalysis, romantic-expressionist literature, transcendental meditation and re-birthing. The meaning that he attributed to the disturbed behavior of his patients naturally varied depending on the combination of which of his inspirations was in ascendance at the time.

In his first book, *The Divided Self: Existential Study of Madness and Sanity* (1960), he focused on the application of existential-phenomenological ideas to the so-called "schizoid condition," a term taken from Kraepelin. Laing recognized that the psychiatric terminology that he had been trained to use actually prevented him from understanding the "meaning" of the patient's existence in any way other than as a clinical category. It is impossible to come to an understanding of patients when the technical terminology either isolates them or attributes a disproportionate importance to just one aspect of their being. Such false dichotomies as mind/body, psyche/soma, psychological/physical, and exaggerated attention to specific aspects such as the self or the personality encourage us to see the person in terms of abstract models. The individual is lost in this process of abstraction. As Laing expresses it:

> How can we speak in any way adequately of the relationship between me and you in terms of the interaction of one mental apparatus with another? ...Only existential thought has attempted to match the original experience of oneself in relationship to others in one's world by a term that adequately reflects this totality. (1960, p. 19)

Further highly influential books were to follow in the years 1957–1964. The companion volume to *The Divided Self* – *The Self and Others* – appeared in 1961, swiftly followed by three co-authored texts. *Sanity, Madness and the Family* (1964), a book Laing co-authored with Aaron Esterson, represented the result of joint phenomenological research on the families of "schizophrenics" at the Tavistock Clinic and was the source of the common misunderstanding that they were claiming that families caused schizophrenia. This was to have major consequences, given the attention that Laing and Esterson paid to the role of mothers, and many feminist writers then and since have been concerned with the notion that it was in some sense the "fault" of the mothers that "caused" their children to become mentally disturbed. Elaine Showalter in *The Female Malady* (1985) charged Laing with being a "manly physician-priest leading another explorer to the heart of darkness" whom he fails when "faced with the obligation to play mother on the psychic journey." Laing's characteristically direct response to this as "total shit from beginning to end" was not helped greatly by his subsequent confession that he had never read the book.

Interpersonal Perception (1966), co-authored with A. R. Lee and H. Phillipson, is less remembered now but nevertheless contained important ideas about social (or interpersonal) phenomenology. *Reason and Violence: A Decade of Sartre's Philosophy 1950–60*, with David Cooper, first published in 1964, dealt with Sartre's later works, which provided one of the main theoretical influences on Laing's thinking in the early 1960s. Subsequent talks and papers were increasingly polemical and were collected in *The Politics of Experience* (1967).

The "psychedelic model" of *The Politics of Experience* introduced the unique conceptualization of mental disturbance not as a breakdown but as breakthrough, a stage in a healing process containing the possibility of entry into a realm of "hyper-sanity" (Laing 1967: 129). Laing – with colleagues known as "the brothers" (Cooper, Esterson, Briskin, and Sigal) – sought to provide a true asylum for those in distress who would otherwise be admitted into a traditional psychiatric hospital. We should not understate the contrast between such asylums and the reality of psychiatric treatment at that time when insulin comas, electro-shock, physical restraint, and lobotomies were often the treatment of (the psychiatrist's) choice. In comparison the asylum that was provided by Laing and his colleagues was, at least in theory, a supportive, democratic environment in which people could journey through their madness into the light of a greater sanity and self-awareness. Berke's explanation of the name "Arbours" for the association he formed in 1970 illustrates well the philosophical and spiritual rather than interventionist medical goals that Laing and those around him were pursuing:

> The temporary dwelling places where the Israelites lived in the wilderness after the exodus from Egypt were called "Arbours" – places of shade or shelter. Arbours communities aim to provide shelter and safe anchorage for people who have been buffeted by internal turbulence or external disturbance whether in fantasy or in actuality. (Berke 1979, p. 116)

The reality of the PA was often somewhat different – staff and residents were clearly distinguishable from each other, referral to psychiatric services was sometimes used in difficult situations, and those who did not make the journey might find themselves lost and alone in their despair. To remedy this problem the Arbours Association set up its own crisis center where it provided a safe holding environment for those going through a period of destabilization.

The fame and notoriety of R.D. Laing acted as a magnet to students from the United Kingdom and internationally who flocked to take part in what, by 1970, had become a formal training in psychoanalytic psychotherapy. Readers are referred to Robin Cooper et al.'s *Thresholds between Philosophy and Psychoanalysis: Papers from the Philadelphia Association* (1989) for a more detailed account of the development of the Association. Laing's appearance at the 1967 Dialectics of Liberation conference, held at the Round House in London under the auspices of the Institute of Phenomenological Studies (represented by Cooper, Berke, and Redler), seemed to place him firmly in the New Left but the already volatile relationship that he had with Cooper was fractured irretrievably when Cooper identified him publicly with what he called "anti-psychiatry." The American psychiatrist Thomas S. Szasz rejected the term "anti-psychiatry" on the grounds that it was "imprecise, misleading, and cheaply self-aggrandising" (1977: p. 3). Not only did Szasz find it unhelpful, he also pointed out that it was not new, having first been employed by Bernhard Beyer in 1912. As a result of his disagreement with Cooper, Laing distanced himself from his erstwhile colleague and instead of going on to write the definitive politics of mental health as had been expected, he withdrew from this field. His interests became progressively more introspective and concerned with schizophrenia, families, and radical psychiatry. In his later work Laing was to move closer to humanistic psychology and the gulf between himself and his colleagues in the PA widened. He finally resigned as chairperson in 1981, but then he supported the development of the Society for Existential Analysis by Emmy van Deurzen in 1987 and agreed to give a talk for its second conference in 1989, entitled "Demystifying Psychotherapy," which was to be his definitive statement on existential therapy. This was not to be as Laing died in France in the summer of 1989. This meant that it was his son, Adrian Laing, who gave a talk about his father's contribution to existential psychotherapy instead.

Though it is not often acknowledged because of the vociferous attacks launched at Laing throughout most of his career by academic psychiatry and the radical myths that have grown up around his memory, he was unique in the United Kingdom in the 1960s and 1970s for his practice and his theories, both of which straddled the worlds of psychoanalysis and existentialism. Though it may initially have been useful to attain the status of a psychoanalyst (in order to attack the institution from within) he never wholly abandoned psychoanalytic theory, as can be seen in a reading of his struggle with "unconscious phantasy" in *The Self and Others.* Certainly most of his followers in the PA appeared to move more towards psychoanalysis after Laing left, except in the case of John Heaton, whose work on Wittgenstein and therapy stands out (Heaton 2010).

Adrian Laing, in his study of his father (1994), claimed that Laing's intention at the end of his professional training was to be able to speak authoritatively as a member of the medical establishment and, at the same time, to challenge in particular the conservative psychoanalytic movement by trying to persuade its members of the relevance of the existential-phenomenological perspective to the understanding of mentally disturbed patients. Zinovieff has asked whether:

> R. D. Laing. and his works (fifteen books, multi-various articles, the formation of the Philadelphia Association as an alternative place of care for psychiatric patients etc. etc.) were merely a symptom of the times? A "reaction-formation" in tandem with the 60s climate of revolt and unrest? What lasting contribution, therefore, has Laing made to the study of human relations and, indeed, to the practice of psychotherapy? (1995, p. 184)

These are questions that must exercise any British existential psychotherapist, particularly because for a large number of psychologists and practitioners from other orientations Laing *is* existential psychotherapy, just as Yalom personifies it in the United States.

Some aspects of Laing's conceptualization of mental disturbance appear overly-optimistic now but they complemented the anti-psychiatry movement which sprang out of the radical and revolutionary political groupings of the late 1960s and the 1970s. As Sedgwick wrote: "The thrust of Laingian theorising accords so well with the loose romanticism and libertarianism implicit in a number of contemporary creeds and moods that it can easily generate support and acquire plausibility" (1982, p. 6).

While he enjoyed limited success in influencing the stance of the medical establishment during his lifetime, his work has not resulted in a substantial change in psychiatric practice (Tantam 1991). His contribution to the development of an existential-phenomenological therapy may have been more significant (Cohn 1994).

Like Yalom, Laing wrote in an accessible, relatively jargon-free style (at least for his time) and the titles of his books intrigue and encourage the potential reader to take the plunge in a way that many of the scholarly tomes do not. More importantly, his work appeared in a period when conventional wisdom was being questioned on all fronts, especially by young people and students who were concerned to redress the wrongs with which they identified the capitalist system and its various agents of social repression and control. It is a tribute to his passion and accessibility that even today if the average psychology student or therapy trainee retains anything about existentialism in the United Kingdom it will be likely to have been culled from the pages of *The Divided Self* or *The Politics of Experience.*

The aspects of Laing's work that many value to this day are his directness in talking to his patients. While he wrote surprisingly little about how to practice his form of therapy, he spoke of therapy as a form of research:

> A search, constantly reasserted and reconstituted for what we have all lost, and which some can perhaps endure a little more easily than others, as some people can stand lack of oxygen better than others, and this re-search is validated by the shared experience of experience regained in and through the therapeutic relationship in the here and now. (Laing 1967, p. 47)

This was a revolutionary way of conceiving psychotherapy. So long as mainstream psychiatry and psychoanalysis are perceived as distant or disempowering, Laing's commitment to the individual and to the pain and importance of relationship will stand out as a beacon. The term "Laingian" has taken its place in the *Oxford English Dictionary* and a whole Laing industry has been built up around his name which attests to the unabated public and professional interest in his life and work, an interest exacerbated by the "guru" image Laing cultivated in the latter half of his career, his enigmatic and combative personality, and his comparatively early death.

As regards the continuing influence of his work on specific psychotherapy and counselling trainings, allegiance to some of his core ideas remains constant and many of his books are still in print – no small achievement in itself in a field in which the number of publications each year seems to grow exponentially and publishers' lists are rigorously pruned of dead wood. An in-depth examination of Laing forms a significant part of the curriculum in only a handful of training courses – those offered by the Arbours Association, the Philadelphia Association, Regent's University, and the New School (all in London). Appreciation of Laing's work is limited to a relatively small group of practitioners, trainers, and advanced students.

The Arbours Association was established in 1970 by Drs. Joseph Berke and Morton Schatzman who had worked with R.D. Laing on the Kingsley Hall project from 1965 to 1968. Joseph Berke came to wide public attention because of his work with a patient called Mary Barnes, which led to the publication of *Mary Barnes: Two Accounts of a Journey Through Madness* (1971) and a subsequent play of the case first performed at the Royal Court Theatre in 1979. These, and his book the *Butterfly Man* (1977), later published as *I Haven't Had To Go Mad Here* (1979), have done much to bring the work of R.D. Laing and his associates into the public domain. Perhaps surprisingly, given these links with Laing, the training program, which accepts no more than ten students annually and lasts between four and six years, is primarily concerned with the theory and practice of psychoanalysis. The aim of the Arbours is to provide both in- and out-patients with psychotherapeutic help within long-term communities as an alternative to psychiatric hospitalization.

The Philadelphia Association, like the Arbours Association, restricts the numbers of trainees who enter the training program to approximately 15 each year, and the full training takes four to six years to complete. This training pays attention to the work of psychoanalysts including Freud, Klein, Winnicott, and Bion, as well as Laing, and to philosophers such as Socrates, Plato, Hegel, Kierkegaard, Nietzsche, Husserl, Heidegger, Sartre, and Derrida.

Regent's School of Psychotherapy and Psychology, part of Regent's University and founded by Emmy van Deurzen in 1990, is probably the largest psychotherapy training institute in the United Kingdom after the Tavistock and the Metanoia Institute. It was originally concerned with ensuring that psychotherapy would not neglect its philosophical origins and encouraged an appreciation of these philosophical underpinnings at all levels of training. Interest in Laing continues to be strong among a number of the staff. The New School of Psychotherapy and Counselling at the Existential Academy, also founded by Emmy van Deurzen, is unique in offering masters and doctoral programs that are entirely based in existential therapy, and this organization has now established itself as the world's epicenter for existential training, with programs in existential coaching and existential pastoral care alongside large doctoral training programs in existential psychology and existential psychotherapy.

While the interest generated by Laing et al. and the anti-psychiatry movement of the 1960s has never died away, its strong resurgence was generated and is evidenced by the number of major British publications over the past two decades that were directly derivative of the founding of the Society for Existential Analysis by van Deurzen in 1988. There the disparate, and not so disparate, bodies and individuals which we have considered, however briefly, in this chapter have had a forum for discussion and development of the existential-phenomenological approach. The journal of the society has numbered such distinguished authors and practitioners as James Bugental and Thomas Szasz from the United States, and Gion Condrau of the International Federation of Daseinsanalysis in Switzerland on its editorial board, as well as Dan Burston of Duquesne University and, from the United Kingdom, John M. Heaton of the Philadelphia Association and Andrea Sabbadini of the Arbours Association.

The growth in the dissemination of the existential-phenomenological approach to therapy is likely to have exciting repercussions for the delivery of mental health care in the United Kingdom in the future. When Emmy van Deurzen was the first chair of the United Kingdom Council for Psychotherapy, she ensured that existential psychotherapy was part of the approved methods for registration from the launch of the voluntary UK psychotherapy register at the House of Lords in 1993. Existential therapy is taught or mentioned, be it in a minimalistic way, on most training programs in psychotherapy, counselling, and counselling psychology in the United Kingdom. Those who have chosen to pursue a career within the medical establishment, whether NHS or private, may be free to critique labelling and treatment but, in the final analysis, are expected to work as part of a team for whom the medical model provides, by and large, a bedrock of certainty about their role in relation to patients who are conceptualized as in need of treatment and, where possible, cure.

But in some important respects existential psychotherapy, far from being out of step with current shifts in attitudes to both mental health and mental illness, can be seen to be prominently in the vanguard of such new developments. A number of commentators, among them Samuels (1993) and Smail (1993) have noted that a better-educated, information-rich, largely secular society suffers as much if not more from psychological problems as did those of the century that witnessed the advent of psychoanalysis. As Smail notes, the origins of unhappiness are to be found among both the haves and the have-nots; anxiety, stress, depression, all seem endemic to our present ways of life. And so it is that we begin to recall Kierkegaard's hard-earned lesson that when everybody is bent on making life easier and easier perhaps the wisest, most authentic course is to make things more difficult, or at least to address the question of whether these endless examples of "progress" really do add anything worthwhile to human existence. Life may be vastly easier for the majority in terms of consumerist culture but the problem of how to live one's life is as burgeoning today when each is said to be free to invent him/herself as it was in ancient Greece 3,000 years ago. *Eudaimonia*, or the good or flourishing life, is of concern to us as it has never been before and a philosophical approach to these problems is just as relevant.

Van Deurzen's contribution

The relevance of existential-phenomenological therapy in the United Kingdom and Europe has been much augmented by the work of Emmy van Deurzen. Having been trained in philosophy in France and having worked in a psychiatric environment for many years, van Deurzen retrained as a clinical psychologist and as a psychotherapist before coming to the United Kingdom in response to an invitation to come work with the Arbours. She lived and worked in an Arbours therapeutic community for a year as well as working in their crisis center. She taught existential phenomenology on the Arbours training program and began to develop existential courses for the Antioch University MA in Humanistic Psychology from 1978 onwards. This program was transformed into an existentially based master's program in 1982 under her leadership, and it was moved to Regent's College in 1985. It formed the basis of the school of psychotherapy she created at Regent's in 1990, after merging the course with the College.

Van Deurzen gathered a group of dedicated existential practitioners around her and was able to bring together the Philadelphia Association, the Arbours Association and some independent practitioners with Regent's existential staff and students to form the Society for Existential Analysis in 1988. This was a milestone for existential therapy in the United Kingdom, which established existential therapy as a credible alternative to other forms of psychotherapy.

Van Deurzen's first book *Existential Counselling in Practice* (1988, 2012), had been published earlier that year and this became the spur from which many other publications were to follow. Van Deurzen's clinical work in France and in the London therapeutic communities, together with her training in existential phenomenological philosophy, formed the basis of her writing from the outset. She had been trained in philosophy with Michel Henry, a well-respected French phenomenologist at Montpellier University and had written about applying phenomenological ideas to psychotherapy. She had lived and worked for five years in various therapeutic communities and had developed distinct ideas about how to work practically and concretely with people who were feeling lost and confused without putting them through hoops or theoretical mazes. In her work she demonstrated in which ways Laing's practice fell short of implementing phenomenological principles and how it misunderstood the fundamental existential givens and limitations that all human beings are subjected to. Laing's allegation that ontological insecurity is something experienced by schizophrenics alone was replaced by the contention that all human beings struggle with the insecurities of the human condition and that there are many ways in which people make adjustments that turn out to strangle their freedom and possibilities. Van Deurzen had an in-depth knowledge of Husserl's work and a wide-ranging philosophical expertise on Athenian philosophy, Spinoza, French philosophers such as Rousseau and Descartes and an ever-increasing thirst for a deeper understanding of Heidegger, Sartre, de Beauvoir, Merleau-Ponty, Camus, and many other existential philosophers. She was later to earn a British PhD for her work on existential psychotherapy in terms of the concept of self-deception. This commitment to philosophical depth in understanding human existence inspired her clinical work as well, where she aimed to pierce through to the actual experience of the person who is asking for help so that a new way of living can be slowly evolved in a very mutual conversation where technique is in the background and human contact and resonance are in the foreground.

Van Deurzen was to tackle the controversy over her way of working and the conflicts it elicited with the more psychoanalytic methods of her fellow existential therapists in the PA and the Arbours Associations, in her second book *Everyday Mysteries* (2010), which gave a précis of the contributions of the most relevant existential philosophers and existential practitioners as well as a phenomenological alternative to many of the established ways of interpreting in psychotherapy.

When van Deurzen was unfairly dismissed from Regent's College, after challenging its financial practices, Ernesto Spinelli took control of the movement, both in the College and at the Society for Existential Analysis. Van Deurzen, with her husband Digby Tantam, had to create a new foundation, the New School of Psychotherapy and Counselling, in order for her to continue her work.

Her book *Paradox and Passion in Psychotherapy* (2015) was a much more personal version of existential therapy, in which she celebrated the need for a phenomenology that is deeply philosophical and personal in nature and that emphasizes self-reflection, self-disclosure, and understanding. She became increasingly bold in her way of working and illustrated this in many co-edited and co-authored books to follow, focusing on important areas that existential psychotherapists needed to develop expertise in, such as existential and human issues (Deurzen and Arnold-Baker 2005), existential supervision (Deurzen and Young 2009), existential coaching (Deurzen and Hanaway 2011) and existential relationship therapy (Deurzen and Iacovou 2013). She also co-authored a *Dictionary of Existential Psychotherapy and Counselling* with Raymond Kenward (2005), to firmly establish and give access to the philosophical roots of the approach. She co-authored a practical guide to existential therapy with Martin Adams in *Skills in Existential Counselling and Psychotherapy* in 2011 and this became so popular that it saw its second edition in 2016 (Deurzen and Adams 2016).

All of van Deurzen's 16 books remain in print and have been translated into more than a dozen languages. She has written many book chapters and papers and has given talks on every continent over many decades, by doing so spreading her existential approach far and wide. It is perhaps her book on *Psychotherapy and the Quest for Happiness* (2009) that allowed her work to become noted by a wider audience, as it tackled the societal misunderstanding of the desire for human happiness from a firmly philosophical perspective. She showed the importance of meaning over happiness and took on the new movement of positive psychology, advocating firmly for a realism that is based in observations of the way in which people actually experience human existence and its wide-ranging troubles and problems.

Van Deurzen contributed significantly to the movement of philosophical consultancy and has always encouraged the collaboration between philosophers and psychologists, arguing that both need to engage with each other as the depth for human existence can only become fully understood if we combine philosophical and psychological insights, to create a therapy of life. In this she aimed to merge scientific observation and an emotional felt sense of rightness whilst searching for truth.

It is interesting to note that while Laing was able to command a provocative authority in the field by thrusting himself into the limelight and making controversial statements, van Deurzen's work has consisted of patient and careful writing, international teaching, and unbroken therapeutic work for 45 years. Van Deurzen has trained and encouraged thousands of people over the many years of her long-standing career. Most of her colleagues have been able to establish authority of their own instead of teaching van Deurzen's work or referring to it as their source of inspiration. This is an interesting existential phenomenon in its own right which is relevant to existential therapy and its understanding of oppression, freedom, human relationships, societal forces, individuality, and gender roles.

Van Deurzen's work has contributed many existential insights that have been widely adopted. In her teaching she foregrounds the importance of philosophical thinking and exploring, alongside a patient tracking of the multilayered phenomenological, eidetic, and transcendental reductions. She is perhaps best known for her contribution of the four worlds of existence and their paradoxical tensions at each level, the physical, social, personal, and spiritual dimensions, also known as *Umwelt*, *Mitwelt*, *Eigenwelt*, and *Uberwelt*, the latter a concept she created. Her emotional compass and the way in which it enlightens and illustrates a person's values, is an instrument that is now widely used by existential therapists and which is complemented by a sensory, thought, and moral compass. These are all examples of the way in which her work has enabled existential therapists to formulate their clients' predicaments in new and more robust ways. These ideas have also blossomed into her Structural Existential Analysis (SEA) methodology, which can be used for both praxis and for research. Her illustrations of her own work in the many case studies she has written across her publications demonstrate her deeply personal engagement and resonant approach with her clients. This will be evident in Chapter 10.

Van Deurzen has shown how, as practical philosophers, existential psychotherapists are attuned to cultural changes and are able to engage with the problems of what Foucault (Foucault and Sheridan 1973) termed the post-modern era. She has argued that we are post-post-modern and have now entered into the era of virtuality, where imagination and virtual reality are a new layer of experience. Not only is truth obviously multiple and varied, but phenomenological investigation of what people experience, can now also be done by using the new social media at our disposal. Van Deurzen has founded numerous organizations and was instrumental in creating a Europe-wide online training program for existential therapists, with Digby Tantam. They also organized the first World Congress for Existential Therapy in London in 2015, which was another landmark in the history of existential therapy, with 650 existential therapists attending over four days from all over the world. This congress led to the formation of a World Confederation of Existential Therapy (WCET) and a second world congress in Argentina in 2019. The London Congress was also the crucible for the creation of the Federation of Existential Therapy in Europe (FETE).

Van Deurzen and Tantam together also founded the Existential Academy, which, as a not-for-profit community interest company provides a space where ordinary people can find out how to include philosophical and practical understanding in their own lives. The Existential Academy runs a popular low-cost existential therapy clinic in conjunction with van Deurzen and Tantam's clinical practice, Dilemma Consultancy.

While other approaches, most notably the psychoanalytic, have altered immeasurably in response to cultural changes and are now better able to address the social malaise rather than situate pathology in specific individuals or groups, the existential approach is increasingly recognized as the most relevant to address the era that Rieff has called that of psychological man (Rieff 1966). Van Deurzen has said that:

> A lot of distress is generated by post-modern society, now that humankind has reached a position of potential self-destruction through atomic war or overpopulation of the planet. Mass communication increasingly rules our lives, endangering personal relationships whilst little solace is expected from the old structures that used to safeguard human values. People often feel that they have a choice between either becoming commodities themselves as slaves in the production process or focusing so much on achievement in producing more commodities that they will not have time to enjoy the commodities that they have accumulated. (Deurzen-Smith 1994, p. 7)

The exhortatory tone of these words should by now be familiar: it is that of a tradition, which we have traced from Kierkegaard and Nietzsche, through to Heidegger and Sartre and Laing. It may be found in the schools of ancient philosophy, which inspired much of their work, and it is alive in the writings of Camus and de Beauvoir, among others. Each urges humans to rise above the herd, to use their talents to the full and to strive to live authentically. And recalling our opening remark, to do so they must face the fact of their finitude, of the impending death, which gives meaning to their actions in the world. This tone and tradition is in marked contrast to the technocratic style of much Anglo-American philosophizing, less abstract and distant from the problems of living with which we all struggle on a daily basis, and thus far better able to provide an intelligent guide to enable us to chart a course, though always open to what life brings, rather than stumble blindly from crisis to crisis.

These aspects of the existential-phenomenological approach which are most often criticized – its willingness to speak of values and to make statements about moral actions, its flexibility and unwillingness to label and to pathologize – in fact, constitute its best strengths and are embodied fully in van Deurzen's work. As people increasingly realize, particularly in the West, that no matter how much they concern themselves with "feel-good factors" what is important is that what underpins these, in psychotherapy as in any other area of our society, is a genuine exploration and appreciation of what it means to be human. What matters is, as Husserl termed it, a return "to the things themselves" and as van Deurzen would say a return to a reflective and meaningful way of life where we face our limits and celebrate our possibilities whilst carefully considering our values and purposes, without omitting to take responsibility for our choices and the consequences of our actions.

Spinelli's contribution

Ernesto Spinelli is, arguably, alongside Emmy van Deurzen, the best-known existential therapist working in the United Kingdom. After training as a psychologist, Spinelli joined the faculty at Regent's College in 1989. He built up a considerable body of publications in the form of case studies, existential-phenomenological reformulations of classic therapeutic perspectives, and, in recent years, developments of phenomenological psychology.

He has in 1992 identified himself as a "phenomenologically oriented" therapist, and this makes his contribution distinct from that of van Deurzen, who is more clearly concerned with directly engaging with problems of living via the application of insights from existential philosophy.

For Spinelli the main value of existential-phenomenological thinking for therapists is that it offers them a way of being which they can attempt to embody (see Spinelli and Marshall's *Embodied Theories*, 2001), rather than providing a framework by which to understand clients, or as a blueprint for living. Since an attitude of openness lies at the heart of this existential-phenomenological attitude, it follows that Spinelli is concerned with helping therapists reflect upon and question the assumptions they hold which limit their availability for being with clients. While it is never possible for us to completely bracket our own biases and assumptions we can, he argues, signal our willingness to be as present as possible.

Spinelli (1994a, 1994b, 2001) has challenged a number of widely adopted but un-reflected upon assumptions held by therapists. In his book *Demystifying Therapy* (1994) he presents a radical critique of transference, the unconscious, and the notion of a fixed, thing-like self. Like Bugental (1981) and Rogers (1959), Spinelli distinguishes between the way individuals develop a particular sense of self – what he calls the "self-structure" – and the actuality of their lived-experience. On this basis, he argues that human beings will tend to disown, or dissociate from, those experiences that do not fit in with the believed-in self. An individual, for instance, who has constructed a notion of himself as strong and invulnerable may not acknowledge his feelings of vulnerability. The more fixed – or what Spinelli, drawing on Merleau-Ponty, terms "sedimented" – an individual's self-structure, the greater the number of experiences that are disowned.

Unlike proponents of the Daseinanalytic, logotherapeutic, or existential-humanistic approaches, Spinelli does not assume psychological health is promoted by people being open to the world, meaning-orientated, or facing up to the givens of existence. Nor does he, as van Deurzen does, assume it is better to face rather than seek to evade the challenges life brings. He is more concerned that therapists respect and truly accept the client's current way of living, than that they seek to do something to clients. The aim of therapy then, is to help clients reflect on their way of experiencing their being-in-the-world so that they can either truly chose their current way of being or decide to change.

Ultimately, Spinelli (1994b) even questions the value of therapy itself, arguing that much of the "magic" of therapy is brought about by therapists' belief in their theories and techniques, rather than the theories and techniques themselves. He terms this the "Dumbo effect," after the Disney cartoon character who mistakenly believed that he needed a magic feather to help himself fly.

For Spinelli (1994b, 2001), the self-structure is not an independent entity, but something constructed and maintained in relationship with others. He argues that an individual has four, inter-related foci, or realms of encounter, that can be examined at every encounter: they have developed some sense of themselves, some sense of the other that they are encountering, they have some sense of what goes on between the two of them, and they have some sense of how that other relates to further others in their world. Within the therapeutic relationship, Spinelli (1994b) suggests that clients can be encouraged to explore each of these realms, as well as the extent to which their experiences of self, other, we, and they in the therapeutic relationship are representative of self, other, we, and they in relationships beyond therapy. For Spinelli the particular specialness of therapy is that it provides client and therapist an opportunity to explore "the various *conjunctions or points of contact* between the participants' relational realms" (1994b, p. 332).

Spinelli's approach emphasizes the relational and the contextual. He focuses in this way for two reasons. First, he states that from an existential, inter-subjective perspective, client's experiences and choices cannot be isolated from the experiences and choices of those around them. Second, he argues that a therapeutic approach that ignores the relational realms of those outside the therapeutic relationship relinquishes social responsibility in favor of self-serving individualism.

Spinelli's work makes little explicit reference to existential philosophy and with its focus on lived-experience, distinction between self-as-experienced and self-as-construed, and emphasis on empathy, congruence, and acceptance might be considered to be more relational than existential.

Hans Cohn's contribution

If van Deurzen infuses British existential therapy with a passion for bringing a rigorous philosophical perspective on the problems of everyday life, and Spinelli emphasizes the importance of embodying an existential-phenomenological way of being, Hans Cohn (1916–2004) is notable for the way in which he returns us to a certain bedrock for therapeutic practice. Coming from a psychoanalytic training, he was very aware of the need for existential therapists to hold fast to their philosophical origins in the work of seminal writers, in particular Martin Heidegger.

His two books, *Existential Thought and Therapeutic Practice: An Introduction to Existential Psychotherapy* (1997), and *Heidegger and the Roots of Existential Psychotherapy* (2000) together provide a remarkably concise and concentrated way into the world of existential theory and practice. In his lifetime many therapists and trainees came to feel that when they read these texts, or his various journal articles, or met him in person, they had a direct link to the life source of the existential perspective. While his meticulous reading of psychoanalytic and Daseinsanalytic work has enabled later therapists to understand the arguments from which existential therapy emerged, he has also contributed significantly to our thinking about the significance of phenomenology, and ways of working existentially with groups.

Existential philosophers have always been concerned with the relationship between the individual and his or her context and existential psychotherapists have underlined, and their work has reinforced, the understanding that humans cannot be talked of meaningfully separate from their society – to attempt to do so, as some other approaches have, invariably impoverishes our understanding of what it is to be human and leads us down the cul-de-sac of labelling and pathologizing the individual. Just as it makes no sense to talk of human beings without their societies, so it is pointless to attempt a rigorous examination of life without a corresponding awareness of death. Similarly, any wish, no matter how well intentioned, to extend individual freedom without re-evaluating individual responsibility is deeply flawed. The debate between humanists and existentialists on the meaning of "authenticity" is important here. Humanists think it is about self-assertive living – being true to the essential self. Existential therapists consider authenticity to be about being open and truthful to life: accepting its limitations and boundaries and allowing it to manifest as fully as possible through one's own transparency.

The result of such an approach as utilized in much humanistic therapy, and especially in the human potential movement, is that everybody loses: those with access to individual therapy become more egotistical, less connected to the wider society, and therefore more isolated from reality, while the poor and otherwise disadvantaged end up labelled as under-achievers. Worse, in these dog days of political correctness, they are likely to attract the sort of euphonious terms which actually do violence to them in that they patronize and typecast while denying the political, philosophical, or economic facts of their situation.

Conclusions

Psychotherapy and counselling are now in crisis as the conflict becomes more apparent between those who pursued "feel-good" short cuts to psychological health, those who cling to intellectual theories of a functional kind, and those who are attempting to develop deeper philosophical foundations for their work in recognition of the creative dynamics in individuals. The ancient philosophies sought to know the world as a whole, by reason and by studying the nature of things in their entirety. Modern science substitutes an abstract picture of the world for the world itself – seeking to master it in this way, leaving nothing other than a universal science. As we have seen, the existential-phenomenological approach, though its core characteristics endure, is articulated differently in the United Kingdom, the United States, and continental Europe. As it spreads to other parts of the world – flourishing practices are now springing up in Australia and New Zealand, South America and China as well as the rest of Asia – it is probable that new strains will emerge as some aspects of the tradition are emphasized and others relegated in keeping with the perceived needs of new client groups.

The work of the Society for Existential Analysis in facilitating contact and debate between all existential theorists and practitioners has been an important factor in the strengthening of this approach. The remit of the Society, though based in the United Kingdom, has been to provide a forum for the expression of views and the exchange of ideas amongst those interested in the analysis of existence from philosophical and psychological perspectives. Its work is now extended into the work of the FETE, which is eminently representative of existential-phenomenological therapy in Europe, though it also represents logotherapy and Daseinsanalysis. All these developments are furthermore stimulated by the creation of the World Confederation of Existential Therapy since the first world congress of existential therapy in London and the second congress in Buenos Aires.

There is no doubt that this new, worldwide interest in existential therapy will greatly enhance the deeply rooted tradition of existential-phenomenological therapy as developed in the United Kingdom and spread around Europe. We are aware that all of these methods and ways of working will continue to evolve and change in that process over the coming years.

References

Barnes, M. and Berke, J. (1971). *Mary Barnes: Two Accounts of a Journey through Madness.* London: Hart-Davis MacGibbon.

Berke, J.H. (1977). *Butterfly Man: Madness, Degradation and Redemption.* London: Hutchinson.

Berke, J. (1979). *I Haven't Had To Go Mad Here.* Harmondsworth: Pelican.

Bugental, J.F.T. (1981). *The Search for Authenticity: An Existential-Analytic Approach to Psychotherapy.* New York: Irvington.

Cohn, H.W. (1994). What is existential psychotherapy? *British Journal of Psychiatry 165* (5): 699–701.

Cohn, H.W. (1997) *Existential Thought and Therapeutic Practice.* London: Sage.

Cohn, H.W. (2000). *Heidegger and the Roots of Existential Psychotherapy.* London: Continuum.

Cooper, D.L. (1967). *Psychiatry and Anti-Psychiatry.* London: Tavistock.

Cooper, D.L. and Laing, R.D. (1964). *Reason and Violence: A Decade of Sartre's Philosophy.* London: Tavistock.

Cooper, R., Friedman, J., Gans, S. et al. (1989). *Thresholds between Philosophy and Psychoanalysis: Papers from the Philadelphia Association.* London: Free Association Books.

Deurzen, E. van (1998). *Paradox and Passion in Psychotherapy,* Chichester: Wiley.

Deurzen, E. van (2009). *Psychotherapy and the Quest for Happiness.* London: Sage.

Deurzen, E. van (2010). *Everyday Mysteries: Handbook of Existential Therapy,* 2e. London: Routledge.

Deurzen, E. van (2012) *Existential Counselling and Psychotherapy in Practice,* 3e. London: Sage.

Deurzen, E. van (2015). *Paradox and Passion in Psychotherapy: An Existential Approach,* 2e. Chichester: John Wiley and Sons, Ltd.

Deurzen, E. van and Adams, M. (2016). *Skills in Existential Counselling and Psychotherapy,* 2e. London: Sage. (Original work published 2011.)

Deurzen, E. van and Arnold-Baker, C. (eds.) (2005). *Existential Perspectives on Human Issues: A Handbook for Practice.* Basingstoke: Palgrave Macmillan.

Deurzen, E. van and Hanaway M. (eds.) (2011). *Existential Perspectives on Coaching.* Basingstoke: Palgrave Macmillan.

Deurzen, E. van and Iacovou, S. (2013). *Existential Perspectives on Relationship Therapy.* London: Palgrave Macmillan.

Deurzen, E. van and Kenward, R. (2005). *Dictionary of Existential Counselling and Psychotherapy.* London: Sage.

Deurzen, E. van and Young, S. (2009). *Existential Perspectives on Supervision.* Basingstoke: Palgrave Macmillan.

Deurzen-Smith, E. van (1988). *Existential Counselling in Practice.* London: Sage Publications.
Deurzen-Smith, E. van (1994). *Can Counselling Help?*, Occasional Paper. Durham: University of Durham.
Foucault, M. (1961). *Madness and Civilization. A History of Insanity in the Age of Reason.* New York: Vintage Books.
Foucault, M. and Sheridan, A. (1973). *The Birth of the Clinic: An Archaeology of Medical Perception.* London, Tavistock.
Fromm, E. (1980). *Beyond the Chains of Illusion: My Encounter with Marx & Freud.* London: Sphere Books.
Heaton, J.M. (1994). *The Talking Cure. Wittgenstein's Therapeutic Method for Psychotherapy.* Basingstoke: Palgrave Macmillan.
Husserl, E. (1962). *Ideas: General Introduction to Pure Phenomenology.* New York: Collier. (Original work published 1913.)
Laing, A. (1994). *R.D. Laing: A Biography.* London: Peter Owen.
Laing, R.D. (1960). *The Divided Self: Existential Study of Madness and Sanity.* London: Tavistock.
Laing, R.D. (1961). *The Self and Others.* London: Tavistock.
Laing, R.D. (1967). *The Politics of Experience.* New York: Pantheon Books.
Laing, R.D. and Cooper, D. (1964). *Reason and Violence.* London: Tavistock.
Laing, R.D. and Esterson, A. (1964). *Sanity, Madness and the Family.* London: Tavistock.
Laing, R.D., Phillipson, H., and Lee, A.R. (1966). *Interpersonal Perception.* London: Tavistock.
Masson, J.M. (1984). Freud, Fliess, and Emma Eckstein. In: *The Assault on Truth: Freud's Suppression of the Seduction Theory* (ed. J.M. Masson), 55–106. New York: Strauss & Giroux.
Rieff, P. (1966). *The Triumph of the Therapeutic.* New York: Harper & Row.
Rogers, C.R. (1969). A theory of therapy, personality and interpersonal relationships as developed in the client-centred framework. In: *Psychology: A Study of Science*, vol. 3 (ed. S. Koch), 184–256. New York: McGraw-Hill.
Samuels, A. (1993). *The Political Psyche.* London: Routledge.
Sedgwick, P. (1982). *Psychopolitics.* London: Pluto Press.
Showalter, E. (1985). *The Female Malady.* Princeton, NJ: Princeton University Press.
Smail, D. (1993). *The Origins of Unhappiness.* London: HarperCollins.
Spinelli, E. (1994a). Riding shotgun for Freud or aiming a gun at his head? A reply to David Smith. *Existential Analysis 5*: 142–156.
Spinelli, E. (1994b). *Demystifying Therapy.* London: Constable and Company.
Spinelli, E. (2001). *The Mirror and the Hammer: Challenging Orthodoxies in Psychotherapeutic Thought.* London: Sage.
Spinelli, E. and Marshall, S. (2001). *Embodied Theories.* London: Sage.
Stein, E. (1922). Individuum und Gemeinschaft. *Jahrbuch für Philosophie und phänomenologische Forschung 5*: 117–283.
Szasz, T.S. (1977). *Anti-psychiatry: The Paradigm of the Plundered Mind.* London: The New Review.
Tantam, D. (1991). The anti-psychiatry movement. In: *150 Years of British Psychiatry, 1841–1991* (ed. G. Berrios and H. Freeman), 333–347. London: Gaskell Press.
Zinovieff, N. (1995). R.D. Laing: A biography by Adrian Charles Laing. *Existential Analysis 6*(1): 183–185.

8

Existential Phenomenological Therapy

Philosophy and Theory

Helen Hayes and Martin Adams

Introduction

As we have seen in the previous chapter, existential-phenomenological therapy is characterized both by its adherence to phenomenology as a method of enquiry into human experience, and by its engagement with existential philosophy as an account of the characteristic features of that experience. In insisting on a philosophical, rather than psychological or medical, foundation for the development of its theory and practice, existential-phenomenological therapy refutes the natural scientific foundations of much psychotherapeutic theory. This problematizes psychotherapeutic notions such as the unconscious, the unitary self, and the idea of psychopathology as quasi-physical phenomena affecting an individual mind. A resistance to the pathologizing language of psychiatric discourse is a persistent theme in existential-phenomenological therapy. In the United Kingdom, as we have seen, its development was influenced by the work of R.D. Laing, and consequently its epistemological challenge to natural science is accompanied by an ethical and political resistance to the practices of medical-model psychiatry. In this chapter, we will review the main philosophical ideas that inform existential-phenomenological psychotherapy in the United Kingdom, concentrating on the work of Husserl, Kierkegaard, Heidegger, and Sartre. We will then discuss how these ideas are applied in the particularly philosophical model of therapy developed in the United Kingdom by Emmy van Deurzen. We will also discuss the contributions of other UK-based existential therapists, including Hans Cohn and Ernesto Spinelli.

Phenomenology: Husserl

The philosopher Edmund Husserl initially developed phenomenology as an attempt to establish a sound epistemological foundation for science and mathematics. Husserl

---

The Wiley World Handbook of Existential Therapy, First Edition. Edited by Emmy van Deurzen, Erik Craig, Alfried Längle, Kirk J. Schneider, Digby Tantam, and Simon du Plock.

sought to answer the Cartesian conundrum of how to integrate knowledge derived from the exercise of human reason with that arising from fallible sensory experience. His objective was to establish a method for the human subject to attain reliable knowledge about a world of other entities with a material existence independent of the perceiving and enquiring subject. This led him to study the nature of human consciousness and to develop an account of the operation of consciousness in the acts of perception and meaning making.

Husserl's earlier work remained within the bounds of pure mathematics and logic. However, he subsequently developed his ideas beyond this domain to offer an account of human consciousness and the process of knowledge formation. In Husserl's account, the question of the ultimate nature of reality is left unanswered, insofar as the object of human knowledge can only ever be the phenomenal object, that is, the object as apprehended by the perceiving subject; the object's noumenal existence outside human perception remains unknowable. However, the assertion that it is only the phenomenal object that can be known by the knowing subject does not necessarily result in a solipsistic or subjectivist grasp of the world. Rather, it is the task of the subject to engage in a methodical procedure for the continual expansion and refinement of its knowledge, until it can establish a claim to know the "essence" of the thing perceived.

This brings our attention to the nature of the subject, that is, consciousness. From a phenomenological perspective, human consciousness is characterized by intentionality, a sense of direction in its activity in the world. Consciousness is itself empty until it apprehends an object and seeks to make sense and use of it. This is an active process, consciousness grasps the objects which are of interest to it, it grasps them in a way that speaks to its interests, and its initial understanding of them is situated in its prior knowledge and experience. Husserl then offers a sequential and iterative process, by means of which consciousness transcends these initial limitations or biases, to reach a more complete grasp of its objects. This process comprises the three reductions or *epoché*, which Husserl terms the phenomenological reduction, the eidetic reduction, and the transcendental reduction. In the phenomenological reduction, the subject attends to their own consciousness, noting and attempting to suspend their habitual biases in perceiving and understanding the world, in order to attend more fully to the particular experience of the moment. In the eidetic reduction, the subject focuses on the objects of their observations, resisting any tendency to form premature conclusions that would foreclose further investigation. The subject might also attempt to perceive, or imagine, the object in different states, so as to reach an understanding of what is essential to it and what is only contingent or variable. In the transcendental reduction, the subject's attention focuses on their own thoughts and feelings in response to the object perceived, seeking to move beyond the limitations of their own observations and knowledge.

In his later work, Husserl turned his attention towards a concern for the social and political world in which he lived. This led him to reformulate phenomenology not as simply intellectual or philosophical but as a descriptive understanding of the lived experience of the human being as a being with agency and subjectivity, active and engaged in the world (*Lebenswelt*). The question then becomes less how to eliminate the inevitable biases of perception through the reductions, and more how to acknowledge and inhabit our situated grasp of our world. As we will see below, this shift in emphasis is taken up by Heidegger and Merleau-Ponty in their developments of phenomenology as an approach to understanding human experience.

Existential Philosophy: Kierkegaard, Heidegger, Sartre

The Danish philosopher Søren Kierkegaard, often termed the "father of existentialism," is significant for his opposition to the Hegelian rationalism of the great system builders of Enlightenment philosophy and insistence on attending to the lived experience and search for spiritual truth of an "existing person" or "existing subject" (Kierkegaard 1846/2000, pp. 204–205).

For Kierkegaard, this search for personal truth is always inflected with existential anxiety, an experience of paralysis and self-doubt at the moment at which the human being is faced with the possibility of becoming an individual, and especially with the recognition of one's temporal nature. The process of becoming fully human, recognizing one's unique capabilities, possibilities, weaknesses, and limitations is equated with falling into sin and then finding one's way to salvation and faith (Kierkegaard 1844/1980). This pivotal moment of claiming one's own individual existence means accepting one's mortality, realizing the enormity of owning the freedom of choosing one's own life at the same time as recognizing its temporal limitation. Anxiety is experienced as a fainting away from one's own existence, overawed, and overwhelmed by the magnitude of the moment. Kierkegaard sees the path to selfhood and spiritual growth in reflecting on this vertiginous experience of anxiety, embracing our weakness in order to harness our strengths and make the "leap of faith" across the abyss of nothingness.

> This is an adventure that every human being must go through- to learn to be anxious in order that he might not perish either by never having been in anxiety or by succumbing in anxiety. Whoever has learned to be anxious in the right way has learned the ultimate. (Kierkegaard 1844/1980, p. 155.)

Heidegger takes as his starting point Husserl's later work on human lived experience to develop an account of human being (Dasein) which emphasizes our inter-relationship with our material and social environment as an *a priori* existential structure. Our existence is always embedded in a web of relationships which gives meaning to our perception, understanding, interpretation and action: "Being-with is an attribute of one's own Dasein" (Heidegger 1927/1996, p. 113). However, the particular world in which we find ourselves is not initially of our choosing. We are "thrown" into a "factical world," we do not choose the circumstances of our birth, our gender, ethnicity, physical attributes, family relationships, and many other factors in our immediate environment. "Everyday Dasein" immerses itself totally in the world in which it finds itself, "falls prey to" pre-established norms, surrendering its own possibilities and its own being to the "others" amongst whom it has been thrown. These "others," the generalized mass of public opinion, social norms, cultural expectations, are referred to by Heidegger as "the they." In inauthenticity, Dasein settles for what "the they" assert regarding "what is proper, what is allowed, and what is not. Of what is granted success and what is not" (Heidegger 1927/1996, p. 119). Life amidst "the they" is safe, dull, and mediocre: "the they is essentially concerned with averageness .... The care of averageness reveals ... an essential tendency of Dasein, which we call the *levelling down* of all possibilities of being" (Heidegger 1927/1996, p.119).

For Dasein to discover itself and come into itself, it has to be jolted out of the complacency of everyday living by the "call of conscience" which brings Dasein back from listening only to "the they" to listening to itself. The call of conscience reminds Dasein of its possibilities, it "calls the self of Dasein forth from its lostness in the they" (Heidegger 1927/1996, p. 253). If Dasein heeds the call, it is confronted with its guilt, or indebtedness, that is, its failure to grasp its possibilities. Experiencing its existential guilt and the accompanying Angst, Dasein discovers its "resoluteness" and can take charge of its life authentically, recognizing its possibilities and limitations in the world in which it lives. Echoing Kierkegaard, Heidegger's account of what it means to grasp one's existence as a being-in-the-world emphasizes the experience of existential anxiety (*Angst*), a sense of unease and heightened awareness experienced when the individual recognizes her responsibility for her existence as a relational, free, temporal, and mortal being. It is through the encounter with *Angst* that the individual has the opportunity to grasp her life authentically, to open herself to the fullness of her experience of the world and to take ownership of her life.

Sartre, the philosopher who was first described as "existentialist," refers back to Husserl's account of consciousness as intentionality to develop an account of human existence (for-itself) which emphasizes the radical freedom of a being whose life is not determined by origins, circumstances, innate essence, or divine purpose. Human consciousness is empty, a pinpoint of nothingness shining into the world. It can never be a solid entity, since it can never quite be captured by the chains of causality. It is a subjectivity that forms desires and motivations, generating action in the world, engaging with its phenomenal objects, and creating projects. The paradox at the heart of human being is that its inherent nothingness and indeterminacy is the source of both its freedom and its anguish. "In anguish I apprehend myself at once as totally free and as not being able to derive the meaning of the world except as coming from myself" (Sartre 1943/2001, p. 40). Unlike Kierkegaard, Sartre is a humanist and an atheist; there can be no divine guidance or salvation to sustain us in our search for personal truth beyond the vertiginous apprehension of our emptiness, freedom and responsibility.

Sartre offers an account of the many ways in which as human beings we seek to evade the anguish of our groundlessness whilst retaining our status as free beings. The "useless passion" (Sartre 1943/2001, p. 615) which characterizes human existence is the paradoxical desire both to make ourselves into entities with the solidity and certainty of inanimate objects (the in-itself) and at the same time retain the free will which is our unique human attribute. His descriptions of "bad faith," our self-deceptions, and our evasions of freedom, demonstrate the inevitability of our flight from the radical freedom and emptiness at the core of human being. The unresolvable paradox of our situation is not a conclusion of defeatist passivity, but rather an acknowledgment that our impossible desire for certainty and solidity is the source of human activity and production, personal identity, and relationship. Our intentional actions form a project, a coherent strategy to form a sense of personal identity and purpose, so that it is in what we do that we form a sense of who we are. Such a self-definition is always partial, however, since it is only in hindsight that we can identify our productions and self-creation: "man first of all exists, encounters himself, surges up in the world – and defines himself afterwards. [...] He will not be anything until later, and then he will be what he makes of himself" (Sartre 1948, p.22). At the same time, the apprehension of our activities and projects by others means that we become objects in their phenomenal field and, as such, who we are becomes defined by what others make of us. Sartre shows how as human beings we are ambivalent in our relationship to our definitions of ourselves derived both from our own past projects and also from others' perceptions of us. We flee in anguish from the freedom which we not only desire, but which is actually the only foundation of our being, our only inescapable quality: "man is condemned to be free" (Sartre 1948, p. 29).

We will now discuss how the phenomenological method developed by Husserl and the existential philosophies of Kierkegaard, Heidegger and Sartre are utilized in the British school of existential-phenomenological psychotherapy, as developed by Emmy van Deurzen. We will also consider the different emphases in the therapeutic approaches offered by Hans Cohn and Ernesto Spinelli

Emmy van Deurzen's Model of Existential Psychotherapy: Existential Anxiety and the Search for Truth

Emmy van Deurzen's model of existential-phenomenological therapy, as mentioned, has developed through extensive clinical practice, teaching, and research and has been documented in a series of books since 1988.

In working with clients, Deurzen adopts Husserlian phenomenology as a method of investigation of the client's world, their dilemmas and difficulties. The methodical procedures of the phenomenological reductions are applied in the context of psychotherapy. Alongside the suspension of assumptions and foreknowledge, the therapist emphasizes descriptive clarification of the emerging phenomena and a gradual sense-making process as the dialogue between therapist and client develops (Deurzen 2014; Deurzen and Adams 2016). The stages and process of the phenomenological reductions in the context of therapeutic practice are discussed in further detail in Chapter 9.

This systematic application of the phenomenological method elicits an account of the client's experiences and difficulties that Deurzen understands within her existential philosophical framework. Her approach to therapy rests on the premise that the difficulties that bring clients to therapy originate in questions about human life, which are fundamentally philosophical. Distress and difficulties arise when a person is unable to clarify and live in accordance with her values, find meaning in her life, negotiate the competing demands of others, or develop a way of living fruitfully within the constraints of her circumstances. Deurzen's personal view of human life is that it is inherently paradoxical and challenging, and often tragic. Suffering is inevitable, the threat of losing all that we value is ever present; and yet it is in the struggle to transcend crises and traumas that we have the possibility of developing courage and wisdom. As she says: (2012, p. 30) "Clients are not considered to be ill but rather to be sick of life or clumsy at living."

Deurzen emphasizes the philosophical foundations of her work, naming as her philosophical antecedents not just the specific existential philosophies of Heidegger or Sartre, but rather situating her work in the context of Western philosophy from the Ancient Greeks onwards. Her interest is in identifying philosophers whose work contributes to the questions of meaning, values, identity, emotions, life goals, or ethics, which concern psychotherapy clients.

Deurzen pays special attention to Kierkegaard, in whose work she finds her inspiration to take seriously the struggle of the individual to find her own way in life, to form a sense of meaning and purpose, and in so doing, to develop a sense of self. Kierkegaard's account of selfhood as a continuing dialectical struggle between the polarities of necessity and possibility, finitude and infinity, temporality and eternity (Kierkegaard 1849/1989) is reflected in Deurzen's work which sees the self as a fluid process rather than a fixed entity, always searching for the overarching principle or meaning to transcend the polarities of existence in a synthesis of self-realization. Whereas Kierkegaard reframes the notion of Christian faith as the source of ultimate value and meaning, Deurzen leaves it open for the individual to define the overarching value which enables her to mobilize her energies and follow her direction in life. A non-specific belief in some sort of transcendent possibility beyond the realm of the human characterizes Deurzen's work and sets it apart from other contemporary existential approaches.

Deurzen follows Kierkegaard in seeing existential anxiety as fundamental to human existence. Like Kierkegaard, she asserts the value of anxiety as an indication of human vitality and potential, and the need to make a relationship with our own anxiety, to understand it and channel its energy, rather than either allowing ourselves to be paralyzed by it or else seeking to tranquillize it.

Deurzen emphasizes that the significance of an existential perspective on anxiety is that it discloses what is of most importance to the individual, her concerns in her lived existence, her direction in life, her values, goals and desires. Anxiety is the "dizziness of freedom" (Kierkegaard 1844/1980, p. 61) the opening of our possibilities, and also the acknowledgement of the inherent uncertainty and limitations of human existence:

> To live is to never be completely safe and it is this engagement with the paradoxes and dilemmas of living that gives human existence its excitement and sense of aliveness. It is in this tension that we find the source of all true creativity and vitality. Anxiety is a teacher, not an obstacle or something to be removed or avoided. (Deurzen and Adams 2016, p. 30)

Alongside Kierkegaard, Deurzen sets the rigorous demands for self-examination and self-transcendence asserted by Nietzsche. She views Nietzsche's contributions to existential psychotherapy to lie in his call to grasp our courage and stretch ourselves to be more than we are, in the course of which we are exhorted to accept and embrace the inevitability of suffering, not in a spirit of piety or resignation but rather one of vitality and excitement, *amor fati*. Nietzsche's emphasis on creating our own values also plays a part in Deurzen's perspective (Deurzen 2010).

After Kierkegaard and Nietzsche, Deurzen's most significant philosophical influence is Heidegger. She takes from Heidegger the sense of wonder at existence, alongside our uneasiness (*Unheimlichkeit*) at finding ourselves thrown into a world of activity, relationship, temporality, and mortality. She views Heidegger's emphasis on our inevitable connectedness and relatedness as a necessary counterbalance to the individualism of Kierkegaard and Nietzsche. At the same time, she follows all three philosophers in considering the human tendency for absorption into the crowd as something to be resisted. Again, it is the experience of existential anxiety, *Angst*, which is central to the development of personhood, as the individual realizes that her life is her own, with the freedom and responsibility, which accompany that knowledge, and that, she is always moving inexorably towards death. The Heideggerian call of conscience is an invitation to free ourselves from our absorption and grasp our unique existence in its possibilities and limitations. Anxiety thus makes possible the choice of authenticity:

> Existential anxiety or Angst is that basic unease or malaise which people experience as soon as they are aware of themselves and of their own responsibility in making something out of nothing. It is the sensation that accompanies self-consciousness and awareness of one's vulnerability when confronted with the possibility of one's death or one's failure. Anxiety is the life energy required to create something out of nothing. It is therefore the sine qua non of facing life and finding oneself. (Deurzen 2012, p. 47)

Although she emphasizes authenticity and self-ownership as a core existential concern, Deurzen sets this in the context of the individual's relationships and life situation, rather than promoting an individualistic notion of personal freedom. She is as much concerned with the limitations of a situation as with its possibilities. She also considers every specific human dilemma or difficulty to be situated within the "boundaries of human existence" (Deurzen 2012, p. 64), holding that "a basic principle is that human existence is a struggle between opposites" (Deurzen 2012, p. 65). All experiences and conflicts can be located on a spectrum between two opposed polarities, such as activity/passivity, dominance/submission, inclusion/exclusion, giving/receiving. Existential-phenomenological therapy aims to enable the client to face truthfully the inevitable paradoxes and contradictions of human existence.

Deurzen develops a sophisticated understanding of the self derived in part from Sartre's work (Deurzen 2015). She refers to the existentialist motto that "existence precedes essence" (Sartre 1948, p. 22), as offering consolation that the human sense of emptiness is an existential given rather than a personal failure, and that in our efforts to make ourselves into something we find our resources and creativity (Deurzen 2010). She notes the usefulness of Sartre's formulation of human relationships, although she tempers the account of conflictual ways of relating described in *Being and Nothingness* with the possibilities offered by Beauvoir (1948) and extended in Sartre's later work, for the development of genuine mutuality and reciprocity (Deurzen 2010). She makes reference to his notion of the "original project" in relation to challenging clients' narratives of their lives (Deurzen and Adams 2016) and considers the importance of a person finding some kind of overarching project or purpose in life. Sartre's early phenomenological work on emotions (Sartre 1939/1994) contributes to her formulation of the "emotional compass" (Deurzen 2010, pp. 306-314). She finds value in Sartre's account of consciousness, its forms of unreflected and reflective states, and its alternative to a psychoanalytic model of unconscious mental life (Sartre 1943/2001; Deurzen 2010).

She also refers to Merleau-Ponty's account of human existence as relational and embodied (Merleau-Ponty 1945/2002; Deurzen 2010).

Other Contributions: Hans Cohn and Ernesto Spinelli

Hans Cohn developed his version of existential therapy independently of Emmy van Deurzen. From his experience of and disillusionment with psychoanalysis, his model is firmly based on Heideggerian existential phenomenology and therefore has something in common with Daseinsanalysis. He is concerned mainly with showing how adopting this as the foundational basis for therapy results in a radical rethinking of concepts of the unconscious, the self, the psyche, projection, transference, and other concepts important to psychoanalytic psychotherapy. He frames an understanding of the origins and nature of clients' difficulties in a Heideggerian perspective: "From an existential perspective, there is at the core of many (perhaps all) psychological disturbances a conflict between the 'givens' of existence and our response to them" (Cohn 1996, p. 125). Cohn then demonstrates how a Heideggerian perspective might inform therapeutic work with particular client concerns, including anxiety, depression, obsessional states, and sexuality.

Cohn addresses the difficulty that can arise for therapists in considering Heidegger's account of inauthentic and authentic ways of living. As we have seen, Heidegger presents an account of human existence as initially inauthentic, in Dasein's "lostness in the They" (Heidegger 1927/1996, p. 274). Authenticity means individuating oneself and living with a truthful relationship to the givens of existence. The potential for a more authentic way of being arises in response to Dasein's encounter with Angst. Heidegger claims to be offering a descriptive account of human existence, not proposing that one way of living is superior to the other. He describes human existence as a continual oscillation between authenticity and inauthenticity, as we repeatedly struggle to define ourselves and then fall back into the state of absorption in "the They." As we have seen, in Deurzen's work, authentic living is prized and encouraged, albeit with a realistic grasp of the person's relational context. Cohn, however, is hesitant about making authenticity an explicit aim of therapy:

> It cannot be the therapist's task to judge the degree of a client's authenticity. However, if the client's distress indicates that it might be rooted in a conflict with unavoidable aspects of existence itself or in the paralyzing feeling that he or she has neither choice nor responsibility, the therapist can attempt to open up the ontological dimension pervading the ontic manifestations of the conflict. This may lead the client to a new understanding and the possibility of a new response. But in the end it is the client who determines the aim of psychotherapy (Cohn 1996, p. 127).

Cohn's resistance to the imposition of authenticity as a normative goal for therapy is echoed in a series of works by Ernesto Spinelli that span almost 30 years. Spinelli emphasizes the importance of phenomenology as an epistemological and methodological approach to various aspects of psychological research, theory, and practice. He makes only passing reference to the precursors of existential philosophy, Kierkegaard and Nietzsche, but emphasizes the phenomenological method developed by Husserl and aspects of the existential phenomenology of Heidegger. Sartrean ideas are considered "extensions of Heideggerian thought" (Spinelli 1989, p. 116) and little reference is made to Merleau-Ponty. In considering the practitioners who have influenced him, Spinelli places most emphasis on Laing for his application of phenomenology and unsettling of the assumptions of psychiatry (Spinelli 1989). He acknowledges the contributions of aspects of Carl Rogers' approach (Spinelli 1990), Buber's concepts of I-thou and I-it relating (Buber 1923/1996), and also refers to Binswanger, Yalom, and Deurzen (Spinelli 1989).

Spinelli's model of therapy is based on three foundational principles: relatedness, uncertainty, and existential anxiety. He derives these principles from the phenomenology of Husserl and Heidegger. In Spinelli's account, the principles are not equiprimordial, but rather are derived from one another sequentially.

Spinelli emphasizes the primacy of relatedness in any phenomenological account of human being, contrasting this with the individualist focus of many Western psychological models. An individual's primary unreflected experience of being in a relational world is termed by Spinelli as "worlding" (2007, p.18), by which he means the flow of experience and the activity of the human being in living in her relational world. Worlding includes the encounter with existence tensions, which are common human dilemmas experienced as polarities between competing needs or values in human existence. The construction of individual selfhood is a secondary process, in which this flow of experience is reflected on, consolidated and, defined as a "structural focus point" (2007, p. 19), a vantage point on the world, and in the world, from where the individual can organize her experience. This structuring of the experiential flow of worlding results in the formation of the individual's worldview, a synonym for both selfhood and meaning-creation. The worldview is the set of fundamental beliefs about self, others, and the world on which the individual seeks to base her life choices and actions. It expresses her awareness of and negotiation with the existence tensions.

Spinelli derives his second principle, uncertainty, from the human being's apprehension of her fundamental relatedness: "if all of one's reflective experience, knowledge and awareness of self, others and the world in general arises through and within relatedness then what is revealed is an inevitable and inescapable *uncertainty or lack of completeness in any and all of our reflections*" (Spinelli 2007, p.21; italics in original).

Uncertainty arises out of the partial and incomplete nature of the individual's perspective on existence. Uncertainty is also linked to temporality, since the flow of experience is necessarily temporal and continually threatens to render the perspective of the worldview inaccurate and outdated. Our unreflected worlding, our existence, perpetually outstrips our secondary constructions of who we think we are and how we believe our world to be.

The tension between worlding and worldview brings Spinelli to his third fundamental principle, existential anxiety. In his account, existential anxiety arises from the recognition that all attempts to create a static structure to our experience, that is, to establish certainty and meaning in the face of the ever-changing flow of being, can only ever be provisional: "That is to say, all meanings are subject to the threat of becoming meaningless" (Spinelli 2007, p. 26). The fundamental difficulty of human life, therefore, is that we need to build some structure for ourselves, to have an anchor in the flow of our worlding by constructing a worldview, whilst at the same time knowing that this is a precariously poised position, vulnerable to being swept away in the vicissitudes of experience:

> If the worldview provides persons with the basis with which to construe meaning in their experience of being, worlding constantly challenges and expands the limits of such meaning and by doing so directs the person toward the experience of meaninglessness. (Spinelli 2007, p. 39)

If we adopt a worldview with as much openness and flexibility as possible towards the lived experience of worlding, the risk is that we accord ourselves too little stability in our constructions of self, other, and life meaning, and so are vulnerable to collapsing into meaninglessness. On the other hand, if we place greater emphasis on maintaining a firm structure to our worldview, the cost is an overly rigid approach to our lived experience in which an increasing amount of experiential flow has to be excluded from our awareness. In the latter instance, we resort to a range of dissociative or defensive strategies to exclude from awareness any experiences that are not consistent with the worldview we seek to maintain, so that there is an increasing disjunction between the defensively maintained worldview and the actual experience of worlding. Although Spinelli avoids normative judgements about individuals' ways of living, he does consider that there are more or less truthful ways of engaging with existential anxiety, and that the individual's response has implications for their psychological, emotional, and relational well-being:

> those "untruthful" responses to existential anxiety which seek to avoid or deny the experiential consequences of relatedness and uncertainty, will serve to "fix" and focus existential anxiety so that it expresses itself through the "structures" of symptoms and disorders. (Spinelli 2007, p. 29)

Spinelli draws on personal construct psychology to describe the worldview as a tripartite structure, consisting of core beliefs, assumptions, and attitudes regarding the self, others, and the world. He refers to these as "sedimentations" or sometimes more fully as "sedimented dispositional stances" (Spinelli 2007, p.34), an idea derived from Merleau-Ponty's work. For Spinelli, therapy entails the descriptive clarification of the client's worlding and sedimented worldview, so that the tensions between them are exposed. This offers the client the opportunity to modify the ways in which she manages these tensions and understands her personal ways of living her relational, uncertain, and inherently anxiety-creating existence.

Phenomenology, Truth, and Authenticity: The Philosophical Aims of Existential-Phenomenological Therapy

In this section, we will examine the significant philosophical differences amongst the therapeutic models discussed. These differences are concerned with both the understanding of Husserl's phenomenological method and the place given to existential philosophy.

Deurzen considers phenomenology as a way of gaining access to truths, not just about the client's life in particular, but about human life in general. She is quite sure that truth can be discovered, through the systematic application of all aspects of the phenomenological method (Deurzen 2014), as discussed in Chapter 9. This includes the therapist taking ownership of her expertise, and in particular, her philosophical understanding, as a significant resource to be utilized in the service of the client.

For Deurzen, therapy faces out into the client's life, rather than inwards into the client's inner world or into the therapeutic relationship itself. Existential therapy entails a philosophically informed examination of the client's difficulties, based on an underlying assumption that the client's fundamental need is to make sense of her existence:

> The aim of existential counselling and psychotherapy is to clarify, reflect upon and understand life. Problems in living are confronted and life's possibilities and boundaries are explored. [...] The focus is therefore on life itself, rather than on one's personality. (Deurzen 2012, p. 30)

The influences of Kierkegaard and Heidegger are evident throughout Deurzen's writing. Existential anxiety is crucial in disclosing to the client her responsibility for her own existence.

The paradoxes and tensions of fundamental existential dilemmas are the substance of psychotherapy. The therapist aims to enable the client to face up to these dilemmas and find her unique way of living with them. Deurzen expresses certitude that the client has the necessary resources and skills to do so, with the encouragement, guidance, and challenge of the therapist's philosophically grounded understanding. Life is recognized as a challenge, often as struggle, but one for which the client can be well equipped: "The goal of existential work is to enable clients to enter a new phase of development of their talent for life" (Deurzen 2012, p. 35).

In contrast with both Cohn and Spinelli, Deurzen does not shy away from stating her position on the desirability of facing existential anxieties and grasping life with wholehearted commitment to some purpose. Cooper (2016) identifies a tension between Deurzen's personal beliefs in striving towards authentic existence and her commitment to maintaining a phenomenological openness to clients' various choices of ways of living. Deurzen herself acknowledges that: "There is an undeniable implicit exhortation in an existential approach for people to stand up for what they feel ready to make sacrifices for and to claim their rights to live a life as full as is humanly possible" (Deurzen 2012, p. 239).

As we have seen above, Cohn is critical of the merit of adopting authenticity as a therapeutic goal. His approach to therapy is consistent with a more descriptive phenomenological reading of Heidegger. For Spinelli, the principles of relatedness and uncertainty require the therapeutic stance of "un-knowing," his term for the attitude necessary for *epoché*. In fact, Spinelli stays almost entirely with a descriptive phenomenology which does not encourage the therapist to make substantive use of the contributions of existential philosophy. Through the process of descriptive phenomenological clarification, the client's experiences and self-structures (worlding and worldview) are understood as disclosive of her particular encounters with the fundamental existential principles of relatedness, uncertainty, and existential anxiety. Therapy entails the provision of a particular relational space in which the client's experiences and worldview are described and explored. By attending to the experience of the therapeutic relationship itself, the client learns about her relatedness in the world.

The aim of this exploration of the therapeutic relationship is the modification of the client's worldview in order that she might have the opportunity of living with less dissociation and distortion of her experiential flow of worlding:

> Ultimately, existential psychotherapy seeks to allow clients the means to diminish that gap or dissonance between their maintained worldview and their experience of worlding, in such a way that the worldview is a more adequate (if still incomplete and imperfect) expression of the client's direct experience of worlding. (Spinelli 2007, p. 86)

Spinelli does not go so far as to say that this entails a more truthful grasp of existential givens or is a way of more skillfully managing existence tensions. His vision for the possibilities of existential therapy is framed by the exclusion of any normative judgement of therapeutic goals or desirable ways of living. He remains committed to the stance of un-knowing and openness. While his model of therapy is in many ways closer to a person-centered approach in its use of non-directive descriptive phenomenology, it is a model that does draw on existential principles of fundamental relatedness, uncertainty, and anxiety.

Conclusion

When Deurzen, Cohn, and Spinelli's philosophical and theoretical approaches to therapy are considered alongside one another, the differences amongst their models become evident. In Deurzen's work, we find a robustly philosophical existential-phenomenological model in which the systematic acknowledgment of all three of Husserl's reductions enables the disclosure of the truths about human life, at the same time as the insights of existential philosophy inform the process of grappling with these truths in the quest for a more authentic way of living. Cohn contributes a thorough and coherent model of a Heideggerian approach to therapy which is concerned to establish itself on sound epistemological foundations, but is circumspect about Deurzen's normative stance on the aims of therapy. In Spinelli's approach, we find an almost limitless descriptive phenomenological openness and un-knowing, but it is one in which comparatively less use is made of the contributions of existential philosophy in informing the therapist's work.

References

Adams, M. (2006). "Towards an existential phenomenological model of life span human development," *Existential Analysis 17* (2): 261–280.

Adams, M. (2013). *A Concise Introduction to Existential Counselling*. London: Sage.

Beauvoir, S. de (1948). *The Ethics of Ambiguity* (trans. B. Frechtman). New York: Citadel Press.

Buber, M. (1996). *I and Thou* (trans. W. Kaufmann, 1970). New York: Touchstone. (Original work published 1923.)

Cohn, H.W. (1996). *Existential Theory and Therapeutic Practice*. London: Sage.

Cohn, H.W. (2002). *Heidegger and the Roots of Existential Therapy*. London: Sage

Cooper, M. (2016). *Existential Therapies*, 2e. London: Sage

Deurzen, E. van (2010). *Everyday Mysteries: Existential Dimensions of Psychotherapy*, 2e. London: Routledge.

Deurzen, E. van (2012). *Existential Counselling in Practice*, 3e. London: Sage.

Deurzen, E. van (2014). Structural Existential Analysis (SEA): A phenomenological method for therapeutic work. *Journal of Contemporary Psychotherapy 45* (1): 59–68.

Deurzen, E. van (2015). *Paradox and Passion in Psychotherapy: An Existential Approach*, 2e. Chichester: Wiley Blackwell.

Deurzen, E. van and Adams, M. (2016). *Skills in Existential Counselling & Psychotherapy*, 2e. London: Sage.

Heidegger, M. (1996). *Being and Time* (trans. J. Stambaugh). New York: SUNY Press. (Original work published 1927.)

Kierkegaard, S. (1980). *The Concept of Anxiety*. Princeton: Princeton University Press. (Original work published 1844.)

Kierkegaard, S. (1989). *The Sickness Unto Death*. London: Penguin. (Original work published 1849.)

Kierkegaard, S. (2000). Concluding unscientific postscript to *Philosophical Fragments*. In: *The Essential Kierkegaard* (ed. H.V. Hong and E.H. Hong), 187–246. Princeton: Princeton University Press. (Original work published 1846.)

Merleau-Ponty, M. (2002). *Phenomenology of Perception* (trans. C. Smith). London: Routledge. (Original work published 1945.)

Sartre, J-P. (2001). *Being and Nothingness* (trans. H. Barnes). London: Routledge. (Original work published 1943.)

Sartre, J.-P. (1948). *Existentialism and Humanism* (trans. P. Mairet). London: Methuen.

Sartre, J-P. (1994). *Sketch for a Theory of the Emotions*. London: Routledge. (Original work published 1939.)

Spinelli, E. (1989). *The Interpreted World. An Introduction to Phenomenological Psychology*. London: Sage.

Spinelli, E. (1990). Phenomenological Method and Client-Centred Therapy. *Existential Analysis 1*: 18–26.

Spinelli, E. (2007). *Practising Existential Therapy: The Relational World*. London: Sage.

9

Existential-Phenomenological Therapy

Method and Practice

Martin Adams

As said, the existential-phenomenological field of vision reaches beyond the purely individual to life itself and considers the person as a being-in-the-world in its wider philosophical and socio-political context. Its focus, and therefore the focus of existential-phenomenological therapy, is on the nature of truth, reality, and the generation of personal meaning within the parameters of human existence, rather than on personality, illness, or cure. As we have also seen, Binswanger (1963), Yalom (1980), and Deurzen (2010), among others, have talked about four basic experiential worlds; the physical, the social, the personal, and the spiritual or moral, each of which manifest themselves in everyday life as unsolvable paradoxes and dilemmas, and Spinelli, who also considers relatedness as primary, has talked about the way our identity, or self-structure as he calls it, is embodied in the four relational realms of the I, You, We, and the They (2015). One of the tasks of therapy for Deurzen, as well as for Spinelli, is to enable the connections between these four realms or worlds to be better understood. Therefore, existential-phenomenological therapy prefers to think in terms of the ways people meet the challenges that life inevitably presents them with between birth and death.

Skills and existential-phenomenological therapy

Existentialists have long been suspicious of technique and with good reason. In its simplest form a technique is an action that is done in a given circumstance to achieve a particular purpose, and an action becomes a technique when there is a gap between enactment and belief; when we are doing something without full attention or personal commitment.

Rather than concentrating on the mutually dehumanizing consequences of technique, existential-phenomenological therapists tend to rely instead on the

The Wiley World Handbook of Existential Therapy, First Edition. Edited by Emmy van Deurzen, Erik Craig, Alfried Längle, Kirk J. Schneider, Digby Tantam, and Simon du Plock.

authority of their own experience, their integrity, and their values. A more accurate and consistent term here would be "skills" or alternatively "practice," and an action becomes a skill when we are able to enact and own our beliefs. Following Sartre, skills are what Laing refers to as praxis (Laing and Cooper 1964; Laing 1967, 2013). And as Heidegger reminds us (1962, p. 98), a hammer is only useful if we have the skill to use it. Otherwise it is either useless or dangerous. Therefore, techniques are tools, whereas skills are owned ways of being.

Successful living is in fact a process of learning skills rather than of technique acquisition (Adams 2018). This distinction is important in psychotherapy because the presence of technique results in the mutualizing and dehumanizing strategies so easily recognized in many limited-contract models. In our work the danger of slipping from skills into technique is ever present and existential-phenomenological therapists are certainly not immune from it; it is a human failing that we can fall into when looking for short cuts. But if we adhere to existential and phenomenological principles we will reduce the danger and also increase our awareness of its occurrence, as well as treat our clients ethically.

Phenomenology

Theories are like maps, they are out of date as soon as they are made and are never the same as the territory. In psychotherapy what is more useful than a theory to follow is a way of developing a theory. But because the research method will always produce findings in accordance with the assumptions of the research method, the assumptions of the research method must match the nature of what is being researched.

The assumptions of natural science; causation, replicability, and the existence of objective truth, work well for the physical world, but not for the human world, because human meaning is dependent on context, freedom, and personal responsibility. For this reason, and following Kant and Hegel, in the early-twentieth century Edmund Husserl developed phenomenology as a research method for the human sciences. Where natural science asks the question "Why?" that always gets "Because…" as an answer, phenomenology asks the questions "What?" or "How?" that get further description. This is the origin of the familiar injunction "Describe don't explain." Phenomenology does not focus on objectivity as natural science does, or subjectivity as introspectionism does, but attempts to find the link between the two; to find a correlation between consciousness and the objects of consciousness. In this sense it is concerned with intersubjective truth. Phenomenology aims to arrive at an understanding of individual human experience by returning us to embodied lived experience and opening out to the richness and mystery of life by successive description. It stays experience-near.

However, intersubjective meaning is never simple or obvious because our assumptions about our experiences are contextual and will always constrain and restrict our understanding. Husserl called these assumptions our "natural attitude" and he proposed phenomenology as a way we can reduce and hence become aware of their influence. To put it another way, phenomenology asks the question, "*How can we understand anything without first understanding that which does the understanding?*" This is an implication of his principle of intentionality; that we can never simply be observers, we are always participant-observers. In order to "*understand that which does the understanding*" Husserl proposed three interlinked ways we can reduce the effect of our natural attitude and see the world and our interaction with it more clearly. These "reductions," as described in Chapter 8, are the phenomenological, the eidetic, and the transcendental, and they all have direct relevance to the practice of existential-phenomenological therapy.

The phenomenological reduction focuses on our attitude towards whatever it is we are attending to. It is about how we are attending. Therapeutically we know this as our process. The way we attend, our background emotional tone, or what Heidegger (1962) called our "mood," will always color our receptiveness and lead us to come to conclusions that will inevitably have more to do with our expectations and prejudices than the richness of what we are attending to.

By describing and not explaining we embrace ambiguity and uncertainty and become more able to identify what we usually call the content. This is the eidetic reduction, when we become aware of the meaning of what we have identified to focus on. This also allows us more accurately to distinguish common from specific features. Although they are talked of here as separate, they are never separate; they cannot exist apart.

Reflexivity is the way we continually monitor the interlocking of the "how" and the "what," in order to grasp the many ways our natural attitude intervenes. When done consistently, this will lead to the third reduction, the transcendental reduction. In examining the world and our responses to it we are more able to understand and experience our intersubjective relationship with the world. We get to understand that rather than it being given to us by the world, we are the source of our meaning as a part of the world. By gaining a sense of perspective we come to realize not just the limitations of our own point of view but also the potential of alternatives.

The aim of existential-phenomenological therapy is to show that this can be done by providing an experiential model of relatedness and understanding. It will lead to moments where therapist and client can connect together in a surprising and very special sense of togetherness of lived inter-subjectivity.

Principles of existential-phenomenological practice

Husserl was a philosopher and did not concern himself with phenomenological practice, and the philosophical principles of phenomenology have been developed and operationalized into a set of systematic and characteristic actions and interventions for therapy (Spinelli 2015; Langdridge 2013; Adams 2001, 2013; Deurzen and Adams 2016), as well as for research (Giorgi 1970; Langdridge 2007; Smith, Flowers, and Larkin 2009; Finlay 2011).

It is flexible enough to be able to be used in short, fixed-term work as well as in long-term, open-ended work. And also with all human issues (Deurzen and Arnold-Baker 2005; Deurzen and Hanaway 2012; Deurzen and Iacovou 2013; Milton 2014).

The overall task of the existential-phenomenological therapist is to facilitate the discovery and understanding of the assumptions that influence a client's decisions and actions, so that new choices can be made and owned more deliberately. As we are permanently in the world with others, there is a reflexive demand on ourselves to identify and understand how our own assumptions constrain and restrict our perception. In this way we ensure ethical practice by simultaneously acknowledging both our autonomy and that of the client.

The existence of assumptions embodies a paradox because we need these assumptions not only to make sense of the world but also to remind ourselves of how we usually make sense of the world; what our own personal natural attitude is. We can never be free of assumptions and to claim to be so is to deny our humanity. Heidegger calls this being inauthentic and Sartre calls it being in bad faith. Although Hans Cohn maintained a strong link to philosophy, particularly to that of Heidegger, he was also a psychotherapist and with respect to authenticity he says (2002, p. 124): "However great Heidegger's reluctance may have been to tell us what to do, there can hardly be any doubt that he considered 'choosing existence' to be a choice of surpassing value." Authenticity can therefore be an aim of existential-phenomenological therapy as long as we remember first, that it is a general statement of intent and direction rather than an expectation of a particular end result, second, that it is not a norm, third, that we can never rid ourselves of inauthenticity, and any claims to have done so are inauthentic and fourth, that it should not be the therapist who defines it.

With respect to our assumptions; our clients need us to have them, but only if we know what to do with them. Our attempt at self-awareness, our reflexivity, is the protection our clients have from our assumptions taking over and turning existential-phenomenological therapy into a sophisticated form of suggestion.

Life is continuous, so reflecting on our evolving assumptions is continuous. It begins before, is present during, and continues after the session. The client's own distress and the questions they have about their life indicate that their assumptions are flawed, inconsistent, or unexamined. What is important is not so much whether their assumptions are correct, but what they mean to the client and how they inform the client's decisions about their life, and whether these choices are satisfactory to them.

Following Husserl, there are two parts to phenomenological practice called epoché (or bracketing) and verification. Although the overall aim of existential-phenomenological therapy is to promote understanding, in order to do this we first need to attend, and the entire therapeutic process begins with and is sustained by attention. This kind of attention facilitates openness both to ourselves and also to the client's unfolding meanings. Spinelli (2015) refers to it as un-knowing, but in phenomenology it is better known as an attitude of wonder or not knowing. Our ability to attend is correlated with our ability to live with ambiguity and uncertainty. If our attention wanders or we find we are searching for an explanation or a theory it probably means that we are not attending well enough. But as long as we attend we will become increasingly aware of our assumptions and the reductions will follow.

Epoché – discovering meaning through clarification

There are two elements to the first part of phenomenological practice – description and equalization – we do them simultaneously and the skills we use are those of clarification. The questions "how?" and "what?," which request further description are far more appropriate than "why?" which will invariably lead to defensiveness and a narrowing down of the field of vision. The question "why?" says more about the therapist's unexamined assumptions than the questions the client has come to explore.

There are many characteristic clarifying descriptive interventions, for instance:

- "How do you mean?"
- "What's that like?"
- "Can you give me an example?"
- "Can you say a bit more about that?"

These will need to be translated into the existential-phenomenological therapist's own context sensitive language and be responsive to each different client's perspective and experience.

In equalizing we consider that each part of the content and the process is of equal significance until we are told otherwise. We have to resist and bracket our tendency to create a hierarchy of meaning. Our ability to listen will always be influenced by our life experience, so it is inevitable that our natural attitude will be present. Again, reflexivity will monitor this.

However, as long as we are describing it, if only to ourselves, we will become aware of our mood enough to reflect on it and step aside from it, bracket it, and sooner or later certain elements will begin to stand out.

Horizontalization – discovering meaning through gaining perspective

The beginning of existential-phenomenological therapy is largely about attending and clarifying, and leads on to the interpreting and challenging skills of verification. Horizontalization is a process described by Husserl (Moran 2000) as the bridge between the two, when what is becoming known is placed against a horizon, in a context. It is when we start to understand our particular viewpoint, our perspective. Understanding that we always have a perspective on the world enables us to understand that there are things we cannot see, things that our current view obscures. Understanding the context of our experiences is vital and the client needs to find a way, facilitated by us, to stand back from their immediate issues and see them in the context of their whole life – past, present, and future. The existential-phenomenological therapist will be able to move the focus of the work from the general to the specific and vice versa so that the client gets to see their life in perspective. Often, just being a different person who is fully attending and trying to understand can facilitate the emergence of a sense of perspective.

Verification – discovering meaning through challenging and interpretation

Attention and requests for further description can be extremely powerful and on many occasions can rekindle genuine philosophical perplexity and personal questioning, but on some occasions it is not enough. This can lead to a morbid going round in circles when almost literally, nothing happens. Both are busy finding out things they already know.

Existentially we are always interpreting because we are meaning-making creatures. Following Husserl (Ihde 1968; Langdridge 2007), we can call this verification. The overall aim of verification is to explore hidden meanings and to make links between them, to look for recurring themes that can then be owned, questioned, and re-evaluated; to verify. It is where we break the principle of equalization and it is necessary for the therapy to progress. It is also in verification that we explicitly shed light on the way the client is struggling with the givens of existence, death, relationality, freedom and responsibility, and morality. It is where we do something with the questions derived from clarification and use our intuition and the knowledge of life we have derived from our own struggles.

Verification in a manner that is sensitive to the client's being is almost a definition of effective therapy. It gives a person a feeling that their experience matters and is taken seriously and can be understood and perhaps even transcended. Spinelli (2015) calls these interventions, strategic questioning and descriptive challenges, and for him they tend to focus on one of the four relational realms.

There are four characteristic verifying interventions

- "What is your part in this?" This brings present personal responsibility into the dialogue.
- "Is this feeling familiar?" This brings past experience, into the dialogue and begins to find repeating patterns.
- "How is this leading you to what you say you want?" This introduces the future, hope, and change, into the dialogue.
- "On the one hand you feel [...] but on the other hand you feel [...]." This introduces dilemma, paradox, and the tension between opposites into the dialogue.

As with the clarificatory interventions, for these to become owned as embodied skills rather than as disembodied and therefore disowned techniques the existential-phenomenological therapist will not only need to translate them into their own context sensitive language but also to discover the subtleties of timing and placing that can only come about through sustained and accurate attention.

Open dialogue as the agent of change

As we are permanently in the world with others, our identity is tied up with others whether we like it or not. It follows that the relationship between therapist and client is central to existential- phenomenological practice.

Existential-phenomenological therapy takes place primarily in the social world, in which the challenge is to work out what other people are there for and how to get on with them. It is through dialogue, through cooperation, that we are able to take each other into account and so reduce our narcissism. Open dialogue is more than just a conversation; it is a joint search for meaning while keeping the wider context of existence in mind.

Existentially, dialogue means that no matter how much the therapist and client feel they understand each other, they are always aware that the other is a separate autonomy. Clients can try to solve this tension either by merging, for example by agreeing with everything the therapist says, or by separating, for example by disputing everything the therapist says.

That cooperation is difficult is shown by how often people enter therapy because of relationship difficulties. When people can tolerate the inherent paradox of relationships they will be able to discover the freedom that intimacy can offer. This both/and solution to the question of personal autonomy in relationships can be summarized as: "I have the responsibility to do what I want in a world of others, but so does everybody else and it works best if we take each other into account."

Dialogue is not simply another word for conversation – there is a difference between a monologue, a duologue, and a dialogue. Both a monologue and a duologue are evidence of our natural attitude while a dialogue can only come about when the phenomenological reductions are in operation.

Monologue

A monologue is when the talker's main concern is to talk and has little concern about how he or she is received. The listener will often feel talked at rather than talked to or with.

Duologue

A duologue is when the two people are talking but only superficially listening to each other. They may well take it in turns to talk and even respond but neither is really hearing what the other is saying. They are more likely to be listening to what they want the other person to say. Heidegger (1962, p. 211) calls this "idle talk."

Dialogue

A dialogue is when the two people genuinely attend and listen to each other, not for what they assume the other is saying, but for what is actually being said and often what is only hinted at. It involves a reflexive openness to the other and also to oneself. There is a trust between the therapist and client such that their separateness and difference is not felt to be a threat. Heidegger (1962, p. 158) referred to this by the somewhat awkward phrase "leaping-ahead" (Karban 2017).

In existential-phenomenological therapy, there will always be a certain amount of anxiety because we never know what will happen next. This may be felt as excitement if we are comfortable with it and fear when we are not. In this sense both the therapist and the client should always be feeling apprehensive and if not, there will be a monologue or a duologue pretending to be a dialogue.

As existential-phenomenological therapists one way we are responsible for the development of dialogue is by knowing how to maintain a balance between support and challenge. Often this will mean that we say relatively little, at least at the start of therapy. Clients may not be immediately ready to enter into dialogue; they may initially find monologue or duologue easier to deal with.

The route from monologue or duologue to dialogue will be different for each therapeutic relationship but all successful work will end with dialogue.

Working existentially with presenting issues

Working with dilemma and paradox

In existential-phenomenological therapy, the questions clients come with always relate to a human dilemma that needs exploring and all life's dilemmas and paradoxes can be linked to one or more of the givens of existence. In everyday life trying to solve dilemmas with an either/or decision actually makes the issue more rigid and narrow, so we need to open it out instead, phenomenologically.

Our aim is always to promote a stronger engagement with the complexity, ambiguity, and continuity of experience. We do not work on change as such, we work on stopping people obstructing change. Consequently we will invariably use the present tense as this reinforces the principle of the past-in-the-present and helps the person focus on the immediate aspects of their dilemma. It can usually be more valuable to paraphrase, to reformulate the clients' story as a dilemma so that it can be explored and solved dialectically. We will also refer to feelings as "important" or "significant" rather than as "interesting." "Important" or "significant" indicates the presence of passion, whereas "interesting" indicates something worthy of note but of no great meaning. We connect emotionally with the client, as well as cognitively. Moreover, describing the conflicting thoughts and feelings they have without trying to justify them will eventually bring hidden facets of the dilemma into perspective.

On other occasions we may sense that the client is evading some issues that could benefit from consideration and on some occasions, it may seem to us that the client is actually preventing him or herself from making a decision. They get something from not making a decision. They may hope they will not have to give anything up, and they can avoid choosing by not choosing, by getting someone else or circumstances to make the decision for them.

Acknowledging that there can be two apparently opposite feelings can be at first confusing and then freeing when it is realized that it was the tension between the feelings that was causing the problem all along. As is seen in Chapter 10, ultimately such dilemmas are only resolvable by choice and commitment.

A greater contact with the emotional meaning of a dilemma will often lead to an expression of feeling, to catharsis, but this is not an end in itself. Its meaning has to be processed before it can be understood. Insight follows action, it does not precede it.

Every choice involves a sacrifice and we have to recognize them for what they are, and encourage further exploration by pointing out the dilemma they put themselves in and wondering what the advantages are for them. It will often be found that the reason the solution could not be found was because the question was posed wrongly.

A paradox is that in the risky process of getting to know our desires and committing to a choice, life becomes more meaningful than it ever was before

Working with themes and issues

What is meant by existential themes and issues is not simply what is being talked about, it is the way a person engages with the givens of existence.

Clients are always talking about what is important to them although initially the detail may be unclear. It is up to the existential-phenomenological therapist to listen for the existential dimensions of the clients concerns and to paraphrase these into specific concrete issues that can be worked on. All the while taking the lead from the client.

We are not just noticing what is being talked about, but also what is not being talked about. We notice what is significant by its absence. Something may impact on a client without them realizing its importance, for example, a client raised in a family that gave preference to survival through competitiveness, may see cooperativeness as a weakness and not realize its benefits.

The existential-phenomenological therapist will note,

- How is a theme represented within the present topic?
- How are the givens being evaded or denied?
- How the client is trying to become alive and fulfilled?
- What are the risks and how are they being avoided?
- How resilient are the themes and which situations do they occur in and not occur in?
- What does the theme say about the client's worldview and their experience of life?

Simply identifying the issues is likely to be of little value unless we do something with it. We do this by referring to the paradox and dilemma embedded in the issue.

Working with values and beliefs

One of the values of existential-phenomenological therapy is that people be encouraged to discover and choose a value system to live by and to understand why it is important to them. In the same way, the existential-phenomenological therapist must be able to question their own value system. If we cannot do this we will have no ethical right to challenge our client's value system. The word "values" is an appropriate word because it refers to what we value, what is important to us.

Values and beliefs will generally be less explicit than themes and issues because they relate to the ethical principles we live by. Everything we do and say says something about what we value. By identifying ourselves as existential-phenomenological therapists we are saying that we value the principles of openness and autonomy.

We tend to think of our values as fixed, but actually they are personal creations based on our understanding of our life experience to date, and the realization of the relativity of values will evoke anxiety because it means that we are responsible for finding our own. This is the starting point of a fuller life because it means our values can be the result of personal choice and reflection rather than accident or history.

Values and beliefs are intimately linked to emotions and existential-phenomenological therapy aims to understand the link between what we do and how we feel so that we may act more deliberately and with greater ownership.

Focusing on the immediacy of a client's emotional life will lead to a greater clarity about this link and the limitations they place on themselves. This can best be done by using dialogue to bring the relationship we have with the client into focus. This can be seen clearly in Chapter 10.

A coherent value system which is flexible enough to adapt to new circumstances will give us the feeling of integrity and make living worthwhile. Clients often come to a therapist when there is a conflict within their own values, or between their own and other people's values. This can be distressing because they are forced to decide perhaps for the first time whether something is worth sacrificing something else for.

Because values are implicit we are most likely to find out about a client's value system from how they run their lives. Our focus is always on the client's specific experience and the way in which their values and beliefs are linked to actions and their consequences. All the assumptions underlying such conflicts can be examined and if clients do not bring up their unease with their values and beliefs, it may be necessary to bring it to their attention.

We do this by considering

- Which values are useful now? Which belong to an earlier time of life?
- What feelings are evoked by each value?
- Are there contradictions between different values?
- Which values have been accepted without reflection and choice and which have not?

Another clue is the way clients talk with us. Sometimes we are asked for our judgement on how the client says they were treated. If we feel drawn to agree or disagree with a client it means there is a strong value that needs to be brought out and examined either with the client or in supervision.

Working with choice and responsibility

In everyday life we are overwhelmed with choices, choices of where to go, what to buy, what to do, and so on, and we can easily get confused about what we want. But existentially these are not choices at all but options.

Existentially, choosing is nothing to do with selecting between options because much of the time it seems there is only one alternative on offer. Choosing means being able to own and commit ourselves to whatever decisions we take. Existentially we become alive by committing to our decisions and existentially we die by denying our commitment.

The existential choice therefore is whether to own the consequences of our decisions, or whether to deny them and blame someone else. In fact we do this all the time in small ways when we act half-heartedly, or blame someone else for how we feel. Sartre (2003, p. 55) gives us an example of a woman on a date making her hand go limp when it is held by a man she does not want to be with. Passively not choosing has just as strong a consequence as actively choosing. The consequence of disowning our actions is that we feel powerless and depressed. Much existential-phenomenological therapy is to do with establishing a resilient understanding of what I have come to call the Law of Existential Consequence (Adams 2013); that when I do something, something follows from it that I have responsibility for.

Making choices and taking responsibility is at the center of everything we do and the root of all existential problems of living is when we take responsibility for things we have no responsibility for and/or deny responsibility for those things we do have responsibility for.

People learn best when they use their autonomy, although a client at the beginning of therapy will probably have little confidence in their autonomy. If the existential-phenomenological therapist can believe in it though, the client will reflexively start to believe in it. By rescuing, by "leaping-in" (Karban 2017; Heidegger 1962, p. 158) we undermine the clients' autonomy. When we care for someone, what we care for is his or her autonomy. Staying with the tension of the dilemma will allow a new solution to emerge.

A principle of all existential work then is to introduce, or re-introduce the client to the reality that not only did they contribute to the situation they find themselves in now, but that they also have responsibility for it changing. By doing this we link the past, the present, and the future, which is to say that only when we discover the meaning of our past, can we make our own future.

Working with endings and termination

Considerably more has been written on the start and the maintenance of therapeutic relationships than on endings, and it is hard not to put this down to a universal avoidance of the issue of death, which is the final ending. But we need to remember that like death, the termination of existential-phenomenological therapy is not just a cessation of activity, it is a process that if worked through can give meaning to our lives (Adams 2018).

Many clients come with issues of unsatisfactory endings or losses, and it is important that the end of the work is not experienced as something else that ended unsatisfactorily. It is therefore the existential-phenomenological therapist's responsibility to know how to work so that they get to the end of the work at the end of the available time (Deurzen and Adams 2016). The existential-phenomenological therapist will also need to know when they either prolong or shorten the ending for their own reasons and supervision is valuable in throwing light on these blind spots.

Although with a fixed-term contract the decision of when to stop is taken away, what remains in common to all contracts is to work out how to evaluate and end the work, and clients who have a particular sensitivity to loss and endings will need more time and care in working this through.

Given that endings are universally difficult, with an open-ended contract the issue for both the therapist and client is to arrive at an ending which is at the right time for both of them, bearing in mind that since life is constantly unfolding there can be no point at which any therapy can be said to have finished – it can only ever be enough for the time being.

This point can only be known by the two people on the basis of their work together, but it is useful to bear in mind the signs of poorly managed endings, which can be characterized by:

- the client leaving suddenly;
- leaving when either the outcome of the task and/or the relationship has not been evaluated;
- leaving with a denial of feelings of loss;
- ending after a specific goal has only been partially met; and
- leaving before the work has had a chance to establish itself.

It is not the job of the existential-phenomenological therapist to advise the client to stay or to go but to ensure that the reasons for staying or for going are sufficiently understood. This cannot be known unless the issue is discussed. To this end, if a client is reluctant to discuss a sudden departure, the likelihood is that the ending will not be well managed, but if it is discussed, the likelihood is that it will be well managed. Thinking about endings becomes important as soon as we engage with new beginnings.

As therapy is about task as well as relationship, the client will probably wish to know that the therapist will remember them, and this is more likely to be reinforced by the quality of the therapist's attention over the whole time and especially at the end. The better the ending, the more the work will be remembered as valuable and the gains sustainable, and vice versa. But a good ending does not mean that all loose ends have been tied up. On the contrary, it means that both therapist and client have confidence that the client has learnt enough about self-reflection and the philosophical understanding of living so that they will be equal to the further challenges that life will inevitably throw their way.

The skills learning process

As said, successful living is a process of skills acquisition and this applies to making the most of the therapy experience (Adams 2018). A principle of all existential-phenomenological therapy is to introduce, or re-introduce, the client to the reality that they have an active part in their learning. But as well as learning the skills of living more resourcefully, clients also have to learn the skill of using existential-phenomenological therapy. We need to remember this.

The skills learning process is marked by a characteristic sequence of thoughts, feelings, and actions that can evolve backwards and forwards through qualitatively different but interconnected phases, dependent on the nature of the adversity. In addition, each phase requires something different from us as existential-phenomenological therapists (Adams 2016; Deurzen and Adams 2016).

The first challenge begins even before the first meeting. For the client, it begins when they start to ask themselves questions about the way they are living. Our task at this point is simply to attend, and as we listen and clarify, we begin to find out about how they usually meet adversity. Gradually, the client starts to understand that he or she is the thread that connects everything together. This can be as frightening as it can be exciting. If frightening, the client may believe that no good can come from it and wish to leave.

Our task here is to try to understand and tolerate these feelings and facilitate the client to understand their experience in a new way in the light of ambiguity, dilemma, and paradox. The challenge for the existential-phenomenological therapist is to stay with the client as they find the courage to persevere. As long as we guard against seeking easy solutions gradually the client will get used to the new experience of facing adversity with a different outcome.

Our task is then to try to consolidate the changes made so they can be integrated into the client's idea of who they now are. We need to affirm their learning at the same time as acknowledging that the uncertainty of existence can be exciting as well as terrifying. As the client gets used to living differently, they also become more resilient.

Our task here is to encourage the emerging competence and confidence while at the same time guarding against over-confidence. A challenge for the therapist is that their knowledge and experience can lead them into complacency and arrogance. When this happens what were once skills become techniques. This is dangerous for both therapist and client.

Persevering against adversity is a given of existence and each part of the skills learning process presents a different sort of adversity which is there to be met, not avoided. It is in this sense that what is learnt in therapy is transferable to everyday life.

Conclusion

This chapter has described how the method and practice of existential-phenomenological therapy is related to its underpinning philosophy. Every therapy can be seen as a unique research project and phenomenology is the most appropriate research method to use in the human sciences because acknowledges and respects the context sensitive dynamic co-constituted nature of human meaning.

References

Adams M. (2001). Practising phenomenology: Some reflections and considerations. *Existential Analysis* 12 (1): 65–84.

Adams, M. (2013). *A Concise Introduction to Existential Counselling*. London: Sage.

Adams, M. (2016). Existential therapy as a skills learning process. *Existential Analysis* 27 (1): 58–69.

Adams, M. (2018). *An Existential Approach to Human Development: Philosophical and Therapeutic Perspectives*. London: Palgrave

Binswanger, L. (1963). *Being-in-the-World: Selected Papers of Ludwig Binswanger* (ed. J. Needleman). New York: Basic Books.

Cohn, H. (2002). *Heidegger and the Roots of Existential Psychotherapy*. London: Continuum.

Deurzen, E. van (2010). *Everyday Mysteries: Existential Dimensions of Psychotherapy*. London: Routledge.

Deurzen E. van and Adams M. (2016). *Skills in Existential Counselling and Psychotherapy* 2e. London: Sage.

Deurzen, E. van and Arnold-Baker C. (eds.) (2005). *Existential Perspectives on Human Issues: A Handbook for Therapeutic Practice.* Basingstoke: Palgrave Macmillan.
Deurzen, E. van and Hanaway, M. (2012). *Existential Perspectives on Coaching.* Basingstoke: Palgrave Macmillan.
Deurzen, E van and Iacovou, S. (2013). *Existential Perspectives on Relationship Therapy.* Basingstoke: Palgrave Macmillan.
Finlay, L. (2011). *Phenomenology for Psychotherapists: Researching the Lived World.* Chicester: Wiley-Blackwell
Giorgi A. (1970). *Psychology as a Human Science. A Phenomenologically Based Approach.* New York: Harper & Row.
Heidegger, M. (1962). *Being and Time* (trans. J. Macquarrie and E.S. Robinson). New York: Harper & Row. (Original work published 1927.)
Ihde, D. (1986). *Experimental Phenomenology.* Albany, NY: SUNY Press
Karban, B. (2017). Leaping-in and leaping-ahead: An exploration of Heidegger's notion of solicitude. *Existential Analysis* 28 (2): 106–117.
Laing, R.D. (1967). *The Politics of Experience and The Bird of Paradise.* Harmondsworth: Penguin.
Laing, R.D. (2013). The use of existential phenomenology in psychotherapy. In: *The Evolution of Psychotherapy* (ed. J.K. Zeig), 203–210. Hove: Routledge.
Laing, R.D. and Cooper, D. (1964). *Reason & Violence: A Decade of Sartre's Philosophy, 1950–1960.* London: Tavistock.
Langdridge, D. (2007). *Phenomenological Psychology: Theory, Research and Method.* Harlow: Pearson Education.
Langdridge. D. (2013). *Existential Counselling and Psychotherapy.* London: Sage.
Milton, M. (ed.) (2014). *Sexuality: Existential Perspectives.* Ross on Wye: PCCS.
Moran, D. (2000). *Introduction to Phenomenology.* London: Routledge.
Sartre, J.-P. (2003). *Being and Nothingness: An Essay in Phenomenological Ontology* (trans. H.E. Barnes). London: Routledge. (Original work published 1946.)
Smith, J., Flowers P., and Larkin, M. (2009). *Interpretative Phenomenological Analysis: Theory, Practice and Method.* London: Sage.
Spinelli, E. (2015). *Practising Existential Psychotherapy. The Relational World.* London: Sage
Yalom, I. (1980). *Existential Psychotherapy.* New York: Basic Books.

10

Existential-Phenomenological Therapy Illustration

Rahim's Dilemma[1]

Emmy van Deurzen and Claire Arnold-Baker

The client

Rahim is a Persian man of 42. When I first meet him in my consulting room, he is extremely carefully dressed, in classic European style. I am struck by the way in which his white shirt, with high collar, sets off his smooth, mat-brown skin and hazel colored eyes. He is elegant and comes across as confident and affluent and this image is completed by a sharply cut navy-blue three-piece suit and wine-red tie. He is of average height and weight. He is extremely polite and smiles affably and lightly bows to me upon entering the room. He immediately comes across as someone who is comfortable being in charge and he moves with ease and grace. I try to match his good manners and instinctively act somewhat more formally than I would normally. As he takes the seat that I point to, I notice his poise in taking possession of the space he occupies. I now see just how carefully groomed he is: clean-shaven, with a backcombed hairstyle and apparently perfectly manicured nails. He wears several large stones on his fingers, which he displays by posing his hands on the armrests. It is a gesture that seems to indicate a certain sense of entitlement.

CLAIRE: The way in which Rahim presents himself, both physically and socially, has quite an effect on you. I wonder how his formality and sense of entitlements impacts upon the way you respond to him.

EMMY: This is very true. I am always deeply touched by the presence of my clients and find myself tuning in to their mode of being in the world. I make myself aware of how each person affects me and allow myself to feel this deeply before reflecting on my own response. Rahim's presence was quite imposing initially as he, deliberately, projected confidence and poise. I felt briefly as if I might be lacking in these qualities myself,

[1] The case study is contributed by Emmy van Deurzen and commented on by Claire Arnold-Baker

The Wiley World Handbook of Existential Therapy, First Edition. Edited by Emmy van Deurzen, Erik Craig, Alfried Längle, Kirk J. Schneider, Digby Tantam, and Simon du Plock.

> before appreciating the immense and constant effort he was making to hold himself together to continue to create that impression of pristine control. Becoming aware of this gave me an immediate sense of both his courage and underlying insecurity. Having taken the time to let him affect me in this way, I could resonate better with his mode of being and I could begin to understand it, and sense it in myself, so that I could join his world and begin to feel into the words he was going to speak even before he had told me what the issues were.

After a pause, during which we make eye contact, the top layer of his social varnish cracks like a mirror. He slumps somewhat and seems to sink into sadness, perhaps even despondency. As I invite him to tell me what it is that he has come to talk to me about, his face seems to become paler and he looks nervous. He produces a clean, cream, silk handkerchief from his pocket and wipes his brow meticulously. I can now see that hundreds of tiny droplets of sweat continuously form and accumulate on his forehead. An ocean of compassion wells up inside of me, unbidden, as I begin to sense his tension and apprehension. I can literally smell his fear and I nod encouragement with as much reassuring and warm friendliness as possible and he promptly begins to speak in a deep voice that trembles with emotion.

> CLAIRE Your rich description of Rahim shows that you are noticing and recording what you see rather than making judgements or suggestions. Instead you seem to be connecting to his emotions and the anxiety he is exuding.
>
> EMMY Yes, this is true. I search for connection and emotional resonance with the person I am with, trying to locate their vulnerability and the pulse of their life. My observations tend to begin after I have calmed myself enough to focus on the other rather than on myself. I seek to sense their central concern and try to understand their position and way of being present in the world before I begin to speak. My understanding comes from my senses first and then gets refined by my feelings and reactions, and then it is adjusted and corrected by my reflection, and by our exchanges of words and the mental images I am forming and articulating.

The first thing he tells me is that he is a professional man, a management consultant. He says that he owns and runs his own company, in Iran. This statement seems to give him back some of his poise and he completes this self-validating presentation by adding, proudly, that he is part of a well-established business family, with aristocratic heritage in Iran. He briefly looks a little bit conceited as he shuts his eyes, then peers at me from below his lashes.

It is as if he is reminding himself of his caliber and status by referring to the standard of his forebears. In my imagination, I see a crowd of family members standing around him. I nod appreciatively, lightly smiling my respect at him and his family, exactly as I imagine he expects me to do. Rahim smiles back at me gratefully and, after a short pause, tells me that his name means "merciful." He has striven all his life to live up to this name and to the expectations his family had of him. I make a mental note as I am certain this theme will be of great importance later.

He tells me without further prompting that he has come to see me to understand how he can solve his dilemma of wanting to be a good and just person, whilst being aware that he has deeply disappointed and shamed his family. He fears he may never be in a position to see his family again.

CLAIRE I wonder what he means by being a "good and just person," it feels like a dilemma he is unable to solve himself and I wonder what his expectations are of you and the therapy?

EMMY Really good questions which I was dying to ask, but which I decided to postpone till later, trusting that his story would start to reveal the answers to these queries without me needing to probe too much at this stage.

I express my surprise at the rather dramatic statement he has made by saying "aha?" in typical therapeutic mode, signaling my interest and puzzlement. Rahim accepts the cue and continues to tell me his story, describing the way in which his entire family live at home in Tehran, while he has had to flee to save his life. "Your life is in danger? How come?," I say, somewhat dismayed and openly showing my curiosity and my desire to get the details. I am aware that I am struggling with a bit of internal skepticism as well, but I shall soon be humbled and stripped of any such comforting cynical thoughts. Rahim tells me he is an asylum seeker and wishes to remain in the United Kingdom and apply for British citizenship. He is too frightened to return home. "But why?," I say, still puzzled, and self-conscious of my own naiveté and lack of cultural perspicacity. I am now feeling very concerned at the enormous vehemence of suppressed emotion I am picking up in him and I realize the situation is a grave one. I prepare myself to receive a shock and muster both my strength and inner softness.

Rahim takes a deep breath, which he holds on to for a while with closed eyes, before he tells me of the events that have devastated him and his life and that have alienated him from the rest of his family. He paces himself very carefully, going slowly. He constantly suppresses his emotion, but he is nevertheless visibly upset and terrified and occasionally scans my consulting room, as if he is checking for the presence of some unknown threat, as if he suspects there may be hidden cameras or recorders. At first he is a bit hesitant to speak, saying he is never sure whom to trust, but when I assure him of the exact rules of our confidentiality and invite him to tell me what it is that frightens him so much that he has had to leave his country, he decides to take a leap of faith and shares every detail of his awful experience.

CLAIRE Rahim seems to be struggling between needing to talk about his experience and the need for self-protection, wondering whether he can trust you. The leap of faith reminds me of Kierkegaard's view of the self and I wonder whether you used that term because it resonated with you too?

EMMY Kierkegaard did come to mind when I spoke about the leap of faith, as I had an instinctive sense of Rahim's struggle to affirm his individuality in the face of the worldview of the society around him. However I kept this private as I would not want to impose my mental images on my client, so early on, especially not when my personal associations or interpretations may be culturally or socially alien to my client. Meanwhile my intuitive image of Kierkegaard's struggles helped me enormously in my understanding of Rahim's plight.

Rahim at this point tells me that he is gay, avoiding my gaze. I stay quiet as I am guessing that this is not the issue he is presenting. He wipes his forehead again and then reminds me that homosexuality is illegal in Iran. He says that while he has no compunction in sharing his sexual orientation with me, as a Western therapist, used to tolerance, he would not be able to make this statement in Iran. He clearly reads me as liberated but also as needing to be reminded that homosexuality is punishable in his home country. He is right on both counts. I am shocked when he tells me that when he was caught in a homosexual act by the police as a teenager this led to him being punished with 76 lashes. When he hears me sigh in reply to this horror, he says: "it was a terrible thing that broke me." He goes on to say that he abstained from sex for many months as he recovered from this assault. He smiles a little bit when he says that his family forgave him on condition that he would go away for a while. So he came to the United Kingdom to study and this is why his English is so good. He made many friends and he felt free and emboldened to have sex again, and often. He wondered if that was what his family wanted him to do, in order to "get it out of his system." He kept telling himself that he would be able to suppress his sexuality after he turned 30 and when his father decided that it was time for him to return to Iran to marry a young, attractive and eligible woman, who was the daughter of a close family friend and whom he had always been very fond of, he genuinely thought he could go back and turn his life around. But upon his return to Iran things did not work out as planned. Within days he fell desperately in love with Firouz, a much older man and colleague of his father's, whom he had known previously and had thought about frequently when he lived in the United Kingdom. He tells me that this name means: "victorious" and when he says this word, his voice holds a tremor and two tears start running down his cheeks. It takes him a while to collect himself and blow his nose in his silk handkerchief.

CLAIRE The meanings of names seem important for Rahim, as if they signify more to him than just a name.

EMMY This is very true and it is frustrating not to be able to use the real names of the people I have named Rahim and Firouz, Their names connected them very strongly in a way I can't disclose and this link between their names was part of the initial passion between them. They were both proud of writing poetry and wrote poetry to each other around the link between their names as well. The secretive nature of their relationship and these kinds of rituals as well as the sacrifices it involved in the end made the love between them very romantic and quite other worldly and gave it a kind of supernatural, religious meaning. I realized that Firouz had taken on an almost saintly status for Rahim and perhaps this had once been true vice versa too. They had created a deeply meaningful relationship together. I could have challenged this as a form of idealization but was not inclined to do so, as it was evident to me that Rahim's entire life's purpose was wrapped up in the love he felt for Firouz. Any mention of idealization would have tarnished this sentiment and would have alienated him from me.

Rahim now tells me how careful Firouz and he had to be to always meet under the cover of business as they had to keep their love well hidden. Though this mysterious aspect to the relationship was undoubtedly part of the romance, the two of them suffered greatly from not being able to be together more often. Their relationship carried on like this for a long time. But one day, when they were celebrating the tenth anniversary of their first ever meeting, they became careless and spent the night in a hotel together where they had booked separate rooms. The hotel was raided in the night as they slept in the same bed. Rahim and Firouz were both arrested, but Rahim's father was able to get his son out of prison within hours because of his connections in the courts. Rahim only discovered later that his father had achieved his release by claiming that Firouz was the guilty party, while his son was blameless. Rahim felt deeply miserable to discover that his freedom was bought at the expense of a lie. Initially he blamed this on his father, but later in the therapy it became a huge issue for him to take responsibility for the happenings in his life. Only then did it become clear how much shame Rahim was carrying for having hidden behind his father's actions, like a little boy, leaving his lover to die. This was so the worse for him as it had made him not only abandon his lover but also disrespect his father, whom he actually, in good Persian tradition, held in great esteem.

CLAIRE The concept of freedom is paradoxical here, he is aware that he is physically free as he is not in a prison but seems not to be able to experience his freedom. How did you conceptualize this paradox?

EMMY Yes, the paradox was damning. Rahim had chosen life and freedom over death and imprisonment, but ended up with a complete lack of inner freedom and an inability to live his life. Of course it worked the other way as well: as soon as he began to claim responsibility for his plight, he started to make some room for himself. He told me how dreadful it was to think of Firouz when the latter was still in prison. On the one hand his heart was with his lover behind bars, on the other hand he was scared and intensely relieved to be safely in his parents' home. It was bewildering. He felt like a coward. He felt disloyal. This is when his true plight began: the terrible tension of cherishing Firouz, ferociously, whilst at the same time abandoning him in fear.

Later in the sessions Rahim begins to elaborate a new understanding of his own actions. He can see how he chose life over love. Put like this it doesn't seem as offensive. He also sees how he has inflicted a deep wound on himself by choosing to live on beyond the suffering. He believes he has condemned himself to living with an inability to ever truly love again. The price he has paid for saving his own skin is to have become a pathetic figure, he says. He feels that being an outcast is appropriate punishment for his sins. He often states that it would have been easier to die. He wishes he had stayed in prison and had died with Firouz. And yet it is not hard to help him admit that he is also desperately pleased and relieved to be free and to have the chance at living in relative safety in England. It is hard for him to make sense of these contradictory feelings. He thinks it makes him evil and feeble.

As he is working his way through his contradictory emotions he can allow himself to recollect more of what happened. He speaks to me in later sessions of the impossible tension he felt on the day of Firouz's execution and describes the situation to me with great emotion. He trembles as he tells me that on that day he went to the square where the hanging took place and he hid behind some cars, wearing a large cape. He saw how four gay men, including Firouz, were hanged from a special crane on a truck in the street, for all to see. Shockingly, it was a spectacle that many welcomed and applauded. Firouz was wearing a blindfold over his eyes and Rahim, without thinking about it for a second, shouted out to Firouz that he would always love him. At least he had done that, quite spontaneously. It was some proof that he still loved Firouz, forgetting his self-interest. Nevertheless he had made a quick exit after this and had not seen Firouz's moment of dying. Fortunately, he tells me, he had been invisible to the police when he shouted and so he had got away. I point out that his instinct for survival had been really strong all along. He had chosen to live another day. Rahim still struggles with his shame over this as to him it is a mark of egoism and exposes his lack of love for Firouz.

What followed made this conflict in him worse. The next day Rahim had left his home country. His parents had phoned him at a safe house where he was staying to tell him they would not be able to be secure until he had left and had cut all ties with his family. This was when Rahim discovered that his father had told the police that the relationship with Firouz had been non-consensual. That is how his life had been saved: by his father blaming his great love on Firouz's bad behavior and making his lover seem like a criminal, an exploitative man, a pedophile, a pervert. He spits out these words in anger. As we talk about this in more depth he acknowledges that he had always known this must be what his father had said to the authorities. He had simply hidden the knowledge from himself, because it was too painful. He had protected his affection for his father and he had also saved his own face. But now that he faces up to this he feels shattered at the thought that Firouz was executed because of this lie that he had seduced and raped Rahim. He wonders even if he should go back to Iran and give himself up, to pay his debt to his lover. It helps to remind him of the further pain and shame and perhaps danger this would bring upon his family and he decides to remain in the United Kingdom and find another way to pay what he considers now to be a debt of honor.

He weeps at the memory of his parents saying their last goodbyes to him, telling him they will never be able to be in touch with him again. He misses them bitterly but understands that by cutting that tie he has at least saved their lives. It is a small price to pay. He wants them to live without the shame he has brought upon them, he wants them to be free of it for the sake of their other children and grandchildren. We acknowledge that his sadness at being cast from his entire family is in this way, almost satisfying, as it allows him to pay back the enormous debt he feels he holds, not just towards Firouz but towards his parents as well. There is no way to stop him believing that he owes this debt. We go forwards and backwards over it. He will not accept that he is blameless in the face of hypocrisy and cultural habits that are outdated. In his value system that is how it works and he needs to sort it out for himself in a dignified manner.

CLAIRE Rahim is experiencing a number of emotions, which he has previously tried to hold back. Guilt being the overriding emotion and I wondered how you saw that in terms of the compass of emotions?

EMMY Interesting question. From almost the first moment I met Rahim, I was aware of his conflicting emotions and values, but it took me quite a few weeks to disentangle all this. It was confusing to me. He was flipping between many feelings: shame, guilt, grief, humiliation, confusion, disappointment, sadness, and sometimes briefly a bit of anger and resentment. Sometimes there was some hope and pride at the way in which he may have done something right, but only if I pointed it out to him. There was, at first, an overriding and damning sense of despondency and despair. The way I am describing his experience has the benefit of hindsight that we were eventually able to arrive at much greater clarity. But initially he was very troubled and despairing. As you know the emotional compass guides us towards what it is that the person values most. Each emotion tells us how the person is positioned in relation to what matters to them. Rahim's despair over Firouz's death indicated that his deepest commitment was to his love for Firouz: the love they had created together, the closeness they had had. This seemed more important to Rahim than the person of Firouz himself, who now was dead. The love was holy. The guilt was about having betrayed that love. He saw himself as not having been on the level of such a gift, as having somehow purloined it. After a while however Rahim realized that this love they had for each other was still alive in him. It was not lost. It was something they had achieved, something of value he would be able to value and hold forever. Nobody and nothing, not even death itself, could take this away from them. And this was when he began to see the possibility of his own redemption. For this love was reinforced, not annihilated, by Firouz's martyrdom for him. And his personal survival, in exile, was a means of making this love last in the earthly world as well. It was not just cowardice, but a deliberate choice for him to have opted to continue to live his life. It allowed him to honor the memory of Firouz and what they had had together. It meant that while he felt a deep grief at losing the love of his life he also felt a new pride in having risked his own life for this love. He also felt a new obligation to do something with it.

Of course, many greater complexities emerged over the weeks and months of our work together. His values were not simple or straight forwarded. His shame and guilt towards his family remained painfully present. But there were other struggles too. His sense that he had betrayed Firouz and his humiliation in having allowed his father to save him by presenting him as a victim of pederasty both tortured and humiliated him. This suggested that he also strongly valued loyalty, truth, and courage, all of which he felt he had failed in. It helped somewhat when he realized how much loyalty and truth and courage mattered to him, but initially it made him more ashamed. The only way this shame would go away is if he could do something concrete to be equal to those values and honor Firouz in some way. He began to think of collecting the poems they had written to each other over the years and this lightened his life a bit. It was not an easy thing to do, as he had to access some hidden papers, which cost him much effort and created many complications. But it helped him in reclaiming some honor again. And now the shame shifted to a different area. He felt bad about not having been a "good man." And this was hard to deal with, for his father had always treated him as if he were not a proper man and this had humiliated Rahim. This facing up to the idea of what "manhood" was became quite central after about nine months of therapy. As he began to define for himself who he was and how he wanted to live a whole new raft of ideas came to the fore that he had previously hidden from me: his religion and his deeply contradictory personal views about his homosexuality.

Now the hardest part of the work began. For his religion was deeply rooted in him and was in conflict with his feelings, becoming a constant source of confusion and self-recrimination. The enemy was not just out there, in the form of the law and the state, and its religion, it was within himself in the shape of his own belief system that told him he had sinned and was an unworthy person. He was the one who thought he was bad for loving men and for not being strong enough to die for his love if he must love a man. It wasn't his Islamic faith that was somehow to blame for his suffering: his personal values were at odds with his desires. It was his self-condemnation that really was the true enemy, which we had to tackle and tame.

CLAIRE It feels as though Rahim's guilt is the prison he has made for himself. In terms of Minkowski's zone of activity in time Rahim seems stuck in the immediate past, the zone of remorse or guilt.

Emmy That's true but what I began to realize at this stage is that this was not just about the past, for he saw his future as impossible, because it could only ever bring him more of the same guilt and despair. When I first met Rahim he was a man in a state of torment and regret over what had happened. My heart went out to him. He avoided my gaze because he was so ashamed of what he had to say and he was filled with self-condemnation over what he saw as his "weakness and bad behavior." His self-loathing was obvious throughout his tale in that first session. It was an attempt at making a connection between the regretted past, and the uncertain present in the United Kingdom. He was trying to make the past alright by confessing it. There was a glimpse of hope that he would have a chance to create a new future for himself. But later we became aware that this future was always going to contain further contradictions and self-loathing, unless he tackled his internal conflicts. He admitted to me early on that he came to see me rather than someone from his own background and religion because he wanted to have a break from condemnation and wondered if he might be able to take a leap of faith into a different worldview. But this turned out to be impossible. He had to face up to his own worldview and resolve it.

Claire I wonder how you were left feeling and how you formulated his dilemma for yourself, using SEA and the four dimensions?

Emmy I had a strong sense of the complexity of his different values and emotions and the tangle this represented. I was aware of the blockage of his presence in time, and how the past held his attention totally, because he felt his future had been cut off with the loss of everything he valued: his partner, his parents, his culture, and his home country as well as his self-esteem. I was less immediately aware of his presence in the four world dimensions. It took me a lot longer to work this out and I think this was telling of Rahim's predicament as well. From the start, there was ambiguity about his physical presence, as he was so obviously poised, whilst sweating and being physically more insecure and anxious than he wanted to own up to. It took a while before Rahim felt comfortable enough to talk to me about his physical self-loathing, which coincided with his loneliness and guilt-ridden masturbatory practice, which was very private and ritualized and connected to self-harming and hanging. When he finally did talk about this, it helped us understand how the paradox of life and death was woven into his very physical existence. Every pleasure he had must be punished with suffering. His sexuality could only be solitary and had to connect to Firouz's death in some way, as some kind of penance. His life could only blossom when he remembered and honored death. Interestingly he connected this to the practice of sport and he began to take some pleasure in activities like going to the gym and playing rough games of football. This helped much with his shame issues and allowed him to start enjoying other physical activities that were less hard and punishing. He started taking classes in cookery, after we spent a session exploring the things he used to take pleasure in without feeling obliged to suffer. He became unashamedly proud of his cookery and relished telling me about his expertise in preparing a well-known Persian dish (Baghali Polo) for a group of friends from his football practice. This is when I saw Rahim relaxed and smiley for the first time and this greatly reassured me of his vitality and commitment to life.

Socially the tensions were even greater. Initially he shared a flat with a female friend, whom he avoided speaking to. He had no contact with his family in Iran and felt deeply frustrated about this, but assumed it was necessary. Talking about this helped us pinpoint some of his cultural assumptions and I began to understand more fully how his identity was interwoven with his relationship to his family. He could not separate himself from them, and yet he had to. This was like torture to him and it made it very hard for him to esteem himself, not having the esteem of his parents and siblings and family networks. He kept his social relationships in the United Kingdom to a strict minimum. He had some casual sexual relationships occasionally, but this always made him feel terribly guilty towards Firouz. It also brought on self-loathing as he judged it wrong in relation to his family and his religion. His relationships in his job were formal and to him they were of no significance and no consequence. He admitted that he had thought initially that therapy would be the same: a professional exchange from which he could return untouched. The depth of our therapeutic relationship and his own capacity for honesty in it was a revelation to him that allowed him to deepen his relationship with his flat mate and some of his other friends as well.

At the personal level, Rahim was very entangled in his inner contradictions as we have seen. He wasn't sure whether he would ever be able to respect himself for having survived a situation so dire and so damning. He was proud of being an entrepreneur, like his dad, and he shyly admitted he thought of himself as an intelligent and fair-minded person. Nevertheless, this was all erased by him perceiving himself as having messed up his career by banning himself from Iran. As his work caused him much more tension than he wanted to admit he didn't get the benefit from the considerable success he had in his job. He slowly began to accept that his attitude to his work was important and that he was recreating himself by the way he was in the world every day. He realized that many of his everyday tensions could be tackled by changing the way he was at work. It was particularly his painful feelings about the way others treated him that led us to unravelling his hidden and contradictory feelings towards his parents and other family members in Iran. He loved them so much and yet he was so disappointed in the way they had misunderstood and judged him at the same time. He began to be able to speak of his deep feelings of hatred and betrayal. But even then, Rahim would constantly return to his worries that all the faults lay entirely with him. He was the one who was bad and who had failed everyone. He had hurt so many people and it was best for him to stay away from others for fear of hurting and wronging them again. His deep and unending sorrow at his fate had plunged him into isolation. Step by step he began to remedy this.

All of this slowly moved us towards probing his spiritual beliefs and his values. It was clear that he took life extremely seriously and that he was a very devout person, but the extent to which he struggled with the implications of this religious devotion was taboo for many months and he would only really get to the core of this, after exploding against me for pushing him into examining this.

Rahim and I were establishing a good basis for our relationship. There was much trust and affection between us. But he remained tactfully secretive with regards to the subject of religion. I knew he absolutely did not trust my secular stance and was deeply suspicious of my philosophical background, as he passed occasional negative comments on it. We were good at working on the slow process of naming his emotions and understanding their provenance. We were making progress on him immersing himself more in the world and connecting more with other people in it as well. Rahim became more confident in his capacity for being able to plumb and name that darkness in his life. His battle to retrieve some self-understanding and respect was profoundly moving. The moments where Rahim would slowly reflect and suddenly understand something were points of light and liberation for both of us. They always led to him feeling emboldened to reconnect to the world some more.

Even so the taboo topics remained taboo. We never really spoke about his Islamic belief system during the first months of our work at all. If I named it, he would turn his face away from me, as if I were offending him. We both accepted the importance of this tenderness, but we left it aside, referring to it as "his religion," acknowledging it had shaped his fate and life, but never seeking to understand how or why. As our philosophical discussions gathered speed he started asking for reassurance about my ability to accept his faith and some of its culturally specific concepts, such as putting family before the individual. I knew he treasured this and did not find it hard to respect and validate it, even when he appeared to challenge me on not sharing those values. I was less sure than Rahim that I did not share those values, but when I pointed out to him that I was closely in tune with my own family while he lived as a single person in the United Kingdom, he waved this away as insignificant, as he may not even be able to stay.

This was a whole other area of difficulty in working with Rahim, as he had originally applied for asylum in the United Kingdom but had his claim rejected as it wasn't accepted that his life was at risk. He was now working on sorting out his British citizenship by showing his financial independence and this was quite a tricky business that he talked about occasionally in our sessions. Having to work so hard at becoming British made him feel even guiltier: he felt that taking on another nationality was another form of betrayal of his origins. And when he eventually succeeded in becoming British, this made him feel all the more Persian. He began telling me that though he didn't practice his religion publicly, he did so in private. He admitted to me that he had thought that I would disapprove of his beliefs and would try to persuade him to become an atheist. We had some rather vehement debates about gods and religion in which he reproached me for not accepting the superiority of his God over other gods. I saw a side to Rahim that had been previously well hidden. He was hostile and spoke disdainfully as if he felt quite superior to me, a Western woman. We were okay together as long as our conversations were psychological or political, as he respected my academic and professional status and we were united in our desire for a liberal and open society. But in our religious conversations, we hit some very hard obstacles and no-go areas. The conflicts at the ideological, or spiritual, level turned out to be the most difficult for us to master together.

This became most intense and vehement when we started to talk about the religious nature of his sexual relationship with Firouz. One day Rahim told me, shyly, and with some amount of trepidation that it was his physical closeness to Firouz that had made him feel truly close to God and that he could not understand this. This confession emerged from his realization that he had in fact risked himself and everything he had in order to be true to Firouz. I remarked that it sounded as if Firouz had been like the representation of God on earth and this left a deafening silence between us. Rahim told me that my words had struck fear and awe in his heart, for it made him wonder whether he had offended God through his love. He could see that what he had felt for Firouz had offended God, as he had felt strong enough about Firouz to disobey God's rules. Now he felt he had betrayed and abandoned Firouz as he had also betrayed and abandoned his God. But as we remembered together how he had actually sacrificed an easy life for the sake of shouting his love out loud at Firouz as he was dying, suddenly something shifted in Rahim's mind. For a long time he had overlooked this sacrifice, thinking he had been cowardly and stupid and lame in his attempt at being with Firouz at the end of his life. Remembering and accepting that overwhelming feeling of loyalty and love he had felt for Firouz and seeing the sacrifices it led to, finally allowed him to weep for both himself and his lover. His life now looked like a tragedy instead of a farce and a crime. He allowed himself the fleeting thought that Allah might forgive him for loving another man so much. Perhaps his sacrifice had been enough. For the first time he could glimpse the possibility of Firouz approving of him and praising him from heaven above and still loving him rather than feeling disappointed by him. He was certain that God would have forgiven Firouz for having given his life for loving a man. I remarked that if God could be forgiving of homosexuality in this way, this would apply to himself as well. This was an epiphany for him, briefly. For in feeling reunited with Firouz and feeling the possibility of being redeemed by God, his closed down life suddenly re-opened once more in front of him.

It was as if this initial acceptance of redemption made new room for Rahim. He started to take a little more interest in the business he was building up: a business located in London rather than in Iran. He became stronger and much fiercer and more outspoken. I met a different person the day he told me he had started meeting other men, but still he would not talk to me about it. He now came to sessions in jeans and shirts instead of in impeccable business attire. He told me he was going to live a new life in line with the changes he had made for himself.

CLAIRE There seems to have been a shift in Rahim's values and how he understands his culture. But has he also changed his views on religion?

EMMY Good question and one I underestimated. For it soon became clear to me that in spite of his changed attitude, externally, internally the contradictions and tensions were growing. Rahim had not changed his religious views. Far from it. He was just testing himself. His new flexibility and movement enabled him to launch himself back onto the gay scene. But with this came a whole new guilt in relation to both Firouz and to God himself. This lead to a fierce exchange between us.

As I see Rahim struggling with his guilt about his religion all the time I become aware that I may need to press him on the issue that he is not confronting. It seems to me that he is keeping himself in a stranglehold and that he cannot let go of his own judgements on himself. As he acts in a more liberated way, his guilt is increasing and he is tying himself into knots. Rahim has found a group of Muslim gay men who regard religion in a rather different way than he does himself. He tells me that these guys are living lives of hypocrisy. Most of them are married with children and they live sham married lives. They are, unlike him, happily worshipping at the mosque, whilst betraying their principles. It reminds him uncomfortably of his own hypocrisy in the past as he used to worship with his father, whilst thinking of Firouz. He longs for another committed relationship, one in which he can live with another person he loves, openly. He won't go to mosque to worship, nor would he be prepared to enter into a sham marriage. He speaks of his sexual partners with both envy and derision. But one day he comes to the conclusion that they are only free of guilt because they don't actually take their religious beliefs seriously. He could never be like that. He is full of bottled up anger and resentment. He says: "These guys have no integrity. They have no idea what I have been through for my God. Most of them don't even realize that there are countries where you get murdered for being homosexual."

"But **you** do," I say, very quietly and affirmatively. I can feel the portent of the moment heavily in the room.

Rahim's voice is full of controlled rage when he replies: "I do. I have to live with those memories every day. Those dangers and memories torture me. The thoughts hurt me more than the lashes did when I was 18. I still feel like a criminal. They got to me. I feel a bad person and always will. It has been tattooed on my skin. These guys I meet in the park don't even accept they are doing anything wrong. It's just a game for them. Most of them were born in England and they have no idea what is going on, in the countries where their families come from. Not one of them knows how I feel about it."

I say softly: "You know things about being gay and Muslim that they will never know?"

Rahim: "And that they don't care about, don't want to know."

I wait a bit but he stays silent, so I probe a little bit further: "Perhaps they don't want to feel guilty as you do."

Rahim nods and I take my cue from that to confront him: "But you think that it is better that you do know and that you do feel guilty."

Rahim: "I know that my religion thinks me a bad person for doing what I do and my country thinks I am a criminal."

I nod and ask him if he agrees with his religion and country about this. This is too much of a challenge and Rahim lashes out at me for offending him.

Rahim: "Of course I do. I can't just change my mind about that. I am not some kind of gay hero, who can liberate Muslims. I don't share your perverse perspective on the world."

I am somewhat taken aback at the vehemence of his words and speak very tentatively when he falls silent, as he is looking angry and upset. I sense that he has made me into the enemy together with the guys he meets in the park. He is back in hiding and all alone again.

Claire This was quite a challenge! I wondered how you felt about what he said, his judgement on you and how that affected your relationship with Rahim and your own views.

Emmy I always find it hard when a client gets angry at me, even though I may be aware that I have deliberately pushed beyond a boundary that I have previously observed and respected. It takes me some courage to make up my mind to do so, but I do it when I feel that someone is stuck with their own anger and outrage and needs to find a way to express it, safely. I think that I usually err on the side of warmth and kindness and that it is often when I do push the other person into conflict with me that new progress emerges. But I don't stick with the controversy for long. I try to get to the bottom of it without being defensive or unnecessarily aggressive. I make sure there is enough trust and warmth between us before I hazard it.

So I say to Rahim: "Perverse?"

I think my voice is a bit hesitant and tentative, as I am shocked at his change of tone with me. I feel under suspicion and under attack, but I am also aware of the importance of what is happening and at the same time feel a fierce and genuine curiosity to know where this will lead us.

Rahim responds immediately with deep outrage and yet with tearful emotion: "Yes, of course. You are a liberated, tolerant Western intellectual who will try to accept and welcome almost anything. But that is a problem, is it not? That's how the world descends into chaos. Liberal philosophies are the enemy of order and morals and religion." His voice stops but his eyes continue to scrutinize me in a way that has been rare before this moment. It is as if he has overcome his reticence and no longer treats me with kid gloves. He is aggressive and hostile.

My response is genuine and spontaneous: "Ah, I had not realized you were so doubtful about me and my views of human nature." I think I must sound disappointed and a bit hurt, for that is also how I am feeling.

Rahim takes the conversation immediately back onto himself: "But it is not about you. You know that I think that God will damn me. Allah sees all and knows everything. I cannot hide what I do from him. I know you forgive me and even encourage me."

I nod meekly.

Rahim: (looking fiercely at me): "But that just means you will be damned too. There is nothing that will change that."

CLAIRE Another challenge! It feels like an attempt to bring you into the same predicament that he finds himself in. Quite a powerful statement especially accompanied with a fierce look. Rahim is pitting two worldviews against each other. But both views are at either ends of the spectrum. Is this how you saw it?

EMMY I felt a certain amount of fear and an equal amount of excitement at seeing Rahim expressing himself with complete confidence and authority for the first time ever. I knew in my bones, it was good that he was standing up to me and speaking his truth. I also saw an opportunity for us to now speak truthfully about things that had been previously taboo. And yes, of course there had been intrinsic and unspoken contradictions between him marching down the path of existential explorations with me without ever mentioning Islam for a moment. But I felt something else too, I think: I felt that for the first time he was uniting us. I was no longer the one who was in judgement of him, together with God and others. I was a faulty human being, like himself and we were suddenly in the same boat together.

So, I bring out the contradiction that I sense, in the best way I can grasp it in that moment and I challenge him back; "If that is truly your view, why did you come to me for help?" I imagined I would come across as curious and fair-minded in my exploration of what was really going on. But I can't be sure about that, for memory can be rather flattering and self-deceptive. Perhaps I was more forceful than I remember and when I read this now it sounds also quite hurt and self-protective. There is a bit of special pleading in it too. I think that Rahim had truly broken through my poised professionalism and had aligned me with him, in the bench of the accused, for the first time ever. I think this is why it mattered.

My question and my dismay sober him up and plunge him into reflection for a while.

After this pause for thought Rahim says: "I think I hoped you might find a way around my pain by seeing a path for reconciling your liberalism with my religion."

This makes me laugh out loud a little bit, with the relief of not being seen in quite the damning way that I was fearing. I feel pleased that he was expecting so much of me, but I realize that I am unable to deliver. His beliefs are affecting me greatly. I have begun to think that I may indeed be too tolerant and not God fearing enough to work with someone like Rahim. I am deeply aware of my assumptions about the world and how they are at odds with his. I feel doubtful and guilty about this: I am finally feeling the same way he is. I want to be able to give him more than this, but I also know that I can only give what I truly am. And Rahim has just challenged my limits.

Claire The therapy has taken an interesting direction, where you now question your own views on religion and culture; that must have been quite unsettling?

Emmy Yes, as is often the case when therapy gets down to brass tacks, Rahim had definitely got under my therapeutic skin. I felt that I was lacking in cultural sensitivity and awareness, until I realized it was not why I was so unsettled. I felt as if my own morality was in question and I wondered, what I often wonder, whether our society is too secular and lacking in spiritual humility. I always think of myself as a spiritually aware person, but now this was suddenly in question. Far from me regretting this, it made me feel more real in my relationship with Rahim and more truly connected to him. I think it makes a huge difference when I allow a person to affect me and change me. Of course, I protect myself from this until I feel safe enough, then I feel ready to enter a new chapter. As is usually the case when this happens, this episode changed the way we were together very much for the better.

The exchange ended with me noting that we would clearly need to return to this controversy between us, as both of our nerves had been touched and some very important things had been said. I was inspired to start reading about the philosophy and psychology of religion again, something I had neglected for quite a few years, having been more preoccupied with Western philosophy. I realized how much I had to learn. It had been all too easy for me to feel empathic of Rahim's bad experiences whilst feeling safely ensconced in my own worldview and way of life. I had been quite blind to my presumptions about this, complacent in the superior belief that I was on the right side of the equation. I had perceived myself as an agent of liberation. Now that status was in question.

After plunging myself into the Koran and other texts and commentaries, I began to contemplate for the first time what it would really be like to be Rahim and to have been raised in a family and a country that made my beliefs so sacred and so central, that I could not escape from them, even if they were damaging to my safety. I did a philosophical experiment, imaging the Muslim community finding out about my work with Rahim, to help him accept and claim his gay rights. That was alright until I pictured myself travelling to Iran to give a lecture and being outed there as a traitor to God and state. Suddenly my peace of mind was gone and for the first time I truly got it. I got the feeling of being trapped and threatened and of being caught between two cultural realities. I realized I had been taking the idea of religious freedom totally for granted. I had felt that my scientific view of the world gave me a firm base in truth. Spiritual truth took no notice of my certainties. I felt quite shaken.

When I share a bit of this discovery with Rahim at the next session, it leads to a very interesting conversation where he begins to tell me how I should read the Koran. He acts in an almost tutorial capacity all at once and it is immediately obvious to me that he is hoping to have an impact and even perhaps convert me to Islam. Now, I become truly aware of his plight at last. His religious beliefs are such a deep part of him and he feels condemned by his god and torn asunder with guilt and regret. He lives in a persecutory universe where there is no safety. In his struggle between his love of God and his love of men, he loses on both sides and cannot reconcile one with the other.

The idea that he might convert me to his religion gives him more hope than anything we have said to date.

CLAIRE This exchange had obviously had a great impact on you and caused you to think about your own values. It also made me think about how our beliefs are created and how we create beliefs around things that are beyond/unknown to us? What conclusions did you draw from your own self-reflection?

EMMY My main discovery about myself was that my belief in the search for truth is very much my backbone. I had little difficulty with the religious fervor and demands of the Koran. What disconcerted me was how lives were put at risk for the sake of the mundane beliefs that come with that religious fervor. It seemed to me that there is much good in people seeking a connection with transcendence, however they may conceive of this. It seems to me that many people lack such connection totally and that this is a deprivation of something special. I can be moved by the way in which such a connection is sought in many different religions, including in Islam. What I cannot abide by is the worldly consequences of such beliefs, especially not when they seem to me to be based in historical judgements rather than in something divine or transcendental. I could never accept that people are killed for the way they experience sexual love or for the way in which they wish to establish equality between men and women. I cannot picture any god who could be so bigoted, so bloodthirsty and punishing. Having thought this through for myself, I was able to bring the conundrum to Rahim as a heuristic question and he responded very thoughtfully.

He said: "And that's why I came to you rather than speaking to an Imam. Not just because you would understand that moral struggle, but also because I thought that if I could convince you, of all people, of the importance of my religion, then perhaps this would bring me peace and resolution."

I try to grasp what it is he is saying: "You meant to convert me, so that I would condemn you for being gay?"

Rahim shook his head: "No. I meant to save you, to bring you back to God. I thought you would find a way through the contradictions if I did that. For you, you could sort things out with God on my behalf." We both smile, inwardly laughing, knowing this will not happen. That moment of humor brings new lightness in the room.

I say: "How could you save me if I am not in danger and I don't need saving? And how could I intervene between you and god, or between anyone and god? Ever?"

But I become aware that I have not understood it accurately yet and Rahim counters me with confidence: "Perhaps there are things I understand through my religion that you are unable to get." I am still skeptical and say: "Like what for instance?"

Rahim really speaks from the heart now: "Like there is no way to be saved unless we find God again."

I say: "Is that what you believe? That you can't really get through your guilt and pain and self-loathing until you make peace with God again?"

Rahim nods and I am with him. There are tears in his eyes and I think he has put his finger on the essence of his problem. It is not me who needs to intervene. It is him who needs to be back in touch with God, directly for himself and face up to all the questions this leaves him with.

I ask him if he prays and as I expected he says he can't pray until God forgives him. He says: "God won't accept my devotion until I let go of my inclination" and it feels utterly damning. It tells me more about his predicament than anything he has said about the state or his family. It is his relationship with God and his beliefs that are central to his well-being. And now he is beginning to find his way back to open up to that authority that he feels is elemental.

We now talk about the ways in which he might reconcile with God without giving up on his love for Firouz, which, as I remind him, brought him closer to God than anything else. It is important for him to be true to himself, his love, and his God. It is a challenging discussion where we both have to be aware of our very fundamental disagreements about religion. It is deeply satisfying to meet him at the center of his concerns and to gradually find a shared way to speak about the love of God. We agree that what he calls God is the utmost power in the universe. We agree that this power is a fair and lawful power, not one that seeks to punish individuals. Rahim is beginning to explore new ways of practicing Islam that may allow him to be less damning and more open to reconciliation between West and East, science and religion. It is an investigation that I find personally fascinating and that applies every bit as much to other religions as well as to radical atheism.

Claire This feels like a big shift to be able to start this type of discussion. Where you were both able to reframe Rahim's values so that he could find some flexibility in what he believed. Rahim's solution to his dilemma seemed so linked with you. It seems that he needed you to experience what it is like for him before he could explore his relationship to his religion.

Emmy Yes, all of this is the case, I think. And this is always true: therapy is always deeply personal and depends on the therapist's ability to plunge profoundly into someone else's existential predicament and philosophical exploration. Each one of us is having to solve some riddles and mysteries in our lives that might burn us if we get stuck with them. As therapists we need to be prepared to stand in this life or death, truth struggle, next to the other person. My humble investigation of his religion has inspired him to humbly re-investigate his own perspective as well.

This is the crucial moment where Rahim begins to see some light at the end of the tunnel of his self-condemnation. He knows he can't give up his religion and he can't give up on his tormented love for Firouz either. Both these commitments are essential to him. He has sacrificed so much for them that it is now possible for him to imagine he can go through the eye of the needle. He knows another way has to be found and he does so, quite quickly, and all by himself, by finding a different group of gay men who devotedly practice Islam in London. Amongst them are men from Islamic countries like Albania, Bosnia, and Turkey who are much more liberal in their interpretation of the Koran and Hadith. He discovers medieval Islamic verses that sing the praises of homosexuality. He is enchanted. As his views relax so does his whole way of being with me.

Claire Rahim was really stuck when he first came to see you and could find no solution other than condemning himself. His values and beliefs seemed quite sedimented. Yet once he allowed himself to explore this area he realized that there was some flexibility and he was able to find his own solutions.

EMMY Yes, self-condemnation was his initial way of coping with the feeling of having brought death to Firouz and shame on his family. It was his way of grieving for all he had lost. Self-blame was the only way for him, within the framework of his beliefs. All of that had hardened, had become mineralized in him. I think this is why we had to have some violent explosions between us to loosen the stones and rearrange them. Now he felt it was possible to be honorable again, as he had found a way to be both devout and self-respecting. When we discuss this it is clear that his guilt will only be alleviated if we interpret it as existential guilt, that is, if he can accept the challenge that fate has placed in his lap. Something more is expected of him. He has a task to do, not just in terms of easing his own conscience, but in terms of the plight of so many people around the world who are caught in the same trap as he was.

Rahim does not need much help in finding a way forward, once he is able to move into the future once more. He finds new ways of accommodating the holy texts. He learns to separate out the legal side of the Qur'an from its religious side. He decides homosexuality is only to be condemned if it is casual, violent, and oppressive, not when it is loving and tender. He finds new ways of cleansing himself so that he can feel able to show his devotion and go back to pray in a mosque. This brings him the peace he has been so lacking and it becomes possible to start grieving with tears for Firouz, something that was not possible when he felt so guilty. As he weeps for Firouz, he also weeps for his own suffering. We start talking more about how he might come to terms with his parents' actions and his own actions towards his parents, but much of his improvement comes from his being part of a new community of likeminded people. Before too much longer he finds a special friend, who is, like him, from a country where homosexuality is punished severely and who is devout as well. This support is invaluable and changes the therapy a lot. It is clear that Rahim is ready to make a new life for himself.

I realize how challenging my work with Rahim has been and how I often doubted my ability to do right by him, lacking his Islamic background. I feel a deep sense of relief when his new soul mate becomes his companion. I feel happy when I see Rahim's joy in being able to share his qualms and yearnings with someone he trusts, totally.

CLAIRE For me this case highlighted the way in which we are not detached in the therapeutic relationship; we are interconnected beings and therefore we learn something about ourselves from our clients' struggles. I often wonder with my own clients – what do they have to teach me or what do I need to learn? In this case Emmy I wonder what you have learnt, or how this client has changed your worldview?

EMMY Where do I start? I learnt so much about my own intellectual and religious limitations, but also discovered that despite the fact that I am non-religious, I am deeply devout and respect other people's spiritual choices completely as long as they do not imply any kind of violence or condemnation of others. I became very clear about that in working with Rahim and he shared that view with me, in the end. We came together in that way, both learning something new, as is always the case when therapy touches the depth of our shared human existence. There is something extremely satisfying about such human communion as is possible in therapeutic work. I think it has its own, pastoral and philosophical depth that is quite special and rare. To me it feels like a complete privilege and rare pleasure to experience it.

11

Key Texts in Existential-Phenomenological Therapy

Laura Barnett

Introduction

Selecting "key texts" for this chapter has been both a thought-provoking and invidious task, as to make one choice is to exclude another. There are the keynote speakers who have their allocated place at the table of British existential therapists – Laing, van Deurzen, and Spinelli, and there are the many who have been influenced by them. There are, for instance, the various authors in the British section of this book; numerous influential teachers at the two bastions of existential therapy in the United Kingdom: the New School at the Existential Academy and Regent's University. There are also erudite voices such as the therapist and historian of psychotherapy Anthony Stadlen, who, in his Inner Circle Seminars, has engaged in existential questioning and dialogue with scholars, novelists, and other therapists – from Hilary Mantel to Thomas Szasz; and others who, developing one particular strand of existential thought, have straddled the boundaries of existential therapy and other disciplines in a mutually enriching process, as Todres and Madison have done for instance with Merleau-Ponty's perspectives on embodiment and Gendlin's Focusing.

This chapter therefore takes an alternative approach to the selection of "key texts," specifically highlighting those key characteristics that may distinguish it from its American and Continental counterparts, namely: the importance of various philosophical roots within the British schools; a critique of the Freudian unconscious and its processes; and a skeptical attitude to, and avoidance of, the use of psychiatric diagnoses. Contrasting articulations of each theme illustrate the divergence of views that flourish within the British Schools of existential-phenomenological therapy.

This selection necessarily represents this author's personal dialogue with existential therapy as taught and practiced in the United Kingdom, and as such, some texts and topics will receive an emphasis that other authors may not have chosen to give them.

The Wiley World Handbook of Existential Therapy, First Edition. Edited by Emmy van Deurzen, Erik Craig, Alfried Längle, Kirk J. Schneider, Digby Tantam, and Simon du Plock.

Laing: text and critique

R.D. Laing

The following extracts were selected from *The Divided Self, An Existential Study in Sanity and Madness* (1959/1990). London: Penguin; they highlight the thesis and philosophical premises that underpinned Laing's psychiatric/psychotherapeutic work, in particular his work with those to whom he refers as schizoid and schizophrenic persons.

> To look and to listen to a patient and to see "signs" of schizophrenia as a "disease" and to look and listen to him simply as a human being are to see and to hear in ... radically different ways... (p. 33).
>
> The most serious objection to the technical vocabulary currently used to describe psychiatric patients is that it consists of words which split man up verbally in a way which is analogous to the existential splits we have to describe here. But we cannot give an adequate account of the existential splits unless we can begin from the concept of a unitary whole, and no such concept exists, nor can any such concept be expressed within the current language system of psychiatry or psychoanalysis.
>
> The words of the current technical vocabulary either refer to man in isolation from the other and the world, that is, as an entity not *essentially* "in relation to" the other and in a world, or they refer to falsely substantialized aspects of this isolated entity. Such words are: mind and body, psyche and soma, psychological and physical, personality, the self, the organism. All these term are abstracta. Instead of the original bond of *I* and *You*, we take a single man in isolation and conceptualize his various aspects into "the ego", "the superego", and "the id". The other becomes either an internal or external object or a fusion of both. How can we speak in any way adequately of the relationship between me and you in terms of the interaction of one mental apparatus with another? This difficulty faces not only classical Freudian metapsychology but equally any theory that begins with man or a part of man abstracted from his relation with the other in his world. We all know from our personal experience that we can be ourselves only in and through our world and there is a sense in which "our" world will die with us although "the" world will go on without us. Only existential thought has attempted to match the original experience of oneself in relationship to others in one's world by a term that adequately reflects this totality. Thus existentially, the concretum is seen as man's existence, his *being-in-the-world*. Unless we begin with the concept of man in relation to other men and from the beginning "in" a world, and unless we realize that man does not exist without "his" world nor can his world exist without him, we are condemned to start our study of schizoid and schizophrenic people with a verbal and conceptual splitting that matches the split of the totality of the schizoid being-in-the-world. Moreover, the secondary verbal and conceptual task of reintegrating the various bits and pieces will parallel the despairing efforts of the schizophrenic to put his disintegrated self and world together again. (pp. 19–20)
>
> Psychotherapy is an activity in which that aspect of the patient's being, his relatedness to others, is used for therapeutic ends. The therapist acts on the principle that, since relatedness is potentially present in everyone, then he may not be wasting his time in sitting for hours with a silent catatonic who gives every evidence that he does not recognize his existence. (p. 26)

> the therapist must have the plasticity to transpose himself into another strange and even alien view of the world. In this act, he draws on his own psychotic possibilities, without foregoing his sanity. Only thus can he arrive at an understanding of the patient's *existential position*. (p. 34)

Yet entering and understanding the ontologically insecure patient's world in this way may still backfire:

> To be understood correctly is to be engulfed, to be enclosed, swallowed up, drowned, eaten up, smothered, stifled in or by another person's supposed all-embracing comprehension. It is lonely and painful to be always misunderstood, but there is at least from this point of view a measure of safety in isolation. (p. 45)

Laing proceeds to describe patients who seek to create for themselves a strong, watertight distinction between a "false" and a "true", "inner" self: isolating and splitting themselves to seek to stay in control and deny outer reality any access to their phantasy world.

> [Yet] [t]he *inner honesty, freedom, omnipotence and creativity*, which the "inner" self cherishes as its ideals, are cancelled … by a coexisting tortured sense of self-duplicity, of the lack of any real freedom, of utter impotence and sterility. (p. 89)
>
> [Meanwhile] [t]he observable behaviour that is the expression of the false self is often perfectly normal. We see a model child, an ideal husband, an industrious clerk. This façade, however, becomes more and more stereotyped, and in the stereotype bizarre characteristics develop.
>
> …
>
> Indeed, what is called psychosis is sometimes simply the removal of the veil of the false self. (p. 99)

Laing concludes:

> It is the thesis of this study that schizophrenia is a possible outcome of a more than usual difficulty in being a whole person with the other, and with not sharing the common-sense (i.e. the community sense) way of experiencing oneself in the world. The world of the child, as of the adult, is "a *unity* of the given and the constructed" (Hegel), a unity for the child of what is mediated to it by the parents, the mother in the first instance and of what he makes of this. …
>
> But what can happen if the mother's or the family's scheme of things does not match what the child can live and breathe in? The child then has to develop its own piercing vision and to be able to live by that – as William Blake succeeded in doing, as Rimbaud succeeded in stating but not in living – or else become mad. (p. 189)

John Heaton's reflects on Laing

Next, John Heaton reflects on "authenticity" in relation to therapy and to Laing, in all its lived (in)congruences and paradoxes. These excerpts were taken from Heaton, J. and Thompson, M.G. (2012) R.D. Laing Revisited: a dialogue on his contribution to authenticity and the sceptic tradition. In: *Existential Therapy, Legacy, Vibrancy and Dialogue* (ed. L. Barnett and G. Madison), 109–126. London: Routledge.

John Heaton was a close colleague of Laing's (as was Mike Thompson) and Chair of the Training Committee at the Philadelphia Association.

> Should the aim of existential therapy be to make us more authentic? Many philosophers and most existential therapists take this moralizing attitude to authenticity, certainly Laing did, most of the time, as Mike shows. We and our patients *ought* to be more authentic, follow Laing the model of authenticity. I disagree and think the relation between authenticity and inauthenticity is far more subtle than the simple-minded dichotomies of conventional morality. Heidegger, if read carefully, took a very nuanced view of these concepts. He did not think it correct to be authentic.
>
> Heidegger wrote: "*Authentic-Being-one's-Self* does not rest on an exceptional condition of the subject, a condition that has been detached from the 'they'; *it is rather an existentiell modification of the 'they' – of the 'they' as an essential existentiale*". So authenticity is not separated from inauthenticity in any simple way, but is a modification of inauthenticity
>
> […]
>
> We cannot have it as an aim of therapy. Thus, for example, to search for a true self is a fantastical undertaking.
>
> Authenticity is not a position that can be arrived at, possessed, and taught.
>
> […]
>
> Authenticity and inauthenticity differ from one another perspectively, they are not metaphysical opposites, like good and bad. They are foci rather than polarities. They are orientational and perspectival within the structure of human living. They depend on one another, along with other terms and meanings in a person's life. That an authentic person is nevertheless inauthentic is the quintessence of practice … (p. 117)
>
> Laing's hierarchical and teleological attitude to it [the authentic "moment of vision"], his tendency to classify some people as superior, as they are authentic, whereas most of the world is wretchedly inauthentic, is deeply antagonistic to the tradition to which he gave verbal support. (p. 118)

Heaton concludes by giving a characteristic example of Laing's uncanny ability to make authentic human contact:

> He was being shown round a mental hospital and came across a young girl, diagnosed as schizophrenic, who was naked and rocking herself, refusing to speak to anyone, in a corner of her room. He immediately undressed, went into her room, and sat beside the girl. Soon she started to speak to him, a human contact had been made. (p.123)

Emmy van Deurzen and Structural Existential Analysis

In the article from which this passage was taken, van Deurzen explicates Husserl's phenomenological method and, with the help of examples, describes her rigorous way of applying it to psychotherapy. From: Structural Existential Analysis (SEA):

A phenomenological method for therapeutic work. *Journal of Contemporary Psychotherapy* 44 (3): 1–12.

When speaking about phenomenology I refer back to the original formulations of Edmund Husserl. Husserl's work needs to be read and studied before we can fully appreciate how much his methodology can contribute to psychotherapy. His books, from *Formal and Transcendental Logic*, through his *Ideas*, to his *Phenomenological Psychology* are essential reading for those who want to do phenomenological psychology or therapy. If you are just starting to explore phenomenology Husserl's *Cartesian Meditations* is a good place to begin. Otherwise try an introductory text like that of Moran. Phenomenology is not just the foundation of qualitative research, a technique to rival with statistical analysis, but a new way of looking at the world for both therapist and client. Practicing phenomenology teaches you systematic observation and self-observation. It demands that you challenge yourself in your affective and experiential life and that you are prepared to become aware of your usual assumptions, values and biases, in other words, it requires you to see how you make sense of the world and how you situate yourself in it. This is an essential pre-requisite for doing phenomenological therapy. We cannot understand other people's worldviews unless we have learnt to consider our own.

What is Phenomenology?

Though many people have at least heard of phenomenology these days, they often have misconceptions about it. Phenomenology is the study of phenomena as we experience them. It is not, as many people imagine, the study of subjectivity. It is the study of all conscious phenomena: a methodical study of the process of human awareness and the experiences we have. Brentano's concept of intentionality is its starting point. Brentano was both Husserl's and Freud's teacher. Husserl carefully elaborated Brentano's original idea, that human consciousness is always related and directed towards something outside of itself.

The objective of phenomenology is to refine intentionality. As a mathematician Husserl aimed to provide a better method for dealing with human consciousness than mathematics or logic, since he considered these methods to be inadequate in capturing the essence of human experience and its objects.

Husserl observed that any statement we make or any experience we have includes three elements: a subject, a predicate and an object. These are inseparable and constitute the intentional arc of consciousness. Each act of consciousness has a subject, a predicate (which is our intentionality in action) and an object:

subject > predicate > object

As Husserl put it:

"in perception something is perceived, in imagination something is imagined, in a statement something is stated, in love something is loved, in hate something is hated, in desire something is desired etc."

Phenomenology proceeds by considering each aspect of consciousness by setting aside any prejudice and bias through a process known as the "Epoche", or suspension, sometimes better understood as the act of "bracketing" our assumptions. Phenomenology is a search for true observation, by clearing our minds of any obstacles that come from previous knowledge. In this search for truth, we remain aware that truth is complex and can be approached from many directions. Phenomenological observation can never make any claims to absolute truth.

> What we aim to grasp in phenomenological therapy is the complex reality of what a person experiences and how this person makes sense of the world. There is an ongoing loop of verification, to remind us to check our observations against reality. In phenomenological therapy dialogue is the vehicle for this checking. (pp. 3–4)
>
> All our observations about our clients need to be verified with them continuously, until a more and more true picture emerges. We aim for coherence and simplicity. Interpretation is always hermeneutic, i.e. it ensures that meanings correspond to the meaning that was intended by the subject of the experience. We do not translate clients' experiences into theoretical concepts or symptoms of pathology. We do not impose or suggest meanings. It is the client who is the judge and jury. We look for the essence of their experience and know this has been found when they get an intuitive sense of rightness that feels whole, simple, consistent and familiar. We keep returning to the process of verification until this is achieved.
>
> In entering into dialogue we aim for transparency and clarity, viewing each phenomenon from many different angles. We constantly keep clearing and polishing the lenses of our perception. We elucidate, throwing light where darkness is. We aim for greater perspective. (p. 4)

Having explicated Husserl's phenomenological, eidetic, and transcendental reductions, van Deurzen develops her structural framework for the phenomenological process of working with the client's four worlds (physical, social, personal, and spiritual) as well as with time, and here below, space, and the emotions.

> Structural existential analysis has many aspects and many layers, and we do not necessarily apply all of its capacities in each session. What we always do is to be clear and systematic in our observations.
>
> Working with space in a structured manner is one way of seeing to it that we cover all bases of a person's actual existence. Human space is multidimensional. Human beings move and act in relation to a physical world, in which they move forwards towards things, or backwards away from things, where they interact with the material world in specific ways, creating a particular kind of intertwinement and interaction. They also move in an inter-personal, inter-subjective way, where they engage with others or disengage from them. Where they open to some people and close off to others, where they try to connect with some and disconnect from others at the same time as being welcomed by some and rejected by others. They also have the experience of an inner world, where they can retreat into a sense of personal privacy and intimacy and they can be more or less open or closed to that and in which they can move in time, by recollecting the past, focusing on the present or imagining and anticipating the future. They also have a world of ideas, or a spiritual world, where they create meanings and organize their understanding of and purpose in the world. To pay attention to these different dimensions will provide a first framework of organization of the data we collect. We need to learn to observe carefully and systematically at which level the studied phenomena take place and what movement the person is making in relation to this. Are they located in the physical dimension, the social dimension, the personal dimension, or the spiritual dimension? And if so, what are the tensions, the desires, and fears at each level? And how do all these layers affect each other and weave together?
>
> The four relational layers can be represented in many different ways. We can show the layers and their tensions in a hierarchical fashion, with the main conflicts that we have to approach in each dimension (Figure 11.1).

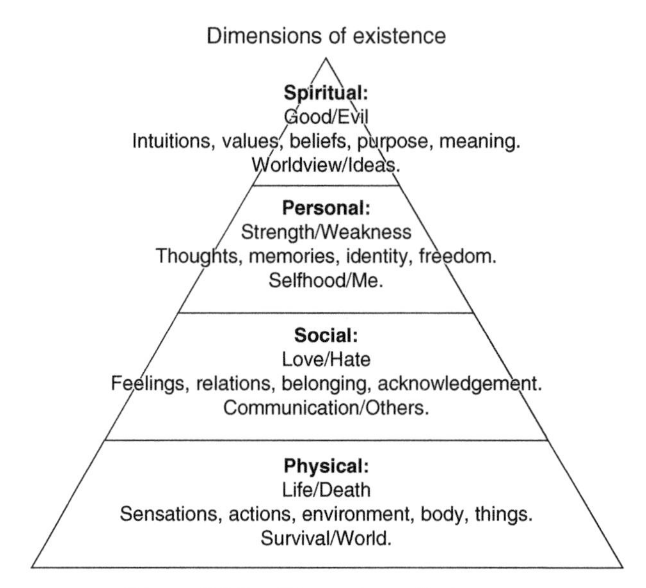

Figure 11.1 Dimensions of existence.

This representation is a simple heuristic device to facilitate our observations and understanding of where each person is struggling. But we should never mistake the map for the territory. Human existence is a lot more complex than this and we face challenges on every level at once, and all dimensions are woven and knotted together.

[…]

It is possible to experience challenges as contradictions, or as conflicts, or dilemmas, but we can also learn to recognize them as polarities and creative tensions. The paradoxical nature of life is pretty obvious. None of us can avoid having to deal with both sides of the equation and we get better at living when we stop trying to avoid the negatives and recognize that dealing with negatives effectively is the only way to experience positives. Learning to balance between opposites to find enjoyment and satisfaction in that dynamic gravity is the dialectical way forward.

Working with the Movement of Emotion, Mood, Attunement, Values and Actions

The same can be said for focusing on the issue of emotion, which is so essential in psychotherapy, as all human life happens in a mood and with a certain attunement to the world in which we find ourselves. Heidegger had a lot to say about affectedness, or *Befindlichkeit*, which is the way in which I find myself in relation to the world. Attunement is elemental and happens in a preverbal manner. Emotions are always already there when we become aware of our connection to the world. Sartre spoke of values as partridges springing up in the world as soon as we act in it. Indeed we cannot live or exist without uncovering these values and we cannot stop feeling the emotions they evoke in us. The movement of our lives follows that of our attraction to the things we value and our repulsion from the things we dislike. Being able to see clearly through the lens of our emotions to the values they relate to is particularly important.

The model of the compass of emotions can help us understand this connection between emotion and value. It shows us where the person is moving from being on top of their value to the bottom of their despair. The model is simple, but needs some practice for full

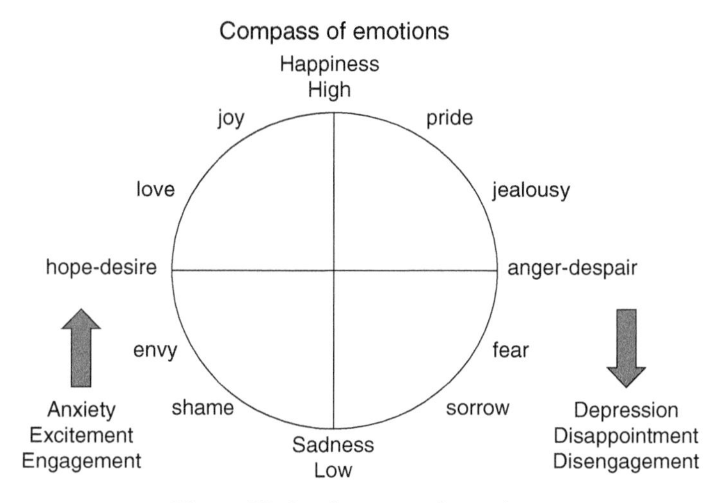

Figure 11.2 Compass of emotions.

understanding. The basic compass of emotions, above, shows the top of the compass, indicating the magnetic north of happiness, which occurs when a person is united with their value. The bottom of the compass indicates the point of greatest loss, when the value is forsaken or out of reach. The movement around the compass is clock wise, with the mid points between ownership of value and loss of value leading to anger, and the regaining of hope of achieving value leading to desire and love (Figure 11.2).

Ernesto Spinelli

This section explores Spinelli's three key Principles of Existential Therapy as well as his concepts of worlding and worldview, and the alternative perspective they offer on the Freudian unconscious and on psychopathology. From: Spinelli, E. (2015). *Practising Existential Therapy, The Relational World*, 2e. London: Sage.

The pivotal principle of Existential Relatedness

At its simplest, surface level, relatedness argues that everything that exists is always in an inseparable relation to everything else. From this understanding of relatedness, every thought, feeling and action experienced or undertaken by me is said to arise not only from the interaction of systems and components *within* me as a boundaried organism, but also from the interaction *between* boundaried organisms (which is to say, between self and others and between self and world). (p. 16)

Far more significantly, what it is proposing is that *seemingly separate beings exist only because of a foundational precondition of relatedness*. Each being stands out in a wholly unique and unrepeatable way of being *and* is able to be and do so through a foundational relatedness that is not only shared by all beings but which is also the necessary condition through which individual beings emerge. (p. 17)

Viewed in this way, subjectivity does not arise or exist in contrast to, nor is it distinct from, relatedness, nor can it be placed alongside relatedness as a separate and alternative mode of *being* and experiencing. Rather, subjectivity is seen as a particular, perhaps culturally specific, emergent consequence of relatedness. (p. 19)

Uncertainty
The second foundational Principle of existential phenomenology, *uncertainty*, arises as an immediate consequence of relatedness. Uncertainty expresses the inevitable and inescapable openness of possibility in any and all of our reflections upon our existence. (p. 22)

Existential anxiety
The principle of existential anxiety follows as a direct consequence of the first two Principles in that it expresses *the lived experience of relational uncertainty.* (p. 29)

Spinelli develops two useful concepts, Worlding and Worldview:

I employ the term *worlding* as that mode of existence which is always-becoming, ever-shifting, process-like and linguistically elusive. Worlding is the experience of existence at a pre-reflective level. As such, *any* attempts to convey worlding can only be indirectly expressed through allusion and metaphor. (p. 58)

the use I make of it [the term "worlding"] should not be confused with Heidegger's, even though some points of similarity do arise. As inadequate and clumsy as it still is, worlding, as I employ the term, suggests an action rather than an essence and, in this way, may be more adequate than other terms that have tried to express this mode of existence.

In contrast, when, as human beings, we experience our existence reflectively, we do so through imposing of linguistically derived, structural limitations so that our experience of existing is essentialised and appears as "thing-based", and hence as separate and distinct, if still relational, constructs such as self and other and world. This structural "thingification" of our experience of being is expressed via the term *worldview*. Unlike worlding, the worldview's reflective experiences of existence are open to direct linguistic expression. However in order to be able to do so, the worldview requires that our experience of existence must be split or separated into discrete entities or structures that retain an adequate degree of "fixedness" or stability in space and time. (p. 59)

At a worlding level, existential anxiety is the response given to the experientially open possibilities of *being*-always-becoming. This experience can be one of liberating acceptance of relational uncertainty that welcomes its de-structuring anxiety. But worlding experiences of existential anxiety can also be terrifyingly debilitating, as in those instances most commonly labelled as psychosis, when this experiential openness is an undesired outcome of the inability to generate and maintain sufficiently stable worldview structures. As an expression of the worldview, existential anxiety refers to the inevitable unease and insecurity that accompanies the worldview's partial and limiting attempts to reflect relational uncertainty from a structural, meaning-based perspective. As such, existential anxiety necessarily permeates all reflective experiences. It is neither avoidable, nor is it an aspect of pathology, but rather a basic given of our worldview experience of human existence. (p. 61)

Sedimentation and dissociation
In its embodied response to the experiential challenges of existence, the worldview may either be open and flexible to its reconstitution or may resist restructuring and continue to maintain the existing structure's experiential inadequacy or inconstancy. Those instances of structural inflexibility can be said to be *sedimented.* (p. 74)

> Sedimentation in the worldview can only be maintained via the strategy of dissociating the challenging experience either from the whole of the worldview or from that structural component whose sedimentation is under threat. *Dissociation*, in that sense, refers to the worldview's maintenance of a sedimentation by its distancing from, denial or disownership of the impact and consequences of experiential challenges upon it. (p. 74)

> De-sedimentation of inadequate fixed stances and re-ownership of dissociated experiences might logically appear to be attractive and sensible options. But what is being missed is that the consequence of such strategies is the destabilisation of the worldview as well as the unpredictability of the extent and duration of that destabilisation. (p. 75)

An alternative to the Freudian unconscious

Spinelli gives the example of Aretha, a client who views herself as heterosexual (sedimented worldview) and has to explain away the incongruence of finding herself in bed after a passionate night with a woman.

Of Aretha's narrative:

> It is that narrative which, from a psychoanalytic perspective, is called "the unconscious", and which from an existential phenomenological perspective, is the narrative of divided consciousness – sedimentation and dissociation. Its value, ultimately, is that it obscures, rather than fully removes, the anxiety that appears when the worldview is challenged by those confrontations with the relational uncertainties of existence that threaten to destabilise its very structuredness by making it too consonant with worlding. Under such circumstances, it is not surprising that our most commonly chosen course is that of maintaining the sedimentation. (p. 80)

> Viewed in this way, symptoms are considered to be principally rooted in socio-ethical tensions arising from the dilemmas of relatedness. *Every symptomatic disturbance is also an attempted solution to the irresolvable "problem" of existential anxiety.* The client's presenting symptoms, therefore, are the starting point for the existential therapist's investigations in that they are the way in to the clients presenting worldview, rather than alien obstacles that attack it and which require expulsion. Any attempt to remove, reduce, amend, or re-shape the presenting symptoms will have is unpredictable impact upon the whole of the worldview. Consequently, any enterprise of symptom removal should be avoided without prior clarification of the co-maintenance of symptom and worldview. As disturbing as the symptom may be, it may also be the one available means by which either the worlding openness of *being*-always-becoming or the structural security and continuity of the worldview, or both, can be either accessed or adequately maintained. (p. 95)

The Heidegger Controversy; Why Heidegger?

While many of Heidegger's philosophical concepts are central to Existential therapy today, in some academic circles, particularly in France and Germany, his name has become taboo, with participants walking out of conferences at its mention. The publication of his *Black Notebooks* in 2014 exacerbated reactions, and caused dismay among some existential therapists, although the facts were already there for all to see.

So before reading Hans Cohn's personal reflections on the controversial issue of grounding therapeutic practice in Heidegger's philosophy, it is important to set out the historical facts. (The following remarks are a summary of Barnett, L. (2008). *When Death Enters the Therapeutic Space*, 19–23. London: Routledge).

That Heidegger had a five-year affair with Hannah Arendt, and entertained warm relations with most of his brilliant Jewish students, who, beside Arendt, included Levinas, Marcuse, Löwith, and Jonas, should not blind us to the fact that Heidegger was a card-carrying member of the Nazi party until 1945 and never explicitly recanted (other than calling it his biggest Dummheit, "stupidity") or apologized. His words and actions throughout the decades attest his cultural anti-Semitism and his allegiance to Nazism: by 1919, in a letter to his fiancée, Heidegger speaks of the "growing Jewish contamination" of the German universities. His philosophy lectures of the 1930s are permeated with a vocabulary of Volk and Kampf, Boden, Stamme, und Blut (people, struggle, soil, root, and blood). After Hitler's ascent to power in 1933, and his election to the post of Rector of the University of Freiburg, Heidegger prevented all Jewish doctoral students of his from gaining their doctorate and forbade all Jewish students from "ever" receiving bursaries. His speeches as Rector are peppered with references to the Führer's "resolve" (being "resolute" is a characteristically "authentic" attitude in *Being and Time*).

As he later admitted in 1948 to Marcuse: "Concerning 1933: I expected from National Socialism a spiritual renewal of life in its entirety." Even in his post-war publications, Heidegger displayed an ambivalent attitude: in some texts, he sought to put a more acceptable slant or alter what he had said earlier, while deceitfully alleging that these alterations were part of the original texts; whereas in 1953, when the Introduction to Metaphysics was published, he did not see fit to expunge admiring references to Nazism such as "the inner truth and greatness of this movement," even though he was recommending this book as an appropriate introduction to his thought.

For existential therapists, to engage with Heidegger's Nazism may be unsettling, but to ignore it could be argued to put bad faith at the center of the therapeutic enterprise.

Why Heidegger?

From: Cohn, H. (1999). Why Heidegger? *Journal of the Society for Existential Analysis* 10 (2): 2–9.

> As a German Jew who was fortunate enough to escape the fate of six million other Jews and had become an existential therapist, I had to face some difficult questions.
>
> The problem can perhaps be formulated like this: can a person's creative contribution as a thinker … be taken seriously when there are indisputable reasons to question or reject his personal actions? When we believe that a person's "self" is, so to speak, of one piece, and that every aspect of it is necessarily reflected by any other aspect so that a person admirable in one way will be admirable in any other way, then Heidegger cannot be acceptable as a thinker. (p. 3)
>
> I came to see this as a very understandable view which reflects our deep desire for harmony and wholeness – but it is an idealistic rather than a phenomenological view. I do not think that Heidegger's political attitude can or should be defended. This is not the place to show its connection with some of his philosophical ideas – and there certainly is such a connection. But this connection, in my view, is not one in which the philosophy

validates the behaviour but rather it is one in which the behaviour is a gross betrayal of the philosophy.

For me the question was, in the end: are Heidegger's ideas worth thinking about, are they illuminating, helpful? Or more particularly: are they relevant for psychotherapy? My answer to this was: yes, they are. For me they were liberating. They made and still make my work understandable to myself in a way in which no other theoretical framework has done. (pp. 3–4)

Basic Ideas

It is often said, and is, of course true, that existential ideas have always been with us and have not had a specific origin. What I suggest and wish to show … is that Heidegger has expressed these in a richer and often more concrete form than they had been expressed before, and that our neglect or over-simplification of his formulations is our loss. (p. 6)

Cohn goes on to explicate the Heideggerian concepts of "existence" and "time":

In conclusion I wish to say something about Heidegger's description of existence as Being-in-the-world. This seems to me, in some ways, his boldest formulation and the clearest opposition to the Cartesian dualism which completely separates the thinking mind from the world

…

The meaning of the "in" in "Being-in-the-world" is crucial: human beings are not in the world as the wine is in the bottle or the driver in the car. The wine can be poured out, and the driver can leave the car. But there is no world without human beings, and human beings cannot be defined without a world.

The world includes other people, it is a "with-world". Being-in-the-world always means Being-in-the-world-with Others. Our relatedness to others is always based on this fundamental understanding and it can take many forms – from relationships to the rejection of relationships

…

This has, of course, deep-reaching relevance for an existential psychotherapy. The therapeutic space to explore is my relation to the world, and the world's relation to me, and particularly my relation to others and the relation of others to me. (p. 8)

This takes the place of an exploration of a structured individual psyche with its intra-psychic processes. There is no need to construct bridges between a person's "inner" world and what is "outside" it – the person is always "in" the world outside. "Being-in-the-world" establishes a context for what we are and do and makes this context inescapable […] If we eliminate the hyphens in "Being-in-the-world", we water down, even destroy its meaning.

[…]

[I can now] remove the question mark from my question. I do not think we have to say "yes" to Heidegger's ideas but I think we need to confront them. When we disagree we need to say how and why. One of his concerns was the relation between what is given and how we respond to it. In existential psychotherapy, Heidegger is a given to which we need to respond. (p. 9)

Response to Cohn

Following Cohn's invitation, I would like to respond briefly to his sentence: "But this connection [of Heidegger's Nazism with his philosophical ideas], in my view, is not one in which the philosophy validates the behaviour but rather it is one in which the behaviour is a gross betrayal of the philosophy." I do believe that, sadly, some of Heidegger's philosophical concepts can be used to validate his behavior.

Heidegger's erstwhile student Löwith reports saying to him in 1936: "I was of the opinion that his partisanship for National Socialism lay in the essence of his philosophy. Heidegger agreed with me without reservation, and added that his concept of 'historicity' was the basis of his political 'engagement'."

As Heidegger's concept of "authenticity," lying outside the categories of good and evil, lacks any guiding ethical principle, his own "open and resolute" choice, as he stared into the abyss of a world in crisis and followed his "hero," qualifies, according to the criteria of *Being and Time*, as an "authentic" historical act – as indeed, arguably, does Hitler's own "unprecedented resolve."

Similarly, subsuming the traditional Aristotelian correspondence theory of truth under his concept of the "primordial essence" of truth, with which untruth is "equiprimordial," allows him to speak of the "inner truth" of National Socialism. And once it is Being that unfolds as truth and "destines," then Dasein is exonerated: Heidegger can try to elude his personal guilt, claiming Being has "destined" this for Germany.

Hence it can be argued that Heidegger's concepts of historicity, authenticity, and truth validate his behavior – and that which his behavior betrayed is not so much his philosophy as his "ownmost potentiality-for-being."

Should we therefore condemn Heidegger's philosophy as a whole and discard it as a suitable foundation for existential therapy? With Cohn, I would argue against this. While I believe that Heideggerian "authenticity," free from any ethical constraints, is severely compromised for therapeutic practice, I concur with Cohn that Heidegger's description of human existence as being-in-the-world is masterly and of fundamental value for the practice of existential therapy today. Indeed it is an awe-inspiring way of conceptualizing and experiencing one's own existence.

Embodiment

The following text shows the impact of the notion of embodiment and its impact on therapeutic theory and practice.

Dr. John Heaton, in an impressively broad-ranging and scholarly paper of which this is but a short excerpt, addresses the so-called mind–body problem. This illustrates how some existential-phenomenological therapists work at the intersection of philosophy and embodied presence.

From: Heaton, J. (2002). The human body is the best picture of the human soul. *Journal of the Society for Existential Therapists* 13 (2): 309–330.

> The aim of this paper is to show that the so-called relation of body to mind can never be understood by psychology. The phrase psycho-somatic is nonsensical and has caused endless confusion in medicine and psychotherapy. Psycho-somatic medicine endeavours to synthesize two things which simply do not exist and the hyphen is a meaningless mark. (p. 309)

Heaton first asks us to take a naïve attitude and "attend rather than think. Just carefully attend to a human being who is speaking or to yourself who is listening. You will find it very difficult to disentangle body from mind." (p. 309)

Then, starting from Heidegger's premise that "The question of the psychosomatic is in the first place a question of method," Heaton turns to Heidegger and Wittgenstein's interest in transcendental logic – the fundamental logic of ordinary language, that goes beyond our understanding of language, is prior to it, yet speaks through it.

> It is our understanding of the logic of language [Heidegger argues] which shows us the need for primordial thinking and this need compels man dispositionally into the basic disposition of wonder …
>
> Wonder simply strikes us, we are moved by it. It is not brought about by our will nor is it caused by any particular entity in the world. It sets us before the ordinary itself precisely as what is the most extraordinary. This is why it is thought by Heidegger to be a basic attunement that disposes man into the beginning of thinking. (p. 314)

And Wittgenstein agrees: "In order to marvel human beings – and perhaps peoples- have to wake up. Science is a way of sending them to sleep again." (p. 315)

However, they argue, we are losing this sense of wonder.

> With the loss of wonder it is as if we are asleep and so we see ourselves and others as ghosts in a bodily machine.
>
> How is it that the basic attunement of thinking is lost? How can we understand this loss of wonder that we had as children? What happens "*after the primordial phenomenon of Being-in-the-world has been shattered, the isolated subject is all that remains, and becomes the basis for being joined together with a 'world'*" (Heidegger). It leads to a transformation of thought. We fall into the assumption that the essence of truth is the correctness of an assertion made by an isolated subject and so our understanding of human being is lost. We move into the realm of know-how and knowledge, of measurement, correctness and consciousness. In terms of the body we begin to think of it solely in terms of extension, what can be observed and measured. Then we are left with what cannot be measured – the psyche – and so we now have a psyche and soma which we can't put together. For how can we unite an extensive thing – the body – with something non-extensive – "ghostly" – like the psyche?
>
> We now become fixed in asking how things are and have lost sight of the wonder that they are. We have lost the human being, the being of the human which is not some sort of combination of mind and body. The sole pursuit of the question "how?" prevents one from seeing where the problem lies. This is one of the consequences of psychologism. (pp. 315–316).
>
> So the body can be measured but the psyche cannot; and even more important we can never be certain about the psyche in the same sense of certainty as is required for measurement. So we get the notion that the soul is merely subjective; that is, any truth about it is uncertain and it is even uncertain whether it exists or not; after all we cannot measure it.
>
> **Bodying-forth**. The soul is mysterious; if it exists at all it seems to be hidden and we cannot measure it. As the soul has been made totally mysterious by thinking of the body

> as being a purely measurable object it is replaced by the mind. I now want to consider the myth of the body as a veil somewhere inside of which is the mind. This myth includes the belief that the mind is an immaterially constituted organ located in the head or perhaps in the brain. (p. 318)
>
> But is the mind hidden by the body or is it within it? In the first we are tempted by a type of idealism so we look beyond the body to find the mind – some anorexics do this, they may try to minimize their body by starving it to reach a pure mind. In the second we are tempted to search within it – to the pineal gland if we are Descartes or nowadays to the brain – to find the mind. But neuro-physiologists who examine and test the brain do not find any soul or mind there, only electrical impulses, biochemical changes.
>
> What is the relation between "I" and my body? Am I my body or am I in my body? I look in the mirror and I see myself – do I just see my body – or my self - but where am "I" that sees "me"?
>
> [...]
>
> My body is not a possession that I can grasp in the way that my money and my clothes are. You could take away my money and clothes and I would still be here although somewhat embarrassed. You could take away many parts of my body and I would still be here but you could not take the whole of my body from me and have me still here.
>
> [...]
>
> My body is not a possession of mine but expresses me. If I move it is my movement, I move myself. I manifest myself. If I point to something then this gesture of pointing to something that I perceive is named bodying forth (*leiben*) by Heidegger. (p. 319)

After asking us to consider the question of body/mind/soul in relation pain, "Is pain – bodily pain and the pain of grief – somatic or psychical?" (p. 320), Heaton turns to "gestures" such as smiling to further explicate bodying forth, and then to language:

> Language is not a body onto which we impose our thoughts and feelings but rather we inhabit language, it is natural for us. Language, once it is there, becomes the form of life that is lived. Our involvement with linguistic expression conditions all our actions and responses. Words have value in their own right, they express us; we are not something behind the words anymore than our soul is behind our somewhere in our bodies. In psychotherapy interpretations often actually distort or trivialize what the person has said, patients may actually mean just what they say! My language expresses me and to substitute a technical language such as psychoanalysis is a subtle way of degrading me [...]
>
> We human beings have the capacity to say, to see, to make manifest, because we live in the world. He/she stands in the openness of being, the unconcealedness of what comes to presence. All comportment as being in the world is determined by the bodying forth of the body which does not enter the indifferent, geometrical space of extension but is gesture. Gesture reveals the ecstatic nature of human being, it helps us recognize the soul. This is why most religions develop rituals, which are creative elaborations of gesture, for they are the best way of reminding people of the nature of the soul. And this is why Freud who had no understanding of ritual, reducing it to obsessional behavior, had no understanding of religion. (p. 323)

In conclusion, following Heidegger and Wittgenstein, Heaton reminds us that:

1. "Being with one another means being-with-each-other-in-the-world. It is not a relationship of a subject with another subject." (p. 328)
2. Listening to philosophers such as Heidegger and Wittgenstein is not about gaining further knowledge but about changing "our way of seeing or approaching things and this we have to do ourselves; they are trying to help us think." (p. 328)

12

Challenges and New Developments in Existential-Phenomenological Therapy

Claire Arnold-Baker and Neil Lamont with Martin Adams, Joel Vos, Chris Blackmore, Digby Tantam, Edgar Correia, Alison Strasser, Sasha van Deurzen-Smith, and Ann Lagerström

Introduction

Neil Lamont and Claire Arnold-Baker

We live in a world in which the political, economic, and social landscapes are constantly changing and evolving. We have witnessed exponential technological advancements, and the development of the internet has become an omnipotent presence in so much of what we do and how we live. We now have unparalleled access to information of every hue and this has changed the way we connect with the world, with others, and to their experiences. This world is very different to the one that Socrates, Plato, and Aristotle inhabited or indeed Kierkegaard and Nietzsche. It is also even incalculably different to the more recent days of Heidegger and Sartre.

The great challenges that we face at the current time – the immense uncertainty and profound insecurity of displaced peoples, wars, poverty, political and social polarisation, climate change, to name a few – are unequivocally existential in nature. Engaging with philosophical questions such as how we live and how we can live well has never been more vital than it is now. Existential therapy therefore, has considerable relevance and potential for helping people to understand themselves, their relationships with others, and their place in the world better; ultimately to find meaning in these confusing and uncertain times.

A key question and challenge for us as a profession as we move forward, is how do we respond to this need and realize the potential of existential therapy in mainstream provision? This inevitably means engaging with the demand for research-based evidence by service commissioners. The existential approach needs to evolve and adapt

The Wiley World Handbook of Existential Therapy, First Edition. Edited by Emmy van Deurzen, Erik Craig, Alfried Längle, Kirk J. Schneider, Digby Tantam, and Simon du Plock.

to meet these challenges and crucially, to meet the needs of clients as well as therapists. We highlight in the first part of this chapter the tensions that are created in balancing political and economic policy with philosophical rigor.

Martin Adams and Joel Vos explore the importance of existential philosophy in helping people to create meaning for themselves. They tackle fundamental questions about our existence; such as how can we lead meaningful lives, and how can we make sense of our experiences? Developments within meaning-focused therapy and its relevance to everyday living are also considered.

A major development for ourselves personally and more recently for the therapy profession, has been the burgeoning use of online platforms and social media as a primary means of communication. As part of this, there has been a steadily growing trend towards conducting therapy online, using instant messaging, video conferencing, and various other applications. This has undoubtedly brought many advantages, most notably, that people are more readily in touch with the world and have greater access to (often less expensive) therapy services. However, it has also associated difficulties, often imbuing a profoundly isolating effect for some by amplifying a sense of remoteness. Chris Blackmore and Digby Tantam elucidate some of the tensions that technological developments have had on our well-being and on our work in therapy settings.

Increasingly the existential approach has developed a truly global reach and is now practiced in approximately 130 countries worldwide. Edgar Correia discusses his research on the British School of existential therapy and how it has been a leading influence internationally and has impacted on the way the existential approach has developed in many countries throughout the world. This is complemented by Alison Strasser's portrayal of the specific developments in Australia.

The final section of this chapter relates to how the existential approach has been applied to other allied disciplines, namely coaching and pastoral care. Sasha van Deurzen-Smith and Ann Lagerström explore the emergence of the existential coaching field and how its inception has allowed the approach to have yet further reach and in a variety of ways.

That existential philosophy is as relevant today as it was to the ancient Greeks, demonstrates the importance and unique need to understand and find meaning in our existence, and that is at the core of being human. These fundamental aspects of our existence transcend nationality, time, culture, and technology and so the existential approach has much to offer as we move forward to the future.

Philosophical and Political Challenges to Existential-Phenomenological Therapy

Neil Lamont and Claire Arnold-Baker

The existential-phenomenological approach has steadily grown and developed, and is now, more than ever, widely acknowledged as a powerful method of engaging with problems in living. However, we should be in no doubt that we face some formidable challenges ahead if our aim is to secure recognition as an effective therapy option with large-scale service providers, such as the United Kingdom's National Health Service

(NHS). Indeed, as several leading commentators (e.g., Deurzen 2010; Cooper 2011; Woolfe 2012, 2016) have warned, we face a crisis for the profession's identity and survival. The very underpinnings of our profession; plurality, subjectivity, and the relational, philosophical, and contextual understanding of human living, are all at risk by a drift towards homogeneity and a "one size fits all" approach, so readily shown by the current omnipotence of the empirically supported, cognitive-behavioral therapy.

Certainly, proof of effectiveness is an explicit criterion set by the National Institute for Health and Clinical Excellence (NICE) for determining which psychological therapies should be provided by the NHS (Guy et al. 2012). In assuming the medical model as a framework for understanding mental health, therapeutic orientations that do not concur – including existential therapy – have been largely excluded from its' recommendations for service provision (Mollon 2010). This is all, of course, in large part driven by economic constraints and the associated political pressures and while we can surely lament these, we must recognize that this is the environment in which we find ourselves and, crucially, one that is unlikely to change anytime soon.

Therefore, the question we must address is whether existential therapy should seek to claim its place as a viable treatment option and so ensure that those who could perhaps benefit most from it have that choice. The philosophical and political dilemma we continue to face is how this can be done while remaining true to our phenomenological heritage and rejection of the Cartesian paradigm. This has caused tensions in the past (e.g., see Hoffman et al. 2012) and surely will continue to do so but this is a defining moment in the history of existential therapy. How we engage with this will shape our reach in the years ahead.

Existential therapy is essentially anti-establishment in nature representing a questioning, critical attitude towards the mainstream view of objectivist, evidence-based, research (Manafi 2010, Miller 2006; Woolfe 2012, 2016). Phenomenological researchers are particularly interested in what goes on in the *intentional* relationship between ourselves and our world (Langdridge 2007; Deurzen 2014). At its core, is the veneration of the subjective lived experience with the aim to expose the hidden essential features of the complex reality as it has been experienced. This is done by examining as many different perspectives as possible, in order to arrive, as objectively as possible, at a subjective truth. While of course the research purpose and data output is fundamentally different for qualitative research, this does not mean it should be considered any less robust. Indeed, assuring the quality of future qualitative research will be of fundamental importance if we are to protect the existential interests of our clients.

However, while some have pointed to an invigorated embrace of post-modernism over the past decade (e.g., Smith 2008), we would be unwise to anticipate a paradigm shift anytime soon. From his interviews with several influential policymakers, Mick Cooper found that at the senior levels, there was "*no postmodern turn just around the corner*" (2011, p. 10); Far from it. This is further compounded by the gravitas afforded to randomized control trials, the bedrock of traditional science research, in determining the commissioning of empirically supported treatments (Elkin 2007; Cooper 2011; Frost 2012).

However, we must also remember, that while some approaches have been more extensively researched than others, and most notably cognitive-behavioral ones, this does not mean that those that have not yet been researched are less effective. In fact, comparative studies have revealed in many ways parity in beneficial outcomes across orientations (Norcross 2002; Watson et al. 2003; Cooper 2008). What we do know, however, is that the demands for proof of efficacy and value for money means that only with such evidence will an approach deemed to be fit for purpose.

Our challenge then, if we are not to confine existential therapy to the realms of private practice, is how to enter the fold. Hoffman et al. (2012) suggested that rather than dismissing evidence-based practice (EBP) on practical or epistemological grounds, existential therapists should be actively finding ways in which to engage with EBP. This requires a debate on how we could define EBP in a broader, more inclusive manner. Neimeyer proposed an interesting alternative solution at the Existential World Congress (2015), turning the focus towards practice-based evidence by investigating what defining features expert practitioners possess and producing guidelines for best practice. Both have demonstrated the evidence-based practice of existential therapy. To be able to compete in the world of service provision we may also need to accept the pragmatic demands for time-limited existential therapy (Strasser and Strasser 1997; Langdridge 2013). In all cases, the key will be in demonstrating their effectiveness through outcome-focused research while of course ensuring we avoid any homogenization of the therapy itself.

The point here is that we need to think creatively about how we engage for the benefit of expanding the choice available to those in need. We argue that it is our ethical commitment to our profession that compels us to do all that we can to ensure that existential therapy is being extensively researched and ultimately included as an appropriate treatment option, where it can be of particular value. For this, it must be shown to be effective and that requires an acknowledgement that the qualitative research we do needs to be robust and outcome-based if we want those with influence to take notice.

A growing number of researchers are beginning to address the dearth of existential outcome research (e.g., Vos et al. 2015). There is also an interesting new development in showing that the benefits of existential therapy are educational and personal in nature rather than symptomatic or medical (Sorenson 2015). This is an important new exploration, as existential therapy aims to address a person's whole being, enabling them to gather a greater understanding of what may be possible for them to change in their life. By transcending the narrow scope of other therapies and showing our capacity to reframe problems in living in a way that is beneficial to both individual and society, we shall establish this paradigm all the more firmly.

With the development of dedicated existential doctoral programs in the United Kingdom and with new initiatives such as the Existential Research Academy (ERA) emerging, there is certainly considerable momentum. It could not be a more important time than now for us to engage and show the potential of existential therapy and what it can offer this anxious world. We are confident that the existential approach as it continues to evolve and develop to meet the particular needs of the twenty-first century, will make a very substantial and necessary contribution to the therapy profession, and in doing so, to social justice.

Meaning and existential-phenomenological therapy

Martin Adams and Joel Vos

Existential-phenomenological therapy is fundamentally interested with meaning and meaning-making, evident in that most fundamental question for us all: *How can I live a meaningful life?* A question that cannot be conclusively answered once and for all for it is an ongoing and ever-evolving exploration (Deurzen 2008). We are all in the same boat. That there are different strands within existential-phenomenological therapy in how to attend to this most fundamental quest is no surprise. This is both a strength and also a challenge since paradoxically a dialectical consideration of the ambiguity of meaning is more valuable in the long run.

Phenomenologists have described how individuals in modern society hope we can ascribe ready-made meanings, just as from the shelves in a shop (Vos 2014). Clients may become frustrated on discovering meaning cannot be that easily accessed. Frankl (1988) warned us not to envision meaning as discrete objects from which we could choose one or other, since it would deny the totality of our socially, historically, and embodied lived experience. This technical approach only presents meaning as steps or goals, and not as process (Frankl 1988; Vos 2014). There may be similar tensions between therapeutic practices aiming to investigate meaning primarily through successive descriptions, and those aiming to investigate meaning interpretively. The former tends to align itself with the principles of descriptive phenomenology, the latter with interpretive phenomenology. While there are valuable distinctions to be made and opportunities for productive dialogue it is important to note that they have phenomenology in common.

There has been debate between existential-phenomenological therapists about the metaphysical foundations of meaning. For example, the term meaning has been criticized for being too essentialist. Could phenomenological practices help us identify relatively stable meanings like Husserl and Heidegger suggested ("eidetic reduction")? Could we differentiate between ethically better and worse meanings? Is self-transcendence possible? Or instead, is the term meaning merely an adjective to describe fluctuating states? Existential-phenomenological practices seem to focus more often on the process than on providing metaphysical answers. Therefore, practitioners may merely offer clients the opportunity to phenomenologically examine and unpeel what matters to them. This process itself seems beneficial to clients, and it may be irrelevant for practices whether the result of this process is that clients identify core meanings or not (Vos 2014, 2016). This implies strong self-reflection and reflexivity from therapists, to bracket their metaphysical assumptions when working with clients.

Another issue for development is highlighted in the distinction between skills and techniques. Put simply, techniques are tools to be used whereas skills are owned ways of being that will inevitably incorporate discrete types of interventions but do so in ways that are sensitive to the qualities of the therapeutic relationship (Deurzen and Adams 2016; Adams 2016). This distinction relates to Heidegger's (1962) distinction between objects in the world as the present-at-hand; nearby, and ready-to-hand; owned (Dreyfus and Wrathall 2014). Coming with its increasing popularity, a challenge for the integrity of existential therapy is to ensure that therapeutic practice remains anchored in the owned dialogical skills of phenomenology and do not become manualized into a set of mutually dehumanizing techniques. This point is particularly relevant as models of focused short-term work are developed. Meta-analyses of existential therapies support the above view of skills as owned ways of being that incorporate specific focused interventions. Existential practices that are merely based on phenomenological and experiential foundations have little effectiveness, while practices that (also) explicitly and systematically address meaning largely improve the quality of life and psychological well-being of clients (Vos, Craig, and Cooper 2014). Thus, it has been suggested to combine meaning-centered, phenomenological and relational skills in our practices and training (Vos 2016). More reflection is needed on how such a combination would look.

Another area that is significantly under-represented in current existential-phenomenological practice is a consideration of existential developmental processes from birth through to death. It is curious that this has been overlooked because with the exception of Heidegger, whose project was ontological and who had little personal or professional interest in biography, both Kierkegaard, Nietzsche, Sartre, Beauvoir, and Merleau-Ponty all wrote about it and considered that how things come to be the way they are to be a philosophical problem and Beauvoir is known particularly for her work on both gender and old age. A consequence of this has been that existential-phenomenological theory and practice has been middle-aged adult-centered. There are however some exceptions to this, Scalzo (2010) has written on work with children and Adams (2013, 2018) has developed an existential model of human development than can be used in therapeutic practice.

As noted and questioned by Langdridge (2013) among others, another strand which is present in much existential philosophy, particularly Sartre and Beauvoir, but curiously is yet to find its way into existential-phenomenological practice is that of the wider world of political policy and socio-economics. Issues of national identity, conflict, global ecology, and genderized politics affect us all. The only difference between the person of the therapist and the job the therapist does is in the constraints of the setting (Deurzen and Adams 2016). The personal, the philosophical, and the political are intertwined in each person's being-in-the-world. If existential-phenomenological therapy is going to stay true to its philosophical roots, and not become simply another therapeutic modality, it will need to find a way to incorporate the political dimension to its practice. The core of this is the skill of reflexivity; the ability to be aware of how our own meanings and historical-social positions inevitably influence our therapeutic relationships.

Online Developments

Chris Blackmore and Digby Tantam

Implications for well-being

The advent of the internet, and its integration into everyday life, has taken place at a dizzying rate. The theory and practice of psychotherapy has struggled to keep pace with the rate of change. The impact of being online on our ways-of-being-in-the-world is still being considered, and we don't as yet have a clear sense of how to characterize this new state of being-in-a-virtual-world. But one of its key features is the connectivity brought about by ever smaller and ever faster devices, connected to the World Wide Web, and our increasing use of these for business, pleasure, and education.

The benefits of this connectivity are many, but the harms have taken longer to appreciate. Whilst the use of social media may be great for keeping in touch with a wide range of people, this also allows us to compare our experience with many others, and there is evidence that such social comparison is not always a good thing, for example, the association between social media use and depression among US young adults (Lin and Utz 2016) and the relationship between the amount of time spent on Facebook and depressive symptoms as mediated by Facebook social comparisons (Steers and Wickham 2014). Similarly, Facebook use appears to predict a decline in subjective well-being in young adults (Kross et al. 2013).

There are many other ways in which people are using the internet for malicious purposes, such as cyberbullying, fraud, and hacking. Some of these hazards are made possible by the ways that being online changes behavior and social dynamics; others are examples of malicious actions, mediated by computers, intended to cause disruption and distress. Any of these hazards can have implications for mental health, and for how existential therapy can respond.

New conceptions of intersubjectivity

There is no doubt that the internet has vastly widened our ability to access other people's range of experience and viewpoints. From the safety of our homes, we can view video footage and pick up live messages on social media from people in places around the world affected by war, revolution, famine, or flood. This content was sometimes available previously through TV news programs, but now we can hear directly from people themselves in situ. We can also search for, and find, people engaging online in dialogues on virtually any topic we care to imagine. Thus our access to others' experience has increased since the arrival of the internet in the 1990s, and along with it, our ability to gain an insight into their world.

But is this really inter-subjectivity? It is a relationship of mental connection, using the kind of connectedness that is termed "theory of mind" or "cognitive empathy." Inter-subjectivity in the phenomenological tradition is embodied (Taipale 2015). Although players in a virtual game may incorporate their avatar into their own bodily schema and it has been claimed that this follows Merleau-Ponty's scheme (Crick 2011), the avatars of other players are not incorporated as actual bodies as in face-to-face interaction. There is no "relationship tissue" (Verissimo 2012) that links avatars together, as it links together actual bodies. Inter-subjective experience in a game therefore rests on simulations of the other plays via theory of mind, rather than the immediate knowledge that comes from what one of us calls "the interbrain."

New conceptions of authenticity

In the early days of the internet, it was thought by some that the possibilities of disembodiment online would have huge implications for people's ability to adopt personas, change identity, and even alter their consciousness, and whilst these may not have come to pass as anticipated, there are a number of ways in which lack of physical co-presence does seem to impact upon human behavior.

One important facet of the experience of being online is the absence of what Sartre terms "the look," that is, "feeling the scrutiny of others and being influenced by the awareness of how what one does looks to them" (Tantam 2006, p. 373). This raises questions about authenticity – is the person I am talking to online who I think they are? It can also be a disinhibiting factor – "The absence of the look may enable a person to talk about their problems to another person on the internet although they would feel too ashamed to talk in the flesh" (Tantam 2006, p. 373). "The look" induces self-consciousness and the possibility of shame, but "the absence of a normal level of shame may be one factor that leads to the disinhibition (Suler 2004) that is characteristic of internet users" (Tantam 2006, p.373). However, invisibility/ lack of eye contact may have a negative effect on people's ability to understand one another, and conflicts due to misunderstandings (lack of contextualizing non-verbal information) are not only more common online, but harder to clear up online without the reassurances provided by language (Munro 2012). As Balick notes, "unlike with online relating, interpersonal cues in offline relationships provide a context in which a lean towards intersubjectivity is encouraged" (2013, p. 102).

Along with the ability to connect to more people has come the realization that these connections may be of a different nature. Social media platforms use terms such as "friends" or "followers," but these may be people we have never met in person, and indeed people we would not have any connection to were it not for the internet. Given that the internet often affords a high degree of control over our presentation of self, and how we enable others to perceive us, this naturally raises questions about the authenticity of online interactions, in our minds and in others.

New challenges for existential therapy practice

Existential therapy views well-being, inter-subjectivity, and authenticity as key issues to be considered on the journey to meaning, and the changes to these brought about by the internet poses a challenge for the existential therapist who will need to understand these dynamics and the way they change therapy. For the existential practitioner who decides to work online, there are challenges to face, including how to establish a trusting relationship with someone who is not physically co-present. The therapist also needs to know that the other person is who they claim to be, and the same is true for the client. Once identity has been established, the therapist and client need to understand how the online medium changes their experience of one another, and themselves; can one trust in the authenticity of the other? One of the challenges of working online is also an opportunity, that of the potential for disinhibition, and the possibility for discussion of topics which would otherwise not be explored due, for example, to feelings of shame. The internet can facilitate discussion of these issues, but with that potential comes the possibility for harm through over-sharing.

There are also challenges for face-to-face therapy, such as the client coming to therapy with pre-conceived notions of what therapy is, or about the therapist themselves. This may not be specific to the era of the internet, but information about conditions, therapeutic approaches, and therapists is so much easier to access now. Clients may even find it harder to be "present" in therapy, having got so used to their online presence being ever-present, and super-imposed on their embodied presence. Some of the issues that clients face in therapy are specifically related to the internet, such as the impact of social media, the possibility of exclusion and bullying, and so on. And in a more general sense, clients may find themselves lost in this new world of online interactions, and struggling to find meaning in an online world.

Edgar Correia and Alison Strasser

Authors have claimed the influence of the British School on existential therapy's evolving worldwide scene (Cooper 2012, 2017; du Plock and Deurzen 2015; Groth 2000). But no systematic evidence has been presented to substantiate this claim. A brief historical account may help us to understand the nature of the British School's influence and data from a worldwide study which looked at, amongst other things, what existential practitioners consider their most influential authors and texts, may help us to clarify this influence on an evidence-based footing.

The existential and phenomenological traditions in psychiatry and psychology were already present and well established in several European, North- and Latin-American countries, long before the arrival of the British School (see Besora 1994; Halling and Nill 1995; Martínez and Signorelli 2014; Spiegelberg 1972; Straus 1959). But most of these developments were focused on the phenomenological and anthropological understanding of human (psychopathological) experience (Besora 1994; Spiegelberg 1972). The psychotherapeutic practice was not their main concern (Straus 1959) and, where it was, the existential intervention was not considered a truly independent therapy (e.g., Yalom 1980), with its own therapeutic techniques (e.g., Boss 1963), that could be taught and applied.

In the 1980s, when the existential popularity in therapy seemed to be declining (Norcross, Prochaska, and Farber 1993), a heterogeneous group of existential therapists (Cooper 2003) developed what is nowadays one of the most dynamic existential therapy schools in the world (du Plock and Deurzen 2015; Groth 1999; Martínez and Signorelli 2011): the British School of Existential Analysis (Cooper 2003). Despite an already long tradition of existential thought, the British School's founders did not identify themselves with the psychotherapeutic practice of the different existential schools until that point (Deurzen 2015). They aimed for a new and alternative therapeutic approach – based in existential philosophy – that could be taught and applied (Deurzen 2015). This concern for a psychotherapeutic applicability of the existential tradition is probably the most revolutionary aspect of the British School, as its European predecessors were, until that point (except for Viktor Frankl), more concerned with the psychological-analytical dimension of existential therapy.

Since the late 1990s until now, practitioners worldwide – many perhaps disappointed with mechanistic and reductionist visions of the prevailing psychotherapeutic systems – have been attracted by the applicable existential-phenomenological perspective presented by the British School. These contemporary clinical psychologists, counsellors, and psychotherapists are not so interested in a purely theoretical existential-analytical psychological understanding, but on a trainable and practicable therapeutic intervention; the British existential school appeared as a practice-minded school focused on the therapeutic work.

Evidence of the impact of this applicable existential-phenomenological school can be found in Correia's worldwide study of existential practitioners (Correia 2016; Correia, Cooper, and Berdondini 2015, 2016). Almost 1000 participants, from 48 countries affiliated with different existential schools and with different geographical and cultural roots, were asked to identify the authors and texts on existential therapy that had most influenced their practice. Data showed that six UK-based authors were among the 20 most influential, with nine of the 20 self-reported most influential texts of their authorship (Correia et al. 2015, 2016). Two leading figures of the British School – Ernesto Spinelli and Emmy van Deurzen – were, respectively, the third and the fourth self-reported "most influential author," their books being reported as the third, fifth, sixth, and seventh most influential (Correia et al. 2015, 2016). These authors were among the six most influential, independent of respondents' experience (years of practice), training (having had, or not, institutional training in existential therapy), or continent of practice, except for the American continent and in particular for South America, were these authors were barely cited (Correia 2016).

Data from Correia's (2016) study indicated that the British School was considered influential by Asian practitioners, but it was the Australian respondents who cited the most UK authors, with Ernesto Spinelli and Emmy van Deurzen accounting for 43.8% of their choices, and four of their six most influential books being from the British School. Since 1994 the Existential-Phenomenological approach has become a small but growing field of psychotherapy in Australia. The existential approach is now included in most training programs and is offered as an elective in some of the larger colleges.

The Australian school emanated from Alison Strasser's training at Regent's College, London: one that seamlessly intertwined the Existential philosophies of Sartre, Heidegger, Boss, Merleau-Ponty, and other, as taught by Emmy van Deurzen with the Phenomenological understanding as described by Husserl and imparted by Ernesto Spinelli. More recently, it has incorporated the influence of narrative therapy with its construction and reconstruction of our personal stories; the notion of hope to counter the pervasive presence of existential despair; the putting into practice of the "both/and" concept that encompasses the necessity of living with the paradoxical nature of life. The theme of Time and how we each live with the knowledge of endings and our final death is also a strong component of the teaching philosophy.

Other therapists in Australia arrived at an Existential approach to therapy via the study of philosophy and, similarly, base their professional practice on "helping people with their challenges in living." This work has a focus on making sense of the client's life, the human condition within specific social, economic, and political contexts. It is an approach that is strongly connected to the cultivation of meaning and to deepening one's understanding of, and relationship to, values.

European respondents' choice of authors and texts in Correia's (2016) research were similar to the overall results (see above), with the British authors being considered among the most influential in almost every country (North – including the Baltics and Russia, South and some Eastern European countries), except for the German-speaking countries (Central Europe) where British influence was residual and Viktor Frankl's Logotherapy and Alfried Längle's Meaning Centered therapies predominated (Correia 2016).

The influence of the British School on North American existential practice was present but minor, according to Correia's (2016) data and, except for Mexico, was almost non-existent in Latin American countries. South American countries, in particular Argentina and Brazil, developed in the 1970s and 1980s (respectively) their own independent existential-phenomenological schools (Martínez and Signorelli 2014, 2015), which have been dynamic and prolific, but somehow isolated, probably due to linguistic and cultural barriers, until the First World Congress of Existential Therapy.

Several authors have addressed the relevance of the British School on the worldwide panorama of existential psychotherapy. Both historical and contextual reasons explain this phenomenon, and recent empirical data seems to corroborate this claim.

Coaching and Pastoral Care: What is Existential Coaching?

Sasha van Deurzen-Smith and Ann Lagerström

What is it to be a human being? What is it, in particular, to be me? And how can I live a meaningful life? Existential coaching is a way of exploring such key questions whilst also addressing more practical life concerns. Described by van Deurzen (2012) as a "focussed conversation dealing with specific issues, conflicts or dilemmas," coaching is a forum for robust and mentally healthy clients to explore pressing issues and to work towards specific goals. Originally used to create more psychological awareness in sport, coaching developed into a corporate activity designed to help workers and executives to flourish and address specific problems in business. Eventually, this developed into what is often referred to as life coaching, and various niche markets such as career coaching and redundancy coaching.

Existential coaching, on the other hand, has the same roots, and attends to the same kinds of questions as existential psychotherapy. Deeply rooted in philosophy and phenomenology, it not only concentrates on the client's expressed immediate goals, but also on the subtle philosophical questions that they are asking, of which they may be less aware. To explore the client's dilemma by means of existential perspectives, and couple that with understanding of the client's way of living and their unique worldview, we can broaden and sometimes even change the outcome of the coaching. This takes the focus away from purely practical or cognitive goals, and into the realm of meaning-making, psycho-education, and philosophical awareness of one's life.

Existential coaches are familiar not only with traditional coaching techniques but also with extended philosophical knowledge. This knowledge can be used to help the client examine his or her lifestyle and perspectives, not only in terms of the current situation, but also in relation to the fundamental question of what it is to be a human being. Introducing traditional existential dimensions, such as freedom, meaning, relatedness and uncertainty presents new dimensions that can give the client new angles on old questions, and can lead to unexpected solutions to problems that the client may have assumed were merely of a practical nature.

From an existential perspective, having dilemmas during your lifetime is a natural part of being a human. Some dilemmas are profound and hard to handle and may require professional psychotherapy or even in some cases psychological or psychiatric intervention. This does not mean that coaching issues are by nature superficial, or somehow less profound than traditionally psychotherapeutic ones. Am I doing the right thing? How can I handle my relationship? Can I do what I want? What does it mean to lead other people? Such questions when explored together with a well-educated existential coach can provide deep insight into an everyday problem, and create new pathways into a more authentic, considered life.

Settings and Applications

Kim is a manager for a smaller company and is concerned about the question of authority. What right does she have to govern others?

Tim's life is hectic. How can he handle demands from his job and his partner, while also dealing with his own deep longing for solitude?

Sam is diagnosed with autism. How can she understand herself in relation to others?

Existential coaching is used in many different ways. Traditional coaching issues such as leadership, career planning, conflict, and personal dilemmas can all be explored from an existential perspective in order to gain new insights. But existential coaching is also used to address areas that coaches will often avoid, such as fundamental existential questions about death and meaning, emotionally charged situations, or specific client groups such as adults with autism.

Practitioners working existentially will sometimes combine their approach with more traditional coaching techniques such as NLP, mindfulness, or positive psychology. Others may take inspiration from more specific existential approaches such as ontological coaching or Logotherapy.

The first initiatives in existential coaching practice began at the start of the twenty-first century, led by established existential psychotherapists. Emmy van Deurzen, Freddie Strasser, Monica Hanaway, and Ernesto Spinelli made the first strides in Europe, and Alison Strasser established training and delivery in Australia. Today, several international institutions offer training in existential coaching, from short courses to certification programs and even post-graduate degrees, creating a global community of existential coaches from the United Kingdom, Sweden, Israel, the United States, and Australia to name a few.

Literature on existential coaching is scarce but is expected to grow in the near future. Van Deurzen and Hanaway (2012) and Hanaway and Reed (2014) form the key books on the subject, in addition to chapters by Spinelli in *The Complete Handbook of Coaching and the Handbook of Coaching Psychology*.

The Future of Existential Coaching

Existential coaching, with its aim to help the client to a deeper understanding of his or her dilemma and possibilities, is starting to establish a unique position in countries across the globe as an alternative to traditional coaching, whose foremost objective is to help the client to achieve a specific personal or professional goal in an as effective way as possible.

The coaching profession is still woefully unregulated, and needs careful, considered development as the field progresses. Current initiatives from the United Kingdom and Sweden to implement an international accrediting body for existential coaches is evidence of the growing need for regulation, ethical codes, and a pool of knowledge and professional expertise. That sort of development is essential for the progress of existential coaching, and will support its establishment as a robust, thoughtful, and professional modality.

In Sweden, a certificate in existential coaching has been introduced through collaboration between The Institute of Existential Practice and The Society of Existential Psychotherapy. The New School of Psychotherapy and Counselling, based in London, introduced an MA in Existential Coaching, for the first time giving professionals the possibility to gain a niche post-graduate qualification in the field. Furthermore, the introduction in 2017 of the first ever MA in Existential and Humanist Pastoral Care (also delivered by NSPC) is an exciting new development in the field. Inspired by the humanist chaplaincy movements in the United Kingdom and the Netherlands, and the existential coaching movement in the United Kingdom, the program will create a place for existential coaching skills to be used across a variety of sectors, from healthcare and education, to the armed forces and prison services. Existential chaplains who use philosophy rather than religion will provide pastoral support and guidance, where previously only religious alternatives were available.

In time, as the coaching industry increases in popularity, existential coaching could stand at the forefront as a method of developing skills, strategies, and a philosophical understanding of one's life that promotes the sort of philosophical and psycho-education that is slowly becoming more valued in society. Existential coaching is a way of training us to cope with the complexities of being human before we reach a crisis point. It is a way of approaching life's everyday dilemmas in a more considered, reflective, and philosophical way. It promotes a more thoughtful, gentler way of living that does not shirk the responsibilities and challenges of being human.

References

Adams, M. (2013). Human development from an existential phenomenological perspective: some thoughts and considerations. *Existential Analysis 24* (1): 48–56.

Adams, M. (2016). Existential therapy as a skills learning process. *Existential Analysis 27* (1): 58–69.

Adams, M. (2018). *An Existential Approach to Human Development: Philosophical and Therapeutic Perspectives.* London: Palgrave.

Balick, A. (2013). *The Psychodynamics of Social Networking: Connected-up Instantaneous Culture and the Self.* London: Karnac Books.

Besora, M.V. (1994). Las psicoterapias existenciales: Desarollo historico y modalidades conceptuales. In: *Fenomenologia e psicologia* (ed. J.A.C. Teixeira), 11–23. Lisbon: ISPA.

Boss, M. (1963). *Psychoanalysis and Daseinsanalysis.* New York: Basic Books.

Cooper, M. (2003). *Existential Therapies.* London: Sage.

Cooper, M. (2008). *Essential Research Findings in Counselling and Psychotherapy. The Facts Are Friendly.* London: Sage.

Cooper, M. (2011). Meeting the demand for evidence-based practice. *Therapy Today 22* (4): 10–16.
Cooper, M. (2012). *The Existential Counselling Primer: A Concise, Accessible and Comprehensive Introduction*. Ross-on-Wye: PCCS.
Cooper, M. (2017). *Existential Therapies*, 2e. London: Sage.
Correia, E.A. (2016). Practices and characteristics of existential counsellors and psychotherapists: A worldwide survey and observational study. PhD Thesis, University of Strathclyde, Glasgow.
Correia, E.A., Cooper, M., and Berdondini, L. (2015). Existential psychotherapy: An international survey of the key authors and texts influencing practice. *Journal of Contemporary Psychotherapy 45* (1): 3–10.
Correia, E.A., Cooper, M., and Berdondini, L. (2016). Existential psychotherapy: An international survey of the key authors and texts influencing practice. In: *Clarifying and Furthering Existential Psychotherapy* (ed. S.E. Schulenberg), 5–17. Bern: Springer.
Crick, T. (2011). The game body: Toward a phenomenology of contemporary video gaming. *Games and Culture 6* (3): 259–269.
Deurzen, E. van (2008). *Psychotherapy and the Quest for Happiness*. London: Sage.
Deurzen, E. van (2010). Foreword. In: *Therapy and Beyond: Counselling Psychology Contributions to Therapeutic and Social Issues* (ed. M. Milton), xv–xviii. Chichester: Wiley-Blackwell.
Deurzen, E. van (2012). Forward. In: *Existential Perspectives on Coaching* (ed. E. van Deurzen and M. Hanaway), xv–xix. Basingstoke: Palgrave Macmillan.
Deurzen, E. van (2014). Structural Existential Analysis (SEA): A phenomenological research method for counselling psychology. *Counselling Psychology Review 29* (2): 55–64.
Deurzen, E. van (2015). *Emmy van Deurzen: About Emmy's life and writings*. https://www.emmyvandeurzen.com/?page_id=50 (accessed January 16, 2019).
Deurzen, E. van and Adams, M. (2016). *Skills in Existential Counselling and Psychotherapy, 2e*. London: Sage.
Deurzen, E. van and Hanaway, M. (2012). *Existential Perspectives on Coaching*. Basingstoke: Palgrave Macmillan.
Dreyfus, H.L. and Wrathall, M. (2014). *Skillful Coping: Essays on the Phenomenology of Everyday Perception and Action*. Oxford University Press: Oxford.
Du Plock, S. and Deurzen, E. van (2015). The historical development and future of existential therapy. *International Journal of Psychotherapy 19* (1): 5–14.
Elkins, D.N. (2007). Empirically supported treatments: The deconstruction of a myth. *Journal of Humanistic Psychology 47* (4): 474–500.
Frankl, V. (1988). *The Will to Meaning: Foundations and Applications of Logotherapy*. New York: New American Library.
Frost, C. (2012). Humanism vs. the medical model – can pluralism bridge the divide for counselling psychologists? A trainee's perspective. *Counselling Psychology Review 27* (1): 53–63.
Groth, M. (1999). The background of contemporary existential psychotherapy. *The Humanistic Psychologist 27* (1): 15–22.
Groth, M. (2000). Existential psychotherapy today. *Review of Existential Psychology and Psychiatry 25* (1–3): 7–27.
Guy, A., Loewenthal, D., Thomas, R. et al. (2012). Scrutinising NICE: The impact of the National Institute for Health and Clinical Excellence guidelines on the provision of counselling and psychotherapy in primary care in the UK. *Psychodynamic Practice 18* (1): 25–50.
Halling, S. and Nill, J.D. (1995). A brief history of existential-phenomenological psychiatry and psychotherapy. *Journal of Phenomenological Psychology 26* (1): 1–45.

Hanaway, M. and Reed, J. (2014). *Existential Coaching Skills.* Henley-on-Thames: Corporate Harmony.

Heidegger, M. (1962). *Being and Time* (trans. J. Macquarrie and E. Robinson). New York: Harper & Row. (Original work published 1972.)

Hoffman, L., Dias, J., and Soholm, H.C. (2012). Existential-Humanistic Therapy as a model for evidence-based practice. Paper presented at 120th Annual Convention of the American Psychological Association.

Kross, E., Verduyn, P., Demiralp, E. et al. (2013). Facebook use predicts declines in subjective well-being in young adults. *PLoS ONE 8* (8): 1–6.

Langdridge, D. (2007). *Phenomenological Psychology: Theory, Research and Method.* London: Pearson Education.

Langdridge, D. (2013). *Existential Counselling and Psychotherapy* London: Sage.

Lin, R. and Utz, S. (2015). The emotional responses of browsing Facebook: Happiness, envy, and the role of tie strength. *Computers in Human Behavior 52* (Nov.): 29–38.

Manafi, E. (2010). Existential-phenomenological contributions to counselling psychology's relational framework. In: *Therapy and Beyond: Counselling Psychology Contributions to Therapeutic and Social Issues* (ed. M. Milton), 21–39. Chichester: Wiley-Blackwell.

Martínez, Y.A. and Signorelli, S. (eds.) (2011). *Perspectives en Psicoterapia Existencial. Una Mirada Retrospectiva y Actual.* México: Ediciones LAG.

Martínez, Y.A. and Signorelli, S. (2014). Breve Repaso a la Historia de la Psicoterapia Existencial en Latinoamérica. *Revista Latino Americana de Psicologia Existencial, 9*: 38–40.

Martínez, Y.A. and Signorelli, S. (2015). Brief review of the history of existential psychotherapy in Latin America. *International Journal of Psychotherapy 19* (1): 89–94.

Miller, R. (2006). A long time in (counselling psychology): Memoirs of a BPS junkie. *Counselling Psychology Review 21* (1): 4–7.

Mollon, P. (2010). Our rich heritage – are we building upon it or destroying it? Some malign influences of clinical psychology upon psychotherapy in the UK. *Psychodynamic Practice; Individuals, Groups and Organisations 16* (1): 7–24.

Munro, K. (2012). Conflict in cyberspace: How to resolve conflict online. http://kalimunro.com/wp/articles-info/relationships/article (accessed December 30, 2018).

Norcross, J.C. (2002). Empirically supported therapy relationships. In: *Psychotherapy Relationships that Work: Therapist Contributions and Responsiveness to Patients* (ed. J.C. Norcross), 3–16. New York: Oxford University Press.

Norcross, J.C., Prochaska, J.O., and Farber, J.A. (1993). Psychologists conducting psychotherapy: New findings and historical comparisons on the psychotherapy division membership. *Psychotherapy: Theory, Research, Practice, Training 30* (4): 692–697.

Scalzo, C. (2010). *Therapy with Children: An Existential Perspective.* London: Karnac Books.

Smith, J.A. (2008). *Qualitative Psychology*, 2e. London: Sage.

Sorensen, A.D. (2015). *Exploring learning outcomes in CBT and Existential Therapy in Denmark.* DProf. Thesis. Middlesex University/New School of Psychotherapy and Counselling.

Spiegelberg, H. (1972). *Phenomenology in Psychology and Psychiatry: A Historical Introduction.* Evanston: Northwestern University Press.

Steers, M.N. and Wickham, R.E. (2014). Seeing everyone else's highlight reels: How Facebook usage is linked to depressive symptoms. *Journal of Social and Clinical Psychology 33* (8): 701–731.

Strasser, F. and Strasser, A. (1997). *Existential Time-Limited Therapy: The Wheel of Existence.* Chichester: Wiley.

Straus, E. (1959). The Fourth International Congress of Psychotherapy Barcelona, Spain, September 1–7, 1958. *Psychosomatic Medicine 21* (2): 158–164.

Suler, J. (2004). The online disinhibition effect. *Cyberpsychology & Behavior: The Impact of the Internet, Multimedia and Virtual Reality on Behavior and Society 7* (3): 321–326.

Taipale, J. (2015). Beyond Cartesianism: Body-perception and the immediacy of empathy. *Continental Philosophy Review 48* (2): 161–178.

Tantam, D. (2006). Opportunities and risks in e-therapy. *Advances in Psychiatric Treatment 12* (5): 368–374.

Verissimo, D.S. (2012). On the threshold of the visible world: The notion of body schema in Merleau-Ponty's courses at the Sorbonne. *Psicologia USP 23* (2): 367–394.

Vos, J. (2014). Meaning and existential givens in the lives of cancer clients: A philosophical perspective on psycho-oncology. *Palliative & Supportive Care 12* (9): 1–16.

Vos, J. (2016). Working with meaning in life in mental health care: A systematic literature review and meta-analyses of practices and effectiveness. In: *Clinical Perspectives on Meaning: Positive and Existential Psychotherapy* (ed. P. Russo-Netzer, S.E. Schulenberg, and A. Batthyany), 59–88. New York: Springer

Vos, J., Cooper, M., Correia, E. et al. (2015). Existential therapies: A discussion and review of research methodologies and the evidence base to date. *International Journal of Psychotherapy 19* (1): 47–57.

Vos, J., Craig, M., and Cooper, M. (2014). Existential therapies: A meta-analysis of their effects on psychological outcomes. *Journal of Consulting and Clinical Psychology 83* (1): 115–128.

Watson, J.C., Gordon, L.B., Stermac, L. et al. (2003). Comparing the effectiveness of process-experiential with cognitive-behavioral psychotherapy in the treatment of depression, *Journal of Consulting and Clinical Psychology 71* (4): 773–781.

Woolfe, R. (2012). Risorgimento: A history of counselling psychology in Britain. *Counselling Psychology Review 27* (4): 72–78.

Woolfe, R. (2016). *Mapping the world of helping: The place of counselling psychology.* In: *The Handbook of Counselling Psychology*, 4e (ed. B. Douglas, R. Woolfe, S. Strawbridge et al.), 5–19. London: Sage.

Yalom, I.D. (1980). *Existential Psychotherapy.* New York: Basic Books.

Part III

Existential-Humanistic and Existential-Integrative Therapy

Edited by
Kirk J. Schneider

Introduction

Deriving primarily from the works of Rollo May (1958, 1981), James Bugental (1976, 1987), and Irvin Yalom (1980), the chief aim ofexistential-humanistic (EH) therapy is to set clients free. This freedom is contextualized within the natural and self-imposed (e.g., cultural) limits of living, and phenomenologically can be experienced along a "constrictive-expansive" continuum (Schneider 2008). The chief means by which this approach is facilitated is via whole-bodied presence – or the holding and illuminating of that which is palpably significant between therapist and client and within the client. Akin to a mirror, presence helps guide the EH therapist (in collaboration with the client) toward two – often implicit – questions: "How is the client *presently* living?" and "How is the client *willing* to live"? at every point of the encounter.

In contemporary EH therapy, these guiding questions lead to an essentially integrative (or "existential-integrative" [EI]) approach to clients' struggles (Schneider 2008; Schneider and Krug 2017; Shahar and Schiller 2016; Wolfe 2016).[1] Given that clients exist at a variety of "liberation levels" or levels within which they are

[1] Although "existential-humanistic" therapy is still the dominant perspective in US considerations of existential therapy, "existential-integrative" therapy is gaining rapid acknowledgment (particularly in mainstream psychotherapy circles) as a bona fide offspring of the former (Schneider and Krug 2017; Shahar and Schiller 2016: Wampold 2008). Therefore, in order to recognize the transitional nature of this development, we the contributors to this section, have titled it "Existential-Humanistic and Existential-Integrative Therapy." Finally, it should be stressed that the chapters to follow are but "snapshots" of a much larger EH and EI practice literature. For an elaboration on this literature it is strongly recommended that readers consult the original sources upon which the chapters in this Part are largely based – as well as the chapter on key texts.

The Wiley World Handbook of Existential Therapy, First Edition. Edited by Emmy van Deurzen, Erik Craig, Alfried Längle, Kirk J. Schneider, Digby Tantam, and Simon du Plock.

presently and potentially willing to live, the EH therapist is prepared to work with the client in accord with that client's desire and capacity for change. This means that the contemporary EH therapist attempts to be acutely present to the need, at any given moment, for a range of bona fide therapeutic engagements. These engagements range from supportive/advisory to psychophysiological to cognitive-behavioral and psychoanalytic as appropriate; however the foundation of the approach (given clients' desires and capacities) is availability to the "being" or experiential level of contact. By experiential level of contact we mean an emphasis on the immediate, the affective, the kinesthetic, and the profound (or cosmically significant). This level of contact is characterized by four basic stances that serve as active and passive mirrors for clients. These mirrors support clients to "see," close up, how they've constructed their personal and interpersonal worlds, and the degree to which they are willing to transform (that is, enlarge) those worlds. The stances are: *presence*, which is the method and ultimate aim of the EH/EI approach; *invoking the actual*, which is discerningly and creatively inviting clients *into* fuller presence (generally by helping them to attend to experiential processes, forms of embodiment, demeanor, affect, as much if not more than verbal content); *vivifying and (judiciously) confronting self-protections* (or blocks to embodied presence); and *rediscovering meaning and awe* (or the overcoming of blocks to self-protection such that not only new projects, goals, and aspirations can be attained, but fresh ways of experiencing life as a whole). This overarching attitude is often linked to a sense of the humility and wonder – or adventure – of being human. I call this sense of adventure an experience of *awe* (Schneider 2004, 2008, 2009). Put another way, optimal EH/EI therapy provides a staging ground for the rediscovery of meaning and awe. The more fully clients are able to experience their worlds, the greater their ability to "decide" how it is they're willing to live. This willingness, ideally, leads to a sense of enhanced meaning along with a deepened capacity for awe – the experience of both the fragility, smallness of one's life as well as the resilience, boldness of one's life. While the capacity to experience both smallness and greatness/fragility and boldness may seem antithetical to some notions of the "positive" life, it is core to the tenets of EH/EI therapy; for EH/EI therapy fosters the paradoxical vitality of life over the unidimensional models of "happiness" conventionally prevalent in mainstream psychology (Diamond 1996; May 1981; Seligman and Csikszentmihalyi 2000; Waterman 2013).

While EH/EI therapy is not for everyone, and is far from fulfilling its ideals, it is gaining in prominence for an increasingly diverse clientele (Hoffman, Jackson, and Cleare-Hoffman 2015; Shahar and Schiller 2016). Specifically, EH/EI therapy is being engaged with a wide range of ethnic, multicultural, and diagnostic clientele, and, due in large part to its stress on relationship, is seen as a key "evidence-based" modality (Angus et al. 2015; Wampold 2008).

With that background then, we will examine the history, theory, practice, key texts, and new developments of EH/EI therapy. Each chapter is written by leading EH/EI practitioners drawing on a wide range of viewpoints. These viewpoints form a rich tableau, illuminating both the diversity and cohesion of this resurging American modality.

References

Angus, L., Watson, J., Elliott, R. et al. (2015). Humanistic psychotherapy research 1990–2015: From methodological innovation to evidence-supported treatment outcomes and beyond. *Psychotherapy Research 25* (3): 330–347.

Bugental, J.F.T. (1976). *The Search for Existential Identity: Patient–Therapist Dialogues in Humanistic Psychotherapy*. San Francisco: Jossey-Bass.

Bugental, J.F.T. (1987). *The Art of the Psychotherapist*. New York: Norton.

Diamond, S. (1996) *Anger, Madness, and the Daimonic*. New York: SUNY Press.

Hoffman, L., Jackson, T., and Cleare-Hoffman, H. (2015). Humanistic psychology and multiculturalism: History, current status, and advancements. In: *The Handbook of Humanistic Psychology: Theory, Practice, and Research*, 2e (ed. K.J. Schneider, J.F. Pierson, and J.F.T. Bugental), 41–55. Thousand Oaks, CA: Sage.

May, R. (1958). The origins and significance of the existential movement in psychology. In: *Existence* (ed. R. May, E. Angel, and H. Ellenberger), 3–36. New York: Basic Books.

May, R. (1981). *Freedom and Destiny*. New York: Norton.

Schneider, K.J. (2004). *Rediscovery of Awe: Splendor, Mystery, and the Fluid Center of Life*. St. Paul, MN: Paragon House.

Schneider, K.J. (2008). *Existential-Integrative Psychotherapy: Guideposts to the Core of Practice*. New York: Routledge.

Schneider, K.J. (2009). *Awakening to Awe: Personal Stories of Profound Transformation*. Lanham, MD: Jason Aronson.

Schneider, K.J. and Krug, O.T. (2017). *Existential-Humanistic Therapy*, 2e. Washington, DC: American Psychological Association Press.

Seligman, M. and Csikszentmihalyi, M. (2000). Positive psychology: An introduction. *American Psychologist 55* (1): 5–14.

Shahar, G. and Schiller, M. (2016). A conqueror by stealth: Introduction to the special issue on humanism, existentialism, and psychotherapy integration. *Journal of Psychotherapy Integration 26*, 1–4.

Wampold, B. (2008). Existential-integrative psychotherapy comes of age. [Review of the book *Existential-Integrative Psychotherapy: Guideposts to the Core of Practice*]. *PsycCritiques 53*, Release 6, Article 1.

Waterman, A. S. (2013). The humanistic psychology–positive psychology divide: Contrasts in philosophical foundations. *American Psychologist 68* (3): 124–133.

Wolfe, B.E. (2016). Existential-humanistic therapy and psychotherapy integration: A commentary. *Journal of Psychotherapy Integration 26* (1): 56–60.

Yalom, I. (1980). *Existential Psychotherapy*. New York: Basic Books.

13

The History of Existential-Humanistic and Existential-Integrative Therapy

Louis Hoffman, Ilene A. Serlin, and Shawn Rubin

Existential-Humanistic psychology, and what can now be termed "Existential-Integrative psychology," as will be discussed later, originated in the United States blending ideas from European existential philosophy and psychology with an American perspective, particularly humanistic psychology. The founding of this school of thought can be traced to the publication of the book *Existence* by Rollo May, Ernest Angel, and Henri F. Ellenberger in 1958. The bulk of *Existence* was a translation of three papers by Ludwig Binswanger along with two important chapters by Rollo May, who quickly became the leading figure in existential psychology in the United States. May was also very influential with the development of the humanistic movement in the United States; however, he used the label "existential" for his approach to psychology. The label "existential-humanistic" can be attributed to James F.T. Bugental, who was strongly influenced by May and the humanistic movement. Despite many still using just the label of "existential psychology," the term "existential-humanistic" gradually became more commonly used to refer to this unique American existential psychology.

Given this early history, it is difficult to differentiate existential-humanistic psychology from the development of humanistic psychology in the United States. This is particularly true in the early history of existential-humanistic psychology. Yet, still today, it is common for the labels "humanistic" or "existential" to be used when referencing what is referred to here as existential-humanistic psychology. This ambiguity in language reflects, in part, the resistance of many in existential-humanistic psychology to be pinned down by a label. This also provides a challenge in writing a history of existential-humanistic psychology.

The Wiley World Handbook of Existential Therapy, First Edition. Edited by Emmy van Deurzen, Erik Craig, Alfried Längle, Kirk J. Schneider, Digby Tantam, and Simon du Plock.

Early History (1958–1979)

Humanistic psychology, including existential-humanistic psychology, is sometimes known as the Third Force in contrast with two prior major orientations in US psychology, behaviorism and psychoanalysis, which, along with the biomedical model, are generally considered by humanistic psychologists to be reductionistic, mechanistic, and dehumanizing in regard to human beings as whole persons. Since the early development of the Third Force, and partially due to the influence of the Third Force, there have been a number of trends in the first two Forces that reflect a more inclusive and holistic understanding (see Grogan 2013). Many psychologists played a vital role preparing the ground for what emerged as the Third Force; however, three stand out: Abraham Maslow, Carl Rogers, and Rollo May. Maslow founded the psychology department at Brandeis University in 1951 with a strong humanistic orientation even before the movement was thus named. Originally working within experimental psychology, Maslow (1954) developed a research program and subsequent humanistic theory of motivation. He argued that people are motivated not only reactively by the "deficiency needs" with which psychology had hitherto been concerned, but also proactively by "being needs," ultimately including such motives as self- actualization.

Rogers (1951) sought ways to facilitate clients' yearning for self-actualization and fully functioning living, especially via person-centered therapy and group work. He was one of the first researchers to study psychotherapy process using tape-recordings and transcripts, and he and his students also made extensive use of Q-sorts to study self-concept and change. He explored the necessary conditions for therapeutic progress and emphasized congruence, presence, and acceptance on the part of the therapist.

May, Angel, and Ellenberger (1958) built a bridge from interpersonal psychoanalysis to European existentialism and phenomenology, having been influenced by Harry Stack Sullivan, Ludwig Binswanger, and Medard Boss. May's books integrated creativity, the arts, mythology, and the humanities with psychology, and encompassed the tragic view of life and the daimonic forces. According to May (1969), the daimonic is "*any natural function which has the power to take over the whole person*.... The daimonic can be either creative or destructive and is normally both" (p. 123, italics in original). Therefore, while existential-humanistic psychology shared with humanistic psychology a valuing of human potential, it balanced the understanding of human potential with human limitation and innate forces that had the potential to be destructive. Charlotte Bühler, Erich Fromm, and Viktor Frankl also contributed European perspectives to this stream, including a concern for values in psychotherapy, human development over the whole course of human life, humanistic psychoanalysis, social issues, love, transcendence of evil, and the search for meaning.

Although less publically prominent than Maslow, Rogers, and May, we would be remiss to overlook the notable contributions of Clark Moustakas to the founding of existential-humanistic psychology. Moustakas's early literary contribution to the field was his edited volume entitled *The Self* (1956), which led directly to his early collaboration with Maslow. This collaboration was followed up when Moustakas hosted the first meeting of humanistic psychologists at the Merrill Palmer Institute in Detroit where Moustakas, Maslow, May, Rogers and others first worked jointly to bring a genuinely humanistic psychology into existence. In addition, Moustakas edited

Existential Child Therapy: The Child's Discovery of Himself (1966), which included contributions by other existential and humanistic scholars such as Charlotte Buhler, Eugene Gendlin, and Hanna Colm. Finally, Moustakas's classic work, *Loneliness* (1961), was the first to make a distinction between loneliness anxiety and existential loneliness which was very much in keeping with Rollo May's existential interpretation of anxiety and Medard Boss's existential interpretation of guilt.[1]

In the 1960s, many isolated voices began to gather momentum and form a critique of US culture and consciousness. Massive cultural changes were sweeping through the United States. That larger movement was an expression of a society eager to move beyond the alienating, bland conformity, embedded presuppositions, and prejudices that had characterized the 1950s return to "normalcy" after the Second World War. In psychology, adjustment models were challenged by visions of growth, and the human potential movement emerged. T-groups, sensitivity training, human relations training, and encounter groups became popular. The goal was greater awareness of one's own actual experience in the moment and authentic engagement with others, goals not well-served by academic psychology, clinical psychology, or the culture in general. Growth centers sprang up across the country, offering a profusion of workshops and techniques, such as transactional analysis, sensory awareness, Gestalt encounter, body work, meditation, yoga, massage therapy, and psychosynthesis. These developments in the culture and in "pop psychology" paralleled changes in clinical and academic domains. Existential and phenomenological trends in continental psychiatry affected the Anglo-American sphere through the work of R.D. Laing and his British colleagues. His trenchant critique of the prevailing medical model's reductionistic and pathological view of schizophrenic patients began a revisioning of even psychotic processes as potentially meaningful and growth-seeking. Various American psychiatrists also contributed to the elaboration of this alternative, most notably John Perry, Leston Havens, and Thomas Szasz. At the same time, Gestalt therapy was developed and popularized especially by Fritz and Laura Perls.

Meanwhile, from the academic side a rising tide of theory and research focused attention on this nonreductive, holistic view of the person. As the 1960s unfolded, new books by Rogers (1961, 1969), Maslow (1968, 1971), and May (1967, 1969) were enormously influential in this more receptive era. May pointed out that to study and understand human beings, a human model was needed. He advocated a science of persons, by which he meant a theory which would enable psychology to understand and clarify the specific, distinguishing characteristics of human beings. Many new voices also now began to be raised. Amedeo Giorgi (1965, 1966, 1970) criticized experimental psychology's reductionism, and argued for a phenomenologically based methodology that could support a more authentic human science of psychology. Giorgi argued that psychology has the responsibility to investigate the full range of behavior and experience of people in such a way that the aims of rigorous science are fulfilled, but that these aims should not be implemented primarily in terms of the criteria of the natural sciences.

[1] This passage on Clark Moustakas has been adapted from a personal communication from Erik Craig (October 6, 2018). The authors wish to thank Professor Craig for the elaboration on Moustakas's important contributions to EH psychology history.

As previously indicated, humanistic psychology as an organized movement grew out of a series of meetings in the late-1950s initiated by Abraham Maslow and Clark Moustakas and included Carl Rogers and Rollo May, all members of the American Psychological Association. They explored themes such as the nature of the self, self-actualization, health, creativity, being, becoming, individuation, and meaning. Building on these meetings, in 1961 an organizing committee including Anthony Sutich launched the *Journal of Humanistic Psychology* (*JHP*), which included May and other existential scholars.

The new journal's success in coalescing a responsive subscriber base quickly convinced its founders that a professional association could also meet a need. With the assistance of James Bugental, who served as its first president, and a grant arranged by Gordon Allport, the inaugural meeting of the Association for Humanistic Psychology (AHP) was held in Philadelphia in 1963. Among the 75 attendees were many who would later play prominent leadership roles in this movement. In 1963 Bugental published a foundational article, "Humanistic Psychology: A New Breakthrough," in the *American Psychologist* that was adopted by AHP as a basic statement of its own orientation. This statement was amplified in Bugental's 1964 article, "The Third Force in Psychology" in the *JHP* and appears, in the following slightly amplified version, in each issue.

1 Human beings, as human, are more than merely the sum of their parts. They cannot be reduced to component parts or functions.
2 Human beings exist in a uniquely human context, as well as in a cosmic ecology.
3 Human beings are aware and aware of being aware—i.e., they are conscious. Human consciousness potentially includes an awareness of oneself in the context of other people and the cosmos.
4 Human beings have some choice, and with that, responsibility.
5 Human beings are intentional, aim at goals, are aware that they cause future events, and seek meaning, value and creativity. (Bugental 1964, pp. 19–25)

Although these five statements were intended primarily for humanistic psychology, Bugental's existential sensitivities can be seen in these statements as well.

The second AHP meeting took place in Los Angeles in 1964, with about 200 attendees. As Bugental observed, this group already included the four major subgroups that have characterized and sometimes strained the association ever since: therapists, social/political activists, academic theorists and researchers, and "touchy feely" personal-growth seekers (deCarvalho 1991a, 1991b). To develop the philosophy, themes, and direction of AHP and humanistic psychology theory, The Old Saybrook Conference was convened in 1964 at a Connecticut country inn. It was an invitational conference sponsored by AHP that again included many who would become pillars of the existential-humanistic movement.

In subsequent years, a number of graduate programs in humanistic psychology were founded, including Masters' programs in humanistic psychology at Sonoma State University (then Sonoma State College) in 1966, and the State University of West Georgia (then West Georgia College) in 1968. A Masters' program in existential-phenomenological psychology was created at Duquesne University in 1959, and a PhD program was added in 1962. Several free-standing institutes also initiated humanistic graduate programs. In 1971 the Association for Humanistic Psychology created the Humanistic Psychology Institute (now known as Saybrook University, named after the famous conference), which has since served as the cornerstone university of the existential-humanistic movement.

Despite the close connections of humanistic and existential-humanistic psychology, some distinguishing factors began to emerge in this early period. For example, beginning with an open letter from Carl Rogers, May and Rogers engaged in a debate on the psychology of evil. For Rogers, evil was something external to the individual located in culture. May disagreed, emphasizing the importance of each person recognizing his or her own potential for evil, which was closely connected to May's concept of the daimonic.

Similarly, Bugental, May, and others spoke of various givens of existence. While these are often attributed to Yalom (1980), whose categorization of the givens are the best known today, his conception of the givens was not the first. The existential givens are not ultimate truths, but rather aspects of human existence that everyone must face. Existential-humanistic psychology does not offer any answers to these givens, and even acknowledges that the answers are dependent upon the individual and his or her culture. Yet, the givens are difficult realities that reflect the fact that human nature is paradoxical and limited. While humanistic psychology focused strongly on human potential, existential-humanistic psychology balanced the emphasis on human potential with attention to human limitation. Although the distinction between humanistic and existential-humanistic psychology is often subtle, and a matter of emphasis rather than disagreement, the two modes began to characterize Third Force psychologies.

The Middle Years (1980–1999)

Although 1980–1999 represented a period of declining influence, many notable developments emerged in these years. Central to any discussion of existential-humanistic psychology during this period is the enduring vision and contributions of Rollo May, who continued to publish many important books and articles. It was May's commitment to write, not for a "limited number" of psychologists and colleagues, which he considered a poor use of time, but rather he wanted to reach many open-minded and intelligent people in the general public as well. This is reflected in his important contributions of this period, including *Freedom and Destiny* (1981), *The Discovery of Being* (1983), and *The Cry for Myth* (1990), which all had appeal beyond the psychological audience. In the middle years, May's protégés, including Ed Mendelowitz, Stephen A. Diamond, Ilene A. Serlin, and Kirk J. Schneider, broadened and extended May's work and existential-humanistic psychology in enduring ways. Mendelowitz, in particular, carried forward the literary tradition of May's work. Diamond further developed May's conception of the daimonic. Serlin made important contributions to trauma applications, dance and the creative arts therapies, and whole person healthcare. Schneider, who stepped into the role of the leading figure in existential-humanistic psychology after May's death, further developed the clinical applications of existential-humanistic psychology, as well as contributing to many different areas of theoretical development. *The Psychology of Existence* (1995), which Schneider wrote and edited with Rollo May, was the beginning of existential-integrative psychology (a way of understanding and coordinating a range of bona fide modalities within an overarching existential or experiential context).

Bugental, who emerged as a central voice in the early years, continued to broaden his influence as well. In addition to contributing important new scholarly works, Bugental made a number of videos with demonstrations of existential therapy. These videos, along with his training programs, were highly influential in the development of the clinical applications of existential-humanistic psychology. The 1980s also witnessed the emergence of Irvin Yalom as a central figure. Yalom quickly became a highly recognized figure in the field because of his contributions to group psychotherapy as well as existential psychotherapy. Along with teaching, training, and scholarly contributions, Yalom became a popular writer with appeal to many in the field of psychology who did not identify as existential as well as to a growing lay audience. Although Yalom is arguably the best known therapist identifying as existential across the different schools of existential therapy, there are challenges in placing Yalom within a school. His approach most closely aligns with existential-humanistic psychology, and he was heavily influenced by May; however, in some ways Yalom's existential therapy represents an approach of its own. Furthermore, Yalom (1980) did not conceptualize existential therapy as a stand-alone approach, which differs from most others in the existential-humanistic movement, and has not himself drawn much upon other important writers within the existential-humanistic field.

The middle years also witnessed other important voices that had an indirect influence upon the movement, such as Allen Wheelis, Ernest Becker, Ernest Keen, Maurice Friedman, and Paul Stern. While these figures are not always recognized as existential-humanistic therapists, their work has strongly influenced many leaders within the existential-humanistic movement. Similarly, Erik Craig, who studied with Clark Moustakas, Paul Stern, and Medard Boss emerged as an important voice. While Craig's work represents other schools of thought covered in this volume, he was an influential bridge builder between the traditions and his contributions influenced existential-humanistic psychology.

Contemporary Developments (2000–current)

Following a period of decreased influence and declining interest, the foundations for a renewed interest in existential-humanistic psychology began in the early 2000s. The early development of existential-humanistic psychology was dominated by charismatic figures, such as Rollo May and Jim Bugental (Schneider, personal communication, 2016). However, Schneider notes that there was an awareness that for the movement to sustain itself, there was a need for formalized structures and training. In the early 2000s, several key developments began to emerge that would help to sustain the existential-humanistic movement. Some of these were closely connected with the development of structures in humanistic psychology in the United States, in which existential-humanistic perspectives were popular. These developments fall into three primary categories: scholarship, institutes and training, and conferences.

Developments in Scholarship

First, two important new handbooks were published in 2001. Kirk J. Schneider, James Bugental, and J. Fraser Pierson published *The Handbook of Humanistic Psychology* with Sage. Although the title refers to "humanistic psychology," existential-humanistic perspectives were primary in this text, making it the most important publication in existential-humanistic psychology since the early writings of Rollo May and James Bugental. The handbook did not just summarize existential-humanistic ideas, but also addressed innovations and new directions, which had been missing in much of the scholarship through the middle years. This allowed *The Handbook of Humanistic Psychology* to become the foundation for new directions in existential-humanistic scholarship.

In the same year, Cain and Seeman (2001) published *Humanistic Psychotherapies: Handbook of Research and Practice.* This handbook was largely rooted in the client-centered and humanistic tradition, but did include an important chapter on existential therapy. Combined, these two books set the foundation for renewed scholarship in humanistic psychology, and existential-humanistic therapy.

Institutes and Training

Along with the renewed scholarship, several institutes formed in the late 1990s and early 2000s. In 1997, the Existential-Humanistic Institute (EHI) was founded with an intent to foster training in existential-humanistic psychotherapy. The institute was inspired by the encouragement of Bugental as well as a number of Russian scholars who were invited to the United States for two weeks to study existential-humanistic psychology. Following a large opening presentation featuring Bugental and Yalom in 1998, the institute offered a number of smaller presentations in the San Francisco Bay Area. In 2001, Maureen O'Hara, president of Saybrook University, invited Orah Krug, Nader Shabahangi, and Kirk J. Schneider of EHI to begin offering training at Saybrook University's Residential Conferences. Along with Tom Greening, they continued to offer a four-day training once a year with Saybrook through 2010. This led to the development of coursework at Saybrook and eventually a certificate program in the Foundations of Existential-Humanistic Practice that was launched in 2012 and continues today.

In 2002, Myrtle Heery, a protégé of James Bugental, formed the International Institute of Humanistic Studies (IIHS). The focus of IIHS was to provide training in existential-humanistic therapy. Heery, along with Bugental, developed and taught Unearthing the Moment Training as a two-year program with additional advanced training options. IIHS continues to offer a variety of regular trainings rooted in existential-humanistic psychology. More recently, in 2013 IIHS founded Tonglen Press, which publishes books related to existential-humanistic psychology, including *Unearthing the Moment: Mindful Applications of Existential-Humanistic and Transpersonal Psychology*, edited by Myrtle Heery, which is a collection of papers from individuals who have completed the Unearthing the Moment training.

More recently, the Zhi Mian International Institute for Existential-Humanistic Psychology (also called the International Institute for Existential and Humanistic Psychology; www.iehpp.org) was formed in 2010 by Mark Yang, Louis Hoffman, Jason Dias, Trent Claypool, and Michael Moats in consultation with Xuefu Wang, who founded the Zhi Mian Institute of Psychotherapy in China. The purpose of this institute was to provide training in existential-humanistic therapy internationally, particularly in southeast Asia. Mark Yang, who has lived in Hong Kong, Taiwan, and China, has been the primary driving force of the institute, providing regular training workshops. Once a year, Louis Hoffman has brought students from the United States to assist in providing training. In 2014, the Zhi Mian International Institute began offering certificates in humanistic and existential psychology in conjunction with the China Institute for Psychotherapy in Beijing.

It is difficult for any movement in psychology to sustain itself without training institutes to support them. Psychoanalytic, Jungian, and Gestalt institutes have helped for these movements to sustain and flourish over the years; however, the existential-humanistic movement has struggled to develop similar institutes to sustain and advance the movement. The founding of EHI and IIHS, following a period where existential-humanistic psychology was beginning to struggle, served a pivotal role in revitalizing the movement.

Conferences

Conferences play a pivotal role in sustaining and advancing psychology movements as well. Along with promoting scholarship and offering training opportunities, conferences facilitate the development of a broader community and energize movements. For many years, there had been a dearth of conferences that reflected the existential-humanistic perspective. The primary conference was Division 32's programming at the American Psychological Association Convention. The few hours granted were hardly sufficient to sustain the community and energy needed for the movement to grow and thrive.

In 2007, under the leadership of David Cain, the Society for Humanistic Psychology began holding an annual conference. Each year, many of the program offerings represented existential-humanistic psychology. The conference played a primary role in developing a stronger existential-humanistic community, fostered collaborative scholarship, and advanced existential-humanistic theory. Additionally, the conferences drew many graduate students and early-career psychologists. For many years prior to the conference, one of the greatest threats to the future of existential-humanistic psychology was the small number of graduate students and early-career professionals identifying with the movement. In large part due to the Annual Society for Humanistic Psychology Conference, this has begun to change.

A few years later, in 2006, EHI began hosting an annual conference as well. Although smaller than the Society for Humanistic Conference, the programming was exclusively focused on existential-humanistic psychology. Similarly, IIHS has offered a couple of conferences, largely composed of graduates from the Unearthing the Moment Training. These conferences as well have helped to build community.

In 2010, Louis Hoffman, Mark Yang, and Xuefu Wang began the biannual International Conference on Existential Psychology (ICEP). This conference, offered every other year in China, has helped expand an existential-humanistic presence in China. The first conference, held in Nanjing, had several hundred very enthusiastic attendees and was covered in the local media. Many leading scholars from the United States, including Kirk J. Schneider, Ilene Serlin, Ed Mendelowitz, and Erik Craig, attended the first conference. Although Hoffman, Yang, and Wang had already been providing numerous trainings on existential-humanistic psychology in China, Malaysia, and Singapore, the conference added more of a foundation in theory, research, and scholarship to the applied trainings that had been being offered.

Emergent Trends

> But a people unable to reform will not be able to preserve [their] old culture either (Lu Xun 1921/1961, p. 138)

Any movement in psychology that is not able to evolve and speak to the times will inevitably fade from influence, and rightly it should. In the 1980s and 1990s, there was some reason to fear that this could be the fate of existential-humanistic psychology. While there were some important innovative voices, the movement was fading and at times co-opted and adapted into the mainstream (Grogan 2013). The scholarship, institutes, and conferences would not have been successful without being combined with new directions in scholarship. In existential-humanistic therapy, several new directions played a vital role in its revitalization: existential-integrative psychology, multicultural and international influences, and spirituality.

Existential-Integrative Psychology

Although the initial formulations of existential-integrative psychology began to emerge in the *The Psychology of Existence* (1995) by Kirk J. Schneider and Rollo May, it was Schneider's book, *Existential-Integrative Psychotherapy: Guideposts to the Core of Practice* (2008) that formalized it. *Existential-Integrative Psychotherapy* accomplished a number of important achievements that helped solidify existential-humanistic psychology's revitalization. First, it provided a framework for understanding existential-humanistic practice. Schneider, in his overview of existential-integrative theory, identified core aspects of this therapy approach. Second, Schneider showed how existential-humanistic therapy can be integrated with various other approaches to therapy. The essence of an integrative approach is that there is a foundation from which therapists practice. From this foundation, other approaches can be integrated. This "assimilative integration" approach is different than an eclectic approach that does not have a foundation and seeks integration haphazardly. With the foundation in existential-humanistic psychology, the other approaches are integrated in a way that is internally coherent and consistent with the foundation (see Wolfe 2016). To this extent, it is now possible to speak of a transition taking place in existential-humanistic psychology to the title of this section which is called "Existential-Humanistic and Existential-Integrative Psychotherapy."

Third, in moving toward the direction of integration, Schneider showed that existential-humanistic therapy can take a collaborative approach with other therapy modalities. This allows existential-humanistic practitioners to remain rooted in their preferred therapy modality while integrating other approaches that are often encouraged, if not required, by managed care. Connected to this, Bruce Wampold (2008), a leading researcher of therapy outcomes, noted, "I have no doubt that EI [Existential-Integrative] approaches would satisfy any criteria used to label other psychological treatments as scientific" (para. 13; see also Shahar and Schiller 2016 for an elaboration on this point).

International and Multicultural Psychology

Psychological dialogues across cultures drive practitioners and scholars to deeper awareness of their own assumptions and biases, which can help advance psychological theories while supporting them to become more culturally sensitive. Additionally, international dialogues often can energize movements in psychology. Nader Shabahangi's work in Russia in the 1990s along with the visit from many Russian scholars in 1996 was one of the impetuses for the development of the EHI. Additionally, they helped to develop existential-humanistic psychology in Russia.

More recently, existential-humanistic psychology has grown rapidly in Southeast Asia leading to important exchanges that have helped energize and advance the movement. This has been due to many exchanges and training across China by Mark Yang, Louis Hoffman, and Xuefu Wang. Additionally, the Zhi-Mian approach to psychotherapy, which was developed by Wang based upon the writings of Chinese literary figure Lu Xun, became recognized as an indigenous Chinese approach to existential therapy (Wang 2011). Since 2008, the international dialogues have helped existential-humanistic therapy grow in popularity in China with the trainings and conferences in China drawing significantly larger crowds than similar events in the United States. The influence of Chinese perspectives, such as Zhi-Mian therapy, Buddhist approaches to therapy (Schneider and Tong 2009), and Taoism (Craig 2009; Yang 2016), have grown in their influence on existential-humanistic psychology in the United States. More recently, the systematic training programs have further solidified the existential-humanistic approach in China. In addition to the existential and humanistic certificates previously discussed, Ilene Serlin offers a certificate training in movement therapy rooted partially in the existential-humanistic tradition through the China Institute for Psychotherapy.

Multicultural psychology, though related, is different to international psychology. In particular, it considers cultural differences within countries as well as between. As Hoffman (2016) has stated, existential-humanistic psychology was one of the first approaches to voice appreciation for cultural differences; however, it has struggled in actualizing this value. This has begun to change. Schneider played an important role in creating space for multicultural perspectives. In *Existential-Integrative Psychotherapy* (2008), Schneider invited many chapters focusing on multicultural perspectives. Similarly, during his time as editor of the *Journal of Humanistic Psychology*, he worked to diversify the editorial board and include more multicultural perspectives. Through the Society for Humanistic Psychology Conference and various recent publications, existential-humanistic psychology has evolved to address multicultural issues with much greater depth and substance.

Spirituality

Existential-humanistic psychology's relationship with spirituality and religion has been controversial and frequently misunderstood (Helminiak, Hoffman, and Dodson 2012). Commonly, it has been misperceived as being rooted in atheism and antagonistic to spirituality and religion. This, however, is not accurate. While some, such as Yalom, have taken a more antagonistic stance to spirituality and religion, most existential-humanistic practitioners are more open.

Existential-humanistic therapy's religious and spiritual influence has deep roots. Paul Tillich, a theologian, was Rollo May's mentor and dissertation chair. The influence of Tillich, as well as Jewish Theologian Martin Buber, on the development of existential-humanistic psychology is quite evident. More recently, Schneider's (2004) development of the concept of awe has brought renewed interest in examining spirituality from an existential-humanistic perspective. Awe is rooted in mystery, wonderment, and appreciation, concurrently embracing our human limitation and potential. It is evident in various religious traditions, but not bound to any. Schneider's conception of awe is relevant to therapy, but also for broader applications of existential humanistic psychology to education (Schneider 2009) and politics (Schneider 2013, 2019). In many ways, the re-emergence of a spiritual perspective reflects a return to important roots of existential-humanistic psychology.

Conclusion

After a long history of growth and decline, existential-humanistic psychotherapy is again in a period of growth, renewal, and advancement. As this trend continues, it is critical to heed the lessons of history and appreciate the importance of the values, ideas, and, most centrally, people who have helped build the existential-humanistic movement into what it is today.

References

Bugental, J.F.T. (1964). The third force in psychology (Basic postulates and orientation of humanistic psychology). *Journal of Humanistic Psychology 4*: 19–26.

Cain, D.J. and Seeman, J. (eds.) (2001). *Humanistic Psychotherapies: Handbook of Research and Practice*. Washington, DC: American Psychological Association.

Craig, E. (2009). Tao, Dasein, and psyche: Shared grounds for depth psychotherapy. In: *Existential Psychology: East-West* (ed. L. Hoffman, M. Yang, F.J. Kaklauskas et al.), 149–164. Colorado Springs, CO: University of the Rockies Press.

deCarvalho, R.J. (1991a). *The Growth Hypothesis: The Humanistic Psychology of Abraham Maslow and Carl Rogers*. Lewiston, NY: E. Mellen Press.

deCarvalho, R.J. (1991b). *The Founders of Humanistic Psychology*. New York: Praeger.

Giorgi, A. (1965). Phenomenology and experimental psychology I. *Review of Existential Psychology and Psychiatry 5*: 228–238.

Giorgi, A. (1966). Phenomenology and experimental psychology II. *Review of Existential Psychology and Psychiatry 6*: 37–50.

Giorgi, A. (1970). *Psychology as a Human Science: A Phenomenologically Based Approach*. New York: Harper & Row.

Grogan, J. (2013). *Encountering America: Humanistic Psychology, Sixties Culture and the Shaping of the Modern Self*. New York: HarperCollins.

Heery, M. (ed.) (2014). *Unearthing the Moment: Mindful Applications of Existential-Humanistic and Transpersonal Psychology*. Petaluma, CA: Tonglen Press.

Helminiak, D., Hoffman, L., and Dodson, E. (2012). A critique of the "theistic psychology" movement as exemplified in Bartz (2009) "Theistic Existential Psychology." *The Humanistic Psychologist 40*: 179–196.

Hoffman, L. (2016). Multiculturalism and humanistic psychology: From neglect to epistemological and ontological diversity. *The Humanistic Psychologist 44* (1): 56–71.

Lu Xun (1961). Sudden notions. In: *Lu Xun: Selected Works*, vol. 1 (trans. and ed. Y. Xianyi and G. Yang), 138–140. Beijing, China: Foreign Language Press. (Original work published 1921.)
Maslow, A. (1954). *Motivation and Personality*. New York: Harper & Row.
Maslow, A. (1968). *Toward a Psychology of Being*. New York: Van Nostrand.
Maslow, A. (1971). *The Further Reaches of Human Nature*. New York: Penguin.
May, R. (1967). *Psychology and the Human Dilemma*. New York: Van Nostrand.
May, R. (1969). *Love and Will*. New York: Norton.
May, R. (1981). *Freedom and Destiny*. New York: Norton.
May, R. (1983). *The Discovery of Being*. New York: Norton.
May, R. (1990). *The Cry for Myth*. New York: Norton.
May, R., Angel, E., and Ellenberger, H.R. (1958). *Existence*. Northvale, NJ: Jason Aronson.
May, R. and Schneider, K.J. (1995). *The Psychology of Existence: An Integrative, Clinical Perspective*. New York: McGraw-Hill.
Moustakas, C. (1956). *The Self: Explorations in Personal Growth*. New York: Joanna Cottler Books.
Moustakas, C. (1961). *Loneliness*. Englewood Cliffs, NJ: Prentice-Hall.
Moustakas, C. (1966). *Existential Child Therapy: The Child's Discovery of Himself*. New York: Basic Books.
Rogers, C.R. (1951). *Client-Centered Therapy: It's Current Practice, Implications, and Theory*. Boston: Houghton-Mifflin & Co.
Rogers, C.R. (1961). *On Becoming a Person*. Boston: Houghton-Mifflin.
Rogers, C.R. (1969). *Freedom to Learn*. Princeton, NC: C.E. Merril Co.
Schneider, K.J. (2004). *Rediscovery of Awe: Splendor, Mystery, and the Fluid Center of Life*. St. Paul, MN: Paragon Press.
Schneider, K.J. (2008). *Existential-Integrative Psychotherapy: Guideposts to the Core of Practice*. New York: Routledge.
Schneider, K.J. (2009). *Awakening to Awe: Personal Stories of Profound Transformation*. New York: Jason Aronson.
Schneider, K.J. (2013). *The Polarized Mind: Why It's Killing Us and What We Can Do About It*. Colorado Springs, CO: University Professors Press.
Schneider, K.J. (2019). *The spirituality of awe: Challenges to the robotic revolution* (Revised Edition). Colorado Springs, CO: University Professors Press.
Schneider, K.J., Bugental, J.F.T., and Pierson, J.F. (eds.) (2001). *The Handbook of Humanistic Psychology: Leading Edges in Theory, Research, and Practice*. Thousand Oaks, CA: Sage.
Schneider, K.J. and Tong, B. (2009). Existentialism, Taoism, and Buddhism: Two views. In: *Existential Psychology: East-West* (ed. L. Hoffman, M. Yang, F.J. Kaklauskas et al.), 165–176. Colorado Springs, CO: University of the Rockies Press.
Shahar, G. and Schiller, M. (2016). A conqueror by stealth: Introduction to the special issue on humanism, existentialism, and psychotherapy integration. *Journal of Psychotherapy Integration, 26*: 1–4.
Wampold, B.E. (2008, February 4). Existential-integrative psychotherapy: Coming of age [Review of the book *Existential-integrative psychotherapy: Guideposts to the core of practice*]. *PsychCRITIQUES–Contemporary Psychology: APA Review of Books*, 53 (No. 6).
Wang, X. (2011). Zhi Mian and existential psychology. *The Humanistic Psychologist 39* (3): 240–246.
Wolfe, B.E. (2016). Existential-humanistic therapy and psychotherapy integration: A commentary. *Journal of Psychotherapy Integration 26* (1), 56–60.
Yalom, I. (1980). *Existential Psychotherapy*. New York: Basic Books.
Yang, M.C. (ed.) (2016). *Existential Psychology and the Way of the Tao: Meditations on the Writings of Zhuangzi*. New York: Routledge.

14

Existential-Humanistic and Existential-Integrative Therapy

Philosophy and Theory[1]

Kirk J. Schneider

A Thumbnail Sketch of the Founders

Existential-humanistic theory originated in the crucible of the American humanistic psychology movement in the late 1950s and early 1960s. Drawing from the germinal writings of such US theorists as Abraham Maslow, Carl Rogers, and Harry Stack Sullivan on the one hand as well as European thinkers, such as Paul Tillich, Eric Fromm, and Frieda Fromm-Reichman, early humanistic psychology pioneer Rollo May became the pivotal figure in the development of existential-humanistic theory. With the advent of his co-edited book *Existence: A New Dimension in Psychiatry and Psychology* (May, Ellenberger, and Angel 1958), May virtually single-handedly launched the field of American existential-humanistic therapy and psychology.

That said, it took a fateful meeting between May and emerging humanistic luminary James Bugental to consolidate both the theory and practice of what is now recognized as contemporary existential-humanistic therapy. Warmly responding to an invitation from Bugental and his practice group to provide a seminar shortly after the publication of *Existence*, May planted the seeds for a major transformation of the humanistic field.[2] Bugental, like May, had a background in both psychoanalysis and humanistic theory, but also like May, Bugental held concerns about both the style and substance of those modalities. Specifically, Bugental, like May, felt that psychoanalysis as it was practiced in the late 1950s was stunted by an overemphasis on the authority of the analyst to the neglect of the subjectivity of his/her clients; Bugental

[1] Part of this chapter is adapted from K. Schneider and O. Krug's (2017) *Existential-Humanistic Therapy*. Washington, DC: American Psychological Association Press.

[2] Jim Bugental's practice group included the future editor of the *Journal of Humanistic Psychology*, Tom Greening, who for over 35 years ensured a central place for existential-humanistic theory, research, and practice.

The Wiley World Handbook of Existential Therapy, First Edition. Edited by Emmy van Deurzen, Erik Craig, Alfried Längle, Kirk J. Schneider, Digby Tantam, and Simon du Plock.

also had concerns about the tendency of analysts to be hyper-reserved in the therapeutic setting, avoiding in his view the need for greater spontaneity and relational encounter to deepen clients' therapeutic explorations. Finally, he, like May, viewed psychoanalytic theory as overly identified with sexual-aggressive drives rather than the "bigger" issues of clients' encounters with love, the passing nature of life, and the meaning and purpose of their lives. On the other hand, both Bugental and May had significant reservations about what they perceived as the superficiality of aspects of humanistic, and in particular Rogerian forms of practice. For example, they both felt that though Rogerian (or "client-centered") therapy focused importantly on clients' subjective experiences, it left out the intensity of some of those experiences, such as the need for some clients to become angry at their therapists, or to delve more fully into "dark" feelings of hatred and anxiety. Too often in Bugental and May's view, Rogerian therapists seemed to aver confrontation with their clients, or to hold an overly optimistic stance that seemed in some cases to stifle clients' needs to intensively grapple with the rivaling sides of themselves, the core "battles" out of which profound life choices are forged.

Given this convergence, May inspired Bugental to begin a rigorous period of translating May and others' existential theories into practical therapeutic guidelines, which could nurture the emerging generation of (humanistic and open-minded non-humanistic) therapists. Whereas May and European scholars provided much of the philosophy of existential-humanistic therapy, Bugental and some of his students provided detailed applications of the philosophy in the everyday world of therapeutic practice (e.g., see Bugental 1965, 1976).

By 1980, the psychiatrist Irvin Yalom produced a landmark volume called *Existential Psychotherapy* that conveyed principles of existential-humanistic practice to a comparatively larger readership than his predecessors, May and Bugental. With *Existential Psychotherapy* and a series of popular novels elucidating existential-humanistic themes, Yalom (1980, 1989, 1992) had a major impact on the incorporation of the topic by more mainstream modalities such as psychoanalysis (e.g., Shahar and Schiller 2016) and Acceptance and Commitment Therapy (e.g., Bunting and Hayes 2008). Moreover whereas May and Bugental tended to explicate the "here-now" experience of clients, Yalom stressed the "here-now" experience of the therapist–client relationship (Krug 2009).

What, then, is meant by existential–humanistic therapy? Existentialism is concerned with the living experience of becoming and originates from the Latin root exsistere, which literally means to stand forth or to become. Humanism comes from the Greek tradition of "knowing thyself" (Schneider and Krug 2010). Thus, existential–humanism, although a seemingly static term, actually refers to the dynamic process of becoming and knowing oneself.

Current Directions

Increasingly, existential-humanistic (EH) theory is becoming an existential-integrative (EI) framework. The inspiration for this shift can be traced to May's prescient opening lines in *Existence*: "The existential movement in psychotherapy," he wrote,

> does not purport to found a new school as over against other schools or to give a new technique of therapy as over against other techniques. It seeks rather, to analyze the structure of human existence – an enterprise which, if successful, should yield an understanding of the reality underlying all situations of human beings in crisis. (May 1958a, pp. 6–7)

In the spirit of this call then, and beginning with the articulations of Schneider and May (1995) and Schneider (2008), EH principles are indeed becoming viewed as foundational for other bona fide approaches (Schneider and Krug 2017; Shahar and Schiller 2016; Shumaker 2011; Wampold 2008; Wolfe 2016). Put more formally, EI therapy is one way to understand and orchestrate a variety of therapeutic modes within an overall existential or experiential context. The basis for this growing perspective is the realization on the part of many existential-humanistic practitioners that to genuinely "meet" a client, one must draw from a range of approaches. These approaches, from the physiological/medical to the behavioral/analytical may best resonate with a given client's readiness and desire for change (Schneider 2008). Correspondingly, the evolution of EI therapy is also being spurred on by more mainstream practitioners and researchers who acknowledge its foundational value (Bunting and Hayes 2008; Shahar and Schiller 2016; Wolfe 2016). The development of EI therapy is also being bolstered by theorists attuned to multicultural communities (e.g., Hoffman 2008; Hoffman, Jackson, and Cleare-Hoffman 2015). These theorists see in the approach a way to both substantively address emotional wounds in such communities as well as to enlarge and deepen the theoretical structure of EI practice.

EH/EI Theoretical Frameworks in Depth

The aim of EH as well as EI therapy is to "set clients free" (May 1981, p. 19). Freedom is understood as the capacity for choice within the natural and self-imposed limits of living (Schneider 2008). Freedom is also understood as a spectrum of liberations levels, from the physiological to the behavioral, the cognitive to the psychosexual, and the interpersonal to the experiential. The natural limits of living refer to the inherent limitations of birth, heredity, age, and so forth, and the realities of living – often referred to as "the givens of existence" – such as death, separateness, and uncertainty. Self-imposed limits are the boundaries established by humans, such as culture, language, and lifestyle.

The freedom to do or to act is probably the clearest freedom we possess. The freedom to be or to adopt attitudes toward situations is a less clear but even more fundamental freedom (May 1981). Freedom to do is generally associated with external, physical decisions, whereas freedom to be is associated with internal, cognitive, and emotional stances. Within these freedoms we have a great capacity to create meaning in our lives – to conceptualize, imagine, invent, communicate, and physically and psychologically enlarge our worlds (Yalom 1980). We also have the capacity to separate from others, to transcend our past, and to become distinct, unique, and heroic (Becker 1973). Conversely, we can choose to restrain ourselves, to become passive, and to give ourselves over to others (May 1981; Rank 1936). We can choose to be a part of others or apart from others, a part of our possibilities or apart from our possibilities (Bugental and Kleiner 1993).

Recognizing Freedom's Limitations

Notwithstanding the vast possibilities, there are great limitations on all these freedoms. We can only do and be so much. Whatever we choose implies a giving up of something else (Bugental 1987, p. 230). If we devote ourselves to scholarship, we give up a degree of athleticism. If we engage in wealth accumulation, we lessen our opportunities for spiritual pursuits. Moreover, every freedom has its price. If one stands out in a crowd, one becomes a larger target for criticism; if one acquires responsibility, one courts guilt; if one isolates oneself, one loses community; if one merges and fuses with others, one loses individuality, and so on (Becker 1973; May 1981). Finally, every freedom has its counterpart in destiny. May (1981) defines four kinds of destiny, or "givens" beyond our control: cosmic, genetic, cultural, and circumstantial. Cosmic destiny embraces the limitations of nature (e.g., earthquakes, climatic shifts); genetic destiny entails physiological dispositions (e.g., life span, temperament); cultural destiny addresses preconceived social patterns (e.g., language, birthrights); and circumstantial destiny pertains to sudden situational developments (e.g., oil spills, job layoffs). In short, our vast potentialities are matched by crushing vulnerabilities. We are semi-aware, semi-capable, in a world of dazzling incomprehensibility.

How, then, shall we deal with these clashing realities according to existential theorists, and what happens when we do not? Let us consider the latter first. The failure to acknowledge our freedom, according to existential theorists, results in the dysfunctional identification with limits, or repressed living (May 1981). This dysfunctional identification forfeits the capacity to enliven, embolden, and enlarge one's perspective. The "shrinking violet," the knit-picking professor, the paranoid reactionary, and the robotic conformist are illustrations of this polarity. The failure to acknowledge our limits, on the other hand, results in the sacrifice of our ability to discipline, discern, and prioritize life's chances (May 1981). The aimless dabbler, the impulsive con man, the unbowed hedonist, and the power-hungry elitist exemplify this polarity.

Integrating Freedom and Limitation

The great question, of course, is how to help clients become emancipated from their polarized conditions and "experience their possibilities" as they engage their destinies (May 1981, p. 20). Put another way, how do we help clients to integrate freedom and limits? This question strikes at the heart of another existential problem – that of identity. Whereas reprogramming clients' behaviors or helping them to understand the genesis of their polarized conditions leads to partially rejuvenated identities, for existential theorists, experiential encounters with these conditions are the great underappreciated complements to the aforementioned change processes (Schneider 2008,

2013). The EH practitioner believes that if life-limiting patterns are experienced in the present, then clients will be more willing and able to choose life-affirming patterns in the future. Put another way, the path to greater freedom is paradoxically found through an encounter with the ways in which we are bound (Krug 2009).

The experiential modality for existential theorists embraces four basic dimensions: the immediate, the kinesthetic, the affective, and the profound or cosmic (Schneider 2008). The road to a fuller, more vital identity, in other words, is to help clients experience their polarized conditions, to assist them to "embody" those conditions and their underlying fears and anxieties, and to help them attune, at the deepest levels, to the implications of what has been discovered. In so doing, EH therapists help clients to respond to, as opposed to react against, panic-filled material. This work typically results in clients experiencing their polarized conditions as restrictive or self-limiting. Consequently, it not only allows clients to understand their part in the construction of their restrictive patterns, it also helps them accept the givens of existence that may have been avoided, denied, or repressed. However, for the EH practitioner, responsibility assumption is often not sufficient. It is simply preparatory for substantive change evidenced when clients choose more life-affirming patterns for themselves and with others. The net result, according to existential theorists, is an expanded sense of self, specifically an enhanced capacity for intimacy, meaning, and spiritual connection in one's life (Bugental 1978; May 1981).

Varied Interpretations of Experiential Encounter

The experiential mode is diversely interpreted by existential theorists. For example, Yalom (1980) appears to stress the immediate and affective elements of his interpersonal therapeutic contacts, but he refers little to kinesthetic components. Bugental (1987) stresses kinesthetic elements of his encounters – illuminating what is "implicitly present but unregarded" (Bugental 1999, p. 25) – but places lesser emphasis on interpersonal implications of those elements (Krug 2009). Tillich (1952) and Friedman (1995) accent the interpersonal dimension of therapeutic experiencing but convey little about the kinesthetic aspect. Finally, Krug (Krug and Schneider 2016) holds the intra- and interpersonal dimensions of therapeutic experiencing with about equal weight, depending on both context and alliance between client and therapist.

There are also differences among existential theorists regarding verbal and non-verbal channels of communication. May (1983), Yalom (1980), and Friedman (1995), for example, rely relatively heavily on verbal interventions, whereas Bugental (1987), Gendlin (1996), Mahrer (1996), and Schneider (2008) draw upon comparatively non-verbal forms of mediation.

Finally, there are differences among existential theorists with regard to philosophical implications of therapeutic experiencing. Although most existential theorists agree that clients need to confront the underlying givens (or ultimate concerns) of human existence during the course of a typical therapy, the nature and specificity of these givens varies. Whereas Yalom (1980), for example, focuses on the need for clients to experientially confront death, freedom, isolation, or meaninglessness, Bugental provides a more elaborate schema: the need for clients to confront embodiment-change, finitude-contingency, action-responsibility, choice-relinquishment, separation-apartness, or relation-being a part of (Bugental and Kleiner 1993). And whereas May (1981) unites these positions with his notion of freedom and destiny (or limitation), as previously suggested, there is only a vague explication of this synthesis in his work.

A Central Concern: The Present Moment

Despite these differences, each theorist shares a central concern – namely, how is this client in this moment coping with his or her awareness of being alive? The EH theorists address this concern by focusing more on the implicit – moment-to-moment – processes in therapy than on explicit content. EH/EI theorists take an ahistorical approach; that is, the past is integral only insofar as it is alive, within the person, in the present moment. Moreover, EH/EI therapists seek to understand a person as a human being in the world, related to his or her physical, personal, and social worlds. It is assumed that a person is not simply a collection of drives and behavior patterns within an encapsulated self. It is further assumed that each person is more than the sum of his or her parts and that each person constructs a particular world from unique perceptions of the world. Finally, the EH/EI therapist assumes, as May (1983, p. 122) suggests, that "the person and his world are a unitary, structural whole ... two poles, self and world, are always dialectically related."

Consequently, the EH theorist takes a step back from examining a person's drives and specific behavior patterns; with a wider scope, she or he understands these in the context of a person's relation to existence (May 1958a, 1958b; Merleau-Ponty 1962). These relations, which manifest as structures, are not abstract but actual, and though they may be obscured from conscious awareness, they are nevertheless evident (though perhaps implied) in the present moment. They express themselves through bodily gestures, vocal tones, dreams, and behavior patterns, and not so much through words spoken.

The Cultivation of Presence

The existential therapist aims to know the person who comes for therapy at this "structural" level. As May (1958b, p. 38) states, "The grasping of the being of the other person occurs on a quite different level from our knowledge of specific things about him." In order to "grasp the being" of the client, and consequently help the client "grasp her being," the therapist must bring a full and genuine presence to the therapeutic encounter. The Latin root for presence is prae (before) + esse (to be); thus, presence means "to be before." Consequently, presence in a therapeutic setting can be understood as the capacity "to be before" or to be with one's being and/or "to be before" or to be with another human being.

Presence involves aspects of awareness, acceptance, availability, and expressiveness in both therapist and client. Presence implies that the encounter is real. For Martin Buber (1970), it means that the person who is before one has ceased being an "it" and has become a "thou"; it means that we are all humans who include each other in each other's recognition. Indeed, as Gabriel Marcel (1951) suggests, intersubjective presence begins with "we are" as opposed to "I think." If one can be truly present with another, then a genuine encounter has occurred.

Even with this emphasis on presence, EH theorists recognize the influence of the past in their present-centered encounters. They acknowledge, for example, the power of developmental deficits to impact therapeutic processes (Schneider 2008; Yalom 1980). However, the bases of those deficits and the contexts within which they are addressed differ significantly from those advanced by more conventional standpoints. For example, whereas psychoanalytically oriented theorists tend to view ruptures in early interpersonal relationships as the bases for developmental deficits, EH-oriented theorists take a wider view. This view acknowledges those early ruptures but goes beyond them to embrace the fuller experience of rupture or estrangement before being itself (May 1981; Schneider 2008; Yalom 1980). Put another way, whereas psychoanalytic theorists tend to focus on isolable family or physiological factors in the etiology of suffering, EH theorists tend to home in on dimensions that are purported to underlie such factors, such as the experience of life's vastness, the terror of dissolving before, or, on the other hand, exploding into life's vastness and the struggle with the enigma of death (Becker 1973; Schneider 1993, 2008; Yalom 1980).

It should be further understood that presence is core to an existential-integrative approach to therapy. Drawing from one's "whole body" experience of a client, presence helps to illuminate that which is palpably significant between oneself and the client and within the client. Like a barometer, presence signals to the therapist – and through reciprocity to the client – how the particular client is currently living, and how the client is *willing* to live. These revelations spur therapist and client to collaborate on his or her readiness and capacity for change. For example, a grave expression on the part of the client coupled with a sense of desperation in the therapist's resonance to the client, may suggest the need to slow down, consider practical options, such as breathing exercises, or the possible use of medication, and to check in about how best to proceed with each other. There are myriad indicators like this that can help fine tune what is most "authentic" to this particular client at this particular moment.

Alongside a willingness to consider mainstream and even programmatic approaches with clients, EH/EI theorists endeavor to understand the phenomenology of a given client's struggle, and to avoid diagnostic and psychodynamic presuppositions. While such presuppositions can certainly inform theorists' understanding, the aim is to remain as open as possible to the living, evolving person who may or may not conform to preset categorization.

Given this background, it may now be clearer why EH/EI theorists focus on here-and-now experiences of the past (as manifested in body posture, vocal tone, etc.) over discussions about the past. Whereas discussions can help clients to assimilate a specifiable event, such as an abuse memory, experiential awareness can help clients to assimilate the life stance, such as the sense of dissolution that both echoes and transcends the event.

For EH/EI theorists, accordingly, the deepest roots of trauma cannot simply be talked about or explained away; they must be rediscovered, felt, and lived through (Bugental 1987; Krug 2009; Schneider 2008).

ur Core Aims Distinguishing Features of EH/EI Therapy

To summarize, EH/EI theorists share four core aims: (a) to help clients to become more present to themselves and others; (b) to help them experience the ways in which they both mobilize and block themselves from fuller presence; (c) to help them take responsibility for the construction of their current lives; and (d) to help them choose or actualize ways of being in their outside lives based on facing, not avoiding, the existential givens such as finiteness, ambiguity, and anxiety.

Finally, although there is a great deal of overlap between EH/EI and other existentially and humanistically oriented theories (e.g., see Cooper 2017), there are several points on which it can be seen to be comparatively distinct. Among these are (1) EH/EI theory's stress on the relational as well as the personal (*although it must be granted that this distinction, like each one that follows, rests on a continuum and that there are occasional exceptions*); (2) it's emphasis on an existential-integrative rather than an exclusively exploratory focus; (3) its utilization of techniques (e.g., cognitive-behavioral, Gestalt) as they are organically called for, as distinct from a pre-set formula or set of suppositions; (4) its openness to discerning risks, such as the invitation to clients to explore tacit yet potentially illuminating "processes" as distinct from "contents" in the flow of their interactions; and (5) related to the latter, EH/EI therapy's reliance on the therapist's whole-body experience as well as clinical and philosophical elucidations to help guide the therapeutic process.

EH/EI therapy, as with several other humanistic and transpersonal therapies is also increasingly opening to a spiritual or "awe-based" dimension of the work. This dimension appears to be a natural extension of earlier existential-spiritual lineages (such as that of Kierkegaard, James, Rank, Tillich, Buber, Marcel, Becker and others) that have only recently come to a new prominence (Hoffman 2008; Schneider 2008). Moreover, the application of EH theories of personal and interpersonal integrity (à la Buber 1970) is also being demonstrated at the level of community dialogue and arts groups, aimed at healing socio-cultural rifts (Serlin 2017; Schneider 2017). I can think of few more urgent applications of EH/EI theory today than these kind of one-on-one and small-group mediation efforts.

Only the future will determine the lasting power of these emergent dimensions of EH/EI practice. That said, however, if the broad and deep aspirations of the founders are any indication, coupled with the fresh energy of the present generation, EH/EI theorists will not only continue to make inroads at the level of psychology, but with the suffering in societies and communities as well.

References

Becker, E. (1973). *The Denial of Death*. New York: Free Press.

Buber, M. (1970). *I and Thou: A Translation and Notes from Walter Kaufmann*. New York: Charles Schribner's Sons.

Bugental, J.F.T. (1965). *The Search for Authenticity*. New York: Holt, Rinehart, & Winston.

Bugental, J.F.T. (1976). *The Search for Existential Identity: Patient-Therapist Dialogues in Humanistic Psychotherapy*. San Francisco, CA: Jossey-Bass.

Bugental, J.F.T. (1978). *Psychotherapy and Process*. Reading, MA: Addison-Wesley.

Bugental, J.F.T. (1987). *The Art of the Psychotherapist*. New York: Norton.

Bugental, J.F.T. (1999). *Psychotherapy Isn't What You Think.* Phoenix, AZ: Zeig Tucker.
Bugental, J.F.T. and Kleiner, R. (1993). Existential psychotherapies. In: *Comprehensive Handbook of Psychotherapy Integration* (ed. G. Stricker and G. Gold), 101–112. New York: Plenum.
Bunting, K. and Hayes, S. (2008). Language and meaning: Acceptance and commitment therapy and the EI model. In: *Existential-integrative Psychotherapy: Guideposts to the Core of Practice* (ed. K.J. Schneider), 217–234. New York: Routledge.
Cooper, M. (2017). *Existential Therapies*, 2e. London: Sage.
Friedman, M. (1995). The case of Dawn. In: *The Psychology of Existence: An Integrative, Clinical Perspective* (ed. K.J. Schneider and R. May), 308–315. New York: McGraw-Hill.
Gendlin, E. (1978). *Focusing.* New York: Bantam.
Hoffman, L. (2008). An EI approach to working with religious and spiritual clients. In: *Existential-Integrative Psychotherapy: Guideposts to the Core of Practice* (ed. K. J. Schneider), 187–201. New York: Routledge.
Hoffman, L., Jackson, T., and Cleare-Hoffman, H. (2015). Humanistic psychology and multiculturalism: History, current status, and advancements. In: *The Handbook of Humanistic Psychology: Theory, Practice, and Research*, 2e (ed. K.J. Schneider, J.F. Pierson, and J.F.T. Bugental), 41–55. Thousand Oaks, CA: Sage.
Krug, O.T. (2009). James Bugental and Irvin Yalom: Two masters of existential therapy cultivate presence in the therapeutic encounter. *Journal of Humanistic Psychology 49* (3): 329–354.
Mahrer, A.R. (1996). *The Complete Guide to Experiential Psychotherapy.* New York: Wiley.
Marcel, G. (1951). *Mystery of Being – Faith and Reality.* Chicago: Gateway Edition.
Marcel, G. (1956). *The Philosophy of Existentialism.* New York: Citadel Press.
May, R. (1958a). The origins and significance of the existential movement in psychology. In: *Existence* (ed. R. May, E. Angel, and H. Ellenberger), 3–36. New York: Basic Books.
May, R. (1958b). Contributions of existential psychotherapy. In: *Existence* (ed. R. May, E. Angel, and H. Ellenberger), 37–91. New York: Basic Books.
May, R. (1981). *Freedom and Destiny.* New York: Norton.
May, R. (1983). *The Discovery of Being.* New York: Norton.
May, R., Angel, E., and Ellenberger, H.R. (1958). *Existence: A New Dimension in Psychiatry and Psychology.* Northvale, NJ: Jason Aronson.
Merleau-Ponty, M. (1962). *The Phenomenology of Perception.* New York: Routledge Kegan-Paul.
Rank, O. (1936). *Will Therapy.* New York: Knopf.
Schneider, K.J. (1993). *Horror and the Holy: Wisdom-Teachings of the Monster Tale.* Chicago: Open Court.
Schneider, K.J. (2008). *Existential-Integrative Psychotherapy: Guideposts to the Core of Practice.* New York: Routledge.
Schneider, K.J. (2013). *The Polarized Mind: Why It's Killing Us and What We Can Do About It.* Colorado Springs, CO: University Professors Press.
Schneider, K.J. (2017). *The Spirituality of Awe: Challenges to the Robotic Revolution.* Cardiff, CA: Waterfront Press.
Schneider, K.J. and Krug, O.T. (2010). *Existential-Humanistic Therapy.* Washington, DC: American Psychological Association Press.
Schneider, K.J. and Krug, O.T. (2017). *Existential-Humanistic Therapy*, 2e. Washington, DC: American Psychological Association.
Schneider, K.J. and May, R. (eds.) (1995). *The Psychology of Existence: An Integrative, Clinical Perspective.* New York: McGraw-Hill.
Serlin, I. (2017, May). Healing intergenerational trauma with arts and movement therapy. *Trauma Psychology News* (Division 56 of the American Psychological Association). http://traumapsychnews.com/2017/05/healing-intergenerational-trauma-with-dance-movement-therapy/ (accessed December 30, 2018).

Shahar, G. and Schiller, M. (2016). A conqueror by stealth: Introduction to the special issue on humanism, existentialism, and psychotherapy integration. *Journal of Psychotherapy Integration 26* (1): 1–4.

Shumaker, D. (2011). An existential-integrative treatment of anxious and depressed adolescents. *Journal of Humanistic Psychology 52* (4): 375–400.

Tillich, P. (1952). *The Courage to Be*. New Haven, CT: Yale University Press.

Wampold, B. (2008, February 6). Existential-integrative psychotherapy comes of age. [Review of the book *Existential-Integrative Psychotherapy: Guideposts to the Core of Practice*]. *PsycCritiques, 53* (6): Article 1.

Wolfe, B.E. (2016). Existential-humanistic therapy and psychotherapy integration: A commentary. *Journal of Psychotherapy Integration 26* (1): 56–60.

Yalom, I. (1980). *Existential Psychotherapy*. New York: Basic Books.

Yalom, I. (1989). *Love's Executioner*. New York: Basic Books.

Yalom, I. (1992). *When Nietzsche Wept*. New York: HarperCollins.

15

Existential-Humanistic and Existential-Integrative Therapy

Method and Practice

Orah T. Krug

Editor's Preface

While the last chapter focused on the philosophical and theoretical foundations of existential-humanistic (EH) and existential-integrative (EI) approaches to therapy, this chapter considers the processes by which those approaches are applied. It will be noted that in this chapter, the absence of detail about the method and practice of EI therapy is due simply to the fact that this latter perspective is still at a comparatively formative stage, and is grounded largely on the principles Dr. Krug is about to set forth. For more detail on my own articulation of EI application and processes, see Chapter 16 as well as *The Psychology of Existence: An Integrative, Clinical Perspective* (with Rollo May 1995); *Existential-Integrative Psychotherapy: Guideposts to the Core of Practice* (2008); "The experiential liberation strategy of the existential-integrative model of therapy" in the March 2007 issue of the *Journal of Contemporary Therapy;* and *Existential-Humanistic Therapy* (2017).

Kirk J. Schneider

Introduction

Existential-Humanistic therapy is a relational and experiential therapy, which focuses on clients' and therapists' actual, lived experiences. EH therapists desire to know their clients directly as opposed to projecting onto them abstract models of human behavior, be they behavioral or psychoanalytic. A real encounter with their clients' inner worlds cannot be had with standardized instruments or preconceived notions. Consequently EH therapists enter their clients' self-constructed worlds, using their own personal contexts to develop responsiveness to clients' feelings, experiences, and protective patterns.

The Wiley World Handbook of Existential Therapy, First Edition. Edited by Emmy van Deurzen, Erik Craig, Alfried Längle, Kirk J. Schneider, Digby Tantam, and Simon du Plock.

Within a safe and collaborative therapeutic relationship, clients work with their protective patterns and core wounds through experiential reflection and relational enactment. They see "close-up" how they miss a fuller life by constricting or blocking their capacity to live. Consciousness, responsibility, and choice take root in this reflective process – thus supporting the reclamation of previously abandoned ways of being. A reclaiming of one's life is the ultimate goal, but this cannot be achieved until one knows what has been disowned. Unlike other therapies, symptom removal is not the primary focus (although symptom removal often occurs). Rather, this type of change is in the core of one's being; it is "whole-bodied" and transformative.

Increasingly, even the science backs EH therapists' opposition to the standardization of therapy. In a comprehensive overview of the effectiveness of humanistic principles of practice Angus et al. (2015) found that for the majority of problems typically addressed in therapy, humanistic principles of practice, such as an emphasis on the relational and experiential aspects of the work, are on par with – and in some cases superior to – more programmatic principles of practice, such as those of cognitive-behavioral therapy. Leading researchers such as Bruce Wampold and John Norcross have been espousing similar positions for the past several years (Wampold 2007, 2008; Norcross and Lambert 2011).

This chapter begins with a review of the principles of EH practice related to identity formation and personal context. These theoretical principles offer EH practitioners a "map" with which to enter and live in the experiential worlds of their clients. A theory of change, from an EH perspective follows. The concluding section describes the method and practice of EH therapy. It illustrates how cultivating presence to process promotes healing and "whole-bodied" transformation. (For an elaboration on the principles summarized in this chapter, see Edelstein [2015] and Schneider and Krug [2017]).

Principles of Practice Related to Identity Formation and Personal Context

Human beings make meaning from experiences in the external world to create their personal (inner) worlds

Existential meaning making is an intrinsically human process related to identity formation. It is the act of "making sense" of an experience. Existential theory challenges the Cartesian notion of a world made up of objects and subjects who perceive those objects. Instead, existential theory understands that individuals participate in constructing their reality by making meaning (sense) of their perceptions and experiences as they relate to the external world. Thus they are not simply aware, they are conscious – aware of being the ones who construct meanings from experiences.

If individuals construct their personal worlds then within the definition of existence lies: (a) agency (i.e., we are centered in our being and create meanings about our world and our selves); (b) freedom (i.e., we choose how we define our perceptions and experiences); (c) responsibility (i.e., we are responsible for the choices we make); and (d) change (i.e., we have agency to create new meanings about our world and our selves).

Understanding the process of existence through this meaning-making lens underscores the need for therapists to sensitively attune to and explore the personal meanings and associated feelings of clients over and above dispensing a particular treatment or technique.

The constructed meanings result in a set of beliefs about oneself and others (self- and world constructs)

The meanings an individual makes from lived experiences create a set of self- and world constructs, essentially a set of beliefs regarding self, others, and the world. These constructs are understood as an individual's personal world or context that varies, continually influenced by the cultural, historical, and cosmological experiences of each individual.

Quite often these constructs are created outside one's awareness. Moreover these constructs are not constituted as dry abstractions but as embodied meanings, richly laden with personal feelings, thoughts, and opinions. All incoming and outgoing information flows through the lens of one's personal context. One's personal context is always "in process," being shaped and re-shaped.

Rollo May (1975) described this process of shaping and re-shaping reality and consciousness as "passion for form," which results in, as he called it, an "I am" experience, or the formation of one's identity. The following example will illustrate. One individual, let's call her Amy, has shaped and re-shaped her context so that currently she perceives herself as essentially lovable but acknowledges her occasional "unlovable behavior with others." Amy currently perceives her world as generally kind and accepting yet recognizes that, on occasion, her world may be harsh and unaccepting. Amy's "I am" experience is: "I am essentially loveable, my world is generally kind and accepting, and I can be open and accepting towards others." We can describe Amy's self- and world construct system (or her personal context) as fluid and flexible.

Contrast Amy's context with Robert's, who perceives himself as essentially unworthy and his world as consistently judgmental and harsh. Robert's "I am" experience is: "I am unworthy, my world is unsafe, and I must to be wary of others." We can describe Robert's self- and world construct system (likely out of his awareness), as "calcified" and rigid.

Clearly, Amy and Robert experience the external world through very different context lenses. Amy's lens is fluid and flexible. She can take in "raw data" from the external world. Amy is able to have a "primary experiencing" of the external world. Consequently, she can be present in her life, easily engaging in the world with curiosity, acceptance, and openness. Whereas Robert, whose context lens is calcified and rigid has more difficulty taking in "raw data" because it gets distorted as it flows through his context lens. We can describe Robert as "caught in his context," unable to perceive what's really "out there," because he can only experience the world through his rigid set of beliefs about himself and others. Robert is typically limited to having a "secondary experiencing" of the external world. Consequently Robert usually constricts his life and relationships, perhaps avoiding real intimacy. Using Amy and Robert as examples we can appreciate that fluid and flexible construct systems often result in joyful living and close relationships whereas "calcified" and rigid construct systems often result in emotional distress along with deadened living and superficial relationships.

We can assess healthy functioning by evaluating the extent to which a person is able to be truly present with self and others versus a person who is consistently caught in his or her context.

Protective patterns ("spacesuits") develop alongside rigid self- and world constructs

Most of us have difficulty fully facing and accepting some life experiences – especially those that are particularly painful and devastating. If we use Robert again as an example, we can imagine that Robert's past may have included rejecting and abandoning experiences, which wounded and overwhelmed him. These experiences led him to conclude that he is unworthy of love and that the world is cruel and rejecting. In order to cope and live, Robert may have buried or disowned, at an early age, his sense of unworthiness and developed a "workaholic protective pattern" to block him from experiencing this painful core belief and wound. Consequently, as an adult, Robert is consistently stuck wearing his spacesuit, always anticipating rejection from others, behaving in ways that validate his assumption again and again. Today Robert is a successful and powerful company executive, who never stops "doing" and whose relationships are superficial, not intimate. Robert may say things like: "I can't slow down," "I have too much to do," and "I'm fine, I don't need close relationships."

James Bugental (1999) likened protective patterns to wearing spacesuits in outer space: they allow us to survive and function, but they don't give us the freedom to scratch our noses! Robert may come to therapy when some life event makes his "spacesuit" too constricting, thereby causing him sufficient distress to seek help. Robert likely has an internal battle raging between a part of himself that wants to emerge (perhaps his desire for intimacy) and his "spacesuit" that holds the emerging part back to protect him (perhaps from his fear of intimacy or rejection).

Awareness of self- and world constructs helps therapists hone in on their clients' unique perspectives about their natures and relational worlds, as well as on their clients' protective patterns that both constrict and support survival. Awareness of self- and world constructs also focuses the therapist on his or her own personal context that may be impeding therapeutic effectiveness with a particular client.

The client's past is alive in the present moment

In each moment, the client's past – all of the meanings constructed about self and others – flows into the present moment, actual and real. In the therapeutic encounter, clients' self-constructed worlds and protective patterns (spacesuits) manifest concretely in vocal tones, affect, body postures, language, dreams, and relational behavior patterns. These "ways of being and relating" are understood as the *client's process*, an amalgam of feelings, thoughts, and behaviors, which are present in the living moment but are often out of awareness.

Robert, for example, who relates to himself and to the therapist as a machine, also comes consistently late to sessions. As therapy progressed, his objectifications and tardiness were revealed to be concrete manifestations of a core decision: "If I treat myself and others as objects, and if I never allow myself to risk real connections with others, then I'll never get rejected or hurt by others." Another "composite" client, let's call her Renee, won't reach over to take a new tissue, even though hers is shredded from crying. Her behavior, as the work revealed was a concrete manifestation of her core decision: "If I always make do, I'll never have to rely on anyone, and thus, never get let down."

Each of these examples serves to illustrate that not only are the clients before us but so are their lives, and their protective patterns, constructed to insulate them from overwhelming hurt and pain. If we recognize this, then we need not go on an "archeological dig" to find the "actuality" of a client's life – it is, in fact, concretely manifesting in the here and now, visible and kinesthetically felt. Our task is to appropriately respond and reflect back our clients' intra- and interpersonal processes. If we do that, the consequences will likely be clients' expanded experiential awareness of themselves and others. This method and how it unfolds is described in the next section.

Human beings are both free and determined

Humans are free because they make meanings from their experiences, and they are determined because these meanings are limited by natural and self-imposed limitations. In other words, our subjective freedom – that is, our freedom to form attitudes, meanings, and emotions about an experience – is limited by the objective facts of the experience, the givens of existence, and our personal, cultural, and historical context. An awareness of the impact of natural and self-imposed limitations on personal freedom helps the therapist appreciate the challenges inherent in effecting healing and change: the "constancy" of personhood is a powerful counterweight to freedom and change. The tension between constancy (of old, familiar patterns) and change (to new, unfamiliar patterns) often results in internal battles that clients like Robert struggle to resolve in therapy.

Personal context influences perception and contact with others

EH therapists appreciate that one's context is continually influencing one's perceptions and experiences of the external world. As Bonnie Raitt, the philosophical singer-songwriter suggests, "no matter if our glasses are on or off, we see the world we make." In other words, as much as we strive to brush away our biases and to be deeply present, our personal context inevitably limits, to some extent, our interpersonal contact. However, a reality complementing the aforementioned reality is that interpersonal contact is always influencing one's intrapersonal context.

Consequently, our task, as EH therapists is first and foremost to "know thyself," in other words: how is our personal context that is, our biases and worldviews influencing the work with clients? Our second task is to help Robert and Renee (and all of our clients) become curious about how their personal contexts impact their experiences of the external world. Our task is to help them develop "reflective secondary experiencing," in other words, a capacity to non-judgmentally reflect on how their personal context might be clouding their primary experiencing of themselves and of others – us for example. We can cultivate their curiosity because we are a crucial part of our clients' present, external world. This means that how we relate to them can significantly influence how they see themselves and us, helping them to re-evaluate their unconstructive relational patterns.

An EH Theory of Human Change Processes

EH practitioners base their conception of human change processes on their suppositions about human nature, human experience, and human functioning. Human beings are understood to be always in the process of becoming, situated as beings-in-the-world – relating to their physical, personal, and social worlds. Human beings are not simply a collection of drives and behavior patterns within encapsulated selves – human beings are more than the sum of their parts. Human beings continually shape their experiences because they are capable of self-reflection and subjective meaning making. Hence human beings have agency: they are free to change, to make new meanings – yet are bound by the givens of existence and their unique personal, cultural, and historical contexts. We are both free and determined.

The path to greater freedom is paradoxically found through an encounter with the ways in which one is bound. This means EH therapists help clients experience and attune to their polarized, limiting protection patterns and their underlying traumas, fears, and anxieties. In so doing, clients reflect upon, as opposed to react against, evocative material. This work typically results in clients appreciating the "functionality" of their symptoms and experiencing their polarized protection patterns as restrictive or self-limiting. Thus, by encouraging clients to experientially embody their restrictive patterns, clients can face and accept the givens of existence that they may have been avoiding, denying, or repressing. However, for the EH practitioner, responsibility assumption is not sufficient – it is simply preparatory for substantive change evidenced when clients first make new meanings about themselves and then choose more life-affirming patterns for themselves and with others (for an expanded perspective see Krug 2016)

Method and Practice: The Process of Therapeutic Change

The cultivation of presence as ground and method for effecting change

EH therapists aim to know the person who comes for therapy at a structural level of being so as to illuminate the blocks and limiting polarized patterns. To accomplish this, EH therapists employ the cultivation of intra and interpersonal presence to empathically enter their clients' experiential worlds and know them as they are and the meanings they have made about themselves and their lives. Presence involves aspects of awareness, acceptance, availability, and expressiveness in both therapist and client. Presence implies that the encounter is real and that client and therapist include each other in each other's recognition.

The cultivation of presence promotes a real encounter between two individuals; it is not a hierarchical meeting in which one is a shadowy figure holding all the knowledge and power. On the contrary as May (1983) suggests, "encounter [is] a way of participating in the feelings and world of the patient" (p. 66). Yalom (2002) describes it as a meeting of two "fellow travelers" on life's journey together. *Hence presence is both the ground for a genuine encounter and a method for effecting transformational change.*

The intention of the cultivation of presence is to treat clients as individuals and not as diagnoses, classifications, or symptoms. It promotes attitudes of "being with" and "being for" clients, it germinates safe and close therapeutic relationships, which form the foundation upon which other, more challenging, work relies. Presence and curiosity cannot be cultivated when abstract models of human behavior or clinical diagnoses are projected onto clients. EH therapists understand clients' symptoms not as problems to eliminate, but rather as methods to maintain selfhood by shutting out disavowed feelings or experiences. They wonder, "What is the meaning of this symptom at this point in my client's life? What does the symptom want 'to tell' my client?"

Cultivate a presence to process more than content

Although EH therapists value the content (or explicit features) of clients' experiences, they are acutely and simultaneously attuned to the process or implicit aspects of those experiences. Thus, EH therapists carefully cultivate presence to what is most alive in the moment and respond accordingly: it may be to the personal process (of the therapist or of the client) or to the interpersonal process (of the therapist or of the client). They wonder, "How is my client telling me his story?" "Is his voice flat and unemotional or filled with trembling emotion?" "Does he look at me or does he turn away as he tells me his story?" Another way to consider the relationship between process and content is to think of content as the "words" of a song and process as the "music" of a song. The "music" conveys the tone and the mood often at a deeper level than the "words" themselves. Similarly, a focus on process will often reveal meanings of a deeper nature than does a focus on content.

To the extent that clients are desirous and capable of deeper work, EH therapists focus on the "here and now," as opposed to the "then and there." The "here" refers to the therapeutic encounter and the "now" refers to the present moment. Working in the "here and now" is a powerful tool for therapists because if one assumes the client's past is alive in the present moment, then the therapeutic relationship becomes a microcosm of the client's personal and relational worlds. This makes the therapeutic encounter a "living laboratory," whereby therapeutic process refers not only to immediate interactions between client and therapist, but it also references the underlying personal and relational processes of both client and therapist. Consequently, EH therapists appropriately reflect back clients' implicit personal and relational ways of being that are evident but unnoticed: for example, my focus on Renee's shredded tissue.

They may also attend to how the client occupies personal space – with confidence and ease or with hesitation and constraint? They may comment on clients' relational ways of being, that is, "You seem to not like what I just said." Or they may simply attend to how clients relate to them – in engaged, open ways or in detached, aloof ways? If therapists bring a full and genuine presence to the encounter they can bracket their own world perspective sufficiently to see a person as he or she really lives and relates, and understand his or her unique meanings made from past experiences.

Illuminate the actual but unnoticed protective patterns

Healing and change happens as protective patterns are mirrored to clients allowing them to experience how their patterns are embodied and enacted within the therapeutic relationship. With Renee for example, when I felt she might be caught in her protective pattern with me, I would check in, asking: "Are you 'making do' right now by not asking me for something you need or want?" This "up close" experiencing of self-limiting patterns also highlights the internal battle between the parts that want to emerge and those which need to stop the emerging part. Implicit in my mirroring of Renee's protective pattern is the question: "Is this how you want to continue living?"

By mirroring self-protective patterns, clients begin to develop a capacity to reflect on their protective life stance (their spacesuits) instead of being unaware of them: Renee can notice: "There I go, just 'making do' again," or Robert opens to: "There I go again, showing up late to our session." Reflection requires pausing, that is, slowing down the client and/or the interpersonal process. By pausing, we help clients develop "reflective secondary experiencing." First we help them develop a non-judgmental witness to their protective stance, "Can you notice, without judging how you're 'making do' with me?" Then we may invite them to attend to what's happening in their bodies or to what's happening in the relational field. We invite images, associations about meanings, and past experiences to become more conscious. "Just go slow and see what's there," is something we might suggest to shift clients from a "doing" mode to a "being mode." Cultivating personal and relational presence in this way often allows clients to feel the pain of a wound, no longer numbed by the protective pattern. The belief about self finds expression: For example, Renee might say, "I've never felt worthy of being cared for – I'm damaged, that's why I don't reach out to you." Or, Robert might convey, "I feel unlovable – I'm afraid if I engage with you and let you matter to me, you'll reject me." To the extent appropriate, meanings made about self, others, and world, and the associated hurt and pain are felt and worked through at an embodied, not cognitive level in the safety of the therapeutic relationship. By supporting clients to experientially embody their self-restrictive patterns, clients can face and accept the givens of existence and their core decisions and wounds that may have been avoided, denied, or repressed. Together past relational patterns can be dissolved and new ones developed.

Awareness, responsibility, and choice now become a part of the exploratory, reiterative process: Renee, "Oh, there I go again, just making do! Is that what I want to keep doing? Maybe not." Or, Robert, "There I go again, not thinking I matter to you, showing up late to our session. Maybe I can risk showing up and engaging with you. Maybe you won't reject me." Jim Bugental (1999) likened a person's protective pattern to a mask on one's face, and as therapy progresses, and awareness about the protective pattern increases, the client slowly pulls the mask away bringing it into ever-greater focus.

Responsibility is assumed for constructing the protective pattern, along with a newfound sense of agency and choice. The process of healing and change is by no means linear, nor is it primarily cognitive. Whereas discussions can help a client incorporate, for example, a memory of abuse – deep attunement or presence can help a client *experience the self-limiting stance* created to protect him or herself from overwhelming feelings. The process of illuminating the life stance that both echoes and transcends the event and then helping one to re-claim the disowned feelings hidden behind the stance is the life-changing work of EH therapy. *The deepest roots of trauma cannot be talked about or explained away; they must be discovered, felt, and lived through.*

Emergence of new meanings and new behaviors indicates substantive change

Responsibility assumption is not sufficient – it is simply preparatory for substantive change evidenced when clients first make new meanings about themselves, for example, Renee, "I don't have to just make do, I can lean on others because I am worthy and good enough." Or, Robert, "I don't have to avoid engaging with people, I'm loveable, and not a pariah." *These new meanings about self typically result in the construction of more functional, satisfying, and meaningful patterns of living and relating to others both personally and professionally.*

Conclusion

EH therapists use the cultivation of presence to effect healing and change. Presence involves aspects of awareness, acceptance, availability, and expressiveness in both therapist and client. If one can be truly present with another, then a genuine encounter has occurred in which previously disowned protective patterns and wounds can be faced, dissolved, or managed making room for new, more functional patterns to emerge. This "whole-bodied" transformation can even, at times, lead clients to notably new attitudes toward life in general; such as an attitude of humility and wonder, or sense of adventure that can fruitfully be termed "awe-inspiring" (Schneider and Krug 2017).

References

Angus, L., Watson, J., Elliott, R. et al. (2015). Humanistic psychotherapy research 1990–2015: From methodological innovation to evidence-supported treatment outcomes and beyond. *Psychotherapy Research 25* (3): 330–347.

Bugental, J.F.T. (1999). *Psychotherapy Isn't What You Think*. Phoenix, AZ: Zeig, Tucker.

Edelstein, B. (2015). Frames, attitudes, and skills of an existential-humanistic therapist. In: *The Handbook of Humanistic Psychology: Theory, Practice, and Research*, 2e (ed. K.J. Schneider, J.F. Pierson, and J.F. Bugental), 435–449. Thousand Oaks, CA: Sage.

Krug, O.T. (2016) Existential, humanistic, and experiential therapies in historical perspective. In: *Comprehensive Textbook of Psychotherapy: Theory and Practice*, 2e (ed. A. Consoli and L. Liebert), 91–105. Oxford: Oxford University Press.

May, R. (1975). *The Courage to Create*. New York: Norton.

May, R. (1983). *The Discovery of Being*. New York: Norton.

Norcross, J.C. and Lambert, M.J. (2011). Psychotherapy relationships that work. *Psychotherapy 48* (1): 4–8. doi: 10.1037/a0022180.

Schneider, K.J. (2007). The experiential liberation strategy of the existential-integrative model of therapy. *Journal of Contemporary Therapy 37* (1): 33–39.

Schneider, K.J. (2008). *Existential-Integrative Psychotherapy: Guideposts to the Core of Practice*. New York: Routledge.

Schneider, K.J. and Krug, O.T. (2017). *Existential-Humanistic Therapy*, 2e. Washington, DC: APA.
Schneider, K.J. and May, R. (1995). *The Psychology of Existence: An Integrative, Clinical Perspective*. London: McGraw Hill.
Wampold, B.E. (2007). Psychotherapy: The humanistic (and effective) treatment. *American Psychologist 62* (8): 857–873.
Wampold, B.E. (2008, February 6). Existential-integrative psychotherapy comes of age [Review of the book *Existential-Integrative Psychotherapy: Guideposts to the Core of Practice*]. *PsycCritiques*, *53*, Release 6, Article 1.
Yalom, I. (2002). *The Gift of Therapy*. New York: HarperCollins.

16

Case Illustrations of Existential-Humanistic and Existential-Integrative Therapy

Orah T. Krug, Nathaniel Granger, Irvin Yalom, and Kirk J. Schneider

Introduction

In this chapter, four case illustrations are presented to give the reader a vivid, lived experience of how existential-humanistic (EH) therapy actually unfolds between clients and therapists. The first two cases, one by Orah Krug and her client Mimi, and one by Nathaniel Granger and his clients Mary and Jeff illustrate how EH therapists (a) develop responsiveness to clients' feelings, experiences and protective patterns; (b) develop collaborative and safe therapeutic relationships with clients; (c) assess client motivation, level of functioning and capacity for presence, and (d) work with levels of self-protections and associated wounds by focusing on process over content. The cases also illustrate how EH therapists attain the goals of expanded experiential awareness and real therapeutic change by cultivating genuine encounters in which both clients and therapists are personally and relationally present.

The third case, by renowned psychiatrist Irvin Yalom, is a vibrant example of how "here-now," experiential engagement can be creatively entwined with psychodynamic understanding of subconscious processes. Yalom's supportive yet selectively challenging stance with his client "Elva" is not only emblematic of superb EH encounter, but also, as Yalom himself imparts, "the best hour of therapy I ever gave."

The final case by Kirk J. Schneider provides a brief illustration of "existential-integrative" therapy, discussed earlier in Part III. This case shows how *availability* to in-depth or experiential change can potentially enhance any bona fide approach, which in this instance began with a cognitive-behavioral slant.

In sum, EH therapists cultivate presence to three dimensions of experience and process: (a) the personal or subjective dimensions of both client and therapist, (i.e., a

---

The Wiley World Handbook of Existential Therapy, First Edition. Edited by Emmy van Deurzen, Erik Craig, Alfried Längle, Kirk J. Schneider, Digby Tantam, and Simon du Plock.

focus on "self"); (b) the interpersonal or relational dimension, (i.e., a focus on the "in-between" field of client and therapist); and (c) the ontological or cosmological dimension, (i.e., an existential focus on "the world"). Being present to all three dimensions of experience and process is crucial – all three dimensions are "actual" in the present moment, and provide entry into the feelings and world of the client. Without presence there may be intellectual, behavioral, or physiological change but not necessarily the sense of agency or personal involvement that "whole-bodied" transformation requires.

The Case of Mimi

Orah T. Krug

The case study of Mimi, my client, demonstrates how EH therapy is an experiential journey of personal discovery and embodied transformation (for the full case study see Schneider and Krug 2017, p. 76). This case illustrates how an EH therapist conceptualizes and facilitates change by being present to all three dimensions of experience and process. Three additionally significant aspects of EH therapy are also illuminated in this case: (a) how it can be tailored to be a brief therapy, (b) how it can be the foundation upon which other approaches such as cognitive behavioral and Eye Movement Desensitization Reprogramming (EMDR) therapy can be employed, and (c) how it allows a therapist to enter the subjective world of her client even though she differs from the therapist with respect to country and culture.

This therapeutic encounter began with Mimi and me in a therapy room several years ago. (Mimi is a composite of several clients with whom I worked). Mimi and I are centered in ourselves with a capacity to relate to the other. We relate to each other from our own personal contexts, which means that we are limited, to some extent, to be present and connected to ourselves and to each other. I had been an existential-humanistic therapist for over 20 years at the time; Mimi was a 29-year-old married woman, of Persian descent, who was 8-months pregnant with her second child. We agreed the therapy would be limited to eight sessions because of Mimi's impending due date. Although not central to the therapy, Mimi's Persian heritage, culture, and worldview factored in to the way I related to and worked with her.

My first aim was to cultivate a safe and collaborative therapeutic relationship with Mimi. I also wanted to step into her experiential world so I could attune empathically to her feelings and experiences. By attuning to what was most alive in the moment whether it be within Mimi, within me, or within the interpersonal field, I could reflect the moment, thereby supporting expansion of her experiential awareness. Why do EH therapists work in this way? Because we believe that it is within a safe and intimate therapeutic relationship, co-created by therapist and client, that disowned experiences and relational patterns (of both client and therapist) can be discovered, integrated, or revised. We assume the client will relate to the therapist as he or she relates to others outside the therapy room because the client's past is concretely alive in the present moment. Thus, as Yalom (2002) suggests, working in the here-and now is the "power cell" of therapy. By cultivating personal and relational presence the therapist and client experience the client's real (actual) but often out of awareness (unregarded) experiences and ways of relating. By illuminating these life stances carefully and respectfully, *therapy becomes a project of experiencing one's life instead of talking about one's life*. EH therapists believe, as do other experiential therapists, that this is the basis for real and lasting life changes.

Mimi presented as a highly functioning, attractive, young woman, in deep distress – a woman significantly motivated to change, related in part, to her fast approaching due date. Three weeks prior to this first meeting, a plane had crashed into her home when Mimi and her three year old were eating lunch. I assessed that prior to the incident Mimi had felt generally happy and content with her life and marriage but now her sense of security was badly ruptured. Mimi was drained both physically and emotionally but very motivated to "get her old life back."

In the first session, as I listened to Mimi tell her story, I attended not only to the content but also to *how* Mimi related her story. Being present to Mimi's process, allowed me to hear and see Mimi's life stance (her spacesuit) emerging in her vocal intensity, affect, body language, and attitude toward self and others. Mimi's life stance was present (actual) but out of Mimi's awareness (unregarded), expressed concretely in different ways, summarized here as: "If I'm good and do things right then good things will happen to me and to those I love." Now Mimi's stance obviously has positive value, that is, Mimi believed in her agency and in taking responsibility for her life. Unfortunately, also implicit in Mimi's life stance was her unmediated belief in the power of her personal control to keep herself and her loved ones safe – Mimi does not truly appreciate an existential axiom: one can influence but not control an outcome. So when the plane crashed into Mimi's home, her unmediated belief in her personal power was seriously shaken. Mimi's typically self-assured and confident manner was only faintly present at the first meeting. Three weeks after the incident Mimi was still highly agitated and anxious. As Mimi told her story, she angrily repeated again and again, "it isn't fair." I sensed the phrase was rife with emotion-laden meaning given her life stance. I also sensed that she was "caught" in the experience, as if in the retelling of the story she was relieving the experience.

My work with Mimi was an integration of behavioral strategies within an existential-humanistic context. Our goals, created together in the first session were to: (a) address her post-traumatic stress disorder (PTSD) symptoms, (b) help her to be more present and calm, and c) incorporate constructively the traumatic experience into her life. In the first session I gave her an experience of how I work in the here and now. She experienced how experiential learning could help her develop deeper awareness of her thoughts and behavior patterns that might be blocking her healing process. I asked whether she agreed to work with me in this way. She readily did. I began with Mimi, as I do with all of my clients to build the therapeutic relationship with my self-disclosures and "contracting" with Mimi on how our work will proceed. Getting Mimi to "buy-in" to my way of working gives me a place to stand with her and conveys to her my belief in transparency and collaboration.

In the first session I learned that in addition to the airplane incident, Mimi was stressed by the responsibility of caring for her elderly parents and sister dying of cancer. Mimi allowed that she was carrying a heavy load but said she was okay because it meant she was fulfilling her role in the family. I understood that Mimi's cultural norm was to be "a good daughter" so I supported Mimi's duties on the one hand acknowledging they gave her life purpose and meaning but noting how the duties seemingly added additional stress to her already stressed system. I framed Mimi's situation in this way thereby allowing Mimi to feel supported and not judged. Eventually Mimi decided to delegate some of her duties to a visiting nurse.

With regard to the traumatic incident in the first session, I knew I needed to help Mimi out of her traumatizing loop enacted as she raged at the pilot's stupidity saying, "it isn't fair, I wasn't prepared." I intervened by noting to her repeated expressions of rage, saying, "once again, you say how unfair it is" or "can you hear yourself getting angry again as you tell me what happened?" Fairly quickly she began to agree with my comment that her repetitive statements were gnawing away at her like the mice gnawing on her clothes in her now abandoned home. I tried to help her move out of her "stuckness" by suggesting that she employ a "Stop" technique (Penzel 2000). Whenever she heard herself begin the repetitive litany, she was to say, "Stop, I don't need to go down this road" and go to a place in her imagination where she felt safe and cozy. I asked her to practice the "Stop" technique as many times as she needed in between sessions.

At the next session, she reported that at first she struggled to stop her repetitive thinking but after using the technique for a while, she was able to stop reliving her plight and started to feel better. Given that Mimi was beginning to let go of her anger, now seemed an opportune time to help her experience other feelings associated with her trauma. At this point, then, Mimi was able to release her anger and her replay of the event, not through advising or suggesting, but through inviting her to cultivate personal presence. I suggested she slow down and make space for the phrase, "It isn't fair, I wasn't prepared," to simply reflect on the phrase, saying aloud whatever emerged. I invited her to "go slow" so she might deepen her experience of her anger, and discover what lay behind it, which eventually emerged as her death terror. "There was no place to go and I thought we were going to die" Mimi eventually realized. Yet prior to this, she was blocked from consciousness by her rage at the pilot for not "doing right" by her. This work allowed Mimi to be "with" her experience, and not "caught" in it. By connecting with her subjective experience, she was able to be both with the experience and stand back from it. She reported that she felt separate from her feelings for the first time. Now Mimi could begin to heal and loosen her stance towards life, a stance that had created a sense of invulnerability and specialness, that is, a belief that "bad things happen to everyone else but me." When this traumatic event occurred, Mimi felt oddly betrayed because of this implicit belief, which was out of her conscious awareness. By encouraging Mimi to be more personally present she began to "shake off her spacesuit" and over the next few sessions she gradually shifted from a repetitive expression of anger to her deeper experience of impending death and associated powerlessness in a constructive and healing way.

I also invited Mimi to focus on interpersonal presence, asking her, "How was it for you to have me witness your exploration of your feelings?" She said she felt comforted by my presence and wondered if it was common for people to use anger to cover up feelings of helplessness. Interestingly, before she had raised that issue, I was aware of my own context and how I too have often "led" with anger to cover up my feelings of helplessness and powerlessness. When she turned to directly ask me if I ever did that, I told her I had. My transparency prompted a fruitful exploration of how we all develop self-protective yet constricting patterns, which we can get caught in during times of great stress.

Within the context of a safe therapeutic relationship, healing and change occurred. In each session I checked in with Mimi as to how we were doing, thereby giving Mimi an opportunity to share what was difficult and what was helpful. The "check-ins" also helped me know if I was staying aligned with her, given that our cultural differences could potentially result in misunderstandings. By working in this relational, collaborative way, I gauged Mimi's sense of safety, knowing that the therapist's most important goal is to create a safe and secure therapeutic relationship.

I helped Mimi dissolve her traumatic memories using a modified version of EMDR, as developed by Shapiro (1998) by asking her to call up the memory and view it as if she were on a train and the landscape was moving past her. As she recalled the memory, I told her to tell herself, "this is just a memory, it's in the past, I can let it go by and focus on my safe and cozy place." Two weeks went by between sessions. Mimi walked in looking more relaxed and secure. She reported that she was no longer plagued by the memories and was beginning to feel more alive in her life. She reported that she was sleeping more soundly, was less irritable, and not jumping at loud noises.

Many therapists would be satisfied with Mimi's reported improvement and would likely have no further aims other than to consolidate the learning. But as an existential-humanistic therapist, I sensed that one of the difficulties underlying Mimi's symptoms was her inability to accept a crucial aspect of existence, namely that personal safety and security is an illusion – at any moment it can be shattered. So I decided to use the two remaining sessions to help Mimi experientially face the existential reality that life will deal with her in the same harsh way it deals with others, helping her to work through her feelings of betrayal. We devoted a substantial amount of time working with Mimi's inability to accept the contingencies of existence. As we explored Mimi's feelings about life's uncertainties, she began to realize how she typically coped with uncertainty – by being self-sufficient and by trying to be in control, by being "on top of everything" and "keeping a lid on her feelings."

Her phrase "it isn't fair" re-emerged but now Mimi understood it as her unwillingness to face and accept the harsh contingencies of life. "Go slow," I suggested "and let yourself explore what it means now." This time, as Mimi experientially reflected on it's meaning, a deeper meaning emerged: "It isn't fair that there is no plan, no structure or protection – anything can happen. I don't like it but I guess that's just how life is." By relinquishing her illusion of personal protection, Mimi could now paradoxically accept her vulnerability and finiteness. Mimi let go of old meanings about herself and her world (e.g., "I'm safe if I do the right thing") and made new ones, (e.g., "I'm vulnerable, anything can happen"), which allowed her to cope more consciously and effectively with the realities of life. The therapeutic journey of discovery and transformation for Mimi eventuated as a paradox – Mimi could only affirm her being by acknowledging her limitations. Mimi had to relinquish her illusion of "specialness" so she could embrace more life-affirming patterns.

My work with Mimi illustrates how EH therapists facilitate transformation by: (1) cultivating therapeutic presence, (2) activating deep experiential reflection and enactment, (3) identifying and illuminating polarized protective patterns, and (4) supporting the reclamation of disowned experiences, thus allowing for the creation of new meanings and more constructive ways of being. The net result for Mimi was an expanded sense of self, specifically, an enhanced capacity for intimacy with her husband and children, coupled with more joy and spontaneity in her life. Mimi succinctly summarized her therapeutic journey by exclaiming: "I'm like my old self but better!"

To summarize, EH theorists share four core aims: (1) to help clients to become more present to themselves and others; (2) to help them experience the ways in which they *both mobilize and block themselves from fuller presence* (3) to help them take responsibility for the construction of their current lives; and (4) to help them choose or actualize ways of being in their outside lives based on facing, not avoiding, the existential givens such as finiteness, ambiguity, separateness and freedom.

EH Couples Therapy: A Study of Mary and Jeff

Nathaniel Granger

Editor's Note: The following is a case study of EH couples therapy by Nathaniel Granger. Although this illustration differs somewhat in style from Dr. Krug's, it nevertheless stresses EH therapy's core principles of freedom, experiential reflection, and responsibility. The illustration also represents one of the rare occasions in which EH therapy has been described as it applies to couples. – Kirk J. Schneider

Introduction

Existential Psychology combines the big questions of philosophy with the tenets of psychology and is not concerned with simply reducing various symptomology but addressing how a person finds and defines meaning, purpose, and a life well lived, despite circumstances. Hence, it is not only concerned with "being" but "becoming" and stresses that the freedom to choose "freedom" (that is, choice, possibility) is most liberating. This case study of "Mary" and to a lesser degree, her husband "Jeff," demonstrates that the acquisition of meaning during the process of therapy can be significantly more valuable than through simply diagnosing the problem and "fixing it" as an endpoint.

History

Presenting Problem

Mary, a 23-year-old, White female with a religious background deeply rooted in the Pentecostal denomination, arrived for her first therapy session meticulously plain, donned all in black including hair and fingernail polish. It was soon evident that Mary could easily fit in wherever she went, but more importantly she could just as easily fade into the background. Yet, when she desired, Mary could also stand out and make her presence known (Hoffman and Granger 2009). However, during the past several months this did not happen so often; she preferred to remain hidden, isolated, and in darkness as indicated by her desire to wear black every day. Mary came into therapy at her husband Jeff's request in order to fix a "broken marriage" and to help Mary better manage her symptoms of depression and cope with a recent diagnosis of multiple sclerosis. At the time of therapy, Jeff, a 23-year-old Hispanic male, also presented with a religious affiliation deeply rooted in Pentecostalism.

As her black attire and sullen demeanor would soon depict, Mary was not "Goth" but was in a state of mourning over the loss of a "friend" in the person of her husband. Mary had been best friends with her husband since college, but confessed she was never in love with him. Her religious family along with Jeff's religious family coerced them into marriage after she unwittingly became pregnant by Jeff after a night of partying.

Jeff and Mary were a young couple who had been married for seven years. Jeff and Mary had two sons whom they both adored, Brandon aged six and Matt aged five. Initially, the plan was to treat only the wife in individual therapy but it was later agreed that it would be beneficial if I would see both Jeff and Mary for individual sessions. At the outset Mary expressed her lack of marital satisfaction, however, it wasn't until the third session that issues of infidelity surfaced on both Jeff and Mary's part, and around the fifth session it was revealed that Jeff had had an ongoing sexual relationship with Mary's twin sister Maribeth. After the fallout from Jeff's indiscretions, he retaliated with the admission that he had contracted from his wife Mary the Human Papillomavirus (HPV) with severe outbreaks of genital warts. Because of histrionic behaviors, such as Mary's expressed attraction for me (her therapist) as well as Jeff's exaggerated desire for a "friendship" with me that seemed counter-intuitive to the therapeutic relationship, I informed them that I would like to refer them to another therapist, at which point, both refused stating that I was the only one they could trust and that they felt it was not possible to develop a rapport with another therapist. Accordingly, individual sessions ensued.

Correspondingly, after weeks of therapy, Mary made a courageous step to separate from her husband. She moved into a hotel but later maintained the family home after Jeff moved out. It was also during this time that she confronted her twin sister about the adulteress relationship with her husband as well as confronted Jeff about his indiscretions. This came in the wake of EMDR to establish a "safe space" and to ameliorate some of the trauma relative to her hyper-religious upbringing and the division within her family resulting from her husband/sister affair. It was in this light that Jeff explained that because he loved his wife so much and because she had become increasingly ambivalent towards him, he found intimacy in Mary's twin sister, citing that she was the "closest thing that reminded me of my wife."

Therapy

After several distressful individual sessions, Mary presented as cheerful with colored (pink) nails; as previously stated, Mary was usually in black but had on color for the first time since coming to therapy. Mary expressed "being pulled between God's grace and forgiveness and doing what makes her happy – two doors of absolutes!" I validated the client in that she was actually demonstrating forgiveness and walking in grace without knowing it in that she was spending time with her husband (spent the night with him one week). It seemed to me that Mary needed to delineate what she really wanted without toying with her husband's emotions as she vacillated between wanting him out of her life and wanting his friendship.

Mary opened the session with "I'm searching for wisdom!" Yet she was torn between the polarities (or extremes) of "right and wrong – God and Satan." In Kirk J. Schneider's

The Polarized Mind: Why It's Killing Us and What We Can Do About It (2013, p. 14) the author suggests that

> Polarization begins with fear, and extreme polarization begins with extreme fear. Extreme fear, depth research has revealed, associates not just with loss of values or even loss of life; but with complete loss of orientation – in a word, *groundlessness*. The sense of groundlessness, in turn, can lead to great defensive maneuvers to regain ground, or *significance* – and not just ordinary ground or significance but enormous height *(glory)* to defy even a hint of the former vulnerability.

Apart from her struggle between "right and wrong," Mary stated that she was struggling under her parents' influence, her religious upbringing, her marriage with her husband (which she believes is the right thing), and her own thoughts and feelings to separate from her husband and continue with her adulterous rendezvous, what Mary judged, the "wrong thing," yet the most fulfilling. At the same time, the client denied knowing her "own thoughts" about what was right or wrong for her. So much of her existence was predicated on others' beliefs and societal and religious injunctions. However, in my view, this denial was an attempt at suppression in order to avoid the judgments resulting from past injunctions relative to her attraction to a married man. Mary felt as if she could not be happy without being selfish and that in order to be "right" she had to suffer. Mary felt as if she could not line up with what she knew was "right" (based on the Bible). She was greatly influenced by religious injunctions and torn between such stringent dogma and the unconditional love of God. In reference to prayer, Mary stated that she was afraid to go to God for fear of Him putting her in a box or making her like everyone else. To which I (the therapist) interjected, "God doesn't make clones" and validated the client for being human. I invited Mary to consider the question, "Do you think God makes clones?" Mary expressed having absolutely no desire to be with her husband, but stated that it is the right thing to do, and questioned what it was in her to be drawn to another man. The other man was named Jay, who was married and the "wrong thing" but the one for whom my client exclaimed, "He makes me feel alive." We explored this powerful statement: For Mary, Jay represented power and freedom – glory, whereas her husband Jeff symbolized bondage, fear, and weakness.

A primary treatment goal for Mary going forward was to continue working on accepting herself separate from judgments. Mary stated that when she came into my office she was free, but must go back into her cage upon leaving.

I have come to understand that the therapeutic encounter transcends the psychoanalytic notion of transference, remembering, and explaining (Phillips 1980). Sometimes in existential therapy we must recognize the *obvious* and transcend it. As sessions ensued, Mary began to exhibit attention-getting behaviors. It was becoming evident that she was increasingly attracted to me as her therapist and admittedly I found her attractive as well. The sterility of the white lab-coat approach would not work! We could have operated under the pretense of transference or some other psychological jargon to explain away what was really happening; instead, we owned the mutual feelings and used the attraction to facilitate the working relationship, ever mindful to maintain ethical boundaries. As with my client Anastasia from *Existential Psychology*

East-West (for the full case study see Hoffman and Granger 2009, p. 69), erotic transferences in therapy happen more often than most therapists realize or are willing to admit to themselves. In this situation, it did not appear as if there was an erotic transference; however, Mary was using her sexuality as a defense. Mary was young and attractive and if she was uncertain about everything else in her life, including God, she was certain of this one thing. She had learned to rely on her looks when all else failed – this is what made her feel powerful in pursuit of other men. This pattern emerged after several emotionally difficult sessions. As Mary started to dress up for therapy she also became more resistant. This pattern, particularly when erotic elements emerge, may prove challenging for the therapist as the client often tries to present him or herself in the best light (Hoffman and Granger 2009, p. 78). Likewise, with her husband Jeff and his insatiable desire for my friendship, which seemed like a ploy to get me to side with him against his wife. Jeff seemed to exemplify a God archetype and would go to great lengths to present in a positive light, even at the expense of his wife Mary. Jeff's perceived "friendship" with me was explored and owned by both Jeff and myself to the extent of discussing the dangers of a dual relationship; again, using the disclosure and the "attraction" to creatively facilitate the therapeutic process.

During one session, Mary was reminded that the therapist must maintain a place of neutrality relative to her desires and choices. From an existential perspective, however, I continued to challenge her polarized way of thinking based on religiosity (rules) and continued to validate her in her humanity. You "make your bed you have to lie in it," I suggested, but at least you are making your own decision from a place within your humanity. With freedom there is responsibility. You must be free to choose, to recognize the consequences of your choices, and exercise the willingness to accept this God-given freedom along with its responsibilities and choices.

Outcome

Camus (1991, p. 11) once said, "Man is the only creature who refuses to be what he is." For this reason, it is important to philosophically argue the need for "all this philosophy" as we investigate the "truth" while simultaneously embracing our humanistic freedom to phenomenologically own that truth and live it. The primary goal in therapy was to facilitate in both Mary and Jeff to "be who they are" – to own their individual truths (apart from judgments) and live those truths out. Despite an initial impulse to provide a solution-focused approach, I recognized that with this particular couple, the *process* of therapy was paramount to the end – the journey more meaningful than the destination. Mary and Jeff decided to forgive each other and to try to work out the marriage humanistically. By "humanistically" I mean that they both developed an understanding that a person can be responsible for their own happiness, and that an unhappy or dissatisfied person can make changes to his/her life that will result in their eventual happiness and self-actualization.

Although Mary (and Jeff) are no longer my clients, I am confident that the existential-humanistic approach to therapy will forever guide them on their journey to freedom and "being" – to "becoming" who they are apart from arbitrary and often self-inflicted judgments.

The Case of Elva: I Never Thought It Would Happen to Me

Irvin Yalom[1]

I greeted Elva in my waiting room and together we walked the short distance to my office. She was different today, her gait labored, discouraged, dispirited. For the last few weeks there had been a bounce in her steps, but today she once again resembled the forlorn, plodding woman I had first met eight months ago. I remember her first words then: "I think I need help. Life doesn't seem worth living. My husband's been dead for a year now, but things aren't getting any better. Maybe I'm a slow learner."

But she hadn't proved to be a slow learner. In fact, therapy had progressed remarkably well – maybe it had been going too easily. What could have set her back like this?

Sitting down, Elva sighed and said, "I never thought it would happen to me."

She had been robbed. From her description it seemed an ordinary purse snatching. The thief, no doubt, spotted her in a Monterey seaside restaurant and saw her pay the check in cash for three friends – elderly widows all. He must have followed her into the parking lot and, his footsteps muffled by the roaring of the waves, sprinted up and, without breaking stride, ripped her purse away and leaped into his nearby car.

Elva, despite her swollen legs, hustled back into the restaurant to call for help, but of course it was too late. A few hours later, the police found her empty purse dangling on a roadside bush.

The robbery changed everything. Gone was the coziness, the softness in her life; gone was the safety. Her home had always beckoned her with its cushions, gardens, comforters, and deep carpets. Now she saw locks, doors, burglar alarms, and telephones. She had always walked her dog every morning at six. The morning stillness now seemed menacing. She and her dog stopped and listened for danger.

None of this is remarkable. Elva had been traumatized and now suffered from commonplace post-traumatic stress. After an accident or an assault, most people tend to feel unsafe, to have a reduced startle threshold, and to be hyper-vigilant. Eventually time erodes the memory of the event, and victims gradually return to their prior, trusting state.

But for Elva it was more than a simple assault. Her worldview was fractured. She had often claimed. "As long as a person has eyes, ears, and a mouth, I can cultivate their friendship." But no longer – she had lost her belief in benevolence, in her personal invulnerability. She felt stripped, ordinary, unprotected. The true impact of that robbery was to shatter illusion and to confirm, in brutal fashion, her husband's death.

Yet despite all this, Elva had retained her feeling of Albert's continued existence and thereby of her persisting safety and specialness. She had continued to live "as if," as if the world were safe, as if Albert were there, back in the workshop next to the garage.

But when she was robbed, she felt as though she were starting all over again. Most of all, the robbery illuminated her ordinariness, her "I never thought it would happen to me" reflecting the loss of belief in her personal specialness. Of course, she was still special in that she had special qualities and gifts, she had a unique life history, and no

[1] This case is a slightly adapted and condensed version of *Love's Executioner and Other Tales of Psychotherapy* by Irvin Yalom (1989).

one who had ever lived was just like her. That's the rational side of specialness. But we (some more than others) also have an irrational sense of specialness. It is one of our chief methods of denying death, and the part of our mind whose task it is to mollify death terror generates the irrational belief that we are invulnerable – that unpleasant things like aging and death may be the lot of others but not our lot, that exist beyond law, beyond human and biological destiny.

Although Elva responded to the purse snatching in ways that *seemed* irrational (for example, proclaiming that she wasn't fit to live on earth, being afraid to leave her house), it was clear that she was *really* suffering from the stripping away of irrationality. That sense of specialness, of being charmed, of being the exception, of being eternally protected – all those self-deceptions that had served her so well suddenly lost their persuasiveness. She saw through her own illusions, and what illusion had shielded now lay before her, bare and terrible.

Her grief wound was now fully exposed. This was the time, I thought, to open it wide, to debride it, and to allow it to heal straight and true.

"When you say you never thought it would happen to you, I know just what you mean," I said. "It's so hard for me, too, to accept that all these afflictions – aging, loss, death – are going to happen to me too."

Elva nodded, her tightened brow showing that she was surprised at my saying anything personal about myself.

"You must feel that if Albert were alive, this would never have happened to you." I ignored her flip response that if Albert were alive she wouldn't have been taking those old hens to lunch. "So the robbery brings home the fact that he's really gone."

Her eyes filled with tears, but I felt I had the right, the mandate, to continue. "You knew that before, I know. But part of you didn't. Now you really know that he's dead. He's not in the yard. He's not out back in the workshop. He's not anywhere. Except in your memories."

Elva was really crying now, and her stubby frame heaved with sobs for several minutes. She had never done that before with me. I sat there and wondered. "Now what do I do?" But my instincts luckily led me to what proved to be an inspired gambit. My eyes lit upon her purse – that same ripped-off, much-abused purse – and I said, "Bad luck is one thing but aren't you asking for it carrying around something that large?" Elva, plucky as ever, did not fail to call attention to my overstuffed pockets and the clutter on the table next to my chair. She pronounced the purse "medium sized."

"Any larger," I responded, "and you'd need a luggage carrier to move it around."

"Besides," she said, ignoring my jibe, "I need everything in it."

"You've got to be joking! Let's see!"

Getting into the spirit of it, Elva hoisted her purse onto my table, opened its jaws wide, and began to empty it. The first items fetched forth were three empty doggie bags.

"Need two extra ones in case of emergency?" I asked.

Elva chuckled and continued to disembowel the purse. Together we inspected and discussed each item. Elva conceded that three packets of Kleenex and twelve pens (plus three pencil stubs) were indeed superfluous, but held firm about two bottles of cologne and three hairbrushes, and dismissed, with an imperious flick of her hand, my challenge to her large flashlight, bulky notepads, and huge sheaf of photographs.

We quarreled over everything. The roll of fifty dimes. Three bags of candies (low-calorie of course). She giggled at my question: "Do you believe, Elva, that the more of these you eat, the thinner you will become?" A plastic sack of old orange peels ("You never know, Elva, when these will come in handy"). A bunch of knitting needles ("Six needles in search of a sweater," I thought). A bag of sourdough starter. Half of a paperback Stephen King novel (Elva threw away sections of pages as she read them: "They weren't worth keeping," she explained). A small stapler ("Elva, this is crazy!"). Three pairs of sunglasses. And tucked away into the innermost corners, assorted coins, paper clips, nail clippers, pieces of emery board, and some substance that looked suspiciously like lint.

When the great bag had finally yielded all, Elva and I stared in wonderment at the contents set out in rows on my table. We were sorry the bag was empty and that the emptying was over. She turned and smiled, and we looked tenderly at each other. It was an extraordinarily intimate moment. In a way no patient had ever done before, she showed me everything. And I had accepted everything and asked for even more. I followed her into every nook and crevice, awed that one old woman's purse could serve as a vehicle for both isolation and intimacy: the absolute isolation that is integral to existence and the intimacy that dispels the dread, if not the fact, of isolation.

That was a transforming hour. Our time of intimacy – call it love, call it love making – was redemptive. In that one hour, Elva moved from a position of forsakenness to one of trust. She came alive and was persuaded, once more, of her capacity for intimacy.

I think it was the best hour of therapy I ever gave.

The Case of Janice: An Existential-Integrative Approach

Kirk J. Schneider

The chief and ongoing questions of existential-integrative (EI) therapy are (1) "how is one *presently* living" and (2) "how is one *willing* to live"? These questions, conveyed both through explicit and preverbal expression, serve as mirrors to clients and therapists, signaling and guiding every key juncture of the work (Schneider and Krug 2017). As my client Janice[2] sat across from me one Friday afternoon, I tried my best to appreciate the struggle she experienced, and the awkwardness with which she attempted to convey it. It was the first time Janice and I had met and from the moment we shook hands, I could sense a cloud over her demeanor.

Janice was a 45-year-old White working-class female with a history of severe emotional and sexual abuse. Her father was an inveterate alcoholic with an explosive temper, and her grandfather had sexually molested her when she was eight years old. When Janice was four, she would be regularly left alone with a "schizophrenic" aunt. These visits terrified Janice, but apparently, there was no parental recognition of this sentiment. When Janice was five, her mother suddenly died. This left Janice with her

[2] Janice is a composite of clients I have worked with from an EI point of view. For more information on the EI perspective see Schneider (2008) and Schneider and Krug (2017).

volatile alcoholic father, her rapacious grandfather, and her psychotic aunt. How Janice even partially emerged from these circumstances is still a mystery to me, but somehow she managed.

As Janice and I greeted each other, I was struck by her composure, and bright, articulate style. Janice told me that although she had brief brushes with therapy in her past, she did "tons" of work on her own. I emphatically believed that. Although Janice ostensibly came to therapy because of her lack of assertiveness with men, I sensed – and in her tacit way, she conveyed – that the assertiveness issue was not her ultimate concern.

At first I worked with Janice to help her build confidence when she confronted men. I invited her to engage in role plays with me where I would stand in for the menacing fellow, for example, her boss or husband, and she would play herself in a particular dilemma. I also worked with Janice to cognitively restructure her thinking about how these men perceived her. Would she really be seen as a "bitch" if she clarified her needs to them, I would ask. And even if she was seen that way, would that make her one? As we deepened and rehearsed these scenarios, Janice was gradually able to develop new skills that would help her confront and successfully assert herself with the aforementioned men.

At the same time as she worked with these cognitive and behavioral restructuring skills, however, something else began to happen to Janice: she began to acknowledge, and I encouraged her to stay present to, fears that went beyond feeling intimidated by men. These fears related to a sense of being intimidated by life.

In this context, she began to share powerful dreams with me, like a dream she had recently of feeling like a burned out tree; and another about a monster attacking her home. In time I took the risk to invite Janice, not just to "talk about" such dreams and fantasies, but to experience them here and now with me. I invited her, in other words, to become more present to how she felt, sensed, and pictured these dreams and fantasies. I also invited her to share her responses about what it was like to interact with me, and to experience the difficult sides of herself, like shame or weakness, in my presence. This brought the work alive between me and Janice and significantly deepened our bond. It also enabled Janice to plumb depths only hinted at during our cognitive restructuring exercises. Finally, it moved Janice to realize how her suffering stemmed not just from her relationships with men (and sometimes women), but to her relationship with life's uncertainties, and to the need for courage in the face of them.

In this vein, Janice began to allude to a whole new language in our work together; this was a language that emphasized her concerns about existence, not just specific aspects of existence. For example, she started speaking about "unnamable fears" and a part of herself that felt like a "black hole." She told me she had never acknowledged these feelings with anyone before, but that she had often glimpsed them, especially when stressed. She also began talking about wonderments that she had rarely ever disclosed – such as her fascination with the occult and her resonance with ancient Mayan culture. When I shared my puzzlement about these identifications, given her background, she quipped: "they are freeing, and in tune with the natural world."

In my experience, these ranges of resonance are not all that extraordinary in depth existential therapy. As people feel safer to explore, they begin to unveil the parts of themselves that both torment, and potentially, set them free. These parts are not necessarily Freudian in nature. They don't necessarily evoke sexual or aggressive conflict or frustrated parental attachments, but they do in my experience stir very primordial undercurrents, some of which pertain directly to sexual, aggressive, or attachment conflicts. To put it succinctly: these undercurrents strike me and others who witness them as emphatically existential in nature – pertaining not just to turbulent sexual-aggressive drives or attachments to parental figures, but fears and desires toward the uncontrollability of existence itself. For example, behind the fear (and sometimes attraction) of aggression can be an even deeper anxiety about imminent disarray, uncontrollability, and ultimately chaos. Or beneath the terror of parental devaluation can be the thornier challenge of one's significance in existence.

These were precisely the mooring points I faced with Janice on a fateful afternoon some six months following our initial meeting. Janice was on the brink of a breakthrough, and we both knew it. But she also grappled with great fears and the need to come to terms with those fears. On this basis, I invited Janice to simply close her eyes and become aware of her breathing. As she seemed ready, I then invited her to become aware of any tension areas she experienced in her body – any areas that felt tight or blocked, and that she was willing to describe. She began by identifying a tension in her neck area, which loosened as she stayed present to it. Then she began perceiving an image of a tiny little girl trapped in a well. She couldn't identify where this well was, or how it got there, but she was clear that it felt fathomless with no end in sight. As I continued to invite her to stay present to this well, she began to feel the girl's terror. "It's like she's sinking," Janice told me, "and she doesn't know where she's going." Gently I supported her to continue with the experience, while at the same time reassuring her that if she needed to stop, she could do so at any time. She chose to proceed.

At about halfway into our session, Janice noticed that the little girl was fading, while the darkness around her grew. At times, the little girl struggled to unfold herself and peek out of the darkness, but invariably she sank back in. To this point Janice said very little about her relationship to the little girl, but as she "stayed with" her, her sense of connection grew. Suddenly, Janice panicked. She could no longer find the little girl! Yet at that very same moment, tears welled up in Janice's eyes. I asked her what brought on the tears and after a long silence she whispered: "I reached out into the dark to touch her, and she reached out into the dark to touch me."

With this simple yet profound image, Janice began a remarkable self-transformation. She moved from a position of abject terror to one of wonder to one of love. These shifts echoed movements in the therapy itself, which served as a kind of "staging ground" for the experience of awe – humility and wonder, and sense of adventure toward living. Through embracing the little girl, Janice at the same time embraced the void in which the little girl (as well as adult Janice) had languished for many years; and now she found solace there, and a chance for self-renewal.

I won't say that this moment completely changed Janice's life, but it went a long way toward freeing her and relieving her panic. Although the specifics of Janice's life – for example, her long-time employment and her involvement with her family – essentially remained the same, what she brought to those specifics altered dramatically. She now had an expanded capacity to feel, for example, a deepened experience of the moment, and a broader appreciation of life's possibilities. In the end, Janice learned much more than assertiveness skills, or an ability to think more "rationally." She discovered how to be present to her life; and this presence enabled her to glimpse the awesomeness of her and frankly all of our lives.

References

Camus, A. (1991). *The Rebel: An Essay on Man in Revolt.* New York: Vintage Books.

Hoffman, L. and Granger, N. (2009). An existential therapy case illustration. In: *Existential Psychology East-West* (ed. L. Hoffman, M. Yang, F. Kaklauskas et al.), 69–92. Colorado Springs, CO: University of the Rockies Press.

Penzel, F. (2000). *Obsessive-Compulsive Disorders: A Complete Guide to Getting Well and Staying Well.* Oxford: Oxford University Press.

Phillips, J. (1980). Transference and encounter: The therapeutic relationship in psychoanalytic and existential therapy. *Review of Existential Psychology and Psychiatry 27* (2–3): 135–152.

Schneider, K.J. (ed.) (2008). *Existential-Integrative Psychotherapy: Guideposts to the Core of Practice.* New York: Routledge.

Schneider, K. (2013). *The Polarized Mind: Why It's Killing Us and What We Can Do About It.* Colorado Springs, CO: University Professors' Press.

Schneider, K. and Krug, O. (2017). *Existential-Humanistic Therapy.* Washington, DC: APA.

Shapiro, F. (1998). *EMDR: The Breakthrough Therapy for Overcoming Anxiety, Stress and Trauma.* New York: Basic Books.

Yalom, I. (1989). *Love's Executioner and Other Tales of Psychotherapy.* New York: Harper Perennial.

Yalom, I. (2002). *The Gift of Therapy.* New York: HarperCollins.

17

Key Texts of Existential-Humanistic and Existential-Integrative Therapy

Shawn Rubin, Louis Hoffman, and Mark Yang

Existential-humanistic psychology has a rich literary tradition, beginning with the publication of *Existence* in 1958, which was edited by Rollo May, Ernest Angel, and Henri F. Ellenberger. *Existence* drew from the European existential analytic tradition, particularly Ludwig Binswanger, while at the same time stimulating the development of a uniquely American strand of existential therapy that would become known as the existential-humanistic tradition.

One of the unique aspects of the existential-humanistic tradition is its literary foundation embodied by Rollo May. May was both a scholar well-versed in literature, the arts, philosophy, and psychology, and an exceptional writer who was able to bridge the gap of academic writing with a style that had appeal to those outside academic and professional psychology. May's books, such as *Love and Will*, *Freedom and Destiny*, and *The Cry for Myth* were academically solid, yet applicable to many of the social issues of the time. This backdrop allowed for these books to be widely read and influential beyond the therapy office.

There is little doubt that May's influence went well beyond the development of the essential ideas of existential therapy; he also influenced the literary style of existential writing. While few could claim the literary beauty of May, many have continued to write in a manner that engages the contemporary world. Therefore, many of the books identified as key texts are books that are not typical of traditional professional scholarship, even though they maintain the academic rigor. Many books, such as Schneider's *Rediscovery of Awe* and *The Polarized Mind*, Becker's *The Denial of Death*, and Diamond's *Anger, Madness, and the Daimonic* will appear on the shelves of psychologists and the general public alike. However, there are also important books that are more traditional professional texts, such as Bugental's *Psychotherapy Isn't What You Think* and Schneider's *Existential-Integrative Psychotherapy*.

Another unique aspect of the existential-humanistic tradition is the prevalence of many case histories. While these were also prevalent in the early psychoanalytic

The Wiley World Handbook of Existential Therapy, First Edition. Edited by Emmy van Deurzen, Erik Craig, Alfried Längle, Kirk J. Schneider, Digby Tantam, and Simon du Plock.

tradition, the existential-humanistic texts take a unique twist to these. Yalom is probably the most recognized existential writer having contributed case histories. Although there is disagreement about whether Yalom fits within the existential-humanistic tradition, his case histories, such as *Love's Executioner* and *Mama and the Meaning of Life*, have been influential on existential-humanistic therapists. Yet, Yalom was not the first to engage in this approach to writing about existential-humanistic therapy. May integrated many long portrayals of clients into his books and Bugental wrote an extraordinarily eloquent book in this style, *Intimate Journeys* (originally titled *The Search for Existential Identity*).

While May was the most influential figure on the development of existential-humanistic theory, Bugental was equally if not more influential on the development of existential-humanistic practice. Many of Bugental's contributions were in non-traditional formats. For example, he was very involved in training and supervision. Related to this, there are quite a number of videos of Bugental conducting and talking about the practice of existential-humanistic therapy. While arguably Bugental's most important contributions were through videos, training, and supervision, he also made a number of important contributions to scholarship.

Bugental's scholarship also tended to focus more on the practice elements. In 1965 Bugental published *The Search for Authenticity*, which was subtitled *An Existential-Analytic Approach to Therapy*. Over time, his language shifted to "existential-humanistic therapy," but his general approach remained largely consistent. Early in *The Search for Authenticity*, Bugental brought in humanistic psychology and integrated humanistic psychology in a thoughtful, consistent manner. In many ways, it was Bugental who solidified the integration of humanistic with the existential approach more than May, even though May remained involved in the humanistic movement as well. Bugental's integration of humanistic with existential psychology was much more thorough in his writings. This, too, is part of what sets apart the American strand of existential therapy from other approaches.

In Bugental's subsequent books, including *Psychotherapy and Process*, *The Art of the Psychotherapist*, *Intimate Journeys*, and *Psychotherapy Isn't What You Think*, he continues to develop his ideas and approach to therapy. He was able to dissect and break down the therapy process without becoming reductionistic or relying upon techniques. Instead, he focused on the process and, maybe more than any other writer, clarified how to bring the abstract into the practical realms. Bugental helped the concepts of presence and process become understandable without reifying them as techniques.

While there were other important early influences, including the influence of people outside the movement, May and Bugental were the primary voices that set the foundation upon which existential-humanistic psychology has since been built. With May providing the most important theory developments, and Bugental the therapeutic innovations, existential-humanistic therapy was able to become more complete.

The next generation whose writings and training have, and continue to, shape contemporary existential-humanistic psychology are Irvin Yalom, Kirk J. Schneider, Orah Krug, Ed Mendelowitz, Myrtle Heery, Ilene Serlin, Kenneth Bradford, Erik Craig, and Louis Hoffman. Drawing upon the landmark contributions of their mentors, Rollo May and Jim Bugental, these authors extend the purview of existential-humanistic psychology into the areas of clinical supervision, integrative and depth psychotherapies, clinical work with extreme states, dream analysis, multicultural and international psychology, and spirituality.

A final important consideration when one approaches essential existential-humanistic texts is the reliance upon books as opposed to journal articles. Thelen (2010) conducted an analysis of the *Journal of Humanistic Psychology*. As part of this study, Thelen noted that articles in the *Journal of Humanistic Psychology* tended to cite a higher percentage of books as opposed to journal articles when compared with other journals. This is an interesting finding and quite significant. While there are likely various reasons contributing to this emphasis, two are important to consider. First, while the existential-humanistic tradition does not eschew research, it embraces a broader epistemological diversity that emphasizes the importance of drawing upon various types of scholarship. Within much of professional psychology, there is a privileging of positivist ways of knowing, such as quantitative research, which is more frequently found in journal articles. Thus, in much of psychology there is a bias toward seeing research articles, which are primarily in journals instead of scholarly texts, as more legitimate scholarly sources.

However, there is a second important consideration of Thelen's results. In the existential-humanistic tradition, there is a preference for a depth analysis of concepts, which often draws far more extended consideration of topics. This type of analysis is more consistent with the development of books as opposed to journal articles. When examining the development of existential-humanistic psychology, certainly there have been many important journal articles. However, books have served as a more primary foundation for the development of theory and practice in existential-humanistic therapy.

In attempting to identify the key texts in existential-humanistic therapy, we approached this task with a few considerations. First, we wanted to identify the texts that are frequently cited in the existential literature. This is a more objective basis for the identification of these texts. However, we also wanted to identify important texts that have served to stretch existential-humanistic theory. For example, while Mendelowitz's *Ethics and Lao Tzu* may not be frequently cited in the literature, it is an important text for a number of reasons. First, Mendelowitz embodies the creative genius and literary style of Rollo May perhaps as good or better than any other contemporary existential-humanistic writer. Second, the breadth of this volume is extraordinarily impressive in its reach, bringing together many voices within and beyond the tradition in a fascinating conversation. Last, Mendelowitz discusses the application of existential-humanistic therapy with a client with Dissociative Identity Disorder. His approach is not a step-by-step guide, or even one that clearly identifies what he is doing in his approach to this client. Yet, it embodies the existential-humanistic tradition with a very complex case.

In the Annotated Bibliography below, there are notable influences, such as Friedrich Nietzsche, Soren Kierkegaard, Karl Jaspers, Allan Wheelis, Erich Fromm, and Paul Stern, which are not included, despite their significant influence. In the diverse approaches to existential psychology, there is a diversity of philosophical influences. While in some schools of existential thought Heidegger is the most influential philosopher, Nietzsche and Kierkegaard tend to be more influential in existential-humanistic

psychology (Cleare-Hoffman and Hoffman 2017). While not wanting t
influence of Nietzsche and Kierkegaard, we felt the books below are m
their influence. The two more philosophical books that we did include,
Buber and *The Courage to Be* by Tillich, have more direct implications and
the therapy process. Wheelis and Stern's influence has been important, pa
a few scholars; however, they are not as frequently cited in the literature.

An important limitation that must be addressed with the books selected for the annotated bibliography is that most of the authors and editors of these books are White males. This is consistent with the findings of Cleare-Hoffman and Hoffman (2017) in their survey on the key influences on existential-humanistic psychology. It is important to consider the reasons for and implications of this finding. Serlin and Creswell (2015), Hoffman (2016), and Hoffman, Cleare-Hoffman, and Jackson (2015) noted that the contributions and perspectives of women and people of color are often not recognized. This has a detrimental impact on existential-humanistic psychology and has limited its advancement. It is imperative that the field of existential-humanistic psychology be intentional about addressing this problem in the future.

In conclusion, we have worked to identify what we consider the most influential, important, and extraordinary texts in the existential-humanistic tradition. While we are certain that no other group of three scholars would come up with the exact same list of influential texts, we believe these books deserve the attention of anyone interested in the existential-humanistic therapy tradition.

Annotated Bibliography of Key Works

Becker, E. (1973). *The Denial of Death*. New York: Free Press.

Becker's Pulitzer Prize winning book significantly impacted the development of existential psychology in the United States. Influencing many existential-humanistic scholars, *The Denial of Death* critiques Freud's psychosexual theory and, instead, places the fear of death as a primary motivational source. While acknowledging that some denial of death may always be necessary, Becker also advocated that there is value in facing one's finiteness.

Buber, M. (1972). *I and Thou* (trans. W. Kaufmann). New York: Touchstone. (Original work published 1923.)

Buber's concept of the I and Thou, which differentiates I–Thou relationships from I–It relationships, has deeply influenced existential-humanistic perspectives on relationships. Maurice Friedman's approach to therapy, which was also influential on existential-humanistic therapists, was largely derived from Buber's ideas.

Bugental, J. (1965). *The Search for Authenticity: An Existential-Analytic Approach to Psychotherapy*. New York: Holt, Rinehart, and Winston.

The Search for Authenticity was Bugental's first major work. At the beginning of the book, he provides a basis for integrating humanistic and existential psychology and sets an important foundation for the development of existential-humanistic therapy. Bugental also addresses many psychoanalytic concepts, such as resistance and transference, from an existential perspective.

Bugental, J. (1978). *Psychotherapy and Process: The Fundamentals of an Existential-Humanistic Approach*, 3e. New York: McGraw-Hill.

In *Psychotherapy and Process*, Bugental is more rooted in developing existential-humanistic psychology as a discipline than in many of his other books, as the subtitle of the book suggests.

Bugental addresses many foundations of the existential-humanistic therapy approach, including desirable therapist qualities, the centrality of the therapy relationship, the importance of subjective experience, and the process of inward searching.

Bugental, J. (1992). *The Art of the Psychotherapist: How to Develop the Skills that take Psychotherapy beyond Science.* New York: W.W. Norton and Company.
The Art of the Psychotherapist was not intended just as an existential-humanistic text and focused more broadly on depth therapy applications. Although most of Bugental's work tends to focus primarily on therapy applications more than theory, this is his more technical book.

Bugental, J. (1999). *Psychotherapy Isn't What You Think.* Phoenix, AZ: Zeig & Tucker.
This is the last book written by James Bugental and it encapsulates his experience-focused model of Existential-Humanistic Psychotherapy. The book serves as a nice summary of Bugental's work where he teaches about the importance of the subjective, opening up perceptions, aligning with the resistance, focusing on the actual, and increasing intentionality.

Cain, D., Keenan, K., and Rubin, S. (eds.) (2015). *Humanistic Psychotherapies: Handbook of Research and Practice*, 2e. Washington DC: American Psychological Association.
A comprehensive handbook providing readers with an illuminating overview of humanistic psychology including its historical and conceptual foundations, research methodology, major therapeutic approaches and modalities, and therapeutic issues and applications. The book closes with a final section on analysis and synthesis. The majority of the book is devoted to the practice and application of therapy.

Diamond, S.A. (1996). *Anger, Madness, and the Daimonic: The Psychological Genesis of Violence, Evil and Creativity (SUNY Series in the Philosophy of Psychology).* New York: State University of New York Press.
Diamond's book is an important expansion on May's conception of the daimonic, which was one of May's important contributions to understanding human nature and the potential for what can be termed as evil. This breadth in the scope of this book is important, ranging from distinguishing the daimonic from demonic and spiritual conceptions of evil to considering the role of creativity in dealing with psychological difficulties.

Heery, M. (ed.) (2014). *Unearthing the Moment: Mindful Applications of Existential-Humanistic and Transpersonal Psychotherapy.* San Francisco, CA: Tonglen Press.
This book is a compilation of chapters written by group members who have participated in Mytle Heery's systematic training "Unearthing the moment." Dr. Heery is a protégé of James Bugental and developed her training around the work of James Bugental.

Hoffman, L., Yang, M., Kaklauskas, F., and Chan, A. (eds.) (2009). *Existential Psychology East–West.* Colorado Springs, CO: University of the Rockies Press.
This edited volume is the first of its kind combining the writings of scholars from both the East and the West. The book is divided into three sections beginning with an overview of existential theory and practice followed by East and West perspectives on existential psychology and ends with three chapters on Eastern perspectives on Eastern and Western myths. This book has been updated in a two-volume second edition in 2019.

Krug, O. and Schneider, K. (2016). *Supervision Essentials for Existential-Humanistic Therapy.* Washington, DC: American Psychological Association.
This is the first book to apply the principles of existential-humanistic therapy to the practice of clinical supervision, and is part of the Clinical Supervision Essentials series published by the American Psychological Association. It provides an important overview of how to approach supervision from an existential-humanistic perspective, a discussion of implications for training,

and case illustrations. (The book is accompanied by a companion video on existential-humanistic therapy supervision.)

May, R. (1969). *Love and Will.* New York: W.W. Norton & Co.
This book was one of the first books by May to have a broader appeal and played a significant role in his expanding popularity. In addition to focusing on the concepts of love and will from an existential perspective, this is the work where May introduced and developed the concept of the daimonic.

May, R. (1975). *The Courage to Create.* New York: W.W. Norton & Co.
Creativity was a strong interest of Rollo May. In *The Courage to Create*, May developed an understanding of creativity drawn from existential concepts. This idea was not only influential on existential-humanistic psychology, but also helped identify existential-humanistic psychology as influential in creativity studies and played a role in deepening the connection between creativity, the arts, and existential-humanistic therapy.

May, R. (1981). *Freedom and Destiny.* New York: W.W. Norton & Co.
This is one of the most thorough books written on the topic of freedom as seen from an existential perspective. Rollo May expounds on the crisis of freedom, mistaken paths to freedom, characteristics of freedom, and the fruits of freedom. This work is often identified as the most comprehensive overview of May's theory.

May, R. (1988). *Paulus: Tillich as Spiritual Teacher.* San Francisco, CA: Saybrook Publishers.
Although Paulus is not as cited as frequently as other works of May, it is important for a number of reasons. Tillich was May's mentor, and this book documents much of Tillich's influence upon May. Additionally, the book speaks to the mentoring relationship from an existential-humanistic perspective; and finally, the book is one of the clearer and more concise summaries of Tillich's existential theology.

May, R. (1991). *The Cry for Myth.* New York: W.W. Norton & Co.
If given the choice, would you choose to write the laws or create the myths of a nation? This challenge speaks to the function and power of the myth and Rollo May gives plenty of examples of how the myths in America and of the Western World shift our society in profound and enduring ways.

May, R., Angel, E., and Ellenberger, H.F. (1958). *Existence: A New Dimension in Psychiatry and Psychology.* New York: Simon & Schuster.
This is the most important text in the development of existential psychology in the United States, and possibly the most important book in the development of existential-humanistic psychology. This volume contains translated articles of Binswanger and a number of contributions from people in the United States; however, the most influential chapters were those written by May providing an overview of the history of existential psychology and an overview of existential applications to therapy. Many individuals who became leading voices in the existential-humanistic movement identify this book as the single most important work that inspired them to pursue existential-humanistic psychology.

Mendelowitz, E. (2008). *Ethics and Lao-tzu: Intimations of Character.* Colorado Springs, CO: University of Rockies Press.
Ethics and Lao-tzu is a powerful collection of essays largely drawn from the inspiration of work with one of Ed Mendelowitz's clients, referred to as Kristina. Mendelowitz also draws inspiration from a number of literary figures, artists, philosophers, and psychologists. Kristina was an artist with a difficult past leading to the development of Dissociative Identity Disorder. The book tells her story, including therapy, interspersed with other psychological essays. Through collages of quotes mixed with his own literary approach to psychology, Mendelowitz introduces many of the great existential thinkers to the contemporary reader.

Rogers, C. (1961). *On Becoming a Person.* New York: Houghton-Mifflin Harcourt Publishing Co.
As the title suggests, this foundational book by the founding father of humanistic psychology is a must read for anyone who is interested in how becoming a (caring and fulfilled) person is the prerequisite to becoming an effective therapist.

Rogers, C. (1980). *A Way of Being.* New York: Houghton-Mifflin Publishers Inc.
This book written near the end of Carl Rogers's career serves as a coda to his classic *On Becoming a Person.* This book encapsulates the philosophy behind Rogers's Person-Centered Psychotherapy.

Schneider, K.J. (1999). *The Paradoxical Self: Toward an Understanding of our Contradictory Nature* (Rev. edn.). New York: Humanity Books.
The Paradoxical Self is one of the most important works relevant to personality theory from an existential-humanistic perspective. Schneider discusses hyper-constriction and hyper-expansion, to illustrate the paradoxical nature of being human. Instead of seeking to balance or moderate aspects of one's personality, as is commonplace in psychology, Schneider depicts how to understand and integrate these varying aspects into a dynamic and vitalizing whole.

Schneider, K.J. (2009). *Awakening to Awe: Personal Stories of Profound Transformation.* Langham, MD: Jason Aronson.
In *Awakening to Awe*, Schneider develops an important conception of spirituality from an existential-humanistic perspective. Awe represents an openness to the wonderment – as well as unsettlement – of the unknown and unknowable. For Schneider, developing an appreciation of awe is a critical aspect of fully living in the face of the challenges of the world.

Schneider, K.J. (ed.) (2015). *Existential-Integrative Psychotherapy: Guideposts to the Core of Practice.* New York: Routledge.
Existential-Integrative Psychotherapy is one of the few texts on existential-humanistic psychology that reaches out to the psychological profession as a whole. It provides an overview of an approach to existential-humanistic psychotherapy while, at the same time, expanding the application in new directions showing that existential-humanistic psychotherapy can serve as a foundation for various approaches to therapy, including cognitive-behavioral, psychoanalytic, and brief therapy modalities. With chapters focusing on cultural diversity, this is one of the first in-depth attempts at applying multicultural perspectives to existential-humanistic psychotherapy.

Schneider, K. and Krug, O. (2017). *Existential-Humanistic Therapy*, 2e. Washington, DC: American Psychological Association. (Also accompanied by a companion video illustrating existential-humanistic practice.)
This book is part of the Systems of Psychotherapy Series published by the American Psychological Association, which identified existential-humanistic therapy as one of most influential contemporary approaches to therapy. It provides an overview of existential-humanistic theory, therapy, and case illustrations, along with a strong emphasis on integrative aspects of the approach.

Schneider, K. and May, R. (1995). *The Psychology of Existence: An Integrative, Clinical Perspective.* New York: McGraw-Hill.
The Psychology of Existence was an important overview of existential therapy that, in many ways, was the forerunner to Schneider's *Existential-Integrative Psychotherapy.* One of the distinctive features of this volume is that it includes an overview of the literary and philosophical influences on existential therapy including excerpts from a number of influential figures, such as Kierkegaard, Nietzche, Camus, and Becker.

Schneider, K., Pierson, J.F., and Bugental, J. (eds.) (2015). *The Handbook of Humanistic Psychology: Theory, Research, and Practice*, 2e. Thousand Oakes, CA: Sage Publications.

This comprehensive volume provides readers with a rich overview of contemporary humanistic psychology including its history, theory, methodology, and application to practice, including applications to broader settings. Each section is divided into contemporary themes along with emergent trends. It closes with an epilogue on the direction of future developments.

Tillich, P. (1952). *The Courage to Be*. New Haven, CT: Yale University Press.
The Courage to Be is an important treatise on the existential condition that addresses the anxiety pertaining to death and mortality, guilt, and meaninglessness. Tillich addresses courage as an important aspect of coming to accept oneself and embracing one's own being.

Yalom, I. (1980). *Existential Psychotherapy*. New York: Basic Books.
This book, written by one of the most well-known authors in the field, can serve as an excellent textbook for an introductory, foundational course on existential psychology. The book presents a systematic model of existential psychology integrating various original thinkers in the field. It breaks down some difficult aspects of existential philosophy, written in a highly readable fashion with numerous illustrative cases studies.

Yalom, I. (1989). *Love's Executioner and Other Tales of Psychotherapy*. New York: Basic Books.
This teaching novel can serve as an excellent introductory read for both the professional and the layperson who is interested to learn more about existential psychology. Written in narrative form, the case studies as story are immensely captivating and serve as excellent illustrations for the existential givens that we all must face. The preface of the book begins with an excellent summary of the existential givens as developed by Irvin Yalom.

References

Cleare-Hoffman, H.P. and Hoffman, L. (2017, August). Key influences on the development of Existential-Humanistic Therapy Practice. Poster presented at the 125th Annual Convention of the American Psychological Association, Washington, DC.

Hoffman, L. (2016). Multiculturalism and humanistic psychology: From neglect to epistemological and ontological diversity. *The Humanistic Psychologist* 44 (1): 56–71.

Hoffman, L., Cleare-Hoffman, H.P., and Jackson, T. (2015). Humanistic psychology and multiculturalism: History, current status, and advancements. In: *The Handbook of Humanistic Psychology: Theory, Research, and Practice*, 2e (ed. K.J. Schneider, J.F. Pierson, and J.F.T. Bugental), 41–55. Thousand Oaks, CA: Sage.

May, R., Angel, E., and Ellenberger, H.F. (1958). *Existence: A New Dimension in Psychiatry and Psychology*. New York: Simon & Schuster.

Serlin, I.A. and Criswell, E. (2015). Humanistic psychology and women: A critical-historical perspective. In: *The Handbook of Humanistic Psychology: Theory, Research, and Practice*, 2e (ed. K.J. Schneider, J.F. Pierson, and J.F.T. Bugental), 27–40. Thousand Oaks, CA: Sage.

Thelen, M. (2010). A bibliometic study of the *Journal of Humanistic Psychology* (PhD thesis). Retrieved from ProQuest (UMI #3466603).

18

Challenges and New Developments in Existential-Humanistic and Existential-Integrative Therapy

Louis Hoffman, Theopia Jackson, Ed Mendelowitz, Xuefu Wang, Mark Yang, Ken Bradford, and Kirk J. Schneider

Introduction

The following sections reflect the farther reaches and leading edges of contemporary existential-humanistic (EH) and existential-integrative (EI) psychotherapy. These sections include multicultural, Asian, and transpersonal-spiritual trends. While some of the sections emphasize a more personal and reflective style, such those by Ed Mendelowitz and Ken Bradford, others are more expository in nature. The upshot, however, is that each section reflects discernable threads that form the tapestry of contemporary EH and EI therapy. These threads have arisen organically and are integral to the inquiries, conversations, and applications emerging in our EH/EI community. The final section of this chapter, the Epilogue, provides an overall vision of where the field appears to be heading, particularly as it impacts the larger discipline of psychotherapy itself. – Kirk J. Schneider

Multicultural Developments in Existential-Humanistic Therapy

Louis Hoffman and Theopia Jackson

Although historically existential-humanistic therapy has struggled with multiculturalism, many recent developments have begun addressing this limitation (Hoffman 2016; Hoffman, Cleare-Hoffman, and Jackson 2014). This section highlights some important innovations in considering relationships and identity, self-actualization, and social justice.

The Wiley World Handbook of Existential Therapy, First Edition. Edited by Emmy van Deurzen, Erik Craig, Alfried Längle, Kirk J. Schneider, Digby Tantam, and Simon du Plock.

Relationship and identity

Existential-humanistic therapy is a highly relational approach to therapy; however, it tends to approach relationship from an individualistic perspective. The constructs of individualism and collectivism have been critiqued for good reasons (Oyserman, Coon, and Kemmelmeier 2002; Schwartz 1990). In particular, it is important to acknowledge that individualism and collectivism cannot adequately be understood as different categories or even as a continuum; but more as epistemological foundational differences that can inform worldviews (Nobles 2006). Many different forms of individualism and collectivism exist, as well as many blends of these. Yet, the idea of individualism and collectivism points toward different conceptions and experiences of self and values pertaining to the self and relationships. In this regard, existential-humanistic psychology has historically shown biases toward the individual.

In order for existential-humanistic psychology to be relevant across diverse cultures, as well as being informed by such engagement, it is necessary for it to become aware of the individualistic bias and begin moving beyond it. Without this awareness, therapists are likely to impose a view of self and values pertaining to the self upon clients potentially without recognizing this. The implications of such "clinical blindness" can manifest as *intention versus impact* – potential risks associated with well-meaning practices and interventions that lack cultural consideration can inadvertently lead to adverse impacts. For example, though valuable, the application of co-actualization, which underscores the value of the interdependence of relational contact for self-actualization, should not be interpreted as a humanistic response to multiculturalism. Co-actualization is predicated on the premise of individualism as the desired outcome in the development of one's "distinctive identity mainly through experiences in relation" (Motschnig-Pitrik and Barrett-Lennard 2010, p. 365). Yet this approach is not sufficient for many persons of color or members of certain indigenous groups. To not consider the cultural epistemological conceptualization of collectivism may contribute to psychological alienation from optimal identity formation within the client's cultural context. While it may not be the intention of the therapist, it still can effect a deleterious impact. Recent scholarship in existential-humanistic psychology has begun to point the way beyond the individualistic bias, including through allowing for different conceptions of the self (Hoffman et al. 2015). Hoffman and colleagues (2015) maintained that different conceptions of the self, including various types of individualism and collectivism, all have merit. Furthermore, they argue that different conceptions of the self may be better associated with well-being in different cultures.

In cultures often associated with collectivism, the understanding of the self is of a relational understanding as compared with the idea of the self-in-relationship with others as is commonly emphasized in existential psychology. In other words, existential psychology places the emphasis on the individual choosing to be in relationship, and the desire to be in a relationship as one of the existential givens. However, for some the relationship with family and culture is deeply embedded in the understanding of the self, or their cultural archetype, and cannot easily be separated from it. More specifically, for many indigenous populations (Comas-Dias 2012), particularly persons of African ancestry (Myers 1985, 1993; Nobles 2006), the "self" is experienced as spiritual and connected to all, inclusive of past, present, and future life forces.

Therefore, *to be human is to be spirit-being*. This difference has important implications for therapy and how therapists empower clients in making decisions and exploring their relationships. When considering the humanistic integration of multiculturalism, Comas-Dias (2012, p. 427) postulates that,

> Self-meaning – the perceived effect of an event on identity and contextual meaning – the perceived relationship of an event to its context (Fife, 1994), are dimensions consistent with a multicultural collectivistic orientation. From a multicultural worldview, meaning making involves the development of a relational identity encased in a cultural context. Accordingly, contextualism, holism, and liberation are multicultural humanistic constructs.

Similarly, existential-humanistic psychology has emphasized the freedom of the individual, placing negative connotations on alternatives. For example, it is common to contrast freedom with conformity. Many non-Western countries conceive freedom differently, including emphasizing the freedom of the group and concepts such as social harmony (Chan 2009). Additionally, literature has consistently documented the benefits or protective factor of cultural groundedness and sense of belonging for groups facing marginalization and/or systems of oppression/racism (Reitz et al. 2009) and the role of cultural allies like existential-humanistic therapy. While group freedom and harmony do not necessarily contradict the idea of individual freedom, these former dimensions are experienced differently and have implications for therapy.

It is not necessary for existential-humanistic therapy to sacrifice core values to adapt to these differences (Hoffman et al. 2014). However, it must be willing to engage in critical self-reflection and questioning with particular consideration for diverse ways of being with an openness to having some of its conceptions transformed and re-interpreted in new cultural contexts (Comas-Dias 2012).

Existential-Humanistic Therapy in China

Mark Yang and Xuefu Wang

Many recognize that there are significant roots of humanistic and existential thought within Confucianism, Buddhism, and Taoism, the three primary philosophies that have deeply impacted Chinese culture. This is why there has been so much interest in cross-cultural dialogue and the development of existential-humanistic psychology within China. At the forefront of this effort has been the work achieved by the International Institute of Existential and Humanistic Psychology, which has devoted itself to building bridges between psychologists in China, Southeast Asia, the United States, and beyond. This work has resulted in the creation of three (and counting) International Conferences on Existential Psychology held in China since 2010, a certificate training program, a book titled *Existential Psychology East-West*, and numerous workshops and conference presentations in the United States, Europe, China, and throughout Southeast Asia. This section describes the resonances between Confucianism, Taoism, Zhi-Mian Psychology, and core tenets of existential-humanistic psychology.

Confucius and Existential-Humanistic Psychology

Confucianism, revered by Chinese rulers as the official ideology since the Han dynasty (141 BCE), has been credited as the most important source of Chinese culture. Confucius was the first educator to pioneer private schools in China and was later venerated as the "Model Teacher for All Ages" (萬世師表). Confucius had many disciples. His discipleship espoused many qualities found within existential-humanistic therapy, such as benevolence (unconditional regard), sincerity (authenticity), experience (here and now), wisdom (paradoxical thinking), and following the flow, the result of a deep respect for what is natural. Confucius's thoughts cover almost every aspect of life. Recorded in the four classical texts, *Confucian Analects*, *The Great Learning*, *The Doctrine of the Mean*, and *Mencius*, his teachings find many resonances with principles and practices in existential-humanistic psychology. These include:

1 **The Focus Upon Humanity**: Confucius placed humanity at the center of his concern. He defined *humaneness* (*ren*, 仁) as "to love all men" [12:22] (Confucius 1893/1971, p. 260). This correlates to one of the fundamental concerns of existential-humanistic psychology which is concerned with the crucial question, "What does it mean to be human?"
2 **Actualization-oriented**: Both Confucius and existential-humanistic psychologists believe in the importance of self-actualization. When Confucius (1893/1971) wrote "Now the man of perfect virtue, wishing to be established himself, seeks also to establish others; wishing to be enlarged himself, he seeks also to enlarge others" [6:28] (p. 260), he believed that it is in self-cultivation through service to others that one becomes a superior person (Junzi, 君子).[1] This is akin to what Carl Rogers described as the "fully-functioning person."
3 **Courage, Freedom, and Perseverance:** Living in a troubled time, Confucius devoted his life to perusing and preaching his Way (Tao, 道), taking it as the mandate of heaven. He espoused the qualities of perseverance and bravery resembling what Paul Tillich described as "the courage to be." His admonition of "no foregone conclusions, no arbitrary predeterminations, no obstinacy, and no egoism" [9:4] (Confucius 1893/1971, p. 217) resonates with central tenets of phenomenology. Confucius (1893/1971) also embraced the spirit of Sartre and Camus's tragic optimism, as even a gatekeeper knew of him to comment that, "despite the impossibility of his mission, he would still persist in its pursuit" [14:41] (p. 290).

Existential-Humanistic Psychology and the Way of the Tao

If you consider yourself a scholar of existential-humanistic psychology, it behooves you to be familiar with the way of the Tao for its numerous resonances with the nature of existence. Chinese Taoism was founded by two main sages and literary scholars Lao

[1] "Things being investigated, knowledge became complete. Their knowledge being complete, their thoughts were sincere. Their thoughts being sincere, their hearts were then rectified. Their hearts being rectified, their persons were cultivated. Their persons being cultivated, their families were regulated. Their family being regulated, their States were rightly governed. Their States being rightly governed, the whole empire was made tranquil and happy." (Legge 1893/1971, pp. 358–359).

Tzi (circa 571–471 BCE) and Zhuangzi (circa 369–286 BCE). Zhuangzi is the lesser known of the sages and his tome is titled *Zhuangzi* with 33 chapters. Lao Tzi wrote the *Tao Te Ching*, which has been translated more than any volume in the world with the exception of the Bible. The *Tao Te Ching* consists of 81 chapters and can be translated as the book or canon (Ching) of how or The Way (Tao) things happen or work. All of this is regarded as virtue (Te). The *Tao Te Ching* addresses three topics: leadership, natural law, and a way of life that is in harmony with natural laws.

The Taoist sages had tremendous respect for natural law and non-interference with the natural order of things. It is both as simple to understand and as challenging to put to clinical practice as "following the flow" or getting lost in the Tao. Indeed people are encouraged to live in harmony with nature, and are to be found in nature, albeit just a small part of nature, not dominating nature. Hence an attitude of humility, wonderment, and awe is the natural result of living in harmony with the Tao. As to harmoniously co-existing with nature, the Taoists and many existential-humanistic psychologists hold that everything is interrelated, or mutually arising with no controlling center. Nothing can be experienced without its polar opposite such as good and bad, pain and joy, sickness and health. Death and life are equiprimordial, existing together as equally fundamental. Clients and therapists are simply roles that we play for we are all fellow travelers, wandering in the ways of the Tao. Who can demarcate the source of healing? The question of the chicken and egg is de-emphasized for co-existence and interdependence is accentuated over cause-and-effect. Epistemologically, Taoists contend that knowledge and understanding are always on their way toward *Truth* without ever having the ability to capture it. This is wonderfully illustrated in the famous opening lines of chapter one of the *Tao Te Ching*, "A way that can be walked is not The Way. A name that can be named is not The Name" (Lao Tzi 2003) and the parable of "How Knowledge Went North" (Zhuangzi 2003, Ch. 22).

The Tao – like existential-humanism – encompasses opposites and embraces paradox. However, the Tao also emphasizes or favors the *less desirable* terms as a more useful way of describing Tao. For Taoist philosophers, the weak, the submissive, and the useless are actually preferable in some ways to the strong, the dominant, and the useful. Chapter 76 (excerpts) of the *Tao Te Ching* states: "When life begins we are tender and weak. When life ends we are stiff and rigid. All things, including the grass and trees, are soft and pliable in life dry and brittle in death. So soft and supple are the companions of life, while the stiff and unyielding are the companions of death" (Lao Tzi 2003, p. 89).

Finally, no discussion of the way of the Tao is complete without an explication of the concept of Wu Wei (無爲/无为). Wu Wei means acting without premeditation, the intention and act being simultaneous. Wu Wei is not forcing, not imposing, not interfering. It is about silence, stillness, and emptying ourselves so that we are able to receive. It is not doing nothing. In the words of Zhuangzi (2003, Ch. 33), the mind of Wu Wei flows like water, reflects like a mirror, and responds like an echo.

Zhi-Mian Psychotherapy: An Indigenous Form of Existential-Humanistic Psychology in Contemporary China

Zhi-Mian Psychotherapy is an indigenous form of existential-humanistic psychology developed by Dr. Wang Xuefu who is based in Nanjing, China. It is based upon the writings of the modern Chinese writer Lu Xun (鲁迅) who directed his critical gaze at what he considered the mental escapism of the Chinese people. The term Zhi-Mian (直面), which can be loosely translated as "facing directly," is derived from the following quote from Lu Xun (1981) who championed the Zhi-Mian Warrior as one who "dares to face life as it is, no matter how gloomy it might be" (真的猛士, 敢于直面惨淡的人生) (p. 271). Through recent (since 2010) international dialogue, particularly with existential-humanistic psychologists from the United States, more and more people in both China and abroad have come to understand existence and existential-humanistic psychology through the concept of Zhi-Mian.

The goal of Zhi-Mian psychotherapy is to become oneself through renunciation, which can be understood as daring to refuse and resist those forces and powers that obstruct and damage one's ability to fully become oneself. A Zhi-Mian psychotherapist is one who empathically understands that clients are faced with all sorts of limitations and concurrently support and encourage clients to exercise their will and choice within the confines of such limitations. At the same time, the Zhi-Mian psychotherapist espouses the sensibility to help clients develop relationships that are built upon love and service.

Zhi-Mian psychotherapists nurture clients' development through the following three core principles:

1 **The courage to explore and face reality.** From the perspective of Zhi-Mian, psychological struggles are believed to come about through an overreliance on escape as a defense mechanism. Thus Zhi-Mian psychotherapy is an endeavor to bring people back to the facing of life.
2 **The capacity to rebel and to serve.** In Zhi-Mian Psychotherapy, therapists are attuned to the myriad of cultural elements that mitigate people's courage and capacity to resist. Therefore, a healthy rebellion is a must. Concurrently, in addition to rebellion, the Zhi-Mian spirit also emphasizes relationships built upon love and service.
3 **The transformation of suffering and trauma through meaning-making.** The Zhi-Mian attitude teaches one to face one's suffering directly and transform that suffering through the discovery or construction of one's personal meaning. When we are hurt or even traumatized, we all develop protections that become defense mechanisms when overly rigid. Such defenses often involve compulsively escaping uncertainty and the reach for absolute security which is an illusion. Zhi-Mian Psychotherapists encourage clients to abandon such illusions through the concept of Zhi-Mian. Dr. Wang Xuefu (2009) adopted Lu Xun's metaphor of an iron house to represent those systems that claim to provide meaning and truth, but in fact shackle people. Thus Zhi-Mian psychotherapists endeavor to help their clients develop awareness for it is believed through awakening clients will choose Zhi-Mian in place of escape.

The Contemplative Heart of Existential-Integrative Therapy

G. Kenneth Bradford

Just as an *integrative* emphasis respects the *breadth* of therapies that address existential concerns, a *contemplative* emphasis respects the *depth of* existentially rigorous therapies that allow for varying degrees of subjective immersion, felt attunement, and authentic presence. An integrative sensibility draws upon a wide range of therapeutic understandings and interventions in order to address particular concerns tailored to conditions and capabilities of specific persons. The common denominator for the entire range of particular approaches is the recognition that any depth therapy is based on the capacity for *self-attention*, requiring both the willingness and capability to look within. Rather than seeking to adjust, fix, or build oneself to suit the constraints of others, existentially robust therapies facilitate a person sourcing themselves from their inner, "existential sense," even as this sense can be approached in various ways (Bugental 1976, p. 2). It is in this felt sense of valuing the *existential core* of experience, rather than in any particular theoretical or philosophic sense, that the kind of integrative approach we favor is understood to be *Existential*-Integrative. The inward turn, away from unreflective, compulsive, and objectivizing judgments of self and others, necessitates attuning to the flow of subjective awareness, which is a decidedly contemplative approach to self-inquiry. The search for authenticity – the pearl beyond price for existential-humanistic therapy – will be more or less deep and thorough depending on a person's capability for opening him or herself.

Eugene Gendlin's (1978) research on psychotherapy found that the principal factor enabling therapy effectiveness hinged on a person's capacity for subjective sensing. His research found that the ability to engage in inward sensing need not be inborn, but is a skill of self-attention that can be learned and deepened. Gendlin unpacked this therapeutic skill into a series of practical steps he calls "focusing." Of course, the specific steps of focusing are not the only way to develop the ability of self-inquiry. There are any number of other meditative techniques and relational-skillful means that can be employed to facilitate self-attention and self-liberation. Even though Gendlin was not the first psychologist to discover that meditative skillfulness is essential for *both* client and therapist in the practice of depth therapy, he was among the first to research it. He belongs to a lineage of psychologists and philosophers that work as *contemplative scientists*, forerunners of the *mindfulness-based* approaches so prominent today.

Freud first recognized contemplative attention to be the indispensible keystone of psychotherapy practice as early as 1911. He noted that the various rules governing the practice of psychoanalysis could all "be summed up in a single precept … [that is] a counterpart to the 'fundamental rule of psycho-analysis' which is laid down for the patient … [that of] maintaining the same 'evenly-suspended attention' in the face of all that one hears" (quoted and discussed in Bradford 2007a, p. 57). In spite of his many differences with Freud, Jung remained in accord with him on this crucial point, as have any number of depth-inclined analysts throughout the last century, including Bion (1984), Winnicott (1971), and Boss (1982/1963). Even though meditative attention is not always consistently or thoroughly deployed in analytic practice, it is still the essence of the "analytic attitude." R.D. Laing (1985) stridently declared psychotherapy to be a practice of "interpersonal meditation," serving the purpose of "catalyzing a person into their own existence." He felt that therapy takes place as a "meditative conversation [involving a] coming together in a reflective, meditative mood, [allowing for an] incubation that invites an intuitive response." Laing went on to observe that this "happens rarely; and could happen more if one trusts that process more completely."

Phenomenology likewise privileges contemplative awareness as its prime cognizant function. Recognizing that taken-for-granted social/mental constructs shape and distort how we see things, Husserl (1973/1929) found it prudent to adopt a "phenomenological attitude" that is able to suspend the tacit assumptions of our self- and world constructs in order to see things more accurately as they are rather than how we think they are. The phenomenological suspension of both belief and disbelief, which enhances openness to and in the world, is a meditative skill of non-interfering awareness that can reduce cognitive and emotional distortions, so as to allow "things/others to reveal themselves." Heidegger (1966/1959) fleshed this out further by distinguishing between "calculative thinking," which is our everyday, concept-bound thinking *about* something or someone, and "meditative thinking," which is a non-conceptual thinking *with* something or someone, potentially empowering a non-willful, spontaneous natural release (*gelassenheit*) of conceptual self-limitations.

Existential psychotherapy, as we practice and teach it (see Bradford 2001, 2013; Bugental 1978, 1981, 1987; Boss 1982/1963; Schneider and May 1995; Schneider and Krug 2010; and Schneider 2008, for instance) entwines the streams of psychoanalysis, phenomenology, and existential-humanism, congealing into what Jim Bugental referred to as "an all-American hash." However, in my view, even this rich intertwining leaves out the deeper and most powerful contemplative stream of all, and the one having the most profound healing potential.

More sophisticated, ontologically robust, and time-tested forms of self-inquiry are to be found in Asian wisdom traditions, which are only beginning to be learned and mastered by Euro-American existentialists. And it is no wonder: understanding and applying the thought of European existential phenomenology is already a formidable task. It is no easy thing to comprehend a Husserl, a Buber, a Sartre, or a Heidegger, and still more difficult to apply their philosophical thought to the practice of therapy. On top of this, to study and practice a contemplative tradition such as Buddhism, Taoism, Sufism, or even mystical Judaism or Christianity for that matter, is downright daunting. But of course, just because it is difficult does not mean it is not worthwhile. As Rollo May (1981, p. 164) put it, "In our crisis of thought and religion in the West, the wisdom of the East emerges as a corrective. This wisdom recalls us to truths in our own mystic tradition that we had forgotten, such as contemplation, meditation and the significance of the pause."

A fertile challenge for existential therapists is to deepen our capacity for non-conceptual awareness. In the service of depth, it behooves us to take advantage of the exceptional psychological knowledge and meditative practices of Asian wisdom traditions. Even as "mindfulness" is currently one of the most researched topics in American psychology (Walsh and Shapiro 2006), it remains an entry-level meditative practice, often applied in a rather superficial way that strips it from its broader philosophical context and deeper emancipatory project. In addition to the disciplined cultivation of mindful awareness – whether we refer to this as "evenly-suspended attention," "phenomenological attention," "PRESENCE," "focusing," insight meditation," or so on – lie more advanced contemplative competencies that can empower the capacity for awe and empathic attunement in the direction of selfless compassion and strengthen the capability for nondual presencing in the direction of self-liberation.

In the twentieth century, it was enough for existential psychology to be considered and to consider itself a wholly Western tradition. In the twenty-first century this is a limitation that is being expanded by consulting the advanced contemplative traditions of Asia (For instance, Boss 1965; Bradford 2007a, 2007b, 2013; Craig 2007; Fenner 1994; Hoffman 2008; Hoffman and Yang 2009). Among the major schools of psychology, with its emphasis on the being of human beings, existential therapy is especially well-suited to develop into a transcultural, East/West, truly holistic psychology in the emerging age.

Psychotherapy and the Arts: Becoming Who We Are

Ed Mendelowitz

> As that which completes the primal images, it is called the Creative; as that which imitates them, it is called the Receptive. (The Book of Changes)

"The arts," writes my three-year-old daughter's pediatrician Mark Vonnegut (2010, p. 3), "are not extra-curricular." It seems so obvious a point as to hardly bear mentioning. A feeling for literature, music, film, art, to say nothing of philosophy and religion – these would seem to be quintessential attributes of any psychology worthy of the name. Skeptics inclined to feel that nothing exists aside from the vaunted and avowedly evidence based may now take comfort in research that confirms what some of us have known all along. "Authors were psychologists, you know, and profound ones," proclaimed Eugene O'Neill (cited in Bogard and Bryer 1994, p. 386), "before psychology was invented." Who would we forgo on that desert island of the metaphorically shipwrecked, the novelist or the simultaneously reductive and self-aggrandizing theorist? Melville or Seligman? The pediatrician's storied father, Kurt, or Aaron Beck?

My reverie considers psychotherapy as creative endeavor on both sides of the therapeutic dialectic and recalls a Nietzschean adage ("self-creation, the most difficult art") and the injunction he adapted ever so slightly from the Greek poet Pindar: "*How one becomes what one is.*" The presuppositions and potentials underwriting these thoughts invoke bedrock themes of transience and ultimate insignificance on one hand while holding out for possibility, some semblance of meaning within the void, on the other. These ongoing tensions elicit the apprehension and novelty that inhere in genuine exchange and the fashioning of character out of fragment, chance, and hard work. "Life," Nietzsche once mused, "is only justified as an aesthetic experience." It is this feeling for the intrinsic, albeit difficult, place of self-creation (a beckoning of, and striving for, a Jamesean "more" or "ever not quite") that serves as touchstone and beacon in this briefest meditation on psychotherapy and the arts.

The therapeutic situation, it seems to me, must in some way function as counterpoint to the shallowness and general vacuity of our times. ("Many people, few gestures," observes Milan Kundera [1991] in *Immortality*, a novel damning in its depiction of just what it is we are up against.) It is a meeting and eventual tension of wills, an occurrence that in its novelty, free-spiritedness, and essential beneficence evokes embrace of broader processes of life on both sides of the consulting room and, hopefully, beyond.

The psychotherapeutic encounter ought to function very much as the right book once did for Kafka (1977, p. 16), as he put the matter in a youthful letter to a friend:

> I think we ought to read only the kind of books that wound or stab us. If the book we're reading doesn' wake us up with a blow to the head, what are we reading for? So that it will make us happy…? Good Lord, we would be happy precisely if we had no books, and the kind of books that make us happy are the kind we could write ourselves if we had to. But we need books that affect us like a disaster, that grieve us deeply, like the death of someone we loved more than ourselves, like being banished into forests far from everyone, like a suicide. A book must be the axe for the frozen sea within us. That is my belief.

Several months earlier, the Czech genius Elias Canetti who would one day be called the West's "only Chinese poet," had also written this to his friend: "Some books seem like a key to unfamiliar rooms in one's own castle" (Kafka 1977, p. 10).

This is the sort of "encounter" that is the lynchpin of change as, I think, existentially inclined psychotherapists like to conceive it, however infrequently embodied it may be. It is the sort of thing Rollo May (following in the footsteps of H.S. Sullivan and Frieda Fromm-Reichmann) was able to effect well into old age. I remember witnessing this unique admix of rarified character commingling with what he liked to call "disciplined naiveté" on the very first night of a case conference in psychotherapy that met long ago in May's living room in Tiburon. Thirty-five years later, I recall, very nearly verbatim, the words spoken that evening; so striking was the man and riveting the experience. Despite the innumerably meaningful connections I have subsequently had and made in this profession, I have never quite experienced this again. As a young black student once said in the aftermath of the death of jazz luminary John Coltrane, a hole has been left that threatens, ominously, to become permanent. A lot of good music to be sure, but the experience is not quite the same for those who have known subtler refrains, loftier key signatures and codes. How does one contribute meaningfully to the literature attending the aesthetics of psychotherapy in an atmosphere of logorrhea and flatness, the surrealistic cults of celebrity and regiment, our age of terminal paradox?

I and Thou

In Buber's *Between Man and Man* (1955, p. 175), we read a passage that is at once hallowed and haunting, in its intimation, among so many other things, of psychotherapy as balm for self-becoming already attained and catalyst for that yet to be: "A great relationship … breaches the barriers of a lofty isolation, subdues its strict law, and throws a bridge from self-being to self-being across the abyss of dread of the universe." And in Robert Coles's (2010) *Handing One Another Along*, this Raymond Carver-inspired thought (not so dissimilar, really, to Kafka's) concerning the inevitability of the arts: "How does one live a life? What kind of a life? And for what purpose?" Psychotherapists like May and Coles are, among other things, aesthetes at heart who take their own creative work quite seriously and whose written works trace poetic arches over the courses of their wise, gentle rendering.

Turbulence and the Humanities

I wish, also, to underscore the places of turbulence and struggle in any creative venture worthy of the name. The exemplars quietly informing this reverie were by no means given to insistently upbeat philosophies or easygoingness in either their persons or respective works. James and Rank, it is likely, suffered with bipolar disorders, biological conditions that may have underwritten, in part, their staggering accomplishments no less than their propensities for despond. James's (1902, pp. 127–128) thumbnail sketch of the Frenchman whose "general depression of spirits" suddenly yields to "a horrible fear of my own existence," was an autobiographical account of his own ordeal. Rank (1932) wrote 12 of the 14 chapters of his masterwork, *Art and Artist*, incredibly, in a single month. ("Confusion creates art," mused Rank's patient-turned-muse, Anais Nin, while noting, additionally, that "too much confusion creates unbalance" [cited in Lieberman 1985, p. 332]). Concerning Rank's therapeutic approach, Nin was succinct: "He improvised." May's life was marked by several existential crises that were depressive in nature. As for the medical wreck Nietzsche – well, this is a story unique unto itself. We can see, now that life is winding down, that Robert Coles has, for a long time now, been something of a saint.

We are very close here to May's (in Schneider and May 1995) late-in-life lectures on the "uses of adversity" and the psychotherapist as "wounded healer" and not far at all from the tenor of our present reflection on psychotherapy and the crafting of respective selves. May loved this passage out of Nietzsche's (in Kaufmann 1954, p. 129) *Zarathustra:* "One must still have chaos in oneself to be able to give birth to a dancing star." Imagine expressing one's philosophy so adroitly in a fictional work! Each of these "artist types" knew firsthand the sacrifices engendered by creativity and the inhabitation of loftier mores, images, and ideals. Not one of them got away unscathed.

Psychotherapy is a time-limited endeavor leading parties, at its best, inward and forward toward a fuller embrace of respective lives. "This is my way," urges Zarathustra (in Nietzsche 1954, p. 307); "where is yours?" Even in therapy, the client at a certain point is on her or his own. "The individual completes the creative work vastly relieved and more a person than before—but also maimed," observes May (1969, p. 286); "human progress is never one-dimensional." Rank (1932, p. 430) writes in his masterwork of the renunciation of "artistic expression" in favor of the formation of the self, implying that it is possible for the artist to overdose on art. He advocates the benefits of the artist's placing the "creative impulse directly in the service of [one's] own personality." "Giving style to one's character," as Nietzsche himself (1954, p. 198) so eloquently cajoled, "a great and rare art."

A contemplation of psychotherapy and art, do you see?

Epilogue: Toward an Integrative, Awe-Based Psychotherapy

Kirk J. Schneider

Recently, I returned from a trip to Amman, Jordan where I witnessed the remarkable power of existential-humanistic (EH) principles in action. These principles were expressed by seminars on phenomenologically informed child therapy, experiential engagement with the expressive arts, presentations on non-violent communications, and perhaps most importantly, enthused personal exchanges among culturally diverse participants. The occasion was the 2017 Transgenerational Trauma Conference, sponsored by the Common Bond Institute. This conference, coordinated by longtime humanistic social activist, Steve Olweean, along with colleagues such as the dynamic Ilene Serlin who worked intensively with Syrian refugees, will be forever emblazoned in my heart. "Heart" is the keyword because so much of what was conveyed at that conference came from the genuine goodwill of wonder, curiosity, and awe. In this way, the conference is emblematic of what is happening in the field of EH psychology today. To wit, and as previously intimated, there are fresh new alliances being formed with multicultural communities; there is a bridge-building and integrative spirit toward not only diverse cultural perspectives but also diverse therapeutic modalities. There is a renewed openness to the spiritual dimension of human experience, with an emphasis on the cultivation of humility and wonder, adventure, or, in short, awe toward living in many contemporary facets of EH practice (see also Pierson [2015] for an eloquent synopsis of the latter). Finally, there is a thrust toward social and political applications of EH therapy, as exemplified by the Jordan conference and work with refugees but also recent forays into experientially grounded dialogue groups in local communities, such as those which have been engaged at recent Society for Humanistic Psychology conferences (e.g., see https://www.youtube.com/watch?v=g92cNF5-Tpw) and by kindred organizations such as The Humanitarian Alliance (see https://thehumanitarianalliance.squarespace.com/mission/) and Better Angels (see https://www.better-angels.org).

In short, for all its ongoing challenges, today's EH therapy is notably more multidimensional, culturally diversified, and politically engaged than its predecessor. Although there is a very long way to go, the evolution of EH therapy would seem to be on a path toward fulfilling the democratic aspirations of its founding. This "deep" democracy however extends far beyond conceptions of individual therapy, or even our profession at large; it is a conviction that EH principles of practice can and should contribute to the wide-ranging efforts to salvage our planet, no less our humanity.

References

Bion, W. (1984). *Learning from Experience*. London: Karnac Books.

Bogard, T. and Bryer, J.R. (eds.) (1994). *Selected Letters of Eugene O'Neill*. New York: Limelight Editions.

Boss, M. (1965). *A Psychiatrist Discovers India* (trans. H.A. Frey). London: Oswald Wolff.

Boss, M. (1982). *Psychoanalysis and Daseinsanalysis*. New York: DaCapo. (Original work published 1963.)

Bradford, G.K. (2001). Therapeutic courage. *Voices: The Art and Science of Psychotherapy, 37* (2): 4–11.

Bradford, G.K. (2007a). From neutrality to the play of unconditional presence. In: *Listening from the Heart of Silence: Nondual Wisdom and Psychotherapy*, vol. 2 (ed. J. Prendergast and G.K. Bradford), 55–76. St. Paul, MN: Paragon.

Bradford, G.K. (2007b). The play of unconditioned presence in Existential-Integrative psychotherapy. *Journal of Transpersonal Psychology 39* (1): 23–47.

Bradford, G.K. (2013). *The I of the Other: Mindfulness-Based Diagnosis and the Question of Sanity*. St Paul, MN: Paragon House.

Buber, M. (1955). *Between Man and Man* (trans. R.G. Smith). Boston: Beacon Paperbacks.

Bugental, J. (1976). *The Search for Existential Identity.* San Francisco: Jossey-Bass.

Bugental, J. (1978). *Psychotherapy and Process.* New York: Addison-Wesley.

Bugental, J. (1981). *The Search for Authenticity: An Existential-Analytic Approach to Psychotherapy* (enlarged edn). New York: Irvington Publications.

Bugental, J. (1987). *The Art of the Psychotherapist.* New York: Norton.

Chan, A. (2009). In harmony with the sky: Implications for existential psychology. In: *Existential Psychology East-West* (ed. L. Hoffman, M. Yang, F. Kaklauskas et al.), 307–325. Colorado Springs, CO: University of the Rockies Press.

Coles, R. (2010). *Handing One Another Along: Literature and Social Reflection.* New York: Random House.

Comas-Dias, L. (2012). Humanism and multiculturalism: An evolutionary alliance. *Psychotherapy 49* (4): 437–441.

Confucius (1971). *Confucian Analects, The Great Learning and the Doctrine of the Mean* (trans. J. Legge). New York: Dover Publications. (Original work published 1893.)

Craig, E. (2007). Tao psychotherapy: Introducing a new approach to Humanistic practice. *The Humanistic Psychologist 35* (2): 109–133.

Fenner, P. (1994). The complete fulfillment (Dzogchen) tradition and Existential Psychology. *Journal of Contemplative Psychotherapy 9*: 53–72.

Fife, B.L. (1994). The conceptualization of meaning in illness. *Social Science and Medicine 38* (2): 309–316.

Gendlin, E.T. (1978). *Focusing.* New York: Bantam.

Heidegger, M. (1966). *Discourse on Thinking* (trans. J. Anderson and E.H. Freund). New York: Harper Colophon. (Original work published 1959.)

Hoffman, L. (2008). An existential framework for Buddhism, world religions, and psychotherapy: Culture and diversity considerations. In: *Brilliant Sanity: Buddhist Approaches to Psychotherapy* (ed. F.S. Kaklauskas, J. Nimanheminda, L. Hoffman et al.), 19–38. Colorado Springs, CO: University of the Rockies Press.

Hoffman, L. (2016). Multiculturalism and humanistic psychology: From neglect to epistemological and ontological diversity. *The Humanistic Psychologist 44* (1): 56–71.

Hoffman, L., Cleare-Hoffman, H.P., and Jackson, T. (2014). Humanistic psychology and multiculturalism: History, current status, and advancements. In: *The Handbook of Humanistic Psychology: Theory, Research, and Practice*, 2e (ed. K.J. Schneider, J.F. Pierson, and J.F.T. Bugental), 41–55. Thousand Oaks, CA: Sage.

Hoffman, L., Stewart, S., Warren, D. et al. (2015). Toward a sustainable myth of self: An existential response to the postmodern condition. In: *The Handbook of Humanistic Psychology: Theory, Research, and Practice*, 2e (ed. K.J. Schneider, J.F. Pierson, and J.F.T. Bugental), 105–133. Thousand Oaks, CA: Sage.

Hoffman, L. and Yang, M. (eds.) (2009). *Existential Psychology East-West.* Colorado Springs, CO: University of the Rockies Press.

Husserl, E. (1973). *Cartesian Meditations: An Introduction to Phenomenology* (trans. D. Cairns). The Hague: Martinus Nijhoff. (Original work published 1929.)

James, W. (1902) *The Varieties of Religious Experience: A Study in Human Nature.* New York: Longmans, Green, and Co.

Kafka, R. (1977). *Letters to Friends, Family, and Editors* (trans R. and C. Winston). New York: Schocken Books.

Kaufmann, W. (ed.) (1954). *The Portable Nietzsche.* New York: Viking Press.

Kundera, M. (1991). *Immortality* (trans. P. Kussi). New York: Grove Press.

Laing, R.D. (1985). *Existential Psychotherapy* (Video recording No. L330- CP13). Lecture and clinical demonstration at the Evolution of Psychotherapy Conference, Phoenix, AZ: The Milton Erikson Foundation.

Lao Tzi, (2003). *Tao Te Ching: The Definitive Edition* (trans. J. Star). New York: Penguin Group.
Legge, J. (1971). *The Chinese Classics: The Great Learning*. Oxford: Clarendon Press. (Original work published 1893.)
Lieberman, E.J. (1985). *Acts of Will: The Life and Work of Otto Rank*. New York: Free Press.
Lu Xun, (1981). *Complete Works of Lu Xun*, vol. 3. Beijing, China. People's Literature Publishing House.
May, R. (1969). *Love and Will*. New York: W.W. Norton & Co.
May, R. (1981). *Freedom and Destiny*. New York: W.W. Norton & Co.
Motschnig-Pitrik, R. and Barrett-Lennard, G. (2010). Co-actualization: A new construct in understanding well-functioning relationships. *Journal of Humanistic Psychology 50* (3): 374–398.
Myers, L.M. (1985). Transpersonal psychology: The role of the Afrocentric paradigm. *Journal of Black Psychology 12* (1): 31–42.
Myers, L.M. (1993). *Understanding an Afrocentric Worldview: Introduction to Optimal Psychology*, 2e. Dubuque, IA: Kendall Hunt Publishing.
Nietzsche, F. (1954). Thus spake Zarathustra. In: *The Portable Nietzsche* (trans. W. Kaufmann), 103–439. New York: Viking Press.
Nobles, W. (2006). *Seeking Saku: Foundational Writings of an African Psychology*. Chicago: Third World Press.
Oyserman, D., Coon, H.M., and Kemmelmeier, M. (2002). Rethinking individualism and collectivism: Evaluation of theoretical assumptions and meta-analyses. *Psychological Bulletin 128* (1): 3–72.
Pierson, J.F. (2015). Closing statements. In: *The Handbook of Humanistic Psychology: Theory, Practice, and Research*, 2e (ed. K.J. Schneider, J.F. Pierson, and J.F.T. Bugental), 742–745. Thousand Oaks, CA: Sage.
Rank, O. (1932). *Art and Artist* (trans. C. Francis). New York: Alfred A. Knopf.
Reitz, J.G., Breton, R., Dion, K.K. et al. (2009). *Multiculturalism and Social Cohesion: Potentials and Challenges of Diversity*. New York: Springer Science & Business Media.
Schneider, K.J. (2008). *Existential-Integrative Psychotherapy: Guideposts to the Core of Practice*. New York: Routledge.
Schneider, K.J. and Krug, O. (2010). *Existential Humanistic Therapy*. Washington, DC: American Psychological Association.
Schneider, K.J. and May, R. (eds.) (1995). *The Psychology of Existence: An Integrative, Clinical Perspective*. New York: McGraw-Hill.
Schwartz, S.H. (1990). Individualism-collectivism: Critique and proposed refinements. *Journal of Cross-Cultural Psychology 21* (2): 139–157.
Vonnegut, M. (2010). *Just Like Someone Without Mental Illness Only More So: A Memoir*. New York: Delacorte Press.
Walsh, R. and Shapiro, S.L. (2006). The meeting of meditative disciplines and Western psychology. *American Psychologist 61* (3): 227–239.
Wang, X. (2009). Spiritual warrior in search of meaning. An existential view of Lu Xun through his life incidences and analogies. In: *Existential Psychology East-West* (ed. L. Hoffman, M. Yang, F. Kaklauskas et al.), 149–164. Colorado Springs, CO: University of the Rockies Press.
Winnicott, D.W. (1971). *Playing and Reality*. New York: Tavistock.
Zhuangzi (2013). *The Complete Work of Zhuangzi* (trans. B. Watson). New York: Columbia University Press (Kindle version).

Part IV
Logotherapy and Existential Analysis

Edited by
Alfried Längle

This introduction provides a brief overview of Logotherapy and Existential Analysis (EA). Logotherapy is a meaning-centered approach to counselling, which mainly aims to help people deal with meaninglessness in their lives. Existential Analysis is a psychotherapy that can address a wide range of suffering, be it clinical, psychological disorders, or sub-clinical disturbances, such as despair, hopelessness, meaninglessness, being overstressed, or grieving a significant loss.

The development of Logotherapy originated in reaction to the prevailing depth psychology of the time. In the early 1920s, Frankl (see Chapter 19 in this book) formulated his first attempt to address the inherent reductionism (which was also raised by Jaspers and Husserl) in Freudian and Adlerian psychology. Although respecting their psychotherapeutic work, Frankl faced this reductionism by emphasizing that psychology needed to see and understand human beings in their wholeness. This holistic emphasis involved not only focusing on psychic (libidinal) mechanisms (Freud) or the struggle with feelings of inferiority (Adler), but rather seeing human beings in their striving for a contextual, encompassing understanding of their existence. This attempt is based in the inherent human freedom, accompanied by responsibility and leading unavoidably to finding an orientation through meaning. Human beings are more than just body and psyche but are characterized by being unique *persons*. Humans are pervaded by this "spiritual power" (Frankl 1946/1982), which brings along the need to discover the "why" of their existence, and gives them capacity to satisfy needs, deal with frustrations or suffering, and ultimately face death.

So Logotherapy marks the beginning of humanistic psychotherapy with the specific existential accent. Its main goal was overcoming reductionism and seeing human beings as giving answers to the demands of world and life. Following this task means to find "*logos*," that is, purpose and meaning in each situation. When this cannot be

---

The Wiley World Handbook of Existential Therapy, First Edition. Edited by Emmy van Deurzen, Erik Craig, Alfried Längle, Kirk J. Schneider, Digby Tantam, and Simon du Plock.

performed intuitively, "logo-therapy" is indicated to help people to find their "logos" (meaning), their personal and situational understanding and orientation. Logotherapeutic practice hence opens up the person so that they can be reached and touched by their actual life. This process needs an "*existential turn*" to catch the inherent question of the actual life situation. Clients are encouraged to allow themselves to be questioned by life. Being questioned by life, means giving up or postponing one's own interests, plans, and questioning of what one may personally gain in the situation. Instead Logotherapy understands human beings as being questioned by life itself. Living fully means giving one's best answer to the demands and offerings of each situation. Frankl described *three main roads to find meaning*: experiential values, creative values, and attitudinal values. When working in the clinical field, Logotherapy also applies methods like de-reflection (turning away from the fixation on anxieties, depressive loops, or histrionic needs) towards the values and requirements of the actual situation. Frankl also developed the famous method of paradoxical intention to assist with anticipatory anxiety, and focused on helping clients regain freedom by validating the search for and realization of meaning.

EA describes the development of the next generation of a psychotherapeutic approach. It has broadened the anthropological and theoretical basis and *understanding of existence.* As such, EA considers meaning as one dimension of existence. EA is no longer focused only on striving for meaning and seeing the lack of meaning as the cause of psychopathological developments. This broader view of existence led to an implementation of the use of *phenomenology* in psychotherapy, instead of relying on giving explanations, philosophical knowledge, or interpretations of the patient's or client's experience and motivation. The focus is on openness and understanding, personal presence and dialogical exchange, as well as activating the client's personal resources and potentials.

All this is reflected in EA's central tenet and existential motto: to help people *to live with inner consent* to what they do. This personally felt consent or approval reflects essentially the application of human freedom on the basis of realistic perception, connection with feelings and sensing, authentic resonance and moral conscience, as well as harmonizing with what is actually given and/or needed. To achieve this chief aim of helping people find *inner yes* to actual life, EA works with both a structural and a procedural method.

With the *structural method* the underlying dimensions of existence are explored collaboratively with clients and patients. In EA's understanding, existence is like a table that is based on four legs: the relation to the world and facts, the relation to life and feelings, the relation to oneself and one's authenticity, and the relation to the greater context of the world and time in which one lives (meaning). Therefore, EA works practically with the respective human capacities of:

1. being able to be and to do something
2. being able to like something, to feel, and to relate
3. being able to decide and give allowance to oneself for what one does (authenticity)
4. being able to harmonize and come to a concordance with our surroundings and the challenges and needs from the inside and outside.

When we can, like, may, and should do what we do, then we have a broadly based and holistic *will* with which we are living our existential freedom.

In situations in which the development of this authentic will and responsible action is blocked or inhibited, we make use of the phenomenological *procedural method* of *Personal Existential Analysis* (PEA), or of around a dozen other methods for strengthening the will, searching for meaning, training a phenomenological attitude, or working on the treatment of anxiety, depression, and so forth. The method of PEA has four steps: (1) describing the reality and what happened, (2) looking at the experienced feelings and reactions and implicit understanding of the phenomenal content. After these two steps the attention of the client is directed to finding a personal position, both emotionally and cognitively (3). (4) Out of this position an inner movement of the will – an idea or an action – can arise, which then needs the preparation for a most effective and strategic application in the concrete situation.

The presentation of both Existential Analysis and Logotherapy in this section is carried out with a rationale maintaining the more specific contents (corresponding especially to Frankl's work in Logotherapy). We acknowledge that there are other meaning-centered theorists, who may be assumed to belong in this part, however the focus for this section is specifically on Logotherapy and Existential Analysis. For further reading, the reader is directed to the literature below.

Further Reading

Breitbart, W., Rosenfeld, B., Gibson, C. et al. (2010). Meaning-centered group psychotherapy for patients with advanced cancer: A pilot randomized controlled trial. *Psycho-Oncology 19* (1): 21–28.

Cooper, M. (2017). *Existential Therapies*. London: Sage.

Correia, E., Cooper, M., and Berdondini, L. (2014). Existential psychotherapy: An international survey of the key authors and texts influencing practice. *Journal of Contemporary Psychotherapy 45* (1): 3–10.

Frankl, V. (1982). *The Doctor and the Soul. From Psychotherapy to Logotherapy*. New York: Random House. (Original work published 1946.)

Vos, J. (2016) Working with meaning in life in mental health care: A systematic literature review of the practices and effectiveness of meaning-centered therapies. In: *Clinical Perspectives on Meaning: Positive and Existential Psychoherapy* (ed. P. Russo-Netzer, S.E. Schulenberg, and A. Batthyany), 59–88. Berne: Springer.

19

The History of Logotherapy and Existential Analysis

Alfried Längle

Summary

The chapter begins with a description of Viktor Frankl's Logotherapy and Existential Analysis and his primary intention with the founding of this psychology. His aim was to combat "psychologism," a reductionistic view of the human being that sees motivations as based solely in psychological needs without any objective appeal, and to introduce the spiritual-mental dimension into psychology by making use of philosophy in psychotherapy. The key concepts of Logotherapy are mentioned: the way to discover meaning, an overview of Frankl's therapeutic techniques, and Frankl's special achievements.

Following this, the beginning of the current development of Existential Analysis will be described. This development emerged mainly for practical reasons, based on the experience of the psychotherapeutic application of Logotherapy. This practical experience combined with the difficulties in teaching Logotherapy gave rise to a need to develop additional methods with greater urgency. These first evolutionary steps in development turned into a revolution within the ranks of Logotherapy when practical phenomenological work revealed a broader basis to psychopathology and when open discussion revealed that the causes of psychological disorders cannot be defined solely as a lack of meaning. This critique led to the development of a new phenomenologically based psychotherapy, called Existential Analysis (EA). EA is structured around a broader understanding of existence that includes a complex, four-dimensional motivational system, and which led to the development of specific and unique therapeutic methods. In addition, EA has a coherent psychopathological and diagnostic framework with corresponding interventions. These theoretical advances brought Existential Analysis closer to Carl Rogers' approach and highlighted distinctions to classic Logotherapy.

The Wiley World Handbook of Existential Therapy, First Edition. Edited by Emmy van Deurzen, Erik Craig, Alfried Längle, Kirk J. Schneider, Digby Tantam, and Simon du Plock.

While the focus of Logotherapy is directed towards values and meanings in the world to which the person should be inclined in a self-transcendental way by forgetting themselves, the central aim of EA is the person with their personal capacities which should be activated in psychotherapy. This seemingly contradictory perspective is not too distant from Frankl's anthropological assumptions, since the person mirrors the subjective world and is the fulcrum for existence. The motto of Logotherapy is: to help people *find meaning* – the motto of EA is to help people *live with inner consent* in all that they do, and to see themselves in dialogical relation with the world and themselves.

Frankl's work

There is no better summary of Frankl's contribution to existential counselling and psychotherapy than his reformulation of Nietzsche's phrase: "He who knows a 'why' for living, will surmount almost every 'how'" (Frankl 1967, p. 103).

Logotherapy, often called the "Third Viennese School of Psychotherapy," was founded by the Viennese psychiatrist and neurologist Viktor E. Frankl (1905–1997) during the 1930s in order to supplement the first two Viennese schools, Sigmund Freud's and Alfred Adler's depth psychology (Soucek 1948; Hofstätter 1957). At an early age, Frankl established a personal correspondence with Sigmund Freud. However, Frankl stepped back from his training in psychoanalysis because of fundamental differences between his views and the anthropological understandings of depth psychology. In this early experience of Freud's psychoanalysis, he criticized the lack of understanding and dialogical encounter (for a more in-depth description, see Längle 2013). He moved to Alfred Adler's school of Individual Psychology and was trained by Rudolf Allers and Oswald Schwarz[1] (Frankl 1995; Längle 2013). As early as 1927, Frankl started to combat a trend within Individual Psychology that he identified as "psychologism"; a "pseudo-scientific procedure [that] presumes to analyze every act for its psychic origin, and on that basis to decree whether its content is valid or invalid" (Frankl 1973, p. 15). Frankl's response was to strive for "humanistic goals" in psychotherapy, focusing on purpose, meaning, and values as the noblest aims of any psychotherapy, as he put it. Thus, he considered the "will to meaning" to be the primary human motivation; the active search for orientation along existential values. He often contrasted the "will to meaning" with the psychodynamics of Freud's "will to pleasure" and Adler's "will to power" (Frankl 1963, 154; 1988, VII f.).

Frankl's theoretical shift resulted in his being expelled by Adler himself from the school of Individual Psychology in 1927. Frankl then worked alone and by the 1930s had developed his own view of what a psychotherapy should contain. He named his psychotherapeutic approach "Existential Analysis and Logotherapy." The creation of the term existential analysis was designed to contrast with psychoanalysis; he presented it as a parallel analysis with a different substance: existence in the world instead

[1] R. Allers became a professor at Harvard University and later built the connection between Frankl and Gordon Allport thus establishing a bridge for him to North America.

of intrapsychic tensions. However, Frankl vehemently distanced himself and existential analysis from psychoanalysis thematically, because he posited that psychotherapy should not be about the analysis of the psyche with its instincts and (pre-personal) needs, but rather the elucidating of the conditions for a meaningful existence (Frankl 1959/1987c, 59ff; 1982, 39 ff.). In order to identify the practical application of his existential anthropology, Frankl chose the philosophical term *logos* to denote "sense" or "meaning." The practice of Logotherapy focused on the treatment that concentrated on the discovery of meaning(s) and oriented the patient towards the future. Frankl's intention and belief were to complement the libidinous "depth psychology" with the *search for meaning* centered "height psychology" (Frankl 1987a, p. 18).

During the Second World War, Frankl was imprisoned in several concentration camps, which – in some sense – provided a crucial and existential experiment of his theory (see Frankl 1963). After his liberation in 1945, he actively published many books and articles and lectured extensively across the world. His unique theoretical contributions became widespread throughout North and South America. The first long-lasting scholarly societies were founded in Germany in 1979 and, in 1983 in Vienna, the Society of Logotherapy and Existential Analysis/Gesellschaft für Logotherapie und Existenzanalyse (GLE), with Frankl as honorary president. This society has become the largest existential psychotherapeutic society worldwide to date.

The first professional training in Logotherapy was offered under the supervision of Frankl. Following Frankl's resignation from GLE in 1991, a group of approximately 50 institutes and societies, as well as some activities of individual persons around the world, continued to follow his classical understanding of Logotherapy, both theoretically and practically. In 1994 ABILE (Ausbildungsinstitut für Logotherapie und Existenzanalyse) was founded in Austria as a counterpart to the GLE; it represents and provides training in the original Logotherapy of Viktor Frankl. In addition to some pre-existing smaller training institutions, further logotherapeutic institutes and trainings soon arose around the world, as we will see later.

The origins of Viktor Frankl's Logotherapy

As early as age 17, Frankl had conceived what he considered to be an ideal structure of psychotherapy. Influenced primarily by the philosophy of Kierkegaard, Frankl believed that the combining of philosophy with psychology provided the best access to illuminating the causes and expressions of human suffering, in particular the suffering that emerges from an unchangeable fate. His idea was to equip psychotherapy with a broader understanding of human existence. For this purpose, philosophy was needed. Frankl would later explain this integration as follows:

> What is needed is an immanent critique of the philosophy of life of the patient, with the assumption that we are in principle willing to take the discussion to a pure world view basis. [...] a philosophical worldview [Weltanschauung] [is] a possibility in psychotherapy [...], occasionally also necessary. Similar to the overcoming of psychologism in philosophy by logicism, it will be necessary within psychotherapy to overcome the actual

> psychologistic deviations with a kind of Logotherapy. This would mean the inclusion of ideological confrontation in the totality of psychotherapeutic treatment [...] just in the form of an existential analysis, which starts from the undeniable primary fact of human responsibility, the essence of human existence, [...] in order to contribute, from this point, to the spiritual anchoring, to give him support in the spiritual.
>
> In many cases, such an existential-analytically oriented psychotherapy may quite deserve the description as a non-specific therapy [... because they do not] start at the specific cause of his suffering." (Frankl 1938/1987a, pp. 25f)

Frankl (1938/1987a, pp. 27f) saw the indication of a psychotherapy, such as existential analysis, "in all cases, especially where the patient imposes on us the plight in his worldview, his lack of support and his struggle to find the meaning for his life." And it was further required in cases, whereby the logotherapeutic "approach, so to say, is to throw over-board the burden of light neurotic symptoms from the spiritual center of the person [... or respectively to help those], who suffer substantially from an insurmountable fact, an inevitable fate [...] by dealing with their philosophical questions."

In another publication from 1938, Frankl (1938/1987b, p. 35) gave a more concrete definition of the relation of Logotherapy and existential analysis to psychotherapy:

> Such existential analysis [...] ought in contrast – rather, in addition to the previous psychotherapeutic methods – to include the totality of the human being, that is it ought to consciously transcend the psychic realm; it ought to see the neurosis, as any mental suffering, not only rooted in the psychic or physiologic, but also as much in the spiritual (and ...) ought to follow the conflict up to the spiritual sphere of world-view decisions in order to enable a solution also from the spiritual. Only then, when oriented at the spiritual and having become existential analysis, will psychotherapy exhaust all therapeutic options; when it sees behind the psychic suffering the one who is wrestling spiritually.

While studying at Alfred Adler's School of Individual Psychology, Frankl became acquainted with the philosophy of Max Scheler through his principle teacher, Rudolf Allers. Through the study of Scheler's work (1980), "Der Formalismus in der Ethik und die materiale Wertethik," Frankl found exactly what he was looking for: a philosophical anthropology. Scheler's phenomenology of values, his phenomenological attitude and procedure, his analysis of love and feelings, his view of the human being as a spiritual being resonated perfectly with Frankl's own personal search and convictions, particularly the importance of meaning, an issue which had pre-occupied him since childhood (Frankl 1995, p. 9 (engl. p. 29), Längle 2013, p. 149). Scheler's writings and philosophy had such a great influence on Frankl that he founded his therapeutic practice on it and referenced it directly as he began publishing and practicing Logotherapy. Frankl's Existential Analysis and Logotherapy can legitimately be considered an application of Max Scheler's philosophy (Wicki 1991). Spiegelberg (1985) considered Frankl's condensation of Scheler's theory of values into three main categories (see later) as a specific phenomenological contribution to Scheler's work that made Logotherapy more applicable.

Before encountering Scheler's philosophy, however, a personal experience led Frankl towards humanistic psychology and existential-phenomenological psychotherapy. This was his encounter with Paul Federn, the General Secretary of the Freudian movement in Vienna. Freud was aware of Frankl's desire to be trained in psychoanalysis, and so arranged for a meeting for him with Federn. Frankl rarely disclosed the details of this meeting to the public. He shared this story with Alfried Längle, and thus he felt it was worthy of inclusion in his book on Frankl which was published after Frankl's death (Längle 2013). During the personal acceptance interview, Frankl was profoundly struck by Federn's overtly impersonal and technical behavior which he felt lacked the basics of human encounter. This experience, coupled with his developing formulations on the importance and impact of the human encounter in the therapeutic setting, led to a definitive split with Freud's psychoanalysis and to the commencement of his psychotherapeutic training with Adler. Frankl's intuitive reaction to Federn's behavior – a "technical" attitude towards human relationships and one that inhibited real, or authentic, encounter – was the birthmark of what would later became Frankl's Existential Analysis and Logotherapy (Längle 2013, pp. 46ff).

The Existential Proof – The Deportation to the Concentration Camps

The expulsion from Adler's school in 1927 marked the beginning of a turbulent period in Frankl's life. Adler expelled Frankl because of his constant emphasis on the "spiritual dimension" expressed primarily through an individual's search for meaning. This expulsion deprived Frankl of the basis for his work and removed his opportunities to exchange with a scientific community. These negative consequences were further compounded by the isolation brought on by the growth of the national socialist movement and its hostility towards Jews. During this time, despite being the darkest in Frankl's life, he published his first articles on Logotherapy and Existential Analysis and he wrote his first book on Logotherapy.[2] Just as he finished the book, he and his family were deported to concentration camps. He lost not only the manuscript (having hidden the manuscript in the lining of his coat) but most devastating, he lost his family. Frankl barely survived those years himself. The two-and-a-half years he spent in concentration camps forced him to experience what he had only conceptualized theoretically up to that point: the importance of purpose and meaning in order to overcome difficult life situations. His testimonies and reflections, as a psychologist, from those years in the concentration camps were published as *Man's Search of Meaning* (1946/1963). This book became a long-time best-seller in North-America and one of the most influential books in the United States.

Frankl (1946/1963, 1946/1973) attributed his survival of the horrors in those camps to three values that corresponded with his basic concept of finding meaning. First, his relationship to his family; a relationship he kept alive during those years in his heart and mind and second, Frankl's determination to re-write his lost manuscript.

[2] The re-constructed manuscript was published in 1946 under the title Ärztliche Seelsorge – Medical Ministry. It was published in English in 1955 as *The Doctor and the Soul* (cf. Frankl 1973).

He credited the creative and mental challenge of re-creating this manuscript from memory as an important factor in keeping him alive. And finally, Frankl acknowledged his strong faith in god which he regained during that time.

A worldwide impact

In the decades following the war and in addition to his ongoing writing and publishing activities, Frankl accepted invitations from over 200 universities around the world. Despite his personal success in presentations with, at times, large audiences of several thousand people, and despite his great prestige in public and academic life, Frankl's Logotherapy, although well-known, was infrequently applied. It spread predominantly through the popularity of his essay on his experiences in the concentration camps, which appeared in the appendix of *Man's Search for Meaning*. There was certainly great respect for him personally as a holocaust survivor. But his Logotherapy encountered a lot of critique and resistance (e.g., Jaspers in Fintz 2006; Görres, 1978, p. 33). Critics often argued that Logotherapy was too philosophical, educational, cognitive, and did not fully consider the psychodynamics and non-spiritual parts of the human being. For a brief period, Frankl was in a close contact with Irvin Yalom, who came to see him in Vienna, but no collaboration arose. While Frankl had contacts with many psychotherapists and philosophers, he preferred to work on his theory alone and was resistant to the foundation of societies. Consequently, no school of Logotherapy was developed until the first institute opened its doors in 1979 in Berkeley, California, guided by the immigrant Viennese lawyer and journalist, Joseph Fabry. There was no great luck in the foundation of societies; the societies which were founded in the 1950s and early 1970s soon disappeared.

To conclude Frankl's great contribution, some facts may underline the importance of his work. Frankl was Professor of Neurology and Psychiatry at the University of Vienna Medical School. He received the degrees of Doctor of Medicine and Doctor of Philosophy from the University of Vienna. During the Second World War he spent two and a half years at Auschwitz, Dachau, and other concentration camps. For 25 years he was head of the Vienna Neurological Policlinic. He was also considered by many as a national moral conscience for post-war Austria. He held professorships at Harvard, Stanford, the University of Dallas, and the University Pittsburgh, and was Distinguished Professor of Logotherapy at the US International University in San Diego, California. Frankl's 39 books (although several books were re-edited in different combinations) were translated in the meantime: 50 languages. He received honorary degrees from 29 universities in Europe, the Americas, Africa, and Asia. He held numerous awards, among them the Oskar Pfister Award of the American Psychiatric Association and an Honorary Membership of the Austrian Academy of Sciences.

The Experience of LT in Practice

It was on this basis, and a trust in the effectiveness of logotherapeutic practice, that we, as members of the GLE, continued to work with what Frankl taught and wrote. Frankl always suggested collaboratively applying methods of other psychotherapies with Logotherapy forming "the roof on the house of psychotherapy." He often repeated that psychotherapy was already invented, it simply lacked the spiritual dimension that he intended to include, thereby expanding the therapeutic offering. Indeed, Frankl intended Logotherapy to act as a *supplement* to the psychotherapies of the 1930s rather than be a comprehensive theory on its own. Logotherapy was thought of as a corrective for a growing trend towards "psychologism,"[3] by concentrating on individual suffering from the perspective of a loss of meaning (Frankl 1938/1987a, 1938/1987b, 1946/1973, 1967, 1988).

While adding methods of other psychotherapies to our clinical practices, the common base in our work as logotherapists, however, was the existential analytical anthropology and the logotherapeutic search for lack of meaning. As a consequence, logotherapeutic practice became quite heterogeneous – some applied a more psychodynamic basis but most applied behavioral methods or took some techniques from Gestalt or from the systemic approach. The broadest consensus was around the use of Carl Rogers' (1951) basic conditions for psychotherapy. One person who invested a great deal of time on the therapeutic application of Logotherapy was Elisabeth Lukas. She worked on a specific application of Logotherapy for dealing with life in general (life education), with suffering, and in family dynamics. She combined behavioral methods thoughtfully with Logotherapy and by doing so, developed several new techniques (e.g., the technique of modulation of attitudes) (Lukas 1980, pp. 96ff).

In 1984, after about two years of practicing, members of the newly formed GLE-society in Vienna began discussing their psychotherapeutic experiences openly during and after training in Logotherapy. There was a broad consensus that Logotherapy was useful as an anthropological map and as such it appeared very helpful in counselling. We heard similar assessments from other Logotherapists abroad. However, there were also limitations which we had all encountered: Logotherapy could hardly be used as psychotherapy in a modern sense – it was no more than an anthropological background for the application of other psychotherapies; essentially, it did not provide specific tools.

These realizations were the impetus for a series of broad developments undertaken by the Society for Logotherapy and Existential Analysis in Vienna, particularly in the areas of motivation and methodology, developments which eventually led to the formation of EA as it exists now.

Facing the Problems in the Application of Logotherapy

With the founding of GLE as an organization, the implementation of a training and supervision program, and the attempt of developing and implementing a rigorous and systematic application of Logotherapy in practice, it became obvious that this situation was not fulfilling the modern requirements for psychotherapy. There was a great need to develop practical tools for a better application of Logotherapy and to create the

[3] Psychologism is a theoretical stand which makes amongst others dependent the rightness of an act or saying from merely psychological elements like intention, motivation, or psychological health.

prerequisites for a complete training in psychotherapy, as was intended. Consequently, the interest was explicitly focused on involving as much anthropological basis as possible in the practical work and to reduce the application of methods from outside Logotherapy only to the degree that good help to patients and clients could still be provided.

What proved particularly difficult was the fact that no method for working with people suffering from a lack of meaning had been developed. The first initiative, therefore, was to develop such a method as a basis for genuine logotherapeutic work. The direction was found by stringently applying Frankl's (1982, pp. 21f, 255) definition of existential meaning, enlarged slightly by the inclusion of values. Thus, meaning was understood as "the most valuable possibility in a given situation" (Längle 2008, 48). The method derived from this theoretical foundation was called *Meaning Finding Method – MFM* (Längle 1988). On the basis of this method it was possible to develop a test measuring the degree of lived meaning (i.e, the self-rated meaningfulness of one's life). The test was named the *Existential Scale – ESK* (Längle and Orgler 1990; Längle, Orgler, and Kundi 2000).

Subsequently, a method for the application of logotherapeutic motivation was needed – the will to meaning (Frankl 1963, pp. 154ff; 1988). The next development focused on the will, on the deepening of motivation, and clarification of situations of un-decidedness and weak will. From here, the *Will Strengthening Method – WSM* was born and published (Längle 2000a).

Questioning the Logotherapeutic Foundation in Psychopathology

Following these first stages of expansion (still accepted by Frankl) a new crisis emerged – this time more fundamental and critical to the concept of Logotherapy. The question arose whether all or at least most psychopathology can really be understood by the concept of Logotherapy, that is, through the perspective of a substantial loss of meaning. Was it, as Frankl (1938/1987a, p. 19; 1938/1987b, p. 32) had pointed out, in referencing C.G. Jung among others, that neurosis is the soul which has lost its meaning and nothing more?

Despite Frankl's contention that Logotherapy was important in the healing of all disturbances, clinical experiences revealed that the lack of existential meaning is not so often the cause of psychic suffering as an accompanying result of many different causes. The main reason for lacking meaning was the lack of understanding of the suffering in experiencing deprivation, conflicts, and problems. A lack of existential meaning is often not indicative of a psychopathological state but rather an overall feeling that the direction of life is missing existential values. Thus, it is a measure of the quality of life and contains no further information about the reasons or causes of why it is diminished or improved. There were observations that suffering from a lack of meaning often has to do with an insufficient perception of reality, values, and of oneself; these factors are further compounded by a lack of openness within the individual.

This discovery gave a strong inspiration to look for a dynamic access to an individual in order to work on the development of more openness. If people are sufficiently open, they can be reached by the values of the world, their will can be moved, the meaning of the situation can be found, and the tools to fulfill their meaning can appear in a given situation. The difficulty was in finding a way to develop a better phenomenological capacity in patients. So, the members of the society began to work with a new tool. Instead of the mainly cognitive procedure in working with clients, according to Frankl's paradigm to give them "arguments for a tragic optimism" (Frankl 1990, pp. 79ff), the therapists began to train their patients in opening themselves phenomenologically, in small situations, accompanied by the therapist, through a perceptual exercise of dialoguing with an object. The Phenomenological Dialogue Exercise, or "Chair Method," gained shape and was first presented in 1987 (published by Längle in 2000b).

This method worked not only in *opening* perceptive capacity towards objects but also towards oneself. It also applied constant positioning and dialogue, enhanced by the therapist. It was therefore reasonable to use the same basic dialogical paradigm of EA in the treatment of anxiety and depression. So, the *Method of Personal Positioning (PP)* (Längle 1997) was developed; a resource-oriented method for dealing with anxiety and negative thinking in depression.

Frankl accepted the developmental changes in Logotherapeutic work up to this point (we increasingly referenced these changes as existential analytic work to denote the progression of the development of these methods), although he did not appreciate the development of the phenomenological exercise.

By the end of the 1980s, the critical assessment of the logotherapeutic capacity, strength, and understanding of psychopathology and development of new methods brought about a new level of understanding and access to patients and clients. A substantial change became necessary and turned out to be revolutionary in the field of Logotherapy. In the spring of 1991 Frankl decided he could no longer support these developments and withdrew from the GLE-society. He pointed to three specific reasons for stepping back from his position as the honorary president of the GLE: The biographical work in psychotherapy, the development of the method of Personal Existential Analysis (PEA) and the requirement of more than 200 hours of self-experience (at that time, now it is much more).

The Turn Towards Phenomenology – PEA

The main renewal in the 1980s was a stringent application of phenomenology in practice. This led to a parallel development in both areas, in the *structural understanding* of existence, and in the process model of EA for working through of problems, deficits or trauma: PEA (Längle 1993, 1995, 2000c), and the development of the four *Fundamental Existential Motivations* (for both see Chapters 20 and 22).

The development of the PEA-method took place on the basis of an enlarged theoretical concept of the person. The new perspective was a phenomenological looking at how the person appears in the encounter with the other and how the person shows up in the inner relationship. This more experiential (and less categorical) view of the person was combined with the practical experience of the potential and activity of personhood in working with the patients and clients. The task was simply to look at: What does the person do in daily life? How does the person become active? What is its role in the inner dialogue with oneself and in the outer dialogue with the world? Through this perspective, the dialogical character of the person became determinative in the anthropology of EA. The person appeared to be impressionable, accessible from the outside, as well as in an ongoing inner dialogue, out of which the person generates an inner position to what they are experiencing. This highly evaluative capacity of the person makes the human being a moral being, with responsibility based on the capacity to decide. This capacity also forms the will – bringing it into an inner resonance with the person and provides a means to realize a person's essence. To complete the process and come to an effective existence finally requires an expression of the acquired inner material and bringing it to an effect in the world – one can see how such a procedure changed therapy and was much closer to the client and their experiences. It did not require any explanations or arguments. The clients developed by themselves what was important for them, in close attunement with the person of the accompanying therapist – the formulation and public presentation of PEA in 1990 signified a separation from the classical, guiding, and reflecting treatment procedure of Logotherapy. And Frankl took it as such. The practical work in EA was now performed in a different way – open, accepting, asking, looking – in a phenomenological attitude in which the therapist does not know a priori what is good and correct, but accompanies the client through an intimate understanding and processing of their experiences. The development of this (in great parts phenomenological) method was one of the reasons why Frankl decided that the new EA no longer corresponded to his classical Logotherapy. It was a logical consequence that this led him to split with the GLE-society.

The Substantial Change of EA: The Concept of the Fundamental Existential Motivations

In parallel to the development of the process model, this phenomenological approach revealed a new view of the structure of existence in its application in practice. Instead of upholding the will-to-meaning as the only motivational force and the concept of meaning as the most relevant content of existence (Frankl 1963, 1988), it became evident that there are at least three additional dimensions which form the fundamental structure of human existence and form fundamental movements in motivation (Längle 1999, 2003).

Practical evidence revealed the impact of the basic dimensions of existence on the structure of existence: the world (reality, the "givens"), life (relationship and feelings), being oneself as a person, and being active in and/or contributing to greater contexts. These constitute the four fundamental dimensions of existence. Viewed from a subjective perspective, they become and are experienced as motivations, and are termed the *four personal-existential fundamental motivations* (Längle 1999), or more succinctly, the four fundamental existential motivations (FM). The motivations come to their completion in the attitude of leading a life with inner consent. Having inner consent to what one is doing is considered to be the basis for existential fulfillment in life and the deepest form of happiness. This structure of existence, giving rise to the fundamental human motivations, forms the *structural model* of EA. With this development, EA received a new anthropology and at the same time the understanding of existence was based much broader in being, in life, and in oneself, apart from the previously described basis of meaning.

Existential Analysis today

Today EA can be described as a phenomenological and person-oriented psychotherapy (in many respects it comes close to the concepts of Carl Rogers [1961, 1966]). The word "existence" lies at the core of EA. Existence, from an EA-perspective, denotes an integrated or "whole" life. From this perspective, human existence is characterized by the capacity to make authentic decisions (being conscious of one's freedom and responsibility in a meaningful context).

The aim of EA is to guide an individual toward leading and experiencing their life authentically and freely. This is accomplished through practical methods: by continually bringing "inner consent" into focus while working on the prerequisites of the existential fundamental motivations and by phenomenologically processing the problems, traumas, and conflicts of the individuals through the process model of PEA (setting back the interpretation or explanation of experiences and symptoms – see Chapter 22). In addition, EA has established almost a dozen other specific methods for stimulating personal resources or treating specific disorders (Längle 2008). Although the focus of EA lies on actual experience, feelings, and subjective positioning, the overall integrity of human existence also demands biographical work in order to gain perspective on the future (meaning).

The aim of EA can be summarized as such: to help people recognize and come to terms with their behavior and emotions and to live with "inner consent." Although this description resonates with the Rogerian concept of congruence (Rogers 1961, 1966), EA places more emphasis on the active decisions and commitments of the individual rather than the accompanying mood or organismic feeling.

On the basis of these developments, the GLE society in Vienna renounced the use of the term Logotherapy and after 1982 called this psychotherapy "Existential Analysis." This term has been used by Viktor Frankl (1938/1987a) since 1938 to describe the theoretical basis (anthropology and philosophy) of practical Logotherapy. The Austrian Ministry of Health officially recognized this form of psychotherapy in 1982 after proving the coherence of theory, practice, methodology, and empirical data available to date (official recognition came later in: Switzerland from the canton of Berne; the Czech Republic; and Romania). There are also training institutes and/or societies in other countries, for example, Germany, Poland, Russia, Ukraine, Latvia, Canada, Mexico, Chile, and Argentina. The new and expanded anthropology and understanding of existence together with the development of the methods and the dominant application of phenomenology completely changed the training program. Training in EA required from now on a strong focus on self-experience in order to illustrate this procedure and prepare students to become open and self-aware enough to be able to work with the phenomenological attitude. A full training in EA currently lasts five to six years completed on a part-time basis (www.existenzanalyse.org; www.existential-analysis.org; www.logoterapia.org).

Today, EA is an independent and major development in psychotherapy. Existential Analysis has evolved from "Logotherapy as a supplement to various psychotherapies," as Frankl put it (for an overview see Längle 2013, p. 54), into a full-fledged psychotherapeutic method (Längle and Görtz 1993; Stumm and Wirth 1994; Stumm and Pritz 2000).

Since 1985, the GLE-International has also organized annual international conferences in German speaking countries (and twice in Prague) with an average attendance of 750 participants (for an overview see https://www.existenzanalyse.org/verein/geschichte-der-gle/). Several local conferences take place every year in different countries. Since 1984, the society also publishes a semi-annual, peer-reviewed journal, from 1995 this has been under the title "EXISTENZANALYSE," which is listed in PSYNDEX and SCOPUS (Elsevier). Additional journals are also published annually in Russian (*Ekzistencial'nyj Analiz*) and quarterly in Spanish/English (*Existencia: The Inter-American Journal of Existential Analysis*; www.icae.cl) for both Americas. There is collaboration with many universities for research and teaching. There is now a possibility to obtain EA training in combination with a Masters' degree at several universities, such as the University of Salzburg (Austria), the Sigmund-Freud-University in Vienna, the HSE-University in Moscow, and the UAHC (Universitad de Humanismo Christiano) in Santiago de Chile.

EA concepts and psychotherapeutic methods have been investigated through both basic and outcome-oriented research. Three German-language (with translations) and two Russian psychometric tests are available. For an overview, see Ascher, Bowers, and Schotte (1985), Becker (1985), Görtz (2001), Laireiter et al. (2000; 2013), Längle et al. (2005), and Regazzo, Längle, and Regazzo (2008). In spite of these empirical and psychometric developments, the personality of the psychotherapist retains more weight for this phenomenological psychotherapy.

EA-societies around the world

GLE-International (GLE-I) is the umbrella society for all national societies and is responsible for the maintenance and quality assurance of clinical training in all countries. The training follows the same curriculum and identical conditions in all countries. GLE-I is also responsible for international congresses, for the journal (with mostly German papers, and sometimes some English), and the coordination of research. The society has approximately 1600 members from German-speaking countries, is incorporated as a national society in 14 countries, and is the largest existential society worldwide. Existential Analysis unfortunately remains rather unknown in English speaking countries in spite of its prevalence in German-speaking countries.

Since 1983 there has been ongoing clinical training in Vienna, initially at the Institute of Logotherapy (Kozdera, Längle, Vesely-Frankl). The training centers and institutes of GLE-Austria have spread throughout Austria, with counselling and psychotherapy now taking place in six cities. Both counselling and psychotherapy are officially recognized by the state. More than 100 training cohorts with approximately 1500 students have taken part in the clinical training in EA to date (not all completed the training; currently, there are almost 400 students). The GLE has been the second largest training institution for psychotherapy in Austria for 10 years. GLE-Austria alone has more than 1000 professional members.

There has been regular clinical training in Germany since 1986 and in Switzerland since 1994, as well as national societies in both countries with a combined membership of approximately 500.

Clinical training began in 1993 in Romania and spread to various cities. A Romanian society was founded in 1994. Training and the development of a national society in the Czech Republic began in 1996. Clinical training began in Russia (Moscow, later also St. Petersburg) in 1999 with up to 38 training groups to date. The Russian society also organizes biannual conferences and has been editing a journal since 2007. They are present in many universities. Training in Poland began in 2007, in 2012 in Ukraine, 2014 in Latvia, as well as Russian-language training in 2017 in England (London), including online training. In the Americas the first training began in 1998 in Argentina (Mendoza), in 2000 in Mexico, in 2004 in Chile, and in 2006 in Canada (Vancouver). All of these countries have also established national societies.

Logotherapy today

In the past two to three decades, Logotherapy has undergone a great expansion. There have been noticeable publications, especially around Viktor Frankl's 100th birthday in 2005 with the beginning of a 14-volume edition of the collected works of Viktor Frankl. A moving film "Viktor and I" appeared in 2011 created by his grandson Alexander Vesely. The City of Vienna has been awarding the "Viktor Frankl Award" for outstanding contributions in the field of meaning-oriented humanistic psychotherapy since 2000. A comprehensive website by the Viktor Frankl Institute http://www.viktorfrankl.org along with a video library and access to the impressive amount of literature on Logotherapy has been developed. In 1998, there were more than 1000 published titles on Logotherapy. Currently there are almost 450 books and 400 master and doctoral theses. More than 600 empirical investigations have provided evidence for the effectiveness of Logotherapy, including the development of 15 specific logotherapeutic instruments (Batthyány and Guttmann 2006).

Today, Logotherapy is organized through an International Association of Logotherapy and Existential Analysis at the Viktor Frankl Institute Vienna. This society is active in 40 countries worldwide with 115 accredited institutions (as of January 1, 2018). This makes this organization the most widely spread existential organization in the world. There are ongoing lectures at various universities and training programs in institutions accredited by the Viktor Frankl Institute of Vienna under the guidance of Prof. Alexander Batthyány. The tradition of a Viktor Frankl lecture at the Vienna Medical School is still alive. There are biennial international congresses organized by the Viktor Frankl Institute Vienna (Prof. Batthyány) with several hundred attendants and between 10 to 20 local conferences in different countries around the world every year, as well as an innumerable number of journals. In Austria, Logotherapy is also recognized by the state as an approach to psychotherapy and counselling.

Acknowledgment

Special thanks to Derrick Klaassen, PhD, of Trinity Western University in Langley, BC, Canada, who assisted with the translation and editing of several chapters.

References

Ascher, L.M., Bowers, M.R., and Schotte, D.E. (1985). A review of data from controlled case studies and experiments evaluating the clinical efficacy of paradoxical intention. In: *Promoting Change Through Paradoxical Therapy* (ed. G.R. Weeks), 216–251. Homewood, IL: Dow Jones-Irwin.

Batthyány, A., and Guttmann, D. (2006). *Empirical Research in Logotherapy and Meaning-Oriented Psychotherapy. An Annotated Bibliography.* Phoenix, AZ: Zeig, Tucker, and Theisen.

Becker, P. (1985). Sinnfindung als zentrale Komponente seelischer Gesundheit. In: *Wege zum Sinn. Logotherapie als Orientierungshilfe* (ed. A. Längle), 186–207. Munich: Piper.

Fintz, A.S. (2006). *Die Kunst der Beratung. Jaspers' Philosophie in sinnorientierter Beratung.* Bielefeld: Sirius.

Frankl, V. (1963). *Man's Search for Meaning.* New York: Simon and Schuster. (Original work published 1946.)

Frankl, V. (1967). *Psychotherapy and Existentialism. Selected Papers on Logotherapy.* New York: Simon and Schuster.

Frankl, V. (1973). *The Doctor and the Soul. From Psychotherapy to Logotherapy.* New York: Random House. (Original work published 1946.)

Frankl, V. (1982). *Ärztliche Seelsorge.* Vienna: Deuticke. (Original work published 1946.)

Frankl, V. (1987a). Zur geistigen Problematik der Psychotherapie. In: *Logotherapie und Existenzanalyse. Texte aus fünf Jahrzehnten* (V. Frankl), 15–30. Munich: Piper. (Original work published 1938.)

Frankl, V. (1987b). Seelenärztliche Selbstbestimmung. In: *Logotherapie und Existenzanalyse. Texte aus fünf Jahrzehnten* (V. Frankl), 31–35. Munich: Piper. (Original work published 1938.)

Frankl, V. (1987c). *Logotherapie und Existenzanalyse. Texte aus fünf Jahrzehnten.* Munich: Piper. (Original work published 1959.)

Frankl, V. (1988). *Will to Meaning. Foundations and Applications of Logotherapy.* New York: Penguin.

Frankl, V. (1990). *Der Leidende Mensch. Anthropologische Grundlagen der Psychotherapie.* Munich: Piper.

Frankl, V. (1995). *Was nicht in meinen Büchern steht.* Munich: Quintessenz [English translation 2000: *Recollections – An Autobiography.* Cambridge: Basic Books].

Görres, A. (1978). *Kennt die Psychologie den Menschen? Fragen zwischen Psychotherapie, Anthropologie und Christentum.* Munich: Piper.

Görtz, A. (2001). Weitere empirische Forschungsarbeiten zur Existenzanalyse seit 1995. *Existenzanalyse 18* (1): 59–60.

Hofstätter, P.R. (1957). *Psychologie.* Frankfurt am Main: Fischer.

Laireiter, A.R., Schaireiter, M.M., Schirl-Russegger, C. et al. (2013). Die Wirksamkeit von Existenzanalyse und Logotherapie. Retrospektive Beurteilungen. *Existenzanalyse 30* (1): 4–14.

Laireiter, A.R., Schirl, C.F., Kimeswenger, I. et al. (2000). Zufriedenheit mit Existenzanalyse. Ergebnisse einer katamnestischen Feldstudie zur Patientenbeurteilung von existenzanalytisch-logotherapeutischer Psychotherapie. *Existenzanalyse 17* (3): 40–50.

Längle, A. (1988). Wende ins Existentielle. Die Methode der Sinnerfassung. In: *Entscheidung zum Sein. V. E. Frankls Logotherapie in der Praxis* (ed. A. Längle), 40–52. Munich: Piper.
Längle, A. (1993). Personale Existenzanalyse. In: *Wertbegegnung. Phänomene und methodische Zugänge* (ed. A. Längle), 133–160. Vienna: GLE-Verlag.
Längle, A. (1995). Personal existential analysis. In: *Psychotherapy East and West. Integration of Psychotherapies* (A. Längle), 348–364. Seoul: Korean Academy of Psychotherapists.
Längle, A. (1997). Die personale Positionsfindung (PP) in der Angsttherapie. In: *Klinische Psychotherapie* (ed. P. Hofmann, M. Lux, C. Probst et al.), 284–297. Vienna, New York: Springer.
Längle, A. (1999). Was bewegt den Menschen? Die existentielle Motivation der Person. *Existenzanalyse 16* (3): 18–29.
Längle, A. (2000a). Die Willensstärkungsmethode (WSM). *Existenzanalyse 17* (1): 4–16.
Längle, A. (2000b). Phänomenologische Dialogübung ("Sesselmethode"). *Existenzanalyse 17* (1): 21–30.
Längle, A. (ed.) (2000c). *Praxis der Personalen Existenzanalyse.* Vienna: Facultas University Press.
Längle, A. (2003). The search for meaning in life and the fundamental existential motivations. *Psychotherapy in Australia 10* (1): 22–27.
Längle, A. (2008). Existenzanalyse. In: *Existenzanalyse und Daseinsanalyse* (ed. A. Längle and A. Holzhey-Kunz), 29–180. Vienna: UTB (Facultas).
Längle, A. (2013). *Viktor Frankl – eine Begegnung.* Wien: Facultas.
Längle, A. and Görtz, A. (1993). *Antrag für die Anerkennung der Existenzanalyse als methodenspezifische Ausbildungsrichtung für Psychotherapie.* Vienna: Federal Ministry of Health.
Längle, A., Görtz, A., Probst, C. et al. (2005). Wie wirksam ist existenzanalytische Psychotherapie: ein Projektbericht zur Existenzanalyse. *Psychotherapie Forum 13* (2): 54–60.
Längle, A. and Orgler, C. (1990). *Existenzskala. Handanweisung zum Test.* Vienna: GLE-Verlag.
Längle, A., Orgler, C., and Kundi, M. (2000). *Existenzskala ESK.* Göttingen: Hogrefe-Beltz.
Lukas, E. (1980). *Auch dein Leben hat Sinn. Logotherapeutische Wege zur Gesundung.* Freiburg: Herder.
Regazzo, L.D., Längle, A., and Regazzo, G. (2008). *Efficacia della Psicoterapia Analitico Esistenziale: Esperimento, Studi e Ricerche.* Padua: Cleup.
Rogers, C.R. (1951). *Client-Centered Therapy: Its Current Practice, Implications and Theory.* London: Constable.
Rogers, C.R. (1961). *On Becoming a Person.* Boston: Houghton Mifflin.
Rogers, C.R. (1966). Client-centered therapy. In: *American Handbook of Psychiatry*, vol. 3 (ed. S. Arieti), 183–200. New York: Basic Books.
Scheler, M. (1980). *Der Formalismus in der Ethik und die materiale Wertethik.* Berne: Franke.
Soucek, W. (1948). Die Existenzanalyse Frankls, die dritte Richtung der Wiener Psychotherapeutischen Schule. *Deutsche Medizinische Wochenschrift 73*: 594.
Spiegelberg, H. (1985). Die Rolle der Phänomenologie in Viktor Frankls Logotherapie und Existenzanalyse. In: *Wege zum Sinn. Logotherapie als Orientierungshilfe* (ed. A. Längle), 55–70. Munich: Piper.
Stumm, G. and Pritz, A. (eds.) (2000). *Wörterbuch der Psychotherapie.* Vienna: Springer.
Stumm, G. and Wirth, B. (eds.) (1994). *Psychotherapie. Schulen und Methoden. Eine Orientierungshilfe für Theorie und Praxis.* Vienna: Falter.
Wicki, B. (1991). *Die Existenzanalyse von Viktor E. Frankl als Beitrag zu einer anthropologisch fundierten Pädagogik.* Berne: Haupt.

20

Logotherapy and Existential Analysis

Philosophy and Theory

Claudia Reitinger and Emmanuel J. Bauer

Introduction

Logotherapy and Existential Analysis refer to different philosophers from the field of phenomenology, existential philosophy and dialogical philosophy (Max Scheler, Martin Heidegger, Nicolai Hartmann, Karl Jaspers, Martin Buber, Friedrich Nietzsche, Søren Kierkegaard, Gabriel Marcel). Although there are similarities between different thinkers belonging to these traditions they also diverge in some of their basic philosophical and anthropological assumptions, for example, in the conception of freedom, responsibility, and meaning. This broad philosophical foundation provides an explanation for the differences between Logotherapy (Frankl), Existential Analysis (Längle et al.), and other forms of Existential Therapy (van Deurzen, Yalom).

Existential Analysis (EA), as developed by Alfried Längle, has two main and divergent roots, which are quite contrary: Viktor Frankl's Logotherapy on the one hand, and phenomenology and the philosophy of dialogue on the other. Although EA shares some of Frankl's central concepts, like meaning, values, responsibility, and freedom, the underlying philosophical theory is a different one. For that reason, these concepts have a different meaning in both theories. The anthropology of Frankl presupposes an ontological meaning in the world, which can be discovered through listening to one's inner voice – the voice of one's conscience (Frankl 2011, p. 68). Due to the foundation of meaning in God, Frankl supports a strong metaphysical theory (Rohr 2009, p. 345) and Frankl's anthropology only becomes accessible from that perspective. We find a strict differentiation between the spiritual person, its dynamic, and its orientation towards values and meaning and the psychophysical dimension (Frankl 2005, p. 77). Because of the assumption that values and meaning can be recognized directly by the conscience without a "detour" via emotions, the person's inner life is of minor importance within Logotherapy.

The Wiley World Handbook of Existential Therapy, First Edition. Edited by Emmy van Deurzen, Erik Craig, Alfried Längle, Kirk J. Schneider, Digby Tantam, and Simon du Plock.

EA questions the assumption of an objective meaning and turns towards phenomenology and the person's inner life (Längle 1994). What might seem to be a minor change at first glance brings in fact a fundamental change of all concepts of Logotherapy, and makes EA a different and autonomous theory, from a philosophical perspective. In addition, EA upholds the idea that meaning is not the only motivation that is required to live a fulfilling life, but there are three other fundamental existential motivations that move the person. For this reason, EA is closer to other existential therapeutic schools (Yalom, van Deurzen, Binswanger) and to the Rogerian concept of congruence (Rogers 1961) than to Logotherapy, although there is some overlap with the anthropology of Logotherapy.

This chapter first outlines the main strands of the ontological assumptions of Logotherapy and clarifies its central concepts. Subsequently it shows the similarities and differences to the anthropology of EA. Due to the importance of Heidegger's understanding of phenomenology as a hermeneutic method, we focus on this in greater detail in the subsequent part. Finally, the fundamental existential motivations are explained and the parallels to similar concepts in other Existential Therapy schools are highlighted.

The Anthropology of Logotherapy

Viktor Frankl is best known for his focus on meaning in psychotherapy and his description of the so-called "noogenic neurosis", the phenomenon that people suffer from the feeling of emptiness and meaninglessness if their will to meaning is frustrated. For Frankl, the human being's deepest and most truly human motivation is the will to meaning, the striving to find meaning in all situations of their life (Frankl 1988). Other motivations are subsidiary to this one. According to Frankl, psychoanalysis was not able to address that kind of neurosis in an adequate manner. Due to its focus on psychodynamic mechanisms, depth psychology turns a blind eye to the noetic (spiritual) dimension and the abilities, dynamics, and obstacles that belong to this dimension. Frankl's primary ambition was to avoid all forms of reductionism in relation to human beings. His initial criticism took Freudian psychoanalysis and Adler's individual psychology to task and described them as reductionistic theories. While psychoanalysis tries to understand human behavior on the basis of a utilitarian pleasure/homeostatic principle, individual psychology understands human behavior as an expression of the will to power. Frankl, on the other hand, holds the view that human behavior can and should not be reduced to psychological or biological mechanisms. Human beings are mainly characterized by being spiritual; as spiritual beings they are not determined but are able to act freely and responsibly and to realize value and meaning (Frankl 1986, pp. 23ff).

Frankl adopts this line of thought mainly from Max Scheler, who is his most important philosophical link. He explicitly states that whilst "Binswanger's work boils down to an application of Heideggerian concepts to psychiatry [...] logotherapy is the result of an application of Max Scheler's concepts to psychotherapy" (Frankl 1988, p. 10). There are two main concepts Frankl adopted from Scheler. First, the role of values for a meaningful life and the assumption that values can be recognized directly through intentionality (Scheler 1954, pp. 271f; Frankl 1991, p. 164). Second, human reality can be stratified into body, psyche, and spirit, and the latter opposes psychophysics.

For Frankl, human beings belong ontologically to three dimensions: the somatic (body), the psychic (mind), and the noetic (spiritual) (Frankl 2005, pp. 176ff). Ontologically, these three dimensions are distinct modes of being and therefore not reducible to one another. According to Frankl, the uniquely human phenomena are identical with the noetic dimension. Because Frankl's aim was a re-humanization of psychotherapy, most of his writings are concerned with bringing the noetic dimension to expression. All of his central concepts, including "meaning," "value," "freedom," "responsibility," "self-distance," and "self-transcendence" belong to this dimension.

To understand the philosophical framework of Logotherapy and the changes within EA it is useful to structure his theory according to the following assumptions (Reitinger 2015, pp. 346f).

1. Human beings have three diverse, non-reducible ontological dimensions: The somatic, the psychic, and the noetic, the latter being the specific human dimension.
2. Due to the noetic dimension, human beings are persons.
3. As persons, human beings are not biologically and/or psychologically determined but can act freely and responsibly.
4. As persons, they have the fundamental human capacities of self-distance and self-transcendence.
5. As persons, their motivation is the will to meaning.
6. Meaning can be realized through realizing values.
7. Values and meaning are objectively given in the world.
8. There is only one most meaningful answer to each situation.
9. In realizing meaning the person acts freely and responsibly.
10. Persons are able to find the meaningful answer to a situation by means of their conscience.
11. What is meaningful for a person has a (conscious or unconscious) connection to God, because the subjective meaning is included in the all-encompassing super-meaning.
12. The human person is related to God, either consciously or unconsciously.

The spiritual person

According to Frankl, the spiritual person is an autonomous ontological entity, which can be distinguished from the "psychophysicum," the togetherness of psyche and body. Because human beings are persons, they have the ability of self-detachment; that is, that they can take a step back from their psychodynamics, recognize them, and are able to decide if we want to act according to them or not. At the same time, human beings as persons are able to realize values and meaning by the other fundamental human capacity, self-transcendence (Frankl 2005, p. 47).

From an ontological perspective it seems clear that Frankl supports a substance ontology (Reitinger 2015, p. 347). This means that the person is understood as an essence, which is prior to its relation to the world and is not changeable through experiences and circumstances. The opposite position deals with the view that the person is constituted by their relations. Although Frankl explicitly rejects supporting a substantialist view of the person, it can be shown that he implicitly takes this view. For Frankl, it is important that the person is not misunderstood as something materialistic or something ontic. Frankl (e.g., 2005) often states that the person is not a substance, as it is generally understood, but an ontological entity, pure power. Since the person is not a materialistic substance but an immaterial one, the person is not causally determined and cannot become ill.

Freedom and responsibility

The spiritual person is fundamentally characterized as being free. Frankl understands freedom as "freedom from" and "freedom for" (Frankl 2011, p. 59). As human beings belong to the noetic dimension, they are not subject to their drives, emotions, and dispositions, but have the ability for self-distancing, which is the negative side of freedom. The person can decide to turn the "suggestions" from the psychophysical dimension into actions. The positive side of freedom is realized by self-transcendence, which, according to Frankl, means to intentionally direct oneself towards values and meaning (Frankl 1988, pp. 50ff)

The concept of freedom in Frankl's theory has a distinct meaning. For Frankl, there is an *unum necesse* in each situation, the one thing that is required or even necessary, namely to recognize the most valuable option in each situation, because this means to realize meaning. To choose this most valuable option means to realize the positive side of freedom. Due to the metaphysical background of Frankl's theory – that the subjective meaning is part of a meaningful structure ("Logos") – his concept of freedom has a deterministic touch, which is reminiscent of Hegel's absolute spirit. In contrast to causal determinism, Frankl (2005, p. 122) calls it a "higher form of causality or finalism." There is a kind of meaning, which "intervenes from above" (Frankl 2005, p. 141). As the person corresponds to this noetic dimension, the person is therefore open for that kind of finalism. The noetic dimension and finalism belong together in the same way as the psychophysical dimension and causal determinism.

The assumptions that human existence is intrinsically meaningful, and each situation has one true meaning, which can and has to be discovered, were often criticized from different sides, because of their distinctly authoritarian undertone (Bauer 2012; Cooper 2003; May 1978; Yalom 1980).

Values and Meaning

For Frankl, meaning can be realized through realizing values. He distinguishes three types of value categories (Frankl 1986, pp. 43f):

- Creative values, which are realized through actions and tasks;
- Experiential values, which have a more passive connotation – they are realized, for example, when turned towards nature or arts;
- Attitudinal values, which can be realized whenever a person finds themselves confronted by a destiny towards which they can act only by acceptance.

Which values should be realized depends on the situation. Guidance gives an inner voice, the voice of the moral conscience. If human beings act according to this inner voice, they find their personal meaning in each situation.

Meaning has both an objective and a subjective component (the same can be said for values). For Frankl, meaning is "not something constructed" (Frankl 2011, p. 88) but something that is always present within each situation and "has to be found." In this sense, meaning is objective. It is subjective because what is meaningful in a situation changes from person to person, as every person is unique and has their own way to follow. This makes meaning also relative, dependent on the interconnection of situation and person.

In Frankl's theory, meaning is objectively given as the demand of the situation. When people open up to it by a "Copernican turn" (Frankl 1973, p. 62; 1988, pp. 50ff, 62f) they become receptive to meaning. Seen from an analytical philosophical point of view, this conception ultimately also refers to his concept of meta-meaning. Although Frankl states that we cannot answer the question of ultimate meaning, he introduces the concept of a super-meaning:

> Actually, our interrogation must be confined to the meaning of a part. We cannot begin to question the "purpose" of the universe. Purpose is transcendent to the extent that it is always external to whatever "possesses" it. We can therefore at best grasp the meaning of the universe in the form of a super-meaning, using the word to convey the idea that the meaning of the whole is no longer comprehensible and goes beyond the comprehensible. (Frankl 1986, p. 30)

The connection between personal meaning and super-meaning is that the former is embedded in the latter. Hence Frankl can state that personal meaning is something objective in the world, which can be found. The connection between finality, super- (or meta-)-meaning and personal meaning lies in the assumption that the super-meaning "always prevails with or without our doing" (Frankl 2005, p. 141) and that the final meaning intervenes in our existence.

Super-meaning plays a foundational role in Frankl's anthropology. Due to super-meaning, the person has the possibility of finding personal meaning on the one hand, and is equipped with the will-to-meaning on the other (Rohr 2009, p. 283). Since super-meaning acts causally in the sense of finality and subjects orient themselves towards it, finality is inherent to the orientation on personal meaning.

The role of God in Frankl's anthropology

Philosophically seen, God plays a key role in Frankl's anthropology. His core concepts – "person," "conscience," "value," "meaning," "freedom," "responsibility" – are only made fully comprehensible through reference to a transcendental force.

As Rohr (2009, p. 354) points out, super-meaning refers to a transcendental Unitary principle, a personal image of God. The ultimate justification of meaning through God can be found in his book on *Anthropological Foundations*:

> Insofar as I exist, my existence is towards meaning and value; insofar as I exist towards meaning and value, my existence is towards something that is necessarily higher in value than my own being – in other words: My existence is towards something, which cannot

be a something but must be a someone – a super-person. In a word: insofar I exist, my existence is always directed to God. (Frankl 2005, 232f)

In its self-transcendental orientation towards value and meaning, the person always refers to God, because values and meaning are grounded in God. Each realization of meaning, one could say, is a movement towards God. At the same time this movement has its origin in God. This movement corresponds to Frankl's concept of a higher causality in terms of finality. Frankl emphasizes that all human beings are related to God. However, for non-religious human beings, this relationship to God is unconscious (Frankl 2011, p. 68).

The Anthropology of Existential Analysis

Although EA has its origin in Logotherapy, a great shift took place in the EA of Alfried Längle after the 1980s. The application of phenomenology, existential philosophy, and the philosophy of dialogue became more dominant, both in theory and research. Practical clinical work revealed that meaning often does not play a considerable role in psycho-pathogenesis (Längle 2015, p. 77). The concept of meaning still plays an important role in Existential Therapy, but changes fundamentally since EA waives the assumption of an objective meaning in the world, and meaning is relativized alongside three other fundamental motivations of human existence (Längle 2013, pp. 73ff). The second major change concerns the role of emotions and the person's inner life. Whereas for Frankl one has to self-distance from one's inner life and its emotions in order to be open for the objectively given meaning in the world, EA turns toward the inner world and the person's subjective experience (Längle 2003b, pp. 31f).

In the following sections, the anthropology of EA is described in greater detail. In a first step, the philosophical roots of Existential Philosophy, Phenomenology, and the elements of philosophy of dialogue are described. Then, the fundamental motivations are explained and briefly put into the framework of other Existential Therapy schools. In conclusion, the changes and differences in modern EA are compared with Frankl's theory.

Philosophical roots of Existential Analysis

The role of Phenomenology in Existential Analysis EA adopts Phenomenology on different levels. To begin, it is used in an ontic sense, in line with an attitude of non-interpretative openness towards the patient. The aim is to understand the patient in their world and their experiences. Second, the anthropological basic terms (like value, freedom, will etc.) and the existential fundamental motivations are gained through experience in a bottom-up approach. Thus, existential fundamental motivations are not deduced from metaphysical assumptions. On these first two levels, phenomenology is employed methodologically as an epistemological tool. Third, on an ontological level, EA shares the basic phenomenological assumption that subject and object – person and world – are not separated entities but are mutually constituted.

The relatedness here has ontological priority. This means that EA does not assume any kind of substance or essence, which precedes the existence of a human being. The phenomenological stand on the ontic level can be understood as an application of this ontological background (Bauer 2016).

If we look at the difference between Husserl's and Heidegger's understanding of phenomenology, it becomes clear that EA adopts Heidegger's understanding of phenomenology as a hermeneutic method. Husserl solves the phenomenological idea "about things themselves" in the direction of a transcendental ego, which has the perspective of an observer (Hermann 1981, p. 34). Heidegger, on the other hand, understands phenomenology as a hermeneutic method. Dasein is always being-in-the-world, related and embedded being, that cannot get behind its thrownness. Dasein has an understanding of itself, the world, and the others and interprets itself out of this context. While Heidegger (2001, p. 37f) uses the phenomenological method to disclose the ontological structures of Dasein and being, EA adopts this method on an ontic level to understand the patient's emotions or habits out of his world.

Following Heidegger, the phenomenological procedure has three steps: reduction – construction – destruction (Heidegger 1993, pp. 26ff; Längle 2007c, p. 23):

1 Reduction: The previous knowledge, preconceptions, interest-led claims are put in brackets (epoché) in the therapeutic setting so that the patient and their experience may appear.
2 Construction: The aim of construction is that the phenomenon is recognized as a whole. Single elements – for example, emotions, impulses, gestures, life context – are related to each other in order to receive an overall picture of the phenomenon.
3 Destruction: The picture is questioned once again to uncover possible assumptions or interests in order to converge the phenomenal content.

The method is equivalent to Heidegger's procedure in its movement but diverges in its intention. (For the practical application of these three steps cf. chapter 3).

Elements of Existential Philosophy and the Philosophy of Dialogue as Part of modern Existential Analysis Alongside some of the most important proponents of existential philosophy, such as S. Kierkegaard, K. Jaspers, and M. Heidegger, modern EA shares the conviction that human being, as spiritual being, is constituted through language, rationality, meaning, and relationships and their corresponding capacities. For this reason, we are able to ascertain specific analogies between the structure of existential-realization and self-realization of the person (Bauer 2016).

Following Heidegger (2001, p. 220), human existence is primarily expressed through the fact that Dasein is accessed through our Being-in-the-world. Structurally, this is revealed through three basic conditions of Dasein, namely *Befindlichkeit* (disposedness), understanding, and discourse. EA, however, understands human beings essentially as persons, whose addressability (capacity for being addressed), reason, and capacity of answering enables an existence in freedom, responsibility, and self-determination. Correspondingly, we recognize the three process levels of Personal Existential

Analysis (PEA), namely impression, positioning, and expression, with their emphasis on the analysis of feelings, the determination of a personal position, and the search for adequate action (Längle 2000). Therefore, a certain parallel of substance and a structural analogy between EA and Heidegger's fundamental ontology cannot be overlooked, even if some particular differences are evident.

According to Heidegger, *Befindlichkeit* (disposition) is informed by a corresponding basic attunement. As such, it reflects the fundamental openness-to-the-world of Dasein, as well as its basic disposition or fundamental mood (*Grundbefindlichkeit*) and reveals the existential condition of possibility and the basic manifestation of human emotionality. The attunement of basic disposition (*Grundbefindlichkeit*) is already seen in a primary and pre-reflective disclosedness and understanding of the world. Understanding itself is a fundamental aspect of a specific actualization of being-human. Heidegger points to understanding as the foundational capacity-of-being for Dasein, following from a familiarity with the "for-the-sake-of which" (*Worumwillen*) and the significance of the moments in the world that constitute one's own being. Existing is constituted through understanding and interpretation, that is, the concrete significance of the possibilities that are gained and revealed through understanding. This hermeneutic process does not occur without prerequisites, but always against the background of a given totality of meaning and a common horizon of questions and understanding, which are raised through life and its actors. The understanding of the world is expressed in language as the fundamental "existential constitution of the disclosedness of Dasein" (Heidegger 2001, p. 161). The everyday Dasein limits itself to the mere *Mit-Verstehen* (understanding-with) of the spoken, instead of searching for an original understanding of the discourse and a primary reference to being. Only those who decisively seize their own ability-to-be, may find the *Eigentlichkeit* (authenticity) of Dasein.

In spite of the similarities in understanding existential realization between Heidegger and EA, there remain substantial differences. In one sense there is a difference in focus. Heidegger is concerned with revealing the basic ontological-existential constitution of Dasein, while EA, through its PEA, operates primarily on the ontic-existential level and searches for concrete feelings, which reveal inner positioning and the stirrings of the will. The decisive difference, however, is found in that human beings are not understood as persons in Heidegger and that therefore the personal-existential, in its narrower meaning, does not appear sufficiently. In a sense, Heidegger views original attunement as a resonance of the whole of Dasein, while EA attempts to recover the phenomenal content of feelings, lead these to an understanding, and integrate them with a free and personal position and thereby make them fruitful for one's existence (Bauer 2012). Accordingly understanding in EA is simultaneously a receptive and creative *personal* act, which encompasses all dimensions of experience and insight and forms the living center between impression and expression. Through personal position, understanding experiences its own explication within the horizon of the whole of self- and world-understanding and its coming-to-itself. As such, it can be regarded as the center of the self-realization of the person (Bauer 2016, pp. 12f). After all, the personal-dialogical character is insufficiently explicated in Heidegger's understanding of discourse as the disclosedness of Dasein (Heidegger 2001, pp. 160ff) and language as the house of Being (Heidegger 1978, p. 330) – a fact pointed out by Heidegger's student H.-G. Gadamer (1986).

At this point, the closeness of EA to the Philosophy of Dialogue can be seen, in particular to the thought of Martin Buber. EA shares the view of existential and linguistic philosophy that human beings always think, understand, and act within the horizon of their concrete language. Alongside the Philosophy of Dialogue, however, EA also emphasizes that the realization of existence is permanently embedded within a field of tension of interaction and communication with the physical and spiritual realities of the concrete world. For human beings, becoming and being oneself first and foremost requires the interaction with other persons, that is, the personal encounter between I and You (Bauer 2017). As a creature that is constituted through being as person and spirit, human beings are always already bound into a dialogical relationship of being-addressed and having the capacity or even the requirement to answer. Buber revealed that human beings only "become" persons when their personal being is developed by being addressed by a You as an I (Buber 2012a). Modern EA agrees with Buber on this point but goes one step further. EA points to the missing facet that human beings are not only open as persons towards the outside but are equally dialogically open inwardly. Without such dialogue the I cannot become itself and threatens to fall into a kind of foreign or external control. Authentic being-oneself presupposes therefore a personal dialogue with oneself (in the form of one's own conscience) as well as with the You in the form of another human being and – in the case of religion – also with the You of God. However, it is important to remember with all the weight given to intrapersonal dialogue, that the interpersonal I–You encounter is ontogenetically more primordial and fundamental, which is also construed as such in the developmental psychology of EA.

EA understands itself primarily as a talk therapy and sees in the therapeutic dialogue a place where personal encounter can be experienced, modelled, and personal-being can be developed. Nonetheless, the features and constituents of the I–You encounter, as described by Buber (2012b, 2012c), can only be applied in part, since we are dealing with a fundamentally different setting. Apart from the fact that the illness of the client inhibits full reciprocity, unreserved and mutual openness is only partially possible and even appropriate. However, the awareness of the wholeness of the person of the other, the authenticity, the respect for the dignity, otherness and freedom of the other, the acceptance and Da-sein (being-there) are basic attitudes that are demanded of the therapist. Of great importance for the praxis of EA is Buber's warning that one should not impose oneself upon the other (Buber 2012c, pp. 287ff). True personal dialogue must forgo any kind of suggestion or manipulation. This danger, to insinuate one's own truth, to suggest one's own view of what is best for the other, or to convince the other in subtle ways that one's truth is their own, should particularly not be underestimated in the psychotherapeutic relationship.

Personal-Existential Fundamental Motivations

The strict application of phenomenology in psychotherapy led to the discovery of the basic structure of existence – the personal-existential fundamental motivations. They are called personal-existential fundamental motivations, because the first three turn around the personal foundation in existence, whereas the fourth is the answer given to the requirements of the world, a truly existential factor in our Dasein.

A prerequisite for the realization of existence is the continuous dialogical exchange with the outer and the inner world (Längle 1999, 2016). A closer look at the reality with which each human being is inevitably confronted, and which needs to be fulfilled to come to a full life, reveals phenomenologically four fundamental existential structures, the four dimensions or "cornerstones of existence" (Längle 2011, pp. 40ff):

- The world in its factuality and potentiality,
- Life with its network of relationships and feelings,
- Being oneself as a unique, autonomous person,
- The wider context where to place oneself and the development through one's activities opening one's future.

1 **Being in the World – dealing with conditions and possibilities**
The description of these dimensions will be presented in an existential way, that is, applying the content to one's own existence.

The first condition arises from the simple fact that I am here at all, that I am in the world. I am there, there I am – realizing this given, I am astonished: How is that even possible? It surpasses my understanding. Within this wide (spiritual) horizon the practical question is the *Fundamental Question of Existence*: I am – *can I be?* Such a question takes into account both the concrete circumstances (facts) of one's being here in the first place, as well as one's own power to bear or change the actual conditions of one's life. To do so we need three main prerequisites: "protection" (a secure physical and emotional base), space, and support. A person experiences these to the highest degree when they feel accepted by others. This in turn generates a sense of security about one's very existence and enables a person to endure to develop an accepting attitude towards themselves and others and even develop endurance of unwanted realities. Without the experience of security, a person essentially fights for their very existence. Disturbances at this existential level lead to anxiety problems and form the psychic component of schizophrenia (Längle 1997).

But, in order to be there, it is not enough to find protection, space, and support – I also have to seize these conditions and to make a decision in their favor. My active part in this respect is to *accept* the positive sides and to *endure* the negative sides. To accept means to be ready to occupy the space, to rely on the support, and to trust the protection; in short "to be there" and not to flee. To support means to have the strength to let be what is there (and then to change when it is not good) or sometimes to bear, when it cannot be changed. Life imposes certain conditions on me, and the world has its laws to which I must bend. On the other hand, these conditions are reliable, solid, and steady. We can procure the space we need with our ability to support and to accept conditions.

2 **Life – dealing with relationships and emotions**
Once we have our space in the world, it can be filled with life. Simply being there is not enough, we want our existence to be good, since to exist means more than a mere fact. It has a "pathic dimension," which means that life does not simply happen. Being alive means to cry and to laugh, to experience joy and suffering, to go through pleasant and unpleasant things, to be lucky or unlucky, and to witness worth and worthlessness.

Therefore, we are motivated by the *Fundamental Question of Life*: I am alive – *do I like to live*? Is it good to be there? This question involves one's relationship to life. Do we relate positively to life, are we literally "attracted" to life, to such a degree that we can give our consent to live? It is not only strain and suffering that can take away the joy of life; it may as well be the shallowness of daily life and the negligence in one's lifestyle that make life stale. In order to seize my life, to love it, I need three things: relationship, time, and closeness to what is of value for oneself. Can I feel close and maintain closeness to things, plants, animals, and people? Can I allow the closeness of someone else? – What do I take time for? To take time for something means to give a part of one's life with someone or something. – Do I have relationships, in which I feel closeness, in which I spend time and in which I experience community? If relationship, time, and closeness are lacking, longing will arise, then coldness and finally depression (Längle 2003a, Nindl 2001). But if these three conditions are fulfilled, one experiences oneself as being in harmony with the world and with oneself and one can sense the depth of life, the fundamental value, the most profound feeling for the value of life. In each experience this fundamental value is touched upon, it colors the emotions and affects, and represents our benchmark for anything we might feel to be of worth.

But this is not possible, without my own consent. My active participation is asked for. I seize life, engage in it, when I *turn to* other people, to things, animals, intellectual work, or to myself, when I go towards it, get close, into touch, or pull it towards me. This will make life vibrate within me. If life is to make me move freely, my consent to being touched is necessary.

3 Being a Person – dealing with uniqueness and conscience

In spite of my being related to life and to people, I am aware of my being separate, different. There is a singularity, too, that makes me an "I" and distinguishes me from everybody else. I realize that I am on my own, that I have to master my existence myself and that, basically, I am alone and may even be solitary. But, besides, there is so much more that is equally singular. The diversity, beauty, and uniqueness in all fill me with respect.

In the midst of this world, I discover myself unmistakably, I am with myself and I am given to myself. This puts before me the *Fundamental Question of Being Oneself*, of being a person – *may I be like this*? Do I feel I am allowed to be the way I am and to behave as I do? – This is the level of identity, of knowing oneself and of ethics. In order to succeed here, it is necessary to have experienced three things: attention or respect, justice, and appreciation, the respective prerequisites of this dimension. – By whom am I seen, considered, and respected? For what am I appreciated – for what can I appreciate myself? – If these experiences are missing, loneliness will be the result, hysteria, as well as a need to hide behind shame (Längle 2002; Tutsch 2003). If, on the contrary, these experiences have been made, one will find oneself, find one's authenticity, and one's self-respect. The sum of these experiences builds one's own worth, the profoundest worth of what identifies one's own self at one's core. It enables the person to actively "hold their own," to delineate their own identity from another's and to recognize and respect another person's worth. In order to be able to be oneself, it is not enough to experience attention, justice, and appreciation. I also have to say "yes" to myself. This requires my active participation: to look at other people, to encounter them and, at the same time, to delimitate myself and to stand by my own. *Delimitation* and *encounter* are the two means by which we can live our authenticity without ending up in solitude. Encounter represents the necessary bridge, makes me find my own "I" in the "you." Thus, I create for myself the appreciation requisite for feeling entitled to be what I am.

4 **Meaning – dealing with becoming, future, and commitment**
If I can be there, love life, and find myself therein, the personal conditions are fulfilled for the *Fourth Fundamental Condition of Existence*, the *Existential Motivation*: the recognition of what my life is all about. I am here for a while – but, to what end? For what purpose? In what greater contexts do I see myself? What do I live *for*? What is my prospect in a world and life where all is continuously changing – is there a valuable outcome? – It does not suffice to simply be there and to have found oneself. In a sense, we have to transcend ourselves, of we want to find fulfilment and to be fruitful.
Thus, the transience of life puts before us the question of the meaning of our existence: I am here – for what good? This dimension of existence deals with our inherent longing to become fruitful in life. For this, three things are needed: a structural context, a field of activity, and a value to be realized in the future.

- Do I see and experience myself in a larger context that provides structure and orientation to my life?
- Is there a place where I feel needed, where I can be productive?
- Is there anything that should still be realized in my life – are there worthwhile tasks or experiences waiting for me in the future?

If this is not the case, the result will be a feeling of emptiness, frustration, even despair, inclination to addiction and suicidality (Debats 1996). If, on the contrary, these conditions are met, one is capable of dedication and action and, finally, a personal religious or spiritual commitment. The sum of these experiences adds up to the meaning of life and leads to a sense of fulfilment.

To be successful in this sense, a phenomenological attitude is needed, which provides an existential access to life: an attitude of openness that is concerned with the questions put before me in specific situations (Frankl 1973, p. 62). The important thing is not only what I can expect from life, but, in accordance with the dialogical structure of existence, it is equally important what life wants from me and what in the moment is needed from me: what I can and should do now for others as well as for myself. My active part in this attitude of openness is to bring myself into agreement with the situation (Längle 2016).

EA understands meaning in terms of existential meaning (Frankl 1973): what is possible here and now, on the basis of facts and reality, what is possible for me, may it be what I need now, or what is the most pressing, valuable, or interesting alternative now (Längle 2007a). To define and re-define this continually is an extremely complex task for which we possess an inner organ of perception: our sensitivity as well as our moral conscience. Three fields of activity make it possible: experiential values, the values of creating something good or the value of adopting a positive attitude towards unchangeable situations (Frankl 1973, pp. 42ff).

Besides this existential meaning, there is an ontological meaning. This is the overall meaning in which I find myself and which does not depend on me. It is the philosophical and religious meaning, the meaning the creator of the world must have had in mind. I can perceive it in relating to the divine, in sensing, in intuition, and in faith (Längle 1994).

Fundamental Motivations and other schools of Existential Therapy At this point it is worth noting that different forms of existential therapies describe certain existential fundamental topics of human life and that there are certain parallels across these approaches (Reitinger 2018, p. 206). We can find a common thread from Heidegger over Binswanger to Längle and van Deurzen, who describes "*Umwelt*," "*Mitwelt*," "*Eigenwelt*," and "*Überwelt*" as different dimension of human existence (Heidegger 1993, pp. 34f; Binswanger 1964, pp. 266ff; Längle 2001; van Deurzen 2010, pp. 137).

Following Heidegger, Binswanger argues, that human beings are related to the world in different ways, of which different basic forms of human existence are contrasted distinctly. Human beings are in a caring relationship with the material world (*Umwelt*). The relationship toward other human beings (*Mitwelt*) is in the mode of care (*Sorge*). The "*Eigenwelt*" differentiates itself through the relatedness to and from "*Umwelt*" and "*Mitwelt*." Van Deurzen, like Längle, supplements these three worlds by a fourth dimension, the "*Überwelt*." Although some similarities with Längle's concept of the four existential fundamental motivations are obvious, Längle explicitly includes in the first dimension the body which is therefore more than just *Umwelt*; in the second he refers to life, so that *Mitwelt* is just an aspect of this dimension; the third dimension describes the core of oneself, that what we call "the own" and the encounter of the own with the other; and the fourth dimension in Längle's concept is by no means a "*Überwelt*," but the actual demand of the situation. *Überwelt* in Längle's concept exists in all four dimensions, because they are rooted in a spiritual depth, which surpasses all human capacities of understanding.

Yalom, on the other hand, assumes that human existence is always based on four ultimate concerns (death, loss of freedom, isolation, meaninglessness), which lead to coping strategies due to anxiety.

If we compare these theories of Existential Therapy, the four basic structures are quite parallel, although they are prioritized differently. Längle sees human existence from the perspective of flourishing and its possibilities. Van Deurzen emphasizes the polarities of each dimension, Yalom takes existence from a tragic angle. Here we see that the anthropology of EA, in contrast to Frankl's Logotherapy, is closer to other schools of Existential Therapy.

Basic philosophical concepts of Existential Analysis Similar to the philosophical analysis of the basic concepts of Logotherapy in the first part of this chapter, the basic concepts of EA are now analyzed philosophically. We observe a change of the meaning of the basic terms due to the divergent philosophical theory. In EA the theory is orientated towards phenomenology, which goes along with leaving behind the metaphysical ground (Espinosa 1998). Instead, the orientation towards subjective experience, emotions, and the inner life emerges in all central concepts of EA: Person combined with the phenomenological attitude of perception, values, meaning, freedom, and responsibility.

Person In line with phenomenology, the person in EA is understood in a relational manner from an ontological perspective. That is, the person is not a substance but is constituted in and through its relationships. There is no essence, which is prior to such relationality (Merleau-Ponty 1966, p. 489).

Längle understands the person as the place of the inner vis-à-vis, which enables the dialogical exchange between inner and outer world (Längle 2008, p. 94). The outer world is reflected in the inner world. The inner world is both, the psychophysical dimension of Frankl (affects, moods, fears, psychodynamics, personality traits) and the personal intimacy, attitudes, and beliefs (Längle 2008, pp. 92ff). Human beings as persons do not fuse in this inner world but can take a step back from it through self-distancing. Personal existence has its beginning in this act of self-distancing and the being given to oneself (Buber 2012b), which opens the possibility of a dialogical relation between the I and me (Längle 2016). On the other hand, human beings have the ability to self-transcend towards the outer world, which enables openness to the world (Scheler 1954) and true encounter (Buber 2012a).

The importance of the relatedness to the inner world is the first major change in the anthropology of EA in comparison to Frankl. EA assumes that the feeling of values goes hand-in-hand with an emotional response. To realize a value means to really feel the value, not only in an intentional sense or as a category of meaning-universals (Frankl 2005) but also in being emotionally touched.

The difference to a substantial ontology, however, becomes also apparent in an integrative and holistic view on Frankl's conception of the three dimensions – person, psyche, body. The spiritual dimension is not understood as this complete oppositional entity or dimension, as we know it from Frankl. Längle emphasizes the interrelatedness and unity of these three dimensions and assigns each of them specific tasks (Längle 2009a, p. 15).

Values and Meaning Values and meaning are linked for both Frankl and Längle. By realizing values, one realizes meaning. Nevertheless, the linkage between values and meaning has a divergent understanding for both. For Frankl, "meaning" is the primary concept and values are the place where this meaning can take place (Frankl 1973, pp. 43f, 55; 2005). For Längle, meaning arises from the feeling and realization of values. This difference becomes apparent in the distinction between existential and ontological meaning (Längle 1994, pp. 18ff). Ontological meaning has the connotation, that meaning is something that *really* exists in the world. This position is expressed in the sentence: Everything, that happens, has a meaning in and of itself, although human beings are not always able to discover it. The activity of the self in this kind of meaning is passive; I receive the meaning from outside myself. Existential meaning, on the other hand, is not a fact in the world but emerges from the relation between person and world, more precisely from the interaction between the person and the (subjective) value (Längle 1994, p. 18). If human beings realize their subjectively felt values, they experience meaning. The self in the context of existential meaning is therefore active. The question of an ontological or meta-meaning is an open one in a psychological perspective and has to be answered individually.

This change in the concept of meaning and value goes hand-in-hand with the orientation towards the emotional experience. It led to the existential turn of Logotherapy (Längle 1994, p. 17). Existential meaning cannot be found through a self-transcendental orientation towards the world, but has to include the inner life with its emotions, because otherwise one has no guidance about what is valuable for oneself. Existential meaning also includes a broader context (see earlier) in which the single action and decision is embedded and has its place. Not only are human beings positioned in broader contexts, but they also create such contexts of purpose through their question: For what is my life good?

Values play an important role in answering that question as they form the concrete possibilities to realize meaning in a broader context (Längle 2009b, p. 81).

Freedom and responsibility EA adopts the central claim of Frankl that human beings are more than their psychophysical determination. Due to their personal dimension, human beings have the ability for self-distancing (from psychodynamic mechanisms) – the negative side of freedom – and toward self-transcendence – the positive side of freedom.

The positive side of freedom can be understood not only as the freedom of action but as freedom of will in a compatibilistic way (for compatibilism cf. Keil 2007; Bauer 2007). This does not mean that human beings are able to decide about the will, but that the will is constituted in a special way in order to be free (Bauer 2009). In EA, this criterion can be understood as acting in accordance with one's subjectively felt values and in congruence with the person, who represents the deepest form of freedom, the freedom of one's essence (Längle 2007b, p. 158). This conception can philosophically be understood from a compatibilistic view, especially in the light of Harry Frankfurt (1971, 1992).

The concept of freedom in EA runs parallel to Frankfurt's understanding (Reitinger 2018, p. 217). To recognize the subjective values is not a rational act. Values have to be felt. And if one is able to act according to these felt subjective values one realizes the freedom of the will. And when this happens in accordance with the personal resonance of the moral conscience, the person realizes the freedom of their essence.

Because human beings have this ability of freedom-from and freedom-for, they can be said to be responsible for their actions and for the way of living in general. In every situation they are asked, are able to choose between different options, and in every situation, they have to find a personal answer. Although there is a responsibility for others which is controlled by the "public ego" or "super-ego," according to EA, the final instance of responsibility is one's personal moral conscience, which is nothing else than the person themselves with respect to what is right or wrong, what corresponds to the essence of the values in question and to the essence of oneself – again a phenomenological attunement.

References

Bauer, E.J. (2007). Zur aktuellen Infragestellung von Freiheit und Personalität. In: *Freiheit in philosophischer, neurowissenschaftlicher und psychotherapeutischer Perspektive* (ed. E.J. Bauer), 19–50. Munich: Wilhelm Fink.

Bauer, E.J. (2009). Arbeit am Freiheitsspielraum statt Appellation an einen “Freigeist.” *Existenzanalyse 26* (2): 9–15.

Bauer, E.J. (2012). Wahrnehmen und Nachempfinden von Emotionen in Texten – aus philosophisch-psychologischer Sicht. In: *Emotions from Ben Sira to Paul* (Deuterocanonical and Cognate Literature Yearbook 2011) (ed. R. Egger-Wenzel and J. Corley), 491–513. Berlin: Walter de Gruyter.

Bauer, E.J. (2016). *Verstehen als Existenzial menschlichen Daseins. Existenzanalyse 33* (1): 4–14.

Bauer, E.J. (2017). Personal-existentieller Dialog als Bedingung des authentischen Selbst-Seins bzw. Selbst-Werdens. *Salzburger Jahrbuch für Philosophie 62*: 9–29.

Binswanger, L. (1964). *Grundformen und Erkenntnis menschlichen Daseins*, 4e. Munich, Basel: Reinhardt.

Buber, M. (2012a). Ich und Du. In: *Das dialogische Prinzip*, 12e (M. Buber), 5–136. Gütersloh: Gütersloher Verlagshaus.

Buber, M. (2012b). Zwiesprache. In: *Das dialogische Prinzip*, 12e (M. Buber), 137–196. Gütersloh: Gütersloher Verlagshaus.

Buber, M. (2012c). Elemente des Zwischenmenschlichen. In: *Das dialogische Prinzip*, 12e (M. Buber), 269–298. Gütersloh: Gütersloher Verlagshaus.

Cooper, M. (2003). *Existential Therapies*. London: Sage.

Debats, D.L. (1996). Meaning in life: Clinical relevance and predictive power. *British Journal of Clinical Psychology 35* (4): 503–516.

Deurzen, E. van (2010). *Everyday Mysteries. A Handbook of Existential Psychotherapy*, 2e. London: Routledge.

Espinosa, N. (1998). Existenzanalyse im nachmetaphysischem Zeitalter. *Existenzanalyse, 13* (1): 4–11.

Frankfurt, H.G. (1971). Freedom of the will and the concept of a person. *The Journal of Philosophy 68* (1): 5–20.

Frankfurt, H.G. (1992). The faintest passion. *Proceedings and Addresses of the American Philosophical Association 66* (3): 5–16.

Frankl, V. (1973). *The Doctor and the Soul. From Psychotherapy to Logotherapy*. New York: Random House Vintage Book.

Frankl, V. (1986). *The Doctor and the Soul. From Psychotherapy to Logotherapy*, 3e (trans. R. Winston and C. Winston) New York: Vintage.

Frankl, V. (1988). *The Will to Meaning. Foundations and Applications of Logotherapy* (Expanded edn). London: Meridian.

Frankl, V. (1991). *Der Wille zum Sinn*. Munich: Piper.

Frankl, V. (2005). *Der leidende Mensch. Anthropologische Grundlagen der Psychotherapie*, 3e. Bern: Hans Huber.

Frankl, V. (2011). *Man’s Search for Ultimate Meaning*. London: Ebury Publishing.

Gadamer, H.-G. (1986). *Hermeneutik II. Wahrheit und Methode*. Ergänzungen, Register (GW 2). Tübingen: Mohr.

Heidegger, M. (1978). Brief über den Humanismus (1946). In: *Wegmarken. Zweite, erweiterte und durchgesehene Auflage* (M. Heidegger), 311–360. Frankfurt am Main: Klostermann.

Heidegger, M. (1993). *Grundprobleme der Phänomenologie*. Freiburger Vorlesung 1921/22. (ed. W. Bröcker). Frankfurt am Main: Klostermann.

Heidegger, M. (2001). *Sein und Zeit*. Tübingen: Niemeyer.

Hermann, F.-W. (1981). *Der Begriff der Phänomenologie bei Heidegger und Husserl*. Frankfurt am Main: Klostermann.

Keil, G. (2007). *Willensfreiheit*. Berlin: DeGruyter.

Längle, A. (1994). Sinn-Glaube oder Sinn-Gespür? Zur Differenzierung von ontologischem und existentiellem Sinn in der Logotherapie. *Bulletin GLE 11* (2): 15–20.

Längle, A. (1997). Die Angst als existentielles Phänomen. Ein existenzanalytischer Zugang zu Verständnis und Therapie von Ängsten. *Psychotherapie, Psychosomatik und klin. Psychologie 47*: 227–233.

Längle, A. (1999). Was bewegt den Menschen? Die existentielle Motivation der Person. *Existenzanalyse 16* (3): 18–29.

Längle, A. (2000). Die "Personale Existenzanalyse" (PEA) als therapeutisches Konzept. In: *Praxis der Personalen Existenzanalyse* (ed. A. Längle), 9–37. Vienna: Facultas.

Längle, A. (2001). Gespräch – Kunst oder Technik? Der Stellenwert von Methodik in Beratung und Therapie. *Existenzanalyse 18* (2–3): 7–18.

Längle, A. (ed.) (2002). *Hysterie*. Vienna: Facultas University Press.

Längle, A. (2003a). The art of involving the person. *European Psychotherapy 4* (1): 25–36.

Längle, A. (2003b). Emotion und Existenz. In: *Emotion und Existenz* (ed. A. Längle), 11–27. Vienna: Facultas University Press.

Längle, A. (2007a). *Sinnvoll leben. Angewandte Logotherapie*. St. Pölten, Salzburg: Residenz.

Längle, A. (2007b). Existenzanalyse der Freiheit – Zur lebenspraktischen und psychotherapeutischen Fundierung personaler Freiheit. In: *Freiheit in philosophischer, neurowissenschaftlicher und psychotherapeutischer Perspektive* (ed. E. Bauer), 147–182. Munich: Fink.

Längle, A. (2007c). Das Bewegende spüren. Phänomenologie in der existenzanalytischen Praxis. *Existenzanalyse 24* (2): 17–30.

Längle, A. (2008). Existenzanalyse. In: *Existenzanalyse und Daseinsanalyse* (ed. A. Längle and A. Holzhey-Kunz), 29–180. Vienna: Facultas University Press.

Längle, A. (2009a). Das eingefleischte Selbst. Existenz und Psychosomatik. *Existenzanalyse 29* (2): 13–35.

Längle, A. (2009b). Sinn-Bedürfnis, Notwendigkeit oder Auftrag? Eine existenzanalytische Fundierung der Logotherapie. *Existenzanalys 26* (1): 76–90.

Längle, A. (2011). The existential fundamental motivations structuring the motivational process. In: *Consciousness and Self-Regulation* (ed. D.A. Leontiev), 27–42. Hauppauge, NY: Nova.

Längle, A. (2013). *Lehrbuch zur Existenzanalyse. Grundlagen*. Vienna: Facultas.

Längle, A. (2015). The power of Logotherapy and the need to develop existential analytical psychotherapy. *International Journal of Psychotherapy 19* (1): 73–81.

Längle, A. (2016). *Existenzanalyse. Existentielle Zugänge der Psychotherapie*. Vienna: Facultas.

May, R. (1978). Response to Bulka's article. *Journal of Humanistic Psychology 18* (4): 57–58.

Merleau-Ponty, M. (1966). *Phänomenologie der Wahrnehmung*. Berlin: DeGruyter.

Nindl, A. (2001). Zwischen existentieller Sinnerfüllung und Burnout. *Existenzanalyse 18*: 15–23.

Reitinger, C. (2015). Viktor Frankl's Logotherapy from a philosophical point of view. *Existential Analysis 26* (2): 344–357.

Reitinger, C. (2018). *Zur Anthropologie von Logotherapie und Existenzanalyse. Viktor Frankl und Alfried Längle im philosophischen Vergleich*. Wiesbaden: Springer.

Rogers, C.R. (1961). *On Becoming a Person*. Boston: Houghton Mifflin.

Rohr, W. (2009). *Viktor E. Frankls Begriff des Logos. Die Sonderstellung des Sinnes in Substanz- und Relationsontologie*. Freiburg, Munich: Karl Alber.

Scheler, M. (1954). Der Formalismus in der Ethik und die Materiale Wertethik, 4e. Bern, Munich: Francke.

Tutsch, L. (2003). Of the phenomenology and therapy of narcissistic personality disturbance. *European Psychotherapy 4* (1): 71–85.

Yalom, I. (1980). *Existential Psychotherapy*. New York: Basic Books.

21

Logotherapy and Existential Analysis

Method and Practice

Silvia Längle and Derrick Klaassen

Summary

This chapter provides a survey of the current state of logotherapeutic and existential-analytical methods, with their specific indication and functioning. Viktor Frankl originally developed two main methods that are grounded in fundamental human (spiritual) abilities for self-distancing and self-transcendence: Paradoxical Intention and Dereflection. These were further supplemented by additional logotherapeutic methods, such as Elisabeth Lukas Modification of Attitudes. The specific methods were supported by a more general approach to psychotherapeutic conversations, Socratic Dialogue, which has the aim of disturbing preconceived and fixed interpretations through systematic questioning, thereby enabling greater openness and facilitation in the recognition of truth.

The further development and differentiation of Existential Analysis (EA) by Alfried Längle enlarged the anthropological basis of psychotherapeutic interventions and their methodological procedures and grounded them in a phenomenological understanding of the person and of existence. The resulting processual method of EA (Personal Existential Analysis, PEA), provides a fundamental procedural structure for EA psychotherapy. Within this wider phenomenological approach to psychotherapy, additional and more focused methods, such as Personal Position Finding, the Will Strengthening Method, or the Search for Existential Meaning, were developed to address specific clinical problems or facilitate the development of personal capacities. For such an existential approach the increased implementation of phenomenology is crucial because this is most apt way to come closest to the persons in their openness and freedom.

The Wiley World Handbook of Existential Therapy, First Edition. Edited by Emmy van Deurzen, Erik Craig, Alfried Längle, Kirk J. Schneider, Digby Tantam, and Simon du Plock.

Introduction and Basics

This chapter surveys the methods of Logotherapy (LT) and EA as they are actually used in psychotherapeutic practice and are taught as part of the curriculum and training program for psychotherapy and counselling by the International Society for Logotherapy and Existential Analysis (GLE-International) today. Logotherapy centers, such as the Viktor Frankl Institute in Vienna, only teach the original Franklian methods.

As a psychotherapy, EA works primarily through dialogical personal encounter, although there is a methodological openness for methods (as mentioned below), techniques (such as Paradoxical Intention), and supportive modalities (e.g., imagination, body work, creative methods). In LT the aim is to establish an access to meaning collaboratively, which is specific to the person and to the situation. The therapeutic conversation in LT is mainly cognitive, trying to provide arguments (Frankl 1990, pp. 79ff), while EA varyingly emphasizes different therapeutic styles: cognitive, empathic, constructive-confrontational, and protective-encouraging, which correspond to the phases in the process of PEA. The central aim and therapeutic element in EA is the establishment of an inner and outer dialogical openness, through which the person can actualize their *personal capacities* and can fulfill the *fundamental conditions* of personal existence (cf. the fundamental existential motivations – Chapter 20). Against this background, it is obvious that EA is not applied as a "method" in the sense of a "technique," since the personal encounter, the meeting of the client as a person, or the experience of relationship cannot be reduced to formal structures (Längle & Kriz 2012; Kriz and Längle 2012). Therapy, from this perspective, intends to reach the person's authenticity, although the methodological structures give a guideline for the procedural steps. Frankl employed Socratic dialogue as his main method, as well as Paradoxical Intention and Dereflection. Further logotherapeutic methods were also developed by Lukas and Martinez. EA has access to several methods with detailed instructions in the process management, including Personal Existential Analysis (cf. Chapter 22), work with its fundamental motivations (cf. Chapter 20), the biographical method, the personal positioning method, and numerous diagnostically specific forms of intervention. Some of these methods and approaches are elaborated below.

Indication and Duration

EA can be applied to all psychological, psychosocial, and psychosomatic disorders. Generally, therapy occurs on a weekly basis. The duration of therapy is dependent upon diagnosis, and ranges from a few sessions, in the case of reactive disturbances, to an average of 25 sessions in neurotic disorders and mild addictions, to six or more years of therapy with personality disorders, psychoses, severe addictions, and traumatic personality changes.

LT aims to address meaning-related problems, and is applied in cases in which meaning has been lost or in situations in which clients are suffering from meaninglessness or from an existential vacuum. LT is also employed in a preventive way, especially in education or in mental health related professions. The duration of counselling varies, lasting from a few sessions to a longer time span.

The Anthropological Foundation

Frankl's anthropology is grounded in the question of a personally meaningful life. It is the essential and necessary consequence of the existential freedom of the will. Frankl explicates this anthropology: "As is the case in any type of therapy, there is a theory underlying its practice—a *theoria*, i.e., a vision, a *Weltanschauung*. In contrast to many other therapies, however, Logotherapy is based on an explicit philosophy of life. More specifically, it is based on the three fundamental assumptions which form a chain of interconnected links: 1. Freedom of Will; 2. Will to Meaning; 3. Meaning of Life." (Frankl 1985, p. 2). The anthropology is developed further in Chapters 20 and 23 of this book.

The "Existential Fundamental Motivations" represent the *structural model* of EA (Längle 1999b, 2003b, 2016; see Chapter 20 in this book), taking up the existential themes with which every human being is inevitably confronted. The author describes the goal of existential-analytical psychotherapy as achieving the ability to live with inner consent, which means to find within oneself a "yes" to one's way of acting and living. One might describe this inner consent as the means to act and deal with situations in a way that leads to self-affirmation and to assuming responsibility for one's actions. The ability to live with an affirmation for life, with inner consent to one's form of existing, is the realization of existential freedom in EA.

The access to the free will of the person proves to be the basis of a mature, meaningful life, a life characterized by self- and other-affirmation and responsibility. As a consequence, all methods of LT and EA share the common goal of achieving this personal, existential freedom.

So far we have provided a comprehensive general description of procedures. In order to develop a more detailed structure of methods, we have to take a more internal look at the structure of existential analytical anthropology.

Anthropology of Classical Logotherapy (V.E. Frankl)

Classical Logotherapy, which is based on the anthropology formulated by Frankl (see e.g., Frankl 1985, also Chapter 23; in German Frankl 1959, 1997, 1991), postulates the two basic abilities of the noetic person for *Self-Detachment (or Self-Distancing) and Self–Transcendence* as the *basic conditions for existential being*. Self-Detachment (SD) emphasizes the ability of the noetic person to oppose their psychological and biological mechanisms or, as Frankl says: "Man is free to rise above the plane of somatic and psychic determinants of his existence. By the same token a new dimension is opened. Man enters the dimension of the noetic, in counter distinction to the somatic and psychic phenomena. He becomes capable of taking a stand not only toward to the world but also toward himself" (Frankl 1985, p. 19).

Self-Transcendence (ST) goes further and is grounded in the uniquely human ability to be drawn toward ends that go beyond the immediate and finite, beyond this particular and individual life in this particular and limited situation. Frankl (1985, p. 87) notes that

> It is a tenet of Logotherapy that self-transcendence is the essence of existence. This tenet means that existence is authentic only to the extent to which it points to something that is not itself. [...] Man, I should say, realizes and actualizes values. He finds himself only to the extent to which he loses himself in the first place, be it for the sake of something or somebody, for the sake of a cause or a fellow man, or "for God's sake."

Frankl stresses that human beings are not prisoners of their feelings or their environments, but that they can transcend their solipsism, egocentrism, or self-preoccupations and view the world and their situation from beyond themselves. Human beings are free to choose and decide where to turn, and to be dedicated to something or someone beyond themselves. In Frankl's view, only the process of neglecting oneself, leads to existential being, to personal fulfilment.

In elaborating his concept of psycho-noetic antagonism, Frankl stresses that one has to leave behind the psycho-somatic dimension and conditions and transcend these restraints. Frankl's formulations concerning his anthropology lead to an oppositionality between spirit and psyche/soma, which may also have implications for the person's relation to themselves. This topic, for example, also concerns his refusal of self-experience in the psychotherapeutic training program. (cf. Längle 2001, pp. 20f; Längle 1996)

Anthropology of Personal Existential Analysis (A. Längle)

Frankl has seen a psycho-noetic antagonism as a starting point in every psychotherapy (Frankl 1959, p. 686). In modern EA, this paradigm has changed substantially insofar as the one-sided openness of the person towards the world is supplemented by the "personal turn" which is, as the name implies, a turn to the conditions of the person as well as a "turn to emotionality" (cf. Längle 1999a, 1999b).

Here we have a great change in comparison to Frankl's original LT. In addition to seriously considering reflection, reason, and conscience, PEA, as the principle method of EA, gives equal attention to emotions, impulses, instincts, and corporeality. These aspects of PEA are discussed further elsewhere (e.g., Längle 1993a, 1995, 2003b) as well as in Chapters 20 and 22 of this book. Whenever human beings are active or impressed, being acted upon, through sensations, feelings, impulses, or spontaneous reactions this happens in the unity of the noetic with the psychic and somatic dimension.

This signifies that in PEA the personal resources of SD and ST are complemented by the capacity of self-acceptance (Längle 2013, pp. 90ff), which allows them to overcome the innate antagonism and protect the human self.

This *Self-Acceptance (SA)* comes from an openness towards oneself, which likewise means, to accept the outer reality as well as what occurs in one's inner world, what is going on in oneself, and how one is moved inwardly, and to devote oneself to both dimensions of existence with equal seriousness (see Figure 21.1). As a consequence, human beings remain in continual dialogue with the external world as well as with the internal world.

Actualizing personal freedom, as the general aim of any existential-analytical intervention in psychotherapy and counselling,[1] focuses on SD, ST, and SA as the specific human resources that lead to personal freedom.

[1] We commonly make distinctions between counselling and psychotherapy in German-speaking countries; in fact, there are even legal distinctions between these terms. *Psychotherapy* is a process of elaborating the ground of pain, suffering, and problems that block the emotionality and activity in their freedom. The patient is accompanied by a psychotherapist in a specific trustworthy, close, and personal relationship. *Counselling*, on the other hand, is the problem-oriented (e.g., family, partnership) helping by primarily providing specific information, new perspectives, encouragement, and so forth so that the client can perform the changes by themselves. Clients are relatively healthy and free in their emotionality and activity.

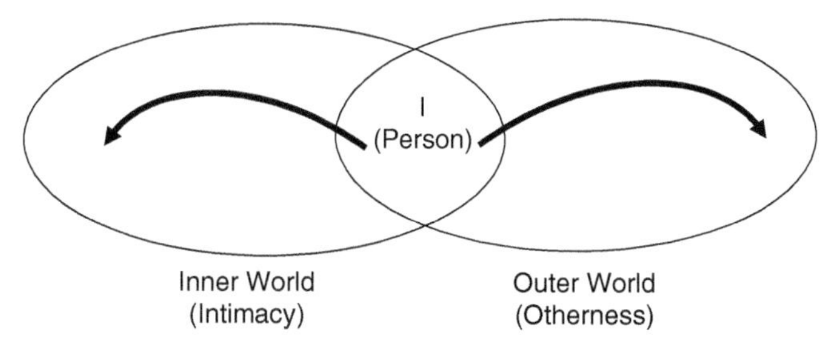

Figure 21.1 Double openness of the person as a result of double relatedness. (Längle 2013b, p. 48).

In these three personal abilities, we find a *structure that grounds the methods of EA and LT* (Längle 2003). The methods differ depending on whether they aim at SD, ST, or SA; for instance, it is commonly understood that Paradoxical Intention aims at SD and Dereflexion at ST, while PEA incorporates SD, ST, and SA.

Specific Methods

In Logotherapy

In LT we find the classical methods as they were developed by Frankl: *Paradoxical Intention* and *Dereflection* (e.g., Frankl 1988, pp. 100ff, 1985, pp. 140ff; see also Chapter 23). These logotherapeutic interventions are complemented by a method developed by Lukas (1984, pp. 43ff) called the *Modification of Attitudes.* The counsellor or psychotherapist leads the client/patient[2] in an internal and external dialogue based upon the assumption that the client/patient will spontaneously find answers and thereby immediately experience their own competence or ability for themselves. These experiences make them aware of their own integrity and authenticity.

The result may be a changed perspective or a fresh look at an old experience, which opens up and widens the received impression. Paradoxical Intention, Dereflection, or the Modification of Attitude may be applied if the client/patient's sense of personal competence has remained intact, but is not freely accessible because of the hindering experiences of problems. In such cases, the patient may be unable to dialogue and reflect with respect to specific topics, but the general ability or competence remains intact. To make personal resources accessible, the patient needs an impulse through an empathic, therapeutic relationship.

These resource-provoking methods have one basic notion in common: They break through a vicious cycle of destabilization, where an anxiety about a certain situation has become fixed, and produce an *openness* to what is essential in the face of difficult

[2] We employ the term "patient" to denote any person who is involved with and receiving psychotherapy, suffering from a clinically relevant diagnosis, and "client" for those looking for help but not suffering from a disease. The terms are commonly employed in German-speaking countries and have legal implications for professions and reimbursement by insurance companies.

situations. Frankl has described such vicious-cycle mechanisms in the case of anxiety disorders, which preserve themselves by alternating between symptom and fear, each producing more of the other and thus leading to increasing avoidance (cf. Frankl 1985, pp. 143ff, 1988, pp. 102ff).

- *Anticipatory anxiety* refers to the experience of an existential threat in certain situations (like blushing in public). Here SD can help to realize that one continues to exist despite this anxiety. The appropriate method is *Paradoxical Intention.*
- *Compulsive self-observation* or *Hyper-reflection* arises from the fear of losing control. Patients with this compulsion are prone to hyper-intention regarding security and control with a guaranteed outcome. ST leads to a new openness to become involved with new experiences, as applied in *Dereflection.*
- *Fixed attitudes* often reveal a fear of change towards that which is perceived as life-threatening. SA leads to a more open view of life; one can dare to go forward with one-self, and to let life come as it may, even if it is not within one's control. This requires a *Modification of Attitude* (for examples see Lukas 1984, pp. 43ff).

All these methods activate the patient's ability to face their own insecurity, and challenge them to move beyond the role of a victim in relation to their anticipatory anxiety or fixations. Frankl gave a classic example for Paradoxical Intention:

> A young physician came to our clinic because of a severe hydrophobia. He had been troubled by disturbances of the autonomic nervous system for a long time. One day he happened to meet his chief on the street, and as the young man extended his hand in greeting, he noticed that he was perspiring more than usual. The next time he was in a similar situation he expected to perspire again, and his anticipatory anxiety precipitated excessive sweating. It was a vicious circle; hyperhidrosis provoked hydrophobia and hydrophobia, in turn, produced hyperhidrosis. We advised our patient, in the event that his anticipatory anxiety should recur, to resolve deliberately to show the people whom he confronted at the time just how much he could really sweat. A week later he returned to report that whenever he met anyone who triggered his anticipatory anxiety, he said to himself, "I only sweated out a litre before, but now I am going to pour out at least ten litres!" what was the result of this paradoxical resolution? After suffering from his phobia for four years, he was quickly able, after only one session, to free himself of it for good by this new procedure. (Frankl 1985, p. 143)

The three methods outlined above do not address the contextual causes of problems and thus do not explicate the background or personal biographical development of problems. Instead these methods provoke fundamental personal abilities directly, which are meant to lead to a stabilization in the life of the client. Paradoxical Intention, Dereflection, and the Modification of Attitudes provide a grounding and give support and result in a freer internal and external dialogue.

In Existential Analysis

The methods in EA focus more on psychological *problems or trauma*. In the process of psychotherapy, unrealistic opinions and prejudices, wishful thinking, avoidance, feelings of helplessness or powerlessness, and so forth frequently emerge in the lives of patients/clients. By working on the emotional state, scrutinizing attitudes, reflecting points of view, or clarifying the life directions, the client/patient enters into a *relationship with themselves and with* their *world* by dealing with the problem. Step-by-step these methods lead to an increased closeness to oneself and others, which in turn allows for an intimate dealing with one's own emotions and may induce a re-affirmation of one's life. This can bring about a re-orientation towards one's experiences of self-worth, replacing the previous orientation towards expectations, wishes, conceptions, or projections.

These interventions are the domain of short-term therapy, which varies between counselling, on one side, and the therapeutic, process-oriented approach on the other side. It is interesting to note that, in this group of existential short-term therapy, we also have three methods, each belonging to one of the fundamental personal abilities SD, ST, and SA.

The *Personal Position Finding* (Längle, 1994a) is a phenomenological method that aims to assist clients in discovering their personal position or attitude towards a given situation. It introduces a more profound process of SD as well as questioning and removal of restrictions and constrictions, which result from an absent personal evaluation (or position) or an entanglement in a situation. Problems in relationships are often indicative of such an entangling structure of getting mixed up or being involved in a way where one does not know how to proceed. But also in cases of anxiety or depression, this method is indicated.

The therapeutic steps in Personal Position Finding involve a three-fold process in which clients are initially encouraged to develop a position towards the *outside*, that is, to evaluate the realistic possibility of a situation. This first step leads to a delimitation of what is realistically possible, as well as greater situational clarity and protection. The second step involves an *inner* positioning, a determination of the client's own resources and capacities, and thus leads towards an inner self-distancing and a clearer self-understanding and inner release. The final step of this method involves a positioning towards a *positive value*, a standing with and for what is good in the situation. This step leads to greater strengthening of the client's intentionality.

The *Will–Strengthening Method* (Längle, 2000b) aims to assist clients in strengthening the decisiveness, endurance, and capacity to follow through on an intended task. This method is indicated in situations in which the client has the will to accomplish a given task, but is frustrated or otherwise unable to follow through with their intention. The strengthening of the will through this method takes place through the two-fold inner and outer dialogue, which clarifies and invigorates the process of realizing one's goals and in turn strengthens ST. The method involves five steps: (1) foundational work on elaborating the facticity of the given situation (e.g., desire to abstain from alcohol); (2) enhancing the awareness of the problem and the reasons for its persistence (e.g., competing intentions or conflicting aims); (3) internalization, that is, strengthening the felt relationship to implicit values associated with the client's intentions; (4) elaborating the horizon of meaning associated with the intention and its relationship to the client's self; and (5) consolidation through decisiveness, preparation, and actualization (practice) of the intended aims. The clinical example serves to highlight this method.

A 25-year-old female client was seen in psychotherapy following a suicide attempt, in which she jumped from a bridge. The young woman spoke openly about the reasons behind her act of desperation. She had been addicted to drugs since age 14, had gone to therapy for the first time at age 16, but had relapsed after two years. For the past 20 months she had increasingly contemplated suicide but had not spoken to anybody about it. Now she was glad that her attempt had failed. She had the chance to live again, but at the same time was fearful about whether she could remain abstinent. She doubted that she could abstain from drugs on her own, but this would be the only way of life that would be worth living for her, which she desired. Although it was an ideal starting point for therapy, only a few sessions were possible since she was to be admitted to a hospital and drug rehabilitation facility in another city. She struggled to see how her wish to remain abstinent could become a reality, since she experienced a subjective lack of willpower. As a result, the woman viewed herself as a weak person, as a victim of her circumstances and infirmities. Moreover, she felt guilty for what she had done, and this in turn further reduced her self-esteem.

To stabilize and support her will to live abstinently, we employed the Will-Strengthening Method (WSM): The *first step* consisted of describing her intentions and the positive consequences expected from the sessions. Her intention to live without drugs was very clear at that moment. She wanted to start a new life. She wanted to lead a normal life, to be capable of enduring endure struggles and difficulties that life brought her way. A life with drugs was too exhausting for her. The *second aspect* of the WSM is the elaboration of negative consequences of her aim. What would she lose by living without drugs? "I used the drugs to close myself off," she said. We looked closely at her pattern of drug use to understand that she sought immediate relief to avoid problems, inner tension, and suffering. By abandoning her lifestyle of drugs, she also stood to lose her well-known milieu. It is the task of this second step to increase the patient's awareness of all the obstacles, of all the reasons which work against her intentions. These obstacles needed to be taken as seriously as the positive outcomes. This step concerned not only a question of handling the limitations but was also a deep encounter with herself, to develop an awareness not only for the positive but also for the negative feelings, to come closer to herself and to significant anxiety. It was arduous for the client to endure the feelings of frustration and isolation. But to have survived, at least thus far, gave her a strong hold and basis for life. The experience of being able to communicate her feelings and to be serious with herself furthered her growing sense of confidence and courage. The more we were able to concretize her hopes and fears the more she could experience the relief of truly being able to remain in her new life. Now she was ready for the *third step* – the intensification of the positive. It entails again a "getting closer" to one's own feelings, which are elicited by the intended goal. This, in turn, leads to an internalization of this goal. In this final step she managed to recall her previous situation: For her the will to live without drugs was originally a decision for or against life. But now she had become more acquainted with herself she had reduced her fear of failure; she could start to trust herself and her gratitude to be alive. The further deepening in steps (4) and (5) was addressed during the client's residential treatment.

The *Search for Existential Meaning* (Längle, 1988; also Drexler, 2016) is a method founded on the ability of SA. On this basis the person is able to perceive (become aware) and answer the situational questions of meaning. The Search for Existential Meaning (SEM) is indicated in situations and states in which meaning is lost or where the search for meaning is failing. This often occurs after a significant loss or transition.

The four steps of SEM have a parallel in the four fundamental motivations, as clients are encouraged to (1) perceive the realities of their world and situation, (2) feel the associated values or their absences, (3) develop their own evaluation of the situation and strengthen their position towards it, and (4) act in accordance with their position. A case example may serve to illustrate this process.

A 56-year-old man was seen for 12 sessions of psychotherapy following a motor vehicle accident, which left him with serious orthopedic injuries. The injuries required a long-term rehabilitation, which included numerous operations. Over the course of the rehabilitation, the man started to experience "depressive" symptoms for which his family doctor referred him for psychotherapy. During the initial assessment it became evident that although the man did indeed suffer from some depressive symptoms – anhedonia, persistent low mood, a lack of energy and motivation, social withdrawal and so forth. However, his suffering was more profoundly grounded in the existential questions that emerged in the course of his rehabilitation. Prior to the accident, the man had worked successfully as a minister and had found great meaning in his work; he felt he was "working for God" and his work was helping people every day. And yet, he had begun to feel dissatisfied with his work. The accident and the persistent severe injuries raised within him the questions of whether he indeed could and, more importantly, whether he wanted to return to his previous work.

The *first step* in the psychotherapy explored the facticity of this man's situation, the physical limitations that he was facing, but also the lack of enjoyment in his work. The therapist aimed to create space for the possibility of asking such questions. It took courage for the man to admit that, although he was doing what was by all accounts successful and evening "godly" work, he had lost the enjoyment and felt meaning of his vocation. Once he could allow for this and could face his situation honestly, he was open to exploring the emotional dimension of his life in the *second step*. It turned out that he not only could not feel the value of his pastoral work, but also more generally disregarded his emotions as secondary to what he was expected to do. As we began to turn towards these losses in therapy, he began to feel sad and grieve over his loss of emotion and meaning, and over the fact that he had neglected and lost himself in his work and life. The felt connection to the losses facilitated movement into the *third step* – the evaluation of the situation. We asked how it could have come to be as it is, that he had gone from being a minister who enjoyed and found meaning in his work, to the current state. In addition to our therapeutic conversations he began a journal and to write about his situation and dialogued with his partner and friends. Reading Frankl's *Man's Search for Meaning* was also deeply moving for him. Over the course of reflection and dialogue he arrived at the position that he had gradually and persistently neglected and devalued his emotional life and himself; his focus had been exclusively on his duties, on what "should do" as a minister and how others perceived him. The accident had afforded him the space to begin to ask the questions about how and why he was not emotionally and personally present in his own life anymore. He came to the firm position that he was not going to neglect these dimensions of his life anymore. In the *fourth step*, we began to work out, and he began to live out, the consequences of this position. One thing was clear, he was not going to continue to live his life without his emotions and without himself. Everyday life offered him opportunities to be questioned, to ask himself, "how do I feel about this situation or this decision?" He began to attend more and more to his emotions, began to value them as an essential part of his existence, and began to feel more connected to his own life. In the end, the accident became a turning point in life, a painful but ultimately fruitful stop to his everyday activities, which had offered him the opportunity to make space for the questions that were emerging in him. Ultimately, he came to the conclusion that he was being called into a new vocation and to a new way of living this vocation and his life.

Developing Personal Capacities for Dialogue

In clients/patients with less ego strength, which is the natural case in neurotic disorders, addiction and, of course, in personality disorders or trauma-related disorders, the psychotherapist moves from resource activation to a *process of development* of yet unrealized potentials.

Personal Existential Analysis (PEA) (Längle 1993a, 1995, 1999a, 2000a; see Chapter 22 for a closer description and case illustration) is the intra/interpersonal, dialogue-predicated process through which the person constitutes themselves in taking a position vis-à-vis a given situation. PEA is considered the core of the existential analytical process and the model of a personal being in the world. Being personal is regarded primarily as process-oriented dealing with oneself while encountering a situation, respectively addressing how to integrate the effect that an event (be it an inner or outer situation) has on oneself. Personal potentials are realized or actualized as the person engages in a dialogical exchange with the world in the three steps of PEA: being impressed, taking a position, and finding an expression. They mark the process-related abilities of the person. They create both an intrapersonal encounter, in which we have an intimate access to what we find in ourselves, and open the way to interpersonal encounter. These processual steps can also be seen from outside the encounter. The three steps appear in the form of being touched and impressed, positioning oneself, and eventually giving one's own answer to the other.

The dialogical process in the personal integration of impression, to position-taking, and finally expression always constitutes a unity. It reveals, respectively, the person's capacity for openness, selectivity, and interactivity. The process has its onset when information produces an impression on the feelings and/or cognition of the person. Impressions can range between soft and intense and are like a wave from outside. With this the person starts to restructure themselves by taking up the inner (counter-) movement (including SD), trying to incorporate and understand the content, taking a *stand* towards it, and finding one's own inner movement (including ST) as the basis for one's will for dealing with the content. Finally, the person prepares their activity and *expression*: choosing the content they want to bring into the world, the context, the means, the time, always considering possible feedback and reactions of the others, and checking back if oneself is able to deal with the expected reactions (including SA).

PEA is a process that binds together SD, ST, and SA which, in this context, are no longer distinct anthropological entities but inseparable domains in the accomplishment of existence. Thus, the realization of personal existence is characterized by wholeness and integrity. Well-known therapeutic procedures in EA, such as biographical work (Kolbe, 1994; Längle, 1994b; Tutsch & Luss, 2000), imagination exercises (cf. Popa, 2001) or the shifting of perspective (Kolbe, 2000) provide a specific access to the holistic approach of PEA and employ the anthropological resources of SA, ST, or SD.

The *indication* of this process-oriented method is all those experiences that are subjectively not understood, are alien to oneself, occupy consciousness and/or feelings or lead to rumination, or simply hurt (i.e., traumatic experiences, deficiencies, overwhelming experiences etc.).

The result of a successful application of PEA is a better understanding of the situation, of oneself and others, finding one's own position, and the freeing of one's own emotionality, which is no longer absorbed or preoccupied by the original experiences. It also leads to the discovery of one's personal will and the motivation for action and planned activity.

Unspecified Methods: Socratic Dialogue and Phenomenology

Both methods, Socratic dialogue and phenomenology, undergird the concrete practical methods described above and are more or less inherent in all of them. The phenomenological attitude, however, is considered to be so fundamental for EA procedures that it gave rise in the form of PEA to the structure of all methods.

Both phenomenology and the Socratic dialogue commonly open up persons to their world and lead to a more comprehensive view and understanding of the reality. But they follow different goals. The *Socratic dialogue* aims primarily at the recognition of truth. Therefore, the knowledge and the convictions (and interpretations) we have about reality are systematically questioned to stimulate the person to have a closer look again to what they take as reality and certainty of knowledge and recognition. Frankl (1982) and later on other authors, mainly Lukas (1984) and Martinez (2015), used this method in logotherapeutic conversations to help people to elucidate possible meanings by "disturbing" their fixed view of their actual situation and "destroying" their conviction of inescapability and impossibility to change their conditions. By questioning the one-sided (sometimes prejudiced) views and destabilizing the structures of the subjective reality (their subjective truth), a new access with new openness is permitted in which meaning can be detected. Along these lines, Socratic methods such as Meaning Perception Training and Meaning Decision-Making have been developed (Martinez, 2013). Socratic dialogue is employed as a means of engaging clinical problems and tends to be one of logotherapists' most-used techniques. For further description and practical examples, as well for the methodological application, see Martinez, (2015).

The *application of phenomenology* has played "the role of a minor auxiliary" in Frankl's original literature, as Spiegelberg (1972, p. 353) stated. According to Spiegelberg (1972, p. 353), the application of phenomenology, however, "helped him in his emancipation from the two earlier forms of Viennese analysis, Freudian psychoanalysis and Adlerian individual psychology, by allowing him to return to a less sophisticated description of immediate experience within a framework of a simplified values theory inspired by, but not simply taken over from, Scheler." In spite of this, Frankl's work is not characterized "as particularly phenomenological" (Spiegelberg, 1972, p. 353).

The application of phenomenology in the practice of psychotherapy and counselling, however, became the central achievement of A. Längle. It was first brought to light in

1989 through the practical method of PEA (1993a, 1994c, 2000a, 2003b) and then through the description of the four fundamental existential motivations (Längle, 1992a, 1992b, 2003a), as elaborated in Chapter 19. Längle and later on Drexler (2000), Tutsch (2001, 2005), Fischer-Danzinger (2013), Steinert (2014), and mainly Kolbe (2016) described the importance of the use of phenomenology in the practice to gain deeper access to the person and to help clients come to a more authentic life. The application of hermeneutic phenomenology (Heidegger, 1975, 2001) is central for EA and the main work in it is based on the two forms of application: the general form, following Heidegger's steps, and the more psychological form of PEA.

Although the phenomenological procedure also assists in opening up and widening the person's view of their world, phenomenology has a slightly different focus to Socratic dialogue. Phenomenology goes a step further. It not only loosens up taken-for-granted views and convictions but radically sets them aside (not even noticing them and working on them as is done in Socratic dialogue). This is called the "epoché" (Husserl, 1984), the bracketing of all knowledge, assumptions, judgments, and so forth. Phenomenology aims to see what is essential and to open up the way to what is basic in existential philosophy: to live authentically and realize fully our being-in-the-world (Heidegger). The aim, therefore, is to detect what is essential, prominent, and really important for this person in this particular situation and in their actual perception. Or, as Heidegger (2001, para. 7) puts it: "to allow the things to speak for themselves."

The general phenomenological procedure of Heidegger's (1975) hermeneutic phenomenology consists of three steps that are applied systematically and provide the basic structure for the existential analytical procedure (their phenomenological structure was described in Chapter 20, section titled "The role of phenomenology in existential analysis"). Here we can simply summarize the methodological application of these three steps:

1. Reduction: *What appears* (spontaneously)?
   This is the phase of ***description***, when the patient describes what moves them. One pays attention to the content, the way it is said, and what appears at the same time to the listener. In this phase of reduction of epoché, the psychotherapist refrains from all knowledge that does not come directly from the person speaking.
2. Construction – *How is it?*
   Single phenomena are interconnected with other phenomena noticing their overall effect on the psychotherapist's own essence (subjective impression), to find out how this is really for oneself.
3. Destruction – *Is that so?*
   The last step of opening after realizing the essential connections is an invitation to question oneself and what one saw, never assuming it to be certain. A phenomenological view does not arrive at final knowledge, never holds the truth, but is always only merely approaching it.

When we come to know what this person is actually concerned with, we arrive at an ***understanding***. This is the final result of a phenomenological process and the solid basis for practical continuation and changes.

The existential analytical method of PEA was developed independently of Heidegger's steps, but it has a striking similarity to it. Bauer (2016; see also Chapter 20) undertook a systematic philosophical comparison of the similarities and differences between PEA and Heidegger's three steps. Apart from the evident similarity, he found that both methods ultimately have different aims and therefore cannot be considered as being the same because of different intentions.

Therapeutic Effect of Logotherapy and Existential Analysis

Logotherapy aims to empower clients to grasp their existential freedom and to actualize the ever-present potentiality of the possibility of meaning. These meanings are available to clients in light of, and in spite of, their physical and psychological limitations. In EA the development of the dialogical capacity and especially of the inner dialogue is seen as the main therapeutic effect. It leads to an explicit development of the *inner consent.* Psychic health, as seen from an EA understanding, arises from the capacity for *inner dialogue* (Längle, 1992c). In this context, it is worth noting the further factors of effectiveness in EA-psychotherapy, which are derived from the application of PEA. They are considered to be (Längle, 1993b): (1) the phenomenological openness of the psychotherapist; (2) dwelling, being-with (*Beisein*) the client as a specific expression of the being a person, which includes confronting and working with paradoxes; (3) relationally stimulating procedures, which assist clients in expressing and enacting their values.

References

Bauer, E.J. (2016). Verstehen als Existential menschlichen Daseins. *Existenzanalyse*, *33* (1): 4–14.

Buber, M. (1973). *Das dialogische Prinzip.* Heidelberg, Germany: Lambert Schneider.

Drexler, H. (2000). Vom Bergen des Verborgenen. Das Heben der Primären Emotionalität in der therapeutischen Praxis. In A. Längle (Ed.). *Praxis der Personalen Existenzanalyse* (pp. 141–144). Vienna, Austria: Facultas.

Drexler, H. (2016). Steps towards meaning: The method of grasping meaning. In S. Längle & C. Wurm (Eds.), *Living Your Own Life. Existential Analysis in Action* (pp. 65–78). London, UK: Karnac.

Fischer-Danzinger, D. (2013). Strafe getilgt – Schuld abgesessen!? Zum schwierigen Weg von der öffentlichen Moral zur persönlichen Stellungnahme. *Existenzanalyse 30* (2): 14–20.

Frankl, V. (1959). Grundriß der Existenzanalyse und Logotherapie. V. Frankl, V. Gebsattel, & J. Schultz (Eds.). *Handbuch der Neurosenlehre und Psychotherapie* (Vol. III) (pp. 663–736).

Frankl, V. (1982). *Ärztliche Seelsorge.* Vienna, Austria: Deuticke.

Frankl, V. (1985). *Psychotherapy and Existentialism.* New York, NY: Washington Square Press.

Frankl, V. (1988). *The Will to Meaning.* New York, NY: The New American Library, Inc.

Frankl, V. ([1975] 1990). *Der leidende Mensch. Anthropologische Grundlagen der Psychotherapie.* Munich, Germany: Piper.

Frankl, V. (1991). *Der Wille zum Sinn.* Munich, Germany: Piper.

Frankl, V. (1997). *Die Psychotherapie in der Praxis.* Munich, Germany: Piper.

Heidegger, M. (1975). *Die Grundprobleme der Phänomenologie*. Gesamtausgabe, vol. 24. Frankfurt am Main, Germany: Klostermann.

Heidegger, M. (2001). *Sein und Zeit, 18*. Unchanged edition. Tübingen, Germany: Niemeyer.

Husserl. E. (1984). *Logische Untersuchungen*. Zweiter Band. Erster Teil, Husserliana XIX/1; Zweiter Teil, Husserliana XIX/2. U. Panzer (Ed.). The Hague, Netherlands: Martinus Nijhoff Publishers.

Kolbe, C. (1994). Stellungnahmen aufgrund biographischer Erfahrungen in ihrer Bedeutung für das aktuelle Handeln. In C. Kolbe (Ed.). *Biographie. Verständnis und Methodik biographischer Arbeit in der Existenzanalyse* (pp. 34–46). Vienna: GLE-Verlag.

Kolbe, C. (2000). Perspektiven-Shifting. Methode zur Arbeit mit primärer Emotionalität und unbewußten Stellungnahmen. *Existenzanalyse 17* (1): 17–20.

Kolbe, C. (2016). Existentielle Kommunikation. Zugänge zum Wesentlichen in Beratung und Therapie. *Existenzanalyse 33* (1): 45–51.

Kriz, J. and Längle, A. (2012). Commentary. A European perspective on the position papers. *Psychotherapy 49* (4): 475–479.

Längle, A. (1988). Wende ins Existentielle. Die Methode der Sinnerfassung. In A. Längle (Ed.). *Entscheidung zum Sein. Viktor E. Frankls Logotherapie in der Praxis* (pp. 40–52). Munich, Germany: Piper.

Längle, A. (1992a). Was bewegt den Menschen? Die existentielle Motivation der Person. Vortrag bei Jahrestagung der GLE in Zug/Schweiz. Published (1999) in *Existenzanalyse 16* (3): 18–29.

Längle, A. (1992b). Ist Kultur machbar? Die Bedürfnisse des heutigen Menschen und die Erwachsenenbildung. In: *Kongreßband "Kulturträger im Dorf,"* (pp. 65–73). Bozen: Auton. Provinz, Assessorat für Unterricht und Kultur.

Längle, A. (1992c). Der Krankheitsbegriff in Existenzanalyse und Logotherapie. A. Pritz, H. Petzold (Eds.). *Der Krankheitsbegriff in der modernen Psychotherapie* (pp. 355–370). Paderborn, Germany: Junfermann-Verlag.

Längle, A. (1993a). Personale Existenzanalyse. In A. Längle (Ed.). *Wertbegegnung. Phänomene und methodische Zugänge* (pp. 133–160). Vienna, Austria: GLE-Verlag.

Längle, A. (1993b). *Die Wirkfaktoren der existenzanalytischen Psychotherapie*. Unpublished training material of GLE-International.

Längle, A. (1994a). Die Personale Positionsfindung (PP). *Bulletin der GLE 11* (3): 6–21.

Längle, A. (1994b). Die biographische Vorgangsweise in der Personalen Existenzanalyse. In C. Kolbe (Ed.). *Biographie. Verständnis und Methodik biographischer Arbeit in der Existenzanalyse* (pp. 9–33). Vienna, Austria: GLE-Verlag.

Längle, A. (1994c). Personal existential analysis. In *Proceedings, 16th Intern Congress Psychotherapy* (pp. 318–355). Seoul, Korea: Korea Academy of Psychotherapy.

Längle, A. (1995). Personal existential analysis. In: *Psychotherapy East and West. Integration of Psychotherapies* (pp. 348–364). Seoul, Korea: Korean Academy of Psychotherapists.

Längle, A. (1996). Kritik, Bedeutung und Stellenwert der Selbsterfahrung in Logotherapie und Existenzanalyse. *Psychotherapie Forum 4* (4): 194–202.

Längle, A. (1999a). Die anthropologische Dimension der Personalen Existenzanalyse (PEA). *Existenzanalyse 16* (1): 18–25.

Längle, A. (1999b). Authentisch leben – Menschsein zwischen Sachzwängen und Selbstsein oder: Wie können wir trotzdem werden, wer wir sind? – Anregungen aus der Existenzanalyse. *Existenzanalyse 16* (1): 26–34.

Längle, A. (2000a). Die "Personale Existenzanalyse" (PEA) als therapeutisches Konzept. In A. Längle (Ed), *Praxis der Personalen Existenzanalyse* (pp. 9–38). Vienna, Austria: Facultas.

Längle, A. (2000b). Die Willensstärkungsmethode (WSM). *Existenzanalyse 17* (1): 4–16.

Längle, A. (2003a). The art of involving the person – The existential fundamental motivations as structure of the motivational process. *European Psychotherapy 4* (1): 25–36.
Längle, A. (2003b). The method of "personal existential analysis." *European Psychotherapy 4* (1): 59–76.
Längle, A. (2013). *Lehrbuch zur Existenzanalyse – Grundlagen.* Vienna, Austria: Facultas.
Längle, A. (2016). *Existenzanalyse. Existentielle Zugänge der Psychotherapie.* Vienna: Facultas.
Längle, S. (2001). Die Methodenstruktur der Existenzanalyse und Logotherapie. *Existenzanalyse 18* (2–3): 19–30.
Längle, S. (2003). Levels of operation for the application of existential-analytical methods. *European Psychotherapy 4* (1): 77–92.
Längle, A. and Kriz, J. (2012). The renewal of humanism in European psychotherapy: Developments and applications. *Psychotherapy 49* (4): 430–436.
Lukas, E. (1984). *Meaningful Living. A Logotherapy Guide to Health.* New York, NY: Grove Press.
Martinez, E. (2009). *El dialogo socratico en la psicoterapia.* Bogota, Columbia: Ediciones SAPS.
Martinez, E. (2013). *Coaching Existencial. Basado en los principios de Viktor Frankl.* Bogotá, Columbia: Ediciones SAPS.
Martinez, E. (2015). Meaning-centered psychotherapy: A Socratic clinical practice. *Journal of Contemporary Psychotherapy 45* (1): 37–48.
Popa, W. (2001). Das existentielle Bilderleben. *Existenzanalyse, 18* (2–3): 62.
Spiegelberg, H. (1972). *Phenomenology in Psychology and Psychiatry: A Historical Introduction.* Evanston, IL: Northwestern University Press.
Steinert, K. (2014). (Wie) Sprichst Du mit dir? – Anleitung zum inneren Dialog. *Existenzanalyse, 31* (2): 46–49.
Tutsch, L. (2001). Existenzanalytische Teamsupervision – Ein Konzept. *Existenzanalyse, 19* (2/3): 31–44.
Tutsch, L. (2005). Supervision and coaching in teams and groups. *Existenzanalyse, 22* (1): 4–18.
Tutsch, L. and Luss, K. (2000). Anleitung für die biographische Arbeit in der Existenzanalyse. *Existenzanalyse, 17* (1): 31–35.

22

Logotherapy and Existential Analysis Therapy Illustration

Personal Existential Analysis in Clinical Practice

Mihaela Launeanu, Derrick Klaassen, and Bruce A. Muir

Joanna's Impasse: A Story of Loss and Betrayal[1]

The client

Joanna is a 31-year-old woman who was referred to psychotherapy by her family doctor for symptoms of depression, sudden bouts of anxiety, and lack of motivation. As the symptoms worsened, Joanna left her teaching job and moved in with her mother and younger sisters who essentially took care of her during this time. She felt alone and had no desire to connect with friends or go out. Joanna was very aware and scared that she was not feeling well, and was eager to get help. She said "I feel empty in here (pointing towards a place deep within her chest), and I see no point to get up in the morning. I don't know why I feel this way, and I am very scared about it." Joanna also mentioned that she did not recognize herself anymore because she used to be cheerful, full of vitality, and outgoing. Although Joanna never contemplated the possibility of not living anymore or taking her life, she felt painfully cut off from life and trapped in her feelings of emptiness and fear.

During the first therapy session, Joanna revealed that her father died ten months previously. Shortly after that, her fiancé left her unexpectedly, just after they had decided a wedding date. Later on, she learned on Facebook that he married another woman shortly after he left her without saying a word. At this point, Joanna pulled a beautiful engagement ring out of her purse; she carried this ring with her since her fiancé left. She asked: "What does this mean now? I just cannot understand anything

[1] This case is based on the clinical work of the first author. The names and other identifying information have been changed to maintain the anonymity of the client.

The Wiley World Handbook of Existential Therapy, First Edition. Edited by Emmy van Deurzen, Erik Craig, Alfried Längle, Kirk J. Schneider, Digby Tantam, and Simon du Plock.

anymore. We were so in love." She said that she felt "devastated" after losing two very important people in her life, but, inexplicably to her, the loss of her fiancé was even more painful than that of her father. Joanna intuitively knew how to grieve for the loss of her father, and with the support of her family and friends, that process moved along quite well. However, every time she spoke about her fiancé, she felt utterly powerless and stuck, "as if a big rock fell in a mountain river and blocked its course." She mentioned that the hardest part was to understand what she called her fiancé's "betrayal," and felt that this was the point where "her life stopped." As a result, she began to feel empty in her chest and nauseous in her stomach, as if "there is something there that I cannot digest."

Joanna had never suffered from any mental health problems, and she was not using any substances or medication. She seemed resourceful and insightful, and mainly coped with her suffering by listening to relaxation tapes, walking in nature, and talking with her family members with whom she felt close. However, it was clear that she was suffering greatly: her eyes were hollow, her skin pale, her curled body sank into the couch, and, at times, she looked dreamy and unreal. She even said a few times "[that] all this seems like a dream and I am waiting to wake up but I don't know how."

After exploring her struggles, it became clear that Joanna's suffering stemmed primarily from feeling stuck and unable to process a significant life event, namely her fiancé leaving her unexpectedly and his marriage to another woman shortly after. She could not grieve that loss the way she was able to do for her father, and she felt trapped. It seemed that Joanna needed help to understand what happened there in order to move on with her life. Hence, the therapist decided to use Personal Existential Analysis (PEA), an existential-analytical method recommended for situations when the client is stuck or has not fully understood a life situation or impasse (Längle 2012).

The Clinical Implementation of Personal Existential Analysis

PEA is considered the central method of Existential Analysis (Längle 1993a, 1993b, 1994, 1999, 2012, 2016). It represents a systematic, phenomenological-experiential and process-oriented approach that also draws upon key principles of Logotherapy, such as self-distancing, self-transcendence, and the search for meaning (Frankl 1985). PEA is meant to support the person in integrating difficult life circumstances or resolving experiences of "stuckness" resulting from situations that were experienced as foreign or difficult to comprehend, such as the one described by Joanna. In these cases, using PEA can help process and integrate that impasse by addressing and activating personal capacities, such as: perceiving reality, feeling and experiencing, evaluating and appreciating, taking a position, deciding, and acting. As therapists, we trust that these capacities of the human person can be activated during psychotherapy work so that they help clients deal with problematic life situations, and this was the main therapeutic intention in using PEA in Joanna's case.

PEA follows three major steps (PEA 1 to PEA 3) preceded by a preliminary step-PEA 0 – meant to provide a *thick description* of the client's impasse. Each step has distinct sub-steps that help elaborate the therapeutic process. Please refer to Figure 22.1

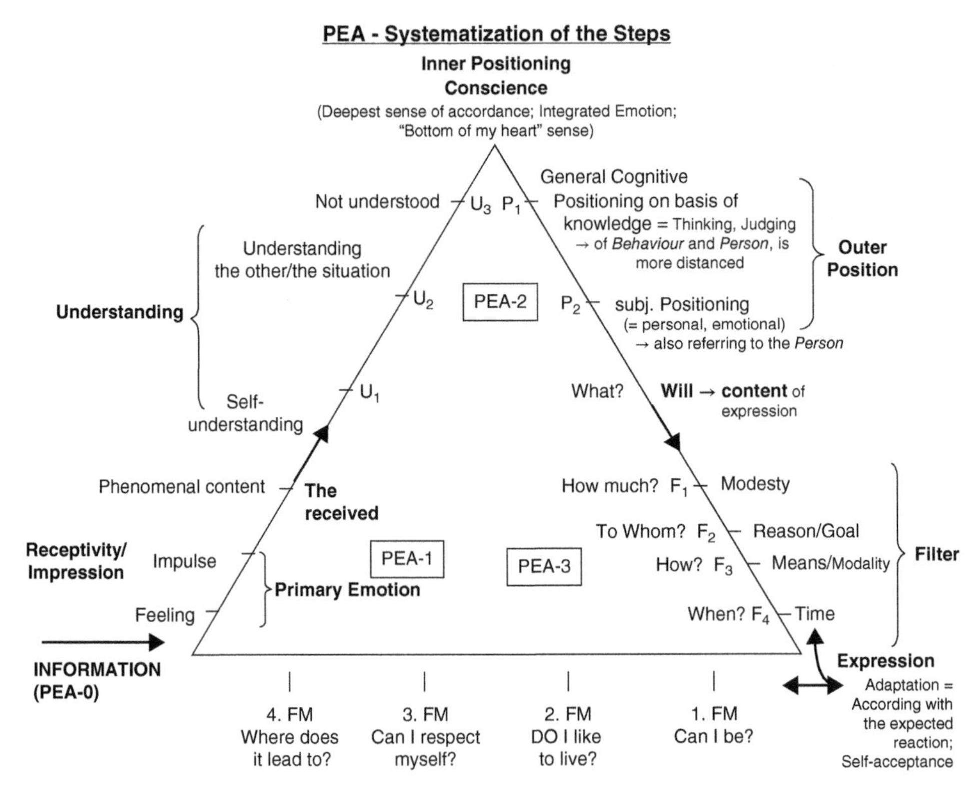

Figure 22.1 The steps of the process of Personal Existential Analysis (Längle 1993a).

for a detailed visual representation of the PEA process. Next, we will describe and discuss how these PEA steps were implemented in the therapeutic work with Joanna over seven 50-minute therapy sessions.

PEA 0: Description

PEA 0 aims to ensure a correct account of what happened, and, as much as possible, an undistorted contact with the concrete facts of the client's problematic situation. The client is asked to describe his or her situation or event in full detail and as concretely as possible. The focus is on gathering information about the client's reality, and the therapist's task is to ascertain that the client provides a report that is factual, clear, complete, realistic, and free of interpretations or fantasies. The main questions of PEA 0 are those able to facilitate a concrete and detailed access to facts: "What happened? When? Where? How? Who was there? Who did what? For how long? What exactly was done/said, by whom, when, etc.? What happened next?" The therapist may periodically encourage the client to search for more information that is not yet uncovered: "Was there anything else that happened? What exactly? How did it happen?" During the description phase, client's interpretations, evaluations, or emotional reactions are discouraged in favour of obtaining detailed factual descriptions of reality.

PEA 0 was a critical step in the process of helping Joanna. She was encouraged to tell the story of what actually happened in her relationship with her fiancé and describe the circumstances in which he left. The therapist kept her focused on the factual information and also tracked the potential signs of emotional dysregulation while she was remembering the facts. Fortunately, for the most part, Joanna was able to describe these facts without becoming overwhelmed, and she paced herself quite well. Although this process of gathering facts seemed a bit tedious and unnatural at the beginning, gradually, Joanna began to realize how much she did not know about her relationship, and how many assumptions she made about it in order to fill in the many gaps. It was very helpful for Joanna when the therapist shared with her when something did not make sense, was difficult to understand, or was simply not there. At these times, Joanna would often pause and comment that "I never questioned that. I just assumed that this is how it must be if people are in love."

As we proceeded in exploring the circumstances related to ending of her relationship, Joanna began to recall several key events. She remembered that when she clearly saw "red flags" in her relationship with her fiancé, she turned a blind eye, and dismissed her perceptions in order to protect her view of the relationship. She recollected that her mom and sisters would tell her that her fiancé was not a good man for her and, how she did not want to listen to them. Slowly, Joanna recounted something that she struggled to admit. Her fiancé told her several times that he was not ready to get married or to start a family. She said "but I wanted that so much and we were so in love that I thought he will eventually enjoy it too." Little by little, Joanna was able to gain some self-distancing, and she was able to see more of the reality that she had previously resisted.

In between our therapy sessions, Joanna decided to write down the facts that emerged to get a better sense of "how things really happened." At the end of the two sessions spent on elaborating PEA 0, Joanna brought her journal to the session, and reflecting on what she wrote, she said that she was "stunned" about how many facts she was missing and how she filled the gaps and silences with her own assumptions and desires. It was during reflecting on these newly retrieved facts that Joanna started to feel more clearly the pain of her loss; not just the loss of her fiancé, but also the loss of her desires and hopes connected with her relationship. This moment marked the transition to the next step of the PEA process: PEA 1.

PEA 1: Impression

During PEA 1, the client's subjective experience of the situation is closely explored with the aim of restoring the ability to access, feel, and accept one's emotions and impulses as they appear phenomenologically. PEA 1 unfolds across three steps: (1) accessing the primary emotions or feelings (what do I feel?), (2) recognizing the spontaneous impulses or urges (what am I moved to do?), and (3) elaborating the phenomenological content or what has client understood to be the message of their existential situation (what does this tell me?). It is important for the client to be able to examine these feelings and impulses first from an inner side and then have an outer gaze. Looking inward, we might ask the client: "What feelings do you get looking at this situation?" "What does it do with you?" "How do you feel with that?" "How does it affect you?" And, looking outward, we might ask: "What does it tell you?" "What is the message that came along to you with what happened?" "What does it mean to you?"

Accessing the primary emotion Once Joanna realized the many distortions that she unwittingly or sometimes intentionally cultivated in her relationship with her fiance's, she started feeling the rumbling stream of her emotions. At the beginning, Joanna felt most intensely sadness and (emotional) pain. Somatically, she described these emotions as heaviness and a sensation of painful squeezing and suction deep in her chest. In spite of the evident discomfort while experiencing these emotions, Joanna began to be more present in sessions, and mentioned that she felt "less empty but in pain" for the first time in the last few months. Whereas Joanna needed her therapist's support to regulate the intensity of these emotions, she was able to experience them fully.

Later, Joanna accessed her anger towards how she was treated by her fiancé. At first, this was a difficult emotion to acknowledge because she still loved him and wanted to protect him. But, gradually, she was amazed at how strongly she felt her anger, an anger directed primarily at her fiancé but also at herself for not standing up for herself. The latter brought up feelings of regret for not speaking up when she noticed that her fiancé was not treating her right, or when he left her with frequent silences and half sentences.

Recognizing the impulse When asked what she would spontaneously like to do in her situation, Joanna hesitated initially and said that "I just want to stop the pain and feel normal again," but she did not feel a clear impulse to do something. On the contrary, she felt somewhat paralyzed. However, as her feelings grew stronger and more differentiated, she had the urge to connect with her fiancé and to confront him. She realized that she was "too weak" and never stood up to him to tell him how much he made her suffer. Joanna felt the impulse to find her fiancé with the help of their Facebook friends and set up a meeting with him. When asked what would she tell him, she appreciated that she probably could not even speak coherently because she felt so emotionally overwhelmed, so she decided to start writing him a letter instead. Moreover, Joanna also developed a strong urge to write about her feelings and thoughts, and she turned to her journal to write down her emotional experience in between sessions.

Phenomenological content As Joanna, together with her therapist, reflected on her writing she began to develop an understanding about what her impasse meant to her and what this life event told her. Specifically, she tried to understand what her former fiancé's sudden leaving meant to her. She reflected that his abrupt cut off meant that he was not really in love with her and that she did not carefully listen to his reluctance to get married. She also commented that perhaps setting up a date for their marriage made him clearly realize that he was not ready for that step, and therefore he ran away to save himself from such a commitment. In addition, Joanna said that the message that she would take from this is "not to trust blindly without checking my understanding." Then, she commented on her "not having had any serious romantic relationships before" and how "maybe I needed this lesson so that I won't act the same way again." Joanna understood just how important it was to have clear communication and to check expectations. PEA 1 took approximately two sessions but Joanna worked hard in between sessions journaling her experiences and allowing her feelings to emerge and to be processed.

PEA 2: Inner Positioning

This step aims to help clients come to a clear understanding of what happened so that they can then find their stance towards the situation. Such a stance moves beyond an initial emotional reaction or reactive opinion and represents a more mature process of synthesizing the information gained thus far with a personal evaluation of the situation. This process of moving from PEA 0 to PEA 2 corresponds to Frankl's notion of self-distancing (Frankl 1985) as the person comes into an optimal distance from first impressions, primary emotions and impulses in order to find his or her own position with respect to the given situation. Inner Positioning takes place over two sub-steps: understanding and positioning.

Understanding The first sub-step of PEA 2 is an understanding of self, of the other, as well as of those aspects of the situation that are not yet understood. Clients grow in understanding by integrating their primary emotions and impulses with the actual constraints of the situation and with their own personal values. The aim is to assist the client in achieving a holistic understanding of what happened. We might ask the client: "Do you understand yourself why you feel this way?" "Do you understand why the other acted that way?" "Is there something that you do not understand in what happened?"

Understanding one's self: During this step, Joanna became aware of how much she wanted to feel worthy and loved, and how much she wanted to have a family with her fiancé, "too much for my own sake," as she would comment. She understood her desire as significantly shaped by her family values and background that emphasized the importance of marriage and family. Joanna also understood that she reacted so intensely because, in fact, she did not connect realistically with her ex-fiancé and did not see him or understand him for who he was. Rather she acted out of her own wishes and desires, and felt disappointed and hurt in the end.

Understanding the other: Gradually, Joanna was also able to understand and at times even empathize with her fiancé. She began to wonder whether he felt pressured by her desire to get married, and whether he did not know how to tell her and eventually ran away. She said that she realized "how important is to speak up and also to listen to the other person."

Not yet understood: Joanna was still struggling to understand why her fiancé left her without a word, and why he agreed to their engagement and then set up the wedding date if he did not want to get married. She also struggled to make sense of how he was able to marry another woman so quickly after he left her, if he truly did not feel ready to settle down. These not-yet-understood aspects made her wonder if there was something about her that pushed him away, and she suggested that maybe she was "too pushy and impatient" to get married and she drove him away.

Positioning The integrative understanding of the previous sub-step forms the basis for the second process of PEA 2: positioning. At its core, PEA 2 entails the articulation of a personal evaluation corresponding to one's moral conscience (i.e., the inner positioning). Then, the outer position is elaborated in two steps: general positioning and subjective (personal) positioning. Positioning entails both an evaluation (e.g., how does the client judge or assess what happened in light of personal and/or shared values) and taking a stance based on that evaluation (e.g., how does the client stand towards what happened). Typically, positioning leads to finding one's will, which marks the transition to PEA 3.

Inner positioning: Evaluation through the lens of one's moral conscience: During this step, the client is encouraged to find his/her deepest sense of justice or what is right by his or her own personal moral conscience. This personally sensed evaluation is the deepest positioning and has a moral quality. Some helpful questions during this step are: "What do you sense at the bottom of your heart about what happened?" "Did it do justice to you?" "Do you feel that it is right for you what happened, that you deserved it?" "What is your own gut feeling about this?" "What do you personally say to all of this?" "What would be right for you to happen in this situation?" "What would seem just to you now?" "What do you feel about your own behaviour?" "Was this right how you behaved toward him?"

Joanna visibly struggled during this step of PEA 2. It took a while to realize what made her struggle so much, but finally she came to a session frustrated saying, "I know that I should just accept this and move on but I just cannot. It is not right." Joanna's statement opened up a conversation about what acceptance meant to her and it quickly became evident that Joanna was using "acceptance" and "agreement" or "moral endorsement" interchangeably. Every time she asked herself to accept what happened, she felt pressured to agree morally or condone what happened, and she felt unable to do so. Hence, again and again, she felt utterly stuck during this step. After she managed to disentangle acceptance from agreement, it became much easier for her to move through PEA 2.

Once Joanna was able to articulate clearly that in her "heart of hearts" she felt that what her fiancé did to her was wrong, and once she was able to take this clearly felt position towards this, she was on solid ground. She also acknowledged that "how I did not say anything at that time was not right either" and this led to feeling deep regret and some empathy for her fiancé, who "maybe did not know how to communicate and felt pressured to get married and settled down."

Outer position: After clients arrive at a personal moral evaluation of what happened (inner positioning), they re-engage with the outer world both cognitively (e.g., thinking, judging) and subjectively (e.g., emotions) in order to articulate their outer position. This double movement in PEA 2 – inner positioning and outer position – illustrates the dialogical nature and double openness of PEA (both towards the inner and the outer), and represents the bridge towards the expression of one's will in the outer world (PEA 3).

General positioning: General positioning entails both a general evaluation of the situation and coming to a clear yet more distant position towards the situation. The general evaluation of the situation refers to knowledge, experience, and information from others and thereby synthesizes the cognitive aspects of the situation and the general knowledge about similar behaviours. It is elicited with questions such as: "What do you think about a person acting like this?" "Is this normal?," "Is it pathological?" "What do you know about this type of behaviour?" "What did other people say about it?"

When asked what she thought about someone who acted the way her fiancé did, Joanna was quick to say that she believed that it was always wrong to cut off from an intimate relationship without a word, especially after getting engaged and already planning to get married. Her cognitive evaluation led to her more general positioning: she was sure that it was wrong if anyone were to act like this in a similar circumstance, and she was able to explain why she thought that way.

Subjective (personal) positioning: This step invites the clients to evaluate subjectively what happened, in the particular context of their personal existential situation, and to take a personal position towards what happened. Sometimes, it is possible that the subjective evaluation and subsequent personal position differ from the general evaluation of what happened. Hence, it is important to work carefully through each of these steps.

Asked what she personally thought of her former fiancé and what her position was towards him and how he acted, Joanna said that she saw him as not ready to commit to marriage, maybe still growing up and inexperienced, and, ultimately unable to assume the responsibilities of a long-term relationship. By articulating her personal spontaneous position, she realized that he was not ready to be with her in marriage.

Will: As a result of PEA 2, a phenomenological check of the inner movement ensues: Is there something coming up that wants to be done? Is there something left to do practically with what happened that is now waiting for the client to execute in order to improve or even resolve the situation on the basis of this new understanding? Is there anything that the client feels that he or she wants to do with this situation?

At the end of PEA 2, after two therapeutic sessions, Joanna was clear that she disagreed with her fiancé's behavior, that she could not forgive it, and, yet, that she could accept that this happened. Now it was a matter of what Joanna would do with this new understanding and clear positioning. Joanna felt clearly that she wanted to do something, that the situation as it did not feel not congruent with her, so she decided that she would like to share her inner position on this situation with her family and friends, and eventually with her ex-fiancé. She felt a strong inner movement that wanted to be expressed in her world.

PEA 3: Expression

The personal process of dealing with one's life situation and conditions concludes with finding one's own expression of free will, namely *what* and *how much* the client wants to do to in the respective situation, as well as *with whom*, *how* (i.e., with what *means*) and *when*. This is the basis for personal action in any given situation and reflects Frankl's (1985) understanding of self-transcendence as acting in the world by realizing the meaning found in a certain context.

In this stage it is crucial to address with the client the following questions: "What do you really want to do?" "What will you do?" "What is better not to do?" "With whom, how, and when?" "What will be the consequences of your action?" "What would be the worst consequence that could happen?" "Can you bear these consequences?" "How will you deal with the consequences of that action?" "What is therefore the best way to take action?" "What will you do if the outcome is different than the anticipated one?"

PEA 3 addresses the following four filters to clarify the strategic procedure of the planned action:

1 Modesty filter or how much should client reveal his or her inner positioning (What is possible to do here and now; How much do I want to reveal; What do I want to keep for myself?).
2 Reason filter referring to the goal or purpose for acting in a certain way. For whom would it be helpful to act this way – For oneself? For the other person? For any group of people? – With whom would it be good to perform it? (e.g., alone, with a friend, with the help of the therapist?).
3 Means filter indicating the means needed to act in the chosen way (How and by what means is the best way?).
4 Timing filter (When shall I do this?).

In stark contrast with her self-described lack of motivation at the beginning of our sessions, Joanna seemed to have an easy time deciding what to do next and made quick progress during PEA 3, which was discussed in one session. She commented that after she got clarity on her position regarding what happened, she felt not only relieved but her energy and motivation significantly increased. Joanna began to look for a new teaching job and for a volunteer position. She began to feel more strongly the desire to live and to experience life again.

Shame/Modesty filter Joanna really wanted now to speak about what happened to her with other people. She felt comfortable to share both what she found wrong about what happened, and to take responsibility for what she understood as her part in it. She did not feel embarrassed now to speak up about what happened. On the contrary, she also found it important to speak about her own mistakes. She formulated what she wanted to say to her former fiancé and what she wanted to ask him.

Reason filter Joanna felt that sharing her inner position with people who were close in her life would allow her to reconnect with them at a deeper level after she had withdrawn from relationships for a while. She thought that it was important to share her position with her fiancé in order to bring this to a close, and even if late, to clarify some of the unspoken expectations and to take responsibility for her part. Joanna decided to implement her decision by herself, but she acknowledged that she hoped that her family and friends would be supportive in dialoguing with her about this. Joanna also felt that "it was time to contribute to others' lives again" and that her decision to find a job and to volunteer was in agreement with her deeply held values.

Means filter Thinking about what exactly to say and how to formulate it, Joanna became aware that she didn't want to meet his fiance personally. She believe that she would be too irritated and was afraid of his insensitive reactions. So she became very clear regarding her position to write him a letter. In terms of finding a job and a volunteering position, Joanna planned to reconnect with some friends and to reach out to community centres.

Time-filter Joanna chose to start implementing her decision right away since there was no reason to wait. By the time of our last session together, Joanna has already drafted a letter that she intended to send to her former fiancé. She anticipated that the discussions with friends and family about what happened may be ongoing and she mentioned that she already started this kind of dialogue with some of her close family members.

In parallel, she started looking into volunteer options and jobs immediately. She mentioned that she would have liked to find a volunteer position within the next month and a new job within the next three months or so.

Reflecting on the PEA Process

At the end of our therapeutic work together, I asked Joanna to reflect on what happened for her during therapy, and some turning points in this process. She quickly identified two branching points: the detailed description of what happened (PEA 0) helped her realize that there were many distortions and false assumptions in the way she lived her relationship, and the differentiation between agreement as moral stance from acceptance of the reality (PEA 2). Joanna mentioned that after each of these moments she felt a surge of new life: after the first moment, the sadness and pain of life, and after the second turning point, the freedom to choose and to live a fulfilled life.

Case Discussion

This section of the chapter offers us the opportunity to reflect on this case and to draw some conclusions about how to implement PEA in clinical practice. First, Joanna was an unusually insightful and high-functioning client who moved relatively smoothly through this process. Hence, in a way she is a "success story" that allows us to see how PEA can progress at its best. Although at the beginning of therapy Joanna displayed some depressive symptoms, she had no mental health problems, many resources, and solid, healthy coping skills. It is very likely that PEA would have looked different with a client with mental health concerns, a lack of resources, and/or poor coping skills. In fact, PEA is not recommended for clients who are suffering from diagnosable conditions, such as anxiety, depression, psychosis, or eating disorders (among others), and whose primary purpose for seeking psychotherapeutic assistance is the amelioration of these conditions (Kwee and Längle 2013). One of the reasons for this limitation is that the process of PEA requires some capacity to both engage with and also distance oneself from one's feelings and thoughts, and to develop a personal position in relation to one's situation. If Joanna's suffering had, for example, developed more fully into a depressive disorder, she would likely have lacked the emotional energy required to engage in this process. She may also have struggled with the capacity to distance herself from hurtful emotions, such as the feelings of betrayal, and may have experienced significant feelings of shame. In such situations, PEA may still be a helpful method to address aspects of her life that were confusing or unresolved, but other therapeutic foci are pre-requisites to rebuild the client's capacities and thus will take therapeutic priority with these clients.

Second, the case highlights some interesting turning points in implementing PEA and how each step builds on the previous one in an organic fashion. The first turning point for Joanna was PEA 0, the step in which clients are encouraged to attend rigorously to elaborating the facts of the situation. While this may seem initially like an easy step, we have found that it is actually quite difficult to refrain from moving to elaborations, theories, interpretations, and fantasies about one's situation. Staying with the facts, with what we actually know about a given situation, is challenging. But, as it was for Joanna, there is often great benefit in being rigorous in this step because clients are able to gain new insights into their situation and can learn to differentiate between these facts and their assumptions or fantasies. For Joanna, she was able to realize how much she took for granted in her relationship (e.g., that they both were equally motivated about getting married) and was able to look at facts that she had previously forgotten or ignored (e.g., the various red flags about her relationship). Ultimately, such clarification can be liberating for clients as they can take responsibility for their own contributions to a situation and let go of unnecessary and misleading fantasies.

A second turning point for Joanna emerged at PEA 2, when she was challenged by the therapist to distinguish between acceptance and agreement. Here Joanna was able to understand that acceptance merely relates to the actuality of a given situation rather than to our moral evaluation of its correctness. This step, likewise, gave Joanna more space; she learned that saying "yes" to the facticity of the breakup did not require her moral endorsement of it. She could maintain the position that this breakup was not right, that it was painful to her, and that it should have been handled in a different way, while at the same time finding a way to be able to endorse the fact that this was how it was. Accepting was not the same as moral agreement.

These therapeutic turning points highlight a third point that bears noting about PEA, namely that it functions as a holistic process that frequently proceeds organically from one step to the next. The organic movement is noticeable as therapists often are not required to prompt clients to move on to the next step in the process; as clients work through one step, they often begin to move on naturally to the next one. Of course, there are times when all of us, including our clients, become stuck. This is where it is particularly helpful to have the company of a therapist who is able to serve as a dialogue partner and assist a client in working through blockages. Therapist's personal feelings and perceptions are equally important throughout the process of implementing the PEA steps. Therapist's sharing of his or her perceptions and feelings in each step (e.g., providing validation or asking for clarification when something is unclear), makes the client feel accompanied and in a close relationship.

Likewise, it is beneficial to follow a process that is holistic and phenomenological; that is, it attends deliberately to the fullness of lived experience, including contextual and factual information, emotional/embodied impressions, cognitive and emotional understandings as well as attending to the client's moral conscience. This latter dimension of human experience – our moral conscience – is frequently avoided in psychotherapy and relegated to the realms of religious accompaniment or philosophical discourse. However, as was evident for Joanna, and it may be particularly important in cases of interpersonal violation, there is a place in which we can and should allow our moral conscience to take its place alongside other dimensions of experience.

Finally, it is worth noting that the process of PEA may be beneficial and transferable to Joanna and other clients in other situations in their lives (Launeanu, Chapman, and Kwee 2014). Once clients have learned the process, they may be able to apply it to other situations even without the assistance and accompaniment of the therapist. Since PEA is applicable in a wide variety of situations, the possibilities for its use are numerous. Additionally, we have found that clients who have worked through PEA frequently feel empowered to attend to and value their own subjectivity more fully and with greater confidence than before. They frequently come to realize that they have access to and can draw upon an inherent wisdom, and that this wisdom, in dialogue with the limitations and affordances of their life world, has much to offer them and their world. As such, clients find themselves often drawing upon this personal and spiritual resource and consequently are more fully and responsibly engaged with their life and their world.

Conclusion

PEA is a phenomenological-experiential and process-oriented method that is intended to support the person in integrating difficult life circumstances and assist in situations when the person feels confused or stuck. PEA: is the central method of existential analysis (Längle 1994; 2000); draws upon key principles from Logotherapy (Frankl 1985); and follows a holistic, dialogical process that includes attention to the facts of a given situation, our phenomenological impression, the development of an inner position, and finally its expression through action. The method of PEA was illustrated through the case of Joanna, a client who was suffering and was unable to move forward after the unexpected and sudden end to a romantic relationship. As the process of PEA emerged over time, Joanna found that she was able to delineate the facts of her situation more clearly, work through unexpressed and confusing feelings, develop a personal position, and was finally able to act congruently on the basis of this position.

References

Frankl, V. (1985). *Psychotherapy and Existentialism*. New York: Washington Square Press.

Kwee, J.L. and Längle, A. (2013). Phenomenology in psychotherapeutic praxis: An introduction to personal existential analysis. http://episjournal.com/journal-2013/phenomenology-in-psychotherapeutic-praxis/ (accessed January 3, 2019).

Längle, A. (1993a) Personale existenzanalyse. In: *Wertbegegnung: Phänomene und methodische Zugänge* (ed. A. Längle), 133–160. Vienna, Austria: Gesellschaft für Logotherapie und Existenzanalyse.

Längle, A. (1993b). A practical application of Personal Existential Analysis (PEA) – A therapeutic conversation for finding oneself. *English translation from Bulletin der GLE 10*: 3–12.

Längle, A. (1994). Die biographische Vorgangsweise in der Personalen Existenzanalyse. In: *Biographie. Verständnis und Methodik biographischer Arbeit in der Existenzanalyse* (ed. C. Kolbe), 9–33. Vienna, Austria: Gesellschaft für Logotherapie und Existenzanalyse.

Längle, A. (1999). Die anthropologische Dimension der Personalen Existenzanalyse (PEA). *Existenzanalyse 16* (1): 18–25.

Längle, A. (ed.) (2000). *Praxis der Personalen Existenzanalyse.* Vienna: Facultas.

Längle, A. (2012). The Viennese school of existential analysis: The search for meaning and the affirmation of life. In: *Existential Therapy: Legacy, Vibrancy, and Dialogue* (ed. L. Barnett and G. Madison), 159–170. New York: Routledge.

Längle, A. (2016). *Existenzanalyse. Zugänge zur existentiellen Psychotherapie.* Vienna: Facultas.

Launeanu, M., Chapman, R., and Kwee, J.L. (2014, July). The personal existential analysis method. Workshop presented at the Constructivist Psychology Conference, Vancouver, BC.

23

Key Texts

From Frankl to Längle

Karin Steinert, Barbara Gawel, and Silvia Längle

These key texts should give an insight into the beginnings of Logotherapy by V.E. Frankl, its development and mature state with its methods, motivational concept, anthropological basics with which the main work in Logotherapy is done. The development of Existential Analysis by A. Längle brought along a shift of the paradigm. Here we attempt to describe this shift with some impacting citations to make clear the new elements in theory and practice.

Why Logotherapy and Existential Analysis?

"The primary motivation to do this work, however, has been my effort to overcome the psychologism in the field of psychotherapy where it usually coexists with a 'pathologism'. But both are aspects of a more comprehensive phenomenon, namely reductionism, which also includes sociologism and biologism. Reductionism is today's nihilism. It reduces a human being by no less than an entire dimension, namely the specific human dimension. [...] In other words, reductionism is subhumanism" (Frankl 1997, pp. 59f).

"A psychotherapy that not only recognizes man's spirit, but actually starts from it, may be termed *Logotherapy*. In this connection, *logos* is intended to signify 'the spiritual' and beyond that, 'the meaning'"[1] (Frankl 1986, p. xvii).

[1] It must be kept in mind, however, that within the frame of logotherapy 'spiritual' does not have a religious connotation but refers to the specifically human dimension. [Original footnote]

The Wiley World Handbook of Existential Therapy, First Edition. Edited by Emmy van Deurzen, Erik Craig, Alfried Längle, Kirk J. Schneider, Digby Tantam, and Simon du Plock.

"At the time we introduced the term 'existential analysis'[2] in 1938, contemporary philosophy offered the word 'existence' to denote that specific mode of being that is basically characterized by being responsible." (Frankl 2000, p. 28)

Frankl's Central Theme: Meaning

"If we were to give a quick account of what led existential analysis to recognize responsibleness as the essence of existence, then we would have to begin with an inversion of the question, What is the meaning of life? I made this inversion in my first book, *Ärztliche Seelsorge* [Frankl 1946],[3] when I contended that man is not he who poses the question, What is the meaning of life? but he who is asked this question; for it is life itself that poses it to him. And man has to answer to life by answering for life; he has to respond by being responsible; in other words, the response is necessarily a response-in-action.

While we respond to live 'in action' we are also responding in the 'here and now'. What is always involved in our response is the concreteness of a person and the concreteness of the situation in which he is involved. Thus, our responsibility is always responsibility *ad personam* plus *ad situationem*." (Frankl 2000, p. 29)

"Ultimately, this responsibleness derives from the existential fact that life is a chain of questions that man has to answer by answering for life, to which he has to respond by being responsible, by making decisions, by deciding which answers to give to the individual questions." (Frankl 1985c, p. 17)

"As is the case in any type of therapy, there is a theory underlying its practice: a *theoria*, that is, a vision, a *Weltanschauung*. In contrast to many other therapies, however, logotherapy is based on an explicit philosophy of life. More specifically, it is based on the three fundamental assumptions that form a chain of interconnected links:

1 Freedom of Will.
2 Will to Meaning.
3 Meaning of Life." (Frankl 1985c, p. 2)

The Freedom of Will

"Needless to say, the freedom of a finite being such as man is a freedom within limits. Man is not free from conditions, be they biological or psychological or sociological in nature. But he is, and always remains, free to take a stand toward these conditions; he always retains the freedom to choose his attitude towards them. Man is free to rise above the plane of somatic and psychic determinants of his existence. By the same token a new dimension is opened. Man enters the dimension of the noetic, in counterdistinction to the somatic and psychic phenomena. He becomes capable of taking a stand not only

[2] Cf. Viktor E. Frankl, '*Zur geistigen Problematik der Psychotherapie*', *Zentralblatt für Psychotherapie*, 10, 33, (1938). [Original footnote]
Viktor E. Frankl, '*Philosophie und Psychotherapie. Zur Grundlegung einer Existenzanalyse*', *Schweizerische medizinische Wochenschrift*, 69, 707 (1939a). [Original footnote]
[3] … (The English version is *The Doctor and the Soul: From Psychotherapy to Logotherapy* New York; Alfred A. Knopf, inc., 1965; London: Souvenir Press, 1969). [Original footnote]

toward the world but also toward himself. Man is a being capable of reflecting on, and even rejecting, himself. He can be his own judge, the judge of his own deeds. In short, the specifically human phenomena linked with one another, self-consciousness and conscience would not be understandable unless we interpret man in terms of a being capable of detaching himself from himself, leaving the 'plane' of the biological and psychological, passing into the 'space' of the noölogical." (Frankl 1985c, pp. 18f)

"Rising spiritually above one's own psychophysical condition might also be called the existential act. By this very act man opens and enters the noölogical dimension of being; nay, he even creates this dimension as a dimension of its own." (Frankl 1985c, p. 136)

Will to Meaning

"the fundamental fact which lends itself to a phenomenological analysis – namely, that man is a being encountering other beings and reaching out for meaning to fulfil.

And this is precisely the reason why I speak of a will to meaning rather than a need for meaning or a drive to meaning. If man were really driven to meaning he would embark on meaning fulfilment solely for the sake of getting rid of this drive, in order to restore homeostasis within himself. At the same time, however, he would no longer be really concerned with meaning itself but rather with his own equilibrium and thus, in the final analysis, with himself. [...]

In fact, it is my conviction that man should not, indeed cannot, struggle for identity in a direct way; he rather finds identity to the extent to which he commits himself to something beyond himself, to a cause greater than himself. No one has put it as cogently as Karl Jaspers did when he said: 'What man is, he ultimately becomes through the cause which he has made his own.'" (Frankl 1985c, pp. 8f)

"[M]eaning must not coincide with being; meaning must be ahead of being. Meaning sets the pace for being. Existence falters unless it is lived in terms of transcendence toward something beyond itself. [...]

Once meaning orientation turns into meaning confrontation, that stage of maturation and development is reached in which freedom—that concept so much emphasized by existentialist philosophy—becomes responsibleness." (Frankl 1985c, p. 12)

Meaning of Life and Meaning in Life

"Let me clarify from the start that meaning as well as its perception, as seen from the logotherapeutic perspective, is something completely down to earth rather than anything floating in the air or residing in an ivory tower." (Frankl 1985b, p. 260)

"A phenomenological analysis reveals that there are three main avenues on which one arrives at meaning in life. The first is finding it by creating a work or by doing a deed. [...] A second avenue to meaning in life is available in experiencing something or encountering someone; in other words, meaning can be found not only in work but also in love. [...] Most important, however, is a third avenue to meaning in life: It finally turns out that even the helpless victim of a hopeless situation, facing a fate he cannot change, may rise above himself, may grow beyond himself, and by so doing change himself. [...] If you really cannot change a situation that causes your suffering, what you still can choose is your attitude." (Frankl 1985b, pp. 271ff)

"However, even apart from this, man is not spared facing his human condition which includes what I call the tragic triad of human existence; namely, pain, death, and guilt. By pain, I mean suffering; by the two other constituents of the tragic triad, I mean the twofold fact of man's mortality and fallibility.

Stressing these tragic aspects of man's life is not as superfluous as it may seem to be at first sight. [...] As a matter of fact, it is my contention, and a tenet of logotherapy, that life's transitoriness does not in the least detract from its meaningfulness. The same holds for man's fallibility. So there is no need to reinforce our patient's escapism in the face of the tragic triad of existence." (Frankl 1985c, p. 15)

"A person's will to meaning can only be elicited if meaning itself can be elucidated as something which is essentially more than his mere self-expression. This implies a certain degree of objectiveness, and without a minimum amount of objectiveness meaning would never be worth fulfilling. We do not just attach and attribute meaning to things, but rather find them; we do not invent them, we detect them." (Frankl 1985c, p. 16)

Frankl's Dimensional Anthropology and Ontology

"How is it possible to preserve the humanness of man in the face of reductionism?" (Frankl 1970, p. 21)

"Conceiving of man in terms of bodily, mental, and spiritual strata or layers [like Hartmann and Scheler] means dealing with him as if his somatic, psychic, and noetic modes of being could be separated from each other.

I myself have tried simultaneously to do justice to the ontological differences and the anthropological unity by what I have called dimensional anthropology and ontology. This approach makes use of the geometrical concept of dimensions as an analogy for qualitative differences which do not destroy the unity of a structure.

Dimensional ontology as I have propounded it, rests on two laws. The first law of dimensional ontology reads: One and the same phenomenon projected out of its own dimension into different dimensions lower than its own is depicted in such a way that the individual pictures contradict one another.

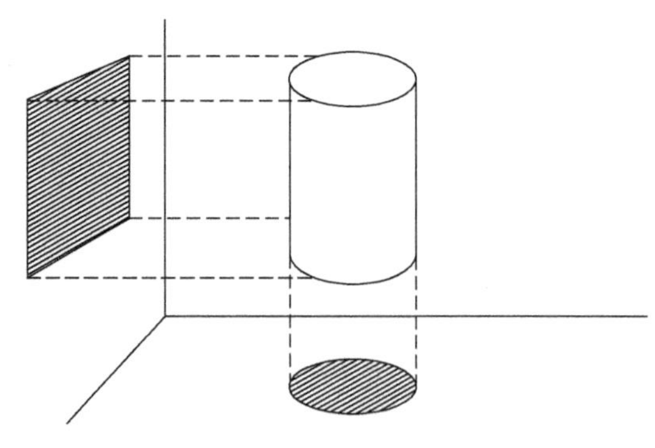

Figure 23.1 First law of dimensional ontology: Inconsistency (Source: Frankl 1970, p. 23).

[…] Now let us proceed to the second law of dimensional ontology which reads: Different phenomena projected out of their own dimension into one dimension lower than their own are depicted in such a manner that the pictures are ambiguous.

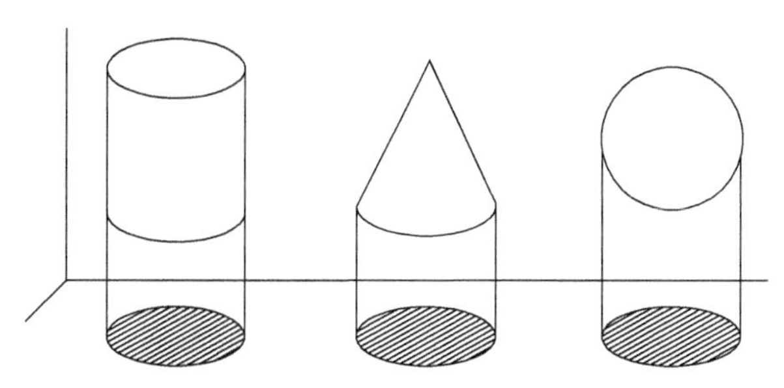

Figure 23.2 Second law of dimensional ontology: Isomorphism (Source: Frankl 1970, p. 24).

Imagine a cylinder, a cone, and a sphere. The shadows they cast upon the horizontal plane depict them as three circles which are interchangeable. We cannot infer from a shadow what casts it, what is above it, whether a cylinder, a cone, or a sphere.

According to the first law of dimensional ontology, the projection of a phenomenon into different lower dimensions results in inconsistencies, and according to the second law of dimensional ontology, the projection of different phenomena into a lower dimension results in isomorphism.

Now how should we apply these images to anthropology and ontology? Once we have projected man into the biological and psychological dimensions we also obtain contradictory results. For in the one case a biological organism is the result; in the other one, a psychological mechanism. But, however the bodily and mental aspects of human existence might contradict one another, seen in the light of dimensional anthropology this contradiction no longer contradicts the oneness of man. Or does the contradiction between a circle and a rectangle contradict the fact that both result from a projection of the same cylinder?

Dimensional ontology is far from solving the mind-body problem. But it does explain why the mind-body problem cannot be solved. Of necessity the unity of man – a unity in spite of the multiplicity of body and mind – cannot be found in the biological or psychological but must be sought in that noological dimension out of which man is projected in the first place."(Frankl 1970, pp. 22 ff)

Self-Distancing

"Man lives in three dimensions: the somatic, the mental, and the spiritual. The spiritual dimension cannot be ignored, for it is what makes us human." (Frankl 1986, p. XVI).

"Taking a stand towards somatic and psychic phenomena implies rising above their level and opening a new dimension, the dimension of noetic phenomena, or the noological dimension – in contradistinction to the biological and psychological ones. It is that dimension in which the uniquely human phenomena are located." (Frankl 1970, p. 17)

"By virtue of this capacity man is capable of detaching himself not only from a situation but also from himself. He is capable of choosing his attitude toward himself. By so doing he really takes a stand toward his own somatic and psychic conditions and determinants." (Frankl 1970, p. 17)

"And it is this very capacity which is mobilized in the logotherapeutic technique of *paradoxical intention* (Frankl 1939b, 1947)." (Frankl 1985b, p. 63)

Viktor Frankl and the Concentration Camp (Self-transcendence)

"I still have nightmares about life in the concentration camps [...] I did not emigrate, and so I ended up at Auschwitz. It was the *experimentum crucis*. The two basic human capacities, self-transcendence and self-distancing, were verified and validated in the concentration camps.

This experiential evidence confirms the survival value of 'the will to meaning' and of self-transcendence – the reaching out beyond ourselves for something other than ourselves. Under the same conditions, those who were oriented toward the future, toward a meaning that waited to be fulfilled – these persons were more likely to survive." (Frankl 1997, p. 97)

"I am convinced that I owe my survival, among other things, to my resolve to reconstruct that lost manuscript. (Frankl 1997, 98) [... The] first draft of *Ärztliche Seelsorge* [*The Doctor and the Soul*] [...] was sewn into the lining of my overcoat, hidden there. [...] upon my arrival at Auschwitz [...] I had to throw everything on the ground [...]." (Frankl 1997, p. 91)

"Any attempt to restore a man's inner strength in the camp had first to succeed in showing him some future goal. Nietzsche's words, 'He who has a why to live for can bear with almost any how', could be the guiding motto for all psychotherapeutic and psycho-hygienic efforts regarding prisoners." (Frankl 1985a, p. 97)

"Man can preserve a vestige of spiritual freedom, of independence of mind, even in such terrible conditions of psychic and physical stress. [...] They may have been few in number, but they offer sufficient proof that everything can be taken from a man but one thing: the last of the human freedoms – to choose one's attitude in any given set of circumstances, to choose one's own way. (...) It is this spiritual freedom – which cannot be taken away – that makes life meaningful and purposeful." (Frankl 1985a, 86f)

Existential Vacuum – Frankl's Diagnosis of the Zeitgeist

"Ever more patients complain of a feeling of emptiness and meaninglessness, which seems to me to derive from two facts. Unlike an animal, man is not told by instincts what he must do. And unlike man in former times, he is no longer told by traditions what he should do. Often he does not even know what he basically wishes to do. Instead, either he wishes to do what other people do (conformism), or he does what other people wish him to do (totalitarianism)." (Frankl 1970, p. ix)

"Struggling for a meaning of life, or wrestling with the question of whether there is a meaning to life, it is not in itself a pathological phenomenon. [...] Above all, it (existential vacuum) is a manifestation of intellectual sincerity and honesty." (Frankl 1970, p. 91)

Frankl's Logotherapeutic Techniques: Paradoxical Intention and Dereflection

"(T)he full-fledged neurosis is caused not only by the primary conditions but also by secondary conditioning. This reinforcement, in turn, is caused by the feedback mechanism called anticipatory anxiety. Therefore, if we wish to recondition a conditioned reflex, we must unhinge the vicious cycle formed by anticipatory anxiety, and this is the very job done by our paradoxical intention technique. [...]

There are cases in which the object of the 'fearful expectation' is – fear itself. Our patients spontaneously speak of a 'fear of fear.' Upon closer interrogation it turns out that they are afraid of the consequences of their fear: fainting, coronaries, or strokes. [...] They react to their fear of fear by a 'flight from fear' – what you would call an avoidance pattern of behavior. [...] In paradoxical intention, the pathogenic fear is replaced by a paradoxical wish. The vicious circle of anticipatory anxiety is unhinged." (Frankl 1985b, pp. 263ff)

"A sound sense of humor is inherent in this technique. This is understandable since we know that humor is a paramount way of putting distance between something and oneself. One might say as well, that humor helps man rise above his own predicament by allowing him to look at himself in a more detached way. So, humor would also have to be located in the noetic dimension." (Frankl 1985c, p. 4)

"In addition to the fact that excessive *attention* proves to be an intrinsically pathogenic factor with regard to the etiology of neurosis, we observe that in many neurotic patients excessive *intention* may also be pathogenic." (Frankl 1985c, p. 145)

"In logotherapy hyperreflection is counteracted by dereflection." (Frankl 1970, p. 100)

"It is a tenet of logotherapy that the more one aims at pleasure the more he misses it. [...] Instead of observing and watching himself [the patient], he should forget himself. [...] In order to counteract the patient's hyper reflection – another logotherapeutic technique has been developed: 'de-reflection'." (Frankl 1978, pp. 151f)

Existential Analysis in Development

A. Längle connected the central position of phenomenology for the development of modern EA with the central attitude of Logotherapy:

"Viktor Frankl (1986, 62) gave a general guide for finding meaning. Finding meaning requires an *attitude* towards the world. Frankl wrote:

> '[...] we must perform a kind of Copernican Revolution and give the question of the meaning of life an entirely new twist. To wit:
>
> It is life itself that asks questions of man. [...] it is not up to man to question; rather, he should recognize that he is questioned, questioned by life; he has to respond by being responsible; and he can answer *to* life only by answering *for* his life.'

This attitude is in fact a *phenomenological* attitude, an openness of the mind free from personal interest, an attitude directed towards the essence of the situation, an attitude that allows one to be reached or even captured by the situation.

[...]

From a more *psychological* point of view, Existential Analysis describes the key for a fulfilling existence in finding a way of living with *inner consent*. [...] This activity consists of a *two-sided dialogue*: one is directed towards the *outside* [...] [See Figure 23.3]

The other dialogue runs *inwardly*. Whatever I decide to do – I cannot leave myself aside to experience meaning. We therefore always live with the question of whether we *agree* with our decisions. To put it more concretely, this inner agreement is a process of contacting the deepest feelings that arise in any situation. [...] *Inner consent* enables us to stand on our own, stand as a unique individual and realize ourselves by meeting the demands of the situation. Meaning, in our definition, creates a harmony between inner experience and outer action." (Längle 2003, p. 16)

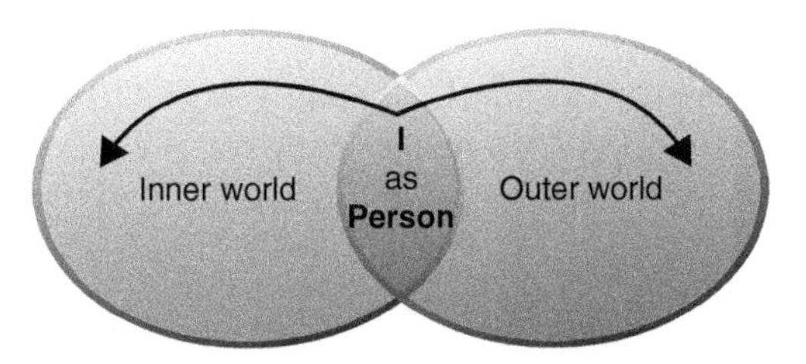

Figure 23.3 The human being as a person is in a continuous inner and outer exchange and dialogue (Längle 2016, p. 58).

Modern Existential Analysis by Alfried Längle

Existential Paradigm

As children of our time, faced with its specific problems, we have to adapt our theories to the needs and sufferings of today. We have, therefore, further elaborated the motivational concept in Existential Analysis into an approach that is by no means less humanistic or less personal, though it follows a different paradigm. As a complement to the individualistic concept of freedom and personal will, which laid ground to the development of this post-modern era, we now need as a counterweight to the shadow of freedom an *interpersonal paradigm*.

This is the line we have adopted in modern Existential Analysis. We have enlarged our motivational concept by basing it on the probably most original activity of personhood: on our being essentially dialogical, prone to and directed towards exchange with others. Being oneself, finding oneself, needs the field of tension of the 'inter-,' the 'between,' the 'aida' as the Japanese say (Kimura 1982; 1995, pp. 103ff.). [...]

Existential Concept of Motivation

From an existential point of view, *dialogue* (or 'communication' as Jaspers says) is an essential constituent in human psychology and in the understanding of the essence of human existence. If we take the capacity for dialogue as a *characteristic* of being a person (i.e., a being with mind and spirit and a potential for decision-making), then humans are always waiting for their completion by a 'partner' in the broadest sense. As dialogical beings, humans expect and look for something or someone 'speaking' to them, calling them, needing them, talking to them, looking for them, challenging them. One gets the necessary *provocation* through everything one is confronted with, one has in front of oneself, one is dealing with. At exactly that moment, the object before us starts 'speaking' to us. Being provoked means being called. This provocation is the *starting point of any motivation.*

In other words: seen from an existential point of view, *motivation means involvement of the person*, initiating the personal processes by provocation in some kind of vis-à-vis. Of course the best vis-à-vis is a partner interacting with us. This processual capacity of the person is described in the theory of 'Personal Existential Analysis (PEA)' (Längle 1994b) and made applicable by its methodological formulation. This method is an application of this dialogical concept of the human being with the goal of engaging personal potentials in a process of dealing with information, thus giving rise to encounter.

The PEA-model is fundamental for any kind of involvement of the person. As such it helps to distinguish *three steps* within the motivational process:

1 *Recognizing* something in its worth or value, insofar as it speaks to us. This is often a challenge demanding action on our part. To see what a situation provokes in us means to recognize the situational meaning involved.
2 *Harmonizing*. Bringing the perceived value, challenge or meaning into accordance with one's inner reality, i.e., examining the consistency with the rest of our values, with attitudes, abilities and capabilities and with our conscience.
3 The final step in the development of motivation is the *inner consent* to one's own *active* involvement. This consent and the act of harmonizing the new value with inner (already existing personal) reality leads to the presence of the inner person in one's actions. It brings up the integration of the new value and the person himself into a *wider context* (meaning).

Without this involvement of the person in the motivational process, human beings would not be dealing with a question of motivation. Instead, there would be a sort of reflex or reaction, but no 'action.' Any act, any deed, is defined as a *decided* act and is therefore *voluntary* and free—which is to say 'personal.'

If we take motivation as a *free* decision to act, then we must also take into consideration the concept of *will*. Frankl (1970, pp. 37–44; 1987, pp. 101–104) saw meaning as the moving part in free will. An existential view of will takes it as the anthropological axis of existence. A *processual description* of will, however, relies on the fundamentals of existence and therefore shows more than just meaning as being basic for constituting will. Free and realistic will is based on three more elements:

1 on the real ability and *capacity* of the subject;
2 on the *emotional* perception of the situational *value*;
3 on the inner *permission* for that act, emerging from an agreement with one's concepts of life and morality.

Before we go into this, let us conclude this part of the exposition dealing with the structure of motivation by adding a reflection on the initial problem of the two basic concepts of motivation. Do people need to be motivated from *outside*, or can the motivation only be shaped, canalized, because people are *intrinsically* motivated? Our theory is that this existential concept results in forming a *bridge between two opposite positions*:

a It is the *interrelation* with the vis-à-vis from which motivation emerges. Being touched and provoked, as well as understanding the situation, is like *being called* on by something or someone. This appeal activates the constitutional 'being-in-the-world' because of a recognition or understanding of what this particular situation is about. This equals the recognition of the situational or existential meaning. Furthermore, this means that we *receive an impulse* from the recognition of the essential message from our vis-à-vis (outer world, but also body, feeling, thoughts).
b By our *understanding* of the context and by our inner agreement, the motivation gets its shape and receives its content.

Seen in that light, the notion of 'being-in-the-world' provides the grounds on which the personal forces are activated. This happens by a perceptive encounter with some form of otherness or with oneself.

Let us now have a closer look at the four fundamental motivations for a fulfilled existence.

The Four Fundamental Conditions for a Fulfilling Existence

For the aspect of freedom in motivation—seeing it as moving a person towards a *free* act within the world—the structure of will has to be taken into account. Will is fundamentally related to the structure of existence, which in turn is shaping the motivation substantially. This—the provocation into dialogue and the relation to the fundamental structure of existence—is the *central hypothesis* of this paper.

If we look more closely, we see that this concept of motivation implies a dialogical *confrontation* with the given facts of our existence. All preconditions of existence can be summarized in four fundamental structures, the 'cornerstones of existence':

- the *world* in its factuality and potentiality
- *life* with its network of relationships and its feelings
- *being oneself* as a unique, autonomous *person*
- the *wider context* where to place oneself = *development* through one's activities, opening one's *future*

Existence in our understanding needs a continuous *confrontation* and a dialogical *exchange* with each of these four dimensions. It is on this basis that the subject forms his specific notions about reality. These four realities challenge the person to give his response, they ask for his inner consent, activate his inner freedom. But they are not only challenging dimensions—they are also structures that, at the same time, allow to entrust oneself to each of these given realities. Their facticity is the fundament of what we call existence. As such, they fundamentally move our existence and can be called 'fundamental existential motivations' (Längle 1992a; 1992b; 1994a; 1997a; 1997b; 1999)." (Längle 2011, pp. 32ff)

References

Frankl, V. (1938). Zur geistigen Problematik der Psychotherapie. *Zentralblatt für Psychotherapie 10*: 33–45.

Frankl, V. (1939a). Philosophie und Psychotherapie. Zur Grundlegung einer Existenzanalyse. *Schweizerische medizinische Wochenschrift 69*: 707–709.

Frankl, V. (1939b). Zur medikamentösen Unterstützung der Psychotherapie bei Neurosen. *Schweizer Archiv für Neurologie und Psychiatrie 43*: 26–31.

Frankl, V. (1946). *Ärztliche Seelsorge*. Vienna: Deuticke.

Frankl, V. (1947). *Die Psychotherapie in der Praxis*. Vienna: Deuticke.

Frankl, V. (1970). *The Will to Meaning. Foundations and Applications of Logotherapy*. New York: New American Library.

Frankl, V. (1978). *The Unheard Cry for Meaning. Psychotherapy and Humanism*. New York: Touchstone.

Frankl, V. (1985a). *Man's Search for Meaning*. New York: Washington Square Press. (Original work published 1946.)

Frankl, V. (1985b). Logos, paradox, and the search for meaning. In: *Cognition and Psychotherapy* (ed. M.J. Mahoney and A. Freeman), 259–275. New York: Plenum.

Frankl, V. (1985c). *Psychotherapy and Existentialism. Selected Papers on Logotherapy*. New York: Washington Square Press. (Original work published 1967.)

Frankl, V. (1986). *The Doctor and the Soul: From Psychotherapy to Logotherapy*. New York: Random House. (Original work published 1965.)

Frankl, V. (1987). *Theorie und Therapie der Neurosen*. Munich: Reinhardt.

Frankl, V. (1997). *Recollections – An Autobiography*. Cambridge: Basic Books.

Frankl, V. (2000). *Man's Search for Ultimate Meaning*. New York: Perseus.

Kimura B. (1982). The phenomenology of the between: On the problem of the basic disturbance in schizophrenia. In: *Phenomenology and Psychiatry* (ed. A.J.J. de Koning and F.A. Jenner), 173–185. London: Academic Press.

Kimura B. (1995). *Zwischen Mensch und Mensch. Strukturen japanischer Subjektivität*. Darmstadt: Wissenschaftliche Buchgemeinschaft.

Längle, A. (1992a). Was bewegt den Menschen? Die existentielle Motivation der Person. Vortrag bei Jahrestagung der GLE in Zug/Schweiz. Published (1999) in *Existenzanalyse 16* (3): 18–29.

Längle, A. (1992b). Ist Kultur machbar? Die Bedürfnisse des heutigen Menschen und die Erwachsenenbildung. In: *Kongreßband "Kulturträger im Dorf,"* 65–73. Bozen: Auton. Provinz, Assessorat für Unterricht und Kultur.

Längle, A. (1994a). Lebenskultur-Kulturerleben. Die Kunst, Bewegendem zu begegnen. *Bulletin der GLE 11* (1): 3–8.

Längle, A. (1994b). Personal existential analysis. In: *Psychotherapy East and West. Integration of Psychotherapies* (ed. International Congress of Psychotherapy), 348–364, Seoul: Korean Academy of Psychotherapists.

Längle, A. (1997a). Das Ja zum Leben finden. Existenzanalyse und Logotherapie in der Suchtkrankenhilfe. In: *Süchtig sein. Entstehung, Formen und Behandlung von Abhängigkeiten* (ed. A Längle and C. Probst), 13–33. Vienna: Facultas.

Längle, A. (1997b). Modell einer existenzanalytischen Gruppentherapie für die Suchtbehandlung. In: *Süchtig sein. Entstehung, Formen und Behandlung von Abhängigkeiten* (ed. A Längle and C. Probst), 149–169. Vienna: Facultas.

Längle, A. (1999). Was bewegt den Menschen? Die existentielle Motivation der Person. *Existenzanalyse 16* (3): 18–29.

Längle, A. (2003). The search for meaning in life and the existential fundamental motivations. *Psychotherapy in Australia 10* (1): 22–27.

Längle, A. (2011). The existential fundamental motivations structuring the motivational process. In: *Motivation, Consciousness and Self-Regulation* (ed. D.A. Leontiev), 27–42. Hauppauge, New York: Nova.

Längle, A. (2016). *Existenzanalyse. Existentielle Zugänge der Psychotherapie.* Vienna: Facultas.

24

Challenges and New Developments in Logotherapy and Existential Analysis

Janelle Kwee and Alfried Längle

Introduction

After several decades of development and focused training activities, there is an active community of practitioners and researchers using Existential Analysis (EA) and Logotherapy in many parts of the world. This geographically, culturally, and linguistically diverse community offers wide-ranging opportunities for continual development and application of EA and Logotherapy. In this community, we also experience unique challenges due to our physical distance, language barriers, cultural and professional differences, and – due to these same factors – somewhat limited opportunities for regular dialogue with each other.

This chapter is organized into three primary sections, including (a) practice developments and challenges; (b) developments and challenges in measurement, research and training; and (c) the future horizon of EA and Logotherapy. There are common threads in each of these sections, as they all reflect the real ongoing activities of the global members of the International Society of EA and Logotherapy. We present this chapter with the aim of offering a realistic glimpse into the ways in which we are developing as a society, both emphasizing the accomplishments of GLE colleagues around the world, and the existing challenges we face in working and growing together.

Practice Developments and Challenges

There have been numerous developments and applications of EA and Logotherapy, each of which bring unique opportunities and challenges. In this section, we first review specific developments in Logotherapy and the development of Meaning-Centered Therapy and Counseling (MCCT), which develops out of Logotherapy and

The Wiley World Handbook of Existential Therapy, First Edition. Edited by Emmy van Deurzen, Erik Craig, Alfried Längle, Kirk J. Schneider, Digby Tantam, and Simon du Plock.

incorporates cognitive-behavioral therapy and positive psychotherapy. Then, we elaborate the current developments of EA in multiple areas, including, (a) educational settings; (b) coaching and leadership; (c) group therapy and workshops; (d) online-based practice and training; (e) mindfulness integration; (f) applications with couples and families; (g) child and youth counselling and psychotherapy; (h) understanding and treating eating disorders and psychosomatic disorders; (i) trauma therapy and integration of auxiliary methods; (j) addictions; (k) personality disorders; and (l) the ongoing refinement of phenomenological access in all applications of psychotherapy, which is at the heart of EA practice.

Developments in Logotherapy

While there is continuity in logotherapeutic theory, there have been significant developments in practice methods and interventions for specific clinical problems.[1] For example, there are currently many therapeutic proposals designed to address personality disorders, including Borderline (Rodrigues 2004), Dependent (Martinez 2011; Rogina and Quilitch 2006), Avoidant (Martinez 2011), Narcissistic (Martinez 2011; Rogina 2004), and Histrionic (Frankl 1995; Lukas 2004; Martinez 2011). The use of Logotherapy in addictions has been explored by Crumbaugh (1980), Henrion (2002), Hutzell (1984), Martinez and Florez (2016), Oscariz (2000), Schippan (1997), and Wurm (1997, 2003). Logotherapy has also been applied to eating disorders (Lukas 2004), intellectual disabilities or mental retardation (Hinsburger 1989, 1990; Schulenberg 2000), sleep disorders (Lukas 2004; Frankl 1995), sexual dysfunctions (Lukas 2004; Frankl 1995), disabilities (Lukas 1998), palliative care (Saunders, cited in Clark 2016) psycho-oncology (Mori 2009), crisis intervention (Lukas 1995), grief (Lukas 2002; Berti and Schneider 1993, 1996, 2003), and trauma (Long 1997). Finally, there are ample applications of Logotherapy for a wide spectrum of clinical syndromes. These include mood disorders such as Major Depressive Disorders (Ungar 2002), other depressive disorders (Lukas 1998, 2001, 2004; Frankl 1992, 1995) and other affect disorders (Henrion 2004). Logotherapy has also been applied to various anxiety disorders (Frankl 1992, 1995), including Generalized Anxiety Disorder (Rogina 2002). Perhaps most specific to Logotherapy is its application to so-called "Existential Crisis" or Noogenic Neurosis, as the term was coined by Frankl (see Pacciolla 2007 and Lukas 2001).

There have also been methodological developments in Logotherapy, moving it past the classical individual methods that reigned in the past. These include development in realms such as couple's therapy (Schulenberg and Melton 2010), working with divorce (Böschemeyer 1997; Fasja 2001), family therapy (Lukas 1992, 2004, 2009; Lantz 1993; Winters 2002), and group-based Logotherapy (Lukas 2006; Martinez 2003; Leon 2001; Fabry 2001; Berti and Schneider 2003). Specialized clinical practices have also emerged to address the unique development needs of people across the lifespan. More specifically, these include, third-age populations (Guttmann 2008; Lukas and García 2002), and adolescents (Almario 2016). While not specifically a form of Logotherapy, William Breitbart's work has been significantly shaped by Frankl and is introduced in Chapters 26 and 27 of this book.

[1] We are grateful to Efrén Martinez for the following compilation.

Meaning-Centered Counseling and Therapy[2]

Another practical development emerging out of Logotherapy is Meaning Therapy (Wong 2010, 2016), also known as meaning-centered counseling and therapy (MCCT). It is based on Frankl's Logotherapy, but extended to integrate with cognitive-behavioral therapy and positive psychotherapy. Thus, it is a pluralistic approach to counseling and therapy that focuses on the fundamental human needs for meaning and relationship, representing a comprehensive way to address meaning-in-life concerns in a supportive therapeutic relationship (Vos et al. 2017).

The motto for meaning therapy is, "Meaning is all we have; relationship is all we need." Meaning therapy assumes that when these two essential human needs are met, individuals are more likely to cope better and to live a more rewarding life. Meaning therapy favors a psycho-educational approach that recognizes the vital role of meaning and purpose in healing, recovery, and well-being (Wong 2012a). It appeals to the client's sense of responsibility to make use of their freedom to pursue a rewarding future. Within this framework, the therapist provides a safe and trusting environment that facilitates collaborative effort. Both assessment and intervention in meaning therapy make full use of empirically validated instruments and findings (Wong 1998, 2015). Recently, mainstream psychotherapy has begun to pay attention to meaning therapy because of its emphasis on meaning-in-life research (DeAngelis 2018; Hill 2018) and existential positive psychology (Wong 2009). The main existential positive interventions (Wong 2016) consist of the PURE[3] and ABCDE[4] strategies.

Another important aspect of meaning therapy is that it practices the dual-system model (Wong 2012b), which takes a dialectic approach to resolving the predicaments of life and creating a more fulfilling future. This approach involves striving to achieve a dynamic positive balance between approach and avoidance systems, and integrating PURE and ABCDE in adaptive ways, depending on the client and the context. Other existential positive interventions from MCCT include: (1) re-orienting from egotistic concern towards an other-oriented larger context of meaning (self-transcendence); (2) reframing problems as challenges (re-appraisal); (3) meaning-focused coping of discovering the meaning and benefits in suffering (existential coping); (4) letting go

[2] We are grateful to Paul Wong for contributing the text for this section on MCCT

[3] PURE is an acronym for (1) Purpose (motivational dimension) – values, life direction, intentions, needs, wants, desires; (2) Understanding (cognitive dimension) – self-knowledge, coherence, comprehension, sense-making; (3) Responsibility (behavioral dimension) – self-determination, commitment, action, doing the right thing, and making self-sacrifices for a worthy goal and (4) Enjoyment (emotional dimension) – satisfaction, sense of significance and fulfillment. Within this framework, a therapist can encourage clients to examine their end values and separate the wheat from the tares; challenge them to stare into the abyss and confront their dark side and vulnerabilities; and work with them to develop worthy goals and action plans (contributed by Paul Wong).

[4] The ABCDE framework focuses on (1) Accept and confront the harsh reality – the reality principle; (2) Believe that life is worth living and they can overcome whatever that troubles them – the faith principle; (3) Commit to achieving the goal through responsible actions, persistence, and flexibility – the action principle; (4) Discover new insights or deeper meaning and significance of the self and situations – the aha! principle; and (5) Enjoy and evaluate both the process and incremental progress through fine tuning and making needed adjustments – the self-regulation principle (contributed by Paul Wong).

and transcending what cannot be changed (existential coping); (5) expressing existential gratitude for life despite sufferings, and (6) re-authoring one's life into a hero's journey and a meta-narrative.

Existential Analysis in Educational Settings

Breckner, Kolbe, and Waibel (Waibel 2012, 2017a, 2017b) have led the exploration of existential anthropology and authenticity in pedagogy and education. Kolbe (2010, 2016) additionally offers training in teaching, leading, and moderating authentically for teachers. Frankl viewed education as a context for the training of conscience and values (Frankl 2005). The actual existential pedagogy translates existential questions into educational thinking and action, with a focus on questions of the development of the person, personal activities, personal values, freedom, and motivation (Aregger and Waibel 2006; Waibel 2012, 2017a, 2017b). Similar to the emphasis in psychotherapy practice on the personal development of the therapist, the development of the educator is the basis for the transformative person-to-person encounter in educational settings. As a context for the development of persons through meaningful companionship, and receptivity of the teacher to the persons of students, educational contexts can be seen as a context for primary prevention where development and strengthening of the person occurs, while psychotherapy is tertiary prevention, when there is already significant emotional suffering (Höfig-Renner 2015). In Russia, over the past 15 years, Dr. Svetlana Krivtsova, in collaboration with Moscow State University, has led a group of existential psychologists and psychotherapists in developing the project "Life Skills" in schools, which is primarily based in the phenomenological method of EA (Krivtsova 2005, 2013, 2015, 2016a). This covers existential themes in school group sessions for children from ages 5 to 15, including dialogue about "likes" and "dislikes," anger, grief, friendship, fear, property, boundaries, and otherness. Teachers or facilitators conduct lessons through games, exercises, and dialogue. Hundreds of schools in Russia and the Russian-speaking world (Odessa, Ukraine, Crimea, Kazakhstan, Israel, and the Baltic states) use the guidance book. A preschool version of Life Skills (Krivtsova 2016b) was also developed based on the developmental stages of children's games, as informed by the structural model of the four fundamental motivations.

Currently, in Mexico, under the direction of the Secretariat of Public Education in Special Education (Martha Alicia Cortés), EA is being applied to educational settings where the focus is on the holistic development of the child as a bio-psycho-social-spiritual being. Also, in Mexico, a program supported by education's private sector has offered training to secondary and high school teachers to develop tutoring and leadership skills for youth in poverty and situations of abuse. This work aims to ensure that teachers help students to be promotors of social change in the marginalized areas from which they come. The design and implementation of these trainings has been led by Silvia Gómez. So far, more than 800 people have received this training. A specific task group within the "Gesellschaft für Logotherapie und Existenzanalyse" (GLE) is also currently exploring opportunities to apply EA within educational settings.

Existential Analysis in Coaching and Leadership

EA has been adapted to the field of coaching and leadership. This work is represented in two books (Längle and Bürgi 2014; Johner, Bürgi, and Längle 2018), and explores change with fundamental consideration of leadership and developmental processes. This practical application of EA to coaching and leadership addresses individual, team, and organizational-level transformation and development. In addition, training applying EA to coaching and leadership has been developed by Kolbe, Krivtsova, Längle, and others. For example, a multi-module training for executives, designed and led by Cristoph Kolbe based on an existential analytic framework, has been offered over 20 times, and training offered by A. Längle have taken place continuously for 17 years.

Existential Analysis in Group Therapy and Workshops

Workshops introducing the main concepts of EA are regularly offered as ways of supporting participants in personal development and in confronting social and existential problems. These workshops are centered on the theme of Authentic Living (in Canada) and topics related to the four Fundamental Motivations (in Mexico). These workshops serve as gateways to extended training in EA, as well as "stand alone" opportunities to disseminate relevant concepts in EA. Similarly, group therapy with therapists in Mexico (carried out by Ma. Elena Ramírez and Beatriz Ávila) has provided an extended opportunity for "group self-experience" for therapists to reflect on and address personal situations from the four FMs. Similar groups also take place in Russia, Germany, and Austria. Also in Mexico, Cecilia Martinez has applied EA as a tool to provide both group and individual psychotherapy to people with motor disabilities. This program provides support to people with low economic resources who suffer with disabilities due to spinal cord injuries, amputations, or degenerative diseases, to grieve for lost value, to find themselves again, to be questioned by the world, and to discover new horizons of meaning.

Online-Based Practice and Training in Existential Analysis

Improving the accessibility of EA for the demands of the twenty-first century, Ryazanova (2014) has forged the application of EA in counselling and psychotherapy in online-based practice, through Skype and written correspondence ("scribotherapy"). Ryazanova describes limitations and contra-indications for distance counseling and therapy. These include high fear and anxiety, blocked motivation, difficulties with verbalization, the presence of over-demanding life situations, and mental and personality disorders. The "virtual twin" in cyberspace refers to the idea that the person in virtual space may be very different than the same person in real life and needs to be considered in online work. Remote therapy offers a sense of safety from the distance it provides, but also provides less intense contact. To be able to translate competence in counseling and psychotherapy provision to conducting distance counseling and therapy through online platforms requires specialized training. This training should address things such as selection criteria for distance-based clients and developing the unique therapeutic frame for online-based counseling. EA, as a dialogical therapy and counseling method, has proven to be suitable for online therapy as well as for online seminars. An exciting development was the launch of a Russian online training in EA in 2018, which has brought together participants from Saloniki (Greece), Sochi, Haborovsk, Rostov, Minsk, Novosibirsk, Saint Petersburg, and Moscow. Online training experiences in EA represent an opportunity for further development and a current challenge given the popular demand for web-based continuing education and professional development opportunities.

Mindfulness Integration with Existential Analysis

Mindfulness concepts have been integrated into the training curriculum in Logotherapy and EA in Mexico. Mindfulness practice has been used to facilitate the therapist's personal contact with him or herself as an approach to self-awareness and personal analysis. Angermayr (2014) offers such workshops in Austria integrating the body. In addition, Roberto Arístegui (2017) in Chile has offered an integrated perspective of Mindfulness and EA, supporting convergence from a meta-theoretical level in psychotherapy. Arístegui identifies points of agreement within a phenomenological hermeneutic vision, specifically applied to the treatment of anxiety.

Applications of Existential Analysis with Couples and Families

Existential-Analytical Couple Therapy has been a specific topic of an international congress (see the many developments in *Existenzanalyse* 2008, 25 [2]). It maintains a focus on enabling the couple to reach an authentic and appreciative encounter (Pointner 2016). This occurs when all parties engage a phenomenological attitude within a structured framework. The activity of the therapist is primarily to ensure the fundamental existential motivations: safe space, emotional involvement, clear personal positioning, and reliable steps of action within a frame of meaning. The partners are primarily strengthened in their capacity for self-caring. They further learn how to understand themselves and their partners' patterns that lurk under everyday conflicts. This understanding includes psychodynamic deficits and protective patterns, as well as personal values and intentions. Further psycho-educational elements or specific methods of EA are also applied if needed (Pointner and Sattler 2014).

The underlying method in Pointner's (2016) couple's therapy is Personal Existential Analysis (PEA) (Längle 2000; see also Kwee and Längle 2013). Partners take turns in the roles of speaker and active listener, guided by the PEA steps. This procedure prevents the development of a hurtful or superficial dynamic between the couple, which is more likely to occur when there is lack of structure in the therapeutic process. A fresh breath of air often enters the relationship when the partners reach a clear view on common meanings and a joined course of development comes into focus. The couple is stimulated to deal with their old patterns in a relationship, leading to a renewal of loving togetherness and shared meanings as a "connecting ribbon" of the relationship, or to a dignified rather than acrimonious separation.

Launeanu, Klaassen, and Kwee (2018) address clinical and theoretical challenges of meaning and meaninglessness in working with bereaved couples and families from an existential-analytical perspective (Längle 1994, 2005). Specifically, the Method of

Life Horizon (Längle work in preparation) illustrates an applied process, which is described as part of accompaniment of bereaved families. In addition, Kwee and McBride (2017) illustrate applications of the four fundamental motivations in a self-help marriage resource, in order to more widely disseminate existential-analytical concepts relevant to couples and families.

Child and Youth Practice in Existential Analysis

What distinguishes existential-analytic therapy with children and adolescents (Biberich et al. 2015) is the use of a phenomenological attitude in order to immerse oneself in the subjective world of the child or young person. Rather than teaching rules or norms to the child, the therapist's stance is focused on maintaining openness to what comes from the child in the child's communication through gestures, body language, language, and play. The aim of existential-analytic therapy with children and youth is to "see" the person in the child, to reach and touch it with the aim of bringing it into life and to strengthen the personal capacities and ego-development of the child. This takes the shape of a sort of pilgrimage with the child on his or her life journey, an enlightened form of caring; rather than imposing something foreign, the therapist accompanies the child or young person in becoming him or herself (Köberl 2015, 68–69).

EA with children and youth makes use of creative methods that allows the young person to freely access the emotional and mental aspects of their own personhood, according to the first step of PEA (Längle 1993). Drawing, painting, role playing, story reading, use of sand tray, and storytelling, are all used to create distance within the child from their primary emotions and spontaneous impulses, helping children and youth to ground themselves in themselves and in that which most matters to them in their world. Several psychologists who are also artists engage the themes of the Fundamental Motivations in expressive art with both child and adult clients as expressive therapy methods easily lend themselves to the phenomenological approach (e.g., Görtz 2003; Jones 2011). The phenomenological procedure leads young clients to understand themselves better and to develop stronger options for difficult life situations. The therapist provides guidance in finding alternative ways to cope (Steinbacher 2016, p. 96).

In order to conceptualize the problems and needs of young patients, we refer to the four Fundamental Motivation (FM) (Längle 2002), which make up the structural model of EA. Conceptualized in the framework of the four FMs, the young person's basic needs and resources can quickly and simply be detected in some detail. Since we also try to include parents as much as possible, a conceptualization based on the child's needs and resources in the four FMs is useful for sharing with them in supporting their efforts to provide a caring relationship for the development of the child or adolescent. Dr. Svetlana Krivtsova (2017) has developed a model of periodization of age development of children from birth to 21 years, which provides a theoretical basis for research and practical recommendations for parents, psychotherapists, and teachers. In this model, Krivtsova applies the structural model of EA to the "layer-by-layer" periodization of Prof. D. Stern, and identifies new topics for phenomenological studies of preschool children (for example, the role of spaces in the life of a child, the experiences of meeting people, and the phenomenology of the "discovery" of objects). It also applied the structural model to the developmental crises of specific ages.

Existential Analysis with Eating Disorders and Psychosomatic Disorders

EA provides a practical framework that has recently been applied to conceptualizing, treating, and preventing disordered eating (Kwee and Launeanu 2018; Launeanu and Kwee 2018) with a focus on the embodied nature of persons. Rooted in Frankl's (1969) tridimensional anthropological model of the human being, the body is understood in EA as a fundamental given of the human being and existence. The body, together with the psychological and noetic dimensions, represents a constitutive dimension of the human being, with each dimension integrated in the lived experience of the body. Consistent with both Heidegger's (1962) and Merleau-Ponty's (1945/2012) affirmation of embodiment as an existential given, the struggles with the body for people suffering from eating disorders can readily be understood as existential struggles to exist as a body in the world (Launeanu and Kwee 2018). EA offers a holistic framework for understanding and treating eating disorders (Längle 2012). The theoretical framework of EA elaborates the paradox of *I am a body* and *I have a body*. EA offers a practical framework for applying interventions that promote embodiment, or integration and expression of the unity of the person's mind, body, and spirit. This embodiment-focused approach contrasts starkly with the status quo of cognitive-behavioral approaches to eating disorder treatment (Kwee and Launeanu 2018).

Similarly, existential-analytical work with psychosomatic complaints takes into account the embodied nature of persons and explores the interplay of psyche and body (*Existenzanalyse* [2009, 2] is dedicated to psychosomatics; Angermayr and Strassl 2013; Angermayr 2014). Specialized training in the existential-analytical approach for working with predominately physical symptoms, such as psychosomatic complaints and somatoform disorders, can be acquired in a continuing education curriculum of GLE-International (Bukovski 2014). In practice, dialogue with physical phenomena and diseases through "mindful" awareness and inner images of body landscapes is supported and stimulated for the client. The perceived message of the body is phenomenologically understood and as such integrated into the person's understanding of one's relationship with oneself and with the world (Angermayr 2010). Conscious guidance of breath (Angermayr 2009) and imagery enable the client to experience deeper appreciation of the physical, support one's own positioning of the person, and activate self-healing powers (Bukovski 2009).

Angermayr (2014) further develops the use of existential grounding and phenomenological bodywork relevant to physical symptoms of distress and to trauma therapy. The corporeal is not only a dimension of being but also provides the condition for us to be in relationship with ourselves. Concrete exercises are elaborated to deepen one's self-experience of bodily existence. The inclusion of the body is strengthened in the inherently bodily psychotherapeutic process.

Trauma Therapy Practice and Integration of Auxiliary Methods in Existential Analysis

An understanding of the specific effects of trauma onto the existential structures and its inhibition of the process variables has been developed for a congress (*Existenzanalyse* 2005, 22 [2]; Längle 2007). The application of EA in the field of trauma therapy is supported by an established continuing education curriculum of GLE-International. This continuing education curriculum addresses theory, practice, and supervision. On the backdrop of existential analytic anthropology, methods from Luise Reddemann's psycho-imaginative trauma therapy (PITT)Reddemann 2007), a phenomenological ego-state approach, is integrated (Tutsch and Bukovski 2016).

The cornerstones of the existential approach, particularly important for integrating and processing traumatic experiences include: (a) stabilization and strengthening of the ego; (b) self-distancing as the pivotal point of stabilization; (c) affection and compassion; (d) grief and fury for processing feelings; (e) developing a personal position of the person towards suffering; and (f) consolation. In the past few years, the method of EA has been extended by the introduction of auxiliary methods, such as PITT, based on practical experience and findings from neurobiological research. Examples of these auxiliary methods include work with music, colors, imagination, and body movement. Application of these methods supports the process of EA, particularly where content and feelings are not consciously accessible, as in the case of traumatization (Drexler 2013).

Matuszak-Luss (2015) specifically explores existential analytical aspects of working with resources in trauma therapy. In resource-oriented work, therapists underline the strength of people, counteracting the deficit-oriented point of view of traumatized patients. She references distinct qualities of inner strengths within the framework of the Existential Fundamental Motivations. These include: (a) stimulating the experience of strength and trust; (b) being related to the world and able to enjoy things; (c) being able to experience self-confidence and pride; and (d) experiences of openness and freedom.

Existential Analysis and Addiction Research and Practice

Substance and process addictions are addressed by the existential-analytical theory of will (Längle 2015, 1997b). Phenomenological research in this area looks at the etiology and pathogenesis of dependence and eating disorders (See Längle 2015; Längle and Görtz 2015; Kohler and Rauch 2015; Drexler 2015; *Existenzanalyse* 2015 [2]). Current research describes the phenomenology of process addictions such as workaholicism, computer-gaming dependence, and internet-dependence. These are all being addressed by psychotherapists practicing EA. The dynamics of the Existential Fundamental Motivations as they are specific to different kinds of addictive behaviors and substances is an area where further research is needed. A program of addiction rehabilitation, particularly for patients dependent on psychoactive substances is running in an inpatient department on the basis of EA and is currently being empirically evaluated.

Applying Existential Analysis to Understanding and Working with Personality Disorders

GLE-International has a specific focus on personality disorders, and there have been four congresses organized around this theme (Narcissism in *Existenzanalyse* 2002 [2 & 3]; Trauma and Personality Disorder in *Existenzanalyse* 2005 [2]; Antisocial Personality Disorder in *Existenzanalyse* 2006 [2]; Borderline in *Existenzanalyse* 2017 [2]). Alfried Längle has been working for the past 15 years on developing a phenomenological understanding and specific existential therapeutic approach to personality disorders. Several publications relevant to personality disorder conceptualization and treatment have appeared from members of the GLE (see, for example Fischer-Danzinger 2010; Probst 2002a, 2002b).

Refinement of Phenomenological Access and Psychotherapeutic Methods in Existential Analysis

The refinement and elaboration of *phenomenological access* and psychotherapeutic methods is ongoing work at the heart of EA (Kolbe 2016). This is taking place in every country in which EA is practiced, in supervision, peer consultation, and clinical practice.

For example, the integration of EA with Systemic Structural Constellation (Sparrer 2004) has proven to be valuable in both individual and group practice. The format of the "Systemic Constellation of the Four Fundamental Motivations" (Lhotski and Artaker 2005) places the client within the framework of the four conditions of existence (Längle 2016), namely the world, life, personhood in its uniqueness, and one's personal role in personal fulfillment and impact within one's greater context. The constellation allows the visualization of this inextricable web of relationships in a physical space. In a group, this is displayed with the aid of persons representing the necessary elements of structure. In individual sessions, the structure is displayed by using objects. In the group, clients are asked to represent each of the four conditions of existence and themselves. When they step back and look at their own "system of existence" they often experience the impression that everything is there, that nothing is missing. In the subsequent process, clients engage consciously with the symbolic representations of their existence, seeing what makes it possible to change poor or insufficient conditions into resources. The creative potential of this method supports clients in developing new insights and fosters their sense of responsibility for their own life (Sparrer 2004).

Another therapeutic development, which has taken place over the past ten years, is the integration of Bert Hellinger's family constellation (Hellinger 2010) with EA. In the framework of the person-phenomenological approach of EA, the goal of the constellation is to find *inner consent* in resonance with oneself. The procedure is applied phenomenologically and excludes interpretations. The practice is now described as *Existential-analytical family constellation* (Barannikov 2015). The focus is on the qualities of the experienced relationship, and their problems in the range of the fundamental existential motivations. The constellation itself gives an additional space of freedom, which allows the activity of the person to be mobilized. The process is accompanied by a facilitator who leads the process following the steps of PEA (Längle 1993) or other methods of EA. This practice can be applied individually and in groups.

Developments and Challenges in Measurement, Research, and Training

In this section, we offer a brief overview of developments and challenges in conceptualization, measurement, research, and training in EA and Logotherapy. Similar to the previous section, we begin with a review of measurement and evaluation specific to

Logotherapy. Following this, we review several areas relevant to conceptualization, measurement, research, and training, including: (a) conceptual developments in understanding the development of the person; (b) research and measurement in EA; (c) the application of existential-analytical methods, particularly PEA to research processes; (d) current venues for dissemination of the concepts of EA; and (e) training and supervision in EA and Logotherapy.

Developments of Measurement and Evaluation in Logotherapy

To date, the greatest progress in evaluation and measurement has been made specifically in the logotherapeutic field, where a wide variety of psychometric tests have been developed. The Purpose in Life Test (PIL) (Crumbaugh and Maholick 1969) is the most used and disseminated logotherapeutic test in the world (Reker 2000; Halama 2009). Its purpose is to evaluate *meaning in life* through a quantitative and qualitative structure. The PIL has been validated in multiple countries on several continents (Schulenberg and Melton 2010; Noblejas 2000) and an investigation that aims to establish a short four-item version of the test has been developed (Schulenberg, Schnetzer, and Buchanan 2011). The Life Purpose Questionnaire (LPQ) was designed by Hablas and Hutzell (1982) with the intention of carrying out a friendlier measure of meaning with a simpler administration (Guttmann 1998) than the PIL.

The Existence Scale (Längle, Orgler, and Kundi 2003) documents the noetic dimension of the person (Landaboure 2002, 2017), specifically in the process of reaching a meaningful life, through four steps evaluated in the scale: (1) self-distancing, (2) self-transcendence, (3) freedom, and (4) responsibility (Halama 2009). There are translations and standardizations of the Existence Scale in seven languages, including a recent adaptation and validation study in Argentina (Ángeles-Páramo et al. 2016); a Spanish language manual has also been developed for this scale (Gottfried 2015; Salazar Lozano 2012). The Logotest, developed by Elisabeth Lukas (1986), includes quantitative and qualitative measures with three parts: (1) values that the respondent sees as possible to be accomplished in his or her life; (2) the manifestation of existential frustration for the respondent; and (3) the respondent's self-valuation of life goals and success and attitude towards them (Halama 2009).

The Personal Meaning Index (PMI) (Reker 1992) is a product of the extended revision of the Life Attitude Profile test of Reker and Peacock (Halama 2009). The PMI aims to evaluate personal meaning, understood as having goals in life, a mission, a sense of direction, and a logical and integrated comprehensive of self, others, and life. The PMI has been evaluated for stability across age and gender groups (Reker 2004).

Other valuable logotherapeutic instruments include: (a) the Life Meaningfulness Scale (Halama 2009), which evaluates the cognitive, affective, and motivational components of meaning (Halama 2009); (b) the Meaning in Suffering Test of Patricia Starck, which measures meaning experienced in suffering (Guttmann 1998; Reker 2000); (c) the Noodynamics Test, which measures noetic dimensions of personality (Halama 2009); (d) the SONG Test from Crumbaugh (1977), developed with the intention of evaluating the concept of *will to meaning* (Halama 2009) as a complement to the PIL; and lastly, (e) the Belfast Test (Giorgi 1982), centered on investigating the difficulty of reaching meaning in states of existential frustration or alienation. Melton and Schulenberg (2008) offer an evaluation and recommendations for using many of these tests.

Two scales have been developed in Latin America, including the Noological Resources Scale (Martinez, Díaz del Castillo, and Jaimes 2010; Martinez et al. 2011), and the Vital Meaning Scale (Martinez et al. 2011). The former was created with the intention of evaluating particular manifestations of Noological resources in both clinical and non-clinical populations. Having a particular interest in formulating treatment processes that are adapted to the person's specific necessities, this scale reflects a dimensional model of human existentiality. On the other hand, The Vital Meaning Scale was created with the clinical objective of evaluating the affective and cognitive perception of values that invite a person to act one way or another in the face of a particular situation, or life in general, conferring the person coherence and personal identity. This scale is used as means of developing therapeutic interventions that would increase the client's perception of meaning.

Conceptual Developments in Existential-Analytical Understandings

Barannikov (2010) has elaborated Bowlby's work on attachment and deprivation with EA theory to conceptualize the pattern of spiritual-personal development of the person. Bowlby's work (1951) made clear the profound impact of parent-child separation on the child's development of psyche and body. Modern EA also provides an understanding of personal deprivation. The main phenomenological content of personal deprivation is the absence of personal encounter as persons (Barannikov 2010). This results in the person's loss (or failure to achieve) encounter with one's own personal essence, or the impossibility of "meeting" oneself as a person. The ultimate devastating result of the deprivation of personal encounter in the developmental period is loss of identity. The concept of personal deprivation allows us, conceptually, to define important conditions of development, and highlight challenges in achieving needed personal encounter in the context of modern life.

Research and Measurement in Existential Analysis

There is an established research group at GLE-International that meets regularly and develops outcome investigations focused on the existential treatment of anxiety, depression, and burnout. An inpatient investigation of the treatment of personality disorders and severe addiction is also in progress.

The phenomenon of burnout has been interpreted by Längle (1997a) from an existential-analytic point of view as the symptom of a non-existential attitude adopted by a person towards his or her life and existence. The empirical results confirm this hypothesis and show a significant correlation between burnout and attributes of personality. Researchers focused on problems of physicians, teachers, psychologists, social workers, parents, and business people (Bucher and Rothbucher 1996; Efimova 2012; Ermakova 2008; Linska 2011; Nindl 2001). Results reveal negative correlations between burnout and existential fulfillment and meaning in life. Analysis of existential attitudes and resources are the central topic of prevention of burnout (Längle 1997a; Meier-Kernen and Kernen 2013) with the aim of restoring motivation. Existential motivations (Efimova 2011; Linska 2011) and decision-making process (Efimova 2012, 2015) are considered.

A new Russian-language instrument (Osin 2009; Ukolova, Shumskiy, and Osin 2014, 2016), which measures existential fulfillment, operationalizes the theory of the four existential FMs. The findings support the convergent validity of existential fulfillment indicators against well-being measures based on different theoretical approaches, as well as discriminant validity of specific existential fundamental motivation scales. The new instrument opens up new possibilities for empirical research in the field of existential psychology, and in a broader context, the field of self-actualization, well-being, and life satisfaction.

Validation studies are in progress for an English-language Test for Existential Motivations (TEM) and a new validation of a new version of this test is also underway in German. Spanish language research on the TEM, specifically with young adults, has also been conducted in Argentina (Gottfried 2017a, 2017b).

Application of Existential-Analytical Methods to Research

A start of hermeneutic phenomenological research in the frame of EA was developed in Vienna by Silvia Längle (2015; Längle and Görtz 2015; Längle and Häfele-Hausmann 2016). Based on the question of how the relationship to oneself and to life changes noticeably through existential analytic therapy, a method of hermeneutic-phenomenological evaluation of qualitative interviews has been developed. For the perception and evaluation of the respondent's statement, the experience from the application of the PEA as to how "understanding" develops plays a specific role in this phenomenological evaluation process. Its process-sequence and systematization of phenomenological procedures has been developed from practical experience for application in qualitative research. After its application in pre-studies it is currently being applied in a pre-post study with addiction patients.

Similarly, Canadian colleagues have recently applied the methodological framework of PEA (see Kwee and Längle 2013) to the process of existential-phenomenological research (Klaassen, Kwee, and Launeanu 2017). While EA is primarily a psychotherapeutic approach, the person-centered, dialogical, and phenomenological tenets encapsulated by its central method – PEA – provide a substantial framework for engaging in a rigorous and systematic research process. This process begins with an attitude of openness towards the object of research, characterized by trying to see anew. Then, the subjective experience of both researcher and participants is engaged in order to understand the lived experience of the researched phenomenon. Next, the researcher and participant seek to sense the essence of the phenomenon, that which resonates deeply and personally for both. This integrated sensing includes paradoxically both an inner knowing on the basis of inter-subjectivity, and a perpetual openness to new understandings. Finally, the essence of the phenomenon is articulated through hermeneutic interpretation and phenomenological writing. The methodological application of EA to this phenomenological research process is applied to an investigation of the lived experience of shame (Klaassen et al. 2018). EA has also been applied to qualitative research in the applied method ofpersonal field reflection (PFR)(Linska 2015), including self-care and self-reflection as tools in qualitative research, particularly participant observation fieldwork.

Dissemination of Concepts in Existential Analysis

The concepts and applications of EA are being disseminated in a variety of ways, including (a) university-based lectures, (b) congresses of the society, and (c) publications.

University-based lectures currently take place in about 12 universities around the world, and regular international congresses are held. Publication opportunities for scholarship in EA currently include two journals, *Existenzanalyse*, the journal of the International Gesellschaft für Logotherapie und Existenzanalyse, and *Existencia: The Inter-American Journal of Existential Analysis. Existenzanalyse* is published mostly in German (some in English) and is based in Austria. It is an international journal for psychotherapy, counselling, and coaching. It publishes full papers (*Originalarbeit*), overview papers, project reports, and case reports with reference to research, anthropology, and practice of EA, which undergo a peer review. In the forum and discussion section, the journal also includes empirical reports and case reports on the application of EA, as well as research inputs, and contributions to the discussion of published articles. The journal *Existenzanalyse* is listed in abstract and citation databases of peer-reviewed literature: PSYNDEX/University of Trier (ZPID) and SCOPUS (Elsevier). The journal is produced twice a year in a print and an online version.

Existencia existed as an exclusively Spanish speaking publication edited by the Chilean Institute of EA until 2017 when collaborators from EA communities in Chile, Argentina, Mexico, and Canada, began to work towards publishing a Spanish-English bilingual journal co-located and co-edited by an editorial committee across North and South America. This resulted in the re-branding and re-naming of *Existencia* as a bilingual, inter-American publication, with four issues per year, which feature brief articles and book reviews appearing in both languages and extended articles appearing in their original language and a translated abstract. The journal *Existencia* (ISSN 0719-8671) is freely accessible via http://www.icae.cl/. The editorial committee of *Existencia* is currently working toward publishing an e-book, which will include a compilation of highlighted articles. Aside from these journals there have been two edited books with a variety of short texts on EA, which are mostly focused on practical applications (Längle and Sulz 2005; Längle and Gawel 2016), and the former has been translated into Czech (Längle and Sulz 2007), Russian (Längle and Krivtsova 2009), Spanish (Längle and Traverso 2013) and English (Längle and Wurm 2016).

Training and Supervision in Existential Analysis

Training cohorts in EA follow a structured curriculum in two main parts, training toward a counselling diploma in EA and Logotherapy, which has a duration of approximately two-and-a-half to three years, with over 50 full days of training. The psychotherapy diploma in EA and Logotherapy requires approximately 40 additional days of training in clinical theory and practice, lasting (including supervision, individual self-experience, practical work and diploma work) in general 6 years. The same structure is applied worldwide with the same contents, according the rules of and supervised by the board of GLE-International. More detail about the training activities is available in Chapter 19.

The Future Horizon of Existential Analysis and Logotherapy

Evidenced in this chapter, the community of practitioners and scholars in EA and Logotherapy is thriving and developing actively around the world. Numerous elaborations and applications of EA and Logotherapy reflect a community that is personally and intellectually vital for its members. These members are innovating current approaches in EA for applications with diverse populations that experience diverse forms of suffering, as well as exploring opportunities to integrate other psychotherapeutic methods with EA while maintaining conceptual coherence on the backdrop of its anthropological, structural, and process models. Moreover, there are ongoing conceptual developments in EA, increasing efforts in research and evaluation, and multiple current venues for dissemination of existential-analytic concepts.

EA and Logotherapy are well integrated options in psychotherapy training and practice in many countries, particularly in Europe. However, in others, our societies and institutes are relatively very young and undeveloped. In the context of psychotherapy training and practice models in some contexts, EA does not easily correspond. In North America, for example, training in EA does not fit within the graduate counselling and psychology degree programs and thus must be undertaken completely outside the primary avenues for professional training required for practice credentialing. As a practice model, EA is not recognized as a viable method of psychotherapy by many third-party payers in North America, and cognitive-behavioral therapy is the common standard.

In spite of the concepts that unite us through our common process of training and personal development in EA, we do not have well-connected dialogue that crosses over the barriers of language and professional practice cultures. We are moving towards this with small steps, such as in collaborating to form the bilingual journal *Existencia*, and we need to continue to take steps toward shared dialogue and advancement of research and practice in EA and Logotherapy.

In considering the future horizon of EA and Logotherapy, we ponder the question, *where do we go from here?* A continued vital future for global collaborators in EA and Logotherapy requires creative efforts to innovate training models (considering such options as partially web-based training), and to demonstrate the effectiveness and importance of existential-analytic therapy to the psychotherapeutic communities where we practice. We need to maintain venues for dialogue and collaboration between local and international colleagues through our journals, congresses, and peer consultation in practice.

The international congresses in Germany, Switzerland, Austria, Russia, and Ukraine, will continue to be a central attraction as a meeting place for people from outside GLE and to develop interest in EA. Because of growing interest, the format of the congresses will be enlarged to a capacity of 1000 participants. The national conferences will continue with smaller attendance of up to 250 people, which lends to a cozier atmosphere and increased opportunities for dialogue. The first Latin American congress was undertaken in Mexico in 2014, organized by the Instituto Mexicano de Análysis Existencial (The Mexican Institute of EA; Dr. Alejandro Velasco and Emilia Escalante). While regular Latin American congresses have not yet been established, the programs of the First (2015 in London) and Second (2019 in Buenos Aires) World Congresses in Existential Psychotherapy have included strong contributions of EA and Logotherapy. We have emerging plans to hold English speaking congresses within the next five years, with the aim to increase intercultural exchange. For the Russian world, we hope to keep up and enlarge both the journal and the biannual congresses. An important endeavor in the future will be to foster ongoing empirical research and to develop and refine the specific phenomenological qualitative research methods that best fit our work.

Once, the wise Japanese philosopher, psychiatrist, and existential psychotherapist Bin Kimura mentioned in a talk to Alfried Längle that the existential approach, according to his perception and with all his love for it, could never be a mainstream psychotherapy. To be a mainstream psychotherapy, he saw the existential approach as too refined and deep in its structure. He suggested it would continue to attract people who are selective, have a deep philosophical sense or an interest in a deeper understanding of what it means to be human and to be in the world. But this group would be a group of special persons. It seems after these few decades of experience in EA and Logotherapy that he was right. In this, we also have a great opportunity: those who are immersed in this existential approach and global community of EA and Logotherapy, have developed professional expertise and grown personally. Together, we form a group in which we have good understanding between us and can be a source of precious influence in the great waves of psychotherapy by always standing for the real human across time, trends, and cultures.

References

Almario, J. (2016). *Una mirada existencial a la adolescencia*. Bogota: SAPS.

Ángeles Páramo, M., García, C., Casanova, J. et al. (2016). *Escala Existencial: Adaptación y validación mendocina*. Mendoza: Universidad del Aconcagua.

Angermayr, M. (2009). Dasein – Atmen – Achtsamkeit, Existenzanalyse und vorreflexives leibliches Erleben. *Existenzanalyse 26* (2): 99–104.

Angermayr, M. (2010). Im Dialog mit der "großen Vernunft des Leibes" Zur Einbindung des gefühlten Körpers in den existenzanalytischen Prozess. *Existenzanalyse 27* (2): 100–105.

Angermayr, M. (2014). Existenzielles Grounding: Das Seinserleben als Ressource der Person. Bausteine zur vertieften Einbindung des gefühlten Körpers in die Existenzanalyse. *Existenzanalyse 31* (2): 41–45.

Angermayr, M. and Strassl, L. (2013). Leiborientierter Zugang zur inneren Stimmigkeit. *Existenzanalyse 30* (2): 55–62.

Aregger, K. and Waibel, E. (2006). Einleitung. In: *Schulleben und Lebensschule – Beiträge einer existenziellen Pädagogik* (ed. K. Aregger, K. and E. Waibel), *8*. Donauwörth/Luzern: Auer/Comenius Verlag.

Arístegui, R. (2017). Hermeneutic phenomenology, existential analysis, and mindfulness. *Existencia: The Inter-American Journal of Existencial Analysis 19*, http://www.icae.cl/?p=3563 (accessed January 4, 2018).

Barannikov, A.S. (2010). *Duhovnaja (personal'naja) deprivacija: fenomenologi sheskoe soderhanie, posledstvija, osobennosti diagnostiki i pomoschi razvitie litschnosti.* Moscow: MPGU.

Barannikov, A.S. (2015). Sistema vo mne ili ya v sisteme (ehkzistentsial'no-analiticheskij podkhod k provedeniyu dukhovnykh semejnykh rasstanovok). *Ehkzistentsial'nyj analiz - Byulleten.- Moskau 7*: 103–122.

Berti, G. and Schneider, A. (1993). Life after the death of a child. *Paliative Care Today 2* (3): 42–44.

Berti, G. and Schneider, A. (1996). La muerte de un hijo. Ayuda mutua en el proceso de duelo. *Archivos Argentinos de Pediatría 94* (5): 323–333.

Berti, G. and Schneider, A. (2003). Cuando un hijo muere. Logoterapia y ayuda mutua en el proceso de duelo: experiencia de los grupos renacer. *Revista Mexicana de Logoterapia 10*: 21–46.

Biberich, R., Kunert, A., Adenbeck, B. et al. (2015). *Existenzanalytische Psychotherapie mit Säuglingen, Kindern und Jugendlichen.* vol. I: *Grundlagen und Konzepte.* Vienna: GLE.

Böschemeyer, U. (1997). Hoffnung nach der Trennung. *Journal des Viktor Frankl Insituts 2* (4): 51–61.

Bowlby, J. (1951). *Maternal Care and Mental Health.* Geneva: World Health Organization.

Bucher, A.A. and Rothbucher, H. (1996). ReligionslehrerInnen: Ausgebrannte Pessimisten oder sinnerfüllte Idealisten. Kurzbericht über eine Befragung in Salzburg. *Christlich-pädagogische Blätter 109*: 47–50.

Bukovski, R. (2009). Frau zu werden. *Existenzanalyse 26* (2): 53–59.

Bukovski, R. (2014). Eine Botschaft des Körpers. *Existenzanalyse 31* (2): 65–72.

Clark, D. (2016). Cicely Saunders and her early associates: A kaleidoscope of effects. In: *To Comfort Always: A History of Palliative Medicine since the Nineteenth Century* (ed. D. Clark), 85–116. Oxford: Oxford University Press.

Crumbaugh, J.C. (1977). *Manual of Instructions: The Seeking of Noetic Goals Test (SONG).* Abilene: Viktor Frankl Institute of Logotherapy.

Crumbaugh, J.C. (1980). *Logotherapy: New Help for Problem Drinkers.* Chicago: Nelson Hall.

Crumbaugh, J.C. and Maholick, L.T. (1969). *Manual of Instructions for the Purpose in Life Test.* Abilene: Viktor Frankl Institute of Logotherapy.

DeAngelis, T. (2018). In search of meaning. *Monitor on Psychology 49* (9): 38–44.

Drexler, H. (2013). *Adjuvante Methoden in der Existenzanalyse.* DVD. Mülheim: Auditorium Netzwerk.

Drexler, H. (2015). Existenzanalytische Therapie von Anorexie und Bulimie. *Existenzanalyse 32* (2): 78–82.

Efimova, I. (2011). Diagnostik und Beratung in der Burnout-Prophylaxe mithilfe des TEM. *Existenzanalyse 28* (1): 94–97.

Efimova, I. (2012). Warum die Beine nicht tragen – wie Burnout den Willen beeinflusst. *Existenzanalyse 29* (2): 71–76.

Efimova, I. (2015). Burnout-Prävention für Eltern – Ein existenzanalytischer Ansatz anhand empirischer Ergebnisse. *Existenzanalyse 32* (1): 13–20.

Ermakova, E. (2008). Existential fulfillment and burnout among school teachers and human resources managers. *Existenzanalyse 25* (1): 81–82.

Fabry, J. (2001). *Señales del camino hacia el sentido. Descubriendo lo que realmente importa.* México. Ed. LAG.

Fasja, R.C. (2001). La logoterapia aplicada al divorcio a traves de un enfoque de genero. *Revista Mexicana de Logoterapia 5* (1): 63–95.

Fischer-Danzinger, D. (2010). Emotionen in der Therapie von schweren Persönlichkeitsstörungen. *Existenzanalyse 27* (2): 55–58.

Frankl, V. (1969). *The Will to Meaning: Foundations and Applications of Logotherapy.* New York: The World Publishing Company.

Frankl, V. (1992). *Teoría y terapia de las neurosis. Iniciación a la logoterapia y el análisis existencial.* Barcelona: Herder.

Frankl, V. (1995). *La psicoterapia en la practica medica.* Buenos Aires: Ed. San Pablo.

Frankl, V. (2005). *Ärztliche Seelsorge.* Vienna: Paul Zsolnay.

Giorgi, B. (1982). The Belfast test: A new psychometric approach to logotherapy. *International Forum of Logotherapy 5*: 31–37.

Görtz, A. (2003). Sandspieltherapie mit einem Scheidungskind. *Existenzanalyse 20* (1): 4–11.

Gottfried, A.E. (2015). *Manual de la Escala Existencial: Evaluación cuantitativa e interpretación cualitativa de la EE Längle, Orgler y Kundi.* Mendoza, Argentian: GLE-International.

Gottfried, A.E. (2017a). *Manual del Test de las Motivaciones Existenciales: Evaluación cuantitativa e interpretación cualitativa del TME de Längle y Eckhardt.* Mendoza: GLE-International.

Gottfried, A.E. (2017b). Las Motivaciones Fundamentales de la Existencia y su relación con el Sentido de Vida en jóvenes universitarios de 18 a 25 años, de la ciudad de Mendoza, Argentina. PhD thesis. Facultad de Psicología y Psicopedagogía, Pontificia Universidad Católica Argentina, Buenos Aires, Argentina.

Guttmann, D. (1998). *Logoterapia para profesionales.* Bilbao: Desclee de Brower.

Guttmann, D. (2008). *Finding Meaning in Life, at Midlife and Beyond.* Westport: Praeger.

Hablas, R. and Hutzell, R. (1982). The Life Purpose Questionnaire: An alternative to the Purpose-in-Life test for geriatric, neuropsychiatric patients. In: *Analecta Frankliana: The Proceedings of the First World Congress of Logotherapy* (ed. S.A. Wawrytko), 211–215. Berkeley: Strawberry Hill.

Halama, P. (2009). Research instruments for investigating meaning of life and other logotherapeutic constructs. In: *Existential Psychotherapy of Meaning. Handbook of Logotherapy and Existential Analysis* (ed. A. Batthyany and J. Levinson), 415–444. Phoenix: Zeig, Tucker & Theisen.

Heidegger, M. (1962). *Being and Time.* Oxford: Blackwell Publishers.

Hellinger, B. (2010). *Das geistige Familienstellen. Ein Überblick.* Berchtesgaden: Hellinger-Publications.

Henrion, R. (2002). Alcohol use disorders: Alcohol dependence. *The International Forum for Logotherapy 25*: 30–38.

Henrion, R. (2004). Logoanalysis: For treatment of mood disorder due to medical condition. *The International Forum for Logotherapy 27*: 3–8.

Hill, C. (2018). *Meaning in Life: A Therapist's Guide.* Washington, DC: APA.

Hinsburger, D. (1989). Logotherapy in behavioral sex counseling with the developmentally handicapped. *The International Forum for Logotherapy 12*: 46–56.

Hinsburger, D. (1990). Relevance of meaning for the developmentally handicapped to spirituality and aging. *The International Forum for Logotherapy 13*: 107–111.

Höfig-Renner, J. (2015). Die Welt des Kindes – Eine vorbereitete Umgebung zur gesunden Persönlichkeitsentwicklung. In: *Existenzanalytische Psychotherapie mit Säuglingen, Kindern und Jugendlichen.* vol. I: *Grundlagen und Konzepte* (ed. R. Biberich, A. Kunert, B. Adenbeck et al.), 141–159. Vienna: GLE.

Hutzell, R.R. (1984). Logoanalysis for alcoholics. *The International Forum for Logotherapy 7*: 40–45.

Johner, P., Bürgi, D., and Längle, A. (2018). *Existential Leadership zum Erfolg. Philosophie und Praxis der Transformation.* Freiburg: Haufe.

Jones, T. (2011). Malen auf dem Hintergrund der Existenzanalyse. *Existenzanalyse 28* (1): 41–46.

Köberl, M. (2015). Die Zentralthemen der Existenzanalyse – Person und Existenz. In: *Existenzanalytische Psychotherapie mit Säuglingen, Kindern und Jugendlichen.* vol. I: *Grundlagen und Konzepte* (ed. R. Biberich, A. Kunert, B. Adenbeck et al.), 49–71. Vienna: GLE.

Kohler, E. and Rauch, J. (2015). Innere leere und sucht. *Existenzanalyse 32* (2): 71–73.

Klaassen, D., Konieczny, K., Launeanu, M. et al. (2018). The lived experience of shame in athletes: An existential-phenomenological exploration. Presentation at the Eleventh Annual Giving Voice to Experience Conference, Seattle University Graduate Program and the Psychotherapy Cooperative, Seattle, WA, March 3.

Klaassen, D., Kwee, J., and Launeanu, M. (2017). Person-centered research: An existential phenomenological approach. Workshop Presentation at the Third Annual MA Counselling Psychology Research Day, Trinity Western University, Langley, BC, October 27.

Kolbe, C. (2010). Wie wirken Gruppen? *Existenzanalyse 27* (1): 4–10.

Kolbe, C. (2016). Existenzielle Kommunikation. – Zugänge zum Wesentlichen in Beratung und Therapie. *Existenzanalyse 33* (1): 45–51.

Krivtsova, S. (2005). *Life Skills. Psychology Lessons in the First to Fourth Grades.* Moscow: Genesis.

Krivtsova, S. (2013). Fenomenologicheskiy metod s pozitsiy ekz1istentsialnogo analiza Problemyi sovremennoy shkolyi s pozitsiy ekzistensialnogo analiza, *Voprosy Psikhologii 6*: 14–23.

Krivtsova, S. (2015). *Life Skills. Trainings for Fifth to Sixth Grades.* Moscow: Genesis.

Krivtsova, S. (2016a). *Life Skills. Trainings for Seventh to Eighth Grades.* Moscow: Genesis.

Krivtsova, S. (2016b). *Life Skills for Preschoolers. Classes-Travel.* Moscow: Clever-Media-Groop.

Krivtsova, S. (2017). Periodization of self from birth before seven years: Existential analysis. *Vosproy Psikhologii 2*: 36–52.

Kwee, J.L. and Längle, A. (2013). Phenomenology in psychotherapeutic praxis: An introduction to Personal Existential Analysis. *Experiencing EPIS, A Journal of the Existential and Psychoanalytic Institute and Society 2* (1): 139–163.

Kwee, J. and Launeanu, M. (2018). Practical strategies for promoting embodiment in working with eating disorders. In: *Embodiment and Eating Disorders: Theory, Research, Prevention and Treatment* (ed. H. McBride and J. Kwee), 342–358. New York: Routledge.

Kwee, J. and McBride, H. (2017). Intimate friendship: How do we get there? In: *Mutual by Design: A Better Model of Christian Marriage* (ed. E. Beyer and L. Nelson). Minneapolis: Christians for Biblical Equality Publishers. (Kindle edition).

Landaboure, N.B. Boado de (2002). *Escala Existencial de A. Lángle, C. Orgler y M. Kundi. Manual Introductorio.* Buenos Aires: Dunken.

Landaboure, N.B. Boado de (2017). Estudio descriptivo-correlacional de las relaciones existentes entre la dimensión noética y las funciones ejecutivas en personas entre 18 y 30 años. PhD thesis. Buenos Aires: Universidad Católica Argentina.

Längle, A. (1993). Die "Personale Existenzanalyse" (PEA) als therapeutisches Konzept, In: *Praxis der Personalen Existenzanalyse* (ed. A. Längle), 9–37. Vienna: GLE.

Längle, A. (1994). Sinn-Glaube oder Sinn-Gespür? Zur Differenzierung von ontologischem und existentiellem Sinn in der Logotherapie. *Bulletin GLE 11*: 15–20.

Längle, A. (1997a). Burnout – Existentielle Bedeutung und Möglichkeiten der Prävention. *Existenzanalyse 14* (2): 11–19.

Längle, A. (1997b). Modell einer existenzanalytischen Gruppentherapie für die Suchtbehandlung. In: *Süchtig sein. Entstehung, Formen und Behandlung von Abhängigkeiten* (ed. A. Längle and C. Probst), 149–169. Vienna: Facultas.

Längle, A. (ed.) (2000). *Praxis der Personalen Existenzanalyse.* Vienna: Facultas.
Längle, A. (2002). Die Grundmotivationen menschlicher Existenz als Wirkstruktur existenzanaltischer Psychotherapie. *Fundamental Psychiatrica 16* (1): 1–8.
Längle, A. (2005). Das Sinnkonzept V. Frankls – ein Beitrag für die gesamte Psychotherapie. In: *Sinn, Sinnerfahrung, Lebenssinn in Psychologie und Psychotherapie* (ed. H.G. Petzold and I. Orth), 403–460. Bielefeld: Aisthesis.
Längle, A. (2007). Trauma und Existenz. *Psychotherapie Forum 15* (3): 109–116.
Längle, A. (2012). The Viennese School of Existential Analysis. The search for meaning and affirmation of life. In: *Existential Therapy: Legacy, Vibrancy, and Dialogue* (ed. L. Barnett and G. Madison), 159–170. New York: Routledge.
Längle, A. (2015). Die Zustimmung in der Süchtigkeit. Ein existenzanalytischer Zugang. *Existenzanalyse 32* (2): 14–23.
Längle, A. (2016). *Existenzanalyse. Zugänge zur existentiellen Psychotherapie.* Vienna: Facultas.
Längle, A. and Bürgi, D. (2014). *Existentielles Coaching. Theoretische Orientierung, Grundlagen und Praxis für Coaching, Organisationsberatung und Supervision.* Vienna: Facultas.
Längle, A., Orgler, C., and Kundi, M. (2003). The existence scale: A new approach to assess the ability to find personal meaning in life and to reach existential fulfillment. *European Psychotherapy 4*: 131–151.
Längle, S. (2015). Methode zur Praxis Hermeneutisch-Phänomenologischer Forschung. *Existenzanalyse 32* (2): 64–70.
Längle, S. and Gawel, B. (eds.) (2016). *Themen der Existenz – Existenz in Themen. Ein Lesebuch zur Existenzanalyse.* Vienna: Facultas.
Längle, S. and Görtz, A. (2015). Lebensqualität vor und nach stationärer Suchttherapie. Quantitative und qualitative Forschungsergebnisse im Vergleich. *Existenzanalyse 32* (2): 51–63.
Längle, S. and Häfele-Hausmann, S. (2016). Übungen zur Phänomenologischen Forschungsmethode. *Existenzanalyse 33* (2): 65–74.
Längle, S. and Krivtsova, S. (eds.) (2009). *S soboj u bez sebja. Praktika ekzistencial'no-analiticheskoj psihoterapii.* Moscow: Genesis.
Längle, S. and Sulz, M. (eds.) (2005). *Das eigene Leben. Ein Lesebuch zur Existenzanalyse.* Vienna: GLE.
Längle, S. and Sulz, M. (eds.) (2007). Mohu se spolehnout na svůj cit? In *Žít svůj vlastní život. Úvod do existenciální analýzy.* Prague: Portál.
Längle, S. and Traverso, G. (eds.) (2013). *Vivir la propia vida.* Santiago de Chile: Mandrágora.
Längle, S. and Wurm, C. (eds.) (2016). *Living Your Own Life. Existential Analyis in Action.* London: Karnac.
Lantz, J. (1993). *Existential Family Therapy: Using the Concepts of Viktor Frankl.* North Vale: Jason Aronson.
Launeanu, M., Klaassen, D., and Kwee, J. (2018). Finding meaning in the aftermath of family bereavement: An existential analytic approach. In: *Existential Elements of the Family* (ed. L.L. Armstrong), 331–354. Walpole: Peeters.
Launeanu, M. and Kwee, J. (2018). Embodiment: A non-dualistic and existential perspective on understanding and treating disordered eating. In: *Embodiment and Eating Disorders: Theory, Research, Prevention and Treatment* (ed. H. McBride and J. Kwee), 35–52. New York: Routledge.
Leon, A. (2001). Grupo logoterapeutico para personas con VIH y Sida. *Revista Mexicana de Logoterapia 6*: 107–138.
Lhotski, B. and Artaker, G. (2005). *Existenzanalytische Aufstellungsarbeit.* Vienna: GLE.

Linska, M. (2011). *Umgang mit psychischer Belastung am Arbeitsplatz. Darstellung eines Weiterqualifizierungsprojektes für Tagesmütter in Oberösterreich unter besonderer Berücksichtigung der existenzanalytischen Grundmotivationen nach Alfried Längle.* Vienna: Univ. Masterarbeit.

Linska, M. (2015). Personale Feld-Reflexion. Überlegungen und Leitfaden zur Einbeziehung von Selbstempathie, Emotion und Selbstreflexion in den Feldforschungsprozess anhand phänomenologischer Methoden der Existenzanalyse. *Curare 38* (1–2): 73–86.

Long, J. (1997). Utilización de la logoterapia para trascender el trauma. *Journal del Instituto Viktor Frankl 2* (4): 23–50.

Lukas, E. (1986). *Logo-Test: Test zur Messung von "innerer Sinnerfüllung" und "existentieller Frustration". Handanweisungen und 20 Testbögen.* Vienna: Deuticke.

Lukas, E. (1992). *Assistencia logoterapeutica.* Petropolis: Voces.

Lukas, E. (1995). *Psicoterapia en dignidad.* Buenos Aires: Ed. San Pablo.

Lukas, E. (1998). *Una vida fascinante. En la tensión entre ser y deber ser.* Buenos Aires: Ed. San Pablo.

Lukas, E. (2001). *Paz vital, plenitud y placer de vivir. Los valores de la logoterapia.* Barcelona. Ed. Paidos.

Lukas, E. (2002). *En la tristeza pervive el amor.* Barcelona: Ed. Paidos.

Lukas, E. (2004). *Logoterapia. La búsqueda de sentido.* Ed. Paidos.

Lukas, E. (2006). *También tu sufrimiento tiene sentido. Alivio en la crisis a través de la logoterapia.* México: Ed. LAG.

Lukas, E. (2009). La familia primero. El significado de amor y familia. *Revista Mexicana de Logoterapia 22*: 5–17.

Lukas, E. and Garcia, C. (2002). *De la Vida Fugaz.* Mexico: Ed. LAG.

Martinez, E. (2003). *Acción y elección. Logoterapia, logoterapia de grupo y abordaje de las drogodependencias.* Bogota: Ed. Colectivo Aquí y Ahora.

Martinez, E. (2011). *Los modos de ser inauténticos. Psicoterapia Centrada en el sentido de los trastornos de la personalidad.* Bogota: Ed. Manual moderno.

Martinez, E., Díaz del Castillo, J., and Jaimes, J. (2010). Validación de la Prueba "Escala De Recursos Noológicos Aquí Y Ahora" Para Personas Mayores de 15 Años. *Revista Argentina de Clínica Psicológica 3*: 257–272.

Martinez, E. and Florez, I. (2016). Meaning in life in the prevention and treatment of substance use disorders. In: *Clinical Perspectives on Meaning: Positive and Existential Psychotherapy* (ed. P. Russo-Netzer, S.E. Schulenberg and A. Batthyanay), 201–222. Geneva: Springer.

Martinez, E., Trujillo, A., Díaz del Castillo, J. et al. (2011). Desarrollo y estructura de la escala dimensional del sentido de vida. *Acta Colombiana de Psicología 14* (2): 113–119.

Matuszak-Luss, K. (2015). Existential analytical aspects on working with resources in traumatherapy. Presentation at the First Existential Psychotherapy International Congress. London, UK, May 16.

Meier-Kernen, G. and Kernen, H. (2013). Sinnerleben und Burnout-Prophylaxe aus Sicht des Ressourcen-Managements und der Existenzanalyse. *Existenzanalyse 30* (1): 80–90.

Melton, A.M.A. and Schulenberg, S.E. (2008). On the measurement of meaning: Logotherapy's empirical contributions to Humanistic psychology. *The Humanistic Psychologist 36*: 31–44.

Merleau-Ponty, M. (2012). *Phenomenology of Perception* (trans D.L. Landes). New York: Routledge. (Original work published 1945.)

Mori, H. (2009). Psico-oncología orientada hacia el sentido en la practica psicoterapéutica. In: *Logoterapia en acción. Aplicaciones practicas* (ed. S.S. Valiente). Buenos Aires: Ed. San Pablo.

Nindl, A. (2001). Zwischen existentieller Sinnerfüllung und Burnout-Prophylaxe Aus Sicht des Ressourcen-Managements und der Existenzanalyse. *Existenzanalyse 18* (1): 15–23.

Noblejas, M. (2000). Fiabilidad de los test PIL y Logotest. *Nous. Boletín de logoterapia y análisis existencial 4* (Fall): 81–90.

Oscariz, A. (2000). Grupo de madres y padres de drogodependientes. Una experiencia de Esqueda de sentido. *Boletín de logoterapia y análisis existencial 4*: 33–42.

Osin, E. (2009). Subjective experience of alienation: Measurement and correlates. *Existenzanalyse 26* (1): 4–11.

Pacciolla, A. (2007). Diagnosi e Disagio noogeno. In: *Il senso come terapia* (ed. E. Fizzotti), 166–187. Milan: Franco Angeli.

Pointner, S. (2016). *Adam wo bist Du? Eva was tust Du? Befreiung aus Isolation und Abhängigkeit in Paarbeziehungen*. Vienna: Orac.

Pointner, S. and Sattler, M. (2014). Therapie 2+: Vom Einzel- zum erweiterten Setting und wieder zurück – Ressourcenorientierte Kurzzeitinterventionen mit Partnern oder Angehörigen von (erwachsenen) KlientInnen. *Existenzanalyse 31* (2): 79–82.

Probst, C. (2002a). Existenzanalytische Therapie bei einem Patienten mit schizoider Persönlichkeitsstörung. *Existenzanalyse 19* (1): 28–31.

Probst, C. (2002b). Therapie eines Patienten mit Borderline-Persönlichkeistsstörung. *Existenzanalyse 19* (1): 32–34.

Reddemann, L. (2007). *Psychodynamisch Imaginative Traumatherapie; PITT – das Manual*. Stuttgart: Klett-Cotta.

Reker, G. (1992). *The Life Attitude Profile- Revised (LAP-R)*. Peterborough, ON: Student Psychologists Press.

Reker, G. (2000). Theoretical perspective, dimensions and measurement of existential meaning. In: *Exploring Existential Meaning* (ed. G. Reker and K. Chamberlain), 39–56. Thousand Oaks, CA: Sage.

Reker, G. (2004). Meaning in life of young, middle-aged, and older adults: factorial validity, age, and gender invariance of the Personal Meaning Index (PMI). *Personality and Individual Differences 38* (1): 71–85.

Rodríguez, R. (2004). Borderline personality disturbances and logotherapeutic treatment approach. *The International Forum for Logotherapy 27* (1): 21–27.

Rogina, J. (2002). Logotherapeutic mastery of Generalized Anxiety Disorder. *The International Forum for Logotherapy 25*: 60–67.

Rogina, J. (2004). Treatment and interventions for Narcissistic Personality Disorder. *The International Forum for Logotherapy 27*: 28–33.

Rogina, J. and Quilitch, H. (2006). Treating dependent personality disorders with logotherapy: A case study. *The International Forum for Logotherapy 29*: 54–61.

Ryazanova, I. (2014). Therapie über Internet – Behandlungspraxis und Training. *Existenzanalyse 31* (2): 90–94.

Salazar Lozano, H. (2012). *Estandarización de la Escala Existencial en Universitarios Mexicanos: Instrumento para evaluar Sentido de Vida*. Riga: Editorial Académica Española.

Schippan, I. (1997). Möglichkeiten der Beratung, Begleitung und Therapie von Eltern drogengefährdeter und drogenabhängiger Jugendlicher. *Journal des Viktor Frankl Instituts 5* (1).

Schulenberg, S.E. (2000). Depression in mental retardation: An additional direction for Logotherapy. *The International Forum for Logotherapy 23*: 107–110.

Schulenberg, S.E. and Melton, A.M.A. (2010). A confirmatory factor-analytic evaluation of the Purpose in Life test: Preliminary psychometric support for a replicable two-factor model. *Journal of Happiness Studies 11*: 95–111.

Schulenberg, S.E., Schnetzer, L.W., and Buchanan, E.M. (2011). The Purpose in Life test-Short Form: Development and psychometric support. *Journal of Happiness Studies 12*: 861–876.

Sparrer, I. (2004). *Wunder, Lösung und System*. Heidelberg: Auer.
Steinbacher, R. (2016). Die Entwicklung des Sinnerlebens und der Sinnvollen Lebensgestaltung. In: *Existenzanalytische Psychotherapie mit Säuglingen, Kindern und Jugendlichen*. vol. II: *Entwicklungsthemen und Diagnostik* (ed. R. Biberich, A Kunert, B. Adenbeck et al.), 83–107. Vienna: GLE.
Tutsch, L. and Bukovski, R. (2016). Trauma – Dissoziation und Integration. *Existenzanalyse 33* (2): 4–15.
Ukolova, E.M., Shumskiy, V.B., and Osin, E.N. (2014). TEMIR – A Test to Measure Existential Motivations in Interpersonal Relationships: Factorial structure, reliability and validity *Existenzanalyse 31* (2): 4–12.
Ukolova, E.M., Shumskiy, V.B., and Osin, E.N. (2016). What makes a good relationship? – Predictors of existential fulfilment in heterosexual romantic relationships. *Existenzanalyse 33* (2): 102–108.
Ungar, M. (2002). A Logotherapy treatment protocol for major depressive disorder. *The International Forum for Logotherapy 25*: 3–10.
Vos, J., Cooper, M., Hill, C.E. et al. (2017). Five perspectives on the meaning of meaning in the context of clinical practices. *Journal of Constructivist Psychology*. https://doi.org/10.1080/10720537.2017.1390511.
Waibel, E.M. (2012). Erziehung zu Selbstwert und Sinn – Self-Worth and Meaning-Oriented Education. In: *Life and Responsibility in European Education. European Dimension in Education and Teaching*, vol. 5 (ed. P.M. Rabensteiner and E. Ropo), 103–131. Hohengehren: Schneider.
Waibel, E.M. (2017a). *Erziehung zum Sinn – Sinn der Erziehung. Grundlagen einer Existenziellen Pädagogik*. Weinheim: Beltz (new edition).
Waibel, E.M. (2017b). *Erziehung zum Selbstwert. Persönlichkeitsstärkung als pädagogisches Anliegen*. Weinheim: Beltz (new edition).
Winters, M. (2002). A logotherapeutic treatment for relationship therapy: Early explorations. *International Forum for Logotherapy 25*: 11–23.
Wong, P.T.P. (1998). Implicit theories of meaningful life and the development of the Personal Meaning Profile (PMP). In: *The Human Quest for Meaning: A Handbook of Psychological Research and Clinical Applications* (ed. P.T.P. Wong and P. Fry), 111–140. Mahwah: Erlbaum.
Wong, P.T.P. (2009). Existential positive psychology. In: *Encyclopedia of Positive Psychology* (ed. S. Lopez), vol. 1, 361–368. Oxford: Wiley Blackwell.
Wong, P.T.P. (2010). Meaning therapy: An integrative and positive existential psychotherapy. *Journal of Contemporary Psychotherapy 40* (2): 85–99.
Wong, P.T.P. (ed.) (2012a). *The Human Quest For Meaning: Theories, Research, And Applications*, 2e. New York: Routledge.
Wong, P.T.P. (2012b). Toward a dual-systems model of what makes life worth living. In: *The Human Quest For Meaning: Theories, Research, and Applications*, 2e (ed. P.T.P. Wong), 3–22. New York: Routledge.
Wong, P.T.P. (2015). Meaning therapy: Assessments and interventions. *Existential Analysis 26* (1): 154–167.
Wong, P.T.P. (2016). Integrative meaning therapy: From Logotherapy to existential positive interventions. In: *Clinical Perspectives on Meaning: Positive and Existential Psychotherapy* (ed. P. Russo-Netzer, S.E. Schulenberg, and A. Batthyany), 323–342. New York: Springer.
Wurm, C.S.E. (1997). Definitionen, Diagnostik und Behandlung von alkoholbedingten Problemen. In: *Süchtig sein. Entstehung, Formen und Behandlung von Abhängigkeiten* (ed. A. Längle and C. Probst), 51–62. Vienna: Facultas Universitätsverlag.
Wurm, C.S.E. (2003). Is addiction a useful concept? An existential view. *European Psychotherapy 4* (1): 153–160.

Part V

Existential Group Therapy

Edited by
Digby Tantam

Introduction

Group psychotherapy draws on two aspects of being human-being an autonomous individual, and being a unit in a social world. Kierkegaard and Nietzsche addressed the former and Scheler addressed the latter, and Heidegger, Sartre, and de Beauvoir addressed them both using the phenomenology of Brentano as enriched by Husserl to conjoin the two perspectives. I have argued elsewhere that a useful characterization of the two perspectives is that our brains interact with other human brains to create a social world, and that our minds enable us to imagine being alone, and independent of this social world (Tantam 2017).

Kierkegaard replaced the social world with God as Nietzsche would have done if he could (or so argues Lou Salomé in her biography of him [Andreas-Salomé 2001]). Instead Nietzsche intermittently found it in an imagined community of "Ubermenschen," the forerunner of whom had been Richard Wagner. Stein did find God and a community. Her and Scheler's application of phenomenology to communities (see Chapter 25) is directly relevant to the use of large groups, for example to the kind of therapeutic community described in the case study in this section by Ansell et al. (Chapter 28), although it is rarely acknowledged in the theory underlying therapeutic communities. It is also relevant to logotherapy. Frankl's injunction (Frankl 1949/1964) "man should not ask what the meaning of his life is, but rather must recognize that it is he who is asked. In a word, each man is questioned by life; and he can only answer to life by answering for his own life; to life he can only respond by being responsible" might have been written by Stein.

For many people being an individual does not conflict with being part of a family, work group, or community but as Sartre argued, these two perspectives on being human may sometimes lead to conflict in how to be human (conflict between what Sartre called l'être-pour-soi and l'être-pour-autrui). Sartre and de Beauvoir who

The Wiley World Handbook of Existential Therapy, First Edition. Edited by Emmy van Deurzen, Erik Craig, Alfried Längle, Kirk J. Schneider, Digby Tantam, and Simon du Plock.

assumed that the conflict was rarely resolved proposed that this conflict might be addressed by a person falsely believing ("mauvaise foi") that they could be entirely self-sufficient ("l'être-en-soi" being in itself).

The implication of Sartre's treatment of living-in-itself was that it was a failure to live up to one's potential, a stultifying compromise, a form of inauthenticity. Authenticity has got a bad name since Sartre wrote. His life contributed to the contemporary idea that authenticity was a kind of self-indulgence. We consider psychiatric practitioners of group therapy who described themselves as "existential" in a later chapter. Their group behavior seems more self-indulgent than developing their ownmost potential, as Heidegger intended the term "authenticity" to mean.

The fixity of being in itself has been of particular interest to group psychotherapists, from Lewin's idea of a "metastable" position in the social field in his field theory, through Ezriel and Stock Whitaker's idea of "required relationships," to Foulkes and Antony's description of the "neurotic" position in which a person communicates their wishes and desires in a "mumble" that designedly fails as a communication.

There is a strand of existential philosophy that holds that living for others may not be as inauthentic as Sartre thought it was. It is an aspect of living in community or in a family, as I discuss in more detail Chapter 25. This goes further than psychological and sociological theories of community and has obvious applications to group therapy, particularly the therapy of large groups. Frankl's "meaning therapy," which is discussed in Chapter 27, could be considered a development of this existential theory of community although Frankl did not acknowledge the philosophical basis for his hypostatization of meaning.

Heidegger, as is well-known, founded his ontology on the integration of each human being with a world known to them (and knowing them, too) through action. The world is, before it is perceived as an assemblage of objects and before self-consciousness develops, made up of beings that are "ready-to-hand." The founder of group analysis also had this insight although he derived it from Gestalt theory and not from Heidegger's hermeneutic phenomenology. He thought of the individual and the constituent of a group as like one of the illusions beloved by Gestalt psychologists. The individual and the social unit are intermingled. One can see one or the other and just occasionally we can fuse both of them together.

Heidegger's concept of Dasein was an answer to a question that had bothered Heidegger as a teenager. What did it mean "to exist" or rather "what does it mean to exist as a human being?" This kind of question will be familiar to many adolescents. "Dasein" presupposes that existence requires a self-conscious being and "equipment," a world that is "ready to hand." Another way to put this is that men and women are social animals whose emotions and focus of attention are non-verbally and reflexively shareable by other humans in their vicinity (via what I and others call the interbrain; Tantam 2017). This connection is primarily motoric, as is the connection that Heidegger outlines, between ourselves and a world that is ready to hand. We realize that other people are smiling at us because we find ourselves smiling back.

Language use provides access to a community of ideas, and we access it sensorily. It allows the development of a narrative about ourselves and other people (a "theory of their minds") and, presumably, the development of self-consciousness. The interbrain is out of the reach of this introspection. It is only its consequences that are disclosed to us, but it is quite possible to consciously block these consequences. So the involuntary smile that rises to our lips and eyes when people smile and which we might become aware of before we even notice them smiling, can be suppressed if the person smiling at us is an enemy.

What, though, if people are not ready to hand? This might arise because we are socially and emotionally isolated. It might arise also because the whole world feels like an enemy, in which case our interbrain connection can be shut down by our conscious evaluation of the world. Or the world of other people may not be ready to hand because the internet connection does not function as it should, for example, or because a person has an autistic spectrum disorder. Heidegger considers equipment (including other beings) that are not ready to hand, but "unready to hand" as only present through theory of mind, through our ability to consciously attend to them (Dotov, Nie, and Chemero 2010). Being present at hand disrupts our ready to hand engagement (that, when it concerns other people, would normally be mediated by our interbrain connection with them). Our existence then becomes dependent, according to Heidegger's model of Dasein, on an imaginary world of our making, a world that could readily collapse into no world or "'nothing."

Heidegger's emotional concerns about nothingness may have emerged around the time that he first left home to go to seminary where he developed anxiety symptoms and had to leave and go back home. Not, I suppose, an unusual experience for an adolescent, alone, disconnected from other people, or shamed and rejected by them. On the one hand dismissing the world around him or her, and on the other feeling judged and found wanting by that same world and either way leading to a feeling of "nothingness." But his conditions for establishing a human existence, a Dasein, were to have a being and to be in a world with others (Mitsein) that were "ready to hand." Without both of these we are nothing. So nothingness is a condition that may result from the world annihilating us, or from us annihilating the world. There is always the possibility of this nothingness supervening (a state that Frankel was to describe as "meaninglessness" and Durkheim had previously described as "anomie") although we may not be so aware of it after adolescence. I shall argue in Chapter 25 that this consciousness of the threat of nothingness was a common factor in the philosophers that we recruit to the existential banner. Another common factor was phenomenology, which even with all of the conditions that Husserl added to it in terms of the transcendental reduction could not quite avoid the threat of solipsism, and therefore did not entirely deal with the threat of nothingness, either.

Nothingness, whether produced by a sense of being rejected by the world or disconnected from it, is a cause of existential anxiety. But that anxiety is also associated with the freedom that comes from feeling no longer controlled by the restraints that the world places on the possibilities of being. Nothingness is the concomitant of freedom, as Sartre and Kierkegaard argued. There could be no step change in personal development without risking it. As the famous novel, the *Journey to the West*, has Gautama Buddha say, "the true scriptures are written on blank pages." Certain life experiences that Jaspers called "limit situations" are also associated with a brush with nothingness that may either lead to a positive transformation, or finish with falling into an unending abyss.

Of course my speculations about Heidegger's feelings as an adolescent are just that, speculations. But they are intended to demonstrate that the common core of nothingness is finding the world no longer ready to hand, whether because of bullying, trauma, autistic spectrum disorder, loneliness, or alienation. Nothingness has been a preoccupation of all the existential philosophers, arguably because they each, with the possible exception of Jaspers, lived through one or other of these experiences. Jaspers may have been aware of nothingness vicariously through the experiences of his brother who may have had attention-deficit hyperactivity disorder, who could never settle in a job or a relationship and who committed suicide in his 40s.

Group practitioners are aware of the anxiety that many of their clients experience when offered group psychotherapy. Indeed, many clients offered group therapy refuse it at first. But group psychotherapy theorists have widely ignored the existential insights into the nothingness that may underpin this anxiety. Using anxiety as an energy for change is a familiar strategy for many existential therapists, but this fundamental concern has not been addressed in the published literature on group psychotherapy before. In the following chapters this will be seen from a philosophical and historical perspective before a phenomenological account of existential group work is developed around a theoretical framework (Tantam 2017).

Emmy van Deurzen has described her existential group therapy before but not in as much detail as in Chapter 27 where she demonstrates how she *has* been able to incorporate all of the strands of the existential philosophers mentioned in this brief introduction, including that of nothingness.

References

Andreas-Salomé, L. (2001). *Nietzsche* (ed. and trans. S. Mandel). Urbana: University Of Illinois Press. (Original work published 1894.)

Dotov, D.G., Nie, L., and Chemero, A. (2010). A demonstration of the transition from ready-to-hand to unready-to-hand. *PLoS ONE 5* (3): e9433.

Frankl, V. (1964). *Man's Search for Meaning*. London: Hodder & Stoughton. (Original work published 1949.)

Tantam, D. (2017). *The Interbrain*. London: Jessica Kingsley.

25

History and Philosophy of Existential Group Therapy

Digby Tantam

One way of looking at the aim of all group therapies is to reduce the conflict inside ourselves and with others, and to increase our harmonious relations with other people and, if we believe in such ideas, within ourselves. Naturally, interpersonal tensions are often greatest during war time when the state intrudes into private life. The philosophers who we nowadays count as existential were understandably preoccupied with ontological issues, including our relations with other human beings. The existential philosophers who made the most contribution to ontology in the early part of the last century were in a Germany that was gearing up for a way to cement an identity as a newly unified country based on the supposed cultural and physical unity of the Volk. Many philosophers of the time were attracted to this notion, perhaps believing like Heidegger that there was a dimension of being, the ontological, that could exist in a separate dimension from the ordinary, everyday bustle of the social world. This proved to be a disastrous mistake leading as it did to the justification of genocide.

The Second World War also provoked a reconsideration of the same issues, but this time not so much from the point of view of a triumphant nation, but from the point of view of the vanquished.

In France, the impossibility of genuine relations with others colored the existentialism of Sartre, de Beauvoir, and Camus (I am omitting Marcel, who coined the term "existential" but lampooned the existentialists, and Merleau-Ponty, a much more sanguine character whose contribution was to phenomenology). Sartre rejected the bad faith of the person who gave in to society's expectations although to some degree was forced by his Marxism to recognize the solidarity that created social institutions. De Beauvoir did not entirely reject community if it was based on reciprocity. Both of them engaged with the challenge that Heidegger made to everyday existence.

In Austria, Frankl emerged from the concentration camps with a newly sharpened focus on "meaning" as the best defense against the constant threat of extinction in the

The Wiley World Handbook of Existential Therapy, First Edition. Edited by Emmy van Deurzen, Erik Craig, Alfried Längle, Kirk J. Schneider, Digby Tantam, and Simon du Plock.

camps. Extinction dulled the spirits of inmates who felt themselves to cease to be individuals but become "nothings," numbers without attachments. Spiritual annihilation, Frankl thought, was the first step on the road to the gas chamber, death by starvation or illness, or being shot by a guard.

In the United Kingdom and the United States a community psychiatry movement was developing that translated during the war into a new approach to the growing rate of psychiatric casualties. These combatants, whom Grinker called sufferers from trauma, turned on the Army, Navy, or Airforce in which they had been serving, distrusting the morale that held their comrades together in units that looked after each other. Therapeutic communities like the Naval Hospital in Oakland or the Rubery Hill and Hollymoor hospitals in the outskirts of Birmingham in the United Kingdom, which had been requisitioned by the Army and named Northfield, implemented self-governing communities of 'shell shocked" combatants in order to recreate morale. Many of the psychiatrists involved in Northfield went on to make major contributions to psychotherapy. They include Main through his championing of the therapeutic community movement, Bion for his development of basic assumption theory, Bieber through his development of the first psychiatric day hospital, and Foulkes through the creation of group analysis.

Each of these strands has a right to be considered a part of the history of existential group psychotherapy. Frankl's legacy is the most explicit as it has directly inspired meaning-centered groups. These have been mostly short-term groups, focusing on people with a shared fate, most often that of terminal illness or bereavement. Several of the case histories in this section provide details of meaning-centered groups, and we also discuss these groups in Chapter 28.

Therapeutic communities have good reason to be considered existential or at least applied phenomenologist since their principles can be found in Stein and Scheler, but this has not been explicitly acknowledged. Anglo-Saxon descriptions tend to be based on interpersonal psychology, using concepts like social adaptation, fellowship or to use a term used by Patrick de Maré, another Northfield staff member, *koinonia*. Classen et al. (Chapter 28) provide a case study of a therapeutic community outside the confines of a hospital ward, but their case is based on pragmatic rather than philosophical principles as seems to be the case for most if not all descriptions of the effectiveness of "the community." Therapeutic communities have focused on social adaptation (Antonsen et al. 2014), which is perhaps why their theoretical basis although extensive, has focused on systems theory, psychoanalysis, and management theory (Campling 2001).

The negativity of group experience emerged early on at Northfields, when the unit was being managed by Bion and Rickman. Their experiences, sometimes termed the first Northfield experiment, probably influenced Bion's treatment of groups that lost sight of their "primary task" and became preoccupied by their own survival (Bion 1961).

Foulkes succeeded Bion, in the second "Northfield experiment," and the same issues were circumvented. One wonders whether having a commanding officer who had been a British tank commander in the First World War, as Bion had been, was crucially different from having a recent emigreé from Germany (as Foulkes was). It has been a common criticism of Foulkes, and of group analysis generally, that it has not accounted effectively for negativity and hatred (Nitsun 1991). Bion did not develop his ideas about groups further, although they were taken up by Turquet and others in the Tavistock Institute of Human Relations and applied to business.

Critics of group therapy teaching have sometimes complained that its theoretical basis has failed to free itself from psychoanalysis. Foulkes saw his work as a replacement of psychoanalytic theory, notably the Kleinian approach, with an interpersonal theory, much as Ronald Laing did. But a recent monograph on group analysis that has received plaudits from contemporary therapists has reverted to Kleinian explanations of group phenomena (Schlapobersky 2016).

Laing found his inspiration in Sartre whose work would probably not have been known to Foulkes although they were contemporaries. Cohn (2002) finds many of Heidegger's ideas in group analysis, too, but the missing element is the profound skepticism about groups that is to be found in both Sartre and Heidegger.

Without this integration, there cannot be, in my view, an entire account of an existential group therapy. There can be groups with a focus on meaning, or a focus on community, as I have indicated, but not groups drawing on the paradoxes that the existential approach lays before us. This is about the struggle of the individual against the desire to submerge her, him, or their self in the community, and the ability to find meaning even in the face of what Camus called absurdity.

The chapters in this Part will therefore start with a review of the philosophical treatment of these topics, followed by a sketch of how this philosophy could be the theoretical foundation of an existential group psychotherapy. This precedes a review of the work of therapists who consider their work to be existential, even though it is not always clear why they adopted this label, and a more detailed description of an existential group whose principles have been developed and applied over many years by the doyenne of existential therapy, Emmy van Deurzen. These chapters are therefore less a chronicle of achievement and more of a work in development.

Given the ubiquity of groups, one might have expected that existential philosophers would have paid more attention to them. One reason that they did not might be that the more famous existential philosophers sooner or later, ran afoul of the societies in which they live and avoided group participation. Many of them (Kierkegaard, Nietzsche, Heidegger, even Sartre in his later life) wrote about the damage that groups can do to individual development with little compensatory emphasis on the contribution that groups make.

Aloneness

Aloneness might seem an usual starting point for a consideration of groups. It is after all the antithesis of what therapy groups set out to achieve, which is to give their members a feeling of belonging or of cohesion as group therapists often term it.

The aloneness of the founding philosophers of what became existential philosophy was chosen, not factitious. Their reasons for choosing a lonely existence eschewing group participation provide us with the first existential account of group membership, albeit a negative one.

The young Kierkegaard was a fashionable man about town, with significant private means after the death of his father. He was known for his wit, and erudition. He reviewed plays, went to the theatre a lot, and enjoyed after-theatre parties. He got engaged. Then he broke the engagement off, spent less time in society, and began to take long walks round Copenhagen, getting into conversation with people that he met. After he was lampooned in a fashionable magazine, he began to avoid company altogether, moving to a flat in an unfashionable area of Copenhagen opposite the abattoir. He poured out a flood of pamphlets and articles usually under a pseudonym and printed at this own expense. Regina Olson, his fiancée, married another man, and Kierkegaard is not known to have had another intimate relationship. By the time of his death he had broken with the Church of Denmark, although he was an ordained minister, and all of his immediate family had died, except for a brother who lived far away (who later committed suicide). He no longer saw his former friends although his writing did have its admirers. Kierkegaard (1849/1983, pp. 5–6) described his lonely life as an act of "Christian heroism – a rarity, to be sure – to venture wholly to become oneself, an individual human being, this specific individual human being, alone before God, alone in this prodigious strenuousness and this prodigious responsibility."

Schopenhauer, too, started life as an energetic and sociable young man. He travelled for his father's business, which he inherited when his father died, possibly by suicide. Schopenhauer's mother moved to Weimar where she started a famous salon and became a novelist. Schopenhauer did not approve and distanced himself from her. He sold the business and lived off the proceeds for the rest of his life. Schopenhauer began an academic career and had a liaison with a younger actress, who had his child. The child, a daughter, died. Schopenhauer refused to marry the mother, and the relationship broke up. Most likely this was Schopenhauer's last intimate relationship although he did have an infatuation for a woman much younger than himself when he was older. He left Berlin where he had a University post, possibly fleeing cholera and thereafter did not return to employment but ended up living alone with a succession of poodles and his flute, which he played assiduously every day, studying and writing. Schopenhauer, like Kierkegaard, thought that being alone was to be welcomed. He wrote, "A man can be himself only so long as he is alone; and if he does not love solitude, he will not love freedom; for it is only when he is alone that he is really free. Constraint is always present in society, like a companion of whom there is no riddance; and in proportion to the greatness of a man's individuality, it will be hard for him to bear the sacrifices which all intercourse with others demands" (Schopenhauer 2006, section 9).

Nietzsche also had a University career and belonged to the inner circle of the fashionable group around Richard Wagner. But a mysterious illness prevented Nietzsche from continuing in his University post and he took medical retirement at the age of 35, never to be in regular, paid employment again but living mainly on his pension. He also distanced himself from Wagner's circle, possibly because he discovered that Wagner attributed his symptoms to too much masturbation. This came out in a medical assessment, presumably much to Nietzsche's mortification. But this was not the first time, or last, time that Nietzsche was humiliated. There was, for example, the occasion during his military service, when Nietzsche smartly mounted his horse only to sail over the horse's back and fall with enough force to cause injury, onto the ground.

Nietzsche is not known to have had an intimate relationship, although some detractors have argued that he had tertiary syphilis and must have caught this in a brothel. He did have infatuations, notably with his first biographer, the redoubtable Andreas Lou-Salome. Nietzsche spent some holidays in the homes of his patrons but preferred to be in lodgings in towns where he could observe life from a distance. He was restless and moved from place to place. His main correspondence was with his mother, whom he abjured in a grossly misogynistic attack in his book "Ecce Homo," and his sister whom he also slandered. Nietzsche ironically spent the last ten years of his life in a catatonic state, cared for by his mother until her death, and then by his sister.

Being alone was the inevitable consequence of rejecting the group and a welcome price to pay for Kierkegaard for whom the crowd represented untruth, for Schopenhauer for whom it represented unfreedom, and for Nietzsche for whom it was the cradle of ressentiment, that pulled down great men to its own level.

But there is a positive spin to be given to these dangers, too. Being the member of a group means pressure to share the same beliefs. This may be bad if, like Kierkegaard, you think that these beliefs are damaging to spiritual health but not if they are healthier than the beliefs that an individual might have had before joining the group. Similarly, members of groups who want to retain their membership have to restrict their actions to a group code of conduct. This might be perceived as a lack of freedom if one is inclined to act in ways that are not deemed socially acceptable – and there is evidence from Schopenhauer's prosecution for assault by an elderly lady that he pushed downstairs that he did occasionally act on such inclinations – but old ladies might consider it salutary to have such inclinations restrained by social pressure. Finally, groups often do not take kindly to members who perceive themselves as heroes or heroines who are a cut above other group members, but the same impulse to pull down the self-regarding is also a source of resistance to tyrants or idolaters who would otherwise abuse their unresisting acolytes.

These early existential philosophers were some of the first intellectuals to recognize the emergence of "me," the "individual," as a salient locus of identity and to consider, quite rightly, the implications of this for the person who identified themselves or others as members of a family, a nation a religious community, an organization, or a social group. Maybe it is inevitable that they saw this as a freedom struggle for individual consciousness. But perhaps, too, they were influenced by their own family experiences. Kierkegaard's mother, Ane Sørensdatter Lund Kierkegaard, was the housemaid before her mistress, who was childless, died. Kierkegaard's father married her scandalously soon after his first wife had died, and even more scandalously, she was pregnant at the time. Kierkegaard is said never to refer to her in his papers or published work, suggesting to commentators that he was ashamed of her. Another possibility was that she loved him, but was over-awed by him too. Or perhaps she was just worn out. He was the youngest of her seven children, born when she was 45 years old. In one of his few references to mothers, Kierkegaard writes of mothers being the most faithful disciplines of their sons in "The Present Age." [When]: "the generation has rid itself of the individual and of everything organic and concrete and put in its place 'humanity' and the numerical equality of man and man … the sharp scythe of the leveller makes it possible for every one individually to leap over the blade – and behold, it is God who waits. Leap, then, into the arms of God.' But the 'unrecognizable' neither can nor dares help man, not even his most faithful disciple, his mother, or the girl for whom he would gladly give his life: they must make the leap themselves, for God's love is not a second-hand gift."

Kierkegaard may have considered his mother powerless. Schopenhauer was embarrassed by his, and Nietzsche thought his mother was obnoxious. Perhaps it was this that made the feminine aspect of groups, their ability to care for and nurture their members, inconceivable to these early existential authors.

Husserl's phenomenology

Nietzsche famously announced the death of god to a world that soon became willing to share his vision. He foresaw the challenge that this would pose to ethicists, but it was Husserl who first tackled a comparable philosophical challenge that the death of god re-ignited, that of solipsism. Descartes had relied on the existence of god, whose nature was truth, that if he could strip away all of his own assumptions what would be left would be god-created, and therefore truthful. Descartes was famously able to base his exploration of his own thoughts and perceptions on this fact – that he existed by virtue of his faith in a truthful god. In the absence of a god to provide an epistemological foundation to his ideas, Husserl followed a rather similar method to that of Descartes, terming it a phenomenological method, but applying it not to objects but to thoughts and "Ideas." At first, he thought that ideas about people would naturally turn out to be dependent on other people existing. But it soon became apparent that Ideas can be had about imaginary objects or people, and that his approach was becoming dependent like that of Kant, on a version of Platonic ideas. This "transcendental" turn provoked strong reactions in two of Husserl's research assistants and their different responses are keys to subsequent developments in an existential approach to group psychotherapy.

Ontology

Heidegger mocked Husserl's transcendentalism (in letters to Jaspers) and, in any case, was less concerned with epistemology than with what it means to "be" that is, ontology. Heidegger's ontogeny was mixed. He was brought up in a close-knit family of Old Catholic believers, who had split with the main congregation in dissent to the doctrine of papal infallibility voted in at the First Vatican council in 1870. His father was a cooper, and also sexton of the church building, which was in a rural town close to the Black Forest, Germany. Heidegger's brother Fritz spent his whole life there, working in a bank. Initially, Martin Heidegger planned to be a monk and joined a Jesuit house as a novice, but he developed heart symptoms (thought to be psychosomatic, and presumably related to anxiety as his heart was strong enough to keep Heidegger going until he died at the age of 86). He then went to another seminary but with no intention to become a monk. This seminary was in Freiburg and Heidegger also attended the University there, reading theology. He was called up in 1914 but discharged for ill health, although he was called up again in 1917 to serve as a meteorologist. Heidegger married a Protestant woman but even before the marriage told his confessor that he had lost his faith in Christianity. His later philosophy has been said to be close to mysticism and was influenced by Buddhism.

Heidegger's starting point in what remains his most famous work, *Being and Time*, was that Dasein finds itself in a world of others (*Mitsein*), which might suggest that the connections between members of human groups would be important to him. But it is not clear what status these others have. Gadamer (2004, p. 23) wrote "Mitsein, for Heidegger, was a concession that he had to make, but one that he never really got behind."

Relations between human beings in Heidegger's work, as in that of Sartre, are based on a foundation of exploitation. We know other people as we know "equipment," because they are "ready to hand" (Heidegger does refer to Others we encounter but does not develop this at all). Brogan (2005) links this to Heidegger's early interest in Aristotle (one of the first books of philosophy that Heidegger is known to have read was Brentano's *On the Several Senses of Being in Aristotle* 1862/1975). Aristotle raised what was the fundamental question for Heidegger at the time: "what is it that makes me aware of my being?" (which became more generalized for Heidegger later when he famously asked the question, "What is metaphysics?": "Why is there something, rather than nothing?"). Heidegger decided that Aristotle located the process by which we become aware of our own being (or rather, as Heidegger put it in abstract, of the Sein of Dasein) in mutual production with other people, "techne."

Sartre, too, is fascinated by techne or, as he terms it, praxis. His fundamental concept is not Dasein though, but consciousness. Heidegger thinks that what lifts Dasein out of its web of task-based interaction, of facticity, is the awareness of death and particularly in the ability of the death of a particular Dasein. Sartre offers two models, one based on Hegel's master-slave dialectic (put forward in Hegel's Phenomenology of Spirit) and the other his own, most famous contribution, the lowering, shaming watcher of Being and Nothingness whose look both creates the psychological experience of self-consciousness and the bad faith that leads us to live for others.

Heidegger and Sartre, like their predecessors Kierkegaard and Nietzsche, are both preoccupied as is Aristotle, according to Heidegger (Brogan 2005), with the nothingness that they think lies at the heart of being. Sartre explicitly refers to this in his most famous philosophical work, "Being and Nothingness." Heidegger tried to formulate his preoccupation with this issue in "What is metaphysics?", which was an attempt to address the doubts that he was already having about his own *Being and Time*: "What is to be investigated is being only and—nothing else; being alone and further—nothing; solely being, and beyond being-nothing. What about this Nothing? ... Does the Nothing exist only because the Not, i.e. the Negation, exists? Or is it the other way around? Does Negation and the Not exist only because the Nothing exists? ... We assert: the Nothing is prior to the Not and the Negation.... Where do we seek the Nothing? How do we find the Nothing.... We know the Nothing.... Anxiety reveals the Nothing.... That for which and because of which we were anxious, was "really"—nothing. Indeed: the Nothing itself—as such—was present.... What about this Nothing?—The Nothing itself nothings" (Carnap 1932, p. 69). Heidegger's inarticulacy about nothingness led to mockery, for example by Carnap, who quotes this passage as an example of the meaninglessness of Heidegger's prose.

It is easy to formulate the psychological problem that both Heidegger and Sartre faced. Self-consciousness emerges sometime after birth, in most children somewhere between the ages of two and four. It emerges as it were from nothing although a developmentalist would not say that. They would say that it emerges from interactions with others from the minute that the child is born, or even before when the activity of the fetus reflects what the mother is doing or even listening to. Both Heidegger and Sartre rejected or were cut off from their earliest family life. Sartre's father died when Sartre was aged two, and he and his mother moved back to his mother's parents' home. Little appears to be known about Heidegger's early life. It is known that on his eighth birthday, his father, the sexton, handed him the keys of the church, and that he later rejected his patrimony.

Both of them became avid readers, and presumably developed relationships with the authors whom they knew through their written words. Sartre entitles his autobiography "Les mots," whose connotation of "writing" is not obvious in its English translation, "Words," and there describes reading as replacing playing with friends.

There is a clear assumption in both Heidegger and Sartre that there are other people, at least insofar as they recognize that the books that they read have had authors. In the second section of *Being and Time*, Heidegger refers to cultural inheritance from these authors as "historicity." Sartre does not doubt that there is an other who looks and judges (although he accepts that we can be mistaken that there is someone looking at us when we feel self-conscious). Clearly the world must be full of people. Sartre notes manifested in the tickets for queues for buses or for service in supermarkets are clear evidence of that. Sartre also imagines the possibility of seeing others working together unknowingly and being the "mediating third" who links them (Sartre 1960/2004).

Nothing and annihilation

Heidegger and Sartre both start from the premise that the task of philosophy is to explain the philosopher, as well as the philosophy. How do we get to think about thinking about philosophy, about what matters, about what comes first, about our place in the universe? So they start with explaining Dasein or "L'être," Being. Heidegger's focus on the Greek αὐθέντης (authentes), whose roots are "self" and "doing" is an indication of this. "Authentic" might be translated as accepting agency. Sartre supposed that true reciprocity in human relationships might come only from giving up agency. In his story about storming the Bastille, no-one knows who says "To the Bastille" because individual agency has disappeared in the "fusion" of the group, a fusion that can be recreated by "terror" – hardly a benign image.

Sartre never seems to have seen a good side to this terror, but Heidegger had, at least inasmuch as he had assimilated some of the views of the Kyoto school of Japanese philosophers (Krummel 2018) who visited him after the publication of *Being and Time*. They included Tanabe, Tsujimura Kōichi, and particularly Nishitani (Heisig 2001). All of them combined study of Continental philosophy with the study of Mahayana Buddhist doctrine including the Buddha's teaching of "absolute nothingness" or anatta. The Buddha explicitly rejected the Hindu idea that there was a permanent soul, or atman, but did not explain what it was that was reborn or was freed from the cycle of suffering. In fact, he taught that it was only possible to be free of suffering when the doctrine of anatta had been fully accepted. Heidegger required hospital treatment for a psychiatric disorder after the Second World War, perhaps brought on by his anxiety about his stepson, Herman, whose fate was uncertain as he was detained after the war ended in a Soviet camp for German prisoners of war. Perhaps as a result of this experience, Heidegger turned to a rejection of technology, and to a new philosophy based on poetry, with parallels to Eastern mysticism, as a possible future way for philosophy (Döll 2011). His interest in Zen re-emerged and he corresponded with D.T. Suzuki who was at the time the exponent of Zen who was the best known in the West, and who had been at University with the founder of the Kyoto school, Nishida Kitaro.

Suggestibility: Great men, and large groups

It is possible that the Buddha considered the dissolution of the self as the prelude to toti-potentiality, and not annihilation. But this is only possible if there remains some connection with the created world even after the individual dies. Obviously this is possible imaginatively but there is no opportunity for the authentic self, the agent, the remorseless pour-soi to experience it. It is, according to Heidegger, the prospect of annihilation by death that summons authenticity.

Yet this experience of transcending the limits of one's own individuality, and of delighting in the agency of a collectivity, is precisely the experience that differentiates immersion in a group from working with a team or being in a family. The latter are experiences that a self-aware individual can usually tolerate without fearing engulfment. The former is, as I have tried to show, a reversion to an infantile, or atavistic experience.

It is impossible to re-experience mergence of the self in a greater wholeness by an act of will although possibly being in a therapy group, taking a serotoninergic drug, going to a rave, haunting romantic spots in nature, meditating, being with a loved person, or running ultramarathons might provide the right conditions for it to happen spontaneously. Nietzsche found it, as a young man, in the music of Wagner. Spontaneous surrender of the self is particularly unlikely if the person itself fears that it will annihilate their unique being, as I have argued Kierkegaard, Nietzsche, Heidegger and Sartre all did.

There is another phenomenological tradition, the Munich phenomenological circle, that did not assume that there would always be conflict between individuality and community. I will be discussing them below after considering one way that autonomy and self-surrender can be combined. This is by a voluntary act of surrender, leading to a servile relationship. Becoming the slave to the master, or to use the terms that Hegel actually used, the bondsman of a Lord gives the bondsman esoteric knowledge and power that seems to enhance the bondsman's will and disguises the loss of freedom that it entails.

The fact that many people do this is perhaps an indication that most of us have a yearning to give up our autonomy. Heidegger and Sartre were no exceptions.

Both of them placed their trust in tyrannical but powerful leaders: Heidegger in Adolf Hitler, and Sartre in a series of them, starting with Stalin. Heidegger's views of Hitler (which he much later described as his greatest mistake in life) are summarized in an address he gave to 600 beneficiaries of the National Socialist "labor service" (Arbeitsdienst) program (1934 and republished in Wolin 1993). Heidegger was Fuhrer-Prinzip (roughly equivalent to Vice-Chancellor in the United Kingdom, or President of the University in the United States) of the University of Freiburg when he gave the address, a position to which Hitler had appointed him (and from which he was soon to be dismissed):

> For this reason, neither for you nor for us can the will to build a living bridge [between workers and students] remain any longer an empty, hopeless wish… this will must be our innermost certainty and never-faltering faith. For in what this will wills, we are only following the towering will of our Führer. To be his loyal followers means: to will that the German people shall again find, as a people of labor, its organic unity, its simple dignity, and its true strength; and that, as a state of labor, it shall secure for itself permanence and greatness. (Heidegger 1933, p. 12)

Inter-subjectivity

I have concentrated so far on the development of phenomenology and then existential philosophy as interpreted by its best-known theoreticians, all of them male. Their preoccupations with individuality and self-development have taken up a large part of this chapter.

But phenomenology, revived by Brentano in Vienna, did not just take root in Göttingen, where Husserl first obtained tenure, and Freiburg where Husserl and then Heidegger spent most of their careers. There was also a parallel phenomenology group in the University of Munich. The Munich school was influenced by Theodore Lipps, a psychologist and philosopher, who had developed the aesthetic theories of Vischer (possibly influenced by Herder) into an interpersonal theory of Einfühlung misleadingly renamed "empathy" by George Titchener who was unaware that the Greek word "εμπάθεια" or empathy, is best translated as "malice." Lipps considered that there was a direct connection between one person and another based on imitation. So if we watch a tight-rope walker, we find our body also swaying as the funambulist sways to maintain his or her balance. Lipps's work was rejected by Weber amongst others on the basis that it did not capture the tension between the funambulist's experience and the observer's experience. So when it came to historiography, historians who wanted to capture the viewpoint of historical figures ran the risk of imposing their own experiences believing them to be those of the historical figures they were writing about.

Husserl's *Logical Investigations*, written whilst he was in Göttingen, captured the attention of the Munich school and several of them moved to Husserl's new department in Freiburg. However they did not entirely give up Lipps's ideas about the primordiality of Einfühlung.

Husserl had driven himself into the same corner as Kant, that of "transcendental idealism." He had broken away from the passive notion that we know about the world through the images that objects – or representations – create in our minds by his great intuitive leap that our relations with the world are intentional rather than receptive. So we can entertain thoughts about objects because we act on them, for example, by grasping them (an idea later adopted as a theory of perception by J.J. Gibson [Gibson, Shaw, and Bransford 1977]). Unfortunately this great leap became a free fall. Husserl could not find any reason to distinguish between, say, acting in response to a hallucination and acting in response to a veridical voice. Both, he thought, could equally be something for and about which we had intentions. All we could know therefore was the object of our intentions, which he called the noema (an unfortunate term since its previous use for three centuries in English had been to apply to things that were deliberately obscure and had to be puzzled out with great effort). Since there was no necessary relationship between the noema and an object, event, or relationship in the actual world, we could have no knowledge of the real work other than what had been prewired in our brains (time, causality, space, and so on).

Einfühlung was the shrub growing on the side of the precipice that Husserl and Husserlians could hang on to. Einfühlung provided a direct connection, according to Lipps, between that which did not require a prior noema of the other person. This directness had been termed "inter-subjectivity" by the Victorian philosopher (Ward 1902). My own term for it is an interbrain connection (Tantam 2017) for reasons that I will describe later. The person who introduced Einfühlung to Husserl was his first research assistant, the predecessor of Martin Heidegger, Edith Stein, who was probably influenced by Max Scheler who had amalgamated Husserl's and Lipps's ideas (see Zahavi [2014] for a review of the details). Stein did not attend the University of Munich but became friends with several of those in the Munich phenomenology group who moved to Freiburg. Husserl did not formally acknowledge Stein's work on empathy until the 1930s, well after the date on which he had failed to give her a reference to pursue her academic career and after she stopped working for him as a research assistant. Stein had, by this time, given up her hope of a University career and had become a nun.

Stein wrote three major theses whilst hoping to get a tenured position, using her own Einfühlung-based phenomenology (Stein 1989). One, her doctoral thesis which Husserl published in his journal of phenomenology was on Einfühlung itself (usually translated as the "On the problem of empathy"), another on the relevance of her phenomenological theories on psychology and the humanities, and the last on groups or least large groups ("An Investigation Concerning the State"). Stein's work is making a comeback, and the last two theses have only been translated into English recently.

Stein does not entirely pull off the twin requirements for a naturalistic theory of Einfühlung, which are to bring together primordially sharing the experience of another person, and yet also knowing that those experiences are different from one's own. But she does go further than her predecessors in establishing that there are connections between us and other people that are not purely imaginative – a rejection therefore of solipsism, too – and that these connections can change our perception of ourselves. Neuroscience has provided considerable evidence for emotional and attention-directing connections between one, two, or more people in line of sight of each other (summarized in Tantam 2017). I claim in that book that a theory of empathy that meets all of the requirements must consist of the combination of a direct connection between people who are co-present, mediated by the brain, and an imaginative connection produced by a narrative about the other person.

Scheler's typology of groups

Scheler was highly productive, like Kierkegaard, and wrote on a wide range of subjects. He had several important university posts but did not retain them because of scandals about his love life. He was reportedly a charismatic speaker, and work as a lecturer was his main income for many years. Scheler influenced Stein and she based her theory of groups partly on his. Scheler continued to develop his group theories well after Stein moved from phenomenology into early feminism, and theology.

Scheler's approach to the connections between people was more taxonomic than Stein's. In his scheme, there are at least five different types of shared or co-feelings. He distinguished: (1) sharing the same feelings with someone else in the same situation (*Miteinanderfühlen*); (2) grasping what another person feels without feeling it oneself (*Nachfühlen*); (3) pity or sympathy (*Mitgefühl*); (4) emotional contagion (*Gefühlansteckung*); (5) identification, for example the trance-like connection that Heidegger had with Hitler (*Einsfühlung*).

Scheler's typology of groups was based on his classification of connections. Scheler's classification was: (1) The Herd or Mass held together either by *Gefühlansteckung* or *Einsfühlung*; (2) Life-Community *(Lebensgemeinschaft)* based on *Mitgefühl* but with an element of structure independent of connection since each individual has the authority to act on behalf of the community; (3) *Gesellschaft* based on *Nachfühlen* and mutual convenience; and (4) Collective Person or the "love-community" based on solidarity and *Miteinanderfühlen*.

Reciprocity

Simone de Beauvoir's reputation has suffered, as Sartre's has, because of their relationship. De Beauvoir's ground-breaking feminism, following in the tradition of Edith Stein, has been trashed by contemporary feminists who are disgusted by what they see as her pandering to the sexual demands of Sartre. Philosophers like Mary Warnock dismiss her as a philosopher because they think that her ideas are just second-hand Sartre (Warnock 1996). Yet the evidence is accumulating that some of Sartre's ideas came from de Beauvoir. Her first novel, *She Came to Stay*, was published in 1943 but written in 1934–1935 when Sartre was still working on *Being and Nothingness* and it tackled themes that he was to take up in that book: violence and freedom for example. But de Beauvoir arrived at different, and arguably better, formulations to some of these key concepts. For example, she argued that freedom is never unconstrained, but is always "situated" and limited by circumstance although there is, she argued in "Pyrrhus and Cineas" her philosophical essay of 1944, always choice and so "subjective freedom." Scholars now think that it was de Beauvoir who influenced Sartre more than the other way around, in particular in her treatment of the relations of self and other (Fullbrook 2009).

De Beauvoir's acceptance of Sartre's demands on her to fit in with his lifestyle – living separately, never marrying, his casual affairs, his fame overshadowing hers – has seemed masochistic to commentators. Her philosophical response, that the freedom of one person to act has consequences on the other who must therefore be taken into consideration, were perhaps a response to this. But de Beauvoir had had a similar previous experience. Her father, who was making a good living in the law, speculated on the stock market. Perhaps he wanted to emulate his father-in-law, a wealthy banker. Instead, his shares lost value, leaving the family in much more straitened circumstances. George Bertrand de Beauvoir's decision was not made in consultation with his family but impacted all of them. His freedom came at the expense of their freedom – but then, was he himself free? Perhaps his wife's family's wealth oppressed him, and he was trying to escape that oppression.

Why *should* we take account of other people in our choices, so long as we have the power to control them and so deny them their freedom to act? This question was sharpened for de Beauvoir as she experienced Parisian life during the German occupation. She addresses it in her next book, *The Ethics of Ambiguity*. She supposes that if we demand our freedom then we must grant the freedom to others. But since our freedom to act impinges on the acts of others, our freedom is affected by the freedom of others who have the power to restrict our freedom. "To will oneself free is also to will others free" she wrote in the *The Ethics of Ambiguity* (1948/1976, p. 73). De Beauvoir terms this "interdépendance." It is clearly a highly relevant idea to existential group psychotherapy.

In *She Came To Stay*, she had already introduced a similar concept, terming it "reciprocity" and this term appears throughout her philosophical writing, and in the *Second Sex* where she uses it to explain why a woman might choose to be a lesbian. Interestingly, it was the one mode of relation that Sartre left out of *Being and Nothingness* although he included de Beauvoir's other two and it does figure in his later work.

Why though should we take others into account? Like Kierkegaard, de Beauvoir considers in the *Ethics of Ambiguity* (as she was later to do in the *Second Sex*) a range of human types none of whom experience interdependence and so fall short of their full ethical potential. De Beauvoir concludes that it is our ethical values that determine whether or not we live a fulfilled life in "joy." De Beauvoir never gave birth, but she considers the relationship of a mother to a child, and supposes that mothers, unlike fathers, aim to give their child greater freedom than they had themselves. She implies that what might need explanation for a solipsistic man as to why he should care for others might be apodictic for a woman (Bauer 2001). De Beauvoir, it has been suggested, was inspired to write the *Second Sex* because she believed that this kind of reciprocity was only possible between two women. De Beauvoir may have been inspired in this by the love that she had for her younger sister, Helene, (who was the only person to understand de Beauvoir's speech when they were both infants) and her best friend, Zaza (Ward 2009).

Conclusion

De Beauvoir's demands, put into the mouth of her alter ego Xavière in her novel *She Came To Stay*, are that she should have the freedom to speak, and that there should be others who hear. These are not bad mottos for existential group psychotherapy, where participants come to speak about themselves and be heard by others, who also speak about themselves and hope to be heard in turn.

References

Antonsen, B.T., Klungsøyr, O., Kamps, A. et al. (2014). Step-down versus outpatient psychotherapeutic treatment for personality disorders: 6-year follow-up of the Ullevål personality project. *BMC Psychiatry 14*: 119–119.

Bauer, N. (2001). *Simone de Beauvoir, Philosophy, and Feminism*. New York: Columbia University Press.

Beauvoir, S. de. (1976). *The Ethics of Ambiguity*. New York: Citadel Press. (Original work published 1948.)

Bion, W. (1961). *Experiences in Groups*. London: Tavistock.

Brentano, F.C. (1975). *On the Several Senses of Being in Aristotle*. Los Angeles: University of California Press. (Original work published 1862.)

Brogan, W. (2005). *Heidegger and Aristotle*. Albany, New York, SUNY Press.

Campling, P. (2001). Therapeutic communities. *Advances in Psychiatric Treatment 7* (5): 365–372.

Carnap, R. (1932). The elimination of metaphysics through logical analysis of language. *Erkenntnis 3*: 60–81.

Cohn, H.W. (2002). *Heidegger and the Roots of Existential Therapy*. London: Continuum.

Döll, S. (2011). Ueda Shizuteru's phenomenology of self and world: Critical dialogues with Descartes, Heidegger, and Merleau-Ponty. In: *Japanese and Continental Philosophy: Conversations with The Kyoto School* (ed. B.W. Davis, B. Schroeder, and J.M. Wirth), 120 –138. Indiana: Indiana University Press.

Fullbrook, E. (2009). She Came to Stay and Being and Nothingness. *Hypatia 14* (4): 50–69.

Gadamer, H.G. (2004). *Truth and Method*. London, Continuum.

Gibson, J.J., Shaw, R.E., and Bransford, J. (1977). *The Theory of Affordances*. Hillsdale, NJ: Lawrence Erlbaum.

Heidegger, M. (1933–1934). Labor Service and the University, June 20, p. 12. http://la.utexas.edu/users/hcleaver/330T/350kPEEHeideggerTractsTable.pdf (accessed January 6, 2019).

Heidegger, M. (1934). Arbeitsdienst. *Der Alemann: Kampfblatt der Nationalsozialisten Oberbadens*, February 1.

Heisig, J. (2001). *Philosophers of Nothingness: An Essay on the Kyoto School (Nanzan Library of Asian Religion and Culture)*. Honolulu, University of Hawai'i Press.

Kierkegaard, S. (1955). *The Present Age*. Cassell: London. https://www.goodreads.com/quotes/337993-and-so-when-the-generation-which-itself-desired-to-level (accessed January 6, 2019).

Kierkegaard, S. (1983). *The Sickness unto Death*. Princeton NJ: Princeton University Press. (Original work published 1849.)

Krummel, J. (2018). On (the) nothing: Heidegger and Nishida. *Continental Philosophy Review 51* (2): 239–268.

Nitsun, M. (1991). Destructive forces in the group. *Group Analysis 24* (1): 7–20.

Sartre, J.-P. (2004). *Critique of Dialectical Reason*, vol. 1 and 2. London, Verso. (Original work published 1960.)
Schlapobersky, J. (2016). *From the Couch to the Circle*. London, Routledge.
Schopenhauer, A. (1890). *Counsels and Maxims* (trans. T.B. Saunders). New York: Macmillan.
Stein, E. (1989). *The Collected Works of Edith Stein*. New York, Springer.
Tantam, D. (2017). *The Interbrain*. London, Jessica Kingsley.
Ward, J. (1902). *Naturalism and Agnosticism. The Gifford Lectures Delivered Before the University of Aberdeen in the Years 1896–1898*, 3e. London, Macmillan.
Ward J.K. (2009). Reciprocity and friendship in Beauvoir's thought. *Hypatia 14* (4): 36–49.
Warnock, M. (ed.) (1996). *Women Philosophers*. London: Dent and Co.
Wolin, R. (1993). *The Heidegger Controversy: A Critical Reader*. Cambridge, MA: MIT Press.
Zahavi, D. (2014). *Self and Other: Exploring Subjectivity, Empathy, and Shame*. Oxford, Oxford University Press.

26

Existential and Phenomenological Theories of Group Relations

Digby Tantam

Introduction

Some years ago (Tantam 2002) I speculated about how group therapy brings about change, and suggested that it happens through changing the past. By this counter-intuitive notion, I meant that as we re-narrate our pasts, we discover new and sometimes more benign meanings. Narrative is therefore important to group psychotherapy, especially as it is co-created by the members of the group given the basic facts provided by each member. J.-P. Sartre, the first philosopher to embrace the term existentialist, was so committed to this method that his first serious work was a novel (Sartre 1964a) and his last a biography (Sartre 1971). The mother of existentialism, Simone de Beauvoir, first made her name as the author of a novel, *The Mandarins*, which won the Prix Goncourt.

Karl Jaspers in an earlier generation applied a kind of narrative approach, which he called "genetic understanding," to psychological disorder (Häfner 2015). He urged that psychiatrists should try to understand how one mental phenomenon leads to another in a meaningful way. Jaspers could have written, "I can follow the story of how things went leading you to this impasse" as an alternative to meaningful connections. Jaspers stuck to this idea up until the fourth edition of his textbook on psychopathology (the only English translation is of the seventh edition) in which the meaningful connections have become a cut-off for psychosis. Genetic understanding is a kind of witnessing as well as a kind of explaining. Witnessing requires that the story being witnessed is not just understandable but also matters to the witness. Mattering is synonymous with another usage of meaning that is, relevant and important to me, as in the expression "Thanks for saying that. It means a lot." This second usage of meaning was of particular importance to another of the important theorists for existential group therapy, Viktor Frankl. Indeed, another way of looking at Jasper's intuition – that the most severe psychological disorders are ones where meaning has

The Wiley World Handbook of Existential Therapy, First Edition. Edited by Emmy van Deurzen, Erik Craig, Alfried Längle, Kirk J. Schneider, Digby Tantam, and Simon du Plock.

broken down – is that it is not just the witness for whom meaningful connections have broken, but also for the hopeless, despairing, or psychotic person themselves

Groups can either provide meaning or break it. There is more to this than narrative, but the psycho-biographical, narrative, method espoused by Sartre provides a useful start.

Psychobiographies

Karl Jaspers went his own way, trying the law, and qualifying in medicine, before becoming attached in a non-clinical position to a professorial unit in psychiatry. He left this to teach psychology and then philosophy. He and his wife became close friends of the Webers, and he seems to have supported Weber through Weber's mood swings. Perhaps Max Weber replaced the father to whom Cally Jaspers had been so close. Apparently, he was a frightening supervisor to have, but he was well-respected. Even during the war, when Jaspers had been sacked from the University and banned from publishing because of his Jewish wife, local shopkeepers would give him small gifts of food so that they could survive without an income (Walter Leibrecht, personal communication). After the war, Jaspers matured into an elder statesman of post-War German political and ethical philosophy, a career path quite at variance with the philosophers who would now be recognized as "existential." Jaspers was resolutely socially embedded: in loving family, in a University, then in the elite of post-War Germany.

Heidegger and Jaspers were friends initially, but Jaspers broke off their friendship when he realized how anti-Semitic Heidegger was. Heidegger, for this part, did not consider that Jaspers was a proper philosopher and, reading him, one can understand why. Like Merleau-Ponty, Jaspers is just too balanced, and too lacking in that extreme originality that led Heidegger to teach in *Lederhosen*, and Sartre to climb on lorries to exhort strikers at Renault to continue their struggle against capitalism. Kierkegaard, Schopenhauer, and Nietzsche were in their own way extremists, too. Kierkegaard punched the primate of the Church of Denmark in the face to show his contempt for the established church. Schopenhauer was taken to court for pushing a woman down the stairs and had to pay her compensation for the rest of her life (when she died, he wrote "Obit anus, abit onus" [the old woman dies, the debt is lifted]). Nietzsche proclaimed the doctrine of the super-man and counted himself as one.

Awakening

But although existentialism's antecedents have often been over-shadowed by these extremes (and by its reputed obsession with death), the critics should take into account the impulse behind them: that existential philosophers had a common belief that we all need to be shaken out of complacency if we are to be able to fully reflect on ourselves. Husserl's notion of reduction seems to be kin to this awakening that both Heidegger (Heidegger 1966) and Nietzsche (Nietzsche 1883/2006) described as a more comprehensive, life-altering process.

Groups certainly have the capacity to wake up people. Some schools of group psychotherapy have even incorporated this into their therapeutic approach. Group psychodrama incorporates an awakening exercise, for example (Karp, Holmes, and Tauvon 1998). But sudden awakenings can, as Heidegger also noted, lead to "nothing," to the removal of old certainties without anything to take their place.

Another way of looking at "awakening" is that it involves the injection of non-lethal elements of nothingness, or perhaps, to arrive at a stage of emotional resilience at which nothingness can be contemplated as plenitude as well as abyss. Pascal captures this ambiguity in the Pensées (Pascal 1995, sect. II, 72):

> For in fact what is man in nature? A Nothing in comparison with the Infinite, an All-in comparison with the Nothing, a mean between nothing and everything. Since he is infinitely removed from comprehending the extremes, the end of things and their beginning are hopelessly hidden from him in an impenetrable secret; he is equally incapable of seeing the Nothing from which he was made, and the Infinite in which he is swallowed up.

In *The Concept of Dread*, Soren Kierkegaard (1844) claims that nothingness wells up into our awareness through moods and emotions. Emotions are intentional states; they are directed toward something. If angered, I am angry *at* something. If amused, there is something I find amusing. Free floating anxiety is often cited as a counterexample. But Kierkegaard says that in this case the emotion of angst is directed at nothingness.

According to Heidegger, we have several motives to shy away from the significance of our emotional encounters with nothingness. They are premonitions of the nothingness of death. They echo the groundlessness of human existence. Kierkegaard and Sartre thought similarly, Kierkegaard famously using dread as a pointer towards freedom.

Small groups, too, may evoke feelings of nothingness in individual members who might feel unheard, or insignificant. Some people may be referred to groups because they feel nothing in the first place. There is a risk that "anhedonia" of this sort may be exacerbated for a new member in a group feeling that they are an "outsider," or an established group member who makes what they take to be a cathartic statement to the group, only to find that it is greeted with apparent indifference or mockery. Joining a group is a kind of limit situation, in Jasper's terms. Whether or not a heightened experience of nothingness leads in a positive or negative therapeutic direction depends on the psychological factors that were deliberately neglected by many existential philosophers who, like Husserl, were unprepared to accept the authority of psychology that, as they thought, masqueraded as a science. But it seems clear looking at their personal reactions to nothingness that some factor linked to their own sense of being valued that psychological factors play a part. This is for example what Sartre, that denizen of café society, said of himself after his mother died, "I … live alone, entirely alone. I never speak to anyone, never; I receive nothing, I give nothing…" (Sartre 1964b/1976).

Deliberately inducing a feeling of nothingness has sometimes been used in group therapy, usually when it involves large groups. "Synanon," "Phoenix House," and other now outmoded residential drug and alcohol rehabilitation programs all had a preliminary stage during which responsibility was removed from the new entrant with the exception of the responsibility to stick to the program, and its rules. This turned out to be a dangerous recipe for Synanon, at least, which closed down amid accusations of violence and financial malfeasance.

Shame

Shame is probably the emotional experience most closely related to feeling nothingness and, correspondingly, not being easily shamed may be the main source of emotional resilience when faced with limit situations that engender a feeling of nothingness. According to Pettersen (2012) Kierkegaard uses the Danish word for shame 59 times in *The Works of Love* (Kjerlighetens Gjerninger 1847, CW 12). Nietzsche refers to the "Shame, shame, shame – that is the history of the human" (Nietzsche 1883/2006). Heidegger is an exception: one person knowledgeable about his work has argued that Heidegger never used the term (Stolorow 2013) and that this was because argues Stolorow, Heidegger viewed shame as the mood of inauthenticity, of being "held hostage by the eyes of others, belonging not to ourselves but to them" (Stolorow 2013, p. 456).

Sartre on the other hand made shame one of the organizing principles of *Being and Nothingness*. The look of others is what, he thought, could not just induce shame, but could and does create a new consciousness of ourselves, because in response to the look we become aware of être pour autrui – being for others. This consciousness leads us too readily to acting to conciliate other people and protect us against that shaming gaze, a kind of bad faith that Sartre especially excoriated because it replaces our freedom to act as we will. Shame therefore produces, in Sartre's view, the destruction of individual potential.

Being in a group potentially multiplies the critical gaze that is directed at an errant group member, reducing the possibilities of individual freedom – if Sartre is correct – even more than in the two-person encounter that he described in *Being and Nothingness.*

Meaning

One of the most significant figures in the development of existential therapy in the twentieth century was Viktor Frankl. His focus on meaning, and finding meaning in life, has directly influenced the development of group therapy for people who share a common fate in being terminally ill or bereaved (Breitbart 2015) and (Lichtenthal and Breitbart 2015). It is difficult to determine the influences on Frankl other than that of the physicians who trained him in psychiatry and neurology. He had already written an essay on the meaning of life whilst at school and was also very drawn to psychoanalysis. His interests in meaning had therefore formed early. But another early interest was the philosophy of Arthur Schopenhauer, who was the subject of the essay that he wrote on graduation from high school. Schopenhauer, like the existentialist philosopher Camus, had concluded that the universe lacked meaning, and so his work seems an unusual interest for Frankl to have. Schopenhauer (1883/1819) – and Camus – fall into that group of nihilists who reject the possibility that there is meaning to be had in the universe, arguing instead that life is absurd (Metz 2013).

Despite this, neither Schopenhauer nor Camus denied that an individual could experience their personal life as having meaning, but they did deny that there could be a formula for this. Schopenhauer eventually arrived at a rather conventional morality but did so on the basis that it was the struggle of wills that caused suffering (he was influenced by the newly translated Upanishads). He assumed, like the Epicureans, that the purpose of life is to reduce suffering, and offered suggestions about how this might be achieved by reducing the conflict of wills. These include playing music (he was a flautist himself), asceticism, and compassion for others.

Frankl refers to Schopenhauer once in his best-known book, published in English as *Man's Search for Meaning*, twice to Nietzsche, and once to Lessing (best known as a dramatist and advocate of religious tolerance). Frankl does not describe life as absurd but is clear that for him the world does not create meaning, it is the individual who has to find it. In a famous passage, he writes about what one would say to a person who said "I have nothing to expect from life anymore" (Frankl 1949/1964).

> What was really needed was a fundamental change in our attitude toward life. We had to learn ourselves and, furthermore, we had to teach the despairing men, that it did not really matter what we expected from life, but rather what life expected from us...Our answer must consist, not in talk and meditation, but in right action and right conduct. Life ultimately means taking the responsibility to find the right answer to its problems and to fulfill the tasks which it constantly sets for each individual. (Frankl 1949/1964: pp. 76–77)

Frankl's survival in the various concentration camps into which he was placed is remarkable. He attributed it to the spiritual experience of his wife being close to him (they had married days before they were deported, separately, to the camps after a whirlwind courtship but she may already have been killed in one of the camps to which she was taken before he first experienced her presence), and to his determination to publish the book whose manuscript had been ripped away from him when he arrived at the camp. He harbored the hope that he would find it again. He did later on find a greatcoat that resembled the one that he had been wearing, but this contained a Hebrew prayer in its pocket, and not his manuscript. Frankl did retain notes on scraps of paper of the points that he had made in the book, and eventually did re-write and publish it.

Frankl does give one instance of the application of what came to be called "logotherapy," in a group setting, in *Man's Search for Meaning*. The men in his camp were being punished by having their rations stopped because no-one would identify the prisoner who had stolen potatoes from the store. Morale was falling in the hut in which he was living, and the senior block leader asked Frankl to address the other men. He describes the points he made in *Man's Search for Meaning*. First, he said that although they had all experienced loss, there were many who had lost more – and anyway, they could potentially look forward to their losses being restored to them after the war (in fact, Frankl returned to find that his wife, and his parents had both died in the camps). Then he said that although the future looked bad, no-one could say for sure what it would bring. There were still grounds for hope. He said that no-one could take away what each of them had already experienced, and perhaps achieved. I am not sure how this would have been taken, but then Frankl moved on to his main point about meaning. No human situation was without meaning – even the suffering that they were all undergoing had a meaning if only as a test of their dignity. There was a witness, Frankl said, who knew how they were dealing with suffering – someone was looking down on them, whether it was a parent, a wife, or their god. Finally, Frankl told them that their suffering was not a pointless sacrifice, even if they died. Perhaps god would accept it as a reason to spare a loved one, for instance.

I doubt that these arguments in themselves convinced anyone. But clearly Frankl was filled with some kind of inspiration, and he communicated this as a feeling and not through a set of arguments. Camus was synchronously describing in his novels and essays, notably the "Myth of Sisyphus," that meaning was linked to affective appraisal. He instructed the reader to imagine that Sisyphus was happy as he rolled his boulder up the hill in Hades only to see it roll down again as it nearly reached the summit.

Two modes of relating

Buber's (2003) short book, *I and Thou* made a considerable impression when it was published. Buber argued that there were two fundamental relations between people, I–Thou and I–It. I–Thou relations are, in Buber's estimation, a pale shadow of the religious person's relationship with their god. Buber supposed that infants experience "I–Thou" encounters (Begegnung – the word is taken from Moreno but is clearly influenced by Dilthey's conception of Zusammenhang, or connectedness). Buber did not trace the philosophical origins of the I–Thou himself, but its description is similar to that given by late-nineteenth century philosophers like Ward (1902) who began to use the term "inter-subjectivity," possibly under the influence of Schleiermacher. I have already discussed the development of the concept of empathy that is assumed to be a condition for inter-subjectivity. The formulation of empathy by Edith Stein is perhaps the closest to Buber's. Stein particularly considers empathy to be a kind of involuntary fellow feeling, which is most like a kind of sensation of another person's thoughts and feelings (Svenaeus 2018).

Inter-subjectivity is currently receiving unusual attention, partly because of a rediscovery of the work of Merleau-Ponty and partly because of the growth of interest in it by developmental psychologists (Kokkinaki et al. 2017; Trevarthen 1979), philosophers (Zahavi 2016), and by neuroscientists (Shamay-Tsoory and Lamm 2018). I summarize this in my book on the "interbrain" (Tantam 2017), my word for inter-subjectivity that I coined to emphasize that inter-subjectivity is not mediated by language, or narrative, or indeed any mental process, but by an in-built potential connectivity of brains, mediated by non-verbal communication.

Buber has been criticized for not clearly defining what he means by I–Thou and I–It relationships. He writes:

> Man travels over the surface of things and experiences them. He extracts knowledge about their constitution from them: he wins an experience from them. He experiences

> what belongs to the things. But the world is not presented to man by experiences alone. They present him with a world composed of *It* and *He* and *She* and *It* again. (Buber 2003, p.12)

I interpret Buber to mean that, unlike the I–Thou relationship in which "I" and "Thou" are incompletely differentiated, in the I–It connection "man" is already differentiated from "things" and gains knowledge of these things by "experience" (Dix 2017).

In my own work I contrast interpersonal understanding by means of "cognitive empathy" making use of "theory of mind," and the involuntary reciprocity of what I call the interbrain. This distinction is not new to the phenomenological field. Schutz makes a similar distinction between "consociates," with whom we have a we-relationship, and others with whom we have a relationship based on what we know of them (Schutz's examples are Contemporaries, Predecessors, and Successors). My concept of the interbrain is very similar to Merleau-Ponty's (1945/1962) description of "pre-personal forms of consciousness" (Merleau-Ponty 1945/1962, p. xii). In my book (Tantam 2017), I present evidence that cognitive empathy or "theory of mind" (not that either of these terms are used consistently between authors) is based on the use of language to create a narrative about other people that is updated with experience and on which we make judgements about our own and other people's beliefs, actions, and emotions. This requires conscious deliberation. The interbrain is mediated by a constant traffic of non-verbal communication, that is, near simultaneous emotional contagion and mutual gaze and gaze following (plus vocal and postural interchange very often) that links us to what those around us are feeling and on what they are attending (and of course links them to us). These two kinds of relating are mediated by different areas of the brain (Vogeley 2017) (see also Tantam 2017 for supporting evidence including that from developmental psychology, phenomenology, and neuroscience).

World and Objects

Western Europeans became progressively more aware of their place in a multifarious and multicultural world from the seventeenth century onwards. The world seemed to offer almost unlimited opportunities for colonialization and empire building. As the centuries progressed, the limits of this world-straddling approach became apparent. Kierkegaard is an early example of someone who rejected this kind of intellectual colonialism. He particularly objected to Hegel's imperialistic claims about his philosophical system. Kierkegaard's own emphasis was on the personal relationship between the man of faith and God, which was unique to that individual man or woman. But Kierkegaard (1941, p. 382) also characterized the man of faith as someone who had stopped reflecting but was called by something outside him or herself: "The externality is the watchman who awakens the sleeper; the externality is the solicitous mother who calls one; the externality is the roll call that brings the soldier to his feet; the externality is the reveille that helps one to make the great effort…."

An appealing but simple paradigm was provided much later by the Estonian biologist von Uexkull who proposed that every organism would have a different view of their personal world (Umwelt) according to their particular sensory apparatus. His description of the Umwelt of the tick particularly caught public imagination although it is now usually quoted in a version by Giorgio Agamben (2010, p. 46) rather than in von Uexkull's:

> This eyeless animal finds the way to her watch post with the help of only her skin's general sensitivity to light. The approach of her prey becomes apparent to this blind and deaf bandit only through her sense of smell. The odor of butyric acid, which emanates from the sebaceous follicles of all mammals, works on the tick as a signal that causes her to abandon her post and fall blindly downward toward her prey. If she is fortunate enough to fall on something warm (which she perceives by means of an organ sensible to a precise temperature) then she has attained her prey, the warm-blooded animal, and thereafter needs only the help of her sense of touch to find the least hairy spot possible and embed herself up to her head in the cutaneous tissue of her prey. She can now slowly suck up a stream of warm blood.

A self-reflective tick might have stayed for years on its blade of grass unaware that it would have this savage capacity for blood sucking until the right stimulus triggered the action sequence. So we cannot just understand others by introspection, we must understand what actions our world can draw out of us.

Husserl and others were influenced by this analogy with the human situation. Husserl used the analogy of a perceptual world to introduce his concept of a horizon that borders it, and therefore limits what we can intend or reach out to. Heidegger adopted the term, defining it to be the totality of things, including other beings, and so on, that are ready to hand.

Von Uexkull's concept of Umwelt pairs a sensory response – to butyric acid – to an object in the world, the mammalian sebaceous gland. Anyone wanting to know why ticks release their hold on vegetation would need to consider butyric acid as the stimulus. Anyone who wanted to understand a person's startle response might similarly need to know that it occurred shortly after the sound of a rifle-shot and that the person has been in a gun fight recently that had left them "traumatized." Most, if not all, therapists assume that to understand other people we have to understand their "world," historically (in the example, having survived an experience of being in a gunfight) and currently (hearing the sound of a shot in the example that I have given).

Cohn (1993) considers the Heideggerian concept of Umwelt as an important contribution to group psychotherapy for this reason and applauds group analytic psychotherapy's emphasis on connections between group members ("the nexus") as well as connections outside the group ("the plexus"). Although Foulkesians often attribute Foulkes's model of the nexus to Goldstein's ideas about the mass action of the nervous system, it seems likely that he must have been influenced by Moreno and Moreno's work on sociograms or, as we would now say, social networks.

Ticks are not known to learn. The butyric acid reflex is wired in. Modern theories of neural networks have developed considerably since Goldstein's clinical intuitions and do accommodate learning. In fact, the trainability of neural networks is what makes them so interesting because it is not often clear what they have learnt only that they have. What is true of neural networks has, *a forteriori*, to be true of how we think, since memory places an inextricable role in the accumulation of experience that thinking relies on. Heidegger did not complete the section of *Being and Time* on "Time" and his views about how the Umwelt changes with time are not known.

Freudian theory apparently handles the question of time readily: "objects" are internalized and relationships with them are updated with life experience. Lacan even called this the "Innenwelt." Most of the existential philosophers who comment on Freudianism were skeptical, as Heidegger was, but none of them seem to have addressed the temporal development of the Umwelt.

Foulkes claimed that there was no need of an "intrapsychic" account of emotional relationships, and by this he meant that he could do without object relations therapy. But then what changes with development?

The later Husserl's account of the Umwelt (Husserl 1989), on the other hand, does seem to leave room for development, but without creating a fictional world of inner objects, and relationships with them. His full development of Umwelt was not published until *Ideen II*, which was published posthumously. Husserl's thought of the Umwelt as those entities in our environment that are "meaningful" to us. Many of these will be meaningful to others, too. He wrote:

> I see coal as heating material; I recognize it and recognize it as useful and as used for heating, as appropriate for and as destined to produce warmth. [...] I can use [a combustible object] as fuel; it has value for me as a possible source of heat. That is, it has value for me with respect to the fact that with it I can produce the heating of a room and thereby pleasant sensations of warmth for myself and others. [...] Others also apprehend it in the same way, and it acquires an intersubjective use-value and in a social context is appreciated and is valuable as serving such and such a purpose, as useful to man, etc. (Husserl 1989, pp. 196–197)

The Umwelt, for Husserl, is therefore an abstraction based on the many wars in which our use of the world – our intentions towards it – create the world, including a world with others. Partly this is done through shared narrative. Suppose, instead of coal, Husserl had described cow dung. For many Indians in rural parts of the country, a cow pat connotes not just excrement, but a dried disk of fuel. This connection is unlikely to be made by anyone who has not seen disks of cow dung being traded as fuel. Anyone who has will have an altered Umwelt that is now, in one small corner, shared with an Indian farmer. Sharing narratives in a group is one way to widen the Umwelt of all the members of the group, to who get involved in those narratives, and therefore to increase the connections between group members without supposing, as object relations theorist do, that there is an Innenwelt.

Therapeutic Groups and the Interbrain

Jacob Moreno (1945, 1952) may have been one of the first group therapists to apply Lippsian ideas about inter-subjectivity to groups, but he was also aware of a potential for violence in the extreme mergence that an unrestricted interbrain connection might bring. Moreno (1952) wrote a poem, "Invitation to a meeting," as a medical student whose first stanza is:

> Meeting of two: eye to eye, face to face. And when you are near I will tear your eyes out and place them instead of mine, and you will tear my eyes out and will place them instead of yours, then I will look at me with mine.

This destructive potential is what existential philosophers from Kierkegaard onwards have warned about and it has been manifested in some encounter groups run by charismatic leaders. Adverse effects of group therapy are also common in attenders at in-patient groups (Schneibel et al. 2017) perhaps because the setting exacerbates the loss of autonomy that is a required potential for involvement in any therapy group.

The development of mind, and its capacity to consciously simulate the behavior of other people through narrative, has enabled these destructive features of emotional cohesion, panicky escape, or contagious rage, to be controlled. The prefrontal areas that are required for social cognition have been shown to have pathways to the right temporal lobe and these are, plausibly, the medium through which stories can inhibit empathic responses. But the interbrain is also what mediates involuntary empathic responses, and the inter-subjectivity that Husserl considered foundational in human relations.

Inter-Subjectivity and Group Analytic Psychotherapy

Scheler's last post before his death at the age of 54 was in Frankfurt, at the Frankfurt Institut für Sozialforschung, His work was highly valued by the director, Max Horkheimer, who had little time for Husserl (Türker 2013). The sociology department in Frankfurt rented rooms from the Institute and these were taken from 1929 by Karl Mannheim and his research assistant Norbert Elias. Elias had attended Husserl's Goethe seminar and was a friend of Edith Stein (Korte 2017) and had philosophical discussions with Karl Jaspers. However, he does not seem to have incorporated phenomenology or existentialism directly into his work on the civilizing process, or into his influence on the development of group psychotherapy. Another Frankfurt student, located in the Frankfurt Psychoanalytic Institute was Sigmund Fuchs. Fuchs was working on Gestalt neurology with Goldstein, who was demonstrating that neuronal excitation could be best modelled by looking at (what we would now call) the behavior of neural nets, rather than the behavior of individual neurons.

Fuchs moved to the United Kingdom, changing his name to S. "Michael" Foulkes, and joined with Elias in creating the Group Analytic Society in London. It was Mannheim who had coined the term group analysis. He, too, had moved to London and met Foulkes once for tea (Winship 2003) but had little direct contribution to the development of group analysis into one of the most influential group therapy approaches in the United Kingdom. One of the key theoretical elements of group analytic psychotherapy is the "matrix," Foulkes's term for the intersubjective connection that develops between the members of a therapeutic group (Foulkes 1973). Although Foulkes originally termed group analysis a "psycho-analytic approach" (Foulkes and Anthony 1957), Hans Cohn, an existential psychotherapist as well as a group analytic psychotherapist, recognized that it was an application of existential philosophy, based as it was on the phenomenological ideas about inter-subjectivity (Cohn 1993).

Cohn considered that the description that Foulkes left of a group analytic group (Foulkes 1975) could just as well be taken as the description of an existential group therapy. Van Deurzen and I will consider this proposal in more detail in the next chapter.

Conclusions

Traditional existential philosophy has focused on guarding the individual from the baneful effects of groups. This is increasingly seen as an aberration of its celebrated male proponents whose personal histories have made them particularly susceptible to fears of engulfment. But there is another existential tradition with mainly female exponents, who have accepted that freedom cannot be taken for ourselves without consideration of its impact on the freedom of others. I have considered de Beauvoir's arguments for this, and also her formulation of an underlying principle of "reciprocity" in human relations that links with the work of Edith Stein and Max Scheler, both of whom I have considered in detail.

This is not to say that freedom is not an important value, and the ruthlessness with which many male existential philosophers pursued it, courting feelings of annihilation along the way, is an important model for change processes in psychotherapy. However, without the values of inter-subjectivity and reciprocity, a purely freedom focused existential philosophy has not proved applicable to group psychotherapy.

But clearly there is potential for an expanded existential philosophy, from which the perspective of female existential philosophers are not excluded, to be applied to groups. There have been practitioners who have considered their work to have been inspired by existential approaches, including the practitioners that we include or refer to in subsequent chapters, but no systematic theory of existential group therapy. Perhaps it has been blocked by the schizoid fears of male existential and phenomenological philosophers. Times are changing and I hope that readers of this chapter might be inspired to create a systematic existential group psychotherapy.

References

Agamben, G. (2010). *The Open*. Palo Alto, CA: Stanford University Press.

Breitbart, W. (2015). Creating your soul in every moment: Meaning, creativity and attitude. *Palliative & Supportive Care 13* (5): 1139–1140.

Buber, M. (2003). *I And Thou: A New Translation, With A Prologue And Notes*. New York: Touchstone.

Cohn, H.W. (1993). Matrix and intersubjectivity: Phenomenological aspects of group analysis. *Group Analysis 26* (4): 481–486.

Dix, A. (2017). I in an other's eye. *AI and Society*: 1–19. https://doi.org/10.1007/s00146-017-0694-7.

Foulkes, S. (1973). The group as matrix of the individual's mental life. In: *Group Therapy 1973 – An Overview* (ed. L. Wolberg and E. Schwartz), 223–233. New York: Intercontinental Medical Book Corporation.

Foulkes, S.J. (1975). *Group-Analytic Psychotherapy: Methods and Principles*. London: Gordon and Breach.

Foulkes, S. and Anthony, E. (1957). *Group Psychotherapy: The Psycho-Analytic Approach*. Harmondsworth: Penguin.

Frankl, V. (1964). *Man's Search For Meaning*. London: Hodder & Stoughton. (Original work published 1949.)

Häfner, H. (2015). Descriptive psychopathology, phenomenology, and the legacy of Karl Jaspers. *Dialogues in Clinical Neuroscience 17* (1): 19–29.
Heidegger, M. (1966). Conversation on a country path about thinking. In *Discourse On Thinking* (pp. 58–90). New York: Harper & Row.
Husserl, E. (1989). *Studies in the Phenomenology of Constitution*. Dordrecht: Kluwer.
Karp, M., Holmes, P.S., and Tauvon, K. (eds.) (1998). *The Handbook of Psychodrama*. Hove: Routledge.
Kierkegaard, S. (1844). *The Concept of Dread*. Copenhagen: Reitzel.
Kierkegaard, S. (1941). *Concluding Unscientific Postscript*. Oxford: Oxford University Press.
Kokkinaki, T.S., Vasdekis, V.G.S., Koufaki, Z.E. et al. (2017). Coordination of emotions in mother–infant dialogues. *Infant and Child Development 26*(2): e1973.
Korte, H. (2017). *On Norbert Elias*. Wiesbaden: Springer.
Lichtenthal, W.G. and Breitbart, W. (2015). The central role of meaning in adjustment to the loss of a child to cancer: Implications for the development of meaning-centered grief therapy. *Current Opinion in Supportive And Palliative Care 9* (1): 46–51.
Merleau-Ponty, M. (1962). *Phenomenology of Perception*. London: Routledge. (Original work published 1945.)
Metz, T. (2013). *Meaning in Life: An Analytic Study*. Oxford: Oxford University Press.
Moreno, J.L. (1945). Scientific foundations of group psychotherapy. *Sociometry and Group Psychotherapy: A Symposium 8*: 77–84.
Moreno, J.L. (1952). Some comments to the trichotomy, tele-transference-empathy. *Group Psychotherapy 5*: 87–90.
Nietzsche, F. (2006). *Thus Spoke Zarathustra: A Book For All And None*. Cambridge: Cambridge University Press. (Original work published 1883.)
Pascal, B. (1995). *Pensées and Other Writings*. Oxford: Oxford World Classics.
Pettersen, K. (2012). Shame as a sickness of the Self. *Practical Philosophy*. http://kaaretorgnypettersen.blogspot.com/2012/05/shame-as-sickness-of-self.html (accessed January 6, 2019).
Sartre, J.P. (1964a). *Nausea*. New York: New Directions Publishing.
Sartre, J.P. (1964b/1976). *The Critique of Dialectical Reason* (English edition). London: Methuen.
Sartre, J.-P. (1971). *The Family Idiot: Gustave Flaubert 1821–1857*. Chicago: University Of Chicago Press.
Schneibel, R., Wilbertz, G., Scholz, C. et al. (2017). Adverse events of group psychotherapy in the in-patient setting – results of a naturalistic trial. *Acta Psychiatrica Scandinavica 136* (3): 247–258.
Schopenhauer, A. (1883/1819). *The World as Will and Idea*. London: Routledge and Kegan Paul.
Shamay-Tsoory, S. and Lamm, C. (2018). The neuroscience of empathy – from past to present and future. *Neuropsychologia 116* (Pt. A): 1–4.
Stolorow, R. (2013). Heidegger and post-Cartesian psychoanalysis. In: *The Bloomsbury Companion To Heidegger* (ed. F. Raffoul and E. Nelson), 451–458. London: Bloomsbury.
Svenaeus, F. (2018). Edith Stein's phenomenology of sensual and emotional empathy. *Phenomenology and the Cognitive Sciences 17* (4): 741–760.
Tantam, D. (2002). *Psychotherapy and Counselling in Practice: A Narrative Framework*. Cambridge: Cambridge University Press.
Tantam, D. (2017). *The Interbrain*. London: Jessica Kingsley.
Trevarthen, C. (1979). Communication and cooperation in early infancy: A description of primary intersubjectivity. In: *Before Speech: The Beginning of Interpersonal Communication* (ed. M. Bullowa) 307–321. Cambridge: Cambridge University Press.

Türker, H. (2013). Horkheimer's criticism of Husserl. *Philosophy & Social Criticism 39* (7): 619–635.

Vogeley, K. (2017). Two social brains: Neural mechanisms of intersubjectivity. *Philosophical Transactions of the Royal Society B: Biological Sciences, 372*(1727).

Ward, J. (1902). *Naturalism and Agnosticism. The Gifford Lectures Delivered Before The University Of Aberdeen In The Years 1896–1898*, 3e. London: Macmillan.

Winship, G. (2003). The democratic origins of the term "group analysis": Karl Mannheims' "third way" for psychoanalysis and social science. *Group Analysis 36* (1): 37–51.

Zahavi, D. (2016). Second-person engagement, self-alienation, and group-identification. *Topoi*: 1–10. https://doi.org/10.1007/s11245-016-9444-6.

27

Existential Group Therapy

Method and Practice

Digby Tantam and Emmy van Deurzen

Introduction

Participation in a group with other people is such a daily and mundane activity that we take it for granted and rarely reflect on it. We are all part of a family group and we learn to find our place in the pecking order in our school life as well. Without realizing it this experience of family and school life induces remarkable shifts in our state of mind. Throughout our lives we encounter this phenomenon of having to insert ourselves into existing groups of people, at work, in our leisure activities, in further or higher education, and in many other situations (Deurzen 2013). Presenting ourselves to a new group creates, for many people, anxious self-consciousness. But the inverse, that is, the experience of pleasant merging and a sense of belonging, can also be induced by groups. Singing in a choir, working in a team, marching in a regiment can all induce a state of selfless compliance with the group task that is experienced as uplifting and brings relief from our sense of personal responsibility. Being with others is such an essential part of human existence (Heidegger 1927; Husserl 1925) that experimenting with the way in which we are with others can be an important existentially therapeutic activity (Tantam and Deurzen 2005).

Existential group therapy is however not widely established as a recognized method of group therapy, but many people who work in groups in mental health or educational settings have found the emphasis on existential themes important to their work (Yalom 1980, 2005; Tantam 2005).

Different forms of existential group therapy

As we saw in the previous chapter, though no systematic existential group psychotherapy exists as yet, there have been group psychotherapists who have identified strongly with the existential tradition.

The Wiley World Handbook of Existential Therapy, First Edition. Edited by Emmy van Deurzen, Erik Craig, Alfried Längle, Kirk J. Schneider, Digby Tantam, and Simon du Plock.

Thomas Hora, a Hungarian psychiatrist who established a practice in New York, for example, sought a spiritual basis for his group therapy and found it in existential and phenomenological philosophy. He created something he called "metapsychiatry" and a foundation, the PAGL foundation, still exists to disseminate his ideas. They are drawn, according to him, from Zen, Christianity, Existential ideas, and other spiritual sources. PAGL stands for Peace, Assurance, Gratitude, Love, and Hora's work is something of an indiscriminate mix of religious and existential ideas. Metapsychiatry, according to the Winter 2018 newsletter of the PAGL foundation, is a response to two questions: 1. What is the meaning of what seems to be? 2. What is what really is? (Anon 2018, p. 4).

Hugh Mullan was another psychiatrist who felt dissatisfied with the conventional practice of group psychotherapy and pioneered existential ideas in his work. These were known to him through the work of Rollo May. The humanist take on the existentialism of the time was mainly interpreted to mean facing up to choices (Mullan 1992) and being "authentic." These early humanist group therapists often interpreted "being authentic" as being spontaneous and lacking in inhibitions. Mullan encouraged this in the members of his groups, too, and termed the results "mutuality." Mutuality could be encouraged, Mullan thought, by a reduction in the therapist's authority, and an increase in care by other group members (Anon 2018). Of course, when a therapist claims that they are no more than an ordinary group member but retains the authority to retain or remove group members, mutuality may be a sham or even a means to gain greater control over members of the group. Mullan's behavior in his groups has been described by Wright (2014) as "'quite unorthodox'. He would tell his own dreams, disclose feelings, make non-logical associations, and, at times, act in a fashion that was puzzling, 'not nice', and even weird from a conventional perspective" (Wright 2014, p. 25).

Bernard Frankel considers key existential ideas for group psychotherapy (his list is very similar to the headings of the previous chapter) and then provides examples of them from his own groups. His existential orientation is apparent in the contents and process that he selects from the groups as being of importance. But the impact of existential ideas on his interventions seems anomalous. Interventions that he cites as being inspired by existential ideas include shouting at a group member, speaking for the group, implying that getting paid is the primary motivation of himself as a group therapist, and tacitly encouraging group members to hide their assets in contested divorces (Frankel 2002). We should be very cautious in accepting such interventions as being described as "existential." They are more usually seen as belonging to the humanistic tradition in psychotherapy and are in line with the movement of encounter groups where such interventions were common in the 1960s and 1970s.

Ronald Laing was also a psychiatrist, although he opted for psychotherapy rather than general psychiatry in his higher training. Like Mullan, Laing was known for his unorthodox and uninhibited approach to patients. Laing had a private practice as an individual psychotherapist and did not, so far as we know, have any specific training in group psychotherapy despite his work at the Tavistock. But he was influenced by the therapeutic community movement to which he had been introduced as a trainee psychiatrist at Gartnavel Hospital in Glasgow, Scotland, and used community groups and community living in his experiments in social psychiatry conducted under the aegis first of the Philadelphia Association that he co-founded and then, after being excluded from that, other organizations. He referred to his group work as "social phenomenology" and the idea was to create safe havens (asylums in the literal sense of the word) where people could experiment with the way they wanted to live with each other, without this leading to a diagnosis or a prescription of anti-psychotic drugs. Kingsley Hall was the first of these communal therapeutic experiments. Here too it was much more about disinhibition and spontaneity than about any formal or structured existential group work. Laing wrote (with David Cooper) an introduction to Sartre's later work (Laing and Cooper 1964), which was especially focused on human beings' social roles, competition, and scarcity. He was explicitly influenced by this work and by existentialist philosophy in general, specifically by Sartre's analysis of human relationships in *Being and Nothingness* (Sartre 1943/1956) and his later work in *Search for a Method* (Sartre 1960/1968). Laing combined this philosophical insight with early (and as it turned out flawed) studies of family communication patterns that he did whilst working at the Tavistock Institute of Human Relations. He began to use his observations in his book the *Self and Others* (Laing 1961), to create a new interpersonal theory (Laing, Phillipson, and Lee 1966). He used this new theory to illuminate extracts from, amongst other fields, group psychotherapy. Laing took from Sartre the importance of what we think other people think about us. Cooper has suggested that "interpersonal perception theory" is particularly applicable to group psychotherapy, as this brings these "meta-perceptions" into the foreground and also provides the opportunity for a group member to compare their meta-perception of another group member with what that other member says that their perceptions are to compare them with what other people say that they are (Cooper 2007). Laing's book *Knots* (1970) was a summary of the patterns of communication and social exchange he had observed in people within his sessions of family and group psychotherapy. It illustrates the negatives of human communication to perfection, especially the phenomenon of the double- bind, where we are damned when we do or say one thing and also damned if we do or say another thing. It was Bateson who had introduced the idea of the double bind and Laing applied it successfully to his descriptions of pathological interactions. His work at the Tavistock also led to his publication of his book with Aron Esterson, *Sanity, Madness and the Family* (Laing and Esterson 1964) but this is often said to have been much influenced by Esterson. Laing's own views of the interactions in family groups were more accurately described in his book on the *Politics of the Family* (Laing 1971), where he made it clear that he thought that families often affected children very badly. In this book he spoke of families as a system or a group in which people are exposed to complex power structures that affect and condition a person's relationship to himself. It is a dark view of the impact of groups and families on an individual typical of that era.

Contemporary group psychotherapists who describe their work with long-term groups as existential often look back to the period when Mullan and Laing were at their most influential, describing it as a high-water mark in group psychotherapy in general. They cite the frequency of group therapy's appearance in the five million books digitized by Google, as found by its search-related API Ngram viewer (Frankel 2002; Vitemb 2018). References to "group psychotherapy" were most frequent in the 1960s and 1970s and have declined since. The former enthusiasts for group psychotherapy who wrote about it in the 1960s and 1970s are now seniors and more and more preoccupied by the salience of death and dying in their lives, or so Vitemb (2018) argues. Existential writing on mortality may therefore be more important in this age group than concerns about autonomy or freedom. She may be right. The use of "existential," in this same corpus of books, reaches a peak in 1969 in Ngram viewer, falls to a low in 1985, but has steadily risen ever since. Vitemb (2018) describes a group that she runs along existential lines for seniors in which concerns about isolation, loss of value in other people's eyes, and dying are common topics for discussion.

Irvin Yalom, a psychiatrist who worked in group psychotherapy (Yalom and Leszcz 2005), before he discovered that existential issues were a vital part of group interaction and who then became an existential psychotherapist (Yalom 1980) has also become more interested in issues surrounding loss and death. He reports (see Chapter 28), becoming more and more interested in clients who are dying as he has aged himself. He has made a significant contribution to therapy for the terminally ill, including in short-term group therapy (Yalom and Greaves 1977; Spiegel and Yalom 1978), but although he is probably the most well-known existential psychotherapist at the time of publication of this chapter and also the author of a well-known book on group psychotherapy, he has admitted in an interview and in his recent autobiography (Yalom 2017) that he made few cross-links between the two. Yalom's group approach is strongly influenced by Harry Stack Sullivan, who developed his interpersonal method out of the mainstream of European philosophy. A replication of Spiegel and Yalom's group psychotherapy for women with metastatic breast cancer has been carried out by Leszcz and Goodwin (1998) and they summarize some of the group themes that emerged. Two out of eight were about practical issues about treatment; two were about relationships with family members and with medical staff; one was about group functioning; and three were existential, changing life priorities and values, dealing with changing body image and the basis of self-worth, and confronting death. Family issues were addressed in monthly family meetings and with existentially influenced interventions that they used. Concerns about death and dying often turned out to be about the process of dying, for example, fears of being in pain or dying alone. These were addressed by encouraging group members to make specific plans for dying, for example, by choosing the music for their funeral.

As noted in Chapter 26 and in the introduction to this book, Hans Cohn is one of the few practitioners who have written explicitly about the links between the English existential tradition, and that of group therapy as exemplified by "group analysis," a practice whose origins have been considered in Chapter 26. He has noted parallels between the methods used by S.H. "Michael" Foulkes and the theories of Heidegger in particular (Cohn 1996). An extract of this paper is included in the key texts chapter. One of us (DT) has similarly argued for the existential relevance of group analysis, but on somewhat different grounds (Tantam 1991; Tantam 2005).

Logotherapy, the existential approach developed by Viktor Frankl from his clinical and personal observations on the experience of meaninglessness, has begun to establish itself as the method of choice in group therapy for people facing crises in their life brought about by bereavement, terminal illness, or other catastrophes. Alfried Längle has spoken about this in Part IV and there will be some further reference to it in Part VI, Chapter 35.

Ernest Becker applied Heideggerian ideas about existential anxiety and developed what has become known as "terror management theory." Terror management theory has been widely applied to individual psychology, but its application to psychotherapy is much more limited (Lewis 2014) and it has not, to our knowledge been applied to group psychotherapy.

Themes of existential group psychotherapy

Limits and frontiers

Dorothy Stock Whitaker was a practicing group therapist and Professor of Social Work. Her training was an unusual blend of Bion's Kleinian approach to group analytic therapy, and the T-groups inspired by Kurt Lewin. Her very practical textbook of therapy (Whitaker 2001) inspires experienced therapists more than trainees. The latter may be put off by the reference to giving "help" in its title, or by the absence of any obvious affiliation to a theoretical modality. Whitaker does not mention existential therapy in her book but uses a concept "frontier" that is very similar to the idea of "limit situation" as used by Jaspers, "ultimate concern" as used by Tillich and Yalom, or "horizon" as used by Husserl. Her description of it in an individual is that it is the boundary of a person's life space but as she explains this, its relationship to Lewin's concept of the equilibrium between restraining and motivating forces comes to mind. Her definition of limit changes somewhat from the first to the second edition of her book. In the first edition, transcending a person's boundaries is a dangerous thing to do, because of the anxiety that it provokes. In the second, Whitaker recognizes that some people want to go beyond their boundaries and she implies this may be a positive thing. She does not consider the condition of boundaries having been broken down, or knocked down from within, but this may be what happens to people whose limits had been exceeded by being placed in a limit situation.

Whitaker argues that effective change or therapy can only occur when the anxiety of group members is within therapeutic limits – not too great, and not too little. She covers a number of structural factors that might increase or decrease anxiety and argues that getting these right is an essential prerequisite of any kind of effective group work.

Freedom to learn

Existential groups usually emphasize that they offer an opportunity for participants to enhance their freedom by experimenting with what they are capable of being and becoming. People enter into real relationships with others in the group to explore their own experiences of life and to discover something about their responses to the world of others. In this they come upon their personal limitations and possibilities. Existential group work initially grew out of the training groups and encounter groups of the 1940s, 1950s, and 1960s (Lieberman, Yalom, and Miles 1973; de Board 1978). Kurt Lewin's work opened a wide realm related to the encounter movement and especially his understanding of the need to run groups democratically, rather than either in a laissez-faire or autocratic manner was invaluable to the search for a new type of existentially based group work. Carl Rogers' work on encounter groups (Rogers 1970) provided a blueprint for an existential way of facilitating such a group. He found that people learn to express themselves more authentically with each other gradually, provided that the facilitator engages directly, fairly, and respectfully, but also genuinely with the group members, instead of staying at a distance. Rogers showed that this leads to:

1. The possibility of change in personal attitudes and behavior towards others and also toward themselves as individuals.
2. People hear each other and learn from each other to a great extent. They build a learning community together, in which they feel safe enough to experiment.
3. Increase in feedback as people learn about the way they appear to others and the effect they have on others.
4. New ideas, concepts, and a sense of possibility start to emerge from improved communication and greater interpersonal freedom.
5. Learning gets carried over into outside relationships.

He described the stages that each existential/humanist group goes through as follows:

Stages:

1. Milling around: people just get to know each other in a superficial manner, trying to figure out who each person is and what they can expect from the group and each other.
2. Resistance to personal expression and exploration: people are defensive and self-protective, hiding behind social niceties or silence.
3. Description of past feelings: some people in the group start to refer to personal past experiences in a more in-depth manner. This is the phase of storytelling.
4. Expression of negative feelings when participants start to say how they feel about the group and the facilitator, this usually starts as criticism.
5. Expression and exploration of personally meaningful material, when the facilitator is skilled and attentive enough to allow the exploration of discomfort to go more deeply.
6. Expression of immediate interpersonal feelings in the group, as people begin to trust each other, having heard a bit more about the way in which others in the group live their lives and feel about the world.
7. Development of a healing capacity in the group, as people begin to care for each other and start recognizing and respecting their similarities and differences.
8. Cracking of facades with a sense that people dare to show how they really are instead of pretending to be more than they are.
9. Individual receives feedback as true perceptions of each other motivate the way people relate to each other, people can actually start to hear what other people see in them.
10. Confrontation becomes more possible, especially as the facilitator models safe and fair confrontations, both with reality and with personal issues.
11. Helping relationships outside the group begin to develop as participants acquire new confidence and news skills in relating to others.

12 Basic encounter, which is the letting go of the masks and the direct contact between people in a frank and fair fashion.
13 Expression of positive feelings and closeness can now be done with a sense of security and trust. People are often amazed that they can feel so good in the presence of so many others.
14 Behavior changes in group as the group takes on a character and life of its own. People now express a real commitment to the group, which is acknowledged as life changing.

Structural existential analysis

While Rogers' encounter-groups model provides a guideline to the way in which the group is conducted, in a democratic and in depth, personal manner, Yalom and van Deurzen's work has shown the importance of reminding people that many of the issues in groups are existential. Many existential therapists have used an existential model to work with terminal cancer patients, or with people facing a death sentence in other ways (Yalom 1980, 2005). Yalom's illustration of his work in an existential group was successfully dramatized in his novel *The Schopenhauer Cure* (Yalom 2015) as well as in a series of video recordings he did of his group work. This is discussed in more detail elsewhere in this section.

One of us (EvD) has argued that the task of existential group work is to enable people to dig a little deeper into their lives, challenging themselves to do a number of things they would never do in ordinary every day discussions.

- They need to be encouraged to dare to explore philosophical issues and values that underpin their lives. An existential group is a privileged moment to exchange with other people in a respectful dialogue about the things that really matter to them profoundly. If the facilitator keeps on target with this, people learn to exchange with each other safely at a level of depth and breadth that allows them to understand life and their own views about it increasingly better.
- The facilitator will model strength of character, fairness and willingness to engage with whatever is important to people. This allows the discussion to evolve in such a way that participants challenge each other's worldviews, without ever ridiculing or attacking each other or make light of each other's positions. In this process of opening up people become aware of who they are, what they stand for, and what they want to be in the world. Of course this kind of exploration needs to stay real and is always set within the context of given possibilities and limitations of each person.
- The process that the facilitator initiates is therefore often about gently confronting people with self-deceptive habits, enabling people to become more truthful with themselves. It is only when we learn to challenge ourselves to seek truth that we can also become truthful with others. When this happens, the masks we carry start falling and we can engage with the reality of the group and with other people's feelings and experiences in a much more profound and direct way. This process is based largely in the safe, careful, kind, but nevertheless frank giving and receiving of feedback.

- Participants start to get very excited when they dare to start talking about things that were previously taboo, like their religious beliefs or their most secret desires or things they are ashamed of having done or thought in the past. When participants discover that it is possible to talk about the human issues, we all have in common, yet deal with in different ways, a sense of hope in humanity is raised. This can only happen when there is a good balance between an exploration of very personal issues and a philosophical understanding of how each of our experiences are illustrations of universal and human issues that affect us all. We all die, but we think about death very differently when we are confronted with it directly in our lives. Explorations are always specific rather than general.
- There is often a growing awareness in an existential group of the passing of time. People will discuss the different stages of life, whether the group is composed of similarly aged people or of people of a broad range of ages. This sense of time moving on and life being shorter than we ever know, comes to people who have a genuine exchange about their crises and disasters, their losses and disappointments. Participants achieve greater awareness of where in life they are at and get a new sense of direction through discussion of difference and similarity in this respect.
- Hearing so many different examples of the human struggle in such a trusting environment leads to people acquiring a sense of perspective they never had. They understand the challenges of human living much better after a while and become less afraid of them, as they observe others around them valiantly dealing with their challenges and hardship. In this way people acquire an inner map of the human condition as well as more clarity on their own talents and strengths in dealing with it.
- The existential group facilitator will make use of systematic phenomenological description of any person's situation and will ask relevant questions about what is felt and experienced, what things mean to the person and how they have engaged with the situation they are in, and to what purpose they have done this. No judgements are made, but different facets of life and different modes of being are highlighted and discussed.
- The existential group is also a safe place for people to test out new ways of being and experiment with more closeness and greater honesty, without getting punished for it. They can figure out what their personal limits and talents are and by listening to others often learn from their experience with human limitations, possibilities, contradictions, and paradoxes too. The group is a veritable resource of information about what works in life and what leads to disaster and catastrophe.
- Facilitators need to be very flexible and have the capacity for strong resonance with the mood in the group or the emotions of individual members of the group. At the same time they need to be clear minded and strongly anchored in a sense of how to keep things safe. They would not create drama for the sake of something happening in the group, but rather tend to events with calm, acceptance and a good sense of balancing the process in the group.
- Trained as existential therapists group facilitators will often draw on their capacity for individual work as well as group process. Both are equally important in an existential group. Facilitators help recognize people's assumptions, prejudice,

experiences, and worldviews, highlighting blind spots, exposing bias, broadening perspectives by drawing on the presence of other experiences and views in the group. Checking with others about their views on issues enables phenomenological scrutiny in the round. The process of verification is thus automatically built into the group.

- The outlook of the existential group is that the group builds a network of relationships rather than providing a platform for individual selves. The group takes on a life of its own and becomes precious to all its members so the more as it enables cooperation, affection, mutual respect, and support.
- Groups that offer this kind of sanctuary in the world to people who have often felt alone or forsaken, bring people back to a sense that life is possible and invaluable. They often start hearing the call of their conscience: in daring to experience anxiety again and in heeding and speaking about their sense of unease with self and world, they take the first step towards doing things differently. People in existential groups become more engaged with the world instead of withdrawing from it.
- In terms of time there is strong emphasis on the freedom of experiencing all forms of time. The group is not just about the here and now. It is also a place for recollecting the past, exploring how it affects the present, and projecting new ways of being into the future. People may sometimes go on flights of imagination and then come back to the ground of reality again. They are encouraged to bring stories and experiences from their own world and they can bring their dreams to work on if they want to.
- The existential group is inclusive and permissive, but it has clear boundaries of confidentiality, mutual care, decency, and loyalty. Destructive behavior is talked about and challenged, not tolerated. People need to be able to trust that their safety is paramount and that the facilitator and other group members will keep their eye on what it is that really matters. The group will discuss what makes life worth living and will sometimes touch on what makes us want to die. People will get a grasp of their original project, their intentionality, their values, and their beliefs. Sometimes the group will change these, gradually. At other times they will affect other persons in return.
- The existential group is a place to understand the difference between living by default or by deliberation: people often come to see that they had just been going through the motions of life, without any true engagement. Frequently people comment that something important has happened inside them and that they feel inspired to start living with more courage and connection. People gain a sense of belonging and a feeling that new ways of being are possible and that they will never be alone in experimenting with these.

The work is practically pinned on the systematic framework of reference of one of us (EvD): the well-known four-fold "dimensional" heuristic. This provides the facilitator with some clear pointers in figuring out where the group is situated at any one time and where individuals are heading. It also provides a model for being aware of current tensions and conflicts in the group. This method was described in Part II. It is equally applicable to individual therapy, to group therapy, and to research (van Deurzen 2010, 2014). The full structural analysis as applied specifically to existential group therapy involves looking at a number of existential issues as and when they are brought up by participants. In group work it must be remembered that all these elements are to be used as heuristic devices, not as prescriptive or interpretive models. Interpretation proceeds in hermeneutic fashion, that is, by tracing and translating the meanings of all individuals in the situation rather than by imposing a theoretical, external interpretation on what is happening.

1. Time Time is an important issue in life and thus in the group. Paying attention to time starts with the timing of the sessions, which is meticulously observed in order to provide a safe framework for the work. Facilitators will note how time is being spent in the group, how time is being distorted, extended in some ways and curtailed in others. The time taken by each person, or the time spent on individual versus group issues may also be in question. But time will figure in more philosophical ways too. What do we do with the time given to us as human beings? How do we place ourselves in relation to our past, our present, and our future? What is our relationship to eternity? In a group such issues crop up automatically and facilitators can bring out the different ways in which people consider these issues. Groups are the natural locus for phenomenological explorations, for phenomenology seeks to look at matters from both an objective and subjective view. In phenomenology we learn to bracket our own assumptions and look at situations and experiences from a multiplicity of perspectives. In a group this exploration of multiple perspectives is achieved naturally because of the many points of view present in the group. When one person becomes preoccupied with the shortness of time, another may start musing on their own time boundaries and the way they try to make room for themselves in their lives by postponing things. A third person may then realize that they do the exact opposite, racing from moment to moment, doing as many things as they can fit in, often things that are not urgent or important. It may begin to dawn on a person that they are running a race against time, as self-imposed competition, which is exhausting them. The theme of time may now spark another to remember how they have cut themselves off from their memories in order to eliminate the past, while the person next to them on the contrary begins to gain awareness of the way in which they try to deny the need to plan for the future. As people speak their minds and let their own experiences flow into the group, the facilitator aims to keep all experiences in perspective, holding on to the equalization of importance of different aspects of reality. Sometimes time may become absorbed by delving deeply into one person's struggles, but at other times time may expand in front of people as they reclaim the openness of the group to different ways of viewing the world and dealing with time. The fact that all are present, now, in this particular group and owe each other their immediate attention, will create a bond that allows extreme experiences to be absorbed and understood much more easily than in personal therapy where a person often feels alone and isolated in the face of a therapist who is so much more together than they feel themselves. The shared troubles provide companionship and courage to stand in the flow of time, facing doubts, regrets, and worries.

2. Space The group takes place in space as much as it takes place in time. The place offered to the group needs to be as safe from interference as possible.

It becomes a sanctuary for everyone in it and it is good when people look forward to finding themselves in that space again and again. Often members of a group become aware that they carry that safe space inside them after a while and can conjure it up as a source of succor when they are anxious or feeling forlorn. Space is a very expandable concept. We experience space in different spheres: at a physical level, at a social level, at a personal level, and also at a spiritual or ideological level. All these dimensions of space are relevant to groups. People will inevitably explore all of these worlds at various moments. It will become very obvious that there are some people in the group who are currently deeply concerned with their physical existence and therefore their physical space in the world. They may be preoccupied with an illness or a weakness in their own body, or they may be obsessed with sexual thoughts or ideas about having to accomplish a particular physical feat. A person's relationship to space is frequently visibly acted out by the way they hold their space in the group itself. This connects directly to the next dimension of space: as we hold our own in relation to others. Many people in groups find the relationship to others problematic. Their preoccupation with the existence of other people and the way they have to share space with them can be very graphically and personally enacted in the group, by remarking on how they feel about the physical presence of specific others in their space for instance. But the social dimension is also about issues of dominance and submission, inclusion or exclusion and these need to be carefully attended to by the facilitator when they are activated. The social dimension is also simply about communication, the presence or lack of it and the quality and depth of it. It helps people to understand this when they are made attentive to particular ways in which they thwart or take over communication, or how they tend to manage it in various ways. The discussion between people will quickly reveal many different ways in which people relate or are sensitized to experiencing space. Gradually we will speak about these different ways in which people connect with or disconnect from each other, in an attempt to safeguard themselves. This will allow people to start reflecting on their personal connections to the world, contrasting these with the way they see their peers acting and reacting. As more and more awareness of relationships, both physical and social, become known and explicit in the group, the facilitator can start tying these bits of understanding in with the skills people are acquiring. This makes it possible to relax the interactions, experimenting more with space, sitting in different places, looking to others more closely or saying more or less to people in a particular session. People start seeing how each of them approach or avoid others, try to keep them under control or aim to please them or oppose them. Some people will become acutely aware that they frequently, or always, hide from others, trying to negate the contact as much as possible, either by silence, systematic agreement, or by imitating other people's behaviors. All these tensions will be set in the perspective of all the various possible ways of relating. People in a group will find kinship with others and feel supported by that new sense of acceptance and similarity. But they will often gain even more from the conflicts with those who are different and who may initially oppose or even look down on them. Seeing someone use hostility or confrontation can be a revelation for someone who regularly placates people. Learning to use affirmation and practicing with making confident statements about your own experience of such situations can be extremely liberating. The contrast between people can lead to amazing experiences of opening up of new vistas to everyone. This kind of existential adventure is simply not possible in individual therapy, though it can also sometimes happen in existential relationship therapy between two partners.

The personal dimension similarly reveals a lot about different people. Some come into a group boasting about their many accomplishments or strengths of character. Others come into the group full of shame or self-conscious awareness of their inner sense of hollowness. But soon enough it will become evident to all participants that even the cockiest of egocentric members are deeply frightened, at some level, of not being good enough. It will also become clear that each member of the group brings particular qualities that come into their own in specific situations. The person who seemed needy initially may suddenly display a capacity for generosity in the face of one of their peer's disaster when their house is flooded. The person who was initially aggressive to everyone may one day collapse into tears after having found they carry the gene of a life-threatening illness. People discover their own character in a dynamic and changing fashion, as they realize they respond and react differently to different people and are capable of many different ways of being in different situations and circumstances. The group dynamic reveals our existential mobility and capacity for change and difference. Reflecting on such existential insights leads to existential group addressing the ideological, philosophical, or spiritual aspects of human existence as well. As people come closer and become more trusting, they start talking about their beliefs, their values, and their sense of what their purpose in life may be. They start comparing notes about what they learn from difficulties and challenges. They start reflecting on the ways in which they avoid plumbing their own depth, by staying at the surface of life, for instance by watching too much television or ridiculing other people or drinking or taking pain killers. They begin to think about how they are able to make a difference for the better. They begin to get feedback about how they are valuable to the group or to specific individual members. Each learns something about their own abilities and capacity, their personal worth. They realize how badly they want to contribute something of value to the group and to the world. They begin to philosophize about what it is that matters in living a good life. It is an amazing spectacle when people begin to transform in that manner, creating links and connections where none existed beforehand. They thrive and develop rapidly. It's a wonderful thing to watch, for it's a kind of magic.

3. Paradox It is important to stay concrete and keep our feet on the ground as an existential facilitator. In the face of so many special things happening in a group we should never lose track of the importance of balance and bearing in mind that things come in opposites, tensions, and contradictions. When we start to wax lyrical, it is time to expect life to remind us of the tasks and duties that also have to be attended to. When we think a person is wonderful, we should look out for the mistake they are about to make. When we are inclined to judge a person, we must open our heart to the potential they also carry. The paradoxes and tensions of life that we are all dealing with are often hidden to a person. In a group they are immediately brought out, because when we listen to other people's stories we hear the tensions in a way we find much harder to spot when it concerns ourselves. In personal therapy we remain enclosed in our inner world, with another person pointing out what is happening.

In group therapy we become aware of how other people live their lives and make mistakes as well. We learn therapeutic insights that are normally reserved for therapists. In existential therapy all participants become therapeutically attuned to each other, in consequence of the facilitator's stance of open exploration, fairness, directness, and also because of their obvious search for truth and reality. Very soon people will be able to sense the contradictions and dilemmas their peers are struggling with. People's natural ability to speak with kindness and consideration for another person's suffering can be a real revelation about the way in which life does not always have to be such a lonely struggle. One person may candidly remark to another that they seem to be holding back from expressing their need for love, thus making the person spoken to suddenly be (a) aware that they crave that love and appreciation and (b) that they tend to do the opposite of what they need, in that they deny their need for others, rather than reaching out and taking a risk on being rejected and surviving that experience. Contradictions and tensions are boldly addressed. Thus, when people speak of life, death will be somewhere in the background and the facilitator may remark on that and point to where death is lurking. When people worry about the honesty of another person, the issue of self-deception or deception needs to be addressed squarely. Existential group therapists need to be brave in facing the implications of what people are saying and dare to bring out the shadows what people are afraid of, whilst holding on to the hidden strengths or light that they also possess. Thinking in terms of polarities and tensions in each situation can help facilitators to become much more directly existential in their interventions.

4. Emotions Groups would be nothing if they were only about intellectual comprehension or about mutual support and social get together. What makes them coherent and cohesive, and collaborative and communicative, and important is that people dare to share their true experiences and emotions. As always existential work will focus directly on the way in which people are attuned to the world, the way in which they are embodied and immersed in their experiences. It helps to work with the emotional compass (see Part II) to understand where they are coming from and what it is they are aiming for. But we need to remember that some people may express their experience primarily as sensations, others as feelings and emotions, and others as thoughts or intuitions. All of these ways of finding out where we are in the world are equally valid and deserve in-depth exploration. There is no normative process of expecting everyone to become the same. When people become comfortable and mutually respectful in relishing the diversity of human experience a group becomes a much safer place to be than when we feel judged and experience ourselves as having to fit in with a norm. We can learn much from hearing about other people's thoughts, when we are inclined to rush into reactive emotion and we can learn just as much from listening to a person's sorrows and joys when we are inclined to reason about our experiences. To explore the whole range of human experience is of much more value than to be told we have to change and fit in with a specific standard. Human emotions are hugely varied and come in the same range of different wavelengths as the different colors on the spectrum: not all of us cover the entire range of hues at all times. We are entitled to our own patterns and ways of being. But the group will deepen our capacity for attunement and it will broaden our horizons and will teach us a much more in-depth understanding of the connection between feelings and values. Existential facilitators will often prompt people to talk about "what this was like for you," or "how they experienced that," or "what this conjured up for them" rather than simply ask the question "what do you feel?" The invitation to further in-depth exploration of the meaning of people's emotions and the values underlying these can come in many different ways and it is important to show participants many pathways towards depth of feeling and reality.

5. Dialectics Existential group therapy, like all forms of existential therapy are a form of exploration of all the secrets of human existence that are often so hidden from our daily lives that they can sometimes be a little bit pedestrian. The beauty of the existential group is that it provides people with a sense of freedom and adventure. They know that they have come to a place where they are entitled to discovering their inmost inner world and share it with other people. They know they are expected to let things be just exactly as they are instead of pretending to be better or wiser than they are. But they will also soon get this exhilarating sense that they are part of a research expedition: they are on a team that is mutually supportive and that has as its task to explore the deepest depth and furthest reaches of human existence. Almost always this is done by finding the contradictions, the problems, the dilemmas, and oppositions that people are caught up in. And almost invariably this leads, eventually, to moments of sudden understanding of how things fit together and of how the very problems we struggle with make us stronger, more resilient, and more persistent. In talking about these things together and seeing them from different directions, new light is thrown on old issues. Then the possibility of transcending problems by holding on to the tensions and making room for different sides to the question comes into people's vision. They start to see that situations can be many things at the same time and can be viewed and experienced in different ways by different people. When we begin to accept this we find a way to rise above the pain or the aggression or the objections to other people's perceptions and see a way to include rather than exclude different positions. When we do this we free ourselves from our usual blinkers and sedimented ideas or mineralized positions and often this helps us to suddenly see a new way forward when we had been locked in to a prejudiced view or a set and patterned way of proceeding.

In Deurzen's existential way of working with groups, there is an emphasis at the start of a new group on encouraging participants to learn to listen to each other respectfully. The group facilitator models this very actively and is both outspoken and supportive, and always directional in seeking to encourage people in being more reflective on their own experience and more outspoken with each other in a respectful manner. There is an educational element in this, by teaching people to give and receive feedback in a calm, careful, caring manner, about the way in which they are in the world and relate to each other. This enables people to note how reactive they often are and how they tend to jump to conclusions or usual ways of acting. Focusing on greater self-reflection and peer feedback is an effective way of enabling people to learn to be more fully in the world with each other. This allows them to discover that they can be much truer to themselves without getting punished for it. In fact, their experience is invariably that they will be more liked and appreciated the more genuine and self-disclosing they manage to become. All dimensions and emotions are interrelated in real life and thus anxiety – a bodily emotion – has both a personal and a physical presence, and when someone is paralyzed by it in the group, it clearly has a social dimension too. The social manifestation of the threat that provokes anxiety in this instance might be the threat of engulfment or annihilation that Kierkegaard and other existential philosophers were so conscious of. With the right support in an existential group, participants soon learn to monitor their anxiety and become aware of the energy and passion it holds beyond our natural fear of nothingness, destruction, impotence, and fallibility. What about van Deurzen's spiritual dimension? The group makes pervasive anxiety so acceptable and safe, so that participants may begin to see how their fears and doubts correspond to a number of beliefs or existential challenges they have dreaded. These are often related to people's past experiences of failing or having failed, but also to historic or future losses they try to shield themselves from. Many of these have been described by people from different orientations in relation to catastrophe: the failure of the belief in a just world, a loss of faith in agency or personal efficacy, the death of God, the disappearance of personal status and autonomy, an overwhelming apprehension about death, or, to use Frankl's term for all of these things, meaninglessness. This does not mean that anxiety leads to meaninglessness (although it may) or that meaninglessness may lead to anxiety. Each experience can lead to different meanings and has to be traced phenomenologically. Frankl for instance noted that meaninglessness led more often to dissociation and anhedonia. Van Deurzen's existential groups explore people's values, purpose and meanings as much as they explore their physical embodiment in the world, their inter-subjectivity with others, and their inner and most private experiences. Anxiety can be high at times, but it is sustained by the willingness of the group to face up to it in themselves as well as in each other.

Whitaker's advice about structuring groups to keep anxiety at a low level can, if our assumptions are true, provide useful guidance about how to create existential groups that both provide, and challenge meaning. This is about learning to hold anxiety at a level that is tolerable and productive, neither too much nor too little.

Why would this be important in existential therapy? As noted in Chapter 26, existential philosophers set out to answer questions like, "Why are we here?" and "What does it all mean?". Suppose the philosophers are speculating, if we suffer a catastrophe that undermines everything that we have believed, or loved, or wanted and that we can no longer believe that we are living for this or that person, or this or that principle, what would make us want to continue living? As Camus put it, in the *Myth of Sisyphus*: "There is only one really serious philosophical question, and that is suicide" (van Deurzen 2010, 2014, p. 3). Such were the questions that faced prisoners in a German concentration camp who had lost their families, their possessions, their identity, and their status – perhaps forever. This was the question often posed to Viktor Frankl, which he considered could only be answered by a reference to the meaning of life. He discovered that those who could create a meaning to transcend their suffering and sense of futility would survive, whereas those who gave up on finding meaning and purpose would soon die.

Meaning groups based on logotherapy's principles take this issue about the loss of meaning as the common factor that all participants share. This, in itself, may increase meaning since the observation that others take the same issue seriously confirms that it is meaningful. Many successful meaning groups run for a defined period of time, have leaders who are active and sometimes directive, and they tend to use exercises. All of these are factors that reduce anxiety and create meaning through belonging and repetition.

Research findings

Spiegel, Yalom, and Bloom looked at a variety of outcomes in their support groups, lasting up to a year, for women with terminal carcinoma of the breast (Spiegel and Yalom 1978). There was a significant reduction in anxiety in the treated group (Spiegel, Bloom, and Yalom 1981) and this may have been partly attributable to a reduction in avoidance of thoughts of dying. They quote this comment by a group member, who likens thinking about death to looking down at the Snake River from the top of the Grand Canyon: "At first you are afraid to look down (I don't like heights) but gradually, a bit at a time, you learn to do it and you can see that falling down would be a disaster. It would be the end. Nonetheless, you feel better about yourself because you are able to look. That is how I feel about death in the group-I am able to look at it now. I can't say I feel serene, but I can look at it" (Spiegel et al. 1981, p. 532). In a replication of this study Classen et al. (2001) found a similar reduction in anxiety (see also Chapter 28). In a more cognitively orientated group there was high satisfaction with the intervention, but the reduction in anxiety that was produced just escaped significance (Kissane et al. 2003). Perhaps this was because in existential groups people learn to tolerate and even value anxiety rather than seeking to reduce it.

It is sometimes claimed that psychological interventions can change the prognosis of carcinoma, and so the study by van der Pompe et al. (1997) of endocrine changes in women with carcinoma of the breast who received existential group therapy is particularly interesting. The authors report changes in hormonal and immunological status that might be relevant to an improved prognosis, but the study has not, to our knowledge, been replicated nor has a survivor rate over a follow-up period been reported.

Meaning-orientated short-term therapy has also been evaluated. If provided individually it does lead to a change in spiritual well-being, meaning in life, and well-being but that quickly washes out (Breitbart et al. 2012). Meaning-orientated group therapy is more persistent in its effects, and results in an increase in personal meaning and purpose in life but also a reduction in anxiety and hopelessness (van der Spek et al. 2017) or depression and hopelessness (Breitbart et al. 2015). Dignity is another issue that seems to many observers to be important in palliative care, yet a focus of "dignity-therapy" groups on dignity did not result in a positive outcome compared to treatment as usual (Chochinov et al. 2011).

The group intervention used in the van der Spek et al. (2017) intervention was developed by Breitbart and colleagues at the Memorial Sloan-Kettering Cancer Center in New York City and he has described it in some detail in various publications in which he also acknowledges his debt to Spiegel and Yalom. Breitbart summarizes the main principles in an editorial in "Palliative and Supportive Care" (Breitbart 2015). He follows on from Frankl in recognizing that there are multiple sources of meaning for most people, which include: "Creative Sources" of meaning (e.g., work), "Experiential Sources" of meaning (e.g., love), "Attitudinal Sources" of meaning (e.g., turning a tragedy into a triumph), and "Historical Sources" of meaning (e.g., the legacy you are given, the legacy you live, and the legacy you give). When plunged into turmoil by a terminal cancer diagnosis it appears to be helpful for patients to have these sources of meaning delineated, described, experienced, and brought to conscious awareness so that one can "reach" for "each" source of meaning when overcome by a sense of loss or disconnection from the experience of personal meaning" (Breitbart 2015, p. 1319). For his part, Breitbart writes, it is "being loving, and empathic, and generous, and caring to others [that brought him] so much personal reward [and presumably, meaning]" (2015, p. 1320).

Methods of longer-term existential group therapy

Being an existential group leader

Although many group leaders would share Breitbart's list of their desirable characteristics (perhaps with the exception of "empathy," which seems to be turning back into a negative property), the doyennes and doyens of the existential approach have certainly cared for others and had a loving interest into the intentions and desires of other people, but they have also been tough-minded and unwilling to compromise their responsibility. Existential group leaders tend to be frank and outspoken, both about positives and negatives. They do not sit back but provide directness and directionality. They show courage under fire.

Structuring the group

Existential therapists draw on philosophy and particularly on the philosophers who are bundled together under the label, "existential philosophers." These philosophers have, as noted in Chapter 26, been only too aware of the conflict between the individual and the crowd or the herd. In Tantam's book *The Interbrain* (Tantam 2017), the potentially competing demands of the interbrain connections with others are shown to lead to a theory of mind or narrative connection, which is essential to our survival. We base our individuality and our sense of agency on the latter, but we rely on our sense of belonging and therefore a major part of our feeling of living a meaningful life on the former. When we are repeatedly beaten, traumatized, or shamed, our eyes avoid the gaze of others and the interbrain connection, and our sense of belonging, is attenuated. We become isolated.

Although in all of our mixed interactions in the world, it is rare that we find ourselves excluded in so many social settings that we become completely disconnected from human society, it can happen. Existential group therapy is a way to reconnect and reinvigorate those vital connections. A small therapeutic group has the potential to do this so effectively that it can spread outside the group. But people can also feel further disconnected in a group, experiencing an increase in their sense of meaninglessness – especially if this is the feeling that they had before they started in the group. New, or newly distressed, members of a therapy group may need to be protected from too much interbrain connection too soon, perhaps by not challenging their personal narrative too quickly or too vigorously, even if that narrative will turn out to be an obstacle to the goals that they will eventually want to aim for. For this same reason existential groups tend to be small, ranging from just four to ten (maximum twelve) participants.

We can observe how individuals develop in a group through stages of maintaining a barrier, become enticed into being intimately (although not sexually) connected with other group members, to re-develop a personal narrative that is less in conflict with the range and nature of their interbrain connections.

What has been described might follow on from existential philosophy about groups and socialization, but it is hardly unique to existential group psychotherapy. The same developmental principles are to be found in textbooks by experienced group therapists from almost any modality included Stock Whitaker, whose work was already cited, or, as Cohn pointed out, the various practical manuals written by Michael Foulkes and other group analytic psychotherapists. We may conclude from this that group work is inevitably existential in nature and therefore has developed existential methods without necessarily naming them.

The content of longer-term existential groups

Whilst few group therapists, or few leading long-term groups anyway, would set topics for discussion or even repeat the remark that group neophytes might sometimes make that: "What we are talking about does not seem relevant to this group" the interests and preoccupations of the group leader do communicate themselves to the group. Even if they did not, selection of the group by the potential group member and of the group member by the group therapist, is likely to ensure that the process of the group is influenced by the therapeutic factors most valued by the group therapist.

So let us consider whether there are any preoccupations held by existential group practitioners, as opposed to practitioners from other schools, which might influence the content of existential groups rather than others.

According to Mullan (1992, p. 453) "Instead of the usual interpretation, members are encouraged to confront the paradoxes in their lives, their humanness, and especially their finitude. Patients are to be brought up to the threshold of their self-knowledge, so they can choose. Choice, therefore, along with action coupled with responsibility are frequent themes. Unless the individual is incompetent, decisions made for him or her by the therapist or by group consensus are thought to be nontherapeutic." Cohn does not define existential methods positively but picks out group analytic assumptions that help him to at least say what an existential group therapy would not be. It would be one in which the leader was not as connected to the group as any other group member; it would not be one in which a group member was considered an island universe who was detached from a "world"; and it would not be a therapy that focused on the inner experience of the group members at the expense of how and what these members were communicating to each other.

Cohn's emphasis on connection is typical of all group analysts who accept Foulkes's' ideas that the aim of long-term group psychotherapy is free communication within the group matrix. This is an unrealistic goal, and if it were truly instituted would as likely lead to domination by the more powerful or articulate members of a group as it might lead to benefit. This was the view we suggested was held by many existential philosophers, as noted in the previous chapter.

"'Freedom" is a central value of existential philosophy but is as difficult to define as it is inspirational. Any definition of free communication would at least require that an adequate connection with others is available through the interbrain connection as through shared narrative. "Unfree" communication might therefore be entirely solipsistic, I–it, relations with others in which people are characters in an internal narrative rather than originators of shared narratives. But "unfree" communication might equally be solely interbrain based, driven by mood or attention caught from other people, without any narrative about personal agency and therefore without taking responsibility for the values and attitudes apparently so disclosed. "Unfree" communication might also be created by an inability to switch from the language of agency and autonomy to the communication of feeling and intuition, and back again, as the situation demands.

Corey (2010) considers that methods of sharpening the choices that individual group members continue to make, even when they argue that they are trapped without any possibility of choosing, are particularly important in existential group therapy. He gives examples in his sections on "the search for authenticity," "aloneness and relatedness," "the search for meaning," "death and nonbeing," and "self-determination and personal responsibility." The only sections where "the implications for group therapy" did not, according to Corey, require individuals to make choices were "self-awareness" and "existential anxiety."

All group therapists would consider that an optimal level of anxiety –not too little, not too much – was optimal for change in group therapy. Too much anxiety is likely to result in withdrawal for many group members, and in all likelihood, would not be tolerated by existential philosophers either. Too little anxiety would lead to boredom and disenchantment as people felt that they were in a safe situation where nothing new was being learnt. Learning is an important aspect of existential group work. It always implies a certain amount of challenge and hardship that needs to be confronted. The existential facilitator will carefully watch how to ease tension when there is too much anxiety and create a greater sense of importance and urgency when anxiety is plummeting.

Self-awareness, the examination of one's life and purpose, is a common thread in all existential writing. Corey quotes Rollo May who, with his usual accuracy and clarity, points out that until we know what is making us suffer, we cannot do anything about it. Existential groups are a privileged place for figuring out what makes us suffer and how we might benefit from this new knowledge.

Conclusions

One of the principal therapeutic factors in all psychotherapy is that people stick it out, and do not leave before they are ready (Tantam 1995). Frank's (1993) position about this is clear: a method of psychotherapy had to be plausible and the main determinant in group outcome, he considered, was cohesion (Frank 1997) and this has been repeatedly confirmed since his studies of groups (Burlingame 2018). One of us (DT) came to a similar conclusion, following a review of the evidence. Three factors were isolated, namely recognition of the client's preoccupying concern, palatable emotional flavor, and shared values (Tantam 2002).

These three factors are distinctive in the existential approach as will be apparent throughout this book. They are particularly salient in existential group work. The concern about meaning in life, prudential concern about the future, about an approach that respects autonomy, and one that accepts doubt and anxiety are also essential and potentially fruitful. The citations of "Existential' have risen ten times since 1942 to the present according to Ngram viewer. This, one presumes, reflects a substantial increase in public interest in these values, concerns, and emotional status. It may be predictive of a growing interest in existential groups as well.

We have provided practical examples, earlier in this chapter, of turning these factors into practice. But if these are the factors that increase cohesiveness and therefore retention in groups, and so are related to outcome, then what are the factors that change people? Group therapy makes it easy for us to see other people's fudges and self-deceptions – and, if we are minded to, their courage and determination, too – as they have gone through life trying to get what they want and give others what they want, also.

Our clinical experience is that existential group therapy potentially enables members of the group to see each other as a struggling subject, exactly as they feel themselves to be, in other words to learn from what Husserl termed "inter-subjectivity." The phenomenological description and the search for a hermeneutic search for meaning in an existential group create a sense of shared humanity and the importance of reflection on the human condition.

The existential tradition has included detailed discussions of the ontology of inter-subjectivity and we turn to these in Chapter 28 to consider whether the phenomenological analysis of inter-subjectivity can help to further research into, and more systematically apply, the factors that are directly associated with group psychotherapy outcome.

References

Anon. (2018). Winter 2018 issue. *PAGL Newsletter.* http://www.pagl.org/wp-content/uploads/pagl-news-Winter-2018.pdf (accessed January 7, 2019).

Breitbart, W. (2015). Creating your soul in every moment: Meaning, creativity and attitude. *Palliative & Supportive Care 13* (5): 1139–1140.

Breitbart, W., Poppito, S., Rosenfeld, B. et al. (2012). Pilot randomized controlled trial of individual meaning-centered psychotherapy for patients with advanced cancer. *Journal of Clinical Oncology: Official Journal of the American Society of Clinical Oncology 30* (12): 1304–1309.

Breitbart, W., Rosenfeld, B., Pessin, H. et al. (2015). Meaning-centered group psychotherapy: an effective intervention for improving psychological well-being in patients with advanced cancer. *Journal of Clinical Oncology 33* (7): 749–754.

Burlingame, G.M. (2018). Cohesion in group therapy: A meta-analysis. *Psychotherapy 55* (4): 384–398.

Chochinov, H.M., Kristjanson, L.J., Breitbart, W. et al. (2011). Effect of dignity therapy on distress and end-of-life experience in terminally ill patients: A randomised controlled trial. *The Lancet Oncology 12* (8): 753–762.

Classen, C., Butler, L.D., Koopman, C. et al. (2001). Supportive-expressive group therapy and distress in patients with metastatic breast cancer: A randomized clinical intervention trial. *Archives of General Psychiatry 58* (5): 494–501.

Cohn, H.W. (1996). Existential-phenomenological dimensions of groups. *Existential Analysis 7* (1).

Cooper, M. (2007). Interpersonal perceptions and metaperceptions: Psychotherapeutic practice in the interexperiential realm. *Journal of Humanistic Psychology 49* (1): 85–99.

Corey, G. (2010). Existential approach. In: *Theory and Practice of Group Counseling*, 8e (ed. G. Corey), 222–252. Pacific Grove: Brooks/Cole.

de Board, R. (2014). *The Psychoanalysis of Organizations.* London: Routledge.

Deurzen, E. van (2010). *Everyday Mysteries: Handbook of Existential Therapy*, 2e. London: Routledge.

Deurzen, E. van (2013). The challenge of human relationships and relationship therapy: To live and to love. In: *Existential Perspectives on Relationship Therapy* (ed. E. van Deurzen and S. Iacovou), 15–31. Basingstoke: Palgrave Macmillan.

Deurzen, E. van (2014). Structural Existential Analysis (SEA): A phenomenological research method for counselling psychology. *Counselling Psychology Review 29* (2): 70–83.

Frank, J.D. (1993). The views of a therapist. In: *Non-Specific Aspects of Treatment* (ed. M. Shepherd and N. Sartorius), 95–114. Bern: Huber.

Frank, J.D. (1997). Some determinants, manifestations, and effects of cohesiveness in therapy groups. 1957 [classical article]. *Journal of Psychotherapy Practice and Research 6* (1): 63–70.

Frankel, B. (2002). Existential issues in group psychotherapy. *International Journal of Group Psychotherapy 52* (2): 215–231.

Heidegger, M. (1927). *Being and Time* (trans. J. Macquarrie and E.S. Robinson). New York: Harper & Row. (Original work published 1962.)

Husserl, E. (1925). *Phenomenological Psychology* (trans. J. Scanlon). The Hague: Nijhoff.

Kissane, D.W., Bloch, S., Smith, G.C. et al. (2003). Cognitive-existential group psychotherapy for women with primary breast cancer: A randomised controlled trial. *Psycho-Oncology 12* (6): 532–546.

Laing, R. (1961). *The Self and Others.* London: Tavistock Press.

Laing, R. (1971). *Politics of the Family.* London: Psychology Press.

Laing, R. and Esterson, A. (1964). *Sanity, Madness and the Family.* London: Tavistock.

Laing, R.D. (1970). *Knots.* London: Tavistock.

Laing, R.D. and Cooper, D. (1964). *Reason and Violence.* Chichester: Routledge.

Laing, R.D., Phillipson, H., and Lee, A.R. (1966). *Interpersonal Perception: A Theory and a Method of Research.* London: Tavistock.

Leszcz, M. and Goodwin, P.J. (1998). The rationale and foundations of group psychotherapy for women with metastatic breast cancer. *International Journal of Group Psychotherapy 48* (2): 245–273.

Lewis, A.M. (2014). Terror management theory applied clinically: Implications for existential-integrative psychotherapy. *Death Studies 38* (6–10): 412–417.

Lieberman, M.A., Yalom, I.D., and Miles, M.B. (1973). *Encounter Groups: First Facts.* New York: Basic Books.

Mullan, H. (1992). "Existential" therapists and their group therapy practices. *International Journal of Group Psychotherapy 42* (4): 453–468.

Rogers, C. (1970). *Encounter Groups.* Harmondsworth: Penguin.

Sartre, J.P. (1943/1956). *Being and Nothingness – An Essay on Phenomenological Ontology* (trans. H. Barnes). New York: Philosophical Library.
Sartre, J.P. (1960/1968). *Search for a Method* (trans. A. Sheridan-Smith). New York: Random House.
Spiegel, D., Bloom, J.R., and Yalom, I. (1981). Group support for patients with metastatic cancer: A randomized prospective outcome study. *Archives of General Psychiatry 38* (5): 527–533.
Spiegel, D. and Yalom, I.D. (1978). A support group for dying patients. *International Journal of Group Psychotherapy 28* (2): 233–245.
Tantam, D. (1991). Shame and groups. *Group Analysis 23* (1): 31–44.
Tantam, D. (1995). Empathy, persistent aggression, and antisocial personality disorder. *Journal of Forensic Psychiatry 6* (1): 10–18.
Tantam, D. (2002). *Psychotherapy and Counselling in Practice: A Narrative Framework.* Cambridge: Cambridge University Press.
Tantam, D. (2005). Groups. In: *Existential Perspectives on Human Issues* (ed. E. van Deurzen and C. Arnold-Baker), 143–154. Basingstoke: Palgrave Macmillan.
Tantam, D. (2017). *The Interbrain: Embodied Connections Versus Common Knowledge.* London: Jessica Kingsley
Tantam, D. and Deurzen, E. van (2005). Relationships. In: *Existential Perspectives on Human Issues* (ed. E. van Deurzen and C. Arnold-Baker), 121–132. Basingstoke: Palgrave Macmillan
Van der Pompe, G., Duivenvoorden, H.J., Antoni, M.H. et al. (1997). Effectiveness of a short-term group psychotherapy program on endocrine and immune function in breast cancer patients: an exploratory study. *Journal of Psychosomatic Research 42* (5): 453–466.
van der Spek, N., Vos, J., van Uden-Kraan, C.F. et al. (2017). Efficacy of meaning-centered group psychotherapy for cancer survivors: A randomized controlled trial. *Psychological Medicine 47* (11): 1990–2001.
Vitemb, S.A. (2018). Talkin' 'bout my generation: Existentialism, aging, and newly emerging issues in group therapy. *International Journal of Group Psychotherapy: 68* (3): 337–354.
Whitaker, D.S. (2001). *Using Groups to Help People*, 2e. London: Routledge and Kegan Paul.
Wright, F. (2014). Personal reflections on Hugh Mullan: Existential group therapist. In: *The One and the Many: Relational Approaches to Group Psychotherapy* (ed. R.W.D. Grossmark) 12–26. New York: Routledge.
Yalom, I.D. (1980). *Existential Psychotherapy.* New York: Basic Books.
Yalom, I.D. (2005). *The Schopenhauer Cure.* New York: HarperCollins.
Yalom, I.D. (2015). *The Schopenhauer Cure.* London: HarperCollins.
Yalom, I.D. (2017). *Becoming Myself: A Psychiatrist's Memoir.* London: Piatkus,
Yalom, I.D. and Greaves, C. (1977). Group therapy with the terminally ill. *American Journal of Psychiatry 134* (4): 396–400.
Yalom, I.D. and Leszcz, M. (2005). *Theory and Practice of Group Psychotherapy*, 5e. New York: Basic Books.

28

Existential Group Therapy

Therapy Illustrations

Catherine C. Classen, Orah T. Krug, Marie S. Dezelic, Lynda Ansell, Rex Haigh, Sarah Hamilton, Fiona Lomas, Sharon Tizzard, and Hilary Welsh

Case study 1: GyneGals – An online support group for gynecologic cancer

Catherine C. Classen

Sexuality is a profoundly personal and often sensitive topic, and this may be especially true for women who have been treated for gynecologic cancer (Laganá et al. 2005). Gynecologic cancer patients have an array of psychosocial sequelae including psychosexual distress, a common yet undertreated problem (Lindau, Gavrilova, and Anderson 2007), along with existential concerns (Simonelli et al. 2008). Given the unmet needs of these patients, we piloted a face-to-face support group specifically to address their psychosexual concerns (Caldwell et al. 2003). Although women who participated seemed to benefit, most of the women we approached declined participation. We posited that this might have been due to the sensitive nature of the topic that was being addressed and the reluctance to speak in a face-to-face group about their sexual challenges. Based on this experience, my colleagues and I began a program of research that aimed to create an intervention that would better meet the needs of women treated for gynecologic cancer. To this end, we developed an online support group we called "GyneGals," using an online format that has been successful with breast cancer patients (Winzelberg et al. 2003).

GyneGals is a 12-week, professionally-moderated, online support group that utilizes a discussion board (i.e., asynchronous) format that allows women to logon to the discussion forum at any time of the day or night. GyneGals is a closed and private group for 15 to 20 women plus two moderators. Each week a new topic is introduced by the moderators and questions are posed to the participants in order to stimulate a conversation on the topic. A link to a dedicated website that provides more information on that week's topic is also provided. Along with the asynchronous discussion forum,

The Wiley World Handbook of Existential Therapy, First Edition. Edited by Emmy van Deurzen, Erik Craig, Alfried Längle, Kirk J. Schneider, Digby Tantam, and Simon du Plock.

two moderated chat (i.e., synchronous) sessions are offered around the fourth and eighth week. The second chat session also includes two oncologists who are there to answer any medical questions or concerns that women might have. Preliminary findings suggest that women feel comfortable discussing their sexuality online and that it improves body image, reduces distress, and enhances well-being (Wiljer et al. 2011; Classen et al. 2013). A full-scale randomized controlled trial (RCT) is underway to demonstrate the efficacy of this intervention (Classen et al. 2015). Women are eligible if they have completed treatment for gynecologic cancer, are disease free for at least three months, are no more than five years post-diagnosis, and meet the clinical cut-off for psychosexual distress based on the Female Sexual Distress Scale-Revised (Derogatis et al. 2008).

GyneGals is based on the principles of supportive-expressive group therapy (Spiegel and Classen 2000); it encourages open and honest discussion of difficult topics and feelings, including discussion of existential concerns. Although there is a specific topic for each of the 12 weeks, women are free to start new discussion threads on topics of their choosing. The 12 topics include: (1) setting your goals for this group; (2) coping with emotional challenges, (3) what did sexuality mean to you before cancer? (4) how did cancer treatment change your sex life? (5) how to talk about cancer and sex; (6) has treatment changed your body image? (7) coping with sudden menopause and infertility; (8) managing pain, fatigue, vaginal changes, and incontinence; (9) finding a new normal: who am I now? (10) enhanced intimacy and sexuality in your relationship; (11) taking stock; and (12) saying goodbye and looking to the future. As women progress through the group and discuss these topics, existential concerns may rise as women sort through and process their experience in dealing with the impact of being treated for gynecologic cancer. In this illustration, I will demonstrate how existential issues are expressed as well as women's reflections on how the online group helped them with their existential concerns.

As women introduced themselves in the first week, the existential concern of identity was evident. One woman described sitting in the waiting room at the cancer centre, "The whole time I sat waiting and looking at all of the sick people around me, thinking that this can't be me. I am not sick, I don't have the same pallor, the same obvious pain, the same obvious nausea and fatigue but it was me, it is me." Another woman speaking about the impact of cancer in her family said, "The common thread – we all lost ourselves – we struggle to maintain our relationships. Personally, I have lost all desire for any intimate interaction." She goes on to talk about the impact scars and weight gain have had on her body image, "I find it hard to come to terms with going from a size 8 to a size 12. Size 12 isn't even that big a deal, it is the way I see myself and feel fat – my self image won't allow me to accept that I am attractive anymore and feel that I need to hide behind clothing." These comments suggest that women have been struggling redefine themselves.

Isolation was also evident in the first week. One 28-year-old woman said "I don't have many friends that understand my situation and often find myself the line (sic) weirdo." In response to her another women replied, "You touched on an issue that I can relate to and that is that family and friends, they don't understand and (hopefully) never will but it does leave one feeling odd." These posts suggest that having cancer made these women feel set apart, no longer fitting into the mainstream.

Death anxiety was indirectly expressed. One woman stated, "It might be irrational, I don't know but I can't get over the fear that my cancer will come back." Others were more veiled, "I am happy to be alive and grateful for the treatment that I had. Still got a little fear in me though," and "having a cancer diagnosis has been a life-altering experience … it brings out all kinds of issues and fears."

During week 2, women were asked to speak about difficult emotions and this led them to speak more directly about their existential concerns. Death was now addressed more openly. Several women spoke about the fear of leaving their children prematurely, of the cancer recurring, and of dying. For example, "Fear … I've been thinking about this a lot this week. What am I truly afraid of? … saying goodbye prematurely and my son forgetting his mom … wow a hard truth. I do think that this fear outweighs my second biggie – cancer returning." Identity was another topic and it seemed that the previous week's discussion spurred women's thinking about the issue. One woman reflected that "after last week['s topic], I think I have to get used to a new 'normal' which may take some doing. I can honestly say that I am disappointed that the pre-cancer me is gone forever, however I am pleased to know that I am not alone in the challenges regarding weight gain and libido." Another woman expressed existential concerns related to both identity and isolation saying, "Another difficult feeling brought on by this experience is a sense of loss for the person I was before the cancer diagnosis … It is very difficult to talk about such feelings with loved ones." Later that day another woman posted about identity and mortality, "I thought that once I got the 'all clear' I would be back to normal but I am not the same person I was before … I think differently now, I have more serious, real fears and I think about my own mortality more than I ever did." The following day, a woman reflected on issues related to choice, freedom and identity, "I was no longer in control … The life that I enjoyed pre-diagnosis just didn't seem to hold the same appeal. I felt like I was now required to find something deeper … Who am I now and what do I want from the rest of my life? … I guess I'm looking for a way to just enjoy each day without thinking that I'm 'wasting' the gift of survivorship." Interestingly, even though it was only the second week, women were describing the benefit they were already feeling from being in the group; "There's something healing about discovering that other people feel exactly the same as you do." And, "After last week's discussion, I found confidence in myself that I am the 'new' normal … The fact that you ladies have confirmed a number of my concerns, I have re-evaluated my path. Thank you!"

The expression of existential concerns emerged more strongly in some weeks than in others, as might be expected. Thus, in addition to the first two weeks, existential concerns dominated in the weeks devoted to "finding a new normal," "taking stock," and "saying goodbye and looking to the future." In the last two weeks, as women reflected on their experience in GyneGals, the dominant themes were that participating reduced the sense of isolation and that women felt a greater acceptance of their new "normal." One woman's comment suggested that participating helped her to find meaning, "I am honestly looking at my cancer scare as something positive." Some women expressed the importance of this being an online group because it helped them to feel safe enough to talk about the intimate details of their lives, including sharing things that they had never shared with anyone before. Other women stated that they would prefer a face-to-face group but that, nevertheless, they found the group to be beneficial. Although not all of the women who actively participated felt that they derived benefit, "While I was pleased to be part of this group study, in the end, I really don't feel that there was much to be gained from it for me (no a-ha moments, unfortunately.) ... and so, even though I tried to participate, I still often felt like an outsider (not that anyone led me to feel that way – I thought everyone participating was both supportive and brave!)." Perhaps this woman is expressing the failure of this online forum to ameliorate her existential isolation.

For these changes, I have drawn on the discussions in one group over the course of 12 weeks. At the time of writing, we have conducted 22 GyneGals groups (including both the pilot study and RCT), with four more to be completed. Naturally there is some variation across groups, Nevertheless, the group from which these illustrations were taken is representative of other groups that have unfolded. To conclude, although this brief online intervention was primarily designed to help women address the impact of cancer on their sexuality and intimate relationships, it has the added benefit of providing women with an opportunity to share the existential struggles that are evoked by having and being treated for gynecologic cancer.

Case study 2: Supervision Group with Irvin Yalom

Orah T. Krug

Introduction

I was a member of Irvin Yalom's supervision[1] group for 20 years until the spring of 2016.[2] What an extraordinary experience my five colleagues and I had, meeting nearly each month in his San Francisco apartment. Upon arrival, when greetings concluded, I habitually settled into "my spot" on the couch, to the right of Irv's chair, took in the glorious city view, and eagerly awaited the encounter to come. Ever the thoughtful host, Yalom never failed to have healthy snacks laid out on the cocktail table and sparkling soda on the counter. He started each meeting by asking who wanted time, noting our replies to ensure he honored the requests. Sometimes, he would begin by describing either a client's dream or an intriguing here-and-now encounter. His willingness to be a member of our group as well as its leader was noted by all. Yalom did not talk about being a "fellow traveler," he simply was one.

We presented informally, and typically, two or three people offered a case within the two-hour time frame. If it was my turn, I began by describing my client, the therapeutic issues, maybe a relevant dream, and what I wanted from the supervision. I often "brought in" a client with whom I felt blocked, knowing I was caught in my context, but unclear as to the "how and why" of it. I hoped the group would illuminate an

[1] In the United States Yalom's group is understood to be a consultation group because the participants are licensed practitioners but in the United Kingdom, a group like Yalom's is known as a supervision group.

[2] Yalom reluctantly stopped supervision because he found it increasingly difficult to be at his San Francisco apartment with pressing commitments closer to home in Palo Alto. The group continues to meet as a peer supervision group.

aspect of me, my client, and/or our relationship that I couldn't see. The group did not disappoint. With their skill, experience, and artistry – my seasoned colleagues and Irv invariably provided new insights into my client's personality, the nature of our relationship or an unrecognized self-protective pattern of mine.

I kept careful notes on my supervision with Yalom, and they constitute the source materials for this chapter. This section will focus on Yalom's teaching, his process interventions, and his leadership style.

Yalom's Teaching

Yalom's didactic teaching was extraordinary. Topics ranged from ways to illuminate unrecognized existential issues to interpersonal process work and dream work. But even more impactful was when he taught by example. That happened when Irv sensed our group had an unaddressed interpersonal issue. Then he never failed to intervene promptly, with skill and clarity; exemplifying one of his central therapeutic tenets*: The safety and well-being of the relationship takes precedence over all else.* The following vignettes illustrate this point.

Attention to Group Process

I thought I was comfortable with the supervision group when I first started but my sketchy attendance in the first year seemed to indicate a healthy dose of ambivalence. Looking back, I understand that as intellectually stimulating and enjoyable as it was, I still was not fully committed to the group, nor entirely comfortable with Yalom's approach. He did two things, almost in tandem that strengthened my commitment to the group and my respect for him. First, in private he directly raised the issue of my spotty attendance without any judgment or blame. He did not explore my evident resistance but simply asked if I was still finding the group valuable, given the fact that I missed a number of meetings. My answer was yes, and yet attending the meetings was difficult.

On one occasion, I searched for a parking space with no success. Finally, in desperation after half an hour, I called Yalom and told him my dilemma. He immediately offered to open his garage and let me use the guest parking. After my parking fiasco, Yalom offered our entire group the use of his garage on a regular basis. My trust in him grew, as did my commitment to the group, with his generous and immediate response to the parking problem.

It is interesting to reflect on this seemingly insignificant act in light of Yalom's reference in *Existential Psychotherapy* (1980, p. 4) to the significance of the "*throw-ins*" of therapy. "Throw-ins" are "off the record" acts of generosity and caring that a therapist does not consider a part of the "treatment" but which have significantly positive impacts on the therapeutic relationship. Given my reaction to Yalom's parking (as well as his many other) "throw-ins," I would like to suggest that these qualities of "presence," that is, of caring and of extending oneself – so hard to define, much less teach – are also crucial for a successful consultative relationship. After these two events the question of whether I would stay or go became a moot point. I felt safer and more committed to the group, and the fact that I stopped missing meetings lends validity to this assertion.

Several years ago another member began to miss meetings. Noting his absence at the beginning of a meeting, Yalom wondered if perhaps his feelings had been hurt by comments he and other group members had made about his work. We agreed that was possible so we reached out to the absent member, letting him know we missed him. When he came back, Yalom immediately asked if his absence was connected to what had happened in one of the previous meetings. Our colleague (who I'll call Jim) acknowledged feeling confused and hurt not only by the group's feedback but also by Irv's as well. Yalom's group skills were evident. First, he intervened to repair his relationship with "Jim," acknowledging his lapse of empathy, and then clarifying his intentions to "Jim." Then he helped those members involved in the interaction repair their relationships with "Jim" in a similar manner. When we finished, we were pleased to have cleared the air and appreciated Yalom's efforts as well as our own to acknowledge our interpersonal mistakes. Not surprisingly, after that, our absent colleague was consistently present.

Yalom's sensitivity to group process was further demonstrated when he allowed the group's needs to shape his approach, an event that happened early in the group's life. One of us (who I'll call Bob), who had trained with James Bugental, asked Irv to engage in a role-play exercise in which Irv would be the therapist and "Bob" would role-play one of his clients. This was familiar to those of us in the group who had been trained by Bugental. At first Irv declined, saying he was not convinced of its value, believing it to be somewhat artificial. However, we persisted and, as my journal attests, he finally agreed, allowing us to experience his masterful approach to working with interpersonal process. By reversing his position on the value of role-play, Yalom embodied yet another one of his core therapeutic principles, that is, *the therapist must shape the therapy to the needs of the client* – in this case, the supervisor to the needs of the supervisees.

On one occasion another member and I came to a supervision group just having had a difficult conversation about a work-related project. Without consulting me, my colleague brought our disagreement up in our group with the intention to work on it there. I had to decide if I trusted the group enough to open up with them. It came as a bit of a surprise to recognize how willing I was to work on it there. Yalom's immediate support and availability helped me feel safe and confident in my decision. It was a good decision, because in working through the conflict, I had to confront a tendency to take on too many projects and the unintended consequences that, at times, follow. Yalom and the group helped me see this, using their own experiences with me. It was not easy to hear but quite valuable in helping me face this behavior and explore its underlying dynamics. Yalom not only validated my feelings, but also suggested that I reflect on aspects of my behavior that were not serving me. He did this with the utmost respect and care. As a result of his feedback and the group's feedback I felt more open and intimate with the group. I had risked working through a thorny conflict with a group member without being blamed or shamed. Instead I felt supported and accepted by the group when Irv and others shared their experiences of me.

To summarize, Yalom's attention to our group and interpersonal processes cultivated a sense of safety and intimacy within our group. The narrative testifies to the ways in which he embodied his core principles of group and interpersonal process work, for example, being both a collegial leader and fellow traveler. The narrative only hints at the numerous ways he quickly attended to problems within the group resulting from interpersonal issues, most memorably, the respectful and effective ways by which he repaired breeches that arose between group members, himself included.

An Interpersonal Focus: Cultivating Presence in the Relationship

After my first supervision group I wrote in my journal, "I feel off balance, my theoretical footing feels shaken. I hear what Yalom is saying, but I do not get it." I was confused because Yalom's here-and-now focus was quite different from that of my other mentor, James Bugental with whom I had trained for many years. Bugental almost exclusively focused on his clients' subjective here-and-now experiences. Bugental's goal was to germinate his clients' sense of "I-ness," that is, personal agency to increase self-awareness and to mobilize the will (Bugental 1976, p. 5). In contrast to Bugental, Yalom also has an interpersonal focus, which aims is to link an experience of "I-ness" with "you-ness." Why does Yalom value an interpersonal focus? Believing that "human problems are largely relational" (Yalom 2002, p. 48), he surmised that an interpersonal focus in a safe and caring therapeutic relationship could help clients immediately experience how their relational patterns affect the therapist and vice versa, thereby helping them develop more intimate and satisfying relationships beyond the therapy room.

"The here-and-now is the major source of therapeutic power, the pay dirt of therapy, the therapist's (and hence the patient's) best friend," says Yalom (2002 p. 46). The immediacy of working the here-and-now is what makes it the therapist's best friend. He urged us to bring the "then and there" into the "here-and-now." For example, if a client says, "I have difficulty trusting my friend because" Yalom suggested we refocus our client's attention to the immediate relationship by asking, "Do you sometimes have difficulty trusting me?" His intention is to move the individual from "*talking about his life and relationships*" outside the therapy room to "*experience being in his life with another*" in the therapy room.

Time and again Yalom would challenge us to find "here and now" equivalents, to give interpersonal feedback, to cultivate the transference, and to teach clients to express their feelings about us. Yalom implicitly and explicitly reminded us that our task was to cultivate a safe and intimate therapeutic relationship with our clients. According to Yalom (2002) "therapeutic intimacy" is only possible if two factors are in place: (a) the underlying ground of safety that presupposes everything else, and (b) the therapist's willingness to tolerate and deeply engage the client in this deep intimacy that characterizes his here-and-now method. And as the preceding paragraphs illustrate he taught this by example, as he willingly engaged in our group and interpersonal processes.

According to Yalom (2002), it is not the content of the explanations that heal, even though explanations bond the client and therapist together in a joint enterprise. *It is only when the client consistently experiences the safety, acceptance, understanding, and connection with the therapist that healing occurs.* As a result, the client feels increased intimacy and acceptance with self and with others, thus resolving the central problem of estrangement. My personal experience with Yalom validates this assumption. His willingness to engage with me most definitely led to greater self-acceptance, and to a stronger connection with him and with the group.

For the field of psychology this is a truly radical notion – even though research consistently points to the primacy of the therapeutic relationship as the crucial ingredient for effecting change. In my opinion, one of Yalom's most significant contributions to the field is his meticulous examination of how a therapist can use the here-and-now method to cultivate such an intimate, interpersonal relationship.

Working interpersonally was challenging for me to learn. I felt out of my comfort zone, somewhat like flying on a trapeze without a net. But as I became more comfortable with this more personal way of working, I saw how much my clients benefited not only from their newfound self-awareness but also from our more intimate therapeutic relationships, which developed as we focused on our interpersonal experiences of one another. An integration of an interpersonal focus with an intrapersonal focus became my preferred method for therapy (for further explanations see Krug 2009; Schneider and Krug 2010). Working interpersonally also had an impact on my personal life in that I was more able to see the ways in which I created distance instead of closeness in my significant relationships – it challenged me to change that.

Working with Dreams

"Have you asked your clients about their dreams?" Yalom would frequently inquire of us. He relished working with dreams in supervision, believing that dreams "represent an incisive restating of the patient's deeper problems, only in a different language – a language of visual imagery" (2002, p. 226). As I mentioned he often began our group by sharing one of his client's dreams or one of his own, written down I think, as much for future use in one of his books as for his client's file. Despite the challenges, learning to work with dreams has significantly enriched my therapeutic skill set. In the beginning, I was reluctant to work with dreams because I lacked formal training in "dream work." I have to credit Yalom for demystifying it. Yalom admits to being very pragmatic about dream work, his fundamental principle "is to extract from them everything that expedites and accelerates therapy" (2002, p. 228). I decided I could do that, so I began to encourage my clients to dream and share them with me. My clients appreciate our dream work as an additional window into their subjective and relational experiences. Their dreams, rich with visual images provide us with concrete representations of their inner worlds and struggles.

Working with Existential Issues

Helping clients face their existential dilemmas that often lie just below the surface is a cornerstone of Yalom's existential approach. He strongly believes in the significance of this work and, paradoxically, in the difficulty that it presents to therapists. He frequently reminded us that at the heart of many clients' issues are unrecognized existential dilemmas. Sensitized to their presence, we helped our clients brush away everyday concerns to explore them.

As Cooper (2003) and van Deurzen-Smith (1997) acknowledged, Irv Yalom, in his texts and novels, has made the existential approach better known than any existential therapist has been able to do previously. That being said, according to van Deurzen-Smith (1997), Yalom is ironically the least existential because he merely uses the existential concepts to intensify confrontation instead of having them be guidelines for life. My experiences suggest otherwise.

Throughout the years of supervision, Irv has not only urged us to be alert to our client's existential issues but also to our own reactions that may be getting triggered. I recall an occasion when a group member was relating his work with an 80-year-old man. Yalom suggested the group member reflect on how his client's impending death and his associated feelings were affecting him. On another occasion, I "brought" a client to supervision caught in the throes of an existential crisis, deeply regretting the life path she had taken. "Perhaps she senses she will die having left too much life inside of her," Yalom offered. "Instead of constantly looking back, turn her attention to the future. Help her focus on ways to avoid having more regrets two years from now."

The "unlived life" is a concept of Friedrich Nietzsche (one of Yalom's favorite existential philosopher's) who wrote eloquently on the subject. In *The Gay Science* (Nietzsche and Kaufmann 1974) Nietzsche introduced an intriguing vision of life, which for Yalom has held great significance. Twice in supervision, Yalom related Nietzsche's vision of "eternal recurrence." Nietzsche's notion asks: "If you were told you would have to live your life again and again would you rejoice or curse? If one can face such a prospect with enthusiasm, one has successfully created a good and meaningful in life, but if one faces such a prospect with dread, than one has left too much life unlived."[3]

There was a memorable meeting in the fall of 2004, when Yalom shared how he used Nietzsche's idea to help him cope with the prospect of a life-threatening illness. He faced this possibility for an entire month before finding out that the diagnosis was incorrect. He decided he said, "To live my life like the main character in my new book *The Schopenhauer Cure*" (2005). This character, a successful San Francisco therapist, fashioned it would seem after Yalom, is diagnosed with cancer and has one year to live. The therapist asks himself, how will I choose to live it?" Upon reflection he concludes that his life is being lived just as he wants it and decides to continue on, making no changes. Yalom told us that when he asked himself the same question, he realized that his feelings were similar to that of his character, specifically: he was presently living precisely as he desired.

[3] The original formulation of "eternal recurrence" covers not just regret over omissions but also over commissions The relevant quotation, as translated by Kaufman, is, "What, if some day or night a demon were to steal after you into your loneliest loneliness and say to you: 'This life as you now live it and have lived it, you will have to live once more and innumerable times more; and there will be nothing new in it, but every pain and every joy and every thought and sigh and everything unutterably small or great in your life will have to return to you, all in the same succession and sequence – even this spider and this moonlight between the trees, and even this moment and I myself. The eternal hourglass of existence is turned upside down again and again, and you with it, speck of dust!' Would you not throw yourself down and gnash your teeth and curse the demon who spoke thus?... Or how well disposed would you have to become to yourself and to life *to crave nothing more fervently* than this ultimate eternal confirmation and seal?"(Nietzsche 1974/ 1882., section 341, p. 273) [Ed.]

A Focus on Our Own Existential Issues

Reflecting on my journal entries, I realized that 2004 and 2005 were traumatic years for many of us in the group. Collectively we bore the loss of parents, a tragic auto accident, a tumor removed, and an erroneous cancer diagnosis. I was touched by how honestly and lovingly Yalom invited each of us to express our feelings about these experiences, and how he shared his own with us. By doing so he embodied his belief in the value of therapeutic transparency. His disclosures never failed to move me. With each lived experience, our group moved to a deeper level of connection and intimacy. The following excerpts from my journal recorded January 25, 2005 are about my own experiences that illustrate this point. My father died on December 28, 2004, a week after our latest meeting. The entire group knew he had died, but, with the exception of my two closest friends, the group didn't know the whole story. I'd actually found my father dead in his apartment. Unwilling to live his remaining years tethered to a dialysis machine, he'd shot himself.

Driving to the meeting I wasn't sure if I would reveal to the group my excruciatingly difficult experience. It took a leap of faith to trust that they could to handle it. My trust was rewarded as each responded with sensitive understanding, thoughtfulness, and support. Two members followed with disclosures of their own about how their mother and father respectively chose to end their lives instead of being compromised by their illnesses. Yalom told us about a dream he had after his mother had died (also published in *Momma and the Meaning of Life*, 1999). The group ended with hugs all around. It was one meeting I will never forget.

We are all just fellow travelers. The harsh experiences that befell our little group in those years speak to the uncompromising truth of Yalom's statement. We must not separate ourselves from our clients (or supervisees). To do so is to deny that we too must face and bear the harsh realities of existence. Those harsh realities are less burdensome when we create a sturdy community of close friends amongst our colleagues. Over the years, as our group grew closer, we were lovingly there for one another when the inevitable vicissitudes of life knocked at our doors. I am grateful that our supervision group has decided to continue, even without our beloved leader.

Closing Thoughts

Recently I completed a text for APA with my co-author Kirk J. Schneider titled *Supervision Essentials for Existential-Humanistic Therapy* (Krug and Schneider 2016). In one chapter Kirk and I described the mentors who influenced our development as supervisors and teachers of Existential-Humanistic therapy. Not surprisingly I pointed to James Bugental and Irvin Yalom as being "most prominent in shaping my therapeutic values, attitudes, and style…" (2016, p. 111).

Yalom consistently embodied his values and principles in our supervision group. From his engagement with our group process, to his personal disclosures, to his fellow traveler demeanor, to name a few, Irv created a safe and intimate space, a space that nurtured my psychological transformation. At a recent brunch with Irv, I mentioned that he and Jim were perched on each shoulder, reminding me as I wrote, "*that abstract ideas do not transform, but lived experiences do*" (p. 115). Thank you Jim and thank you Irv!

Case study 3: Meaning-Centered Existential Group Therapy: Discovering Meaning in Life after Traumatic Experiences

Marie S. Dezelic

Meaning-Centered Therapy is an existential therapeutic approach that is rooted in and expands on Viktor Frankl's Logotherapy and Existential Analysis (LTEA), which is a philosophical, phenomenological, and anthropological approach to psychotherapy. The fundamental basis of LTEA is the recognition of the unique quality of the human being as depicted in its *Dimensional Ontology* – comprised of *Soma* (Body), *Psyche* (Mind), and *Noös* (Spirit). *The 3 primary tenets of Logotherapy* formed around the central concept of meaning are the main underpinnings of Frankl's theory of personality. *Meaning in Life* refers to a unique significance and purpose, often influenced by cultural values, societal descriptions, and familial purposes; it is entirely personal, yet often shaped by experiences in the world. Although human beings may have similar concepts, definitions, and understandings, *Meaning* is, by its fundamental nature and virtue, a unique, experiential, multidimensional, non-linear, abstract, and exclusively human construct (Dezelic and Ghanoum 2015, 2016). Frankl asserted that meaning is not created but rather, always exists, with the potential to be discovered by all individuals in every moment of their lives, even in the most difficult circumstances (Frankl 1988).

The *three primary tenets of Logotherapy* (Dezelic 2014; Frankl 1978, 1988; Graber 2004):

- *Freedom of Will*: The ability to take a stand toward conditions, and change attitudes in the face of life's difficulties; not freedom *from* the conditions of life such as the situations happening to us and around us.
- *Will to Meaning*: The basic striving to discover meaning and purpose in life; not as a drive or pursuit, but as a choice of direction in life.
- *Meaning of Life*: Meaning (a unique significance and purpose) is always available for us to discover and uncover; we are free to search for and fulfill our unique meaning as we "walk toward" an ultimate meaning.

Therapists can assist clients who are dealing with life's difficult and tragic situations to *lessen the impact*, *mediate reactive responses*, *discover meaning*, and ultimately *modify their attitudes* toward unavoidable circumstances and suffering. This is accomplished by reorienting then toward the *three primary tenets of Logotherapy* (Freedom of Will, Will to Meaning, and Meaning of Life) by helping them activate their *Meaning Triangle* – with *Creativity*, *Experiences*, and *Attitudes* (Dezelic 2014; Dezelic and Ghanoum 2015, 2016; Graber 2004).

According to Viktor Frankl, the *Meaning Triangle* consists of three specific areas through which we have the capacity to discover meaning and purpose in life:

- *Creativity* – the creative gifts we offer to life and others through our innate talents in work, deeds done, creative pursuits, and goals achieved that held and hold meaning.
- *Experiences* – the experiences we receive from encountering others in relationships of all kinds, and from love, nature, the arts, culture, or religion.

- *Attitudes* – the attitudinal values we realize by taking a stance toward a situation or circumstance, that was courageous or self-transcending (e.g., attitudes of meaningful discovery in suffering, trauma, and tragedy) (Dezelic 2014; Dezelic and Ghanoum 2015, 2016; Frankl 2006; Graber 2004).

The *Meaning-Centered Therapy Manual: LTEA Brief Therapy for Group & Individual Sessions* (Dezelic and Ghanoum 2015) provides an eight-session manualized protocol to help clients explore existential topics of the human condition, including despair and existential frustration, as well as discover meaning in life, even in the face of difficult life circumstances and tragic situations.

Sessions 1–8

Session 1: Introduction: Concepts of Logotherapy and Existential Analysis (LTEA)

4 What is Viktor Frankl's Logotherapy?
5 Philosophy of Logotherapy: The Basic Assumptions
6 Basic Concepts of Logotherapy: The Three Primary Tenets

Session 2: Exploring Meaning

7 Discovering Meaning in Life
8 Identity: Doing vs. Being

Session 3: The Human Ontology of Body, Mind, Spirit (Essence)

9 The Human Being's Multidimensional Aspects: Body (Soma), Mind (Psyche), Spirit (Noös)
10 The Human Being's Unique Aspect: Spiritual (Nöetic) Dimension

Session 4: Inner Resources and Strengths

11 Nöetic Dimension: The Medicine Chest of Logotherapy
12 Mind-Body-Spirit: Simple Techniques for Stress Reduction and Healthy Living

Session 5: Existential Aspects

13 The Existential Triangle: From Meaningless to Meaningful Existence
14 Tragic Optimism of Logotherapy: Optimism in the Face of Tragedy

Session 6: Suffering and Meaning

15 "Homo Patiens": Extracting Meaning from Suffering
16 Noögenic (Spiritual) Neuroses: Logotherapy as a Specific Therapy

Session 7: Personal Growth and Transformation

17 Post-Traumatic Growth and Possibilities Activated in Logotherapy
18 The Meaning-Action Triangle: Becoming Existentially Aware
19 The Seven-Step Noögenic Activation Method

Session 8: Living Meaningfully

20 REACH Beyond the Limitations: Sources of Meaning in Life
21 Connect–Create–Convey: Living Life with Meaning and Purpose
Closing Discussion

Box 28.1 Session 2, Handout 4: Discovering Meaning in Life

Ten group therapy clients who had experienced developmental trauma, one-time incident trauma, or traumatic grief were given "Handout 4—Discovering Meaning in Life" (Box 28.1) in Session 2, to enhance their discussions. To aid in the *Discovery of Meaning* experienced currently or previously, the clients were asked to offer their *Reflections* on the following questions:

1 What *creative* gifts have I offered to others through my talents, my work, deeds done, and/or goals achieved that held meaning for me?
2 What deeply meaningful *experiences* have I received from encountering others in relationship of all kinds, and/or from nature, culture or religion?
3 What *attitudinal* values have I realized by taking a courageous or self-transcending stance toward situations or blows of fate?

Additionally, clients were asked to reflect on "The Guideposts to Sources of Meaning," identified by Fabry (1988), which highlights five areas that could enhance the discovery of their unique, personal *Meaning Triangle*, *Meaning in the Moment*, and *Ultimate Meaning*.

The Guideposts to Sources of Meaning:

- *Self-Discovery:* Who am I? What do I want to become?
- *Choice:* Change the situation; change the attitude (Past)
- *Uniqueness*: Creativity; personal relationships
- *Responsibility:* Freedom; fate
- *Self-transcendence:* Toward a person; toward a cause

Specific Case Example (Name and identifying details have been changed to preserve anonymity)

Sarah was a 51-year-old woman who had a childhood sexual abuse history. In addition to presenting with anxiety, throughout her normal day-to-day life she often experienced mood swings, flashbacks of traumatic scenes, and intrusive sensations. Although Sarah was working through her traumatic memories in individual therapy, she was also attending group therapy to increase her positive engagement and connection with others. In spite of her traumatic experiences and feeling as if she would always be afflicted by her past trauma, Sarah was able to derive meaning from the three attributes of the Meaning Triangle. The following examples are Sarah's reflections she shared with the group after completing Handout 4:

In *Creativity*: From the time she was a young child, Sarah wrote poems and created booklets that contained meaningful messages for loved ones and for herself. She kept all of her booklets from childhood through her teenage years, and by looking at her booklets again in group therapy, was able to reflect on her growth as an individual. As an outcome of this exercise, her sense of creativity was ignited once more. As a result, Sarah began to create a new booklet that contained notes, poems, and key phrases for the various aspects she was working through and discovering about herself in her current individual and group therapy.

In *Experiences*: Sarah was able to focus on her loving experiences with certain family members and her boyfriend, her times at the beach with the soothing ocean waves lapping against the shore, and on her deep and intimate connection with animals. She now began to look for daily experiences to recognize meaningful moments, and added these positive events to her booklet.

In *Attitudes*: Sarah worked on changing her attitude from "I am a sexual abuse victim" to "I was a child who was sexually abused, but I am now a woman who has many choices ahead of me; and instead of being someone who cannot do anything for myself, I am now someone who is resilient, and I can manage through some of the greatest difficulties in life." Sarah recorded positive affirmations about herself in the booklet.

Finally, when using the "Guideposts to Sources of Meaning," Sarah took one page for each area, and gave detailed explanations of each one. Sarah shared with the group that completing these exercises helped her to realize that, despite the trauma she endured as a child, she was still able to derive meaning from life, including her new experiences in group therapy and with group members. Once she began to recognize these possibilities, Sarah embraced her new attitude that life is full of meaning, regardless of what we have been through in our past, and that all we need to do is "look for it." These are Sarah's own thoughts and words about her transformation: "I can't believe that I have so many amazing things in my life, I just never knew life could be so meaningful! I don't have to focus on the trauma like I used to, and I can look at it as something that helped me to become a stronger person, something that others don't have and I do. I don't wish it away anymore, it now just is, and I focus on what I have in my life today – and that's me and my meaning!"

Conclusion

Meaning in Life often becomes blocked when we experience the difficult, tragic, and traumatic aspects of life and the human condition. Meaning-Centered Therapy offers clients a clinical approach and direction for discovering meaning opportunities, regardless of diagnoses or situation. Through exploring the dialects and existential aspects of the human condition, we can find our similarities, as well as our unique meaning and purposes in life (Dezelic 2014; Dezelic and Ghanoum 2015, 2016; Frankl 1978, 1988, 2006; Graber 2004).

Case study 4: Existential settings and groups. Our Weekly Greencare Group

Lynda Ansell, Rex Haigh, Sarah Hamilton, Fiona Lomas, Sharon Tizzard, Hilary Welsh

This description of the "greencare group" was planned and written as one of the activities of the group on September 22, 2016. It has been modified and added to in early 2018.

We often have visitors come to spend a day with us, to see how we mix group therapy, therapeutic community and horticulture together – in a way that ends up looking very much like existential psychotherapy. Our weekly Thursday group is ostensibly to support the people with long-term emotional troubles that the mainstream mental health services are unable to support: but we think it does much more. Through connection with each other, and with nature, our members – and that includes staff, trainees, and visitors – seem to find, or at least witness, a new way to be with each other. We aim to live in a creative, active, and reflective way, with each other, and so find new meaning and purpose in our lives. The therapeutic community method (see Pearce and Haigh 2017) emphasizes an emancipatory process in which the individuals in the group are supported to take responsibility for themselves and each other by finding a sense of personal agency and sense of "whole self" (Haigh 2013). In the group, people find their own authority in exploring their life – and the way they want to live it.

When new people drive into the car park at the front of the Environment Centre, they immediately recognize what a calm and peaceful place it is, despite the fact we are less than a mile away from London's M25 motorway and adjacent to a huge electricity distribution sub-station. In fact, if the wind is in the wrong direction, you can hear the motorway – although we kid ourselves that it's the sound of the sea.

A couple of our group members will then guide the visitors around the back of the log cabin, which is actually the classroom block for the environment center, to the edge of a large pond. This is a marshy wilderness that is home to our colony of great crested newts, a protected species, some of whom are often found hibernating in the midst of our potato patch.

To get to our group's yurt we cross the reedy expanse of the pond on a rickety wooden bridge – a real and virtual passage to the interior: the woody and organic circle of chairs that we keep under canvas, and the swirling and often troubled mental contents that we keep under our cranium. The yurt is our spiritual home – and was described as "a good space with no corners to hide in" by Norman Sartorius, on receiving our 2014 award. Yurts of course have a nomadic heritage moving across the plains of central Asia – but ours is fixed, and it is those inside we expect to be "moving" – though is it movement, not of a physical kind, while coming to the same place every week.

The staff team arrives at about 9.30am every Thursday morning. This always includes our integrative psychotherapist and our greencare coordinator cum horticulturalist – who is a therapeutic community "expert by experience" herself. Various others, including post-doctoral researcher, animal intervention therapist, consultant medical psychotherapist, come from time to time and are well known by the group, as part-time members. Professional visitors are always welcome, as long as they arrange it well in advance. The staff team has a monthly supervision afternoon, in the yurt, from a long-experienced transpersonal therapist.

Our researcher has engaged several temporary assistant psychologists, from the associated NHS services, in small qualitative research projects. They have given these as oral presentations and posters at the annual conference of the British and Irish Group for the Study of Personality Disorders (BIGSPD). A focus group study that directly asked participants what they most valued about the greencare groups identified several themes that are well-attuned to the principles of humanistic and existential therapy: therapeutic benefits including calm restfulness with opportunity for stillness, togetherness, and socialization as well as catharsis; a non-clinical environment conveying non-stigmatized safety and a sense of lush, green sanctuary; and activities giving freedom of choice, opportunities for rewarding achievement, and a sense of community and fun (Jones, Maurya, and Green 2014). Some of the most powerful statements about the benefit of this work reflect evanescent qualities that are hard to describe in scientific or positivistic terms. This is a sample gathered from a recent discussion group, as part of an appeal to recruit public support for continuation of the service:

> **Service user L**: "Greencare kept me alive. Without it – the other services couldn't give me as much. Trust, support loyalty, sense of family. Where I was treated as a decent human being, not a psychiatric patient or a "waste of space." Not judged at all, it wasn't like a stereotypical mental health group. Not clinical – this was warm and welcoming. I could be who I was, the real me without a mask."
>
> **Service user S:** "I heard of this group through another service and had no expectations because I had no idea what I was walking into but I was hoping for something that would help. I wanted to feel normal. At the time I had thoughts that I shouldn't be having that haunted me and all I could think of was killing myself. This place saved me from that. I felt accepted, it was a ray of hope."
>
> **Service user P**: "it feels like your 'forever' place. It feels safe for us here, structured without being domineering. A break from all the burdens we carry 24/7. Not alone with our issues. It's not just you. And you get your self-confidence back by joining in with all the tasks."
>
> **Volunteer D:** "Over the years greencare has evolved and changed but it has continued to thrive and means a lot to those who use it. In my experience this is a unique group which demonstrates the best of human connections: trust, support, growth – and lots of laughter."

So, back to the weekly group itself. The rest of the members arrive at about 10.00 am. As we are about five miles outside town, this depends on who gets a lift from whom, and how well the buses are running. Usually by 10.15 am, everybody has had a cup of tea or coffee and sits down around the yurt's circular table for the first fixed event of the day: the "check-in."

The purpose of the check-in is to hear from everybody, and establish the sense that each person feels present for everybody else. Once we are all sitting down with our drinks, there is usually a short reflective silence before one of us says "OK then, I'll start," or something similar. For the check-in, the least anybody usually says is what their week has been like, and how they're feeling right now: sometimes there is much more to say and it brings pain and tears, or laughter and jollity, or all sorts of other things that might be going on for them. We have learned to discourage deeply difficult and unprocessed early memories of trauma, abuse or deprivation, as the group is not designed to deal with those issues, and does not have the time or resources to do so. Staff members and visitors are included in the check-in and can be as personal, or not, as they choose. The procedure we have evolved is for the person who speaks first to pass it on, either to their right or left, and for it to then go all round the circle.[4] One person to "says their stuff" at a time, and there is no discussion before it is passed on to the next person. After the check-in, the group usually allocates some time to "follow-ups," during which time people support each other with what they have mentioned. This also continues throughout the time together during the rest of the day, and sometimes beyond – outside the greencare group, in other therapy groups people attend, or at subsequent weeks' groups. There is no fixed time limit to the check-in, but members are generally aware that it is too long if it goes on for longer than about an hour.

Although the discussion and "music" of this group would not be unfamiliar to most traditional group and therapeutic community therapists – using theoretical ideas such as resonance, communalism, and universality – there is something else in operation. It is an ineffable quality, perhaps about "the nature of relationships" that is very difficult to describe in words – or by using the propositional logic of psychiatry, psychology, or most psychotherapy. Perhaps concepts of existential therapy, such as "facilitating a person's greater awareness of their mode of being in the world, helping them to be more in touch with their concrete physicality, their interactions and relationships, their engagement with their own identity or lack of it, their concept of what grounds their being and the ways in which they may be able to bring the flow and their capacity for transcendence, learning and pleasurable forward movement back to life. It helps people to tolerate and embrace suffering and difficulty to engage with it constructively" (Deurzen 2018) capture the essence of what we do, as well as any other verbal constructions.

After the check-in, we talk about what we all want to do during the day – and arrange ourselves in groups of at least three to do whatever we decide. One task is usually preparing lunch for everybody, and everything else depends on people's inclinations and the weather. In spring and summer, we spend much of the time in the organic allotment. We plant things that we want to grow – and later in the year, harvest, cook, and eat together. We make compost, we put up structures like raised beds, fences, and our garden shed; we also spend quite a lot of time and effort looking after the yurt and doing general housekeeping and maintenance. When it is cold and wet, for many of our winter sessions, we usually spend the time indoors – planning the horticulture, doings art and craft activities, writing things, and making pickles, chutneys and jams in the center's main kitchen. Christmas and midwinter is a time when there is little to be done outside, so we usually spend a few weeks preparing for our Christmas lunch and party, and decorating the yurt until it is quite spectacular. We invite all sorts of people along for this – members of other therapy groups we know, referrers, other clinical staff, and anybody else we want to have with us for the celebrations.

As well as Christmas, we have a few regular special events throughout the calendar year, to mark the passing of the seasons. In spring, we go to a local farm at lambing time – and usually have a group session there where members can hold the infant lambs, bottle-feed the orphans, and sometimes see them being born. A lot of feelings and sometimes discussion about attachment issues usually follows! At Easter we have

[4] A method reminiscent of "circle time" (White 1999)

a traditional egg-rolling contest, often with strange new rules invented on the day. In the summer we invite partners, family, friends, and colleagues to the summer barbeque, on the terrace overlooking the pond and yurt. Between then and midwinter, we usually have an outing of some sort: in the past this has included a Grand Union Canal trip on a "floating classroom" barge, an orienteering treasure hunt in a local park, and a walk along London canals to Camden Lock.

In our regular Thursday groups, we break for about three-quarters of an hour to have lunch together, usually in the yurt, but sometimes outdoors on the terrace or by the pond. Then volunteers wash up, and we get back to the various activities of the day. Lunch isn't at a fixed time, but happens when it is ready, and when everybody is ready to come to it.

The whole experience of doing something together that is emotionally meaningful, as well as producing our own food from the ground we sit upon, through seasons of scarcity and plenty, gives the members of our group the experience – such that many of them have never previously had – of living in a creative, active, and reflective manner, in order to find new meaning and purpose in their lives.

At 3.30 pm, we all go to the yurt to "gather" the day together. The first thing we do is to jointly write a paragraph for our blog, including a photo or two, and then do the greencare journals. Every member has one of these, and it contains many pages of information about greencare together with space for reflective writing, photos, and evaluation questionnaires. We have a printer in the yurt for members to print out photos, which they can physically stick into their journal to remind them of the day

The most unusual outcome measure we are using is the "plants of feeling" or "plant emoticons'" scale, which was developed by our researcher together with the group members (Jones 2017). After several sessions that involved looking at slide shows of different plants and discussing what feelings they aroused, a short list of about 50 was whittled down to ten – each of which represented emotional states that people often felt at the end of a greencare day. The researcher then printed out a sheet of tiny adhesive "stamps" of each of the ten plants, from which all members choose the one to best represent their mood of the day, and put it into the journals. Staff and visitors also choose one, and usually stick it on their shirt or jumper.

After a little discussion about people's choices, we have the last item of the day – the check-out. As for the check-in, this is a go-round that starts with whoever wants to go first. It is much shorter than the check-in, and usually takes only a minute or two per person. Everybody says how the day has been for them, and how they feel to be going home. Nearly always, the members of the group report feeling "calm" or "grounded" – and often comment that they are in a better state than when they arrived. Staff and visitors participate as well and make similar comments – without any judgements or interpretations. It always finishes within a few minutes of 4.00 pm. As well as a general containing function, the check-out is seen as an important risk assessment exercise – and on the rare occasions that it does not feel safe for a member to go home alone, the group makes a plan for how to deal with it. This sometimes involves support by other group members (being physically together, or arranging contact by phone or text), or occasionally contacting staff from the local mental health services (with which all the members are registered). Then the members leave, the staff have a short debriefing session, and everybody goes home – sometimes with armfuls of courgettes (zucchini), beans, tomatoes, or pumpkins, but nearly always with an intention to come again next week.

It is important to mention that this group is part of a network of groups and activities that are available to people registered with the local NHS mental health services – but it is provided outside those services, by an organization that is set up as a social enterprise, as a community interest company. The network of other services includes groups provided by the Community Mental Health Team, the recently formed recovery college (importantly, not part of the national "Implementing Recovery through Organisational Change," which we find rather too corporate in its work), local social service commissioning, and various voluntary organizations. The intention is to provide a true therapeutic community across the town, but one without walls.

References

Bugental, J.F.T. (1976). *The Search for Existential Identity.* San Francisco: Jossey-Bass.

Caldwell, R., Classen, C., McGarvey, E. et al. (2003). Changes in sexual functioning and mood among women treated for gynecological cancer who receive group therapy: A pilot study. *Journal of Clinical Psychology in Medical Settings 10* (3): 149–156.

Classen, C.C., Chivers, M.L., Urowitz, S. et al. (2013). Psychosexual distress in women with gynecologic cancer: A feasibility study of an online support group. *Psycho-Oncology 22* (4): 930–935.

Classen, C.C., Drozd, A., Brotto L.A. et al. (2015). Protocol of a randomized controlled trial of an online support group for sexual distress due to gynecologic cancer. *Journal of Clinical Trials 5* (4): 234.

Cooper, M. (2003). *Existential Therapies.* London: Sage.

Derogatis, L., Clayton, A., Lewis-D'Agostino, D. et al. (2008). Validation of the female sexual distress scale-revised for assessing distress in women with hypoactive sexual desire disorder. *Journal of Sexual Medicine 5* (2): 357–364.

Deurzen, E. van (2018). What is the Existential Approach? Accessed January 21, 2019 at: https://www.nspc.org.uk/about-the-school/the-existential-approach/

Dezelic, M.S. (2014). *Meaning-Centered Therapy Workbook: Based on Viktor Frankl's Logotherapy and Existential Analysis.* San Rafael, CA: Palace Printing and Design.

Dezelic, M.S. and Ghanoum, G. (2015). *Meaning-Centered Therapy Manual: Logotherapy and Existential Analysis Brief Therapy Protocol for Group and Individual Sessions.* Miami, FL: Presence Press International.

Dezelic, M.S. and Ghanoum, G. (2016). *Trauma Treatment – Healing the Whole Person: Meaning-Centered Therapy and Trauma Treatment Foundational Phase – Work Manual.* Miami, FL: Presence Press International.

Fabry, J. (1988). *Guideposts to Meaning: Discovering What Really Matters.* Oakland, CA: New Harbinger.

Frankl, V.E. (1978). *The Unheard Cry for Meaning: Psychotherapy and Humanism.* New York: Simon and Schuster.

Frankl, V.E. (1988). *The Will to Meaning: Foundations and Applications of Logotherapy* (Expanded ed.). New York: Penguin Books.

Frankl, V.E. (2006). *Man's Search for Meaning.* Boston, MA: Beacon Press.

Graber, A.V. (2004). *Viktor Frankl's Logotherapy: Method of Choice in Ecumenical Pastoral Psychotherapy*, 2e. Lima, OH: Wyndham Hall Press.

Haigh, R. (2013). The quintessence of a therapeutic environment. *Therapeutic Communities 34*: 6–15.

Jones, V. (2017). *BIGSPD conference poster* 2017.

Jones, V., Maurya, S., Haigh, R. (2014). *Green Therapies for Personality Disorder*. Poster presentation at BIGSPD conference 2014.

Krug, O.T. (2009). James Bugental and Irvin Yalom: Two masters of existential therapy cultivate presence in the therapeutic encounter. *Journal of Humanistic Psychology 49* (3): 329–354.

Krug, O.T. and Schneider, K.J. (2016). *Supervision Essentials for Existential-Humanistic Therapy*. Washington, DC: American Psychological Association.

Laganà, L., Classen, C., Caldwell, R. et al. (2005). Sexual difficulties of patients with gynecological cancer. *Professional Psychology: Research and Practice 36* (4): 391–399.

Lindau, S.T., Gavrilova, N., and Anderson, D. (2007). Sexual morbidity in very long term survivors of vaginal and cervical cancer: A comparison to national norms. *Gynecologic Oncology 106* (2): 413–418.

Nietzsche, F.W. and Kaufmann, W. (1974). *The Gay Science: With a Prelude in Rhymes and an Appendix of Songs*. New York: Vintage Books. (Originally published in German in 1882.)

Pearce, S. and Haigh, R. (2017): *The Theory and Practice of Democratic Therapeutic Community Treatment*. London: JKP.

Schneider, K.J. and Krug, O.T. (2010). *Existential-Humanistic Therapy*. Washington, DC: American Psychological Association.

Simonelli, L.E., Fowler, J., Maxwell, G.L. et al. (2008). Physical sequelae and depressive symptoms in gynecologic cancer survivors: Meaning in life as a mediator. *Annals of Behavioral Medicine 35* (3): 275–284.

Spiegel, D. and Classen, C. (2000). *Group Therapy for Cancer Patients: A Research-Based Handbook of Psychosocial Care*. New York: Basic Books.

Van Deurzen-Smith, E. (1997). *Everyday Mysteries: Existential Dimensions of Psychotherapy*. New York: Brunner-Routledge.

White, M. (1999). *Magic Circles: Building Self-Esteem through Circle Time*. Bristol: Lucky Duck.

Wiljer, D., Urowitz, S., Barbera, L. et al. (2011). A qualitative study of an Internet-based support group for women with sexual distress due to gynecologic cancer. *Journal of Cancer Education 26* (3): 451–458.

Winzelberg, A.J., Classen, C., Alpers, G.W. et al. (2003). Evaluation of an internet support group for women with primary breast cancer. *Cancer 97* (5): 1164–1173.

Yalom, I. (1980). *Existential Psychotherapy*. New York: Basic Books.

Yalom, I. (1999). *Momma and the Meaning of Life*. New York: Basic Books.

Yalom, I. (2002). *The Gift of Therapy*. New York: HarperCollins.

Yalom, I. (2005). *The Schopenhauer Cure*. New York: HarperCollins.

29

Key Texts in Existential Group Therapy

Simone Lee

I have searched for texts that are pertinent to the practice of existential group work. Few of them are explicitly about existential group therapy (the extracts from Mullan are an exception). The contributions are mainly by group therapists, psychoanalysts and psychiatrists, although having strong relevance to existential theory.

For ease of reading, the texts have been organized into themes, however, the intersections are many: Definition of Group; Role of the Therapist; Existential Approaches; Group Membership; Health and Dialogue and Curative Factors.

A brief biography of each author is given before the first citation of his work

Definition of Group

Hora – Existential Psychiatry and Groups – 1961

Thomas Hora MD (1914–1995) was born in Hungary and fused many spiritual traditions together in his attempt to create a "metapsychiatry" concluding that "all solutions [to psychological problems] are spiritual." His therapeutic method was based on Socratic dialogue. A metapsychiatry organization has carried on after his death.

The group situation illuminates the group personality in a multidimensional way and provides for a deeper understanding of the individual through the quality of his relationships to the other group members and the therapist.

> The group-psychotherapeutic experience is a living, dynamic experience for all participants, including the therapist. In therapy groups the members function not as samples of various psychic mechanisms or disease entities, but as people with specific ways of experiencing life and specific ways of dealing and communication with the environment, that

The Wiley World Handbook of Existential Therapy, First Edition. Edited by Emmy van Deurzen, Erik Craig, Alfried Längle, Kirk J. Schneider, Digby Tantam, and Simon du Plock.

> is, as individually characteristic modes of "being there."[1,2] Thus, in fact, the therapy group represents a microcosmos or a segment of the world, and, as such it is a situation of an existential encounter for all participants. It is a crossroads at which [...] people meet and in this meeting reveal to each other and discover for themselves their particular modes of being-in-this world.[3] When they part, the course of their progression through life is for the most part altered to an appreciable degree. (Hora 1961, p. 58)

Laing – The Politics of Experience – Us – 1967

Ronald David Laing (1927–1989) was a Scottish psychiatrist and psycho-analyst who achieved celebrity as a critic of psychiatry. He inspired a series of alternative residential projects for people with psychological disorders including Kingsley Hall in London in 1965. Group therapy was used in all of these projects and drew on Laing's interpersonal theories. Below Laing defines the syntheses required to make a group. In a footnote to the chapter "Them and Us," from which this excerpt was taken, Laing pays tribute to the influence of J. P. Sartre's *Critique de la Raison Dialectique* [Critique of Dialectical Reason] (1960) from which his ideas are derived.

> The being of any group from the point of view of the group members themselves is very curious. If I think of you and him as together with me and others again as not with me, I have already formed two rudimentary syntheses, namely, *We* and *Them*. However, this private act of synthesis is not in itself a group. In order that *We* come into being as a group, it is necessary not only that I regard, let us say, you and him and me as *We*, but that you and he also think of us as *We*. I shall call such an act of experiencing a number of persons as a single collectivity, an act of rudimentary group synthesis. In this case *We*, that is each of Us, me, you and him, have performed acts of rudimentary group synthesis. But at present these are simply three private acts of group synthesis. In order that a group really jell, I must realize that you think of yourself as one of Us, as I do, and that he thinks of himself as one of Us, and you and I do. I must ensure furthermore that both you and he realize that I think of myself with you and him, and you and he must ensure likewise that the other two realize that this We is ubiquitous among us, not simply a private illusion of my, your or his part, shared between two of us but not all three. [...]
>
> The group considered first of all from the point of view of the *experience* of its own members, is not a social object out there in space. It is the quite extraordinary being formed by each person's synthesis of the multiplicity of syntheses. It is the quite extraordinary being formed by each person's synthesis of the same multiplicity into *We*, and each person's synthesis of the multiplicity of syntheses. (Laing 1967, pp. 71–72)

Friedman – The Essential We – 1963

Maurice S Friedman (1921–2012) was an American interdisciplinary philosopher of dialogue. He co-founded the Institute for Dialogical Psychotherapy. "[U]ntil 1956, when Maurice S. Friedman published a broad survey of Buber's work, few Americans

[1] Binswanger, L. (1948). *Grundformen und Erkenntnis Menschlichen Daseins.* Max Niehans Verlag: Zurich.
[2] Hora, T. (1959). Ontic perspectives in psychoanalysis. *The American Journal of Psychoanalysis* XIX, 2.
[3] Heidegger, M. (1953). *Sein und Zeit.* Tuebingen: Max Niehans Verlag.

besides professors and divinity students had ever heard of him. The book, 'Martin Buber: The Life of Dialogue,' marked the first effort to explain and popularize the humanistic and religious concepts Buber." (Vitello 2012)

> The relation between man and man takes place not only in the "I-Thou" relation of direct meeting, but also in the "We" of community. As the "primitive Thou" precedes the consciousness of individual separateness, whereas the "essential Thou" follows and grows out of this consciousness, so the "primitive We" precedes true individuality and independence, whereas the "essential We" only comes about when independent people have come together in essential relation and directness. The essential We includes the Thou potentially, for "only men who are capable of truly saying *Thou* to one another can truly say *We* with one another." The We is not of secondary or merely instrumental importance; it is basic to existence, and as such it is itself a prime source of value. "One should follow the common," Buber quotes Heracleitus, i.e., join with others in building a common world of speech and a common order of being. [...]
>
> The importance for group psychotherapy of Buber's concept of the common world as built by the common speech-with-meaning can hardly be overestimated. Speech, from this point of view, is no mere function or tool, but is itself of the stuff of reality, able to create or destroy it. "Man has always thought his thoughts as I...but as We he has ever raised them into being itself, in just that mode of existence, that I call the 'the between.'" Speech may be falsehood and conventionality, but it is also the great pledge of truth. Whether he takes refuge in individualism or collectivism, the man who flees answering for the genuineness of his existence is marked by the fact that he can no longer really listen to the voice of another. The other is now only his object that he observes. Only if real listening as well as really talking takes place will the full possibility of healing be present in group psychotherapy, for only thus, and not through any mere *feeling* of group unity, will the full potentiality of the group as a group be realized. "He who existentially knows no Thou will never succeed in knowing a We."[4] One *should* follow the common, and that means that lived speech, "speech-with-meaning," is itself a value. Values are not just the content, the building blocks of speech. They exist in the realest sense, in the "between," in the dialogue between man and man. (Friedman 1963, pp. 610–611)

Laing and Esterson – Sanity, Madness and the Family – 1964

Aaron Esterson (1923–1999) was a British psychiatrist, and a founder of the Philadelphia Association along with R.D. Laing. This book recounts the findings when Laing and Esterson studied 11 families in which one member was diagnosed schizophrenic. Their anti-pathological stance was groundbreaking. Their methodology was to investigate phenomenologically the different permutations of the family interrelationships.

> Each person not only is an object in the world of others but is a position in space and time from which he experiences, constitutes, and acts in *his* world. He is his own centre, with his own point of view [...]

[4] M. Buber (1958). "What is common to All," (trans. Maurice S. Friedman), *The Review of Metaphysics*. XI (3): 378

People have identities. But they may also change quite remarkably as they become different others-to-others. It is arbitrary to regard any one of these transformations or *alter*ations as basic, and the others as variations.

Not only may the one person behave differently in his different alterations, but he may experience himself in different ways. He is liable to remember different things, express different attitudes, even quite discordant ones, imagine and fantasize in different ways, and so on. [...]

If one wishes to know how a football team concert or disconcert their actions in play, one does not think only or even primarily approaching this problem by talking to members individually. One watches the way they play together. [...]

When what is going on in any human group can be traced to what agents are doing, it will be termed as *praxis*. What goes on in a group may not be intended by anyone. No one may even realize what is happening. But what happens in a group will be *intelligible* if one can retrace the steps from what is going on (process) to who is doing what (praxis).

Phenomenologically, a group can feel to its members to be an organism; to those outside it, it can appear to act like one. But to go beyond this, and to maintain that, *ontologically*, it *is* an organism, is to become completely mystified.

The concept of [group] pathology is therefore, we believe, a confused one. It extends the unintelligibility of individual behaviour to the unintelligibility of the group. It is the *biological analogy**[5] applied now not just to one person, but to a multiplicity of persons. [...]

The group is *not* to the individual as whole to part, as hyperorganism to organism. It is not a mechanism, except in the sense that the mechanical action of the group may be constituted as such in and through the praxes of each and all of its members, and is the intelligible outcome of such praxes and can be elucidated[.] (Laing and Esterson 1964, pp. 19–23)

Role of the Therapist

Lewis B. Hill – Being and Doing – 1958

Lewis B. Hill, M.D (1894–1958) was a psychiatrist born in Ohio, and one time President of the American Psychoanalytic Association (Anderson 1958). This paper was published on the year of his death. Proclaiming, "A therapist is what he does," in this paper Hill champions the therapist's need for congruence, robustness, humility and assiduous ongoing self-development. The paper was not written specifically with group therapists in mind, but it was published in the *International Journal of Group Psychotherapy*.

[*B*]*eing* and *doing* in therapy cannot be in fact separated. A therapist is what he does. Conversely put, what the therapist does is an expression of what he is. Being and doing are not two disparate things, separate and isolated from each other. There cannot be a

[5] *See MacMurray, J. (1957). *The Self as Agent*. London, Faber; and Chapter 1 of Laing, R.D. (1960). *The Divided Self*. London, Tavistock Publications; Chicago, Partheon Books.

real choice between being and doing, that is, a choice of one or the other in therapy. The choice of what to do, what patients to treat, what goals to set, what techniques to use, or the choice from moment to moment whether to say something or not, or to do something or not; the choice of strategy for the long pull or the tactic of the moment is a choice which is made by the therapist as a predetermined expression of what he *is*, both as a person and as a therapist. [...]

It is this tendency of ours to separate artificially our being what we are from our doing what we do, and to look for help about doing rather than to question the effect of what we are. [...]

[B]eing a useful therapist means doing constructive things and, conversely, reducing to a working minimum destructive activities. [The therapist] has his own conflicts, problems and status sufficiently in hand that he does not use the therapeutic situation for their solution. This does not mean that he actually effaces himself. It means he presents himself in his one major role of therapist. This is a role in which he can respect himself sufficiently that the patient need not be burdened with the task of building him up and can even afford to knock him down without fear of destroying him. [...] When the therapist's own house is in order it certainly cannot be said that it does not matter what he does with the patient. But it can be said that what he does is likely to be helpful, that is, appropriate, constructive, and sincere. For what he does will no longer be in defense of his own blindness, but will become truly an expression of his understanding benevolence. (Hill 1958, pp. 117–121)

Mullan – The Existential Group Therapist – 1979

Hugh Mullan (1912–2003) was an American psychiatrist and a pioneer of group therapy, influenced by existential philosophy. His idiosyncratic way of thinking challenged the orthodox practice of his day as he did not follow the mainstream theories; he advocated "the therapist's personal subjectivity, striving for mutuality, and nonrational experience in the conduct of psychotherapy" (Wright 2012).

Confronting existential conditions of living

[T]he existential therapist welcomes the tragic as well as the playful sequences in the life of his patient. This focus is particularly important in the group therapy session, that segment of the patient's life shared by the therapist and the other members. It is here too, in the treatment group, where the existential therapist faces his disillusionments and satisfactions. (Mullan 1979, p. 377)

It is only the therapist who is able to conceive the necessary investment and the difficult process required in impelling a patient to face his human condition; the long period of treatment, the arduous hours of group struggle, the intense emotional upheaval, and the despair. I judge it essential and therefore look for patients to say in the depths of treatment, "I wish that I had never started this damn therapy. I was in better shape before I came and submitted to all of this." (Mullan 1979, p.377)

Authenticity, Anti-Intellectualism and Humility

Individuality stands out as the essential characteristic of all existentialists. In varying degrees freedom to choose, human dignity, personal love, and creativity are traits which they extol. These qualities must first be found in the therapist if patients likewise are to discover them in themselves. The existential group therapist ignores contemporary treatment technologies and thus finds himself out of the mainstream of current approaches. Data, quantification, and verification do not appeal to him. He prefers subjectivity to objectivity, connectedness to detachment, and emotionality to intellectuality. He knows that emotion, compassion, kindness and concern cannot be parcelled out by formula. He believes that to attempt to do this would at best be unreal and at worst false [...]

Should the therapist's existential therapy be only academic– that is, learned but not actually put into practice– the therapy that results will be similar to any approach based upon intellectual understanding, except that the words used will be different. Should this be the case, the method will be highly analytical where conflict-ridden members under the direction of the would-be conflict-free therapist search for past causes of their present problems. But when the therapist *lives* his philosophical beliefs, the ambience of the entire treatment is altered. [...]

The whole of group therapy, when practiced existentially, corrects the therapist's concept of his power and his "infinite" knowledge. When the therapist sees himself as little different from the members, (all face the same paradoxes of life together); when he relies upon each group member to help him with the others; and when the therapist, while sitting in the treatment circle, is scrutinized, corrected, interpreted, admired, toyed with, made the butt of jokes, loved, hated, and so forth, all of these elements cause the therapist, hopefully to re-examine himself. The result is that his magnified self-image gradually becomes less distorted. The therapist who is able to deny his expertness gains in his therapeutic acumen and, as well, in his treatment ability. No longer must he be clever, overly intellectual, and isolated. This process, therefore, of the therapist's self-inquiry points to a significant difference between the behavior and existential therapist.

Modelling

Each therapist sets the tone for his group – the traditional therapist, and particularly, the behavior therapist by *doing something*; the existential therapist by *being and becoming somebody*. The existential group leader questions his existence and expresses an unremitting search for the meaning of life and death. More obvious to the members, he brings to the group dedication to face therapy's (life's) paradoxes, to unravel the group's (life's) problems, and to identify the immediate meaning of being together. (Mullan 1979, pp. 380–382)

Spontaneity

The tenuous nature of creativity and freedom, even in the group, must be the therapist's concern. His treatment method, including his group rules, whether he articulates them or not, requires that the patients comply with them, be serious, and come to terms with the therapist's routines Who isn't aware of the abrupt change in the patients' playful mood and light banter when the therapist enters and takes his place in the circle? Does the therapist realize, moreover, when playfulness and laughter cease, that creativity is jeopardised and perhaps lost? At the therapist's intrusion the members forgo their spontaneity, sit quietly, and await his cue. They wait expectantly, risk-free, for the "benevolent" authority to do for them or tell them what to do. Soon, [...], they begin to substitute work for play and the session begins. Does this common occurrence enhance or retard therapy? (Mullan 1979, pp. 380–382)

Meaning of Group to Therapist

I would like to suggest that although the group is extremely important to all members at particular times, it is most meaningful to the therapist all of the time. If this is not so, the therapist might wonder what he is doing in the group. Shouldn't he be elsewhere? Or what might he do to make the group experience more valuable for himself? (Mullan 1963, p. 600)

Hora – Role of the Therapist – 1958

It is quite obvious that the private value system of the therapist unavoidably will make itself felt in the group, no matter how objective, neutral, or nonjudgmental he may strive to act. [...]

A group therapist's unhealthy value system can create a subculture of false values in the group. The impact of a therapist's unhealthy values can be such as to overshadow all the value systems of the group members. At times, the entire group may have to defend itself against the value system of the therapist. This leads to paralysis of group interaction. Similarly, a powerful member can succeed in imposing his value system upon an entire group and immobilize it. It is the function of the therapist to reveal to the group the nature of the forces affecting it and to set an example of courage and understanding in refusing to yield to the unhealthy values emanating from the particular patient. [...]

It is to be emphasized that, in addition to his training, theoretical knowledge and technical skill, the group therapist needs to be imbued with healthy human values so that his influence upon the group may consist not only of *what he does* but also of *what he is* as a person. (Hora 1958, p. 158)

Existential Approaches

Shaffer and Galinsky – The Existential Model of Group Therapy – 1974

Shaffer gained his PhD from Harvard University and was a professor of psychology at Queens College, New York. We draw here from his collaboration with Galinsky in undertaking a methodical description of the various modalities of group experiences used across of range of medical, healthcare, and psychotherapeutic settings to show the current state of the field. Together they examined 12 models of group therapy in their book *Models of Group Therapy* (1974).

[A]ccording to the existentialists, orthodox analysts began to gradually move away from this respectful orientation to resistance, and started instead to become convinced that their interpretations, if valid and properly timed, could not but lead the patient one step closer to insight and therefore to eventual cure. Hence the existential therapist's suspicion that the average psychoanalyst all too easily loses sight of the patient's inherent freedom to resist his therapeutic efforts, however benign in intention and brilliant in execution. It is the recognition of the patient's right to choose his own mode of "being-in-the-world," in the face of any and every therapeutic intervention, that constitutes in this model a major stimulus to continuous grown and individuation. (Shaffer and Galinsky 1974, p. 106–107)

Hans W Cohn – An Approach – 2006

Within the British School of Existential Analysis, Cohn was a (1916–2004) proponent of existential-phenomenological practice. While Cohn is known for his development of Heidegger's ideas (Cooper 2003); he was also a member of the Group-Analytic Society and the Institute of Group Analysis and drew from the theories of S.H. 'Michael' Foulkes, the co-founder, with Norbert Elias, of the Group Analytic Society.

> The following list suggests a skeleton structure for [a detailed existential-phenomenological approach to group therapy]
>
> 1 If "Being-in-the-world" always means "Being-with-others," if the world is essentially a "with-world" – a relational field – then the "individual" is indeed an "abstraction," as Foulkes says, and can only be understood in a context of mutual disclosure.
> 2 What we see as psychological disturbances are then disturbances in this context, disturbances of relatedness and communication.
> 3 The therapeutic group provides a context in which these relational and communicative disturbances can be observed in situ, so to speak. Relational and communicative failure can be experienced, and the possibilities of different ways of relating and communicating can be explored.
> 4 The group therapist is a member of the group with a specific task – to assist in the process of clarifying the relational and communicative disturbances and potentialities of the group. It is important that she or he does not see her or himself as being "outside" and "above" the group. Heidegger's definition of "others" is relevant here: "By 'others' we do not mean everyone else but me – those over against the 'I' stands out. They are rather those from whom, for the most part, one does not distinguish oneself – those among whom one is too" (Heidegger 1962: 154). In an existential-phenomenological group, the therapist does not "stand out" hierarchically "over against" the others
> 5 Interpretations of group events are essentially the task of group members. They are not a reduction of these events to other (earlier) occurrences, though remembering those may enrich and clarify what is experienced in the group now. Group phenomena have, of course, past roots and future possibilities – but these are inevitably part of the present experience. The group therapist's principal task is to keep the group space open for such interpretations to be made
> 6 The reliving of past relationships in the present group situation – what psychoanalysts call "transference" – is not primarily focused on the therapist but dispersed among members within the group. It is an example of the multidimensionality of time, and needs of course to be understood and clarified. Again, the therapist's task is that of an enabler rather than the principal interpreter.
> 7 There is no reason why the therapist should not contribute his or her own understanding and feelings to the group process. The question that will arise is the same that arises whenever the therapist chooses a form of "self-disclosure" as means of intervention: who is it she or he is trying to help – the client(s), or her or himself? Another question arises with any form of helping intervention. Heidegger distinguishes between two kinds of solicitude – "that which leaps in and dominates, and that which leaps forth and liberates".
> 8 Some group therapeutic approaches stress the necessity to focus on what happens "within" the group and ignore what members being into it from "outside". We have

> already seen that the "outside" always penetrated the "inside". In an existential-phenomenological approach, with this emphasis on context, the possibility of such a division does not arise. Whatever group members talk about is talked about in the group and is thus relevant to it. (Cohn 1997, pp. 45–57).

Spinelli – The Major Tasks of Existential Group Therapy – 2015

Ernesto Spinelli (1949–) is a psychologist, psychotherapist, and coach who is noted for the promotion of phenomenology in practice (Cooper 2003).

> [F]rom the standpoint of existential group therapy, it can be seen that what may be the most significant, as well as the most taxing, challenge for both the existential therapist and the clients who, together, make up the membership of the group, is precisely its inter-relational complexity. Undoubtedly, it is the multitude of participants whose differing insecurities concerning their own and/or the group's continuity, dispositional stances and identity impact upon one another that generates this complexity. At the same time, this group-generated complexity arises within a structured and distinct therapy world with its explicit and mutually agreed setting, frame and contractual conditions.
>
> As such, the therapy-world of existential group therapy provides a structure that is both more closely akin to each group member's wider-world relations than any one-to-one form of therapy could ever hope to offer. At the same time, however, this same structure is also sufficiently different from each group member's wider-world relations to be able to provoke the disclosure of, and challenge to, each group member's currently maintained worldview.
>
> It is the enterprise of existential group therapy to "hold the tension" between the therapy-world and the wider-world so that the group-construct generated within the therapy-world is neither too alien nor too indistinct from the group members' various wider-world group interactions. (Spinelli 2015, pp. 243–244).

Yalom – The Theory and Practice of Group Psychotherapy – 1995

Irvin Yalom (1931–) is an American psychotherapist, renowned for his Existential Psychotherapy in which he focuses on the four ultimate existential concerns: Death, Freedom, Isolation and Meaninglessness (Yalom 1995). He has also written a standard text on the *Theories and Practice of Group Psychotherapy* (now in its fifth edition with Molyn Leczcz). His practice has become increasingly focused on working with people in grief or who are terminally ill.

> Therapy groups often tend to water down the tragedy of life. Their natural currency is interpersonal theory; if care is not taken, they will make the error of translating existential concerns into interpersonal ones, which are more easily grasped in the group. (Yalom 1995: p. 93)
>
> In 1974, I began to lead groups composed of patients who lived continuously in the midst of extreme experiences. All the members had a terminal illness, generally metastatic carcinoma, and all were entirely aware of the nature and implication of their illness.
>
> We are all familiar with the centrality of the quality of the therapeutic relationship in the process of change. In group therapy a sound, trusting relationship between therapist and patients and among the patients themselves is a necessary mediating condition; it enhances

trust, risk taking, self-disclosure, feedback, constructive conflict, working through problems centring around intimacy, and so on. But in addition to these mediating functions, the basic intimate encounter has an intrinsic value, a value in and for itself.

What can you do as therapist in the face of the inevitable? I think the answer lies in the verb *to be*. You do by being, by being there with the patient. Presence is the hidden agent of help in all forms of therapy. Patients looking back on their therapy rarely remember a single interpretation you made, but they always remember your presence, that you were there with them. It asks a great deal of the therapist to join this group, yet it is hypocrisy not to join. The group configuration is not you, the therapist, and they, the dying; it is we who are dying, we who are banding together in the face of our common condition. The group well demonstrates the double meaning of the word *apartness*: we are separate, lonely, *apart from* but also a *part of*. One of my members put it elegantly when she described herself as a lonely ship in the dark. Even though no physical mooring could be made, it was nonetheless enormously comforting to see the lights of other ships sailing the same water (Yalom 1995, p. 94).

Mullan – Time and Finiteness – 1979

[In our sessions we] face the passage of time and are always aware of our finiteness. Our direction shifts as we become sensitive to our existence and question the meanings of life. We heighten our struggle by choosing and dealing with the consequences. As we make choices and assume responsibility for these choices, we risk. We embrace feelings of joy and sadness. We express love and hate. It is only under this particular urgency and intensity that fundamental and radical personality change takes place. (Mullan 1979, p. 377)

It is our finiteness which, when faced, demands that we seek immediate solutions so as to change. Time's passage, an ever-recurring theme, confronts the members and also the therapist, as they consider their human condition. (Mullan 1979, p. 377)

Mullan – The Importance of Status Denial – 1963

Psychoanalytic groups are composed of individuals whose initial behavior within the group is governed by certain culturally ascribed statuses. These statuses, upon which each individual relies so heavily, define his state, condition, relative position, and relationships to the other members and to the therapist.

At this early moment in this process, the "psychoanalytic" group is merely a microcosm of society. It has the characteristics, including "advantages" and "disadvantages," of all social groups. It is relatively "nontherapeutic" in its functioning. It is mostly structured around certain statuses and certain role dynamisms which are affixed to these statuses. For the psychotherapeutic potential of the group to evolve, we believe that ascribed statuses and their accompanying roles must be denied (Mullan 1963, p. 592)

With the gradual denial of statuses, role behavior lessens in the psychoanalytic group, and a more fundamental relationship arises. Therapist and patient become being and being; male and female become being and being; the younger and the older become being and being; the infirm and the [sturdy] become being and being; the neurotic and the healthy become being and being. (Mullan 1963, p. 592)

The therapist, in his deep emotional involvement with the individuals in the group, is primarily interested in allowing new behaviours to emerge. Statuses, particularly if fixed, controlling as they do the reciprocal interplay between persons, prevent the emergence of the new behavior. Thus, in a group, as is almost always the case, if a person identifies himself as patient, he is denying his therapist-part or potential. And because of this, behavior which is related to his being therapist does not emerge. And, alas, the therapist who does not undermine the status "patient" in the group establishes himself as "therapist" or "doctor" and mistakenly implies through this adherence to status that he alone needs no help and no direction. (Mullan 1963, p. 593)

The task of status reduction within the analytic group cannot be entered upon lightly. It is of crucial importance as it alters in a most therapeutically significant manner the group milieu. First, through this happening, the group becomes more truly cohesive. Individuals belong because they see themselves and others sub species aeternitatis. The matrix of our relatedness within the group is what we are and not what we are supposed to be or might become. [...]

Secondly, we have found that empathic relatedness is directly proportional to the degree of status reduction. Thus, when a group member committed suicide and I was filled with sorrow, self-questioning, and doubts, my status of therapist or leader was extinguished. I suggested an extra group meeting following this tragic occurrence. During this meeting the "patients" became my "therapist" – that a bond emerged which brought us together and through this crisis. Deep empathic relatedness can only occur in status-free relationships where there is minimal role activity on the part of both therapist and members. (Mullan 1963, pp. 593–594)

The method of status denial in groups

If we see clearly the reciprocal nature of status, that therapist and patient are at fixed positions of opposite polarity, our procedure in status denial becomes somewhat clarified. We need only to alter our status (the therapist's) in order to alter the patients'.

The group psychoanalyst is therapist because he can jettison more easily and more completely the many statuses ascribed to him by his culture and by the group members than can the other group members. This is his leadership. [...] [T]he therapist may not allow himself any measure of self-imposed omniscience or omnipotence. And still more difficult to achieve is the requirement of not allowing himself any significance stemming from either transferred or projected godlike attributes. (Mullan 1963, p. 594)

It seems to me that the superior intellectual status of the therapist, supported by the transferred and projected attitudes and actions of the group members, becomes the most formidable obstruction to status denial within the group. (Mullan 1963, p. 595)

If this be so, a fundamental step that the group psychoanalyst must make is to question the significance of this intellectual competence. This is achieved by allowing himself fully to experience in the group and at the same time to have his interpretative activities dependent upon feeling and intuitions as well as his intellect. The group analyst does not know how to live better than the members although in fact he may be living better that they are. (Mullan 1963, p. 595)

The therapist, in [his] deep (life-span) relationship, must be able within himself to match qualitatively, if not quantitatively, every symptom, "trouble," conflict, fear, anxiety, perversion, emotion, defense, resistance, and so on, expressed and felt by those around him. He must be truly accepting of this, his patient role, as he is of his therapist role. He is therapist because he can better accept being patient than the other members (Mullan 1963, p. 596)

Inclusiveness: a factor in non-rejection

If, as I have indicated, status adherence is detrimental to group psychoanalytical experiencing, statuses which designate certain behaviors may not be used to determine admission or participate in the group. This is so for statuses both biologically and culturally ascribed. Thus, the placement of an unmarried virginal woman with a grandfather is possible as is the placement of a physician (psychiatrist) with an unemployed stenographer.

Status derived from social position cannot be acknowledged in group formation. To allow the social position of a prospective group member to control his group entrance (or to determine the group into which he might be placed) is to admit that the therapist has unresolved problems in this area.

It follows from this that therapy group may be and perhaps should be basically inclusive and not exclusive. (Mullan 1963, p. 596)

Our tendency toward greater inclusiveness limits to a minimum psychological testing of a person prior to his admission to a group. Rather than this, we relate ourselves to a new individual in the hope that immediately or in the near future he will be ready for the group experience. To routinely or spasmodically test individuals is to demand tacitly a certain status of them. In doing this we imply that all of what he is not acceptable to us, and we indicate that we are concerned mostly with adaptation and not creative unfolding. (Mullan 1963, p. 596)

The policy of great inclusiveness in the fabrication of a therapy group is only reasonable if two further conditions are espoused by the therapist. First, the therapist must prevent any procedure from becoming ritualized. Each session and each moment of each session are entirely different and cannot be blunted by a fixed procedure of any sort. Second, the therapist must prevent the group or the individual from behavior which is goal-directed. Behavior which is slanted toward some future accomplishment denies the all important immediate experiencing. (Mullan 1963, p. 597)

Mullan – The Value of Group Experiencing – 1963

The value of the therapeutic venture is entirely different and separate from its validity. The value stems not at all from the results but rather from the momentary our-to-hour, day-to-day happenings. The value for the group members and therapist alike who continue to relate over long periods of time must come, it seems to me, at each second of emotional contact. Thus value is a function of the means. It is not directly related to the ends. And most important, value is rigidly attached to our need, as human beings for satisfaction regardless of our theoretical frame of reference, our value system, or the cultural conceptions of what is normal.

When one is concerned with value, he is in a "status-free state, for he is primarily, if not totally, experiencing the moment at hand, and conditions existing before and after are not present in his consciousness. He cannot, nor does he try to, differentiate sickness from wellness. This is in contradistinction to validity of therapy. (Mullan 1963, pp. 599–600)

Group Membership

Hora – Equitable Exchange – 1958

The integrity of the group depends on certain binding forces. These binding forces underlie group cohesiveness. The nature of these binding forces is again essentially affective. These affective forces must be shared by the majority of the group. The group depends on the presence of an affirmative attitude by the majority of the members. This means that in order for a group to exist, the members must be capable of giving at least to a minimal extent, or at least lending some affect to a group in the hope of a fair return [...]

There are patients whose value system is such that they are intent on exploiting to a maximum possible extent. They seek to take only and give as little as possible. [...] The integrity of the group is also threatened by members who come to the group but do not participate in any way. [...] The survival of the group depends on an equitable exchange among its members, and the members often respond in a manner which is designed to protect the integrity of the group. (Hora 1958, pp. 157–158)

Kociûnas – Openness and Sincerity – 2000

Rimanta Kociunas PhD is based in Lithuania, is Director of the Institute of Humanistic and Existential Psychology and Secretary General of the East European Association for Existential Therapy and has been a key player in building the foundations for existential practice across a range of psychotherapeutic disciplines in the post-Soviet space.

In the group, one may and should speak of oneself. Preference is given to sharing one's personal experience. The aim of participants is not to solve one another's problems, but to disclose to others their own life experience. In the group, it is necessary to express all feelings that we experience, especially recurring negative feelings, like irritation, anger, boredom, etc., which usually should not be shown to others. The group should not tolerate untruth. One can refuse to answer questions or to participate in a concrete discussion, but when one says anything, one must be honest. In the group, it is important to speak about oneself openly, but it is for a participant to decide, how [...] open he will be and which aspects of life he will disclose. Self-disclosure in the group opens the door to [...] self-knowledge and stimulates others to disclose themselves. But this self-disclosure does not mean psychological self-exposition. (Kociûnas 2000, pp. 99–112)

Mullan – Changes in the Patient – 1979

The patient upon leaving is to have a different philosophy of life, or perhaps while in treatment he is to discover a theme of living which makes his life more worthwhile. In any event he is to become a more authentic person, one who realizes the preciousness of time and one who develops an urge to be to be free and creative. He is to be able to risk and, what is more important, to be responsible for these risks when taken and the actions that ensue. (Mullan 1979, p. 377)

Change [...] is based, first, upon the patient's gradual awareness of his human condition and, second, upon *his* painful acceptance of it. (Mullan 1979, p. 378)

During the course of treatment, the "therapist's" significance is to diminish. On leaving, the patient's perception of the therapist is to be much more congruent with who he (the therapist) actually **is**; the therapist's charisma along with his omniscience and omnipotence are to be things of the past. The shift in the patient's view of the therapist is most important, for it reflects an identical change in the departing patient's perception of authority figures, heroes, family members and friends. Upon leaving, therefore, the patient is no longer to attribute to others characteristics and attributes which they do not possess [...]

In group treatment, personality change is never directed toward a restricted common denominator, the "mentally healthy woman or man, or the conflict-free woman or man. Our therapy is to bring out the unique being, confronted by his finiteness Unamuno is clarifying in this connection because he contends that good (change) is simply "that which contributes to the preservation, perpetuation and enrichment of consciousness" ([Mann 1965,] p. 29). This, then, is what the existential group therapist is about. He establishes the conditions for the enhancement of each member's consciousness, directing him to face his *human condition.* [...]

In this atmosphere, the therapist achieves great emotional intimacy with the members; he *does not* bring his past or present personal history into the group. He refrains from answering questions or offering information about his life outside the session. Through this deliberate frustration, anxiety and conflict are increased and fantasy is enhanced. Patients, in the long run, are to identify their therapist from who he *is* and how he behaves in the group (Mullan 1979, pp. 379–381)

Anxiety

The therapist realizes that each patient, with little support except that gained from being with him and the other members, must face head on the paradoxical nature of his life. Faced with a difficult conflict, the upset member finds no technical help available. But he does find that the faithful and persevering member steady him and see him through the painful period. Anxiety, then, is a characteristic of the existential group, where assurance and advice are not commodities in large supply (Mullan 1979, p. 388)

Health and Dialogue and Curative Factors

Hora – Interrelation between Human Values and Mental Health – 1958

We can assume that healthy human values constitute an inseparable aspect of mental health. Indeed it appears that group psychotherapy is a remarkable medium for the study of the interrelation between human values and mental health. It is possible to draw the generalization that patients enter the group in the main with their value systems which are designed to provide them with gratifications of their personal needs. At first they manifest but limited regard or concern for their fellow human beings. They come to the group primarily to get something and they utilize a variety of infantile and magic techniques in their efforts at influencing others to provide them with these personal needs. They often manifest a lack of understanding for the autonomy of other individuals. As they improve and grow in interaction, they begin to alter their value systems in the direction of mutuality. They grow from "I" to "I and you" through the stage of "you and I" to the stage of "we." In Martin Buber's terms they grow from a *monologic* existence to a *dialogic* one.

In the stage of "we," the "I" does not lose itself into an amorphous part of a collective, but the individual becomes capable of preserving his own integrity, while at the same time he has the capacity to interact with others and thus derive the necessary stimulation for a creative fulfillment of his inherent potentialities.

For it is inherent in the nature of man that in a seemingly paradoxical manner he becomes an individual by being a part of others. He finds himself by losing himself. He is enriched by giving. Or as Tillich (1952) puts it: "Man needs the courage to be alone and as part."

> The process of group psychotherapy provides abundant evidence to the fact that positive principles of ethics and morality underlie the conditions of mental health. The implications of all this lead us to a concept of mental health which we can define as a condition of human existence which finds expression and meaning in a capacity of the individual to fulfill his inherent creative potentialities through genuine reciprocal interaction and affirmation of his fellow man.
>
> Thus Martin Buber's philosophical concept of dialogic existence coincides with our concept of mental health. (Hora 1958, p. 159)

Hugh Mullan – Group is the Agent of Change –1979

> In existential group therapy the interacting group is to become the essential agent of change, while the single patient and the therapist are of less significance. Each session, therefore, must be a full, spontaneous, and rewarding experience, not one constricted by a program of games or exercises with some immediate purpose. The therapy meeting, where intense emotional bonds are employed to facilitate personality change, must be different from all others in our culture. [...] Each day I witness and participate in intense expressions of emotion, the taking of risks, the facing of the inevitable by persons intimately connected, all absolutely real! From this contrast, the theatre and therapy group, I developed a respect for the therapeutic possibilities inherent in the patients' meeting together. The group as an entity became an effective vehicle where, under proper conditions, hidden conflicts could emerge and crises faced with benefit to all participants. The intactness of the group, therefore, became preeminent in my thinking. (Mullan 1979, p. 387)

Irvin Yalom – Existential Groupwork – Therapeutic Factors – 1995

Yalom researched the "comparative potency of the therapeutic factors" in group work. When presented with 60 questions which were asked randomly yet which fell within 12 general categories. Patients were asked to rank the factors they regarded "as most salient to their improvement in therapy." Yalom acknowledged that "an absolute rank-ordering of therapeutic factors is not possible." Here are resulting findings, ranked here in order of importance according to the results: Interpersonal input, Catharsis, Cohesiveness, Self-understanding, Interpersonal output, Existential factors, Universality, Instillation of hope, Altruism, Family re-enactment, Guidance, Identification. According to Yalom, "These results all suggest that the real core of the therapeutic process in these therapy groups is an affectively charged, self-reflective interpersonal interaction" (1995, p. 79). What is interesting for this chapter is how the Existential Factors category came to be included.

> The category of existential factors was almost an afterthought. My colleagues and I first constructed the Q-sort [research] instrument with eleven major factors. It appeared neat and precise, but something was missing. Important sentiments expressed by both patients and therapists had not been represented, so we added a factor consisting of these five items:
>
> 1 Recognizing that life is at times unfair and unjust
> 2 Recognizing that ultimately there is no escape from some of life's pain or from death
> 3 Recognizing that no matter how close I get to other people, I must still face life alone

4 Facing the basic issues of my life and death, and thus living my life more honestly and being less caught up in trivialities
5 Learning that I must take ultimate responsibility for the way I live my life no matter how much guidance and support I get from others.

Several issues are represented in this cluster: responsibility, basic isolation, contingency, the capriciousness of existence, the recognition of our mortality and the ensuing consequences for the conduct of our life. What to label this category? I finally settled, with much hesitation, on *existential factors*, although I do not care for the word *existential*. It is a term embedded in its own mystique, a term that means something to everyone, yet nothing precise to anyone.

[…]

Despite the unceremonious origin of this category, it is clear that the existential items strike responsive chords in patients, and many cite some of the five statements as having been crucially important to them. In fact, the entire category of existential factors is often ranked highly by patients ahead of such greatly valued modes of changes as universality, altruism, recapitulation of the primary family experience, guidance, identification, and instillation of hope. Item 60, *learning that I must take ultimate responsibility for the way I live my life no matter how much guidance and support I get from others,* was highly ranked by the patients, and its mean score ranked it *fifth* of the 60 items.

The same findings are reported by other researchers. *Every single project that includes an existential category reports that the patients rank that category at least among the upper 50 percent.* […] It is important to listen to our data. Obviously the existential factors in therapy deserve far more consideration that they generally receive.

It is more than happenstance that the category of existential factors was included almost as an afterthought and yet proved to be so important to patients. Existential factors play an important but generally unrecognized role in psychotherapy. (Yalom 1995, pp. 88–89)

References

Anderson, A.R. (1958). Lewis B. Hill, M.D—1894–1958. *Bulletin of the American Psychoanalytical Association 14*: 740–742.

Cohn, H.W. (1997). *Existential Thought and Therapeutic Practice. An Introduction to Existential Psychotherapy.* London: Sage.

Cooper, M. (2003). *Existential Therapies.* London: Sage.

Diamond, N. (2004). Hans W. Cohn. Obituary. *The Group-Analytic Society (London) 37* (4): 564–566.

Friedman, M. (1963). Dialogue and the "Essential We." The bases of values in the philosophy of Martin Buber. In: *Group Psychotherapy and Group Function* (ed. M. Rosenbaum and B. Milton), 604–613. New York: Basic Books.

Goldberg, C. and Goldberg, M.C. (1973). *The Human Circle. An Existential Approach to New Group Therapies.* Chicago: Nelson Hall.

Heidegger, M. (1962). *Being and Time* (trans. J. Macquarrie and E. Robinson). London: Blackwell.

Hill, L.B. (1958). On being rather than doing in psychotherapy. *International Journal of Group Psychotherapy VIII* (2): 115–122.

Hora, T. (1958). Group psychotherapy, human values and mental health in psychotherapy. *International Journal of Group Psychotherapy VIII* (2): 154–160.
Hora, T. (1961). Existential psychiatry and group psychotherapy. *American Journal of Psychoanalysis 21* (1): 58–70.
Kociûnas, R. (2000). Existential experience and group therapy. *Existential Analysis 11* (2): 91–112.
Laing, R.D. (1967). Us and them. In: *The Politics of Experience and The Bird of Paradise*, 71–72. London: Penguin.
Laing, R.D. and Esterson, A. (1964). *Sanity, Madness and the Family*. London: Penguin.
Mann, J. (1965). Evaluation of group psychotherapy. In: *International Handbook of Group Psychotherapy* (ed. J.L. Moreno), 129–148. New York: Philosophical Library.
Mullan, H. (1963). Status denial in group psychoanalysis. In: *Group Psychotherapy and Group Function* (ed. M. Rosenbaum and M. Berger), 592–597. New York: Basic Books.
Mullan, H. (1979). An existential group psychotherapy. *International Journal of Group Psychotherapy 29* (2): 449–455.
Shaffer, B.P. and Galinsky, M.D. (1974). The existential-experiential therapy group. In: *Models of Group Therapy and Sensitivity Training*, 106–107. Englewood Cliffs, NJ: Prentice-Hall Series.
Spinelli, E. (2015). *Practising Existential Psychotherapy. The Relational World*, 2e. London: Sage.
Tillich, P. (1952). *The Courage to Be*. London: Collins.
Vitello, P (2012). *Maurice S. Friedman, Martin Buber's Biographer, Dies at 90*. https://www.nytimes.com/2012/10/06/books/maurice-s-friedman-martin-bubers-biographer-dies-at-90.html (accessed January 8, 2019).
Wright, F. (2012). Personal reflections on Hugh Mullan: Existential group therapist. *International Journal of Group Psychotherapy 62* (1): 23–42.
Yalom, I. D. (1995). The therapeutic factors: An integration. In: *The Theory and Practice of Group Psychotherapy*, 4e, 69–91. New York: Basic Books.

30

Challenges and New Developments in Existential Group Therapy

Digby Tantam

I noted in an earlier chapter that influential group psychotherapists consider that the high point of group psychotherapy was in the late-1960s and 1970s. It is not entirely clear why its popularity has declined. Cognitive behavioral therapy (CBT) in groups does not appear to be following suit. This may be because therapies conducted *in* groups but not *by* groups are likely to be short-term, and time-limited in contrast to groups where membership of the group is itself the therapeutic medium. I will be focusing on the latter groups in this final short chapter about the future.

The survival of treatment methods

CBT groups, or groups that are the context in which other active therapies are provided are symptom focused and it is appropriate to use symptomatic changes as one of the principle outcome measures. Quality of life measures link readily with symptoms and so quality of life outcomes are applicable to symptom-focused groups, too. Meaning-orientated groups, such as those described in this section, are usually shorter term and this simplifies outcome research as interactions are not complicated by the effects of the passage of substantial amounts of time. Shorter-term outcomes also reduce the impact of contingent life events that are independent of the situation that the group members have in common. The value of meaning-orientated groups has been well-established, and their outcomes are better, apparently, than merely supportive groups and are associated with an increase in scores on meaning in life scales (Rosenfeld et al. 2018). Even so, it remains unclear whether the presumed therapeutic factor is the increase in meaning, leading to a reduction in depression scores, or that a reduction in depression leads to an increased sense of meaning.

The Wiley World Handbook of Existential Therapy, First Edition. Edited by Emmy van Deurzen, Erik Craig, Alfried Längle, Kirk J. Schneider, Digby Tantam, and Simon du Plock.

There is a consensus among group therapists and clients that participants in longer-term, exploratory groups gain more than an improvement in symptoms. Evidence of this has been established in groups to reduce distress in people facing existential crises, such as metastatic breast cancer (Beatty et al. 2018). One suggestion is that they gain more fulfilment in relationships, another that they gain more meaning in their lives. But there is no consensus about what the main outcome might be. This makes research into the therapeutic process problematic as there is no criterion on which to gauge which process factor or factors conduce to a good outcome.

Therapists interpersonal skills do seem to matter (Schöttke et al. 2017) but appear to have very low correlation with outcomes. The therapeutic alliance, which is referred to in group psychotherapy as cohesion since it involves relations with all of the group, matters too. But even though it is the most cited predictor of outcome, ratings of this by therapists and by clients differ, sometimes substantially (Mander et al. 2017).

If longer-term group therapy is to thrive again, it will need to embrace the modernist agenda of "evidence" and economic analysis (Blackmore et al. 2012). Consumerism, another item on the modernist agenda, influences clients, too, to ask what their money is buying. So the future of group therapy, and not just existential group therapy, depends on cracking the problem of what outcomes group therapy uniquely offers, and therefore what the value of the intervention is. This should be, despite its difficulty and cost, high on the research agenda. It will not be an easy sell to funding agencies, who are likely to be influenced by the narrowed view of human motivation that has emerged from the focus on belief/desire theories and the neglect of our grounding in the tissue of existence that Heidegger, Husserl, and others called the Umwelt (Goldie 2007). I will argue later that there are the means to demonstrate this tissue in action when I consider "inter-subjectivity" later in this chapter.

Predictors of outcome, are these the same as therapeutic factors?

Elsewhere in this volume, it has been argued that "meaning in life" might be an important outcome measure that links to an improved quality of life and might be more likely to be targeted by an existential approach. In Chapter 27, van Deurzen and I noted that the fit between each member's way of looking at life and the culture of the group is an important determinant of outcome (see also Van Zyl 2018). Meaning might be a particular concern of many people, but especially those facing a crisis or limit situation (Jaspers 1964; Mundt 2014) but may be only indirectly correlated with outcome. Persistence in the group is a crucial intermediary variable that confounds many outcome studies but is rarely explicit in published data analyses. Resistance to adopting inter-subjectivity in practice is also an important measure.

Cognitive behavioral therapists in groups can afford to ignore group-as-a-whole effects and other non-specific therapeutic factors, and instead focus on target behaviors (or rather actions) such as negative automatic thoughts, avoidance, or ruminations. But longer-term group therapy stands or falls by the validity of its explanation of group interaction. There is no specified aim for this interaction as it is the interaction itself that is thought to deliver the therapeutic effect. This is, for example, what Hugh

Mullan one of the few self-avowed existential therapists of a former generation who practiced long-term therapy, described as the main therapeutic factors in groups:

> (1) To relate more meaningfully (therapeutically) to more than one person simultaneously;
>
> (2) To become more totally involved;
>
> and
>
> (3) To be more completely ourselves, without undue reliance upon either the status "therapist" or "patient." (Mullan 1957, p. 226)

Mullan's third point is a sine qua non for inter-subjectivity. But it is not easy to put into practice without falling into the boundary violations that become ethical violations. Mullan continued a long, but marginalized, tradition, going back to Trigant Burrow and Sandor Ferenczi, of reversing roles at times with their patients, who would become the analyst and they the patient.

Burrow, co-founder and president of the American Psychoanalytic Association, is sometimes described as the first group analyst, coining the term "group therapy" (Burrow 2013). Burrow married one of his patients, and Ferenczi proposed to one of his (he eventually married her mother). Burrows was expelled from the American Psychoanalytic Association with the knowledge of Freud, and Freud's relationship with Ferenczi was severely strained. What would now be condemned as a lack of boundaries was, most likely, a consequence of their belief that the psychoanalytic relationship involved mutual influence. And it did lead them to a phenomenological understanding of what was happening in therapy. Ferenczi used theoretical formulations that would nowadays be recognized as based in the theory of inter-subjectivity (Szecsödy 2007). Although Ferenczi did not use that term or refer to phenomenological investigations, his ideas were similar to those of Scheler and Stein that were discussed in Chapter 26. Burrows thought that humanity had a fundamental unity, but that we are divided by the historical development of a "social neurosis" (Galt 1995). He created a research institute, the Lifewynn foundation, and developed an "eye-movement camera" to study the impact of social neurosis in groups.

What Burrows called the social neurosis is his term for what other people would consider to be the building blocks of society. Social status and role restriction are just some of the manifestations of "social neurosis" that are for most people, the imaginary skeleton of the social organism.

Burrows ideas are similar to those of many people who have founded alternative, egalitarian communities, including therapeutic communities (see also Chapter 28). It is not essential to abolish inequalities in social organization to develop communities that foster inter-subjectivity. Extending the biological analogy of society as an organism, a muscle cell might as well resent not having been turned into a neuron instead of a myocyte as a person born in Kampala resent not having been born in Kensington. The existential approach would, I think, be that there are possibilities of fulfilment in every person, what Heidegger would have called Dasein's own-most potentiality for being a self, that are not restricted by such accidents of being. Sartre and de Beauvoir too would have distinguished between the l'être en-soi, that is, the consequence of brute facts of our existence and the freedom to make something of the essence of ourselves, that ever-escaping limit on our existence that he called the l'être pour-soi. I do not think that it is necessary that therapists behave like clients for them to foster inter-subjectivity. In fact, that often seems like a kind of inappropriate envy of the therapeutic benefits that their clients enjoy.

Developing an inter-subjectively based existential group therapy

My own take on this has been set out in my chapter on history (Chapter 25), where I distinguished between our narrative self that plays a key part in those manifestations of self that we call character, individuality, personality, agency, autonomy, and so on and the individual brain that interacts with other brains in its vicinity in an ever changing social and emotional environment by means of "interbrain" connections. These interbrain connections enable involuntary social learning, emotional modulation, intersubjectivity, and what is currently termed emotional empathy. The history of interbrain interactions is stored in memory to which we do not have conscious access. I have referred to them, neutrally, as "caches" because I have no idea how they are instantiated in the brain. They are clearly not the same storage that emotion researchers refer to as emotion scripts (Fischer 1991), which are supposedly accessible by introspection.

Phenomenologists, especially the alternative group of existential theorists whose work can be traced back to Scheler and Edith Stein, and before them to Schopenhauer, Schleiermacher, and Nietzsche have been path breakers in trying to describe the ineffably indescribable effects of these interbrain connections. Merleau-Ponty's phenomenology of mutual gaze, and his conception of its "reversibility" (Stawarska 2006) is one of the observations that is supported by recent neuroscience that I attribute to the interbrain connection. Group psychotherapists have also acknowledged them, most notably the group analysts and have the systems-orientated group psychotherapists.

Mullan, one of the few group therapists to explicitly embrace existential ideas suggested, as noted above, that the basic principles of group therapy were to relate to more than one person, and to become more totally involved. I take it that here, too, his term "total involvement" was another way of describing being connected with other members of the group through shared stories and intellectual efforts to take their perspective, but also through the openness of shared attention and emotional contagion (the former is similar to what Foulkes called "condensation" and the latter to what he called "resonance").

Conflicting communication

The interbrain and the narrative connections between people are not independent, and generally add to each other. As group therapists often note, absent group members are still present in the minds of the other members, but not in the immediate way that they would be if they had attended. Occasionally, though, the interpersonal impact of another person, mediated through their involuntary, interbrain-mediated, communication does conflict with our consciously constructed narrative about them. Conflict is often taken to be one of the key causes of psychological distress or a failure to develop full potential. The model of conflict that I described in the Interbrain is not based in intrapsychic conflict, but a conflict in communication, between the words that a person speaks and their involuntary interbrain engagement with other people that discloses their emotions and which objects of their attention evoke those emotions.

Foulkes view was that the same kind of conflict is problematized in the small, therapeutic group. In that setting, the "neurotic symptom mumbles to itself secretly," he and Anthony wrote (Foulkes and Anthony 1957, p. 260). One way of interpreting this is, according to some analytically -orientated group analysts (Dalal 1988), is that Foulkes thought that the aim of the group was to turn communication into words. But as Dalal notes, although Foulkes thought that explicit communication was the acme of communicative competence, he also thought that everything that happened in the group had communicative potential.

Psychoanalytically orientated therapists, like Foulkes and Dalal, follow Freud in distinguishing two kinds of cognition, primary and secondary processes, except that Foulkes shifted the location of where he thought these processes took place from the intrapsychic to the interpersonal thus making them two types of communication. Primary process communications are conveyed by, amongst other means, symptoms, artistic production, and dream reports. Secondary processes belong to the ego or as many psychologists would say the mind, at least the part of it that is open to introspection. Secondary process communications are predominantly conveyed in language.

Shifting the focus from some putative intrapsychic apparatus, the Unconscious, to the interpersonal heads off Sartre's pointed critique that to allow the Unconscious to originate thoughts makes it into a kind of semi-autonomous agency. It is counter-intuitive to think of having it lodged within but independent of us, a separate agency capable of initiating actions. But there is some phenomenological sense in this. People with schizophrenia may describe passivity experiences in which their arms or other body parts may be moved by something else that takes them over. I, and Foulkes, would say that the origins of this sense of an agency outside ourselves should be looked for in the interpersonal. I would locate it in the interbrain links with other people along with phenomena like echopraxia, also described in people with schizophrenia.

Theories that we are all exposed to conflicting impulses do not just apply intrapsychically, but in our social world. We readily accept conspiracy theories of cabals of the wealthy or the religious secretly running society. We often find ourselves in conflict. We can be ambivalent, our own worst enemy, fail to think before we speak, cut off our nose to spite our face, and so on. We do often pit dreams against reality. There are sometimes conflicts between our reflexive empathy for others and our cognitive empathy. A child might flinch from the fear in another child when they are going to be punished, but by the time that the child is an adolescent may be able to suppress this reaction and replace it with a feeling of satisfaction if the child is being punished for an infraction for which they are, indeed, guilty.

Sartre, following Hegel and Marx, thought of conflict as being an organizing principle in society. He took the master–slave relationship as the model for interpersonal relations and assumed that this grew out of the scarcity of desirable resources. Historically, there had always been unequal distribution of these, which led to war, revolution, and oppression. Foulkes was not good in factoring this political dimension into group life. He euhemeristically argued that conflicts, or at least the group conflicts that interested him, were due to fear. The particular fear was that demands (for being listened to, for being cared for, for being positively regarded, and so on) would be rejected by other people. Sullivan (Morgan 2014) had a similar model although he located the problem in a child's irrational thinking rather than the distortions of upbringing that are currently the focus. Foulkes thought that we hide our demands in "autistic communication" but these give way to free communication as participation in the group progresses, and members realize that they can get enough of their demands accepted. Many therapists have wondered what he meant by free communication. Just saying whatever comes into your head is not free communication. As de Beauvoir wrote (1948/1976) (see also Chapter 25), "To be free is not to have the power to do anything you like; it is to be able to surpass the given towards an open future; the existence of others as a freedom defines my situation and is even the condition of my own freedom."

Just speaking inconsiderately or inconsequentially cannot have been what Foulkes meant. Interbrain communication is most free when it is not suppressed by top-down control and so the reciprocal interchange of reflexive non-verbal communication with other people who are co-present is not inhibited. One of the delights, and occasional frustrations, of interacting with toddlers is that their communication is free in this sense because their theory of mind has yet to develop strongly enough to suppress their interbrain connectivity. At an older age, interbrain connections are usually inhibited, and spontaneity is absent. An exception is when contagious emotion becomes overwhelming. It is worth remembering that when this happens groups entirely connected by the interbrain may become frightening and dangerous to anyone who is in an out-group and therefore is merely a possible obstacle. When panic overwhelms a group is an example of behavior dictated by the interbrain, as Sartre noted in his example of the fused group in which no-one knows whether it is him or his neighbor who cries out, "To the Bastille."

Most of the time it is our narrative about the motives of other people or about what is good for "me" that determines communication by shutting down the interest in others and the influence on us of their emotions. So perhaps what Foulkes meant by free communication was not that we give unstinted expression to our selfishness, or that we fall into superheated interbrain melding with our in-group, but that there is increasing harmony between these two modes of communication. This does not mean unquestioning positivity for fellow group members any more than connection with them results in unstinting positivity flowing towards oneself. It means though that one accepts what flows in the interbrain connection with minimal distortion or self-defensive processing.

Opening up to inter-subjectivity

Inter-subjectivity as Buber, and many others have indicated since, is essential for close relationships with other people. It is related to other influential ideas about social interaction: attunement, attachment, affiliation, belonging, and so on. It is a precondition for other influential ideas in modern psychotherapy, including compassion, forgiveness, love, positive unconditional concern.

Therapists spend a great deal of time studying narrative. It is readily accessible and feels like it is our natural medium. But if free communication in the therapeutic group is its aim, equal attention should be placed on studying interbrain communication. This might spur theoretical development in what has become a stagnant field. Phenomenology has substantial potential for this investigation. Merleau-Ponty (Merleau-Ponty et al. 1968) provided some tools that might form the basis of observational studies of the phenomena that Stein and Scheler hypothesized: reversibility is an example. Reversibility means that as my face is forming an expression it is also shaping itself into the facial expression that I see in the other person's face, and *vice versa*. Interbrain connection is not so much sequential as simultaneous. An utterance, by contrast, is embedded in a sequence something along these lines: a thought/concept/idea is converted into language and then into a method of communicating, such as speech, which is then transmitted, unpacked by a hearer and this creates a concept in the hearer's mind, which is processed and then translated by a language processing area into a communication, and so on. Interbrain communication is more like two circuits being connected that result in a new state shared by the connected circuits. Meaning comes along after. De Beauvoir's early philosophy also deals with this, by means of her concepts of "ambiguity" and "reciprocity" (de Beauvoir 2004).

One problem with investigating the interbrain directly is that it is a language-free zone. One way round this is the newly developed approach of neurophenomenology. This seeks to integrate a phenomenological interview with neurophysiological data (Bockelman, Reinerman-Jones, and Gallagher 2013). Magnetic resonance imaging has, for example, been used in a study of group identification (Vaughn et al. 2018). One strand of this is studying the effects of social hormones on the therapeutic relationship. This has been restricted so far to studies of the effects of oxytocin insufflation on clients undergoing individual therapy. Not enough is known about the effects of social hormones, such as oxytocin, to know whether or not its effects might themselves be influenced by the emotional climate of the therapy (Flanagan et al. 2018). Another approach is looking at unconscious priming towards or away from social cohesion in underpowered groups and individual therapy (Marchese, Robbins, and Morrow 2018).

Another group of researchers have looked at the widespread use of sweat-lodges, saunas, hammams, and other steam rooms. This provides opportunities to look at the dynamics of context-dependent autonomic coupling. Sweating together increases group cohesion (Colmant et al. 2005) and group satisfaction, presumably as a result of hormonal activation. It also increased imitative behavior, at least it did in one small study of children with oppositional defiant disorder (Colmant and Merta 2000).

Even more direct measures of brain-to-brain connectivity are now possible, either with electroencephalograms (EEGs) (Balconi, Gatti, and Vanutelli 2018) or Functional Near Infrared Imaging (fNIRS) (Balconi et al. 2017). These methods are being used to study group identification already. Perhaps Trigant Burrow was not only a forerunner of group analysis but also of the application of neurophysiological methods to the clarification of cohesion in groups that group psychotherapists of all modalities have considered to be the lodestone of effectiveness in therapy groups.

One important research direction for the future will, I consider, be the use of direct measures of the involuntary communication that subserves inter-subjectivity, measures that will bypass the narrative connections that also contribute to cohesion and go directly to possible therapeutic factors. It will be an exciting period for existential group psychotherapists who will not only need to learn their trade, but to be able to research existential philosophers, and calibrate a variety of neuroimaging machines.

References

Balconi, M., Gatti, L., and Vanutelli, M.E. (2018). EEG functional connectivity and brain-to-brain coupling in failing cognitive strategies. *Consciousness and Cognition 60* (4): 86–97.

Balconi, M., Pezard, L., Nandrino, J.-L. et al. (2017). Two is better than one: The effects of strategic cooperation on intra- and inter-brain connectivity by fNIRS. *PLoS ONE 12*: e0187652.

Beatty, L., Kemp, E., Butow, P. et al. (2018). A systematic review of psychotherapeutic interventions for women with metastatic breast cancer: Context matters. *Psycho-Oncology 27* (1): 34–42.

Blackmore, C., Tantam, D., Parry, G. et al. (2012). Report on a systematic review of the efficacy and clinical effectiveness of group analysis and analytic/dynamic group psychotherapy. *Group Analysis 45* (1): 46–49.

Bockelman, P., Reinerman-Jones, L., and Gallagher, S. (2013). Methodological lessons in neurophenomenology: Review of a baseline study and recommendations for research approaches. *Frontiers in Human Neuroscience 7* (608): 1–9.

Burrow, T. (2013). *From Psychoanalysis to Group Analysis: The Pioneering Work of Trigant Burrow*. London: Karnac.

Colmant, S.A., Eason, E.A., Winterowd, C.L. et al. (2005). Investigating the effects of sweat therapy on group dynamics and affect. *The Journal for Specialists in Group Work 30* (4): 329–341.

Colmant, S. and Merta, R. (2000). Sweat therapy. *Journal of Experiential Education 23* (1): 31–38.

Dalal, F. (1988). *Taking the Group Seriously: Towards a Post-Foulkesian Group Analytic Theory*. London: Jessica Kingsley.

de Beauvoir, S.D. (1976). *The Ethics of Ambiguity*, New York: Citadel Press. (Original work published 1948.)

de Beauvoir, S.D. (2004). *Philosophical Writings*. Urbana, IL, University of Chicago Press.

Fischer, A. (1991). *Emotion Scripts: A Study of the Social and Cognitive Facets of Emotions*. Leiden: DSWO Press, Leiden University.

Flanagan, J.C., Sippel, L.M., Wahlquist, A. et al. (2018). Augmenting prolonged exposure therapy for PTSD with intranasal oxytocin: A randomized, placebo-controlled pilot trial. *Journal of Psychiatric Research 98* (3): 64–69.

Foulkes, S. and Anthony, E. (1957). *Group Psychotherapy: The Psycho-Analytic Approach*. Harmondsworth: Penguin.

Galt, A.S. (1995). Trigant Burrow and the laboratory of the "I." *The Humanistic Psychologist 23* (1): 19–39.

Goldie, P. (2007). There are reasons and reasons. In: *Folk Psychology Re-Assessed* (ed. D.D. Hutto and M.M. Ratcliffe), 103–144. Dordrecht: Springer.

Jaspers, K. (1964). *The Nature of Psychotherapy: A Critical Appraisal*. Chicago: University of Chicago Press.

Mander, J., Neubauer, A.B., Schlarb, A. et al. (2017). The therapeutic alliance in different mental disorders: A comparison of patients with depression, somatoform, and eating disorders. *Psychology and Psychotherapy: Theory, Research and Practice 90* (4): 649–667.

Marchese, M.H., Robbins, S.J., and Morrow, M.T. (2018). Nonconscious priming enhances the therapy relationship: An experimental analog study. *Psychotherapy Research 28* (2): 183–191.

Merleau-Ponty, M., Lefort, C., and Lingis, A. (1968). *The Visible and the Invisible.* Evanston, IL: Northwestern University Press.

Morgan, J. (2014). The interpersonal psychotherapy of Harry Stack Sullivan: Remembering the legacy. *Journal of Psychology and Psychotherapy 4* (1): 62–64.

Mullan, H. (1957). Trends in group psychotherapy in the United States. *International Journal of Social Psychiatry 3* (3): 224–230.

Mundt, C. (2014). Jaspers concept of "limit situation": Extensions and therapeutic applications. In: *Karl Jaspers' Philosophy and Psychopathology* (ed. T. Fuchs, T. Breyer, and C. Mundt), 169–178. New York: Springer.

Rosenfeld, B., Cham, H., Pessim, H. et al. (2018). Why is Meaning-Centered Group Psychotherapy (MCGP) effective? Enhanced sense of meaning as the mechanism of change for advanced cancer patients. *Psycho-Oncology 27* (2): 654–660.

Schöttke, H., Flückiger, C., Goldberg, S.B. et al. (2017). Predicting psychotherapy outcome based on therapist interpersonal skills: A five-year longitudinal study of a therapist assessment protocol. *Psychotherapy Research 27* (6): 642–652.

Stawarska, B. (2006). Mutual gaze and social cognition. *Phenomenology and the Cognitive Sciences 5* (1): 17–30.

Szecsödy, I. (2007). Sándor Ferenczi–the first intersubjectivist. *The Scandinavian Psychoanalytic Review 30* (1): 31–41.

Van Zyl, F.N. (2018). A social constructionist model of therapeutic factors. *Journal of Constructivist Psychology 31* (4): 440–459.

Vaughn, D.A., Savjani, R.R., Cohen, M.S. et al. (2018). Empathic neural responses predict group allegiance. *Frontiers in Human Neuroscience 12* (7): 1–10.

Part VI

International Developments

Theory, Practice, and Research

Edited by

Simon du Plock

31

Introduction

Simon du Plock

When I wrote an overview of what I then termed "the Existential-Phenomenological Movement" for Windy Dryden's edited book *Developments in Psychotherapy, Historical Perspectives* just over two decades ago (1996), I set the scene for my account of what was to become existential-phenomenological therapy by considering, briefly, its philosophical roots in the Ancient Greek and Roman worlds. I went on to discuss the diverse ways in which the approach had manifested itself in, in turn, continental Europe, North America, and Britain. At that time the emergence and proliferation of existential-phenomenological therapy seemed to me to follow a relatively evident trajectory beginning with the emergence of existential philosophy (the work of Kierkegaard and Nietzsche), progressing to the development of phenomenology (Brentano and Husserl), and leading to its application by Heidegger as a method with which to investigate the meaning of being. This led to the first direct application by Binswanger of Heidegger's philosophy to the treatment of psychological conditions, and later refinements by Boss. It was possible to trace links to Sartre, de Beauvoir, Merleau-Ponty, and numerous other theorists and practitioners, show how existential theory was introduced into the North American scene, and to describe how Britain in due course became a fertile ground for the further development of the existential approach when Laing and Cooper took Sartre's ideas as the basis for a reconsideration of the notion of mental illness and its treatment. While the above is only the sketchiest indication of a rich and diverse confluence of theory and practice, it perhaps serves to indicate that at that moment it did not seem unrealistic to attempt to capture the essence of the various existential therapies in a single chapter. With regard to future developments, I wrote then:

> As we have seen, the existential approach, though its core characteristics endure, is articulated differently in Britain, the USA and continental Europe. As it spreads to other parts of the world – flourishing practices are now springing up in Australia and New

The Wiley World Handbook of Existential Therapy, First Edition. Edited by Emmy van Deurzen, Erik Craig, Alfried Längle, Kirk J. Schneider, Digby Tantam, and Simon du Plock.

> Zealand – it is probable that new strains will emerge as some aspects of the tradition are emphasized and others relegated in keeping with the perceived needs of new client groups. (Dryden 1996, p. 58)

In the intervening years I have been fortunate to have had the opportunity to contribute to training programs around the world, most frequently in Eastern Europe and Russia, and in the process I have been exposed to the rich existential traditions which have flourished or are now rapidly developing beyond Britain and the United States. In the light of these experiences, I was involved in 2015 in editing (with Emmy van Deurzen) a "Special Issue" of the *International Journal of Psychotherapy*, focusing on Existential Therapy. In the course of composing our opening paper on the development and future of the orientation, I became much more informed about international initiatives – including those in Latin America, Australia and Asia, and the Middle East and Africa, and representatives of each of these regions gave papers at the First World Congress of Existential Therapy in 2015.

All this notwithstanding, I have been fascinated and inspired in the course of editing this part of this *World Handbook* to discover both entire areas of theory and practice of which I had little awareness – I am thinking here particularly of Xuefu Wang's piece on China and other Asian countries (Chapter 36) – and to read in much greater depth about some remarkable forms of existential practice to be found in Russia. I have felt privileged to engage with the many contributors to this part, each of them a pioneer of their own form of existential therapy, and I hope that we have, together, created perhaps the first comprehensive overview of newly evolving forms of existential therapy around the world. Readers interested in developments in Australia are referred to Alison Strasser's account in Chapter 12 of this book. While what follows provides, I feel confident, a valuable "snapshot" of the international situation, I am aware that each contributor could have elaborated in far greater detail on their own approaches; further, had space permitted it would have been fascinating to have created a dialogue between contributors in order to clarify to a far greater degree the similarities and differences between the theory and practice each describes so concisely. It is my hope that what follows will stimulate a conversation between existential therapists around the world, which has already begun with the creation of the World Confederation and World Congresses for Existential Therapy, and I am sure that accounts of newly evolving approaches to existential therapy that appear in future editions of this handbook will be able to expand on developments in those parts of the world which, necessarily, are only outlined here.

To summarize what the reader will, themselves, discover in this part, it begins with a discussion by Anders Dræby Sørensen, Bo Jacobsen, and Lennart Belfrage of the development of existential therapy in Scandinavia. This is followed by a consideration of Eastern Europe and Russia, which opens with a piece on existential therapy in the Baltic Countries by Rimantas Kočiūnas and continues with two pieces on Russia: the first by Semjon Yesselson, the second by Dmitry Leontiev on the philosophical roots of Russian existentialism. Eugenia Georganda contributes a piece on Southern Europe, with support from Edgar Correia (on Portugal and Spain), Gideon Menda and Yali Sar Shalom (on Israel), Lodovico Berra (on Italy), and Jack Icoz (on Turkey). Next is an account of Latin American developments contributed by Susana Signorelli

(Argentina) and Yaqui Andrés Martínez Robles (México). There follows a piece with the title "An East-West Dialogue: An outline of existential therapy development in China and related Asian countries" authored by Xuefu Wang. In each case, the contributors provide not only an account of recent initiatives, but also great insight with regard to the philosophical, historical, and political contexts that give rise to these developments. In doing so, they enable us to appreciate the breadth and depth of the existential tradition anew. This part closes with a review by Joel Vos of research on existential therapy. It is evident that the growth of existential therapy around the world described in previous chapters within this part has been accompanied by a growing acknowledgement of the importance of research-based, and evidence-based, practice. We existential therapists, with our grounding in philosophy, are ideally situated to develop innovative ways of engaging with research – ways that can enable us to truly explore human being.

References

Dryden, W. (ed.) (1996). *Developments in Psychotherapy, Historical Perspectives.* London: Sage.

du Plock, S. and van Deurzen, E. (2015). The historical development and future of existential therapy. *International Journal of Psychotherapy 19* (1): 5–14.

Martínez Robles, Y. (2015). *Existential Therapy.* Mexico: Círculo de Estudios en Psicoterapia Existencial.

Martínez Robles, Y. and Signorelli, S. (2011). *Perspectivas en Psicoterapia Existencial.* México: LAG.

Martínez Robles, Y. and Signorelli, S. (2015). A brief review of the history of existential psychotherapy in Latin America. *International Journal of Psychotherapy 19* (1): 89–94.

Spinelli, E. (2015). *Practising Existential Therapy.* London: Sage.

32

The Development of Existential Therapy in Scandinavia

Anders Dræby Sørensen, Bo Jacobsen, and Lennart Belfrage

Introduction

Scandinavia is a region in Northern Europe consisting of a group of three countries, Denmark, Sweden, and Norway that are geographically and mentally close to as well as separated from Britain and Continental Europe. Danish philosopher and theologian Søren Kierkegaard is widely regarded as the founder of existential psychology and therapy, making Scandinavia the birthplace of the approach. The easy-going, humanistic, and social-welfare-oriented mentality of Scandinavia has shaped the regional development of existential therapy, heavily stimulated by Continental existential philosophy and phenomenology along with especially British and American schools of existential therapy.[1] Thus, the Scandinavians have an original contribution to the world based on a strong focus on equality, care, and human worth.

Early forms of existential therapy have been found in the Scandinavian countries from around 1970, performed by a number of individual psychologists and psychiatrists. They read existential philosophers and works on phenomenological psychology and psychiatry, integrating these thoughts into their practice. Especially in Norway and Denmark, there has been a long tradition for seeing psychology as a subject field to be explored by phenomenological and hermeneutic approaches as well as qualitative methods. This continental version of psychology was seen as different from the Anglo-American so-called behavioristic or positivistic approach. Because of this continental view of what psychology is, it felt natural to see existential therapy as a continuation of phenomenological and existential psychology. Consequently, many existential therapists tend to perceive existential therapy as founded on the *double* foundation of philosophy and psychology (e.g., Jacobsen 2015). Other existential therapists from

[1] The other Nordic countries include Finland and Iceland. In Finland, the approach of Logotherapy has gained a certain popularity, including The Finland Institute for Logotherapy.

The Wiley World Handbook of Existential Therapy, First Edition. Edited by Emmy van Deurzen, Erik Craig, Alfried Längle, Kirk J. Schneider, Digby Tantam, and Simon du Plock.

Scandinavia are more closely in line with a definition of existential therapy as a philosophically informed approach to counselling and psychotherapy (e.g., Sørensen and Keller 2015, pp. 119–151, 187–209).

Denmark

Unlike Sweden and Norway, Denmark connects with Continental Europe, and Søren Kierkegaard partly based his existential approach on German philosophy. Being a small country in the Northern region of Europe, Denmark receives a lot of international influence from its Continental neighbors as well as from Britain and the United States.

1. The impact of Søren Kierkegaard

Søren Kierkegaard is the father of the existential tradition, and his thoughts have had a significant impact on the development of existential philosophy, psychology and therapy in Denmark. Kierkegaard's writings (2009) were written in Danish and were initially limited to Scandinavia, but as early as 1888, Danish critic Georg Brandes wrote a letter to German philosopher Friedrich Nietzsche, stating that Søren Kierkegaard was to be regarded as one of the most profound psychologists ever (Brandes 1952–1966, p. 448). From the turn of the twentieth century, Søren Kierkegaard's writings were translated into major European languages, such as French, German, and English, and his thoughts have had a substantial influence on Western culture.

Søren Kierkegaard's work crosses the boundaries of theology, philosophy, psychology, and therapy, and several of his writings specifically address psychological issues, including *Repetition* (1843/2009), *The Concept of Anxiety* (1844/2009), *Concluding Unscientific Postscript to the Philosophical Fragments* (1846/2009), and *The Sickness unto Death* (1849/2009). In these writings, Søren Kierkegaard uses the new science of psychology to help him explore the observable psychological phenomena of individuals when faced with life choices. His ontological view of the self as a synthesis of body, soul, and spirit, and his description of the nature and forms of anxiety and despair have influenced philosophers such as Martin Heidegger and Jean-Paul Sartre, and existential psychologists and therapists such as Ludwig Binswanger, Rollo May, and Emmy van Deurzen. Søren Kierkegaard himself considered *Works of Love* (1847/2009) to be a book on the spiritual therapy of existential despair, and this book still has an unexplored relevance for psychotherapy in the twenty-first century.

Several Danish writers have taken an interest in examining Søren Kierkegaard's psychology. From 1933 to 1972, psychiatrist Ib Ostenfeld published two books (1933, 1972) on Kierkegaard's psychology. In 1972, Kresten Nordentoft published *Kierkegaard's Psychology*, including a synthesis of Søren Kierkegaard's psychological work. This comprehensive work covers a wide spectrum of psychological topics such as sexuality, identity, despair, and anxiety. Nordentoft makes several parallels to psychoanalysis and he mentions Søren Kierkegaard's influence on Rollo May and the Swiss school of Daseinsanalysis.

In 1969, psychologist Boje Katzenelson published a major work on anxiety, including a section on Kierkegaard's concept of anxiety. In recent years, Kierkegaard's psychology has especially influenced psychologist Bjarne Jacobsen (2000) who published a significant book on the relevance of Kierkegaard's psychology to the understanding of somatic illness. Furthermore, philosopher and existential therapist Anders Dræby Sørensen (2013; 2015a; 2015b, 2015c) has made several contributions on Kierkegaard's descriptions of anxiety and despair as well as on Kierkegaard's relevance for existential psychopathology, psychology and therapy.

2. The pluralistic scene of Danish psychotherapy

In Denmark, three different professions practice psychotherapy: psychiatrists, psychologists, and other psychotherapists.

Medical doctors wishing to specialize in psychiatry obtain an introduction post, followed by specialist rotations lasting five years. Training in psychotherapy consists of 60 one-hour sessions with patients linked with supervision and theory. Personal therapy is not mandatory.

The undergraduate psychology training in Denmark consists of five years of academic studying leading to a Master of Science degree in Psychology. Psychologists wishing to work with psychotherapy go through an authorization program of at least two years including many hours of supervised client work. Thereafter, they have the opportunity of following a specialization in psychotherapy, including personal therapy, this specialization lasting at least three years, often longer.

The other training in psychotherapy either takes the form of authorized training of nurses and other healthcare professionals or as private training at private institutions. There does not exist any formal accreditation of private training as psychotherapist, and the training programs do not allow for any authorization as a psychotherapist, which is not a protected title in Denmark. However, completing a four-year training program provides the opportunity to become a member of one of the two Danish associations for psychotherapists.

Currently, the scene of Danish psychotherapy is very pluralistic, influenced by many distinct psychotherapeutic approaches. Whereas psychiatrists and psychologists formerly used to specialize in psychoanalysis, they now tend to focus more on cognitive behavior therapy (CBT). Among psychologists as a whole there is a broad variety of orientations and in Denmark psychologists have a free choice of method, even if you are receiving patients referred from medical doctors via the National Health Insurance. Privately trained psychotherapists specialize in a broad variety of psychotherapeutic approaches, ranging from psychoanalysis and CBT to humanistic and existential approaches.

3. The development of Existential Therapy in Denmark

In Denmark, existential therapy has mainly become important since the 1990s. However, Søren Kierkegaard's writings and other influences arrived earlier on a fertile ground.

Fertile ground German philosopher Edmund Husserl's phenomenological study of subjective experience had an early impact on Danish psychology, influencing academic psychologists from the 1910s. Psychological research at the University of Copenhagen gradually became known as "The Copenhagen School of Phenomenology," with Edgar Rubin being considered its founder. This school of phenomenological psychology was very popular until the end of the twentieth century.

From the 1950s to the 1980s, the American school of humanistic psychology and person-centered therapy became popular in Denmark, and several books by Gordon Allport, Charlotte Bühler, and Abraham Maslow were translated into Danish. In the same period, the related American schools of Gestalt therapy and experiential psychotherapy also gained ground in Denmark, and writings by Walther Kempler and Fritz Perls were translated into Danish. These approaches contributed to the interest in existential issues among Danish psychologists and psychotherapists, and they are still popular among some Danish psychotherapists.

In Denmark, the protests and youth rebellion of 1968 led to a widespread anti-authoritarian trend that had a significant impact on Danish culture and welfare institutions. This trend included a criticism of conventional psychiatry and its role in Danish society. From the late 1960s, many key works by British psychiatrist Ronald D. Laing were translated into Danish. Together with the anti-psychiatry movement, Laing's existential approach to psychiatry had a huge impact on the intellectual community, also influencing parts of clinical psychology and the establishment of social psychiatry in Denmark.

From the 1970s, several key writings by Austrian psychotherapist Viktor Frankl were translated into Danish, making Frankl's thoughts on Logotherapy and existential analysis popular among a wide audience. Frankl later received an honorary doctorate at the University of Copenhagen. However, Logotherapy has never gained real ground amongst Danish psychologists and psychotherapists as an independent approach.

From the 1980s psychologist and lecturer at the University of Copenhagen John Smidt Thomsen presented existential psychology and therapy for psychology students in Copenhagen, drawing on Martin Buber, Binswanger, Rollo May, Irvin Yalom, and others.

The 1990s onwards In the 1990s, psychologist Bo Jacobsen was the driving force behind the spread of existential therapy in Denmark. Along with some colleagues, Bo Jacobsen received training in existential therapy at The School of Psychotherapy and Counselling at Regent's College in London. Following this training, the Danish group invited British existential therapists Emmy van Deurzen and Ernesto Spinelli to give several lectures, courses, training seminars, and supervision sessions in Copenhagen. Furthermore, Bo Jacobsen, Bjarne Jacobsen, John Smidt Thomsen, and other existential psychologists established a forum for existential psychology and therapy.

Bo Jacobsen developed his own original and comprehensive approach to existential therapy, which is undogmatic but influenced by the British school as well as by Viktor Frankl, Irvin D. Yalom, and Medard Boss. Bo Jacobsen's originality relates to the fact that his therapeutic approach is based on the double perspective of existential philosophy and existential psychology. He conceives these as separate yet related perspectives. Bo Jacobsen has published several books and articles on this approach, whose fundamental principles he outlines in "Authenticity and our basic Existential

Dilemmas: Foundational Concepts of Existential Psychology and Therapy" (2007), *Invitation to Existential Psychology* (2008), and *The Role of Existential Philosophy and Existential Psychology for Existential Therapy* (2015). Bo Jacobsen has also applied his approach in the development of an original method for existential group therapy with structured exercises, published in the book chapter *Working with Existential Groups* (1997). This method is especially well suited to people who are in need of existential and personal development but who do not consider themselves as in need of psychotherapy proper, for example, cancer patients and other critically ill patients, spouses and other family members of cancer patients, accident victims, parents who have children with psychiatric diagnoses, and a number of other groups facing sudden existential challenges. In addition, both Bo Jacobsen and Anders Dræby Sørensen have published several general introductions and overviews of existential therapy.

From the turn of the twenty-first century, psychologist Karsten Borg Hansen (1998; 2009) developed a different dialogical approach to existential psychotherapy, far more based in the philosophical tradition of existential phenomenology. Lotte Lykke Frederiksen (2013) has worked on a narrative approach also centered in existential phenomenology. Anders Dræby Sørensen and Kurt Dauer Keller (2015) published a comprehensive anthology on psychotherapy and existential phenomenology, including Bjarne Jacobsen's effort to ground therapy in Kierkegaard's psychology as well as Anders Dræby Sørensen's development of a philosophical approach based on the concepts of life-capability and self-transgression. In 2015, Anders Dræby Sørensen completed a doctoral degree in existential psychotherapy at Middlesex University, London and the New School of Psychotherapy and Counselling with a thesis on "Exploring learning outcomes in existential psychotherapy and CBT in Denmark," supervised by Emmy van Deurzen and Rosemary Lodge. In 2013, Line Kamstrup Frederiksen completed a doctoral degree in counselling psychology at Regent's University, London with a thesis on "Exploring the influence of mindfulness meditation training on therapeutic practice: The experiences of counselling psychologists trained from an existential-phenomenological perspective."

Since the 1990s, interest in existential therapy has gradually grown in Denmark, and in recent years, several key writings by Emmy van Deurzen, Ernesto Spinelli, Irvin D. Yalom, and Mick Cooper have been translated into Danish. Currently, Danish development connects closely to the British and American schools of existential therapy, while the Continental schools of Daseinsanalysis and Logotherapy have less impact. Whereas there are only a few Danish psychologists and psychotherapists presenting themselves as existential therapists, many others are integrating existential methods and principles into their practice. Anders Dræby Sørensen and Bo Jacobsen are initiating the establishment of a Danish Society for Existential Therapy as part of the Federation for Existential Therapy in Europe (FETE).

Other existential research and developments in Denmark Since the 1990s, Bo Jacobsen (1998a; 2008) has made a significant contribution to the existential tradition by developing an original and comprehensive Danish approach to existential psychology, unifying different psychological concepts, theories and research on existence. Bo Jacobsen has made a substantial effort, placing existential psychology in the field of modern psychology, and he highlights how existential psychology derives from a holistic understanding of human being as a reflective being that is able to talk about its existence and decide what kind of life it wants to live with its fellow human beings. In recent years, Bo Jacobsen has been working on a substantial psychological and sociological research project on love and existence, following his long interest in this subject. Bjarne Jacobsen has developed a different approach to existential psychology (2012), far more closely based on Kierkegaard's psychology. Bjarne Jacobsen demonstrates how our relationship with our body and other people relate the question about the meaning of life. In 2006, Bjarne Jacobsen published an anthology on existential life-themes, co-edited with psychologists Bjarne Sode Funch and Peter la Cour (Funch, Jacobsen, and la Cour 2006).

In Denmark, existential psychology has had a significant application in healthcare and research. Bo Jacobsen founded the Center for Research in Existence and Society at the University of Copenhagen in 1996, among other involved in existential research on cancer patients, ageing, and education. As part of these efforts, Bo Jacobsen (1998b) has published the results of an extensive research project on cancer and existence, and he (1998c; 2003) has applied the existential approach to the field of education. Currently, anthropologist Hanne Bess Boelsbjerg is working on a PhD thesis on the existential dimensions of dying. Outside the center, Peter la Cour has made existential research into the experience of chronic pain as well as into religious experiences among somatic patients. Casper Feilberg has completed a PhD thesis on the existential dimensions of becoming a psychology student, and Janni Lisander Larsen is working on a PhD thesis on the existential experience of rheumatological illness at the National Hospital.

In recent years, philosophical practice has also become popular in Denmark, and philosophical practitioners Finn Thorbjørn Hansen and Jeanette Knox have worked on highlighting the existential dimensions of the approach. Theologian Pia Søltoft and philosopher Anders Fogh Jensen have presented philosophical approaches to coaching and life-practice, founded in Kierkegaard's thinking, and Anders Dræby Sørensen works on integrating existential therapy with Hellenistic and Roman arts of living. An increasing number of philosophy students are writing their master thesis on existential practice.

SWEDEN

In Sweden, existential therapy became popular from the 1990s. However, there was an early ground for this popularity.

1. Early ground: ideas

Historically there never was an independent school of philosophy on Swedish territory. While at first the outcrops were sketchy within the fields of theology, philosophy, and in the general cultural debate, interest subsequently grew in force and intensity. Interest in existential questions emanated from the renaissance of Søren Kierkegaard's ideas on the continent particularly in Germany. During the 1930s, the existentially characterized ideas by Karl Jaspers found their way into psychiatry. An existential philosophical pattern emerged, although impulses from Martin Heidegger's central work were seldom seen. The first Swedish translation of Martin Heidegger's *Sein und Zeit* did not appear until 1981. In the late 1940s, French existentialism, with the onset of the works by Jean-Paul Sartre and Albert Camus, had a remarkable success with the intellectual elite in Sweden. Hence, a fertile ground had been prepared for a potential growth of humanistic and existential psychotherapy.

2. Early ground: psychotherapy

Psychotherapy in its various forms had a noticeable breakthrough as a treatment method during the 1970s. In Stockholm, psychoanalysis attracted a major interest while in Uppsala behavioral therapy was at the center stage. Only in Göteborg, the humanistic perspective appeared to stir a clear interest.

In the late 1980s, several key writings by Viktor Frankl were translated into Swedish. Viktor Frankl visited Stockholm in 1989 and attracted a record audience. Interest in Logotherapy grew substantially. Hans Åkerberg, professor at the University of Lund, who had initiated the visit of Frankl, conducted several academic research projects with regard to existence and the search for meaning. Today, Logotherapy is hosted by the "Society of Existential Psychotherapy" (SEPT) in Sweden.

American existential psychologist Rollo May visited Sweden in 1988 and was interviewed for a Swedish documentary named "Sagolandet," which covered topics related to life in a modern society. May had a central part in the film, which was critical to contemporary Sweden. From the 1990s onwards, several key writings by Rollo May have been translated into Swedish.

3. Development as reaction against psychodynamic and cognitive-behavioral predominance

Psychoanalysis and CBT still dominate psychotherapy and clinical psychology in Sweden. They are also the only therapy variants that are subsidized by the Swedish government. Both approaches tend to have a deterministic and a one-dimensional perspective on human beings and consider mental suffering mainly as an individual phenomenon. The emergence and development of existential therapy in Sweden is very much a reaction against the predominance of these approaches. Existential therapy is seen as an important alternative to the other mainstream approaches. A widely supported public call for a broader range of therapeutic approaches was recently initiated by SEPT.

4. 1990s onwards

In Sweden, existential therapy started to gain real ground in the 1990s. In 1990, theologian and psychotherapist Owe Wikström published the first Swedish book on existential psychology and psychotherapy, combining a psychoanalytic, existential philosophical and a cultural critical perspective on the psychological function of religion. At that time, Emmy van Deurzen's book *Existential Counselling in Practice* was translated into Swedish and widely spread. The Swedish translation of Bo Jacobsen's (2000) book on existential psychology has further contributed to the growing interest in Sweden

From the turn of the twenty-first century, psychologist Dan Stiwne has been a driving force in the popularization of existential therapy and psychology in Sweden. Dan Stiwne (2008, 2009) has edited two comprehensive anthologies and many papers on the subject, describing a variety of existential methods for therapy that are particularly suitable for modern human beings, feeling alienated in life, and being reduced to a functional being. Stiwne is much inspired by existential phenomenologists such as Martin Heidegger, Jean-Paul Sartre, and Emmanuel Levinas as well as by ancient Greek philosophy.

Swedish psychologist Lennart Belfrage, PhD, was trained in existential psychology at Western Kentucky University, completing his Master's degree in 1975, exploring the concept of death in existential psychology (Befrage 1975). In 2009, Lennart Belfrage published his PhD thesis in existential psychology titled *Clergy Existence Challenged: An Existential Psychological Exploration of Meaning-making and Burnout Related to the Church of Sweden*. The thesis explores stress-related burnout amongst Swedish priests from an existential perspective. It particularly explores whether the theory of the four life worlds, developed by Emmy van Deurzen on the basis of Ludwig Binswanger, can be applied to understand the stress reactions of priests (Belfrage 2009).

Sociologist Ted Schröder PhD published an existential phenomenological approach to dream analysis in 2003, especially influenced by Swiss Dasein analyst Medard Boss and has since made important contributions on the connection between Buddhism and existential therapy. Existential psychotherapist and dance therapist Elisabeth Serrander (2009) has developed a therapeutic approach inspired by E.T. Gendlin and Maurice Merleau-Ponty.

Today, the Center for Practical Knowledge at Södertörn College offers some professional training in existential conversation to psychologists, psychotherapists, nurses, teachers, and other professionals. It aims at practical training on a theoretical foundation of existential philosophy and existential psychology. Associate professor Jonna Bornemark, a key figure in this training program, pursues groundbreaking research in existential philosophy and phenomenology.

5. Linköping University

Dan Stiwne, associate professor emeritus in clinical psychology has been at the frontiers in the development of existential psychotherapy training in Sweden since the 1990s. Over the years, he has published several books and research articles in this area. Dan Stiwne initiated professional connections with a number of key persons in Britain such as Hans Cohn, Emmy van Deurzen, and Martin Adams. Recurring visits at Linköping University and other venues by professors Emmy van Deurzen and Digby Tantam resulted in many appreciated lectures. These lectures, initiated by Dan Stiwne, formed the basis for a future independent society for existential psychotherapy in Sweden.

6. SEPT founded in 2005

SEPT was founded by Dan Stiwne and Gunnar Nilsson in 2005 as a non-profit society with the purpose of promoting existential psychotherapy as well as existential perspectives on the human condition. This initiative was carried out with the support of

Emmy van Deurzen and the Society of Existential Analysis in Britain. Today, psychologist Bo Blåvarg holds the chair of the society, while Dan Stiwne holds the chair of the society's scientific advisory board. The society now has about 150 members and ten times as many are connected to its Facebook site. The society offers courses and education on a regular basis and works actively towards a reintroduction and approval of existential psychotherapy at a national level. In order for a student in existential psychotherapy to receive a formal psychotherapy license from the government, he or she needs to acquire a degree from abroad such as Regent's University, London, NSPC, and Middlesex University.

7. How many existential therapists in Sweden?

Currently, there are about 40 fully certified existential psychotherapists in Sweden, specializing in existential therapy at an advanced level. Moreover, there is a growing interest among psychologists in general for further education within the field of existential psychology. Introductory courses administered by SEPT have attracted professionals from all clinical settings and social contexts. Advanced courses run as net-courses have been going on for many years.

8. Existential research on health issues

Research informed by existential philosophy and psychology has gained terrain over the past 20 years. Notably professor Peter Strang at the Karolinska Institutet in Stockholm has been in the forefront of research and writings related to palliative cancer care. In this context, he has a particular focus on existential loneliness and death anxiety and he continues to publish books on these existential themes.

Lisa Sand at the Karolinska Institutet recently published an important dissertation in the field of oncology and palliative care. The title of this study is *Existential Challenges and Coping in Palliative Cancer Care: Experiences of Patients and Family Members* (2008). Marja Schuster (2006) has published an existential-hermeneutical doctoral study in relation to asymmetry and reciprocity in nurses' encounter with severely ill patients. At Södertörn College, research on continental philosophy issues continues without abating.

At Uppsala University under the direction of professor Valerie DeMarinis an interdisciplinary research is focusing on religion and health, quality of life, and existential need. An emphasis on existential meaning-making has characterized academic dissertations over the past two decades.

The future of existential psychotherapy in Sweden

An impediment to the development of psychotherapy in Sweden is the unaltered education system, which has been the same for more than 40 years. It has contributed to a prolonged inflexibility that prevents new ideas from gaining a foothold in the Swedish society. Furthermore, mental health care is on the whole consistently medical – biologically oriented. Psychological and social factors only allow for a limited impact. Nonetheless, existential psychotherapy invokes a considerable interest and it should therefore be seen as a counter force and a complement to traditional healthcare. However, hopes for a change in a positive direction are within sight. The state authority education system is currently investigating the future guidelines with respect to psychotherapy. Consequently, there are hopes that the issue will get a favorable solution. In order for existential therapy to be fully recognized, as in many European countries, a Master of Arts in Psychotherapy will be required.

NORWAY

In Norway, existential therapy has been less popular than in Denmark and Sweden. This is partly due to the fact that philosophical practice has become a widespread approach in Norway.

1. The development of Existential Therapy in Norway

Søren Kierkegaard's philosophy and theology became popular in Norway early on. This popularity rose after the Second World War, and in 1963, Norwegian philosopher Hans Skjervheim wrote an article based on Kierkegaard's psychological thoughts, opposing the humanities and social sciences to the natural sciences.

From the 1960s to the early 2000s, a number of books by Ronald D. Laing, Rollo May, Viktor Frankl, and Irvin D. Yalom were translated into Norwegian. The approach of Logotherapy did attain a certain popularity amongst practitioners, and several Norwegian articles have been published on Viktor Frankl and his relevance to psychotherapy, medicine and education (e.g., Løvlie 1965; Førland 1966; Skaiå 2003).

In 1993, Anne Louise Lippe and Geir Hørsmark Nielsen edited an anthology on psychotherapy, including an introduction to existential phenomenological therapy. In recent years, psychologist Anne-Lise Schibbye has made several contributions to existential psychotherapy. In 2002, she published a book on the importance of relationships, combining a psychodynamic and an existential perspective. In 2006, Anne-Lise Schibbye published a book on existential psychology, focusing on the awareness in life from an existential and existential phenomenological perspective. In recent years, psychologist and researcher Per Einar Binder has focused on different aspects of relational, emotion-focused, and existential psychotherapy. In 2011, he published a book elucidating the ways in which the existential conditions of life make a background for exploration and changes of relationships and emotions in psychotherapy. The book combines existential psychology with a psychology of relationships and emotions in order to present a perspective on human development and healing, attached to attentive presence.

2. Modum Bad and Viken Center for Psychiatry and Pastoral Care

The existential approach, especially influenced by Irvin D. Yalom, has found application in a number of Norwegian institutions. Modum Bad is a private psychiatric hospital that combines psychiatry and psychotherapy in a holistic approach to patients, integrating psychoanalysis, existential methods, and religious perspectives. Since 1999, the Vita Section at Modum Bad has specialized in treating mental sufferings that relate to existential and religious life themes, and Emmy van Deurzen and other existential therapists have visited the hospital and given lectures.

The Viken Center for Psychiatry and Pastoral Care in Troms integrates different approaches in the treatment of mental patients. The center has an existential team, offering treatment to persons with existential, religious, or identity problems. The team combines existential group therapy with individual therapy with the aim of increasing the patients' insight and understanding.

3. Philosophical practice

In Norway, philosophical practice has had a significant impact, and it bears some similarities with existential therapy, although it integrates a variety of methods for treating everyday problems, distancing itself from being therapy. Norwegian philosopher Anders Lindseth has been the driving force behind the introduction of philosophical practice in Norway in 1990, following his training by German philosophical practitioner Gerd Achenbach. Currently, Anders Lindseth is professor at the University of Gothenburg in Sweden and he has published several papers on philosophical practice. Similar to Kari Martinsen, Anders Lindseth has introduced Danish philosopher K.E. Løgstrup's philosophy of care in Norway, which is having a big influence on Norwegian nursing.

From the 1990s, Anders Lindseth helped to train and organize other philosophical practitioners in Norway, and in 1998 he was involved in the establishment of the Norwegian Society for Philosophical Practice (NSFP). The association offers training to people holding a Master's degree in philosophy. Today, there are around 40 fully trained philosophical practitioners in Sweden. In recent years, NSFP has been involved in the establishment of philosophical practice in Denmark and Sweden.

Henning Herrestad, Anders Holt, and Helge Svare are other significant philosophical practitioners from Norway, and in 2002 they published the anthology *Philosophy in Society*, including contributions from existential therapists Emmy van Deurzen and Digby Tantam. In 2004, Helge Svarre and Henning Herrestad published the first Norwegian book on philosophical practice, focusing on the ways in which philosophy can help make life more meaningful. Pia Axell Hverven was trained in both existential psychotherapy and philosophical practice, and she has among other things applied the approach in elderly care.

Note

The section on Bo Jacobsen was written by the two other authors, the same applies to the sections on Anders Dræby Sørensen and Lennart Belfrage, respectively.

References

Belfrage, L. (1975). The role of the concept of death in existential psychology: From Kierkegaard to Binswanger. Unpublished Masters thesis, Western Kentucky University, Bowling Green, KY, United States of America.

Belfrage, L. (2009). *Clergy Existence Challenged: An Existential Psychological Exploration of Meaning-making & Burnout Related to the Church of Sweden*. Uppsala: Uppsala Universitet.

Binder, P.E. (2011). *Et oppmerksomt liv: om relasjon, kropp og nærvær i eksistensens psykologi.* Oslo: Fagbokforlaget.

Brandes, G. (1952–1966). *Correspondance de Georg Brandes 1–4.* Rosenkilde og Bagger.

Frederiksen, L.K. (2013). *Exploring the Influence of Mindfulness Meditation Training on Therapeutic Practice: The Experiences of Counselling Psychologists Trained from an Existential-Phenomenological Perspective.* London: Regent's University London.

Frederiksen, L.L. (2013). *Helende Historier.* Copenhagen: Frydenlund.

Funch, B., Jacobsen, B., and La Cour, P. (2006). *Livstemaer.* Copenhagen: HRF.

Førland E. (1966). Viktor Frankls utfordring til pedagogikken. *Inter Medicos, 9*: 115.

Hansen, K.B. (1998). *Eksistentiel terapi og meditation.* Copenhagen: Klitrose.

Hansen, K.B. (2009). *Den ligeværdige dialog.* Copenhagen: DPF.

Heidegger, M. (1981). *Varat och tiden* (trans. R. Matz). Göteborg: Daidalos.

Herrestad, H., Holt, A., and Svare, H. (2002). *Philosophy in Society.* Oslo: Unipub Forlag.

Jacobsen, Bjarne (2000). *Den helbredende sygdom.* Copenhagen: DPF.

Jacobsen, Bjarne. (2012). *Eksistentiel psykologi: Mellem himmel og jord.* Roskilde: Samfundslitteratur.

Jacobsen, Bo. (1997). Working with Existential Groups. In: *Case Studies in Existential Psychotherapy and Counselling* (ed. S. Plock). London: Wiley.

Jacobsen, Bo. (1998a). *Eksistensens psykologi.* Copenhagen: HRF.

Jacobsen, Bo. (1998b). *Kræft og eksistens.* Copenhagen: DPF.

Jacobsen, Bo. (1998c). *Voksenundervisning og livserfaring.* Copenhagen: HRF.

Jacobsen, Bo. (2000). *Existensens psykologi.* Stockholm: Natur och Kultur.

Jacobsen, Bo. (2003). *Mød eleven.* Copenhagen: HRF.

Jacobsen, Bo. (2007). Authenticity and our basic existential dilemmas: Foundational concepts of existential psychology and therapy. *Existential Analysis 18* (2): 288–296.

Jacobsen, Bo. (2008). *Invitation to Existential Psychology.* A Psychology for the Unique Human Being and Its Applications in Therapy. London: Wiley.

Jacobsen, Bo. (2015). The role of existential philosophy and existential psychology for existential therapy. *International Journal of Psychotherapy 19* (1): 32–38.

Katzenelson, B. (1969). *Angstteorier.* Copenhagen: Munksgaard.

Kierkegaard, S. (2009). *Kierkegaard's Writings, I–XXVI.* Princeton: Princeton University Press.

Lippe, A.L. and Nielsen, G. (ed.) (1993). *Psykoterapi med voksne. Fem perspektiver på teori og praksis.* Oslo: Tano Aschehoug.

Løvlie L. (1965). Wien-professoren Viktor Frankl: Vi lever i et eksistensielt vakuum. *Universitas 7*: 19.

Nordentoft, K. (1972). *Kierkegaard's Psychology.* Eugene: Duquesne University Press.

Ostenfeld, I. (1933). *Om Angst-Begrebet i Søren Kierkegaard Begrebet Angest.* Copenhagen: Gad.

Ostenfeld, I. (1972). *Kierkegaards psykologi.* Copenhagen: Rhodos.

Sand, L. (2008). *Existential Challenges and Coping in Palliative Cancer Care: Experiences of Patients and Family Members.* Stockholm.

Schibbye, A.-L. (2002). *En dialektisk relasjonsforståelse: i psykoterapi med individ, par og familie.* Oslo: Universitetsforlaget.

Schibbye, A.-L. (2006). *Livsbevissthet.* Oslo: Universitetsforlaget.

Schröder, Ted (2003). *Det omedvetna – en dröm om det äkta.* Stockholm: Brutus Östlings Bokförlag Symposion.

Schuster, M. (2006). *Profession och existens: en hermeneutisk studie av asymmetri och ömsesidighet i sjuksköterskors möten med svårt sjuka patienter.* Uddevalla, Sweden: Bokförlaget Daidalos AB.

Serrander, E. (2009). Det förkroppsligade mötet. Existentiell terapi, intersubjektivitet och arbete med "den levda kroppen." In: *Ompröva livet!* (ed. D. Stiwne), 169–188. Lund: Studentenlitteratur.

Skaiå, A. (2003). Betydningen av mening. *Tidsskrift for den Norske Lægeforening 123*: 1877–1879.

Sørensen, A.D. (2013). Søren Kierkegaards gennemslag i den eksistentielle og humanistiske psykologi, psykoterapi og psykiatri. *Slagmark 68*: 79–103.

Sørensen, A.D. (2015a). Søren Kierkegaard og den eksistentielfænomenologiske problematisering af psykopatologi. In: *Kierkegaard som eksistentiel fænomenolog* (ed. M. Pahuus, J. Rendtorff, and P. Søltoft), 251–273. Aalborg: AUF.

Sørensen, A.D. (2015b). Angst – når hverdagslivet bliver hjemløst. In: *Hverdagslivets følelser* (ed. I. Bo and M. Jacobsen), 115–146. Copenhagen: HRF.

Sørensen, A.D. (2015c). *Exploring Learning Outcomes in CBT and Existential Therapy in Denmark*. London: Middlesex University and NSPC.

Sørensen, A.D. and Keller, K.D. (ed.) (2015). *Psykoterapi og eksistentiel fænomenologi*. Aalborg: AUF.

Stiwne, D. (ed.) (2008). *Bara detta liv – texter i existentiell psykologi och psykoterapi*. Stockholm: Natur och Kultur.

Stiwne, D. (ed.) (2009). *Ompröva livet! Existentiell vägledning och terapi i ny tillämpning*. Stockholm: Studentlitteratur.

Svare, H. and Herrestad, H. (2004). *Filosofi for livet*. Olso: Fagbokforlaget.

Wikström, O. (1990). *Den outgrundliga människan. Livsfrågar, psykoterapi & självård*. Stockholm: Natur och Kultur.

33

Eastern Europe and Russia

Rimantas Kočiūnas, Semjon Yesselson, and Dmitry Leontiev

Existential Therapy in the Baltic Countries

Rimantas Kočiūnas

This chapter in Part VI addresses the development of existential therapy in the Baltic countries, but it mainly deals with the emergence and development of existential therapy in Lithuania, where a strong and influential school of this paradigm has formed. It is from there that existential therapy has spread to Latvia and Estonia, and also to Russia and Belarus.

Beginnings

For many years, the evolution of psychotherapy in our region was restricted and barred from its European and world context, first, by a rigorous ideological framework and the seclusion of the Soviet system, which rejected everything that might be coming from the West, and second, by strict adherence to an extremely medicalized model of psychotherapy. Existential philosophy was considered anti-Marxist, and books by existential philosophers, as well as of most classics of Western psychotherapy, were stored in classified depositories, access to which was possible only with special permission available to very few. Thus, the ideas of existentialism could not be publicly discussed or promoted.

In the Baltic countries opposition to the dogmas of Soviet ideology was always more pronounced as compared to other regions of the Soviet Union. This was determined by the historic circumstances: after being independent for more than 20 years, in 1940 the Baltic states were occupied and forcefully annexed to the Soviet Union; following the Second World War, the Soviet government faced armed resistance in these countries for almost a decade, and the opposing attitudes of at least some part of the general public were always alive. This is why the context of the development of

The Wiley World Handbook of Existential Therapy, First Edition. Edited by Emmy van Deurzen, Erik Craig, Alfried Längle, Kirk J. Schneider, Digby Tantam, and Simon du Plock.

psychotherapy was a little more liberal. Therefore in 1978, at the peak of the stagnation of the Soviet system, and after much struggle with authorities, a psychotherapy seminar was hosted in Vilnius on the initiative of local psychotherapist Aleksandras Alekseičikas. This seminar quickly became an annual and highly popular event attracting crowds of interested psychologists and psychotherapists from all over the Soviet Union. Its immediate appeal was that it presented an opportunity for the exchange ideas more or less freely, to learn more about Western psychotherapeutic paradigms, and to try creatively various formats of psychotherapy. These seminars were always permeated with a distinct humanistic existential atmosphere.

The core events at these seminars were groups of Intensive Therapeutic Life (ITL) – the format developed and facilitated by Aleksandras Alekseičikas who pioneered a professional psychotherapy in Lithuania by starting the first psychotherapeutic clinic in a hospital. Their deeply existential nature was one of the major grounds from which existential therapy, in its present shape, stemmed and further developed. The main category of ITL is *life* and its intense and profound exploration within the context of the lives of the participants of a group. The dynamics of a group move through certain life-related situations that are directed so that the healing powers of life itself would have more space to unfold and would reveal possibilities, unnoticed so far, for freer and more realistic everyday life. Issues of freedom, responsibility, meaning, finiteness, time, and other inescapable issues of everyday life always receive special attention in these groups. This model of group therapy provides space and context for thorough and strictly reality-based analysis of the values, meanings, and worldviews of the participants. This analysis facilitates the "knitting" of the network of the therapeutic process which, in turn, allows both the growth of the group as an integral "organism" and therapeutic changes in separate "cells" of this "organism." The life of the group focuses considerable attention towards participants' understanding of the possibilities that may be found in human nature or offered by life, or hidden in themselves, along with inevitable restrictions and limitations that are related to the imperfection of any human being, or depend on the context of an individual life, while some are determined by the very nature of Being. This comprises one of the most important and most universal goals of existential therapy. ITL is practiced with small and large groups, and also as a model of therapeutic community in a psychotherapy division within a psychiatric hospital (Kočiūnas 2000, 2008, 2015). The ideas of ITL received a great response among psychologists and psychotherapists not only in Lithuania, but also in Latvia, Estonia, Russia, and Belarus. Seminars of ITL are held annually to the present day and continue to be popular among those who are impressed by the charismatic personality of Dr. Alekseičikas and his incredible, impossible to emulate, ability to create in these groups an unyieldingly tense atmosphere of exploration of spiritual values.

Another important source, also notable, was a long-term existential psychology seminar that started in Vilnius in 1984, that occurred on a monthly basis until the collapse of the Soviet Union in 1990. It was dedicated to discussion of the ideas of Carl Rogers, Victor Frankl, Rollo May, as some of their books could be obtained through the help of the Lithuanian emigrant communities in the West, and to exploration of existential issues in the context of personal and psychotherapeutic experience. It was not surprising that in 1991 active members of this seminar founded the Lithuanian Association for Humanistic Psychology – the first community of psychologists in Lithuania that had just regained independence, and the first organization of humanistic psychology in the realm of the former Soviet Union. Within the framework of this seminar, an annual intensive workshop under the title "Life and Psychotherapy" was developed that became the basis for Existential Experience Groups (EEG) – yet another model of group therapy (Kočiūnas 2000, 2015). Compared to ITL, it greatly differs from the latter in the position of the therapist: in EEG, it may be defined as phenomenological, since the therapist is not a director, but much more of an assistant in the process of exploration of complex issues and problems in life.

The Institute of Humanistic and Existential Psychology

All these initiatives and active efforts to employ novel activities and practices called for more thorough theoretical concepts in the field of existential therapy. This, along with lively interest towards such activities in Lithuania and other neighboring countries, was the reason behind founding the Institute of Humanistic and Existential Psychology (HEPI) in 1995 (its founding members were Rimvydas Budrys, Leonas Judelevičius, and Rimantas Kočiūnas), which became the most important event in the development of existential therapy not only in Lithuania and other Baltic countries, but also in Russia. The latter country, in spite of its political perturbations, was and is still quite important due to its many ties and contacts. They started in the 1980s with considerable professional activity in the Russian part of the Soviet Union where we were often invited to give workshops and therapeutic groups. A fair part of academics and practitioners there were impressed by the work based on the existential worldview – this was quite novel and daring at that time and place. Existential therapy training groups gathered many colleagues in Russia, and Russians make up a significant portion of current students. Also quite a few teachers and trainers of the Institute are invited to teach existential therapy at many places in Russia.

Additionally, HEPI was the first independent institution offering training in psychotherapy in the Baltic countries. In 1996, HEPI started a program in existential therapy in Birštonas, a small health resort in the southern part of Lithuania. It proved to be a firm base from which, eventually, a strong and independent center of existential therapy emerged in Eastern Europe that now both actively promotes existential therapy and trains its professionals. Since its start, the student body has always included therapists from Lithuania, Latvia, Estonia, Russia, Belarus, and Ukraine. In such an atmosphere, a unique multicultural context of existential therapy was born and continues to flourish. Thus during the past 20 years Birštonas has become a distinctive "capital" of existential therapy in the vast post-Soviet space.

From the very beginning HEPI sought to integrate a very wide and diverse spectrum of ideas in existential therapy into its training programs. Its programs encompass comprehensive studies of all major schools and their concepts, including Daseinsanalysis (Ludwig Binswanger, Medard Boss, Alice Holzhey-Kunz), Logotherapy and Existential Analysis (Viktor Frankl, Alfried Längle), American humanistic existential therapy (Rollo May, James Bugental, Kirk J. Schneider), and the British School (Ronald Laing, Hans Cohn, Emmy van Deurzen, Ernesto Spinelli). The main point in understanding existential therapy, which the training is based on, is the notion that existential therapy is a process of phenomenological exploration of a person's life-world focused on its especially sensitive and problematic areas and their significant contexts. Difficulties of people seeking help are explored based on the principle of relatedness along with considerations of possibilities and restrictions posed by life. The client's values and his/her relation to existential givens in the context of his/her difficulties are seen as most essential. On the therapist's side, the crucial point is his/her position in the process of development of therapeutic relation and his/her inner attitudes. It is of utmost importance that the therapist's position remains descriptive as opposed to analytic or explanatory, that he/she, while maintaining an "un-knowing" stance, attempts to understand what happens in the client's life and in the therapeutic relationship, and shares his/her understanding with the client instead of trying to explain or give advice. In the therapeutic relationship, the therapist's openness, genuineness, emotional resonance, and respect are especially valued and encouraged.

The Existential Therapy training program consists of two stages or levels – initial and professional. Each stage lasts two years. The curriculum includes existential philosophy and the theory of existential therapy, students have an intensive group therapy experience of over 100 hours, while every student has to undergo not less than 110 hours of personal therapy. Individual and group supervisions have great significance and given lots of attention. Upon successful completion of their studies, students are awarded the Diploma in Psychotherapy (Existential Therapy). Graduates with extensive therapeutic practice may continue studies in the Existential Therapy Supervision program that takes two more years, after which they are eligible to join the team of the supervisors of the Institute.

At present the staff of the Institute includes 40 teachers, trainers, therapists, and supervisors from Lithuania, Latvia, Estonia, and Russia. In the course of almost two decades, the Diploma has been awarded to almost 200 practitioners from a number of different countries – Lithuania, Latvia, Estonia, Russia, Belarus, Ukraine, and Kazakhstan. Since 2000, initial training in existential therapy has occasionally been offered in Russia. During the last 15 years five groups have been organized in various regions of Russia, from Moscow to Siberia. At present a training group in Saint Petersburg is being planned.

In 2015, HEPI was audited by the experts of the European Association for Psychotherapy. They acknowledged that the training programs of the Institute conformed to the standards of the European Association for Psychotherapy (EAP), and it was granted the status of a European Accredited Psychotherapy Training Institute. This means that graduates with the Diploma in psychotherapy studies of the Institute are also eligible to receive the European Certificate of Psychotherapy.

HEPI continues to develop the existential group therapy model, which is hinged on the idea that the dynamics of the group are based on building a common life in the group along with its continuous reflection and solution of problems in the "here and now" in the emerging relationships within the group. The group process is a fragment of life that is finite time wise, but has no pre-set framework or defined content. It grows out of the interactions of the participants and the therapist that revolve around their unique life stories and experiences, and around the situations born directly in the group. Thus the life of the group "materializes" participants' ways of being-in-the-world and their problematic aspects (unrealistic attitudes, inadequacy to requirements of specific situations in life, lack of relatedness to others, incongruity of one's relation to existential givens, and so on).

Since 2007, HEPI has offered a training program in group psychotherapy based on this existential model. The training is performed in a small group of eight to ten students. The program consists of three stages: (1) students participate in therapeutic/ training groups facilitated and supervised by experienced group therapists; experiences of each group are scrutinized in "live" discussions and in written form, through participants' and supervisors' mandatory written analyses of the group and of the therapist's work; (2) students in turn act as therapists in the same group, being supervised by experienced therapists; the work of student therapists is continuously discussed and analyzed, the same way as in stage one; (3) on their own, each student has to organize and facilitate a real therapeutic group, which has to be supervised. This program, in spite of being long-term and complicated, is quite popular. Along with the Existential Therapy program it attracts students from various countries.

The East European Association for Existential Therapy

A milestone in the development of existential therapy in the Baltic countries and also in Russia was the Eastern European Association for Existential Therapy (EEAET) founded in 2003 in Birštonas, Lithuania, by a group of 37 existential therapists. In 2015, this Association had over 300 members in Lithuania, Latvia, Estonia, Russia, Belarus (these countries have their sections represented in the Board of the Association), Ukraine, Kazakhstan, the United States, Canada, Australia, Spain, Serbia, Poland, Germany, and Great Britain. The Honorary Members of the Association include Dr. Aleksandras Alekseičikas (Lithuania), Professor Simon du Plock and Professor Ernesto Spinelli (UK), and Dr. Kirk J. Schneider (US). The EEAET is a member organization of the EAP.

The Association publishes the annual journal *Existentia: Psychology and Psychotherapy* (in Russian and English). It contains theoretical papers, interviews with prominent psychotherapists, case analyses, and discussions of therapeutic practice. Most authors, coming from various countries, belong to the existential therapy community of the Association. Some publications are translated from, and in cooperation with, the psychotherapy.net website. Dace Purena, the editor of *Existentia*, periodically initiates indirect discussions involving outstanding figures of existential therapy in our countries, Great Britain, and the United States (their topics vary from money in psychotherapy, to the image of a therapist, to the experience of encounter in therapeutic relations, and so forth).

The EEAET organizes and stimulates communication and cooperation between existential therapy professionals in Eastern Europe, hosts a biennial conference in Birštonas "The Existential Dimension in Counselling and Psychotherapy," and seminars and workshops by the most prominent figures in the field of existential therapy. Professor Simon du Plock has been a frequent guest at events in Birštonas since 1997. Birštonas has also been visited by Professor Ernesto Spinelli, Dr. Kirk J. Schneider, Professor Mick Cooper, Dr. Greg Madison, and Dr. Alice Holzhey-Kunz. Seminars in Birštonas were given by Professor Emmy van Deurzen, Professor Alfried Längle, and Professor Bo Jacobsen, also by Dr. Gerd Achenbach from Germany whose philosophical praxis in its attitude is akin to existential therapy. Such multifaceted collaboration with eminent representatives of various schools of existential therapy allows us to feel a part of an international existential therapy community, it encourages discussions within our own professional community and ensures that more and more psychologists and psychotherapists get "infected" by the existential "virus."

Currently the Association is also part of the newly founded Federation for Existential Therapy in Europe, which was founded at the World Congress of Existential Therapy in London in 2015.

Conclusion

In the course of the 20 years of its existence, the center of existential therapy training and studies in Birštonas, Lithuania (which one might reasonably call the Birštonas school of existential therapy) has become an important part of the world existential therapy community. It has had and continues to have a very significant influence upon the development of existential therapy in the Baltics, as well as influence on the dissemination of existential therapy in Russia and Belarus through offering training in existential therapy at various locations in those countries and short-term seminars on existential therapy theory and practice. Based on its own distinctive roots, it continuously strives to be an integral part of a wider and extremely diverse field of ideas and notions of existential therapy.

Existential Therapy in Russia and Ukraine

Semjon Yesselson

For over 70 years humanitarian thought in the Soviet Union was separated by the "Iron Curtain" from humanitarian thought in the rest of the world. The works of colleagues from other countries were not translated unless they were considered to be Marxist, while scientific periodicals were kept in special storage at a number of leading libraries and access to them was restricted. These were the conditions in which humanitarian thought developed, largely grounded in its own cultural tradition. This applies to existential praxis as well. The development of existential praxis on the territory of the former Union of Soviet Socialist Republics USSR is connected with two figures: a physician, psychiatrist and psychotherapist Alexandr Efimovich Alexeychik, who lives in Vilnius, in Lithuania, and a physician and psychiatrist Andrei Vladimirovich Gnezdilov, who lives in Saint Petersburg.

The approach to existential praxis connected with Alexandr Efimovich Alexeychik emerged in the late 1960s. Most significantly Alexeychik's worldview was affected by two central figures: Antanas Smalstis and Alexeychik's father. The first was a prominent Lithuanian psychiatrist, student, and follower of Eugen Bleuler who taught us to pay attention to the slightest nuances and manifestations of the patient, and to the whole context of the patient's life. The father of A.E. Alexeychik started his path as a young Belorussian peasant and became a professor of medicine, a surgeon, and survived three concentration camps during the Second World War. His father came to similar conclusions as Victor Frankl did at the same time. He told him that the memory of his one-and-a-half-year-old son, and the conviction that he had no right to die helped him to survive the German camps. He taught his son that the spiritual dimension of our existence is defining in the issues of health and illness, life and death.

Starting in the mid-1970s, Alexeychik led an annual conference ("All-Union" until 1992, and "International" thereafter), which provided the context for the growth of an original school of existential therapy. His approach is called Intensive Therapeutic Life (ITL) and is rooted in Russian existentialism. Its key figures include Fyodor Dostoevsky, and such existentially oriented thinkers and philosophers as: Nikolai Berdyaev, Vasily Rozanov, Sergei Levytsky, Semyon Frank, Ivan Illyin, Lev Shestov, and the Metropolitan Anthony of Sourozh. The pivot of the approach created by Alexeychik is Metropolitan Anthony of Sourozh's proposition that if a person falls very ill it is impossible to recover and live the same life. It is only possible to recover in another different way of living, by turning the steering wheel of your life, because the roots of illness go deep into the ground – into the way one leads his life. Illness in this context is understood as disturbance to the holism of human life as a result of:

- Focusing on its individual aspects.
- Disappearance of entire layers from it.
- Alienation: the estrangement from one's own life.

The key to this approach of therapy is the image of a right (healthy) way of life and God as a source of this image. As a consequence, Alexeychik's school of existential therapy had a semi-underground existence in the atheist USSR and the opportunity to undertake a PhD was blocked for him.

For generations people in the USSR learned not to express their thoughts and hid them somewhere: individuals' thoughts very often did not correspond with their words, and their words did not correspond to their actions. This way of life influenced existential therapy at Alexeychik's school. A great importance is given here to the correlation between the words and actions of the client, while demonstrating to him/her the discovered inconsistencies. The treatment proceeds as follows: the therapist, working with the client, seeks to create a new perspective for him, so that the client sees what different kind of a person he could be. The client is enabled to experience himself in a therapeutic group differently – as a better, stronger, more coherent individual than in his/her everyday life. And such transfiguration in the group therapy begins to influence his "real" life outside the group. Here is an example from therapeutic practice of one of Alexeychik's followers:

> A middle-aged woman came to group therapy. In the course of the group she revealed that her stepfather regularly raped her from the age of 11 to 17 and then she ran away from home. She complained to her mother but her mother was in denial and refused to listen to her. Her biological father was alcoholic and it was meaningless to appeal to him. By the time the group was held, according to her words, her stepfather had divorced from her mother and she was safe and sound and lived a cheerful life.
>
> At first the therapist asked her a question:
>
> - Do you seek protection?
> - Yes, I do.
> - Do you want somebody to protect you?
> - Yes, I do.

Then the therapist started working with the male participants in the group and eventually asked them who was ready to protect this woman. At the beginning the men in the group found it hard to realize that it would be necessary to be truly ready to do something real and not to simply role-play for the duration of the group. Finally one man stood up. He had announced earlier the issue that he did not know how to be a proper father. Very difficult work was going on in his soul. It was evident that in standing up he was overcoming himself. He came to the woman and asked her to give him the address of her former rapist stepfather. He took the address, got dressed, and went to the door. At that moment the woman stopped him. It appeared to be enough for her that at least one man in her life wanted to protect her. When the man returned to his seat, they both looked like different people. Speaking about it after the end of the therapeutic group he said that he felt that it helped him to see what he was able to do. And he began becoming a father. He found his daughter, who lived in another country, thousands of kilometers away, and revived his relationship with her.

This approach is further characterized by:

- The move to the "You," towards compassion, helping one another, payment, or redemption for one another, to being or living for the "You" (for another individual), emergence of the "We," "Us" – in the mutual encounter of beings for the sake of the "You."

Towards the creation of a therapeutic community:

- Encouragement of the emergence of courage to see one's life not in time, but in eternity and in the light of this vision, to reduce the fuss, and to increase the value of one's words and actions.

Sometimes, throughout the course of life, illnesses disappear and wounds heal. In Russia, people say: "Time heals." Spiritual wounds sometimes take decades to heal. In the ITL therapeutic group, the therapist sets him/herself the task of speeding up this process so that wounds heal in days, hours, or minutes. For that purpose, many opportunities are offered to people so that they do not discuss their lives but allow life to manifest itself. The therapist helps to make evident the contradictions in a person's life, helps the person to face both familiar difficulties in his or her life, and those which he or she would have to face if they do not make any changes in their life. Often what happens is that the individual finds him/herself in a parable about their life. In Alexeychik's ITL, jokes and ironic stories are often used to allow clients to see the paradox of their life situation, to understand the self-irony, and to move away from their life positions.

The accenting of Alexeychik's approach in the direction of using texts with descriptions of life (or some episodes of it) of the people, who have a great influence in the client's eyes (mainly the lives of the Saints), has led to the emergence of a new variation of this kind of therapeutic approach called the "narrative tuning fork." It was developed by Alexeychik's follower Semjon Yesselson, founder and head of the Board of the International Institute of Existential Consultancy (Russia-Ukraine). Yesselson starts from the belief that the absence of an internal spiritual and ethical foundation is representative of Soviet and post-Soviet people. For almost 70 years, religious believers were persecuted in the Soviet Union; and as for the believers in the new faith – Communism – they were virtually destroyed by the beginning of the 1950s during Stalin's repression. Soviet people of the second half of the twentieth century based their life decisions on the new ethics of family and social traditions emerging right before their eyes. The collapse of the Soviet Union destroyed those foundations as well. As a result, many life difficulties, for which post-Soviet people seek existential consultants and therapists, relate to the uncertainty characteristic of the ethical dimension of their existence. The introduction of solution models of various difficult life conflicts from the Lives of Saints, or from the Holy Scripture to their therapy, allow clients to correlate with them as with a tuning fork and find the basis for solving their own difficulties. Some examples of themes introduced include: "The price of freedom in our lives and in the life of the prophet Moses," "Friendship and power in our lives and in the life of St. Gregory the Illuminator of Armenia," "Love and death in our lives and in life of St. Xenia of St. Petersburg," and "Patience in our lives and in the life of St. Maximus the Greek."

The second approach to existential practice is linked to Andrei Vladimirovich Gnezdilov and dates back to the 1970s. Andrei Vladimirovich Gnezdilov is a Doctor of Medicine, Professor, and former Head of the Gerontopsychiatry Department of the Bekhterev Institute. He holds an Honorary PhD from Essex University (Great Britain), and is the chair of the Association of Oncopsychologists of Russia. He founded the first hospice in the Soviet Union, and is the author of numerous therapeutic fairy tales. His therapeutic approach is rooted in the "Silver Age" of Russian culture, in the works of representatives of Russian humanitarian culture at the beginning of the twentieth century, primarily in the practice of M. Voloshin. (The "Silver Age" is the name given to the incredible age of development in all areas of Russian culture that occurred in the early-twentieth century before the Revolution of 1917.) Maximilian Voloshin is a poet, a painter, a mystic, a pacifist, and a humanist. At the beginning of the First World War he invented and held "consoling mysteries" in his house in Koktebel, Crimea. He invited people of culture, for example, poets, painters, to participate in the mysteries. With a help of decorations and costumes he created a magical atmosphere and stimulated a kind of a fairy-tale happening, in which people started to be like children. At the same time in his poems Voloshin foresaw and predicted the catastrophe of the forthcoming Revolution. But he did not see what could be done to prevent it. In his mysteries Voloshin tried to teach the participants to be like children and not to fear the inescapable. During the civil war, which unfolded on the territory of the former Russian Empire after the First World War, the poet tried to temper the animosity, rescuing the persecuted in his home in Crimea; first the Red Communist fighters from the White counter-revolutionaries, and then, after the change of government in Crimea, the White fighters from the Red, saving many lives on both sides.

The pivot of Gnezdilov's therapy is the notion of the "miraculous dimension of our being" and the ability to solve problems by appealing to this dimension. A significant number of Gnezdilov's patients are critically and terminally ill patients. The realities of their environment irrefutably prove to them that death is inevitable. Adult consciousness, logic, and experience bring no hope. In Gnezdilov's practice, an existential time shift occurs and the time of childhood, the memories of childhood, come to the foreground.

People become like children, with a child's creative fantasy, openness to the world, and trust in life. The possibility of believing in miracles emerges and problems that appear unresolvable for adults begin to be resolved. Therapeutic tales, puppets, existential theatre, bell therapy (therapy by using church bells, ancient church musical slabs called "Semantrons," and also Tibetian singing bowls), creating a unique antiquary space that includes the clothing of all times and nations, antique furniture, and other antiquities. These help the therapist create a space for the "encounter" of the client with the miraculous dimension of their being. Here is an extract from the story of a psychologist, a participant in a Gnezdilov seminar called "The illnesses of our loved ones":

> At the door we were greeted by a polite gentleman, who was dressed in XIX century clothing (wearing a top hat and a frock-coat). He bowed and kindly invited us to the magic Castle. He elegantly met every woman, kissing her hand and showing the way to the living room. He helped us to take off our coats and offered us a mirror with frozen icicles in it, noting that it was a mirror of the Snow Queen. Warning us not to look there for too long, so that the cold would not creep into our souls. Then we saw a huge number of objects, the purpose of which was a mystery to us. Someone from our group accidentally hit some enormous metal disc, and it began to spin slowly and an old melody started playing. There were lots of shelves in the room, and all the shelves were full of dolls and puppets from all ages and nations. The old butler (Gnezdilov) took my hand gently, led towards the shelves and asked me to choose a doll which I think is looking at me and which had already chosen me. He said not to hurry, as the doll could be shy and could hide from me. Something incredible was happening. I felt as if I managed to get through the Platform 9¾ on Kings Cross Station and found myself in the magic Castle! (Zinevych 2015).

Gnezdilov considers the last stage of life as its culmination. Fear of death disappears and capabilities to endure the inevitable suffering appear. Often, when the fear of death disappears, patients are able to determine what for them is the most important task to accomplish. The specter of death vanishes, time stops and they are able to accomplish their purpose in life.

Training

For many years now, existential therapists and consultants have been trained in three long-term programs in the former Soviet Union. There are three well-established existential therapy long-term training pathways in Russia, Ukraine, and the Baltic states. The first program introduces all the existential therapy approaches that exist in the contemporary world. The program has been on offer since 1996 by HEPI in Birštonas, Lithuania. This four-year-long program is headed by Rimantas Kočiūnas. It also trains supervisors. In accordance with the requirements of the EAP, it was brought into compliance with the European Certificate of Psychotherapy. In 2015, the Institute received EAP's accreditation as an educational institution. At different times, HEPI has offered training groups in Moscow, Ivanovo (Central Russia), and Surgut (Siberia, Russia).

The second program trains in the existential therapy tradition of Alexeychik and Gnezdilov. This four-year-long program has been operating since 1999 at the International Institute of Existential Consultancy (MIEK) and is headed by Semjon Yesselson. Currently it is being reorganized as a six-year-long program. At present, there exist seven MIEK branches: Moscow, Nizhny Novgorod, Rostov-on-Don, and Khabarovsk (Russia); Kiev and Odessa (Ukraine); and Almaty (Kazakhstan). Until spring 2014, there were two additional programs in Donetsk and Sevastopol. The branch in Donetsk was closed because the majority of the students became refugees and departed in different directions to Russia and Ukraine. In Sevastopol some students were from Crimea and some came from the nearer parts of Ukraine. Since January 2015 the railway and bus communication has been interrupted, and people do not dare to cross the no-man's land between the borders by foot in winter. Most students of the Donetsk and Sevastopol branches dispersed to other branches of the Institute. In such a way people reacted to the challenges of life. MIEK's training programs are characterized by a process of constant reorganization according to each training group's features of life, and the differences between programs on different educational platforms. Programs focus less on erudition in the fields of existential philosophy and psychology, and more on world classics in literature and cinema, which help to examine one's own life with all its devastating and sick, creative and healthy tendencies – that is, broadly and more diversely. MIEK's motto is: "Physician, heal thyself." This means that priority is given to therapeutic work with students.

A feature of MIEK is its creative search, and the invention of new forms of existential praxis. One of these new forms is "existential theatre therapy." In this type of practice, the whole theatre process – from decision-making as who to be in the upcoming play (an actor in a particular role, prompter, director, lighting technician, set designer, costume designer, musical director, theatre critic, bartender, etc.), competition for certain roles, and up to the analysis that takes place after the performance – become moments of the existential therapeutic process.

Another form of therapy developed at MIEK is the "existential journey," a mobile existential therapeutic group that prepares its members for a certain event and summarizes the results of the Encounter with this event; for example, a journey to St. Petersburg to Gnezdilov is undertaken on the theme: "The illnesses of our loved ones." The group meeting takes place on the train on the way to see Gnezdilov, the group works on requests for the Encounter with the Master, and on the way back, works on the results of the Encounter.

A third form of existential praxis invented at MIEK is the existential project: "The memory of future generations." For this project, MIEK students and teachers work on creating their own existential family archives based on accounts of their older generation relatives of the key stories of their lives. This work aims to transform the stories into a message to their descendants so that they can draw lessons from preceding lives and correct mistakes. This work includes among other things a transformation of the relationships of project participants with the older generations of their families. The attention of children, grandchildren, and great grandchildren to the life experience of the older people often uncovers new meanings for them and radically improves mental and physical health.

MIEK characteristically adheres to a special position in existential philosophy as formulated by Yesselson and called "the radical existential worldview." In this perspective a clear dividing line between psychology and psychotherapy, between existential therapy and other forms of therapy, and the ontological status of the living world and its consequences for existential therapy is formulated.

In 2015, thanks to the efforts of existentialist academic and psychologist O.V. Lukyanov and his followers, the Siberian Institute of Phenomenological and Existential Psychology was founded in Kemerovo (Siberia, Russia). The Institute plans to establish its own long-term training program for training existential therapists. The work of the Institute will be based on the existential-phenomenologic approach, developed by the British school of existential therapy, and will conduct a dialogue with Eastern-European colleagues, followers of "The intensive therapeutic life" approach.

In addition to HEPI and MIEK's long-term training programs, many other training programs, created in the countries of Central Europe, are unfolding in the territory of Eastern Europe. Since 1999, a long-term program for training existential analysts has been operating in Moscow – GLE-International, Vienna (headed by Alfried Längle). The duration of the program is four years. In 2012, an educational program, GLE-International, started in Kiev (Ukraine) and in Riga (Latvia).

In 2013, an educational project for the training of logotherapists was established in Moscow by the Victor Frankl Institute, Vienna, Austria (headed by Alexander Batthyány). The duration of the program is two years.

In 2015, the Dasein Analysis Institute headed by Dr. Alice Holzhey-Kunz (Switzerland, President of the Swiss Society for Hermeneutic Anthropology and Daseinsanalysis) was founded in Minsk (Belarus). In 2018 it started a one-and-a-half-year-long program for teaching Daseinsanalysis in Russia.

In the 1990s and early 2000s The International Institute for Humanistic Studies carried out training programs in Russia. The seminars were conducted by J. Bugental and his colleagues. The Russian-American program on existential psychology was organized by E. Mazur, PhD. However, the program has not been implemented to date.

Moreover, an original existential praxis has gained followers on the territory of Russia called "existential fencing." Since 2002, the preparation of existential fencing specialists has been carried out by the existential therapist V.V. Letunovsky, a graduate of the School of Existential Education and Initial Treatment of Karlfried Dürckheim (Todtmoos-Rütte, Germany). This praxis is based on the proposition that the way you fence is the way you live. Everything that happens during the fencing session becomes the subject of a detailed existential analysis. The length of the program is two years. In 2018 an Association of therapeutic meaningful fencing was created.

Around the three long-term training programs for existential consultants and therapists (the programs of HEPI, MIEK, and GLE-International), three large societies of existentialist practitioners have been formed:

- The East European Association for Existential Therapy.
- International Confederation for Existential Therapy and Counseling, comprising two associations: National Association for Existential Consultants and Therapists of Russia and Ukrainian Association for Existing Counseling and Therapy.
- The Association of Existential-Analytic Psychologists and Psychotherapists.

The East European Association for existential therapy holds an annual conference in Birštonas (Lithuania). The National Association for Existential Consultants and Therapists of Russia and Ukrainian Association for Existential Counseling and Therapy jointly conduct the annual festival, which had been held on Cape Tarkhankut (Crimea) until 2014 and since then in Belarus. The members of the Association of Existential-Analytic Psychologists and Psychotherapists organize every two years the GLE-International conferences in Moscow with the participation of Alfried Längle, and once a year his Russian followers meet together at "post-congresses," where they watch and discuss the video materials from the international congresses, which Längle holds in different countries.

Each of the societies publishes journals in Russian. Since 2002, MIEK has published the journal *The Existential Tradition: Philosophy, Psychology, Psychotherapy* (editor-in-chief S. Yesselson). It is published twice a year and is a MIEK society journal. It is published with the support of the Institute of Existential Psychology and Life Enhancement (headed by D. Leontiev). Since 2008, the journal of the East European Association for Existential Therapy *Existencia* has been published once a year. Since 2009, *Existential Analysis* has been produced once a year and is a journal of the Association of Existential-Analytic Psychologists and Psychotherapists.

In 2001, the Moscow State University professor and psychologist-existentialist D. Leontiev created the Institute of Existential Psychology and Life Enhancement. The main achievement of the institute has become the organization of Russian conferences on existential psychology with international participation held every three years. These conferences became the only platform where existential therapists and consultants of different approaches, who practice on the territory of the former USSR, as well as existentially oriented philosophers and educators, can meet. In 1992, Professor D. Leontiev founded the publishing house "Smysl" [Meaning], which exists up to the present time. Thanks to him a considerable amount of literature on existential psychology has been translated and published in Russian.

The Philosophical Roots of Russian Existentialism

Dmitry Leontiev

Tracing the philosophical roots of existentialist thought in Russia is a risky and sophisticated enterprise for two reasons. First, the definition and borders of existentialism are still debatable. In its narrow meaning, it is a label attached to a tradition in European philosophy beginning with Kierkegaard and embracing Heidegger, Jaspers, Sartre, and Camus, to name only the most widely acknowledged representatives (though not all of them would accept this label). In its broad meaning, existentialism can be identified with the worldviews opposing the idea of determination, predictability, and orderliness of all human life; its core cannot be defined unambiguously.

Having made several attempts to define an existentialist worldview (Leontiev 2009, 2016), I have come to the inescapable conclusion that it is composed of seven features, none of which (nor even an incomplete combination) would be sufficient on their own:

1 Phenomenological orientation, sensitivity to what is going on here and now, to the immediate reality, to the pulse of life, as opposed to viewing it through the prism of pre-established categories and learned stereotypes.

2 Awareness and recognition of one's being in the world rather than in a situation, and one's interaction with the world as the roots of the inner world.
3 The ultimate unpredictability and changeability of life despite the empirical probability of its successful prediction in some periods. "Existence precedes essence" (Sartre 1948, p. 28); that is, we cannot fully deduce what is actually happening from any pre-existing essences (traits, social class, etc.), though statistically the prediction may be quite successful.
4 The specifically human capacity of self-reflection based on self-detachment (Frankl 1969), the capacity of taking an attitude toward oneself.
5 A philosophy of life elaborated through an awareness of general laws and regularities as the premise for finding answers to more special questions.
6 Openness to the realm of the possible beyond and above the realm of the necessary, the causal laws.
7 The capacity for self-determination, or auto-determination; the control over the course of one's life using the resources of self-reflection and the anthropological capacities of self-transcendence and self-detachment (Frankl 1969). An existential way of living and thinking presumes that my behavior is predictable and controlled by external and internal causes, pressures, stereotypes, drives, and so on, as long as my self-reflection is switched off; when I switch it on, I start seeing meaning and optional possibilities and become capable of making any potentially available choice; nearly everything can be different and can be changed.

The second difficulty is a rather peculiar historical fate of Russian philosophy. Unlike Western philosophy, it is quite young. The Orthodox Christian religion for centuries dominated Russian intellectual life to a much greater degree than its Western European Catholic and Protestant branches; one can hardly trace, in Russia, any attempts of philosophical thought that would exceed the religious agenda, not to mention being independent of it, earlier than the nineteenth century (sometimes an agenda of Russian identity and national destiny was added to this). Great Russian writers (first of all Lev Tolstoy and Fedor Dostoyevsky) were more broadminded and influential than philosophers in raising philosophical, including psychological, issues. This is why many Russian philosophers of the early-twentieth century take as their starting point Tolstoy and Dostoyevsky, rather than the Western European philosophical tradition, and this is why Tolstoy and Dostoyevsky (and to a lesser extent Chekhov and Solzhenitsyn) are referred to much more than any other Russian authors in Western publications related to existentialism.

The short flourishing period of Russian philosophy began at the very end of the nineteenth century and lasted about three decades (the so-called "Silver Age" of Russian culture); soon after the Revolution of 1917, many thinkers had to emigrate and some were forcibly deported. In the early 1930s strict ideological control in Soviet intellectual life became all-embracing, and no non-Marxist work could be published. However, there were some philosophers who pretended to be Marxists and/or non-philosophers and developed highly original existentialist ideas without the opportunity to have them published: Mikhail Bakhtin, Sergei Rubinstein, and Merab Mamardashvili. Their brilliant philosophical works have been published posthumously, since the fall of Communism.

So we shall begin with the highlights of existentialist thinking in the writings of Tolstoy and Dostoyevsky, proceed with the "Silver Age" philosophers, especially Nikolai Berdyaev, and finally present the "underground" philosophers of the Soviet era: Bakhtin, Rubinstein, and Mamardashvili.

Tolstoy and Dostoyevsky

The role of literature in Russian spiritual life through the nineteenth and twentieth centuries has been a defining one; much more so than the role of philosophy, and comparable to the role of religion (among the educated classes). Lev Tolstoy (1828 – 1910) and Fedor Dostoyevsky (1821 – 1881) occupy the first two ranks in the hierarchy of Russian writers, even down to the present day; in a recent survey (http://www.levada.ru/2016/03/02/ko-vsemirnomu-dnyu-pisatelya/) Tolstoy was beyond compare as the leading writer (in an open question, 45 percent nominated him as a prominent Russian writer); Dostoyevsky was second with only 23 percent, followed by Anton Chekhov with 18 percent. Writers were especially influential in the second half of the nineteenth century; no wonder that early writings of many philosophers of the "Silver Age" (Berdyaev, Shestov, Vassily Rosanov, and some others) either took the form of essays or literary criticism, or explicitly sprang from the philosophical analysis of Tolstoy and Dostoyevsky.

Besides their famous novels, both Tolstoy and Dostoyevsky have left a number of non-fiction writings, especially Tolstoy, who had a strong sense of mission to teach and disseminate, and to educate uneducated people. Due to this he was sometimes labeled a moralist. Nevertheless he never ceased his spiritual quest in the depths of his soul. Both writers' agenda were focused, first, around the individual search for God (on individual paths aside from conformist confessional ways), and second, around the ethical problems of social injustice.

"Confessions" was the first non-fiction book in which Lev Tolstoy tried to explicate his existential search for meaning in life. This was probably the first analysis of this problem in European thought. The book was completed in 1882 but was prohibited from being published because of the author's critical position toward the official religion, and it only appeared in print for the first time in 1906. In mature adulthood, at the peak of his success and happiness, financially secure, a very popular writer with growing international fame and happily surrounded by the loving family, the author found himself asking the question "What is the meaning of life?". He described this situation in terms of sudden stops in the course of living, of sudden doubts "as if I didn't know how to live, what to do; then it passed away and I started living as before, and those stops in the course of living were always accompanied by uniform questions 'Why?' and 'What then?', and at first those questions seemed to me quite childish, but it was impossible to do anything without resolving those questions" (Tolstoy 1983, p. 115). After a long period of seeking answers to these questions, he came to the final conclusion: "I found that I was misled not because my thoughts were wrong, but because my life was wrong" (Tolstoy 1983, p. 147). Tolstoy made two main discoveries that he explicated in this essay. First, many thinkers tried to figure out what a good life should be, trying to reach a generally valid answer; Tolstoy also tried (and failed) to find the answer this way before he came to the realization that the question about the meaning of life can be addressed only to one's own individual life. The second insight was that meaning is a matter of real living rather than reflecting on it; meaningful living is primary to the meaning of life. Tolstoy concluded: "What is necessary for making sense of life is, first of all, that the life itself be not meaningless and not evil, and then, after this, the reason to understand it" (Tolstoy 1983, p. 147). These two insights also underlay later psychological theories of meaning in life (Adler 1980; Frankl 1973).

In the final two decades of his life Tolstoy was concerned with finding and compiling recommended readings for those who try to make the best of their lives. He published several anthologies; the last and the most elaborate of them, *The Path of Living*, was published in 1910, the year of Tolstoy's death (Tolstoy 1993). It is a systematized collection of wise thoughts, partly taken from different sources (religious, philosophical, and literary, Russian, Western, and Eastern), sometimes adapted and modified by Tolstoy, partly being his own thoughts and aphorisms. In line with his insight from "Confessions," Tolstoy stated that life as it is, whatever it could be, is the supreme good available to us (Tolstoy 1993, p. 459).

Among the key topics of this voluminous book, some are directly relevant to the existentialist way of thinking. As always, Tolstoy stresses the importance of faith and the search for God within oneself, but rejects confessional church and conventional rituals, trying to turn readers towards their personal way of salvation and liberation instead of attempting to save the world. "Just get used to do what 'all' require – and in a blink you will find yourself doing bad things and considering them good" (Tolstoy 1993, p. 240). Conscience is the only and supreme judge.

Another important topic is that of effort: "To disclose one's own soul to oneself, a person must make the efforts of consciousness; that is why these efforts of consciousness are the main business of the person's life" (Tolstoy 1993, p. 309). "When a person is doing good only because he is used to do good, this is not yet the good life. The good life begins when a person makes an effort for being good" (Tolstoy 1993, p. 314). "Effort makes the difference between humans and animals. Saying that I cannot abstain from doing a bad thing means the same as saying that I am an animal rather than a human being" (Tolstoy 1993, p. 316).

The third existential topic is the importance of the present. "There is no time beyond the present moment," says Tolstoy. "However, all our life resides in this moment. That's why one should apply all one's powers in this single moment" (Tolstoy 1993, p. 322). He further developed this idea: "Time exists only for the life of the body. Human spiritual essence is always beyond time. It is because the activity of human spiritual essence is only in the effort of consciousness. And the effort of consciousness is always beyond time, for it is always in the present, and the present is beyond time" (Tolstoy 1993).

An important topic is the complicated relationships between the spiritual and the bodily parts of the human being. "In order to learn to abstain [from bad things], one should learn to bifurcate into the bodily and the spiritual person and to make the bodily person not to do what it wills but rather what the spiritual person wills" (Tolstoy 1993, p. 337). This bifurcation is one of the most relevant vs. pertaining issues in Tolstoy's later writings. "Self-denial is not the denial of oneself, but rather the shift of my Self from my animal essence to the spiritual one. Self-denial does not mean denying one's life; on the contrary, the denial of the bodily life means strengthening one's authentic spiritual life" (Tolstoy 1993, p. 368).

Probably the deepest source of Tolstoy's philosophical insights is his *Philosophical Journal*, notes he made for himself between 1901 and his death in 1910 (Tolstoy 2003). Here we see the living process of intellectual struggles with the central existential problems of life that are presented in varying, incomplete forms, unlike the finalized clear messages in *The Path of Living*. The starting point is the distinction between inauthentic life, lacking the genuine properties of living, that the majority, however, call life, and authentic life in the awareness of its divine origin. Nikolai Berdyaev, who was generally rather critically disposed toward Tolstoy's philosophical ideas, highly appreciated this distinction of two aspects of life as the mark of his geniality and greatness (Berdyaev 1991a). In fact, more than this, Tolstoy distinguished three, rather than two kinds of life: "(1) vegetative, unconscious life; (2) life in the awareness of oneself as a separate being; (3) life in the awareness of oneself as a divine essence within the limits of a person" (Tolstoy 2003, p. 22). The question *Why live* is the central one; all of a person's beliefs stem from the answer to this question (Tolstoy 2003, p. 30). Tolstoy articulates an overtly existentialist position resonating with his conclusion in "Confessions": "One shouldn't want to live due to wanting to do something, but rather should do it because one lives" (Tolstoy 2003, p. 36); life is the primary thing. However, "life is a serious business" (Tolstoy 2003, p. 39). "Life is a stepwise self-unfolding" (Tolstoy 2003, p. 273).

Later, in his notes of 1903, Tolstoy focused on the problem of our borders. He tried many slightly varied definitions of life such as this: "Life is the awareness of the spiritual (i.e. non-spatial and non-temporal) being restricted within some limits and changing these limits" (Tolstoy 2003, p. 67). It is the awareness of these spiritual, non-spatial, and non-temporal aspects of oneself that urges us to liberate ourselves from the limits within which our spiritual Self is enclosed. "Liberation is implemented only through love. Love is the striving of bringing our spiritual Self from our limits, making the life of other creatures a part of our own Self. This is the essence of morality" (Tolstoy 2003, pp. 74–75).

Tolstoy's views on death logically stem from his views on life. "Life is increasing discovery of the existing things, hence death must be also a discovery, however a discovery of something that we do not and cannot know" (Tolstoy 2003, p. 272). "If you love life, do love death ... Death is the fruit of life" (Tolstoy 2003, p. 170). Later however Tolstoy wrote that "death is not a liberation but rather the termination of liberation process" (Tolstoy 2003, p. 340).

Tolstoy's considerations are in some important aspects similar to Frankl's (1969) dimensional ontology. Their similarity is especially visible in their views on the issue of freedom. Tolstoy states that there can be no freedom for bodily awareness, and there can be no limitations of freedom in spiritual awareness. Hence the answer is that human being is "not free in bodily awareness and free in spiritual awareness. If someone asks, whether human being is free to shift from one mode of awareness to another, the answer would say: life resides only in the spiritual dimension" (Tolstoy 2003, p. 293). "The more you live the spiritual life, the less you depend on the destiny, and vice versa" (Tolstoy 2003, p.78). This distinction of the modes of life and, correspondingly, the modes of self-awareness is critical for the evaluation of egoism. "Egoism is the main law of life. What matters is what you acknowledge as your ego, your consciousness or your body, or, more precisely, your spiritual awareness or your bodily awareness" (Tolstoy 2003, p. 299).

Time also belongs to the most important existential topics in Tolstoy's philosophical journals. While bodily existence proceeds in time and space, spiritual existence proceeds beyond time and space. "Death is the cessation of life in space and time; for those who are not aware of the life beyond space and time, it is the cessation of everything" (Tolstoy 2003, p. 392). Since freedom is related to the spiritual being, it exists also beyond space and time. "In time ... human being is apparently not free; one is free only in the present, in doing beyond time" (Tolstoy 2003, p. 117).

The key idea of Tolstoy's journals can be summarized in his aphorism written a few months before his death: "Human being is aware of oneself as God, and is right, because there is God in them. Human being is aware of oneself as pig, and is right again, because there is a pig in them. But one is badly mistaken when one considers a pig in oneself the God" (Tolstoy 2003, p. 482).

Dostoyevsky's intellectual agenda was partly similar to that of Tolstoy, partly different. As he wrote in one of his letters of 1870, explicating the intention of *The Brothers Karamazov*, "the main issue ... over which I consciously and unconsciously tormented myself all my life is God's existence" (quoted in Rozanov 1989, p. 44). An idea quite similar to Tolstoy's final statement of his "Confessions" can be found in Dostoyevsky's *Brothers Karamazov,* spoken by Alesha, the character mentally closest to the author himself: "Everyone must love life before all the world, before any of its meaning, before any logic, and then the meaning can be found" (Part 2. Book 5. III, quoted in Rozanov 1989, p. 87).

Rozanov was not the only Russian philosopher of the "Silver Age" to be deeply influenced by Dostoyevsky's spiritual inquiries. Berdyaev acknowledged Dostoyevsky's determining impact on his spiritual life (Berdyaev 1991b, p. 26). Berdyaev, however, contrasted Tolstoy and Dostoyevsky, calling the former the artist of what has come to being, and the latter as heading to what is becoming. Dostoyevsky "reveals human nature, investigates it not in its stable core, not in everyday ordinary living, not in normal and normalized forms of existence, but rather in the unconscious, in insanity and crime. In insanity, rather than in sanity, in crime rather than in legitimacy, in unconscious nocturnal rudiments rather than in daily mode of living and in the light of organized conscious soul the depth of human nature can be disclosed, its limits and borders investigated" (Berdyaev 1991b, p. 32). Dostoyevsky was struggling against the ossification of spirit, for restitution of human spiritual depths.

Berdyaev paid special attention to Dostoyevsky's insights of the problems of good and evil through the prism of the issue of freedom. "The good cannot be enforced; the freedom of the good suggests the freedom of the evil. The freedom of the evil leads to the eradication of the freedom itself, to its degeneration into an evil necessity. The denial of the freedom of the evil and the assertion of an exclusive freedom of the good also leads to the denial of freedom, to the degeneration of freedom into a good necessity. But a good necessity is no more good, for the good suggests freedom" (Berdyaev 1991b, p. 58). Dostoyevsky suggests that a person should go toward the acceptance of the truth that would make one free, and this way goes through darkness, tragedy, torments, and doubts; it's the way of trials and experiential knowledge of the good and the evil.

The "Silver Age" philosophers

Tolstoy and Dostoyevsky gave a strong impetus to the generation of philosophers active at the turn of the nineteenth and twentieth centuries. The so-called Russian religious philosophy of the late nineteenth and twentieth centuries grew from Orthodox Christian roots and took the form of a mighty stream of moral philosophy teachings from the 1890s. In the early 1920s, all the outstanding representatives of this tradition were forced to emigrate; among the emigrants this tradition was maintained until the 1950s, though the most important writings cover the period between 1890 and 1930. The most prominent authors from this tradition, who failed to draw a borderline between philosophical and religious discourse were, Vladimir Soloviev, Rev. Sergey Bulgakov, Lev Karsavin, Evgeny Trubetskoi, Semen Frank, Lev Shestov, Vassily Rozanov, Nikolai Losskiy, Nikolai Berdyaev, and others; they represent the whole spectrum of discourse, from mystical-irrational to modern rational ones. Many, though not all, teachings of this tradition explicitly depart from the Christian ideal as the only alternative to utilitarian ethics. A common theme for many of these authors was the criticism of the "striving for happiness" principle of human conduct; the principle of striving for meaning was proposed instead. (In a special paper we analyzed these discussions and their similarity to Victor Frankl's later criticism of the pleasure principle; Leontiev 2005.)

Two authors from this school are more or less consensually classified as existential philosophers: Lev Shestov (1866–1938) and Nikolai Berdyaev (1874 – 1948). The two were close friends and both passed through a number of philosophical influences on the way to their own philosophies: Shestov from the Old Testament through Nietzsche and the existentialist pathos of "groundlessness" to Luther and medieval Christianity, and then to a type of synthetic Judeo-Christian-existentialist philosophy inspired by Kierkegaard (Kurabtsev 2005, p. 35); Berdyaev from Marxism and Orthodox Christianity to the religious existentialist personalism.

Shestov was a person of prophetic nature, he rejected the Apollonian type of rational knowledge (and Berdyaev criticized him for this attitude more than once) and affirmed the changeability, indeterminacy, and groundlessness of everything. The central message of his philosophy was irrationalism, and Camus's *Myth of Sisyphus* was written under strong Shestov influence. Nevertheless, his friends included rationalistic thinkers like Berdyaev, Husserl, and Buber. Trying to summarize Shestov's thoughts – which generally resist any attempt at summarizing – his biographer labeled it "religious-existential anti-intellectocentrismus" (Kurabtsev 2005, p. 268).

Berdyaev was much clearer in his thoughts and writings. Unlike his friend, he did not escape self-labeling, stating that at the center of his studies lay the philosophy of the human person, namely of the existentialist type (Berdyaev 1991c, p. 19). He defined existential philosophy as "the cognition of the meaning of being through the subject" (Berdyaev 1991c). Berdyaev worked very fruitfully at the intersection of religious philosophy and ethics. The issues he considered were those of the human person, freedom, spirituality, creativity, and love. However, he left few if any of the essential problems of human living untouched. His basic anthropology treats human being as "the point of intersection of two worlds" (Berdyaev 1989, p. 296). One is the world of nature; however, human being cannot be fully placed into it; "Human being is essentially a break in the natural world, it cannot be enclosed into it"

(Berdyaev 1989, p. 297). Human being is deeper and more fundamental than one's psychological and biological layers. "Human being may be cognized as an object in the world of objects" (Berdyaev 1999, p. 22). There is, however, another option for human being as aware of oneself as the subject par excellence. Human being does not totally belong to the natural world but rather possesses its own world. "Human being as subject is an act, an effort" (Berdyaev 1999, p. 22). In this sense, Berdyaev called his philosophy existentialist "as the opposition of an objectified philosophy" (Berdyaev 1999, p. 23).

The person is a spiritual, rather than natural, category, not subdued by nature or society (Berdyaev 1999, p. 27). Spirituality coming from one's depths is the power that gives shape and supports the person in human being (Berdyaev 1993, p. 324). The person is holistic and cannot be conceived as a part of any other entity. "Person is opposed to a thing, opposed to the world of objects, it is an active subject, an existential center" (Berdyaev 1999, p. 28). Hence only existential philosophy, not sociological or biological philosophy, is capable of construing a teaching of the human person (Berdyaev 1999, p. 182).

The person is independent of Caesar's kingdom; we are not born from our parents; we are created by God and by oneself. Becoming a person is a human challenge (Berdyaev 1999, p. 28) or a task for an individual (Berdyaev 1993, p. 62). The person is not self-sufficient, having nothing to do with solipsism and ego-centeredness; "fulfillment of the person suggests vision of other persons" (Berdyaev 1999, p. 30). The person is related to superordinate values, to God. "There is no person if there is no superordinate being, no celestial world toward which it is to ascend" (Berdyaev 1999, p. 188). Human self is thus split into an empirical self and an ideal, spiritual self; the whole domain of human ethics emerges from the complicated relationships between these two aspects of self. "Fulfilling a moral law does not mean restricting one's Self for the sake of non-Self; rather it means affirming one's authentic Self; moral conscience means responsibility to oneself, to one's spiritual Self" (Berdyaev 2002, p. 87).

The person is not a substance, it has a dynamic nature; "person is invariance within change" (Berdyaev 1999, p. 28). The life of the person is growing over oneself and overcoming oneself, rather than preserving oneself (Berdyaev 1993, p. 63). "Person is effort and struggle, mastering oneself and the world, overcoming slavery, and liberation" (Berdyaev 1999, p. 181). It is elaborated in a long-term process of choosing and pushing out what is not mine in myself (Berdyaev 1993, p. 312).

Freedom is human creative energy. It is based on the spirit, rather than on nature. "Freedom is first of all freedom of the person" (Berdyaev 1993, p. 81); the quality of life and human dignity is tied up with freedom, hence life might be sacrificed for the sake of freedom, but freedom should not be sacrificed for the sake of life (Berdyaev 1993, p. 83). Freedom is unrelated to society; it has another source that society may only acknowledge. Berdyaev pointed at the inevitable conflict between freedom and happiness (1993, p. 99), at the connection between the striving for happiness and the fear of losing it. "Eudemonistic ethics, be it earthly or heavenly eudemonism, is at the end the ethics of fear, for the person is anxious about the happiness of one's own and of others; the happiness is subject to dangers from all directions and is bought at the price of opportunism in judgments and actions. If I have set happiness as the goal for myself, I am doomed to fear all the time" (Berdyaev 1993, p. 157).

Underground Existentialism of the Soviet period

The Soviet era was the time of the monopolistic Marxist ideology and ideological control, which became total in the early 1930s, though the pressure on non-Marxist thinkers started earlier. In 1922, over 160 Russian intellectuals who disapproved of the Communist regime, among them Berdyaev and a number of other prominent philosophers, were expelled from Soviet Russia (aboard the so-called philosophers' ships). As a result, non-Marxist philosophical thought in the Soviet Union was possible only in private, without any possibility of publication. However, there were three prominent Soviet intellectuals who failed to publish their main philosophical ideas in their lifetime but left a very inspiring existentialist philosophical heritage: Mikhail Bakhtin, Sergei Rubinstein, and Merab Mamardashvili.

Mikhail Bakhtin (1895 - 1973) became widely known and even famous by the end of his life in the fields of linguistics, literary science, and cultural theory. However, his early philosophical manuscripts from the 1920s, and in particular *Toward A Philosophy of Act* that Bakhtin himself called "my philosophical anthropology," were published in Russian only in 1988, with US translation in 1993. Sergei Rubinstein (1889 - 1960) studied philosophy at Marburg; later he made a successful career in the Soviet Union as one of the country's leading psychologists and published only psychological works; however, he has also written a philosophical book, *Human Being and the World*, that was published in its full version only in 1997. Merab Mamardashvili (1930 - 1990) studied Marxist philosophy; however he created a philosophy of his own that many contemporaries rate at the same level as those of Descartes, Kant, Heidegger, and others. He published little during his lifetime, but his legacy consists of a number of audiotaped lecture courses given through the 1980s (ideological control was less strict by then), which were transcribed and published after his untimely death and the collapse of the Soviet Union with its ideological monopolism. Some tenets of his philosophy that may be called radical post-existentialism are presented in Leontiev (2009).

One further common feature of all three authors is that Russian psychology in recent decades has been influenced by them probably more than by philosophers belonging to the classical existential tradition (Kierkegaard, Heidegger, Jaspers, Sartre, Camus, Berdyaev, and others).

Mikhail Bakhtin: From responsible agency to mature dialogism Discussions about the philosophical roots and parallels of Bakhtin's thought usually embrace different versions of the philosophy of language and dialogue. Bakhtin is known mostly for introducing the idea of the dialogical nature of human consciousness, suggesting both an external interpersonal dialogue (he is often compared to Buber) and an inner dialogue, the polyphony of voices within our minds. Bakhtin stated that dialogical relationships are almost universal for all domains of human living: "When dialogue ends, everything ends" (Bakhtin 1984, p. 252). Personal being is always a co-being, a person cannot exist outside a "strained encounter" with another person. A person thus cannot be investigated in objective fashion; "The genuine life of the personality is made available only through a dialogic penetration of that personality, during which it freely and reciprocally reveals itself" (Bakhtin 1984, p. 59).

By the end of the 1920s, Bakhtin had reached his mature dialogism. However, in the early part of the decade he wrote *The Philosophy of Act,* in which he was revealed as an existentialist philosopher. The key ideas of the early Bakhtin's existential account (Bakhtin 2003a) are:

1 "The sole place in being" defining the person's unique viewpoint and unique responsibility; no being can be meaningful if it does not consider its sole place in being (Bakhtin 1984, pp. 39–40). This fundamental fact is essentially an antithesis to Husserl's phenomenological reduction; among being and consciousness, Bakhtin, unlike Husserl, chooses being and shows that we never can get in contact with it unless we acknowledge its fundamental asymmetry.
2 "Particity" ("*uchastnost*"), the form of conscious involvement in events that follows from the unique place in being; this concept is close to existential concepts of presence, engagement, and apartness, but with greater emphasis on responsibility.
3 Responsibility as the conscious acknowledgment of the former, "non-alibi in being" (Bakhtin 1984, p. 39) and as the final implementation of an act once and forever. "One can be responsible for meaning affirmation or nonaffirmation, rather than for the meaning itself" (Bakhtin 1984, p. 42).
4 "Emotional-volitional tone" of an act, the concept close to that of personal meaning: everything I deal with (action or thought), at all moments of the event I am participating in, are given to me colored in an emotional-volitional tone.
5 The act as the sole way of turning opportunities into facticity; this transition is not conceivable within the reality of meaningful contents alone. "It is my signature under the contract rather than its contents that produces obligations" (Bakhtin 1984, p. 37). A meaningful side not associated with the inescapably real oneness is like an unsigned document that does not set obligations for anyone.
6 "'I' as the sole centre from which the act proceeds. From the viewpoint of the acting participatory consciousness, the world is situated around me as the sole centre of my acting" (Bakhtin 1984, pp. 53, 55). "I only depart from myself; all the others I do find" (Bakhtin 1984, p. 67).

To summarize, "Life may be conceived only in its special responsibility. Philosophy of life may be only a moral philosophy.... A life fallen apart from responsibility cannot have philosophy; it is essentially occasional and unrooted" (Bakhtin 1984, p. 51).

Bakhtin's work appears thus as the first coherent (though incomplete) explication of existential philosophical anthropology. Many of Bakhtin's ideas that stayed unpublished until the 1980s have found new birth and elaboration in the writings of other thinkers. However, in many aspects we are still to reach Bakhtin's philosophical anthropology of the 1920s; for instance, to date, human responsibility has nowhere been conceptualized as deeply and thoroughly as in Bakhtin's manuscript.

Another Bakhtin's manuscript, *The Author and the Character in the Aesthetic Activity* (Bakhtin 2003b), which was written a few years after *The Philosophy of Act* and also published posthumously, is a transitional one. He elaborated the concept of meaning, introduced the idea of self-reflection as self-regard mediated by a view from outside, and introduced the distinction of factual me and possible me. This reveals the direction of evolution of his views artificially restricted by the controlling ideological context: from the sole stable point in the world from which I can proceed in my action toward self-transcendence to discover the "outsided" aesthetic position from which I can be given to myself (virtual Other), and to the meaningful possible perspective of my yet-to-be, toward a dialogue with a real Other in the conversational space of interacting meanings.

There is no contradiction between the radical monological existentialism of *Toward a Philosophy of the Act* and the mature dialogism of *Problems of Dostoyevsky's Poetics*, and so forth. Dialogue can develop only between responsible agents. And responsible agency presumes that my action is not based on some truth but rather on something I choose to consider truth and invest myself in while recognizing that this might not be true for another person.

Sergei Rubinstein: Person inside the Being. The general message of Rubinstein's main book is very close to that of Bakhtin's anthropology but with a somewhat different emphasis. It says: "Human being resides within Being, rather than Being residing just outside their consciousness" (Rubinstein 1997, p. 9). Rubinstein opposed his ontological position to the gnoseological view of Descartes and classical German philosophy, in which human being was construed as a being cognizing the world rather than existing in it. This is why for Rubinstein the primary relation is "the one of human being interacting with reality that 'resists' human acting" (Rubinstein 1997, p. 5). The world is also defined by Rubinstein through its relatedness to human being, as "the sum total of persons and things communicating with each other or, more precisely, as the sum total of things and events related to persons" (Rubinstein 1997, p. 10).

Rubinstein avoided labeling his own philosophical approach. His attitude to classical philosophical existentialism was ambiguous. Accepting the primacy of existence over essence, he disapproved of their confrontation and final denial of any human essence in existentialism, because this would deny any determination, any connection to the past. Human essence exists, though it is changeable in the course of existence, which is participating in the process of life. "To live means to change and to reside, to act and to suffer, to maintain and to change" (Rubinstein 1997, p. 23) – change is thus the starting point and the final point of living.

Crucial to Rubinstein's thinking is his distinction between two modes of living. The first one is living as a natural process, which does not transcend immediate vital ties. The second mode of existence is connected with the appearance of self-reflection. It stops or breaks this immediate living process and virtually brings the person beyond its limits. The person takes a position outside it. This is similar to Rollo May's (1981) description of the pause as the location point of human freedom. In this second mode of existence, the human person is not only related to the world and determined by it, but also determines one's attitude to it, becoming consciously self-determined. Here Rubinstein finds the roots of human freedom, again in quite a similar way to May's formulations: "Human being can change the given conditions, but first these must be given to him/her, he/she must depart from them" (Rubinstein 1997, p. 85). This is why "freedom is not only the rejection of the givens, as existentialism declares, but also their affirmation" (Rubinstein 1997, pp. 85–86).

Rubinstein's view of love is rather close to Frankl's view on the meaning of love (Frankl 1973). "Love appears as enforced affirmation of the human existence of the given person for another one … To be loved means to be the most existing creature of all" (Rubinstein 1997, p. 97). In order to exist as a human being I must exist for another one as a human condition rather than an object of cognition. Rubinstein's manuscript is completed by his statement on the meaning of life: "The meaning of human life is being a source of light and warmth for other people. Being the consciousness of the Universe and the conscience of the humankind. Being the centre of transformation of natural powers to conscious ones. Being the changer of living" (Rubinstein 1997, p. 113).

Merab Mamardashvili: The Way Toward Authentic Living Through Responsible Effort. The most philosophically mature and psychologically relevant ideas can be found in two posthumous books: *Lectures on Proust* (Mamardashvili 1995) and *Psychological Topology of the Way* (Mamardashvili 1997). Both books are transcripts of lecture courses read in 1982 and 1984–1985 correspondingly. Only a brief summary of them is presented here; for a more detailed analysis see Leontiev (2009). In many respects, Mamardashvili's later views are close to the existentialist worldview. Their similarity is already seen in their stylistic peculiarities: Mamardashvili's reflections are fluid and cannot be frozen in categories. They resist any structuring on the one hand, and are often quite radical, clear, and unambiguous on the other; "The devil is playing with us, when we are not thinking precisely," was one of his frequently quoted mottos (Mamardashvili 1997, p. 207).

Mamardashvili's starting point was, however, reflexive consciousness of an individual moving in the world; he neither isolated the consciousness from being-in-the-world, nor claimed to describe being-in-the-world analytically. Probably the label he used for these views, *psychological topology of the way*, reflected these points: "topology of the way" referred to real life, and "psychological" referred to the processes in individual consciousness accompanying one's moving along the way (or in other directions). He called his views "real psychology," unlike the psychological science of his days; though Mamardashvili often lectured for psychologists, and had good personal relationships and even joint projects with some of them, he was highly critical of academic psychology in general.

The focus of Mamardashvili's reflections in his *Lectures on Proust* is life. However, what Mamardashvili calls life is "different life" – different from the one that discloses itself to us in our everyday routine. In fact, there are two "regimes," or "registers," of living that account for the fundamental duality of our living. One regime is everyday shallow living on a surface level of existence. It is governed by habits and stereotypes; time flows on here without producing events, it is an unreal fog, or maya as it was called in the Orient. The other regime of living is intermittent, interruptible; Mamardashvili calls it "conscious living." Life at this underlying level has its laws and we may from time to time get access to this level through our conscious efforts. "We are always dual beings," said Mamardashvili, "half sprouted into the real, conscious life, half into something that hides this conscious life from us" (1995, p. 447). Mamardashvili (1997, p. 50) referred to the flashes of "possibility of the other life" that Proust's characters face at different points. Other life is ordered life in terms of its inevitable laws, which can be conceived unless we succeed in hiding this real life from our view and completely dissolve in the surface living, the one of "dispersion and collapse" (Mamardashvili 1997, p. 51). Mamardashvili compared the shallow regime of living with death. "To be alive means the capacity to be different (unlike that what you expect, wish, or demand). The living one can always just go and write another book, or create another idea – on autonomous reasons of one's own" (Mamardashvili 1995, p. 128; see also Mamardashvili 1997, p. 204). However, at every moment life is intertwined with death. What is dead is not your authentic, genuine feeling, but rather something borrowed, which you are just reproducing without experiencing it yourself. There is a dead duplicate for every living state and it is not always easy to see the difference, for not everything apparently living is truly alive (Mamardashvili 1997). Real human psychology is an incessant attempt to make alive that which is dead – dead words, dead gestures, dead conventions; at the same time, there are conditions and limitations that act in us and strive to kill that which must be alive (Mamardashvili 1997). This struggle underlies our living, for being alive is not easy, it requires a constant effort, inner work done by everyone who lives. "But of course not everyone does live ..." (Mamardashvili 1997, p. 61).

Mamardashvili's views on the living and dead elements of our existence are remarkably similar to views developed at the same time by James Bugental. "The *New Yorker* magazine several years ago carried a cartoon which showed a young family of father, mother, and little boy strolling sedately along the sidewalk as the boy asked, 'are we live or on tape?' Out of the mouths of babes can come the most fundamental existential questions!.... Most of us spend the greater portion of our lives on tape. Without awareness we carry out preprogrammed actions, feel preset emotions, and act on predetermined judgments. This taped living comes not because we are helplessly the creatures of our habit systems, our environments, our glands, or our ancestry, but because we have lost our centers" (Bugental 1991a, p. 3). "Living is the fundamental business of life. We all do it only partially. Being alive is a matter of degree; not an either-or proposition" (Bugental 1991b, p. 30).

"The world might open itself only to the engaged person – the one who has courage to stake oneself in the hope that something would happen that will make things clear" (Bugental 1991b, p. 28). "You cannot know anything unless you are engaged (though being engaged makes your knowledge distorted)" (Mamardashvili 1997, p. 130). Being engaged means staking yourself, being concerned for your predestination (Mamardashvili 1997, p. 215). It is this possible movement, along with the laws of genuine life, that Mamardashvili calls "the way" – "the sedimentation of the living particles from the human experience and their collecting" (Mamardashvili 1997, p. 395).

Inasmuch as we move along our way, our actions are not determined. Mamardashvili blamed psychology for its over concern with deterministic explanations. Indeed, this kind of explanation is relevant for the surface level of living that Mamardashvili calls "death" or "sleep," in which events, including mental events, are produced by a cohesion of events and mechanisms (Bugental's "tapes"). But the causation refers to the things in humans that are not humane; in the domain of specifically human phenomena deterministic concepts are of no use: "one cannot causally evoke the human in a human" (Mamardashvili 1997, p. 416). Many times Mamardashvili repeats the idea that good has no causes. We use causal explanations in case of something evil (he has been made angry, offended, hence he is fierce), but in the case of good acts we deny a causal view and say that the person has acted "in good conscience" that is, without reasons (Mamardashvili 1997, p. 349).

The concept of effort is the basic one Mamardashvili used to explain what occurs in genuine life, and how. Mamardashvili calls effort an existential, or a cogital concept having a single modus – intensity (Mamardashvili 1995, p. 30). It may be held by the person and it may last, endure; it cannot be let to some self-sustaining mechanism; it is only our holding the effort that makes it last and produces humane phenomena. "Truth, beauty, virtue, etc. exist to the extent they are at every given moment being fed and permanently reproduced by an effort, reviving and permanently being made anew. The existence of some things is the existence on the ridge of the wave of effort. The wave of effort carries the existence of some things through time and duration, but we as limited mental beings do see the duration and do not see the wave that supports it" (Mamardashvili 1995, p. 318).

The concept of effort allows us to escape the confusion of good deeds and good intentions; "All the world is so arranged that the good in it is not our wish for the good. Justice is not our wish for the justice" (Mamardashvili 1997, p. 238). Moral acts and moral events require much more than the intention to be moral. "What occurs in reality is only ontologically grounded events, rather than feelings-pretensions of half-beings" (Mamardashvili 1997, p. 348). Mamardashvili uses the metaphor of "moral muscles" – a child would not lift up a chair, having no muscles. Special kinds of "muscles" are needed to lift up a thought, to lift up a moral act. "It's only through muscles that something occurs in the world" (Mamardashvili 1997, p. 531).

One of the key tenets of Mamardashvili's thought is treating human beings as artificial, rather than natural, creatures. We are to find and pass our own way of personal salvation. This is the effortful way of our becoming humans; "human being is the effort to be human" (Mamardashvili 1997, p. 119). The result is not warranted; it is up to our efforts. To the extent that we are capable and wish to apply efforts to become human we approach humanity. "We are never humans in the abstract sense, we are humans as we can be humans" (Mamardashvili 1995, p. 502).

More than once Mamardashvili tried to characterize the type of person he considered a philosophical ideal. He spoke of the "inner person," or "person of the Gospel" (as opposed to "person of the Church") (Mamardashvili 1997, p. 104), or "universal person," or "heroic person," or "the classic soul" as the type of person who holds the world independent of norms and past causes, who produces the laws and norms from one's experience, one's life trial. The classic soul needs no supporting environment – it is capable, whatever could be out there, for it possesses "the courage of the impossible": "There are no mechanisms that by themselves, independent of your effort and your courage, provide something in the world" (Mamardashvili 1997, p. 108). Humans are capable of moral actions in principle, when no reason and meaning for being good and doing good is being sought. "I am facing the world alone, and I must hold my loneliness. Whatever the world is, there is something I can and must do" (Mamardashvili 1997, p. 197). Other metaphors for this type of person are "vertical person," "standing person," and "assembled person" (Mamardashvili 1997, p. 146). The idea of self-assembling as the mission of a mature, adult human person has become one of the central ideas of the second course on Proust. Mamardashvili used the Russian words "sobiraniye sebya" that can be translated both as "self-collecting" and "self-assembling"; in fact, he had in mind both meanings. Passing one's way one collects "the particles of living experiences" and then assembles them into a meaningful structure; personality appears as the assembling point. "I am here, at this point, and here and now I am to merge with myself. And I merge with myself through elaboration or processing of impressions" (Mamardashvili 1997, p. 151). The only view similar to this account of the human person is to be found in Carl Jung's theory of personality development. Jung specified that humans project their own psychological properties onto the objects of the outer world; as they mature, they have to collect all these projections again and to return them to their Self, recognizing them as the properties of their own and providing their integration with the Self. It is amazing that Jung also spoke of one's own way, one's own law, and inescapable loneliness as characteristics of a mature, developed person (see Jung 1934/1992, pp. 166–186).

Besides muscles and the courage to withstand loneliness and a lack of support and orientation, the heroic soul has what Mamardashvili calls adult consciousness. On the one hand, it assumes that the world is indifferent to us: "the adult view that requires the courage of the soul is the acknowledgement that things occur in the world by themselves. They have no intentions regarding us. And the intentions they have are those we ascribed them" (Mamardashvili 1997, p. 65). By contrast, infantile consciousness is based on the presumption "that everything in the world occurs either in order to make us happy or in order to make us sad" (Mamardashvili 1997, pp. 64–65). On the other hand, adult consciousness assumes that we are not indifferent to the world and are responsible for the implementation of our intentions. Summing up, "to live in the real life is to live in the world where there are no culprits of your misfortunes and no awards for your virtues and merits" (Mamardashvili 1997, p. 483). Mamardashvili never ceased pointing the direction where the light can be seen: toward the possible person who is always transcending oneself and is capable to make efforts in order to change. "Free is only the person who is ready and really capable for the labour of freedom" (Mamardashvili 1997, p. 94).

References

Adler, A. (1980). *What Life Should Mean to You.* London: George Allen and Unwin.

Bakhtin, M.M. (1984) *Problems of Dostoevsky's Poetics* (trans. and ed. C. Emerson). Minneapolis: University of Minnesota Press.

Bakhtin, M.M. (1993). *Toward a Philosophy of the Act* (ed. V. Liapunov and M. Holquis, trans. V. Liapunov). Austin: University of Texas Press.

Bakhtin, M.M. (2003a). K filosofii postupka [Toward the philosophy of the act]. In: *Sobranie sochinenii* [Collected works], vol. 1 (ed. M.M. Bakhtin), 7 - 68. Moscow: Russkie slovari.

Bakhtin, M.M. (2003b). Avtor i geroi v esteticheskoi deyatelnosti [The author and the character in the aesthetic activity]. In: *Sobranie sochinenii* [Collected works], vol. 1 (ed. M.M. Bakhtin), 69–263. Moscow: Russkie slovari.

Berdyaev, N.A. (1989). Smysl tvorchestva [The meaning of creativity]. In: *Filosofiia svobody. Smysl tvorchestva* [Philosophy of freedom. The meaning of creativity] (ed. N.A. Berdyaev), 251–580. Moscow: Pravda.

Berdyaev, N. (1991a). L. Tolstoy. In: *O russkoi filosofii* [On Russian philosophy], Part 2 (ed. N. Berdyaev), 38 - 43. Sveerdlovsk: Urals University Press.

Berdyaev, N. (1991b). Mirosozertsaniye Dostoevskogo [Dostoyevsky's world view]. In: *O russkoi filosofii* [On Russian philosophy], Part 1 (ed. N. Berdyaev), 26 - 148. Sveerdlovsk: Urals University Press.

Berdyaev, N. (1991c). Moe filosofskoe mirosozertsaniye (My philosophical world view]. In: *O russkoi filosofii* [On Russian philosophy], Part 1 (ed. N. Berdyaev) 19 - 25. Sveerdlovsk: Urals University Press.

Berdyaev, N. (1993). *O naznachenii cheloveka* [On human destination]. Moscow: Respublika.

Berdyaev, N.A. (1999). *O cheloveke, ego svobode i dukhovnosti: izbrannye trudy* [On human being, his/her freedom and spirituality: selected works]. Moscow: Flinta.

Berdyaev, N.A. (2002). Eticheskaya problema v svete filosofskogo idealism [Ethical problem in light of philosophical idealism]. In: *Sub specie aeternitatis: opity filosofskie, socialnye I literarturnye (1900 - 1906)* [Sub specie aeternitatis: philosophical, social and literature essays, 1900 - 1906] (ed. N.A. Berdyaev), 70 - 114. Moscow: Canon+.

Bugental, J.F.T. (1991a). Outcomes of an existential-humanistic psychotherapy: A tribute to Rollo May. *The Humanistic Psychologist 19* (1): 2 - 9.

Bugental, J.F.T. (1991b). Lessons clients teach therapists. *Journal of Humanistic Psychology 31* (3): 28 - 32.

Frankl V.E. (1969). *The Will to Meaning: Foundations and Applications of Logotherapy.* New York: Plume.

Frankl V. (1973). *The Doctor and the Soul: From Psychotherapy to Logotherapy.* New York: Vintage.

Jung, C.G. (1992). *The Development of Personality.* London: Routledge. (Original work published 1934.)

Kočiūnas R. (2000) Existential experience and group therapy. *Journal of the Society for Existential Analysis 11* (2): 91–112.

Kočiūnas R. (ed.) (2008) *Gydyti gyvenimu: Aleksandro Alekseičiko Intensyvus terapinis gyvenimas.* Vilnius: Humanistinės ir egzistencinės psichologijos institutas.

Kočiūnas R. (2015) The existential approach in group psychotherapy. *International Journal of Psychotherapy 19* (1): 95–110.

Kurabtsev, V.L. (2005). *Miry svobody I chudes Lva Shestova* [Lev Shestov's worlds of freedom and miracles]. Moscow: Russian Humanistic Society.

Leontiev, D. (2005). Meaning vs. happiness issue in the history of thought and present-day debates. In: *Viktor Frankl und die Philosophie* (ed. D. Batthyany and O. Zsok), 57–68). Vienna; New York: Springer.

Leontiev, D. (2009). Life as heroic effort: Merab Mamardashvili's psychological topology of the way. *Transcultural Studies 5* (1–2): 74 - 91.

Leontiev, D. (2016). *Zhizn kak tvorchestvo: vvedenie v ekzistentsialnoe izmerenie* [Living as creating: introduction to the existential dimension]. Moscow: Smysl.

Mamardashvili, M.K. (1995). *Lektsii o Prouste: Psikhologicheskaya Topologiya Puti* [Lectures on Proust: Psychological topology of the way]. Moscow: Ad Marginem.

Mamardashvili, M.K. (1997). *Psikhologicheskaya Topologiya Puti: M. Proust "V Poiskakh Utrachennogo Vremeni"* [Psychological topology of the way: M. Proust "In search of lost time"]. St Petersburg: Russian Christian Humanitarian Institute Press.

May, R. (1981). *Freedom and Destiny.* New York: Norton.

Rozanov, V. (1989) F.M. Dostoyevsky's legend on the Grand Inquisitor: An attempt of critical commentary). In: *Sobranie Sochinenii Mysli o Literature* [Thoughts on literature], 41–157. Moscow: Sovremennik.

Rubinstein, S.L. (1997). *Chelovek I mir* [Human being and the world]. Moscow: Nauka.
Sartre, J.P. (1948). *Existentialism and Humanism* (trans. P. Mairet). London: Methuen.
Tolstoy, L. (1983). Ispoved [Confessions]. In *Polnoe Sobranie Sochinenii* [Collected works], vol. 16 (ed. V.G. Chertkov), 106–165. Moscow: Khudozhestvennaya Literature.
Tolstoy, L. (1993). *Put' zhisni* [The path of life]. Moscow: Vysshaya shkola.
Tolstoy, L. (2003). *Filosofskii Dnevnik 1901–1910* [Philosophical journal 1901–1910]. Moscow: Izvestiya.
Zinevych, A. (2015). A journey to fairy tale with Dr. Baloo. In: *Memoirs of Anastasiia Zinevych.* Odessa, Ukraine: Academy of Sciences.

34

Southern Europe

Evgenia T. Georganda, Edgar A. Correia, Lodovico E. Berra, Jak Icoz, Gideon Menda, and Yali Sar Shalom

Introduction

Eugenia Georganda

Although one could argue that the first form of a phenomenological approach to dialogue and therapy was introduced by Socrates somewhere around 300 BCE with his "dialectic inquiry," modern existential and phenomenological traditions in psychiatry and psychology arrived in the 1920s in France and in the 1930s and 1940s in some other southern European countries. Prolific contributions to existential and phenomenological psychology, psychiatry, and psychopathology were made during the following decades, but psychotherapeutic practice was not the main concern of these pioneering authors. It was only at the dawn of the new millennium that existential and/or phenomenological psychotherapeutic societies and training schools started to emerge and spread along the Mediterranean.

Developed mainly by psychiatrists and a few psychologists, the initial period aimed to produce an alternative perspective to the dominant mechanistic and somatic (brain diseases) viewpoint over psychopathology. Following the work of Jaspers, Binswanger, Straus, von Gebsattel, and Boss, southern existential pioneers wanted to include the subjective personal experience of the person who suffers in its diagnosis and understanding.

Psychopharmacological treatments, with their fast and quantifiable results, end up attracting most psychiatrists. The revival of the existential-phenomenological perspective, in the late at late 1990s and at the dawn of the new millennium, is now mainly through psychologists, counsellors, and psychotherapists, whose main interest is no longer the diagnosis and the analysis of the shared commonalties among the lived experiences of the disturbed persons, but the praxis of a psychotherapy that shares with the pioneers the focus on that lived (subjective) experience of the person who suffers.

The Wiley World Handbook of Existential Therapy, First Edition. Edited by Emmy van Deurzen, Erik Craig, Alfried Längle, Kirk J. Schneider, Digby Tantam, and Simon du Plock.

France

French philosophers such as Gabriel Marcel, Jean-Paul Sartre, Emmanuel Lévinas, Simone de Beauvoir, Maurice Merleau-Ponty, Henri Maldiney, Paul Ricoeur, Albert Camus, and Gilles Deleuze, are usually present in the bibliographic references of existential therapists worldwide. The theoretical-philosophical contribution of French authors has been pivotal in the development of existential therapy as we know it. In contrast, French existential therapy authors are barely referred to in the predominant literature (Correia, Cooper, and Berdondini 2015), in particular at the contemporary Anglo-Saxon existential literature (e.g., Barnett and Madison 2012; Cooper 2003; Craig et al. 2016; Schneider and Krug 2010). The hegemonic presence of the French Lacanian psychoanalysis, and language barriers to reading and adopting the work of the few and untranslated French existential psychiatrists and/or psychotherapists, are two plausible reasons for such contrasting phenomena between the relevance of French philosophy and French existential therapy.

Despite this, French existential therapy has had important figures and seminal contributions. Eugène Minkowski (1885–1972), a psychiatrist born in St. Petersburg within a Lithuanian family, immigrated to France and, in the 1920s, started developing his phenomenological anthropology, inspired mainly by Scheler's and Bergson's phenomenology (Spiegelberg 1972). Together with Binswanger, Straus, and von Gebsattel, his work is frequently considered as part of the beginnings of existential psychotherapy (Besora 1994; Cooper 2012; May 1958; Straus 1959).

Henri Ey (1900–1977) was another leading figure in French phenomenological psychiatry and, together with Minkowski, he helped to establish the phenomenological and existential tradition in French psychiatry and psychopathology (Spiegelberg 1972). In the 1960s, Georges Lantéri-Laura (1930–2004) followed and developed several studies on phenomenological psychiatry (Besora 1994), while Pierre Fédida, formerly a student of Gilles Deleuze, developed a psychoanalysis that was inspired and influenced by both existential philosophy and phenomenology.

More recently (the 1970s to the 1990s), Arthur Tatossian (1929–1995), based on the writings of his German and French predecessors, developed a kind of synthesis of their work and established new perspectives for phenomenological psychiatry, sometimes referred as "contemporary phenomenological psychopathology" (Tatossian and Moreira 2012).

Despite their influence (national and international), none of these authors founded a school and their work did not develop into a psychotherapeutic system. Of the three existential therapy institutions found in France (Correia, Cooper, and Berdondini 2016a), two are related to Frankl's Logotherapy (the *Association de Logothérapeutes Francophones* and *L'Ecole Française d'analyse existentielle et de logothérapie*) and another one is related to the daseinsanalytic branch of existential therapy (the *École Française de Daseinsanalyse*). All these institutions offer regular seminars and debates in their fields and both logotherapeutic associations offer recognized training in counselling and psychotherapy. The Daseinsanalytic School has been chaired by Françoise Dastur and Philippe Cabestan, two leading philosophers who have undertaken prolific work on phenomenology and existential philosophy, in particular on the development of a philosophy of psychopathologies.

Greece

Although Greek philosophers and writers have a long tradition in the use and development of existential ideas, there was no similar development in the existential approach to psychotherapy. It was not only ancient Greek philosophers, like Socrates, Plato, Epicurus, and Heraclitus whose ideas, although not labelled as such at the time, were clearly existential, but also later philosophers and writers, such as Costas Axelos and Nikos Kazantzakis who struggled with issues of meaning, life and death, constant change, and responsibility. Despite their influence in the scholarly world some of them were excommunicated by the Church for their radical ideas, while others were characterized as communists, at a time when the Greek civil war rendered leftist ideas dangerous and unacceptable. They were thus marginalized by the establishment, which preferred to emphasize the values of family life and religion over ideas of human freedom, dignity, and personal responsibility.

In the early 1980s the primary orientation of most psychotherapists in Greece was psychoanalytic to such a degree that the general public believed psychoanalysis and psychotherapy to be one and the same. Psychoanalysis was an elitist approach for the upper classes and was practiced primarily by psychiatrists. Psychology and psychotherapy were generally slow in being formally established within the Greek universities (1990s), but private training centers, predominantly Systemic, Adlerian, and Behavioral, had begun to emerge. This was largely due to the initiatives of individual psychologists who, after studying abroad, returned to Greece and set up centers providing training in the approaches in which they had, themselves, been trained. The post-War need for trained volunteers in various organizations was also instrumental in promoting the more socially orientated Adlerian approach, which prepared lay people to work in numerous practical situations such as parent groups, supportive counselling, and end of life support in hospitals.

Upon the return of Eugenia Georganda from the United States in the late 1980s and while teaching psychology in various colleges in Athens, it became apparent that existential theory had a great appeal to most students. The "ultimate concerns" of Irvin Yalom that were brought into the class material touched basic issues of their existence and made the introductory courses quite popular among undergraduate students. In 2001 she was invited to write a chapter on existential theory for a book on the current approaches to psychotherapy in Greece (Georganda 2001) but it was not until 2002 that she started the first seminars in existential thought in her private office. Alexis Harisiadis, whom she had met as a graduate psychology student, was one of the first to attend them, continuing for two years. In 2004 they decided to start a joint project so as to make existential therapy better known to the general public. Evy Dallas, a long-standing friend and colleague of Eugenia Georganda, was approached and she joined the project. She later introduced Katerina Zymnis-Georgalou, one of her psychology graduates, to the group. The four established the Hellenic Association for Existential Psychology and named it "Gignesthai," or "becoming," since they view its development as a generic ongoing process.

For the first five years the four were intensely involved in becoming acquainted with one another, familiarizing themselves with the various existential schools, co-creating a sense of identity and a shared existential language and modality of work. In 2004 a year-long course in existential theory started and Gignesthai came into contact with colleagues in the United Kingdom. Paul Smith Pickard, chair of the Society for Existential Analysis (SEA) at the time, was the first contact person who brought Gignesthai to the United Kingdom for the SEA annual conference in 2005 and introduced them to his colleagues. Since then, Mick Cooper, Ernesto Spinelli, Emmy van Deurzen, and Kirk J. Schneider have visited Gignesthai and have run seminars to coincide with the publication of their books in the Greek language. From the beginning the effort was twofold: (1) to translate important existential texts into Greek so as to make them accessible to the Greek public; and (2) to explore ways of integrating Greek insights and traditions into existing existential theory and practice.

As part of the second endeavor seminars and workshops based on Greek philosophers, writers, and poets were run. This experience led to the emergence and development of a new existential concept, that of "oistros of life," which was presented at the World Congress in Shanghai in 2012, during which Gignesthai had the opportunity to meet and become acquainted with existential theorists and practitioners from the United States. Kirk J. Schneider, Orah Krug, Louis Hoffman, and Erik Craig have been important contact people on the other side of the Atlantic. The presentation on the concept of "oistros" was published in the *Journal of Humanistic Psychology* in 2012 (Dallas et al. 2012). The concept of "oistros" was triggered by the Greek poet Empeirikos and the work of the writer Kazantzakis. His character, Alexis Zorbas, was an inspiration for a purely existential outlook on life, the ability to live life fully despite, or even because of, adversity and the ever-present knowledge of death (Hoffman et al. 2009). This work was also presented at the First World Congress of Existential Psychotherapy in London in 2015.

Furthermore, Gignesthai constantly encourages research and the development of concepts in the field. As an example, the research team has been working on the concept of authenticity, presenting the results at the First and Second Greek-Swedish Conferences in Karpathos in 2013 and 2014, respectively. Since its establishment, Gignesthai has also participated in a number of conferences and congresses, both locally and abroad, and has developed strong ties with the Greek University of Thessaly and the Panteion University in Athens, presenting existential theory to its graduate students.

It slowly became obvious that there was a growing need for a full training program in existential counselling and psychotherapy. Accordingly, Gignesthai started a four-year training in 2009. Initially students were graduates from psychology programs in the Greek universities. The first class graduated in 2013. In 2015 the training program was accredited by the European Association of Psychotherapy (EAP) as a European Association of Psychotherapy Training Institute (EAPTI) eligible to offer to its graduates the European Certificate of Psychotherapy (ECP). The training is based on four basic pillars: (1) familiarization with the most influential existential philosophers; (2) the study of the different existential psychotherapeutic approaches and counselling skills; (3) exposure to clinical practice and supervision; and (4) the optimization of the trainee's personal development through therapy and experiential workshops. At the end of the four years, having completed all academic requirements, the trainee must write a culminating thesis, using a case study to present the way they view themselves as existential therapists. So far 12 students have graduated and another 20 are in training.

The philosophy of Gignesthai is founded on a pluralistic approach to existential psychotherapy that is based not only on different existential theories, but also on the possibility of integrating other perspectives and approaches in order to forge the approach best suited to the personality of the therapist and the needs of the client. Thus, important professionals from other schools and approaches to psychotherapy are invited in order to present their work to trainees. In addition, as trainers, we have each developed our own particular way of understanding and using existential theory. Alexis Harisiadis has developed the "existential-poetic approach," which he has presented in conferences in Athens and in our joint conferences with the Swedish and Turkish Associations. Katerina Zymnis-Georgalos is elaborating an integration of systemic theory, positive psychology, and existential theory and practice, while Eugenia Georganda had the opportunity to present her "existential-developmental" approach to psychotherapy at the Second World Congress of Psychotherapy in Vienna in 2002 and, since then, at numerous other conferences and publications (2003, 2007, 2009).

Portugal

Edgar A. Correia

During the first half of the twentieth century, Germany concentrated major developments of a new vision on psychopathology and psychiatry, where phenomenology was the main method for a comprehensive and anthropological understanding of psychopathological problems, substituting the predominant mechanistic or deterministic vision: Heidelberg Clinic was the main center for this new development (Spiegelberg 1972). In 1936, after two years studying in Germany with Carl Kleist, Kurt Schneider, and Karl Jaspers (Fernandes 2007), Barahona Fernandes (1904–1992) returned to Portugal and had a leading role in disseminating the phenomenological and anthropological perspective within the Portuguese psychiatry, psychopathology, and medicine. Henrique Gomes de Araújo (1914–2000), another psychiatrist based at Oporto, was also influenced by the existential-phenomenological perspective and helped Barahona's task in north Portugal. A few scattered psychiatrists followed in their footsteps: particularly relevant were Raúl Guimarães Lopes, doctored at Heidelberg, and whose prolific studies on existential-phenomenological anthropology (e.g., Lopes 1994, 1996, 2006a, 2006b) helped to disseminate the existential perspective both in hospital psychiatric practice and with his medical and psychologist students; and José L. Pio Abreu, whose writings and teaching stressed the value of phenomenology for a comprehensive psychopathology (e.g., Abreu 1997).

Despite the work of those leading psychiatrists, no existential school or association was developed until the end of the 1980s. In 1989, José A. Carvalho Teixeira, based at Lisbon's *Instituto Superior de Psicologia Aplicada* (ISPA), brought together a group of psychologists and psychiatrists interested in existential-phenomenological psychology and psychopathology (the *Grupo de Estudos de Psicologia e Psicopatologia Fenomenológicas e Existenciais*), in order to learn, discuss and promote existential-phenomenological psychology and psychopathology. During the following years, the group organized conferences, seminars, and published a few papers and books (e.g., Teixeira 1994). Striving for a complete and formal training in existential psychotherapy, two of its newest members went to London to train at Regent's College, with Ernesto Spinelli, Simon du Plock, Lucia Moja-Strasser, among others. On their return to Portugal, the psychologists Daniel Sousa and Edgar A. Correia, together with the psychiatrists José A. Carvalho Teixeira and Víctor Amorim Rodrigues and the philosopher Paula Ponce de Leão, founded the Portuguese Society for Existential Psychotherapy (*Sociedade Portuguesa de Psicoterapia Existencial* – SPPE) in 2006.

SPPE recognizes itself as part of the existential-phenomenological branch of existential therapy (Correia, Cooper, and Berdondini 2014) and its members are deeply influenced by the British school of existential therapy (Cooper 2012; Correia et al. 2014a). The relational, interpersonal, and descriptive British existential tradition is deeply rooted in Portuguese existential practice (Correia et al. 2014a; Correia et al. 2015). Nevertheless, the different backgrounds of its founding members, and the previous Portuguese phenomenological anthropological tradition, makes it more open to a hermeneutic-analytical stance towards clients' problems (Correia et al. 2018) – for example, Sousa's "genetic phenomenological" approach (Sousa 2015) – and, simultaneously, more open to a phenomenological psychopathology (e.g., Lopes 2006a; Rodrigues 2006; Teixeira 1993, 2006b), when compared with its British colleagues.

In fact, Portuguese existential therapy has at its roots a diverse array of perspectives that co-exist in mutual respect and recognition. Among its founding members we can find a Sartrean-dialectical (social and politically minded) existential therapy and psychopathology (e.g., Teixeira 1997, 2006a, 2008, 2017), a Heideggerian ontological-hermeneutic and post-existential understanding of psychopathology (e.g., Rodrigues 2008, 2014; Rodrigues and Montenegro 2013) and practice (e.g., Rodrigues 2006), a Husserlian relational and genetic approach (e.g., Sousa 2014a, 2014b, 2015), and a Levinasian relational approach (e.g., Correia 2005, 2006, 2008).

But SPPE's most characteristic and distinctive feature is its open stance towards empirical research. Portuguese existential therapists have been calling for existential therapists to start developing research about its practice (Correia 2017; Sousa 2004, 2006) and they have been actively developing and publishing both qualitative and quantitative research. They have developed pioneering research in such fields as: significant events (Oliveira, Sousa, and Pires 2012; Sousa 2010; Sousa and Vaz 2017); process research (Alegria et al. 2016; Correia et al. 2018); outcome research (Alegria et al. 2016); existential therapy's theory of practice (Correia et al. 2017); differences and similarities across the main existential branches (Correia, Cooper, Berdondini et al. 2016); existential therapy's worldwide distribution and characteristics (Correia et al. 2014; Correia, Cooper, and Berdondini 2016; Correia et al. 2014a; Correia et al. 2014b); and practitioners' self-reported main influential authors and texts (Correia et al. 2015). New research is now being developed concerning existential therapy supervision (Silva and Sousa 2018), feedback systems applied to existential therapy (still in development by Daniel Sousa), and existential therapy with children and adolescents – a community-based clinical intervention, focusing on choice, freedom and change (Sá Pires 2016).

As a result of this vitality, much production has been made by the members of the Portuguese Society: three books and 47 articles or book chapters were published, both in Portugal and worldwide. In ten years, 16 articles were published in *Existential Analysis* and 12 other articles at several other peer-reviewed international journals. SPPE's members have also been actively participating in national and international congresses and conferences and particularly relevant is an encounter between Portuguese and Brazilian existential therapists, that occurs every two years (Feijoo and Lessa 2014).

Since 2008, SPPE has developed training in existential psychotherapy and eight years later was recognized as an EAPTI by the EAP. In 2016, SPEE counted 16 professional members and 28 trainees. Its course could be situated within the existential-phenomenological branch of existential psychotherapy, but the whole training is developed in order to encourage trainees to find the existential perspective that they best identify with. Different branches and perspectives are presented and several trainers are invited from the United Kingdom, France, and Brazil. Psychotherapy research is also a fundamental component of the Portuguese program that trains existential therapists.

Spain

German psychiatry and psychology has had a strong influence in Spain since the 1930s. Ramon Sarró e Burbano (1900–1993) and Juan López Ibor (1906–1991) were the first two major contributors in the establishment of the phenomenological anthropology and existential analysis at Spain, helped later by Castilla del Pino (Besora 1994).

In the late 1950s, Luis Martín-Santos (1924–1964) started to develop his existential approach largely influenced by Sartre's existentialism (Besora 1994). Besides the analytical dimension of existential analysis (Martín-Santos 2004), Martín-Santos was also interested in the therapeutic dimension and applicability of Sartre's existential psychoanalysis (Besora 1994). The analysis of the client's existence should clarify his/her existential project and, by making it conscious, the client can assume and rework it; allowing for a therapeutic change (Martín-Santos 1964). Martín-Santos died young and his ideas did not develop to found a school of psychotherapy. In the 1980s the psychiatrist Manuel Villegas developed an existential-phenomenological method for discourse analysis based on Sartre's existentialism (Villegas 1981).

Despite the strong tradition phenomenological anthropology and existential analysis had in Spain's psychiatry, the pharmacological approach has seduced the Spanish psychiatrist and it was Logotherapy that came to develop training courses in counselling and psychotherapy. Four existential therapy institutions now exist in Spain (Correia et al. 2016a) and all of then related to Logotherapy (*Asociación Española de Logoterapia*, *Asociación Viktor E. Frankl de Valencia*, *Associació Catalana de Logoteràpia i Anàlisi Existencial* and *Centro Sentido*).

Existential Psychotherapy in Italy

Lodovico E. Berra

In Italy there are different and heterogeneous groups linked to phenomenological-existential psychology, some focused on philosophy and existential psychology (*Società*

Italiana di Psicoterapia Esistenziale e *Istituto di scienze umane ed esistenziali*) others on Frankl's Existential Analysis and Logotherapy (*Analisi Esistenziale Frankliana*,) and others on phenomenological psychopathology (*Società Italiana per la Psicopatologia Fenomenologica*).

A fundamental reference in Italy about existentialism is the philosopher Nicola Abbagnano (1901–1990), who developed an original existential philosophy named "positive" (Abbagnano 1948). Abbagnano's "positive existentialism" conceives existence as Possibility, an existential possibility that opens up the research of its conditions and about what it can offer, avoiding turning it into a negative form, such as "impossibility" or death. The Abbagnano positive existential philosophy strongly influenced the psychiatrist Michel Torre (1917–1986) who was director of the Institute of Clinical Psychiatry at the University of Torino for about 20 years. Torre developed, in the 1970s, an original psychodynamic existential model derived from a direct confrontation and friendship with Abbagnano. This clinical theory is based on the concepts of *Possibility* from the works of philosophers such as Kierkegaard, Heidegger, and Sartre (Torre 1982). This psychodynamic model focuses psychological work on Existential Projection and on the so-called *existential insufficiency*, linked to the feeling of anxiety (*anguish*).

On this practical theoretical basis, at the end of the 1990s Lodovico Berra, former pupil of Michele Torre, set up the first group of psychologists, psychiatrists, and existential philosophers, creating in 1998 the *Italian School of Existential Psychotherapy* (Scuola Italiana di Psicoterapia Esistenziale; SIPE). SIPE is now connected to the *Italian Society of Existential Psychotherapy* (*Società Italiana di Psicoterapia Esistenziale)* pursuing an existential psychological model (Berra 2011) based fundamentally on the thought of Abbagnano and Torre, but also referring to authors like Heidegger, Jaspers, Minkowski, and Binwanger. It organizes training courses for psychotherapists, as well as seminars and conferences. Psychotherapy practice is based on existential projection and possibilities analysis, on worldviews (*Weltanschauungen*), and authenticity, with a specific *philosophical attitude*. The SIPE gave birth, in 1999, to the *Post-graduate School of Philosophical Counseling (Scuola Superiore di Counseling Filosofico* – SSCF) with a three-year Masters degree, based fundamentally on phenomenological-existential philosophy practice.[1] The year 2013 was the founding year for *Dasein*,[2] the official reference journal about psychology, psychopathology, and existential psychotherapy in Italy.

The *Istituto di Scienze Umane ed Esistenziali* (Institute of Human and Existential Sciences – ISUE) was founded in February 1988 by Renato Buffardi, Ferdinando Brancaleone, Fernando Boscaino, and Gianfranco Buffardi. ISUE promotes existential philosophies and an existential psychological model – *neo-existential*. This model joins, for therapeutic purposes, existential anthropological theory with the pragmatics of communication, constituting the so-called Consciential Logoanalysis

[1] SIPE and SSCF are Departments of the National Institute for research and education in Philosophy, Psychology and Psychiatry – (*Istituto di ricerca e formazione in Filosofia, Psicologia, Psichiatria* – ISFiPP), www.isfipp.org

[2] www.psicoterapiaesistenziale.org

or Subliminal Logodynamic. From 1996, the Institute has organized courses for existential counseling and therapy.

In 2014 SIPE with ISUE and the European University of Rome organized, in Rome, the *First Italian Conference of Existential Psychotherapy*, joining together for the first time in Italy the leading groups in the field of existential psychotherapy, Frankl's Logotherapy and phenomenological psychopathology.

The *Associazione Italiana di Logoterapia e Analisi Esistenziale* – ALÆF (Italian Association of Logotherapy and Existential Analysis) was founded by Eugenio Fizzotti during a conference held by Viktor E. Frankl in Rome in 1992. Nowadays it is an internationally recognized institution that collaborates with many countries in the world. It is accredited as a member of the International Association for Logotherapy and Existential Analysis at the Viktor Frankl Institute of Vienna.

ALÆF has a complete three-year training program in Franklian Existential Counseling and promotes research and training in the fields of logotherapy and existential analysis, meaning-centered education and phenomenological-existential approach to healthcare and social work. It publishes the four-monthly scientific review *Ricerca di Senso. Analisi esistenziale e logoterapia frankliana.*

The *Italian Association for Phenomenological Psychopathology* gathered together several leading figures in the field of phenomenology. Recently the association established the *School of Phenomenological-Dynamic Psychotherapy* with a four-year training course for psychologists and psychiatrists, and other courses on phenomenological psychopathology (basic, advanced, intensive) with an original psychological method named PHD (Phenomenological unfolding, Hermeneutic analysis and Dynamic analysis).

Turkey

Jak Icoz

The history of existential psychotherapies is quite complicated, given the fact that until recently there has been no organized movement or practice. On the other hand, it could be safely assumed that existential philosophy has long had a stable audience and an interested readership. Back in the 1970s, first ideas of existential psychotherapies entered into Turkish practice with Engin Gectan, a famous psychiatrist, who wrote more than 20 books on the subject. Yet, somehow curiously, this has never translated into an organized movement, for example, foundation of a society, trainings. However, this changed in 2012.

Other related "cousin" fields of psychotherapy have long been around, for example, Gestalt therapy, psychodrama, or person-centered. In 2012, the very first comprehensive training in existential psychotherapies started to be offered by the Existential Academy of Istanbul, which is also a fairly new establishment. This training is now expanding with more trainers, voices, topics, and perspectives on board. At the Existential Academy of Istanbul, which hosts the training, more than ten therapists are practicing existential psychotherapy under proper supervision. As of 2016, the academy offered training to roughly 80 mental health practitioners.

The Existential Academy of Istanbul's activities have also inspired other centers, which now offer therapy, seminars, and short-term training in the field. In line with these developments, in 2014 a not-for-profit society, EXISTanbul (The Society for Existential Psychotherapies in Turkey), was initiated. Currently the society is focusing on two interrelated aims: first to promote existential ideas to the general public and interested colleagues; and second to serve as a base for existential psychotherapists with a proper training for professional exchanges, ethical guidance, and occupational support as a professional association.

Other Southern European Countries

Beyond the countries mentioned above, Correia's worldwide research of existential therapists (Correia 2017; Correia et al. 2014) found existential practitioners based in four other South European countries: Croatia, Cyprus, Malta, and Slovenia. Existential therapy institutions were also found both in Croatia (the *Logoterapija Hrvatska*) and Slovenia (the *Inštitut Antona Trstenjaka za gerontologijo in medgeneracijsko sožitje* and the *Slovenský inštitút logoterapie [SILOE]*) (Correia et al. 2016a). All these institutes are related to Viktor Frankl's classic Logotherapy and SILOE runs accredited courses to train logotherapists.

The Development of Existential Psychotherapy in Israel

Gideon Menda and Yali Sar Shalom

The roots of existentialism in Israel can be traced back to philosophy and literature focused on the existence of the individual and its particular submersion in the meaning of life.

In 1925, with the establishment of the Hebrew University in Jerusalem, the first university in Israel, philosophy was already being taught. Nevertheless, *existential philosophy* was taught only as part of continental philosophy, which centered on nineteenth- to twentieth-century German and French philosophy. However, with the rise of the Nazi Regime in Germany, some philosophy lecturers refused to teach Heidegger's philosophy during the second half of the twentieth century.

One of the first lecturers to teach philosophy at the Hebrew University of Jerusalem was Martin Buber (1878–1965). Buber, a Jewish philosopher who had escaped Nazi terror in Germany, settled in Israel in 1938. He received academic tenure as a professor in the discipline of philosophy. The fact that Buber was a Haredi (ultra-orthodox) Jew and that his writings also dealt with Hasidism captured the hearts of many during the initial years of Jewish settlement in Israel. This led many to be exposed to the principles of existentialism. Additionally, Buber's contemplation of dialogue was quite influential, especially in the field of education. His book, *I and Thou*, first published in Germany in 1923, was translated into Hebrew in 1959 and was a bestseller in Israel.

Two other prominent scholars contributed greatly to the advancement of existential philosophical dialogue in Israel. These were Samuel Hugo Bergman (1883–1975) and Jacob Golomb (born in 1947). Bergman, an Israeli philosopher born in Prague and highly influenced by Martin Buber, was appointed rector of the Hebrew University of Jerusalem. His book *Dialogical Philosophy from Kierkegaard to Buber*, first published in 1974, is still used by students today.

Golomb, who was appointed professor of philosophy at the Hebrew University in Jerusalem, published several books in Hebrew that focused on existential philosophy. These texts include references to the thinking of prominent phenomenological and existential philosophers such as Kant, Hegel, Kierkegaard, Nietzsche, Husserl, Heidegger, and Sartre.

Additionally, many books on existential philosophy have been translated into Hebrew. Among these, one can find the first translation of Kierkegaard's writings (*Collection of Writings*), which was published in 1954.

The first seeds of existential therapy, moving beyond merely existential thinking, can be found in the translation into Hebrew of the books of two well-known authors who not only focused on existential thought, but also on its therapeutic applications. These authors are Viktor E. Frankl and Irvin D. Yalom. Frankl's recounting of his experience as a Jewish Holocaust survivor and his discussion, first and foremost, of how to find meaning in an experience as harrowing as the concentration camps, made his book *Man's Search for Meaning* highly popular amongst adolescents and adults, and it became required reading in schools. Frankl's book turned the subject of "logotherapy" into a better-known therapeutic concept, although it was taught only in a very narrow manner. Additional books by Frankl were published in Israel in the 1980s, and they are still sold today.

Jewish-American psychiatrist and psychotherapist Irvin Yalom made tremendous progress in disseminating existential psychotherapy in Israel. At least 12 of Yalom's texts, including novels and professional books, were translated into Hebrew, and they were bestsellers. Through Yalom's texts, existential psychotherapy became better known. This enabled many therapists in Israel to identify with its philosophical and therapeutic ideas. Nonetheless, for many years, not one academic institution taught existential psychotherapy as an independent approach in any detailed or comprehensive way, and no trained therapists were committed to existential psychotherapy.

The most accepted approaches within the psychology and psychotherapy milieu were the psychoanalytic and psychodynamic approaches. Within the curricula taught in both undergraduate and postgraduate psychology programs, the existential approach was pushed to the side-lines, often mentioned alongside the humanistic approach.

Finally, in 2007, an Israeli academic institution opened the first three-year postgraduate academic program focused on existential psychotherapy and counselling. The program was inaugurated by Dr. Gideon Menda and Yali Sar Shalom in the Kibbutzim College of Education, Technology and Arts, in Tel-Aviv.

The program was possible due to Menda's return to Israel after his graduation from the New School of Psychotherapy and Counselling (NSPC), which had been opened in London by Professor Emmy van Deurzen and which focused on existential psychotherapy. Menda and Sar Shalom's experience as van Deurzen's students, as well as Professor van Deurzen and Professor Digby Tantam's visit to the Kibbutzim College in 2008, around the time of the opening of the program, meant that the Israeli program would be significantly influenced by van Deurzen's ideas and methods.

The Existential Psychotherapy and Counselling program is still in operation in Kibbutzim College. Its students and graduates have become integrated into many institutions throughout Israel as part of their training, and its graduates are working in private practices, thus making the existential approach is known all over Israel. It has also been recognized by the Inter-Disciplinary Israeli Association of Psychotherapy, established in conjunction with several directors of psychotherapy programs in Israel, including Gideon Menda. The Association aims to expand the accepted/traditional boundaries of psychotherapy in Israel.

Additionally, in 2015, Menda and Sar Shalom established the EPCI – the Existential Psychotherapy and Counselling – Israel community. This community brings together all of the graduates of the Existential Psychotherapy and Counselling program, constituting a platform for the advancement and growth of existential psychotherapy in Israel.

Conclusions

The first steps of the South European existential therapy can be traced back to the 1920s, when a group of Latin European psychiatrists, disappointed with the prevailing mechanistic and somatic – brain diseases – perspective over psychopathology, embraced a new perspective that was being developed by a few pioneers inspired by phenomenology and existential philosophy. Minkowski, one these leading pioneers, together with Binswanger, Straus, von Gebsattel, and the Heidelberg Clinic group, found the subjective experience of the person who suffers as a proper phenomenon to study, distinguish, classify, and to understand the psychopathological disturbances.

This initial period was led by psychiatrists and psychopathologists, whose main interest was the description and understanding of the psychopathological experience of the disturbed person (Besora 1994; Spiegelberg 1972). During this initial period psychoanalysis was still the dominant psychotherapeutic paradigm and the newly existential analysis was still struggling to develop into a proper psychotherapy (May 1958; Straus 1959). But psychopharmacological treatments ended attracting most psychiatrists and the revival of the existential movement in South European countries was mainly developed by psychologists and counsellors (and a few psychiatrists disappointed with the reductionism of a pure pharmacological intervention), whose main interest was the actual psychotherapeutic intervention. The reasons for this revival are still to be studied, but the disappointment (once again) with mechanistic and reductionist visions of the prevailing psychotherapeutic systems (psychoanalysis and cognitive behavioral therapy) is probably a reason for the growing number of counsellors and psychotherapists that turned to a new/old intervention model, that really embraces and respects the full subjective experience of the person who suffers.

Frankl's Logotherapy, with its pragmatic and clearly defined intervention model (Correia et al. 2016b; Craig et al. 2016), was the first existential branch to attract this new generation of Southern European counsellors and psychologists. But, based on a previous existential-anthropological tradition and/or on a more philosophically informed perspective, several existential schools have been developing highly dynamic and creative existential-phenomenological perspectives, in a close dialogue with their culture, tradition, and worldwide developments.

References

Abbagnano, N. (1948). *Esistenzialismo positivo*, Turin: Taylor.
Abreu, J.L.P. (1997). *Introdução à psicopatologia compreensiva*, 2e. Lisbon: Fundação Calouste Gulbenkian.
Alegria, S., Carvalho, I., Sousa, D. et al. (2016). Process and outcome research in existential psychotherapy. *Existential Analysis 27* (1): 78–92.
Barnett, L. and Madison, G. (eds.) (2012). *Existential Therapy: Legacy, Vibrancy and Dialogue*. London: Routledge.
Bergman, S.H. (1974). *Dialogical Philosophy from Kierkegaard to Buber*. Jerusalem: Bialik Institute.
Berra, L. (2011.) *Manuale di psicoterapia esistenziale*. Padua: Libreria Universitaria.
Besora, M.V. (1994). Las psicoterapias existenciales: Desarollo historico y modalidades conceptuales. In: *Fenomenologia e psicologia* (ed. J.A.C. Teixeira), 11–23. Lisbon: ISPA.
Buber, M. (1923) *Ich und Du (I and Thou)*. Berlin: Schocken.
Cooper, M. (2003). *Existential Therapies*. London: Sage.
Cooper, M. (2012). *The Existential Counselling Primer: A Concise, Accessible and Comprehensive Introduction*. Ross-on-Wye: PCCS.
Correia, E.A. (2005). Alterity and psychotherapy. *Existential Analysis: Journal of the Society for Existential Analysis 16* (1): 61–72.
Correia, E.A. (2006). "Oh if only there were heavenly paths by which to creep into another existence and into happiness!" *Existential Analysis: Journal of the Society for Existential Analysis 17* (1): 123–136.
Correia, E.A. (2008). Love is a hell of a job! *Existential Analysis: Journal of the Society for Existential Analysis 19* (2): 267–279.
Correia, E.A. (2017). Can existential-phenomenological theory and epistemology ever be congruent with empirical research and systematizations? *Existential Analysis: Journal of the Society for Existential Analysis 28* (1): 176–189.
Correia, E.A., Cooper, M., and Berdondini, L. (2014). The worldwide distribution and characteristics of existential counsellors and psychotherapists. *Existential Analysis 25* (2): 321–337.
Correia, E.A., Cooper, M., and Berdondini, L. (2015). Existential psychotherapy: An international survey of the key authors and texts influencing practice. *Journal of Contemporary Psychotherapy 45* (1): 3–10.
Correia, E.A., Cooper, M., and Berdondini, L. (2016a). Existential therapy institutions worldwide: An update of data and the extensive list. *Existential Analysis 27* (1): 155–200.
Correia, E.A., Cooper, M., Berdondini, L. et al. (2016b). Existential psychotherapies: Similarities and differences among the main branches. *Journal of Humanistic Psychology 58* (2): 119–143.
Correia, E.A., Cooper, M., Berdondini, L. et al. (2017). Characteristic practices of existential psychotherapy: A worldwide survey of practitioners' perspectives. *The Humanistic Psychologist 45* (3): 217–237.
Correia, E.A., Correia, K., Cooper, M. et al. (2014a). Práticas da psicoterapia existencial em Portugal e no Brasil: Aguns dados comparativos. In: *Fenomenologia e práticas clínicas* (ed. A.M.L. Feijoo and M.B. Lessa), 47–72). Rio de Janeiro: Edições IFEN.
Correia, E.A., Correia, K., Cooper, M. et al. (2014b). Psicoterapia existencial latinoamericana en la actualidad. *Revista Latinoamericana de Psicología Existencial 9*: 26–37.
Correia, E.A., Sartóris, V., Fernandes, T. et al. (2018). The practices of existential psychotherapists: An exploratory study for the development and application of an observational grid. *British journal of Guidance & Counselling 46* (2): 201–216.

Craig, M., Vos, J., Cooper, M. et al. (2016). Existential psychotherapies. In: *Humanistic Psychotherapies: Handbook of Research and Practice*, 2e (ed. D.J. Cain, K. Keenan and S. Rubin), 283–317. Washington: American Psychological Association.

Dallas E., Georganda, E., Harisiadis, A. et al. (2012). Zhi Mian and "Oistros" of Life. *Journal of Humanistic Psychology. 53* (2): 252–260.

Feijoo, A.M.L. and Lessa, M.B. (eds.) (2014). *Fenomenologia e práticas clínicas.* Rio de Janeiro: IFEN.

Fernandes, B. (2007). Autoapresentação de Barahona Fernandes. *Revista do Hospital Júlio de Matos, 20*: 60–80.

Georganda, E. (2001). Existential psychotherapy. In: *Σύγχρονες Ψυχοθεραπείες: Από την Θεωρία στην Εφαρμογή (Current psychotherapies in Greece: From theory to practice)* (ed. P. Assimakis). Athens: Εκδόσεις Ασημάκης.

Georganda, E. (2003). *Τι είναι Ψυχοθεραπεία.* (What is Psychotherapy). Athens: Εκδόσεις Ασημάκης.

Georganda, E. (2007). The DNA of the Soul: Integrating developmental issues with existential-humanistic theory. *The British Journal of Psychotherapy Integration: The Integrative Project in Practice 4* (1): 4–12.

Georganda, E. (2009). *Ταξίδι στο Συναίσθημα: Ο Υπαρξισμός στην Ζωή μου.* (Journey into emotions: Existentialism in my life). Athens: Εκδόσεις Άσπρη λέξη.

Hoffman, L., Yang, M., Kaklauskas, F.J., and Chan. A. (eds.) (2009). The myth of Zorba the Greek and the existential concept of "oistros." In: *Existential Psychology East–West*, vol. 2. Colorado Springs, CO: Universities of the Rockies Press.

Kierkegaard, S. (1954). *Mivhar Ktavim/Seren Kirkegor* [Collection of Writings] (ed. I. Croch and Y. Shechter). Tel Aviv: Dvir.

Lopes, R.G. (1994). Fenómeno e sintoma. In: *Fenomenologia e psicologia* (ed. J.A.C. Teixeira), 25–39). Lisbon: ISPA.

Lopes, R.G. (1996). Projecto existencial. In: *A escolha de si-próprio* (ed. R.G. Lopes, V. Mota, and C. Santos), 150–171. Porto: Hospital de Conde de Ferreira.

Lopes, R.G. (2006a). *Psicologia da pessoa e elucidação psicopatológica.* Porto: Higiomed Edições.

Lopes, R.G. (2006b). Renovação noética: Fundamento da verdade no encontro terapêutico. *Análise Psicológica 24* (3): 323–330.

Martín-Santos, L. (1964). *Libertad, temporalidad y transferencia en el psicoanálisis existencial.* Barcelona: Seix Barral.

Martín-Santos, L. (2004). *Análisis existencial: Ensayos.* Madrid: Triacastela.

May, R. (1958). The origins and significance of the existential movement in psychology. In: *Existence* (ed. R. May, E. Angel, and H.F. Ellenberger), 3–36). Lanham, MD: Rowman & Littlefield.

Oliveira, A., Sousa, D., and Pires, A.P. (2012). Significant events in existential psychotherapy: The client's perspective. *Existential Analysis 23* (2): 288–304.

Rodrigues, V.A. (2006). Psicoterapia existencial: Esboço de uma problematização. *Análise Psicológica 24* (3): 401–403.

Rodrigues, V.A. (2008). Fenomenologia clínica das perturbações da personalidade. *Phainomenon 16*/17: 235–246.

Rodrigues, V.A. (2014). Are sexual preferences existential choices? *Existential Analysis 25* (1): 43–52.

Rodrigues, V.A. and Montenegro, M. (2013). Personality disorders as existential phrenitis: An ontological understanding. *Existential Analysis 24* (1): 36–47.

Sá Pires, B. (2016). Therapy with children and adolescents in the phenomenological-existential tradition: Community-based clinical interventions. *Existential Analysis 27* (1): 93–106.

Schneider, K.J. and Krug, O.T. (2010). *Existential-Humanistic Therapy.* Washington, DC: American Psychological Association.

Silva, S. and Sousa, D. (2018). Existential supervision: The supervisor's perspective. *Journal of Humanistic Psychology*. https://doi.org/10.1177/0022167818802905.

Sousa, D. (2004). A short note underlying reflection on psychotherapy research. *Existential Analysis 15* (2): 194–202.

Sousa, D. (2006). Investigação em psicoterapia: Contexto, questões e controvérsias. *Análise Psicológica 24* (3): 373–382.

Sousa, D. (2010). A descriptive phenomenological analysis of significant events in existential therapy. PhD thesis, University of Wales, London.

Sousa, D. (2014a). Phenomenological psychology: Husserl's static and genetic methods. *Journal Phenomenological Psychology 45* (1): 27–60.

Sousa, D. (2014b). Psicoterapia existencial: Análise genético-fenomenológica da existência. In: *Fenomanologia e práticas clínicas* (ed. A.M.L. Feijoo and M.B. Lessa), 17–45. Rio de Janeiro: IFEN.

Sousa, D. (2015). Existential psychotherapy the genetic-phenomenological approach: Beyond a dichotomy between relating and skills. *Journal of Contemporary Psychotherapy 45* (1): 69–77.

Sousa, D. and Vaz, A. (2017). A descriptive phenomenological exploration of significant events in existential therapy. *Existential Psychotherapy Journal of Humanistic Psychology*. https://www.researchgate.net/publication/266853544_A_Descriptive_Phenomenological_Exploration_of_Significant_Events_in_Existential_Therapy (accessed January 21, 2019).

Spiegelberg, H. (1972). *Phenomenology in Psychology and Psychiatry: A Historical Introduction*. Evanston, IL: Northwestern University Press.

Straus, E. (1959). The Fourth International Congress of Psychotherapy Barcelona, Spain, September 1–7, 1958. *Psychosomatic Medicine 21* (2): 158–164.

Tatossian, A. and Moreira, V. (2012). *Clínica do lebenswelt: Psicoterapia e psicopatologia fenomenológica*. São Paulo: Editora Escuta.

Teixeira, J.A.C. (1993). Introdução às abordagens fenomenológica e existencial em psicopatologia (I): A psicopatologia fenomenológica. *Análise Psicológica 11* (4): 621–627.

Teixeira, J.A.C. (ed.) (1994). *Fenomenologia e psicologia: Actas das 1ªs jornadas de psicologia e psicopatologia fenomenológicas e existenciais*. Lisbon: Instituto Superior de Psicologia Aplicada.

Teixeira, J.A.C. (1997). Introdução às abordagens fenomenológica e existencial em psicopatologia (II): As abordagens existenciais. *Análise Psicológica 15* (2): 195–205.

Teixeira, J.A.C. (2006a). Introdução à psicoterapia existencial. *Análise Psicológica 24* (3): 289–309.

Teixeira, J.A.C. (2006b). Problemas psicopatológicos contemporâneos: Uma perspectiva existencial. *Análise Psicológica 24* (3): 405–413.

Teixeira, J.A.C. (2008). Psicologia da saúde crítica: Breve revisão e perspectiva existencialista. *Análise Psicológica 26* (2): 335–345.

Torre, M. (1982). *Esistenza e progetto. Fondamenti per una psicodinamica*. Turin: Edizioni Medico Scientifiche.

Villegas, M. (1981). Análisis existencial: Cuestiones de método. *Revista de Psiquiatria y Psicologia Humanista 25*: 55–70.

35

Latin American Developments

Susana Signorelli and Yaqui Andrés Martínez Robles

Introduction

Existential Therapy is not a unified approach. Both in theory and in practice it encompasses many styles and different approaches. This is an interesting characteristic, since it has been present from its beginning, and is also present in what is called "existential philosophy." In philosophy, as well as therapy, this movement is characterized by not having a single founding figure, so it is difficult to follow a specific model. At the same time, this approach has always been resistant to orthodoxy. It must be stressed that here we are not talking about therapeutic approaches of a general existential orientation, which would lead us to include Logotherapy and Gestalt Therapy, for example. Here, we are referring specifically to the forms of therapy that identify themselves as Existential Therapy or, Existential-Phenomenological Therapy.

Regardless of the field of knowledge we are referring to, *diversity* is demanding more recognition. The different voices, no matter how much they may seem to be minorities, shine out demonstrating their uniqueness and their special contributions. The twenty-first century is partly framed by the acknowledgment that, paradoxically, the "majority" is actually just a minority when compared to the large number of existent minorities. We might say that there are so many minorities that the concept of a majority position begins to seem absurd. This is the case throughout the world and in every field. Latin America, and the specific field of Existential Therapy, is no exception.

The Latin American movement interested in Existential Therapy has had a complex history, since it began separately in different countries. At that time these different existential movements were not in contact with each other (Martínez Robles and Signorelli 2015). At the dawn of the twenty-first century, the diverse schools in Latin America have begun to communicate with each other organizing academic events, learning from each other, and sharing their different perspectives. The different countries have original developments that are worthy of being made known beyond their

The Wiley World Handbook of Existential Therapy, First Edition. Edited by Emmy van Deurzen, Erik Craig, Alfried Längle, Kirk J. Schneider, Digby Tantam, and Simon du Plock.

geographical borders. Some internationally renowned authors and thinkers have stated that the developments in Latin America augur well for the future of Existential Therapy in the world (du Plock and Deurzen 2015; Spinelli and May 2015, pers. comm.).

In previous texts, the authors of this article have advanced some of the Latin American propositions in the field of Existential Therapy, underscoring both our differences and our similarities (Martínez Robles and Signorelli 2011; Martínez Robles 2015). However, in countries outside Latin America, these proposals are usually regarded as if they were a single perspective. As if it is a single country with one perspective, one idiosyncrasy; even when dealing with countries that are different and have different social and cultural characteristics. Latin America encompasses 20 Spanish- and Portuguese-speaking countries located in North, Central (including the Caribbean), and South America.

There are, nevertheless, some shared traits that the Latin American reality has imposed upon the specific cultures of the different countries. These aspects reach all political, economic, academic, artistic, and cultural spheres. We have shared a history of conquest and colonization for approximately 500 years. We have experienced, and in some cases are still experiencing, struggle and strife, sometimes of a highly bellicose and violent nature, including civil wars, revolutions, and/or dictatorships. We are also undergoing similar social, cultural, economic, and political processes such as poverty, social injustice, differences between social classes in their access to quality services in education, health, and many others. All of this has led to a shared experience of fraternity between our peoples.

These centuries-old, and to varying degrees current, experiences are part of the construction of the national identity in each one of our countries. Latin American therapists have to struggle with these issues constantly, both personally and in our work with clients. However, at the same time, each of our countries has developed separately, which grants them unique identity traits, such as peculiar linguistic qualities, or different ways of approaching conflict.

Nevertheless, occasionally the European countries and/or the United States observe the reality of Latin America making no distinctions. They fail to acknowledge the uniqueness of the different cultures and idiosyncrasies of the different countries, which can often be uncomfortable or even harmful, since there is not a full acknowledgment of each country's identity and culture. Because of this, even though the different Latin American propositions about Existential Therapy have developed through mutual relations that are friendly and fraternal, we believe it is important to point out that *we do not have the same perspective.*

In the face of the wide diversity in the ways of conceptualizing Existential Therapy, in 2010 the Latin American Existential Therapy Association (ALPE) was created, assembling countries and institutions that are interested in sharing, researching, training, and developing the existential and phenomenological perspective in psychology and therapy. We have organized seven international conferences and we publish biannually the *Revista Latinoamericana de Psicología Existencial*, which already counts 11 published numbers.

If there is one thing that unites us, it is our interest in remaining in dialogue and collaboration, learning from both our differences and our similarities. In Mexico,

Existential Therapy parted from the felt need to integrate more philosophy and phenomenology into some humanistic therapies, such as Gestalt or Logotherapy. In Argentina, Existential Therapy is mainly derived from the psychiatric tradition in their search to integrate existential philosophy into their everyday practice. The other Latin American countries where Existential Therapy has a strong presence are Colombia and Brazil. It has some presence in Peru, and is practically absent in the rest of Latin America. In contrast, Logotherapy and Gestalt have a strong presence in most of Latin America.

Finally, before we continue, it is important to explain what we mean when we say "Latin America." That term includes all the countries that have Spanish, French, and Portuguese as their official languages. Thus, Latin America encompasses from Mexico all the way to Argentina and Chile. In other words, it is a cultural and linguistic distinction. Geographically there are some exceptions, such as Guyana where the official language is English, and Suriname were it is Dutch, so they are not considered Latin American countries. Belize, being an English-speaking country, would be the exception in Central America, and the English and Dutch speaking islands in the Caribbean. So culturally, Mexico is a Latin American country, but geographically it is located in North America.

In the following texts we attempt to clarify some characteristics of two of the main Latin American perspectives on Existential Therapy, those of Argentina (written by Susana Signorelli) and Mexico (written by Yaqui Andrés Martínez Robles), underscoring some of the aspects that make them unique.

Existential Therapy in Argentina

Susana Signorelli

The existential approach in Argentina comes from a long tradition. During the 1950s a group of psychiatrists in Buenos Aires, who were interested in applying ideas from the existential philosophers to the therapeutic practice, conformed the Onto-analytical Society. One of its members was Pablo Rispo, a psychiatrist of Italian origin and professor at the University of Buenos Aires, who developed a long career training psychiatrists and psychologists in this field.

With regard to existentialism, a philosophy he always stayed close to because of his personal interest, he began shaping it in his own way. Like every existential thinker, he did not follow only one author's point of view, but he followed many. Among them, he was inspired by: Husserl, Heidegger, and Sartre from a philosophical perspective; and Binswanger and Minkowski for the strictly therapeutic. Other psychiatrists also studied existentialism on their own although none of them were dedicated to training existential therapists.

One of Rispo's students was Susana Signorelli, who much later became his wife. They both planned what would become the therapeutic model taught and applied in Argentina from the Centre of Community Mental Health Activities Foundation (CAPAC), which they founded. This model may be regarded as the Argentinian Existential Therapy School.

This approach favors the therapeutic relationship as an encounter, where the therapist's presence and commitment demonstrate the difference to other doctrines. This encounter is based on a love relationship, where both protagonists are introduced as co-existent. They start distant, as they are strangers who should reach a "therapeutic us" in an emotional intimacy surrounding.

Analyzing the relationship is one of the foundations of Existential Therapy. So as to generate a bond, the therapist should be creative and find a way to be open to the uncertainty of the unknown. The therapist should also be willing to be surprised by the other as much as he or she should surprise the other individual. Repetitions are enemies of changes and opening to new opportunities. The therapist highlights how the patient expresses himself rather than what he expresses, the important fact is how existence is experienced. This therapy values and praises clients to be free individuals responsible for their own existence.

Existential Therapy intervenes in every typical part of existence; "typical" refers to those aspects regarded unavoidable and of which not any other living creature is aware of: life, death, suffering, freedom, social and personal responsibility, bonds, and so forth.

Existential Therapy in Argentina considers the way in which clients perceive time and space and how they build it together with the therapist; given that during the encounter, they create a new time and space. Regarding the core idea of time, it privileges the present and the future because changes from the present outline a different future, and at the same time, the future calls for a change in the current reality. The human being is the only being who builds its future for a moment in which it will not even be alive.

Regarding the symptoms and how to face them, existential therapists start from a phenomenological description of them; and, depending on what they refer to, therapists will attempt to ease them by enquiring into the client's experience in order to find their meaning and understanding of their existence in its entirety.

There is no immediate relief for the symptoms, not even with the use of pharmacological therapy, because nothing or no one may suddenly soothe distress. This is not either the existential therapist's proposal, as they believe that distress may encourage a change. However, it should be considered that in the high levels of grief suffered by some people, any attempt to talk is impossible. A good example would be a person with an intense wish to commit suicide or a person that attempted to commit suicide, a person in the middle of a schizophrenic outbreak or, without being so extreme, a person in the middle of a panic attack. In these cases, other therapeutic methods become necessary, and once this isolated crisis is treated, even at the same time, therapists should continue with their own worldview of existential therapy. One does not invalidate the other. To sum up, although it does not favor the immediate relief of the symptoms, resources that other sciences offer should not be disregarded.

This form of Existential Therapy can be addressed and applied to all sorts of people in any of the circumstances in which existence has been modified to help people recover from the insanity that surrounds them and recover their humanity. In this way, not only can we contribute with them to identify themselves as individuals but also to do so as social beings.

Pablo Rispo and Susana Signorelli designed a therapeutic method based on the existential vision mentioned above. Following Binswanger, Rispo put into words that every encounter has an ethical aspect (every encounter is based on principles), an aesthetic aspect (every encounter has its own beauty and affects the sensitivity), and a historical aspect (every encounter leaves a mark in every person, and even in the future of them and others).

The therapeutic relationship has its foundations according to "here," "now," and "among ourselves." "Here," due to the shared space; "now" refers to the time dimension of the encounter; "among ourselves" is about the dyadic relationship where a web of affection is weaved that also involves the society they both belong to (*vorwelt* and *überwelt*). This way to perform therapy is based on the existential hypotheses about being-with-the-Other and for-the-Other, by giving special importance to the group therapy, without putting aside or devaluing other kinds of therapeutic encounter.

Rispo contemplated that if the human being is born and flung into the world in a social environment, in a world with the others, it was necessary to implement this otherness during the therapy. Since conception there is someone (two Others) who conceived us; some Other who gave us birth; and once we are born, we are accepted into the world. "Accepted" implies a long period in which either a parent or whoever is responsible for us gives us food and affection to let us grow. Without the Other, this is not possible; without the Other who teaches us about the world, we die. Eventually, at best, we will live in a family, in a society, in a place, and a historical moment in the human race.

We will be in contact with others in the course of our life; no matter the quality of these bonds, the Other will always be present even when this presence indicates an absence, and when we die, we generally share space with other dead people. This means that since they are born until they die, human beings are social beings; furthermore, they are beings who co-exist. In order to establish an ego, a previous "you" is necessary and, even in the biological origin of the human being, it is essential to join two cells (sperm and egg cell) coming from two well-distinguished bodies (man and woman). Besides, the fragility of your birth requires somebody to welcome us to transmit the humanity in order to make existence possible; in other words, from the *lebenswelt* there is a "you."

Therefore, if co-existence makes existence possible and, in turn, one cannot separate from the other as they complete themselves in a wider context, which is the community, Rispo and Signorelli asked themselves: Why should we exclude in existential therapy that key aspect in people's lives? Why should we be limited by a two-way relationship? Why should we not give others the same therapy, others who are here and now? Group therapy is no other than the evidence of this human being idea about being-in-the-world-with-others. The beings do not only connect with other beings but with multiple beings that mirror them with different perspectives of themselves, the others broaden the viewpoint of the own being, which allows them to display countless possibilities.

The idea of there-then-and-among-other-selves that tends to happen in other therapies is replaced by the idea of here-now-and-among-ourselves-being-affectionately-together that will make a new origin of meaning easier. *There* refers to other space, something that happens somewhere else; *then* is referred to a time in the past; and *among other selves* refers to the client's relationships with other people that are not necessarily present. Therapists generally offer themselves as a screen or as an active listener, but they are not involved in the relationship with their clients, therapists do not go beyond the transfer analysis, they are not implicated in the relationship, and there is no emphasis in the encounter as the mean of change.

To achieve the among-ourselves in group therapy the use of lights, music, and dramatizations become central. All of them foster other ways of expression in a combination where essential themes of existence are captured. Among these themes, space, lighting (with the lights, a particular setting is created, the space changes into emotions), temporary nature (with music and its rhythm, its sounds and silences, it is spread out in a time that turns to be emotional), corporeality, spontaneity, freedom, authenticity (with dramatizations, without scripts or indications that leads to the body in movement, the experienced body) are used. For example, a client was able to express in group therapy his experience of being tortured when Argentina was under military government during 1970s. The client was invited to express his feelings, he accepted and went to the area available for dramatizations. He stood in the center, and the therapist turned off the lights of the area where the rest of the group was sitting and put the spotlight on him and put on loud music in which people were screaming. Light and music intensified the atmosphere that was already developing. The therapist, seen by everyone, got close to the client who was standing still and abstracted, and held his arms from the back as if the client was trapped. The client desperately shouted as if he was being tortured and broke into tears for a long time. The therapist stopped holding the client and the rest got close to him, some crying, and hugged him. The therapist then turned on the lights and once everyone was calm again the group talked about the experience. The client told the group that it was the first time in his life he was able to share in an affective environment his painful intimacy.

Likewise, clients are encouraged to express themselves creatively on the attempt to introduce them to their world. They can bring to the group therapy their favorite music, photos, paints; they can share sweets or souvenirs after travelling, and so on. The value and meaning given to those situations in their lives is highlighted and shared. We also use humor as a possibility to create an affective atmosphere. Since the relationship between the therapist and the client is spontaneous, humor arises in the same way. Generally therapists promote jokes related to what is being said and then the clients feel they can also be humorous. This makes it possible to ease the pains in life without undervaluing them; this distended atmosphere promotes the development of deeper conversations.

Another possibility offered by this approach is to understand the therapy as a model of social change. When I change with others and I see the other person as part of myself, I commit with all human race. This means that participating in community work outside the consulting room, in many cases with several clients or even them on their own, turns into the vehicle that allows for the being-for-the-other. This is named "open-doors therapy" to the group therapy and the community actions. Being open to the other, being available for the other, being a compromised being cannot be only a nice slogan about the existential therapy. It has to be shown in actions, an "open-doors therapy" makes these aspects easier and the existential therapist can be a promoter of such openness. From CAPAC Foundation, Rispo and Signorelli together with their clients have developed community activities, which emerged from their own initiatives: a school violence prevention program implemented with the support from the UNESCO; participation in the volunteers program at the Posadas National Public Hospital; open talks for parents; cinema debates; production of short educational films; theatre plays with clients and their families; and so forth.

Most therapies are characterized by keeping a private, intimate, and closed-doors space. These are aspects we do not reject, but, we include another aspect, which is opening ourselves to the other as a conscience of our own co-existent being.

The Mexican School of Existential Therapy

Yaqui Andrés Martínez Robles

Considering the different approaches to Existential Therapy, in Mexico we wonder how we could organize the different postures, so that we can sit at the same table in dialogue and learn from one another, even in the face of postures that at a first glance might seem irreconcilable. Before such diversity, we might use a three-part outline[1] to facilitate an understanding of them, making communication and dialogue between our differences easier.

The description shared here is about the way it is practiced in Mexico. The three orientations scheme is used for distinctions and dialogue between the different Latin American approaches. During my participation in the 1st World Congress on Existential Therapy (London 2015), I perceived that an outline, such as this, might aid in the understanding and dialogue between the multiple perspectives that were presented, from all over the world.

The outline proposes three distinct approximations/orientations in the field of Existential Therapy, each of which is distinguished from the others basically in regards to its aims and purposes, which leads it to develop distinct forms of practice.

A CLINICAL. This is the form that is closest to clinical psychology. The interest of this approach is supported by diagnostic criteria and, thus, it can be developed with health institutions. Out of the three models, this is the one that more commonly resorts to the use of techniques, be they original or taken from other psychological models normally adapted so they can be closely linked to existential phenomenology, to aid in the search of its aims, which can be more or less specific depending on the mental health or psychological criteria.

B EDUCATIONAL. Its main interest is in facilitating or promoting forms of existence that are more satisfactory for those seeking therapy. Generally, these "more fulfilling" forms are seen through the lens of existential thought. For

[1] Like any other outline, it is limiting and reductionist, as well as rigid. This is proposed mainly with didactic and organizational aims.

example, it is considered best or more convenient to live confronting the aspects of existence that generate anxiety, such as death and the search for meaning, rather than running away from them. Similarly, it is considered more appropriate to experience authentic interpersonal relations, rather than the opposite. Thus, the therapist's task is to facilitate the client's path towards the aforementioned goals.

C EXPLORATORY. This last approach underscores the therapeutic task mainly as a form of dialogical and collaborative inquiry, based on existential phenomenology and hermeneutics. In other words, an exploration of the client's existential and inter-relational situation as a being-in-the-world where, together with the therapist, the client will review not only her relationships with the world and with others, but also with herself and with her therapist. In this model there is no specific objective to fulfill. The tasks of this model will be described below.

Obviously, the different proposals may encompass two or three orientations. Each model may perform its own combination, emphasizing whatever seems most convenient to each context. There can also be models that develop a single orientation. Most approaches to Existential Therapy use *phenomenological exploration*, although with a different degree of emphasis, be it in relieving symptoms or some type of psychopathology (Clinical); in improving existence or the awareness of existence (Educational); or in exploration in itself, because it is considered a valuable activity (Exploratory).

The Mexican School of Existential Therapy, at least the style we have developed in the Círculo de Estudios en Psicoterapia Existencial,[2] has attempted to develop its approach (almost) exclusively within the Exploratory Orientation. However, some practitioners may find support in any of the other orientations in particular contexts.

This means that we consider Existential Therapy as a *conversation of a philosophical nature*. In other words, its objective is not to "repair." An existential therapist from the Mexican School will renounce any aim to heal, improve, promote maturity, or facilitate more fulfilling or satisfactory forms of existence. In Mexico, the Clinical and Educational orientations are used in most other schools of therapy such as Logotherapy or Gestalt, but the Mexican School of Existential Therapy is an attempt to put a purely Exploratory orientation into practice. In general, the therapist will renounce any wish to lead the client towards any "ideal" point, or to a place that is considered to be "better" in any sense, that is different to the point the client is at. There is no *a priori* objective established for the therapeutic process, beyond the co-construction of a relationship of such a quality that it will allow a joint exploration and analysis of the clien's inter-relational existence.

The tasks of a therapist in this third form of orientation may be summarized in these actions:

[2] The *Círculo de Estudios en Psicoterapia Existencial* was established in 2002, from the wish for an institution in Mexico, it is interested in the study and reflection on existential philosophy and phenomenology, and their application to therapy. Their main activity has been providing training in Existential Therapy through a three-year course. Its founder and director is Yaqui Andrés Martínez Robles.

1. **Exploring**. To explore means to start the therapeutic work through questions that attempt to promote the therapist coming closer to understanding the client's perspective, constantly verifying if her understanding is near to the experience being narrated to her. It is done through a *phenomenological attitude*, with the therapist showing interest and acknowledging that, though she may have studies and experiences concerning the issues placed before her, she will always be a beginner in regard to the client's experiences.
2. **Analyzing**. Through this action, the work is focused on the meanings constructed by the client's experience. It is an *hermeneutic* task not to be confused with merely rational actions. It is an activity that implies an acknowledgement that, in each experience that is narrated in therapy, the meanings contributed by clients and therapists, are influenced by: bodily physiology, collective history and language, personal history, social links, desires, aspirations, beliefs and projects, and the mood or state of mind. The analysis is performed in a *dialogical and collaborative* manner.
3. **Sustaining**. This implies acknowledging that working therapeutically means reviewing some extremely important areas of existence, such as: (a) situations and/or experiences that imply vulnerability; (b) issues that make direct reference to the construction of identity; (c) experiences that make reference to intimacy, or to the need or lack of intimacy; (d) satisfactory or unsatisfactory forms of interpersonal connection; and (e) the worldview, or how the client understands and relates to her relational situation as a being-in-the-world. Reviewing these areas tends to generate intense emotional experiences, which the therapist will attempt to share, remaining in them as long as it is necessary to continue exploring and analyzing them.
4. **Appropriating**. This is probably the hardest aspect of the approach to describe, since it is an action that takes place when the first three first aspects have remained continuously activated for some time. Thus, it is an aspiration, rather than an action. It means having the experience that the situation that we are exploring is ours, it belongs to us, and we can find some distinction in it, as small as it may be. That we are the owners of our existence, not like property in the sense of having or possessing an object or a thing, but rather as an extension of our being, of our identity; and that the inter-relational experience of being-in-the-world is not just a complex philosophical concept, but rather a possible experience for each of us.

These four verbs/aspects are based on the *existential-phenomenological and hermeneutic worldview and attitude* that are fundamental for the Mexican existential therapeutic style. These actions are performed within a post-Cartesian frame, since the work is based on an image of human beings that transcends the typical Cartesian subject–object split. We do not see the human being as separate from his world, nor do we see his body as separate from his mind, nor his emotions isolated from his feelings. We consider the human situation as a *relational situation* (Martínez Robles 2015).

Another aspect of this frame, is that we are parting from the idea that the experience of identity is a discourse, a socially constructed narration that can be repeatedly de-constructed and then re-constructed, and that any feeling of a more or less fixed and stable "I" is a necessary illusion so as to sustain an experience of continuity and coherence, which allows us to manage anxiety at bearable levels. Although this illusion is necessary for an experience of "sanity," occasionally it is intensified to the extreme, which prevents the necessary fluidity that enables us to face the novelty that is natural to existence.

This orientation, at least in the Mexican style, also implies *constantly working* **in, with, and from** *the therapeutic relationship.* This aspects places our proposal amongst the models that are called *relational*, not only because it is based on a paradigm that considers humans as in a *relational* situation, but also because, in congruity with this, we consider that the therapeutic relationship is, on the one hand, the main tool for exploration and analysis, and on the other, part of the social connections the client co-constructs in his/her existence. In this sense, the therapist is constituted as *the other* with whom the patient relates and constructs his/her existence. An important part of the therapeutic process is not only to try to construct a warm, collaborative relationship that facilitates exploration and analysis, but also to review the ways that we facilitate or hinder its construction. In other words, another task in the therapeutic process is to review the type of relationship that is being built by the participants, investigating what type of situations both are constructing, and how the patient faces the aspects of that otherness represented by his/her therapist, in ways that are either similar to what takes place with all the others with whom the clients relates in his/her everyday life, as those ways that are distinct and unique to their particular relationship.

As we can see, the Mexican proposal has to do with phenomenological inquiry performed in collaboration with the client, in which the therapist attempts to generate a close and warm relationship, suitable for the performance of the therapeutic tasks proposed in this orientation. This posture requires the therapist to take on a humble attitude, acknowledging that he cannot fully know his patient's experiences, nor name them with any certainty, nor understand them fully, much less conduct them in a way that is accurately adequate. He is in a position to gradually open himself to the mystery of the other and his existence.

The therapist invites the patient to explore and analyze things such as: How does he experience his existence? What does he like and dislike about it? What would he want to keep and what does he wish to change? How does he know that that is possible? How does he know that it is worth it? Who or what brings him closer or further from this experience? What type of help does he think he needs? Does he believe his therapist is the right person to help him? How does he reach all these conclusions? What is his bodily emotional experience when reflecting about these situations with his therapist?

To achieve this, it is convenient for the therapist to experience certain attitudes, and find a way to transmit them to his/her client as messages that are implicit during their encounters. These messages are:

a *You interest me.* I truly wish to know you and to understand your experience in a way that comes as close as possible to your perspective. I don't want to flee from your experience, no matter how complex, chaotic, confusing, or threatening it may seem to me. I believe whatever you have to say is worth listening to.

b *I am available for our encounter.* I will try to offer you the best of myself. This implies that sometimes I will listen to you attentively and silently, and at other times I'll ask questions to understand you better.
c *I want us to construct an honest relationship and link.* My intention is to talk with you, not about you, to share my impressions, ideas, and emotions with you, not about you. I hope I'll be able to be available to emotionally touch and be touched by our encounters.
d *I acknowledge that we are surrounded by great uncertainty*, and sometimes I will not know how to respond to your experiences. I hope I will remain open before the mystery that envelops us, acknowledging that when discussing your experiences, you'll know more about them than I will.
e *I have the best wishes for you and your existence*, even when none of us really knows what that means for certain.

As we can see, many of the aspects mentioned are part of a phenomenological and hermeneutic approach like that which has been developed in Existential Therapy in different parts of the world, as well as in Latin America. An aspect of the Mexican School that may be noted, is its interest in learning from and integrating proposals from other perspectives (such as that of the so-called British School) and make our own "mestizo" mixture with them. Although our geographical proximity to the United States may facilitate their influence on us, and some of the proposals of the American school have been taken into consideration for the development of the Mexican perspective, we tend to look suspiciously at the tendency of some of these approaches that focus on potentiality development and/or promoting a more "authentic" life.

Recently there has been a fascinating exchange via e-mail around the attempt to answer the question "What is Existential Therapy?" through which a large diversity of approaches has emerged. As has become evident through these exchanges, in Latin America as well as in other parts of the world, some Existential Therapy practitioners work with more educational or reparative orientations. They attempt to teach their clients more "appropriate," "authentic," "right," "real," or even more "existential" ways of living (Educational orientation). Or else, they try to help the client to get in "good terms with their difficulties," or even to build a relationship aimed at the correction of deficits, pathologies, or flaws (Clinical orientation).

Maybe because the Mexican School has been developed separately from psychiatric environments, or from clinical psychology (in contrast to the Argentinean proposal) – although this does not mean we don't work with all kinds of people – we consider our work to be mainly *philosophical*, in the sense that we aim at problematizing our client's narrative; that is, we invite them to question and doubt their certainties. It is important for our proposal that existential therapists part from a post-Cartesian, *relational* posture that invites us to renounce any ideal about human functioning, any pre-established objective of the therapeutic process, and dedicate ourselves to an exploration that may bring us closer, at least a bit, to understanding our relationship with the mystery of existence.

Conclusion

Existential therapy has taken a different course in every Latin American country. Each model shows different points of view, methodologies, and approaches. Obviously, it is impossible to summarize a complete therapeutic approach in the available space. However, we hope that this first outline will help the reader understand some of the basic tenets (and their differences) of two perspectives: the Existential Therapy in Argentina and the Mexican School of Existential Therapy.

We are open to these differences. In ALPE what brings us together is the shared commitment to approach the human being as another human being. We believe in the possibility of getting closer to other people's existence, from the simplest perspective to the most complex of the client's existence and our own. We have to take into account our similarities and differences.

The different Latin American proposals are in full development. ALPE is growing, encompassing more countries that are interested in developing the existential perspective in therapy, beyond humanist or Logotherapy approaches. The number of people that are becoming interested in the existential proposal is increasing, as shown by the growing interest in the different Latin American congresses. For this reason, we are proud to host the Second World Existential Therapy Congress, to be celebrated in 2019 in the city of Buenos Aires, Argentina. It will undoubtedly be a great opportunity to continue presenting the different proposals around Existential Therapy to the world, and a wonderful event to promote Existential Therapy worldwide, with the energy and passion that characterize Latin American countries.

References

Du Plock, S. and van Deurzen, E. (2015). The historical development and future of existential therapy. *International Journal of Psychotherapy 19* (1): 5–14.

Martínez Robles, Y.A. (2015). *Existential Therapy: Relational Theory and Practice for a Post-Cartesian World*, vol 1. (trans. B. Cornejo). Mexico: Circulo de Estudios en Psicoterapia Existencial.

Martínez Robles, Y.A. and Signorelli, S. (2011). *Perspectivas de la Psicoterapia Existencial. Una mirada retrospectiva y actual.* México: Editorial LAG.

Martínez Robles, Y.A. and Signorelli, S. (2015). A brief review of the history of existential psychotherapy in Latin America. *International Journal of Psychotherapy 19* (1): 89–94.

36

An East–West Dialogue

An outline of existential therapy development in China and related Asian countries

Xuefu Wang

An Encounter

September 12, 2007. A Sino-US bilateral forum on the psychology of religion was in progress at a campus hotel of Zhejiang Normal University, Southeast China. During a break, three people were sitting in the hotel lobby, having a casual conversation. They, respectively, were Louis Hoffman, Mark Yang, and Wang Xuefu. Louis Hoffman was a professor of psychology at the University of the Rockies while Mark Yang, born in Taiwan and migrated to the United States at nine years old, held a teaching position with Alliant University's Hong Kong campus. Wang Xuefu was a psychotherapist from Zhi Mian Institute for Psychotherapy, Nanjing China. The conversation went randomly for a while until it shifted to, and then focused on, existential psychology. Obviously the topic allowed them to bond with each other. Immersed in a tacit understanding they shared their zeal for existential psychology and were inspired to explore the possibility of collaboration in the field. The brief encounter of three of them felt like planting a seed and expecting something grow in days to come. "What is the situation of existential psychology in China?" was the question raised by Louis Hoffman and Mark Yang. Wang Xuefu, to the best of his knowledge, gave them an answer, roughly as follows.

Introduction

In academic circles in China there are scholars of Western existential philosophy. Viewed from the perspective of existentialism, a rich resource of likely existential thought can be found in Taoism, Confucianism, and Buddhism, the three major streams of thought that compose Chinese cultural tradition. Chinese literature resonates to a significant degree with Western existentialism. Lu Xun, a brilliant Chinese

The Wiley World Handbook of Existential Therapy, First Edition. Edited by Emmy van Deurzen, Erik Craig, Alfried Längle, Kirk J. Schneider, Digby Tantam, and Simon du Plock.

writer, can be regarded as the most profound existential thinker in modern China. His literary works, such as *Diary of the Madman*, *The Story of Ah Q*, *Kong Yiji*, present a number of typical characters that reveal the profundity of Chinese culture and Chinese psyche. This makes Lu Xun equal to the Western existential writers such as Franz Kafka and Albert Camus. Other writers such as Shi Tiesheng, Yu Hua, Mo Yan, Yan Lianke, Liu Zhenyun, scholars such as Chen Danqing, TV program hosts such as Cui Yongyaun are all exemplary members of a vanguard that have existential quality and touch the deep realm of humanity and human existence.

At the turn of the twentieth century China was in a transition from tradition to modernity. Chinese society, especially its intellectual community, began to critically reflect on Chinese cultural tradition that had been embedded with a long history of deeply set feudalism. Many reform-minded intellectuals advocated a cultural critique movement called the May 4th New Culture Movement, likened to the Western Renaissance. They opened fully to embrace Western thought in the hope of inspiring a social-cultural reform in China. Western existential philosophers such as Friedrich Nietzsche and Søren Kierkegaard, together with many figures in other fields, were introduced in China. Nietzsche, with his thought on the re-evaluation of tradition and calling for heroes (individualistically supermen of high intellectual caliber), had a significant impact upon young avant-garde Chinese intellectuals, including whom Lu Xun, for instance, was regarded as the "Nietzsche of China." With the emergence of Modern Chinese Literature as a form of culture critique, Lu Xun became the most brilliant writer and acute observer of the Chinese psyche. He directed his critical gaze at what he considered the cultural backwardness and the psychological cowardice of the Chinese character. He penetrated deeply into the shadowy realm of the Chinese psyche and exposed what he called the mental escapism as characterized by Ah Q, the most typical character of his literary creation. As an antidote to Ah Q mentality, Lu Xun advocates the Zhi-Mian spirit embodied in a galaxy of heroic individuals throughout West history, such as Socrates, Jesus Christ, Nietzsche, Byron, Shelley, all those he called "the warriors of the Spirit," and the same sort of heroes in Chinese history who were called "the backbones of China." With its strong spirit to liberate humanity from the long feudalistic derogation, the May 4th New Cultural Movement is an age of advocating individualism in the sense of calling for people to live genuinely and fully as human being worthy of respect. Therefore Nietzsche and Kierkegaard came right in time to toll the resonance with the zeitgeist of the age.

In 1949, Chinese communists took power and launched a series of political movements to strengthen the control of the nation. China was closed from the outside world for several decades, during which time Chinese people experienced the so-called Cultural Revolution. It was actually a movement of political power struggle that devastated the country most profoundly and laid a deep wound in the Chinese psyche. In the early 1980s, China was reopened to the world. After a period of intellectual drought when people were only allowed to study and follow Marxism and Mao Zedong thought, Chinese had a deep thirst for the Western thoughts that flew abundantly into China. Existentialism, once again, in the form of philosophy, literature, and psychology, was fervently welcomed by young scholars and students. There was a period of abundant translation of existentialism and psychoanalysis in the 1980s and the 1990s. Existential philosophers such as Friedrich Nietzsche, Martin Heidegger, Søren

Kierkegaard, Paul Tillich, Jean-Paul Sartre, Simone de Beauvoir, and existential writers such as Albert Camus and Franz Kafka, became known in the intellectual circles of China.

In the 1990s, at a number of universities, some psychology professors began to study existential psychology and mentored their students. These pioneers in this field of existential psychology included Che Wenbo, Yang Shaogang, Guo Benyu, Ren Qiping, Feng Chuan, and Ye Haosheng. Then came the next generation of researchers such as Fang Hong, Zheng Shiyan, Gao Jianting, Sun Ping, and Liu Yiyan. They were translators and researchers to begin with and became existentially informed scholars and therapists later on. In their research they traced the origin of existential thought from ancient Europe and the influence of existential philosophy of more recent times. Out of their personal interest and importance they attached to each of the following figures, they studied existential philosophers such as Kierkegaard, Heidegger, Sartre, and existential psychiatrists and psychotherapists such as Frankl, Binswanger, Boss, Laing, May, and Bugental.

More recently, in 2008, Louis Hoffman and Mark Yang initiated a trip to China for existential psychology training. Based on the face-to-face interaction and the supposition of existential richness in Chinese philosophy, literature, and the newly emerging awareness in psychology, a plan for East–West dialogue in existential psychology was synchronized in the minds of Louis Hoffman, Mark Yang, and Wang Xuefu. It actualized in four consecutive international conferences on existential psychology, respectively, Nanjing 2010, Shanghai 2012, Guangzhou 2014, and Hong Kong 2016 with related workshops, courses, publications, and forums. All these threads have come to be woven into the tapestry of existential therapy development in China and other Asian countries and regions.

East–West Dialogue: Existential Psychology East–West

In 2009, Louis Hoffman, co-edited *Existential Psychology: East and West* with Mark Yang, Francis Kaklauskas, and Albert Chan. Alongside the editors who also were contributors to the book, other US contributors included Erik Craig, Kirk J. Schneider, Myrtle Heery, Ed Mendelowitz, and Ilene Serlin. Chinese authors were also invited to make the book an East–West dialogue. Wang Xuefu contributed a chapter on Lu Xun and his Zhi-Mian thinking. Other Chinese contributors included Shen Heyong, Wang Wensheng, and Bao Zaohui. Additionally some overseas Chinese, such as Mark Yang, Albert Chan, Benjamin Tong who bridged the gap between West and East. The book was published in 2009, in which "Differences and difficulties in cultural understandings of existentialism are addressed forthrightly which deepens the reflection process that is a hallmark of existential psychology" (comment by David Lukoff, see Hoffman et al. 2009, p. i).

Existential Psychology Forum

In 2009, a forum on existential psychology, perhaps the first of its kind in China, was held in Nanjing. It was organized by Louis Hoffman, Mark Yang, and Wang Xuefu, in collaboration with the Social Work Department of Nanjing Population College through Yan Fengming. The US delegation was composed of Louis Hoffman, Mark Yang, James Ungvarsky, Michael Moats, Jason Dias, and Trent Claypool. The Chinese audience was impressed with Louis Hoffman's lectures on Western figures in existential philosophy, literature and psychology, the existential concerns, and therapeutic poems. James Ungvarsky presented an appealing theme: psychology of self-deception. In response, some Chinese speakers presented their experience in view of existential psychology. It was a tentative dialogue that paved a way to an upcoming international conference on existential psychology that was then brewing.

The First International Conference on Existential Psychology

The most significant event was the First International Conference on Existential Psychology held in Nanjing in 2010. It was co-organized by Louis Hoffman, Mark Yang, and Wang Xuefu, hosted by Nanjing Xiao Zhuang University through Tao Laiheng of the China Institute of Psychology headed by Sun Lizhe and the Zhi Mian Institute for Psychotherapy founded by Wang Xuefu. Its intention was to promote East–West dialogue in the area of existential psychology/therapy. The conference was highly commemorated as "the unprecedented event in 30 years history of existential psychology in China" (Guo 2010). Numerous existential psychologists from the United States presented on a variety of topics including: "Awakening to an Awe-based Psychology" (Kirk J. Schneider); "Human Existence: What is It? and What's in it for Us?" (Erik Craig); "Transience and Possibility: The Legacy of Rollo May" (Ed Mendelowitz)"; "Whole Person Healthcare" (Ilene Serlin); "Supervision Issues in Existential Psychotherapy" (Louis Hoffman and Mark Yang); "Art Therapy" (Richard Bargdill); and "Introduction to Existential Givens in the West" (Susan Gordon).

Chinese Scholars in existential psychology participated and presented on various topics, such as: "Approaches of Zhi Man and Existence" (Wang Xuefu); "Practice of Existential Psychotherapy" (Tao Laiheng); "30 Years of Existential Psychology in China" (Guo Benyu); "On Binswanger's Existential Analysis" (Ren Qiping); "Ultimate Concerns in Existential Psychotherapy" (Zheng Shiyan); and "Existential Psychology and Contemporary Chinese" (Chen Shiying). Some renowned scholars who may not connect themselves to existential psychology were also drawn to the conference and their presentations contributed to the diversity of the conference: "*Yin* and *Yang*: An Eastern Positive Approach of Counseling" (Zheng Richang); "Cultural Archetype and Soul Healing (Shen Heyong)"; "'Existential' Dilemma and Therapeutic Value of Zen Bhddhism" (Tang Zhongmao); and many more.

The conference was also seen to welcome the overseas Chinese scholars from the United States, Canada, Hong Kong, and Taiwan, including, for instance, Albert Chan (Marriage and Family Issues), Paul Wong (Core Themes of Chinese Existential Psychology), Jennifer Tam (Existential Psychology and the Arts), and Stephen Char (My Life Story).

Presenters from other Asian countries contributed to building the quality and creating diversity in the East–West dialogue, namely: Korea: Chae Young Kim (Religious and Spiritual Issues in Existential Psychology); Japan: Kingo Matsuda; Singapore: Jill Bromely (Movies in the View of Existential Psychology); and Oksana Okhrimenko.

The Second International Conference on Existential Psychology

In 2012, through coordination with Sun Shijin, psychology professor of Fudan University, the Second International Conference of Existential Psychology was held in Shanghai, mainly hosted by the Psychological Research Center of Fudan University. It was a banquet of existential dialogue between the East and the West. The opening speech was given on "Zhi Mian, Acceptance, Harmony, and Civilization" by Zheng Xingxia, followed by keynotes on various existential topics: Brent Dean Robbins' presentation was based on his book (co-authored with Sharna Olfman; 2012) *Drugging our Children: How Profiteers are Pushing Antipsychotics on our Youngest, and What We Can Do To Stop It.* Other keynote speeches included: "The Poetics of Suffering" by Louis Hoffman, and "The Symbol of the Iron House" by Wang Xuefu. Major themes of the conference included: "Existential Psychology and Cultures of East and West"; "Study of Existential Psychology"; "Study of Existential Givens"; "Existential Psychology and Arts Therapy"; "Comparative Studies of Western Existentialism and Eastern Taoism and Buddhism"; and "Existential Psychology and Religion."

Zhi-Mian as the Central Theme of Study

Chinese audiences also felt honored and inspired when they witnessed how Zhi-Mian, the indigenous Chinese approach of existential thinking and practice, was set as one of the central themes for East–West dialogue at the Second International Conference on Existential Psychology in Shanghai and especially recognized by Western colleagues. A rough estimation has found that the presentations in relation to the study of Zhi-Mian count up to almost 20, including, for instance, Erik Craig: "Dreaming as a Path for Zhi Mian"; Al Dueck: "The Cultural Psychology of Lu Xun and Xuefu Wang"; Mark Yang: "The Beauty of Zhi-Mian"; Diane Blau: "Enhancing Zhi Mian through Reflection"; Juliet Rhode-Brown and Betty Frain: "Facing the Invisible Dragon: Finding Meaning with a Special Needs Child in the Family"; Diana Edwards: "Termination and Zhi-Mian in Group Psychotherapy: Catalyst or Stumbling Block"; and also a Korean presenter by name of Christine Myunghee demonstrating her study of "Tao Psychotherapy from the Zhi Mian Perspective."

Presence of the Hellenic Society for Existential Psychology

The conference also welcomed the Hellenic Society for Existential Psychology, composed of Evgenia Georganda, Evy Dallas, Alexandros Harisiadis, and Katerina Zymnis-Georgalous, who presented on the "Application of 'Zhi Mian' for 'Oestrus of Life'," making a fascinating comparative study of the two terms (Zhi-Mian from China and "Oestrus" from Greece) by revealing respectively their existential meanings and implications.

Media Report

The Shanghai local *Xinmin Evening News* gave a full page of coverage of the conference titled "Zhi Mian (Facing) Suffering," subtitled "the Dialogue between Western Psychology and Eastern Philosophy" (2012). It composed of interviews with three people and touched on three topics: "The Interconnection of Eastern 'humaneness' and Western Existentialism" (Tang Liangsu); "Lu Xun's Zhi-Mian Thought Bridges the East and West Scholars" (Wang Xuefu); and "The Chinese notion of 'fluidity' in resonance with the Existential 'presence'" (Wu Fei).

The Third International Conference on Existential Psychology

In 2014, by coordinating with Yang Shaogang, the renowned Chinese existential scholar, the Third International Conference on Existential Psychology was held in Guangzhou, hosted by Guangdong University of Foreign Studies. One noticeable character of the conference was the studies of existential fundamentals and Chinese classics. This indicated that the dialogue had gone to a deeper cultural level. Here are some examples: "Fundamentals of Existential psychology with Comparisons to the *I Ching*" (Richard Bargdill); "Tao Psychotherapy and Existential Psychotherapy" (Erik Craig); "The Tao of Dreams" (Erik Craig); "Riding an Ox, Looking for an Ox" (Todd DuBose); "Junzidao: The Psychological Quest for Peace 'An'" (Meili Pinto); "Exploring the Existential-Humanistic Mentality of *Huang-ti Nei-ching*" (Yan Ru); and "Existential Psychology in *Tao Te Ching*" (Qiu Hongzhong).

Applying Existential Therapy to University Education

One unique character of the conference was the combination of existential psychology with psychological support for university students. The audiences witnessed a group of educational psychologists from France joining the East–West dialogue, which added another perspective. Some presentations show that existential psychology is also part of the Chinese education system, for instance, "The Significance of Existential Psychology to China's Education" (Liu Yuran).

The Fourth International Conference on Existential Psychology

The East–West dialogue is continuing through the international conferences. In June 2016, with the strenuous effort of Mark Yang, the Fourth International Conference on Existential Psychology was held in Hong Kong, a place where Mark Yang had once taught and trained in collaboration with Louis Hoffman and his existential team members. One of his local students, Bruce Lee, is a major promoter of existential psychology in Hong Kong.

The East–West dialogues happened mostly with existential psychologists/therapists "coming in" to China with few Chinese psychological existentialists "going out" to the world. In 2015, a globally unprecedented World Congress on Existential Therapy was convened in London. It was the first time that China had participants (Wang Xuefu and Yang Shaogang) join the worldwide existential gathering. The voice from a fledgling existential psychology in China was heard in the international arena, much strengthened by some US existential psychologists, such as Louis Hoffman, Erik Craig, Kirk J. Schneider, Shawn Rubin, and the overseas Chinese existentialist Mark

Yang, who had been pioneering in China in collaboration with Chinese colleagues. The congress organizers, for example, Emmy van Deurzen, Digby Tantam, Bo Jacobsen, Alfred Längle, and Simon du Plock were very supportive.

Training

While East–West dialogue by way of conferences was proceeding, existential therapy training programs took place in workshops, forums, certificate courses, research projects, and the publication of translated books. Major institutions that offer existential training include Zhi-Mian Institute for Psychotherapy, China Institute of Psychology (CIP), and the recently emerged Huajing Psychology. There are also individuals across China who claim to be existential therapists, such as, Ye Bing in Shanghai, Zheng Shiyan in Hefei, Liu Yiyan in Xi'an, and provide various forms of training to spread existential psychology.

The Zhi Mian Institute for Psychotherapy

The Zhi Mian Institute for Psychotherapy was found in Nanjing in 2002 by Wang Xuefu. With his education and training characterized in existentialism (theology, literature, and psychology), Wang Xuefu claims his existential orientation in practice and develops an indigenous Zhi-Mian therapy; this has been widely regarded as the Chinese existential approach to healing. Very importantly, the Zhi Mian Institute collaborates extensively with Western existential psychologists to offer training. Wang Xuefu, feeling called, took the lead in organizing the China Society of Existential Therapy, the aim of which is to promote existential psychology/therapy through domestic and international collaboration. Since 2008, many existential psychologists have conducted training at the Zhi Mian Institute, and through this they have extended existential psychology throughout China, and to other Asian countries and regions. Those who have lectured, conducted workshops, and initiated courses at the Zhi Mian Institute include Louis Hoffman, Mark Yang, Erik Craig. Kirk J. Schneider, Ilene Serlin, Ed Mendelowitz, and Rob Bageant.

The China Institute of Psychology (CIP)

The China Institute of Psychology, registered by Sun Lizhe in the United States in 2008, is a non-profit organization in education. CIP's major contribution has been to introduce Yalom group therapy training in China. It was also one of the hosting institutions of the First International Conference on Existential Psychology in 2010. With the institution's effective promotion, Yalom group therapy has become widely available in China. Especially, given the institution's strength in publishing, Irvin Yalom's books have become hugely influential. In the eight years since its founding, CIP has certified 39 Yalom group therapists and supervisors from among 3000 training recipients. But it is worthy of mentioning that Irvin Yalom defines his model of group psychotherapy not so much as existential, but rather, interpersonal. Chinese trainees know little about existential psychology because there are very few existential elements in Yalom group therapy training.

In 2012, CIP sought collaboration with Louis Hoffman and Mark Yang to set up a certificate-level existential therapy course, giving quality existential training to people from all across China. Ilene Serlin, the US licensed dance movement therapist, also joined CIP's training system.

HuaJing Psychology

The founder of HuaJing Psychology, Fei Xiaoyi, received her training of Yalom Group Therapy from CIP and started her own training program. She is active in promoting existentially informed group therapy across China. Her training, as she proclaims, traces the existential roots and is centered on the existential givens. Since its founding, two years ago, HuaJing psychology has trained approximately 200 people.

Trainers from the United States

The existential psychology conferences, as fully illustrated above, have acted as a stimulus to existential therapy training in China and related Asian countries. In conjunction with each conference there were pre- and post-conference workshops, not only in the host city but also in other cities across China. In the past decade, many existential psychologists have pioneered existential psychology training. There follows a very brief summary of their respective work.

Since 2008, Louis Hoffman and Mark Yang have worked closely in offering training through workshops and lectures. They have given a lot of lectures and conducted many workshops. Besides organizing conferences, they provided pre- and post-conference workshops. In 2012 they established a certificate course on existential-humanistic psychology at CIP. Since 2008, their training programs have been extended to many cities such as Shanghai, Hefei, Zhengzhou, Guangzhou, Suzhou, Shenzhen, Urumqi, and Hong Kong, and even further afield to Asian countries like Singapore and Malaysia.

Erik Craig came to China to participate in the 2010 conference in Nanjing and became the frequent participant of the subsequent conferences in Shanghai (2012) and Guangzhou (2014). He did not only present at conferences but also lectured at some universities and institutions all across China. Prior to his work in China Erik Craig had known the Korean psychologist Rhee Dongshick (the founder of Tao Psychotherapy) for ten years, and had conducted training programs in existential therapy. By working with Dr. Rhee and his colleagues, Erik Craig trained a group of existentially informed therapists in Korea. Since 2010, Erik Craig has been working closely with Wang Xuefu in conducting a series of workshops on existential therapy with a special focus on the existential analysis of dreams. Mark Yang has also extended his training to other cities in China and other countries and regions in Asia.

Kirk J. Schneider had been invited to conduct training in Japan and Russia before coming to China as an opening conference keynote speaker in 2010. In subsequent years he has given lectures and conducted workshops at the Zhi Mian Institute for Psychotherapy, the Academy of Chinese Culture Studies of Nanjing University, Nanjing Xiaozhuang University, China Institute of Psychology, and Guangdong University of Foreign Studies.

Ilene Serlin, carrying on the heritage from Rollo May, has contributed largely in conducting dance movement therapy in China. Her work has been demonstrated in Nanjing, Beijing, Shanghai, and Zhengzhou and acclaimed by many participants.

Ed Mendelowitz came to China to attend the conference in 2010 and soon after he returned to conduct workshops and give lectures on Rollo May at the Zhi Mian Institute and other universities such as Nanjing Normal University and Nanjing University of Finance and Economics. As a brilliant disciple of Rollo May he carries his teacher's heritage everywhere he travels. Other trainers include Rob Bageant, Shawn Robin, Meili Pinto, and Louise Sundararajjan, to name only a few.

Practice

China

As mentioned above, existential psychology was translated and studied by a group of scholars in China during the 1980s. At this early stage of development, however, it was introduced as a theory without a clinical foundation supported by practice. We had researchers but not practitioners per se. The Zhi Mian Institute for Psychotherapy, founded by Wang Xuefu in 2002, was the first institution of its kind in China that claimed to provide existentially oriented counseling and psychotherapy. Meanwhile, the Zhi Mian Institute also sets its effort in exploring an indigenous Chinese approach to psychotherapy, gradually recognized as Zhi-Mian Therapy. "Zhi-Mian" has resonance with "existence." It advocates facing life directly and questioning life's phenomenon with authenticity. In recent years, some US existential psychologists discovered Zhi-Mian psychology in China. In organizing the second existential conference in Shanghai, Mark Yang and Louis Hoffman recommended Zhi-Mian as the central theme for the conference, with an intention of uncovering "critical dimensions the phenomenon of Zhi Mian and to open up a field for mutual questioning and dialogue" (Craig 2012, p. 23).

Zhi-Mian Therapy has learned much from the West in its foundation, but it is not a repetition or imitation of Western existential therapy. It draws its original inspiration from Lu Xun's existential thought, just as existential therapy gains its source of thought in existential philosophy and literature, and its methodology in phenomenology. Zhi-Mian Therapy evolved from the situation of China, which calls for Chinese people to directly face their own reality. It provides a perspective through which to view, reflect on, and question our own suffering and trauma and seeks to heal our people. It emphasizes courage and sincerity. It opposes the mental escapism that is deep-rooted in our culture and society. It resembles Lu Xun from a century ago who sought inspiration in the new voice from the West but at the same time, creating a voice of our own to bring the Chinese the awareness of our mental escapism bred by feudalistic oppression. Wang Xuefu, in his practice of psychotherapy, finds the similar mental escapism in many sorts of psychological disorders. As perceived by Wang Xuefu, no matter how many forms a client presents as symptoms, they, by essence, can be seen as avoiding life's reality, due to, understandably, fear or sense of insecurity. Zhi-Mian, meaning courageously facing reality, becomes a way paved to aid recovery from escapism.

The tradition of Chinese culture is composed of three major streams: Confucianism, Taoism, and Buddhism. Each has in itself rich existential resources that are ready for a dialogue with Western existential psychology. For Chinese, the tradition of thought is a natural supply for understanding humanity and creating methods for practicing psychotherapy. Integration of Buddhism and psychotherapy has become prevailing phenomenon in China. Paul Yang, born in Taiwan and practice psychiatry in United States, integrates mindfulness into his treatment. Xu Jun, a therapist in Shanghai, also integrates Buddhist elements into his psychotherapy practice. Based on Taoist notions and modern psychotherapy, some Chinese psychiatrists such as Yang Deseng and his colleagues Zhang Yaling and Xiao Shuiyuan founded a Tao-Cognitive Therapy. But the existential resource in Buddhism and Taoism is yet to be explored. Mark Yang published *Existential Psychology and the Way of the Tao: Meditations on the Writings of Zhuangzi* in 2017.

Japan

When examining therapies developed in Eastern Asian countries such as Japan and Korea, we can easily trace their influences from Confucianism, Taoism, and Buddhism. Confucianism and Taoism have developed in Chinese soil while Buddhism originated in India and grew into its prime in China. It was around 4 to 6 BCE that Confucianism, Buddhism, Taoism spread into Japan and Korea and gave influence to nurturing therapies of their own. Morita Therapy, for example, developed by Japanese psychiatrist named Shoma Morita in the early-twentieth century, drew much inspiration from Taoism and Buddhism. Its tenet for therapy is adopting the Taoist way: following nature. NaiKan Therapy, also originated in Japan, it has a direct origin in Buddhism and has an emphasis on meditation as a way to therapy. When it comes to existential psychology development in Japan, the Academy of Counselors of Japan was invited to participate in the 2010 conference in Nanjing. Prior to that, Kirk J. Schneider was invited by the Academy to provide training on existential psychology.

Korea

Tao Psychotherapy was developed by Korean psychiatrist Rhee Dongshick in the 1970s. It is more akin to existential-humanistic psychology than Morita Therapy and NaiKan Therapy. According to Erik Craig, "Tao Psychotherapy is a synthesis of Eastern and Western psychotherapies seeking to integrate psychoanalytic, existential, humanistic, and transpersonal, and Eastern perspectives in a single coherent approach" (Craig 2007, p. 109). In her presentation at the Second International Conference (Shanghai 2012), the Korean presenter Christine Myunghee Ahn also pointed out that Tao Psychotherapy "integrates the Western intellectual traditions and psychotherapy approaches of the humanistic, existential and psychoanalytic views with the central teachings of the Buddhism, Confucianism, and Taoism" (Ahn 2012, p. 26). Jung Kee Lee, another Korean existential therapist, came into contact with existential therapy through Rhee Dongshick's Tao psychotherapy and became the founder of an institute on existential psychology in Korea.

Singapore

In the practice of existential therapy in Singapore, Zheng Liren is recognized as an existential counselor who has great existential perception. He works with students through an existential approach. Having received Western education in English but grown up in a Mandarin-speaking home, he has both a Western cultural perspective and Lu Xun's legacy and feels in himself a connection with the Chinese wisdom tradition. At the Second International Conference on Existential Psychology, on hearing Wang Xuefu's keynote address on Lu Xun and the Iron House, he wrote "When Many Men Pass One Way" reflecting on the wisdom of experience. He said this: "The wisdom opened possibilities for their people to negotiate the tragedies of existence and construct meanings of their experiences. This wisdom connected easily to people because the healers were not aloof from the tragedies of existence afflicting the afflicted" (Liren 2012).

Oksana Okhrimenko, born in Ukraine, works in Singapore as a therapist and claims an existential orientation. She is a frequent participant at the existential conferences in China and presents on different topics. She also practices existential-oriented coaching as a way of facilitating transformation. In Singapore there is also Jill Bromely who brings an existential psychology perspective to working with film.

Malaysia

Evone Phoo has been developing existential psychology in Malaysia and hosted the first conference on existential psychology in Malaysia in July 2018. Louis Hoffman, Mark Yang, and Erik Craig all have set their feet in Malaysia to provide existential training.

India

The developments and innovations of existential psychology in India is yet unknown. Rochelle Suri, an Indian psychologist receiving her education in psychology in the West, presented at the Second International Conference on Existential Psychology arguing that existential-humanistic psychology, if viewed on the surface of Western values, may find no space in India. "But a closer look at Existential-Humanistic psychology and Indian philosophy or Indian psychology indicates the two are compatible in more ways than one could perceive" (Suri 2012, p. 32). She finds that Existential-Humanistic psychology can "address and serve the psychological needs of the Indian psyche in a complimentary fashion" (Suri 2012, p. 32). S.K. Kiran Kumar, an existentially informed Indian scholar, in his communication with Wang Xuefu, had this to say: "The whole of Indian culture and thought traditions have dealt with existential issues in particular life, death, happiness and liberation from a spiritual perspective. So the whole of Indian Psychology has an existential orientation" (pers. comm. December 31, 2015). Gayitri Bhatt, a psychotherapist practicing in Bangalore, India, studied existential therapy at Sheffield University with tutors Digby Tantam and Emmy van Deurzen. She calls herself "an existentially informed therapist" and integrates existential approaches in her counsellor-development program as "an important component."

Reflection

In the field of psychology in China, the mainstream foundation is psychoanalysis, first spread by German psychoanalysts from 30 years ago and now also by US psychoanalysts. The family therapy of Virginia Satir, family constellation, and also Yalom group therapy are marketed widely. However, Al Dueck, the US psychologist, who travelled in China many times to encourage indigenous psychology, has observed that locally constructed psychologies are rare in this country. Only recently, existential psychology has come to China with an intention to facilitate and East–West dialogue. A series of East–West dialogues has manifested a spirit of equality, sincerity, and respect. Chinese audiences were most impressed with the warmth and diversity of the consecutive existential conferences. The variety of topics presented, the demonstrations, workshops, and the round-table discussions have provided many opportunities for existential scholars and therapists to share their respective views. Through the existential dialogues, Chinese participants, in varying degrees, have become existentially informed. Many are inspired to reflect on "Why, in China, do we need a psychology of existence?"

When reflecting on the East–West dialogues, we note the following:

1 The dialogues were mostly between US existential psychologists and Chinese scholars and therapists. There has been a lack of wider participation of existential psychologists from Europe and other parts of the world, making the East–West dialogue less substantially representative. We look forward to future dialogues that are of a deeper level and richer diversity.
2 In the dialogues we have encountered cultural differences and challenges in the understanding of existentialism. In a collectivistic culture, meaning is to be given by a certain respected authority rather than explored personally. Some participants of the conferences would expect that existential psychologists provide a meaning of life. The examination-centered contemporary Chinese education system has enhanced people's expectation of a given correct answer. At the same time, given the fact that existential psychology is new in China, it will take time for Chinese to be comfortable with this new way of thinking and living than to be required to obtain it on a given level of knowledge. As can be predicted, the dialogue, when going on to the deeper level, may cause uneasiness among Chinese, but it would also be just as significant. The dialogue is rather an encounter of cultures, a culture of China that breeds more avoidance and a culture of the West that encourages more direct facing. Chinese may feel more challenged but will hopefully learn more from the East–West dialogue.
3 Many Chinese people have a misunderstanding that existential therapy is not so much a "therapy" as other therapies because it does not have methodologies of its own. This was Irvin Yalom's view some years ago; he regarded existential psychotherapy as representing a quality way of experiencing and reflecting on the human condition. Yes, existential therapy claims that quality but it is also a therapeutic approach no less than other therapies. It creates its own methodologies, not as commonly assumed that it only borrows methods from other therapies. How can a therapy with its profound depth and richness in culture not create methods of its

own? Only that it creates by nature, not by purposefulness; it creates when there is a need, not a pre-set method. It aims to fine-tune in accordance with people, time, and circumstances, and does not act in a procrustean way. Existential therapy is, more than other therapies, a way of creation, including the creation of method.

4 In Chinese culture there is an emphasis on relationship, experience, nature, which resonates deeply with existentialism. Existential psychology also brings us something that our culture seriously lacks: for instance, its emphasis on the respect of the individual, the freedom of choice, and a frank way of reflection. These, hopefully, will become an antidote to the tyrannical elements permeated in our collectivism that oppress the individual. When we think of China and its history, we find that the Chinese have been suffering so much while reflecting so little. This is what Lu Xun once called the mental escapism: we tend to avoid our reality. Existential therapy, as an approach, invites people to reflect on fundamental issues of life, inspiring us to reflect deeper on our condition so that we live an examined life and make wise choices based on awareness of value and meaning. Chinese people need to reflect and question their own history, culture, and reality from the existential perspectives on suffering and trauma, deprivation of humanity, in our pursuit of a life of meaning and awareness. We need to Zhi-Mian (directly face) our life.

References

Ahn, C.M. (2012). Zhi Mian and pointing directly at the nuclear feeling in Tao psychotherapy. In: *Proceedings of the Second International Conference on Existential Psychology Congress* (ed. Sun, S., Gao, S., Chen, K. et al.). Shanghai China: The Society for Humanistic Psychology.

Craig, E. (2007). Tao psychotherapy: Introducing a new approach to humanistic practice. *The Humanistic Psychologist 35* (2): 109–133.

Craig, E. (2012) Facing and fleeing being-in-the-world. In: *Proceedings of the Second International Conference on Existential Psychology Congress* (ed. Sun, S., Gao, S., Chen, K. et al.). Shanghai China: The Society for Humanistic Psychology.

Guo, B. (2010). 30 Years' History of Existential Psychology in China. Presentation at the First International Conference on Existential Psychology, Nanjing, China.

Hoffman, L., Yang, M., Kaklauskas, F. et al. (2009). *Existential Psychology East-West*, Colorado Springs: University of the Rockies Press.

Liren, Z. (2012). When many men pass one way. https://www.saybrook.edu/blog/2012/08/21/08-21-12/ (accessed January 21, 2019).

Olfman, S. and Robbins B.D. (2012). *How Profiteers are Pushing Antipsychotics on our Youngest, and What We Can Do To Stop It.* Santa Barbara: Praeger.

Suri, R. (2012). Bridging Eastern philosophy with Western psychology. In: *Proceedings of the Second International Conference on Existential Psychology Congress* (ed. Sun, S., Gao, S., Chen, K. et al.). Shanghai China: The Society for Humanistic Psychology.

Xinmin Evening News (2012). No. 225: June 6, Shanghai, China.

Yang, M.C. (2017). *Existential Psychology and the Way of the Tao: Meditations on the Writings of Zhuangzi.* New York: Routledge.

37

A Review of Research on Existential-Phenomenological Therapies

Joel Vos

The Historical-Philosophical Context

This chapter gives an overview of research findings on Existential-Phenomenological Therapies (EPT). For any other type of psychological therapy, such as cognitive behavior therapy, a chapter like this would be relatively straightforward, as it would mainly review statistical results from clinical trials and psychological laboratory experiments. However, EPT research is more complex, as EPT is historically rooted in a scientific debate about knowledge and truth (i.e., "epistemology").

The philosopher Sartre (1967) summarized this debate with his famous adage "existence precedes essence." That is, traditional research has tried to explain the complex subjectively lived experience of individuals with categories, labels and numbers. However, for example the score "10' on the Beck Depression Inventory does not tell what an individual client precisely experiences, as this only tells how the individual answered the standardized questions, which may give a general indication of how they feel at this moment compared to a standard, set by researchers. There is much more to their experiences than the number "10." Dilthey (1895) clearly differentiated this essentialist way of "explaining" psychological phenomena with external instruments and objective observation (*erklären*) from "understanding" from within the individual's subjectively lived experience (*verstehen*). Dilthey, and many other phenomenological philosophers and therapists such as Sartre, have tried to turn the scientific paradigm more towards an inside understanding of the subjectively lived experiences from clients, therapists, and what happens in their relationship and in the therapeutic processes.

For example, in his PhD thesis, in 1913, Heidegger described how psychologists reduced ("objectified") the totality of our subjectively lived experiences to discrete objects or labels. For example, psychoanalysts in Heidegger's time reduced the complex subjective experiences of individuals to psychological-emotional drives,

The Wiley World Handbook of Existential Therapy, First Edition. Edited by Emmy van Deurzen, Erik Craig, Alfried Längle, Kirk J. Schneider, Digby Tantam, and Simon du Plock.

Ego and Super-Ego. In line with associationist philosophers such as Hume and Locke, the behaviorists Skinner and Watson wrote how mental health problems are often caused by irrational connections between prior experiences and by reinforcements, like being bitten by a dog can cause dog phobia. According to Heidegger, there can be much more to underlying experiences such as phobias, as our experiences can express the totality and dynamics of our fundamental being: "the view that psychology – which turned long ago in psychoanalysis – is taken [...] as a substitute for philosophy (if not for religion) [...] [they are] representative of modern science which is based on the fact that the human being posits himself as an authoritative subject to whom everything which can be investigated becomes an object" (Heidegger 1987, pp. 94, 310).

To explain this, Heidegger often used the metaphor of a house standing in wider surroundings (Vos 2014). He used this metaphor to explain the experiences of individuals, the role of language, and any type of knowledge – *logos* – in general. Individuals build and live in houses of essences, labels, psychological models, and limited world views, but these houses are embedded in wider environments, which are often ignored. For example, in 2017 many psychologists seem to live in a house of numerical research, clinical trials, and laboratory experiments. They regard this as the sole and only truth: this is the scientific paradigm within which they work, and they need large revolutions in thinking before they would question the walls of their house and would walk into their surroundings to look for other possible research methods outside their house of positivist psychology (cf. Popper 1956).

Thus, most research seems limited as it only focuses on one dominant paradigm and does not examine the relationships with the wider surroundings. According to Heidegger, Binswanger, and Van Deurzen, our experiences – including our research – are always embedded in wider surroundings, such as the worlds of the self, our physical being, social connections, and our spirituality. For example, doing a randomized controlled means that I will relate to individuals as research objects in a physically standardized context, where I reduce the subjectively lived experience of clients in specific questionnaires or categories. These scientific findings may be internally valid – as I have consistently followed all internal rules that count inside my house – but they may not be ecologically valid, as they do not take into account the wider ecology of individuals.

According to Heidegger, knowledge is not only limited by its focus on a specific location within wider surroundings (topology), but also by its focus on a specific fixed time (temporality). That is, every era perceives knowledge in different ways, such as the empirical positivist paradigm dominates modern psychology, and this is likely to change as all paradigms seem changeable. For example, in many countries phenomenological-existential therapies are not included in standard mental health services as these only include therapies of which the effectiveness have been proven in randomized controlled trials. However, it is possible that in a century from now, randomized controlled trials may be regarded as invalid research as we may have developed a different understanding of truth then. Furthermore, Heidegger – and even more Gadamer and constructivist philosophers (e.g., Neimeyer and Raskin 2000) – have examined the process of knowledge creation, such as the relationship between the researcher and the participants, logical reasoning, and abstraction from individual experiences to general statements. Therefore, phenomenological researchers often explicate how their personal perspective may limit their research findings here and now (i.e., hermeneutics), and they reflect on the position of their research within the wider context, via self-reflection and reflexivity.

Thus, Heidegger (1927/2001) suggested that we should not reduce psychological experiences to objectified distinct phenomena ("ontic") such as psychological labels or numbers in questionnaires or laboratory experiments. Instead, we should try to understand subjective experiences from the topological and temporal totality of our being ("ontology"). In his early work, such as *Being and Time*, Heidegger started with showing how current scientific paradigms such as psychologism are limited. However, in his later work, he avoided starting his writing with a criticism on existing paradigms and instead he started from the perspective of the totality of Being. Heidegger showed from the perspective of this totality how specific houses of knowledge evolved at certain places in these wide surroundings for certain periods of time. This transformation in his philosophical writings seemed to go hand in hand with an increasing criticism of therapists such as the Daseinsanalysts Binswanger and Boss who tried to directly translate his work into psychotherapeutic practices, and whose work Heidegger started to criticize for being too essentialist. Many phenomenological-existential researchers and therapists seem to stand in this line.

Epistemological position

Over the years, researchers on EPT have held four different positions on the nature of knowledge ("epistemology"), as described in Vos, Cooper, Correia et al. (2015a).

First, existential-phenomenological therapists have traditionally been reluctant to follow the medical paradigm that focuses on *explaining* phenomena with instruments and observations, such as questionnaires and laboratory experiments. However, recent years have seen more clinical trials (Vos 2016a). This type of research seems to assume that we have direct access to reality and can directly test hypotheses for instance about "whether EPT works." The research findings are regarded to be objective and generalizable in general. Although most research may be characterized as traditional positivism, some authors position themselves in critical realism, which takes into account the contextualized and subjective ways individuals make sense of their world.

Second, most existential-phenomenological therapists seem to reject the idea that the client's reality is directly accessible by instruments, calculations, and observations. Due to our limited senses, we cannot have absolute certainty what is real and true, as we have only access to our *perception* about reality. Therefore we cannot *explain* phenomena objectively, but we can only try to *understand* these from the perspective of the totality of an individual's subjectively lived experience. Consequently, research questions are not about testing hypotheses "whether what works in reality" or about universal structures of human experience, but focus on the subjective/idiosyncratic and inter-subjective/relational experience of a specific phenomenon by clients and/or therapists: how is meaning constructed in a certain context? Such questions have been answered with a wide range of qualitative methods, such as systematic case studies, discourse analyses, conversation analyses, descriptive and interpretative phenomenological analyses, and narrative psychology (Smith, Flowers, and Larkins, 2009), and are often grounded in relativist or postmodern epistemologies (e.g., Loewenthal 2003). Inherent to this methodology is the practice of researchers scrutinizing the generalizability of the findings and acknowledging their own interpretative biasing role. Some authors have argued that this type of research fits particularly well with EPT, as existential-phenomenological practices are usually not standardized but tailored to clients in their unique context and may be best defined as an unstandardized unoperationalizable "existential therapeutic attitude" or "deep intuition" (Van Deurzen and Adams 2011; Yalom 1980). Consequently, from this perspective, "the validation, justification and improvement of therapies can and should only be developed in client-centered ways, for instance by focusing on the client's self-reflection, the unique therapeutic relationship, and the therapist's own development, consisting of intensive training, personal therapy and critical self-reflection" (Vos 2015).

Third, one specific qualitative approach, which is particularly popular in EPT research, regards *fundamental phenomenology* (Vos 2015). On the one hand, it refutes the over-simplistic "psychologicalization" of reality, as there is a reality that we already understand from within our daily life world (Husserl 1901/1975). On the other hand, it also rejects the over-simplistic idea of direct access to "reality": we often cover reality and make it inaccessible for ourselves (Heidegger 1927/2001). Therefore, researchers need to uncover reality and "return to the things themselves" through systematic critical procedures, such as critical self-analyses, which include temporarily setting aside our assumptions and biases ("rule-of-epoché"), neutrally describing the phenomena ("rule-of-description"), avoiding placing any initial hierarchies of significance or importance upon the themes of description ("rule-of-equalization"), and intuitively understanding the true essences in the research data ("eidetic reduction") (Spinelli 2005). Fundamental phenomenology research focuses on the common structure of a phenomenon such as anger (e.g., "what are the main experiential features of being angry?"), in contrast with idiosyncratic interpretative-phenomenological-analyses that focuses on the personal meaning and sense-making for particular individuals (e.g., "how do people who have complained about their medical treatment make sense of being angry?") (Smith et al. 2009). Examples are conceptual, phenomenological, and Daseinsanalytic interpretations of universal experiences such as being a therapeutic practitioner (De Feijoo 2012) or an immigrant (Vos 2005) or having psychosomatic complaints (Condrau 1994).

Fourth, in line with phenomenological and post-modern philosophies, the *pluralistic* methodological paradigm claims that there is neither one method considered best for psychotherapy research nor a given hierarchy of evidence (Cooper and McLeod 2011). In line with the existential adage of "existence precedes essence," it is assumed that absolute true scientific labels may not exist – neither in positivist nor qualitative paradigms – and to reveal our experienced reality we need to use multiple methods, such as qualitative, quantitative, case studies, process-outcome studies, outcome studies, surveys, and experimental designs (Vos, Cooper, Correia, and Craig 2015b). Combining methods can be mutually enhancing: "corroborating, triangulating and elaborating each other, with the possibility of an active, continual process of interpretation and re-interpretation" (Goss and Mearns 1997). Pluralistic research may not lead to one conclusion and one prescriptive-normative recommendation, but often stays with the descriptions of different opinions and research findings.

This chapter is based on pluralistic epistemology, as pluralism focuses on the existence of different co-existing perspectives and their relationships. According to Heidegger we should not only focus on one house of research, albeit the house of positivism or the house of reductionist phenomenological psychology. We need to investigate how our different houses are related, how they came into existence – why did I build my house here and not there where you have your house? – and how they relate to the wider context (Vos 2014).

Effectiveness research

How does EPT sit within the positivist medical paradigm that dominates psychology and mental health services? Positivist researchers often search for evidence for its effectiveness in Randomized Clinical Trials (RCTs). Effectiveness describes to which extent an intervention brings about the desired effect. The desired effect that is focused on in therapy trials usually primarily regards a reduction in symptoms of psychological disorders, such as anxiety or depression. Effects are commonly measured with standardized measurement instruments such as questionnaires. To ensure that the measured effects are caused only by the therapeutic intervention, and not by extra-therapeutic events, the conditions under which the therapy is provided are standardized as much as possible, such as giving therapy to a small selected group of clients with a specific psychological problem, which often do not represent the ecological complexity and subjectivity of mental health care practices.

Given the limitations of this positivist paradigm and the criticism from phenomenology, no controlled randomized trials have been conducted on the effectiveness of EPT. An exception is the non-controlled clinical trial on existential experimentation, which is a short-term therapy applying phenomenological methods in therapeutic practices with clients and considering human potential from humanistic psychology to support recovery and aim for well-being (Rayner and Vitali 2016, 2018). The approach is standardized only to the extent that generic phases in the therapeutic process have been identified, and that therapists are trained and supervised to work in phenomenological ways with clients. The trial shows good ecological validity by including a broad range of clients in primary care settings. Preliminary findings indicate large improvements in questionnaires that measure general psychological stress, anxiety, and depression, with low relapse and dropout rates.

Correia, Cooper, and Berdondini (2015) have conducted a series of surveys in which they asked existential therapists worldwide about their practices. This study also included those who do not merely identify themselves as existential-phenomenological therapists but also for instance, as a Logotherapist. This study showed that EPT cannot be clearly distinguished from other existential therapies, as many self-identified existential-phenomenological therapists use non-phenomenological therapeutic methods and therapists who do not primarily identify themselves as EPT do use similar existential-phenomenological methods. Correia et al. found that existential therapists used four – sometimes overlapping – therapeutic competences: phenomenological skills, relational skills, explicating existential themes, and therapeutic school-specific competences (Correia et al. 2015). Furthermore, there seems to be a trend in publications on meaning-centered and humanistic-existential therapies that integrates phenomenological skills more explicitly (Vos 2018, accepted for publication). Some differences between the different therapeutic schools may also be mainly in terminology, for example, it will be explained below how explicitly addressing different types of meaning in meaning-centered therapies may be similar to phenomenologically exploring different worlds. As the different existential approaches seem to be slowly merging, it is worthwhile examining their research.

In 2015, a systematic literature review and meta-analyses was conducted on any types of existential therapies. This yielded 15 RCTs and 27 other non-RCTs measuring the effects of existential therapy (ET) compared to a baseline measurement but without randomization and/or without control groups (Vos, Craig, and Cooper 2015). Five RCTs described Supportive-Expressive-Group-Therapy, which is a type of US existential-humanistic therapy aiming to help physically ill patients face and adjust to their existential concerns, express and manage disease-related emotions, increase social support, enhance relationships, and improve symptom control (Classen et al. 2001; Spiegel et al. 1989). This demonstrated significant but small improvements in their psychological distress and self-efficacy (resp. *Cohen's* $d = 0.18$, $p < .01$, $n = 6$; $d = .11$, $p < .05$, $n = 1$); follow-up effect sizes were small and non-significant ($p > .05$); non-RCTs showed similar small, non-significant effects. Small non-significant effects were found in one RCT and one non-RCT study on experiential-existential therapy, which is an existential-humanistic approach with a strong experiential-phenomenological focus, supporting clients in openly facing their experiences and existential processes (Van der Pompe et al. 1997). One RCT for cognitive-existential group therapy showed similarly small non-significant effects (Kissane et al. 2003). The meta-analyses suggested a statistical trend, that applying phenomenology without simultaneously explicitly addressing existential themes such as meaning in life is less effective than combining phenomenology with explicating existential themes ($d = .22$, $p = .08$).

Many clinical trials have been conducted on meaning-centered therapies. This type of therapy helps clients in a systematic and explicit way to live a meaningful and satisfying life, despite physical, emotional, social, and practical limitations. Most studies are based on structured brief therapy manuals, describing therapist skills about assessment, meaning-specific issues, existential-phenomenological method, therapeutic relationship, and spirituality/mindfulness. These therapies cover a wide range of didactic techniques, psycho-education, group discussion, Socratic dialogue, guided experiential exercises, and homework. In total, there have been 26 RCTs (total sample $N = 1975$), 22 with non-randomized control groups ($N = 3775$), and 22 uncontrolled pre-post studies ($N = 6547$). These trials show that, compared to baseline measurement only, clients experienced significant large improvements of their quality-of-life and level psychological-stress (resp. Hedges' $g = 1.13$, $SE = .12$, $p < .01$, $N = 49$; $g = 1.21$, $SE = .10$, $p < .01$, $N = 49$). However individual studies varied much between each other in effect sizes, and the effects were significantly larger in non-RCTs than in RCTs. Therefore, further analyses focused only on RCTs, which revealed that, compared to the effects in control conditions, meaning-centered therapies had large significant effects both at termination and at follow-up on quality-of-life (resp. Hedges' $g = .86$, $SE = .01$; $g = .85$, $SE = .13$) and on psychological-stress ($g = .84$, $SE = .08$, $p < .01$; $g = .75$, $SE = .10$). Effects were larger on general quality-of-life ($g = 1.22$, $SE = .12$) than on meaning-in-life ($g = 1.00$, $SE = 07$), hope and optimism ($g = .98$, $SE = .16$), social well-being ($g = .81$, $SE = 13$), and self-efficacy ($g = .75$, $SE = .10$).

Additional meta-regression analyses indicated that the improvement in meaning-in-life strongly predicted a significant decrease in psychological-stress ($\beta = -.56$, $p < .001$); this suggests that meaning-centered therapies reduce psychological-stress *thanks to* explicitly addressing and improving meaning-in-life in therapy. Thematic analyses of the treatment manuals showed that most meaning-centered therapists used meaning-centered assessment, meaning-specific, relational, phenomenological, experiential/mindfulness, and existential skills. Meaning-centered practices had larger effects when these did not include religious-spiritual formulations, had a clear systematic approach, explicitly stimulated clients to set and experiment with achievable goals in daily life, used mindfulness exercises, explicitly discussed one type of meaning per session (cf. the four worlds of Heidegger, Binswanger and van Deurzen), addressed self-worth, discussed existential limitations, mentioned the coherence of time, and focused on creating a positive therapeutic relationship. There was no evidence that the stronger therapists focus on phenomenological skills, the more effective the therapies become; this lack of effect could be due to research limitations.

Pluralistic counselling and psychotherapy may be described as a more integrative version of EPT (Cooper and McLeod 2011). This approach starts with the assumption that every client is unique, and therefore different clients may have different needs at different moments in time. There is not one best way of working with clients, and therefore pluralistic-therapists bracket their assumptions about the therapeutic method and outcomes, and instead use phenomenological methods to focus on the experienced needs and preferences of the clients. To facilitate this client-centered approach, therapists use meta-therapeutic talk and questionnaires. Therapists can use existential and also other therapeutic methods to address the needs and wishes of clients. Several ongoing clinical trials on the effectiveness of pluralistic counselling indicate positive results on psychological well-being (e.g., Cooper et al. 2015).

Humanistic therapies are another group of therapies that have some similarities to EPT, particularly given their client-centeredness and focus and on the therapeutic relationship. A meta-analysis of 86 studies showed large short-term and long-term effects on psychological stress, anxiety, and depression (Elliott 2002). This review did not specify the extent to which phenomenological skills improved the effectiveness.

In summary, there is only one on-going non-controlled trial that focuses specifically on EPT. The findings from other existential and humanistic therapies suggest that in combination with other therapeutic skills, phenomenological-therapeutic skills could be beneficial to clients. There is no evidence (yet) that phenomenological-existential competences alone are sufficient to create significant therapeutic change.

Fundamental research on phenomenology

Phenomenology has its roots in Ancient Greek philosophers such as Plato and in religious traditions such as Taoism (Vos 2018, accepted for publication). Its more recent conception in the West can be found in medieval mystics such as Meister Eckhart who identified the steps of purgatio, illuminatio, and unio. These mystic steps implied that individuals focused on their relationship or attitude towards God or the Holy, via which they set aside their mundane approaches that blocked their relationship; after they had emptied themselves from these blockades, the Holy could be revealed to them or they could become one (cf. Visser, Garssen, and Vingerhoets 2010). Kierkegaard reformulated these mystic steps as aesthetics, ethics, and religion. Schopenhauer and Nietzsche further developed this phenomenological tradition, but started to leave out the explicit religious context. This is similar to the atheist trend in several religions, such as Buddhism, which says that if you meet the Buddha on your road you need to kill him, or like Meister Eckhart who said that we need to let go of God to become one with Godness. Brentano and Husserl developed a secular version of phenomenology, which Heidegger and others further elaborated. For example, for Sartre, phenomenology seems to be about understanding our freedom and nothingness of being. Instead of the Holy being communicated to the individual or the individual becoming One, secular phenomenology helps to empty ourselves from unhelpful intentions and attitudes so that we can perceive our worlds as they appear with the least possible interference from ourselves. The secularization made phenomenology accessible not only as an existential method but also as a therapeutic and scientific method. Instead of focusing on the most holy of the holiest, EPT focuses on challenges in everyday life, breaking down our self-deception by creating dreams and myths telling that life can be challenge-free, and instead accepting life as it comes and realizing our freedom.

Like all scientific methods, the basic assumptions of the phenomenological method cannot be proven. These are postulates, like a philosophy or religion. This does not make phenomenology less sound than for instance positivism, as the latter is for instance based on the assumption that reality is directly accessible via measurement and quantification but this assumption cannot be proven. From a phenomenological perspective, all scientific positions are limited, as long as they do not embrace the totality and dynamics of Being. Countless texts have argued the conceptual consistence and ontological soundness of the phenomenological method, including other chapters in this book.

However, it seems difficult to argue that certain specific phenomenological models or steps are "better" than others. A fundamental debate is to which extent eidetic and transcendental reduction are possible. Eidetic reduction is about "seeking for the essence of something," and transcendental reduction is about "finding the truth of something by keeping going with verification and universalisation until it fits" (Cooper 2017, p. 143). It is difficult to prove whether it is possible for clients, therapists, and researchers to discover true essences or know what fits best. This statement is not falsifiable. For example, can clients discover what is ultimately meaningful for them in life? Can clients ultimately know their best way of living? Or can we only pretend as if we know what matters? Questions like these seem to occupy many texts and conferences from phenomenological-existential therapists. In line with the later work of Heidegger, this debate could be explained as a topological debate that ignores the temporality of the phenomenological method. It has been argued, that a more pragmatic phenomenological approach could be used by focusing on the phenomenological process instead of on a fixed end result:

> the core phenomenological process is unpeeling our experiences like an onion or a mango. Of course, we cannot be totally certain that when we start unpeeling our experiences that we will arrive at a core like in a mango. That is, we cannot be sure that "authenticity" and "true self" exist, like Buddhists claim; possibly our self-experiences are nothing else than covers and there is no core, like an onion. Thus, the unpeeling process could lead to an 'essence' or 'reality', but it could also be the case that we continue unpeeling until nothing is left: we may not know what the end point will be. This philosophical question where our unpeeling will end is pragmatically irrelevant. As the unpeeling process itself has shown beneficial to individuals. Whatever the result of unpeeling is, clients seem to benefit from this unpeeling process [according to empirical research]: they experience their lives as more meaningful, experience a better quality-of-life, lower psychological stress and better physical well-being. (Vos 2018)

The phenomenological process in EPT often involves exploring the different ways in which clients relate to their world (van Deurzen 2010, 2012). In line with Heidegger and Binswanger, van Deurzen describes four different but interdependent dimensions of worldly being that clients can explore. These are the physical, social, personal, and spiritual dimensions. Similarly, the existential analyst Alfried Längle (2013), who bases much of his work on phenomenological approaches, speaks about the four fundamental motivations of existence, values, self, and meaning. These authors do not argue that these worlds exist as absolute separate entities, but that these are interlinked and that this is a non-essentialist categorization to facilitate exploration of our relationships to our surroundings. Thus they do not make any scientific claims about the absolute existence of these worlds or dimensions.

This categorization was confirmed by a systematic review of 109 studies in over 45,000 individuals worldwide who were asked to describe what they experience as meaningful, important, or valuable in life (Vos 2018). This empirical review showed that individuals find meaning in materialistic-hedonistic, self-oriented, social, higher, and existential-philosophical types of meanings. This parallels the four worlds of van Deurzen, although in this categorization higher and existential-philosophical meanings are separated. Meaning-centered therapists explicitly explore each of these groups of meanings with their clients, similar to van Deurzen who explores the different worlds. Research shows that therapies are significantly more effective when these explicitly address a broad range of different types of meanings (Vos 2018). Clients who focus more on social, higher, and existential-philosophical meanings experience a significant better well-being (Vos 2018), which confirms van Deurzen's hypothesis that spirituality is central to the development of individuals.

Spinelli (2006, 2015) seems critical about the idea that therapists should focus on explicitly exploring or developing the worldviews of clients – such as their views of the four worlds or different types of meanings. He aims to stay with the worlding process of clients, which is the process of immediate unrepeatable embodied flow of experiencing. Therapy aims to de-sediment fixed stances and re-own dissociated experiences, although this aim should not be enforced and clients may decide not to consider alternative ways of seeing themselves and their world. Thus, Spinelli suggests staying with the client's existence as it is currently being lived.

To some extent Spinelli's approach is similar to van Deurzen's, who hypothesizes that while clients explore each of these dimensions, they could discover tensions and paradoxes. Instead of finding a solution or running away from tensions, van Deurzen stimulates clients to stay with these tensions. Thus, van Deurzen stimulates clients to develop a dual attitude, in which they learn to live with different, apparently incommensurable, positions. Some empirical studies indicate that individuals experience a better well-being when they are able to tolerate tensions and ambiguities (Vos 2014; Vos et al. 2015a, 2015b). However in contrast with Spinelli, van Deurzen (2012) may also use a more directional approach by explicitly supporting clients in finding new paths. Research suggests that relatively structured and directional therapeutic approaches are – without necessarily being rigidly directive – more effective than therapies without any structure or direction (Cooper 2009; Craske, Maidenberg, and Bystritsky 1995).

To some extent, Spinelli does use a systematic approach as he has described how therapists could explore four inter-related realms of encounter. He explores relationships in the I-focused, you-focused, we-focused, and they-focused realms (Spinelli 2006). As will be shown below, the focus on social relationships and particularly the therapeutic relationship has been shown to improve the effectiveness of therapy. It may be argued though that his mere focus on social meanings is limited, as it leaves out other types of meanings that have shown beneficial for clients, and it has shown that combining different types of social higher and existential-philosophical meanings is important for well-being (Vos 2018).

In summary, many fundamental assumptions in phenomenology cannot be proven but conceptual research indicates its conceptual coherence and ontological foundations. There is little empirical evidence that identifies the most effective specific therapeutic steps, or describes the desirable end state of EPT. However, research indicates that clients benefit from a phenomenological process in the therapeutic encounter, and particularly from a systematic exploration of different parts of their experiences, albeit formulated in terms of worlds, meanings, or other terms.

Applied phenomenological research

Many phenomenological-existential therapists stand in line with the later work of Heidegger, such as Cohn, Spinelli, and van Deurzen. They aim to address the individual in the wider surroundings, by phenomenologically bracketing our assumptions and essences about the individual that could limit the clients. For many decades, this critical perspective seemed to imply a complete rejection of all empiricist research. EPT rejected precise definitions, operationalizations, categorizations, and measurement with standardized research instruments. Some therapists seemed to reject any academic research at all, as they argued that any research summarizing the practices and outcomes of EPT is incomplete and there will always be remaining questions and paradoxes. Additionally, they argued that any research process can be detrimental to clients, as standardization of procedures and effect measurement are likely to influence the therapeutic relationship, burden the client, and affect the extent to which the therapy is tailored to the unique skills and needs of the client (Vos 2014). Existential-phenomenological therapists seemed to justify and validate their therapeutic practices mainly on the basis of their theoretical training, personal and clinical experience, and, most of all, the unique relationship and therapeutic process with the client.

To overcome the reductionism in research, Giorgi (2009) developed a descriptive phenomenological method in the 1970s. Researchers are encouraged to bracket their assumptions by refraining from positing a static sense of objective reality for oneself and the research participants. This helps researchers describe the subjectively lived experiences of the clients without forcing the meaning of the descriptive units into pre-defined categories. This method includes both description and interpretation of the findings, where the researchers immerse themselves emphatically with the participants, in line with Husserl who wrote that "being given and being interpreted are descriptions of the same situation from two levels of discourse" (Mohanty 1985, p. 117). In the United Kingdom, Smith (2009) developed an applied phenomenological method that pays more attention to the hermeneutic circle, and how knowledge is constructed. This method takes explicitly into account how researchers construct their own interpretations of the participants' stories, while being critically aware of the influence of their own perspective on the research process and embedding this in the wider worlds. Several other phenomenologists have further developed phenomenological methods which can be used in research, such as Vos (2005) and van Deurzen and Iacovou (2013).

Over the years, hundreds of studies with usually relatively small samples have applied phenomenological methods. This has yielded a deeper understanding of the therapeutic relationships and processes, although given the nature of this research these findings are difficult to generalize. There are no known systematic reviews of phenomenological research. Most phenomenological studies have been conducted by students, and it seems doing applied phenomenological research can improve their phenomenological understanding of the clients, which can help the therapeutic relationships and processes.

However, applied phenomenological research does not always seem to overcome the criticisms of research, as researchers can use phenomenology while ignoring the topological and temporal surroundings of their research. That is, there is the danger that an applied phenomenological researcher quickly rejects all positivist methods, without critically describing their own methods and relating this to other research paradigms. They can use Interpretative Phenomenological Analyses as a simplistic step-by-step method, while lacking thorough bracketing of their own perspective and systematic reflexivity regarding the position of their research in the wider context of their physical, personal, social, and spiritual worlds. Consequently, their research only internally validates their own methods and findings, and creates their own solipsistic house of research and therapy. Therefore, it has been argued that conducting a mixed-methods study on the basis of a pluralistic epistemology may be more consistent with phenomenological philosophy, as researchers may need to cast light from many different angles to understand as many facets as possible from the multifaceted diamond that is EPT (Vos 2014).

Research on existential themes

Is EPT a bona fide therapy? To answer this question, it seems important to not only examine whether clients improve in therapy, but also whether the underlying existential-therapeutic model is valid and reliable. That is, it has been argued that "the difference between quack-therapies and evidence-based-therapies is not only that outcome-studies prove their effectiveness, but also that there is empirical evidence and conceptual coherence for the underlying clinical and aetiological models, and that the therapeutic mechanisms are logically built on these clinical-aetiological models" (Vos 2015, p. 2; Kazdin 2005, 2008). A clinical-etiological model summarizes and specifies key clinical concepts, classifications, and contexts of existential-therapists and answers the question "why does which individual in which context develop which psychological experience/problem which existential-therapy focuses at?" (e.g., Goossen, Goossen-Baremans, and Zel 2010). In a bona fide therapy, the therapeutic mechanisms follow logically from this clinical-etiological model (Vos 2015). For instance, a stereotypical cognitive-therapeutic model says that cognitive biases cause psychopathology, and to cure clients from pathology the therapists helps them to overcome these biases.

However, based on the before-described epistemological positions, EPT does not have one unified clinical-etiological model, and most existential therapists reject the idea of a universal etiology or clinical model. Despite a lack of consensus, some trends may be identified amongst existential therapists. The following fundamental clinical-etiological assumptions were most frequently reported during a discussion with a network of leading existential psychotherapists, primarily based in the United Kingdom, about their implicit understandings and definitions of existential therapy. These assumptions are further elaborated by thematic analyses of discussions amongst existential-therapists about the definition of ET, during and after the First World Conference for Existential Therapy hosted in London 2015. These assumptions as visualized, in Figure 37.1, are the author's reflection of these discussions, and have not been confirmed by the debaters; it is likely that differences exist between individual therapists and between clients. These steps should not be regarded as one-directional or separated from each other, but as an integrated holistic process. Each of the steps will be presented alongside supportive empirical evidence.

First, many existential-phenomenological therapists state that every individual is thrown into the world, which is defined in four parts: physical, social, psychological, and spiritual worlds (Binswanger 1963; Yalom 1980; van Deurzen-Smith 1984). The reality of being-there includes our human capacity for freedom and choice, and inevitably facing paradoxes, limitations, and challenges in life, such as being-mortal. As these assumptions are philosophical in nature they cannot be empirically verified (Lukas 1986/2014), although support comes from research on the five types of meaning (Vos 2018).

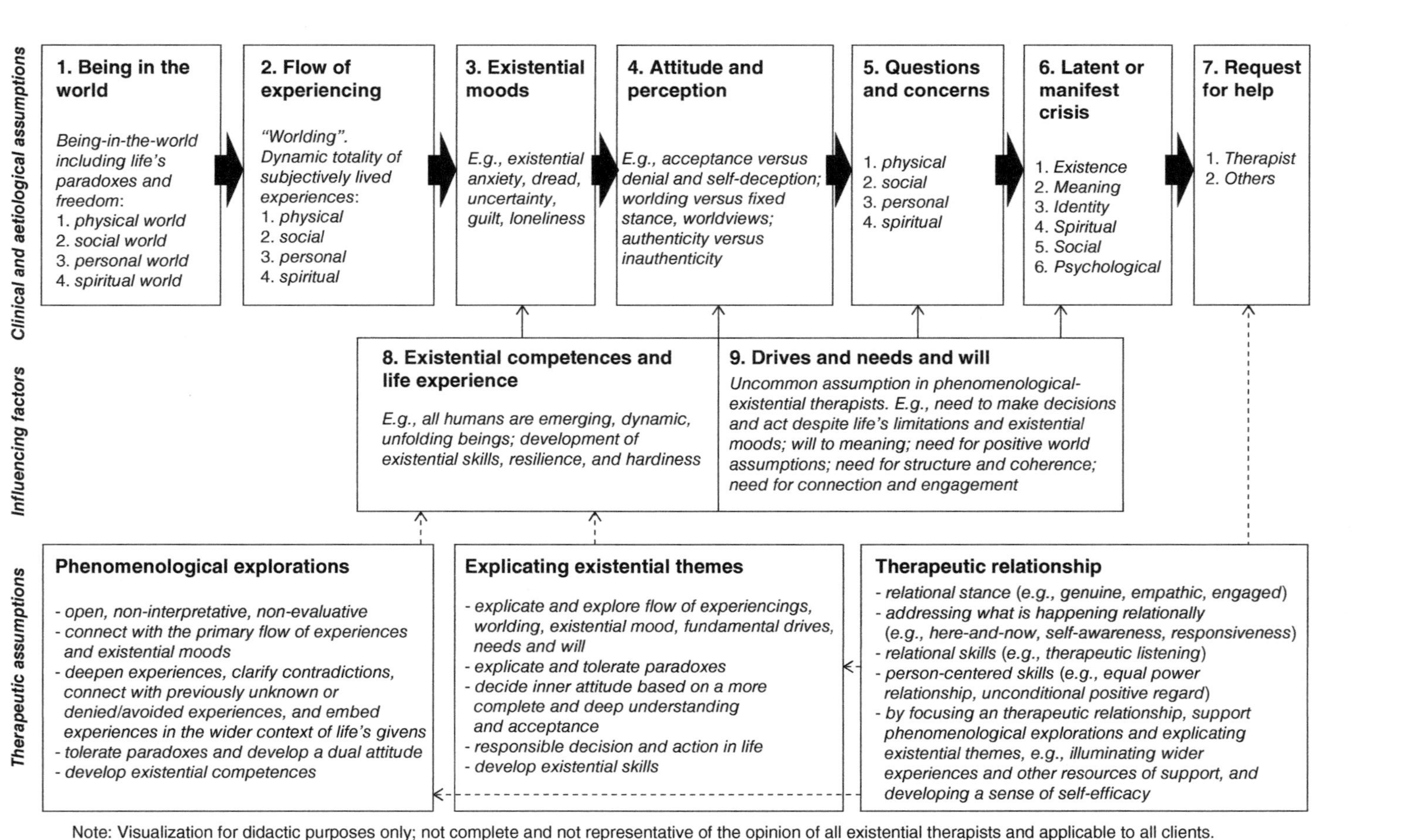

Figure 37.1 Visual overview of clinical, etiological, and therapeutic assumptions mentioned by phenomenological-existential therapists.

Second, individuals experience their *being-there* in their primary subjective phenomenological *flux of experiencing* their daily life world. For instance, an uncountable number of qualitative studies have described how individuals relate to their physical, social, personal, and spiritual worlds, and how they experience life's givens as important and relevant to themselves (e.g., Frankl 1998; Spinelli 2005; Yalom 1980). However, phenomenologists describe how individuals often cover these primary experiences by attaching meaning/interpretation (e.g., Spinelli 2005; Wrathall 2010), and they have therefore developed measures to describe this stream of consciousness and distinguish it from secondary interpretations (e.g., Smith et al. 2009). Additional neuropsychological research suggests that consciousness starts with a primary "feeling of what happens," even before it enters our awareness and we interpret this (Damasio 1999). Research suggests that when clients are supporting in deepening their experiencing and staying with their flow – such as focusing (Gendlin 1986) – they experience better general well-being (Hendricks 2002; Orlinsky, Ronnestad, and Willutzki 2004).

Third, the primary experience of being-there has often been described in terms of *existential moods*, such as death anxiety, existential guilt, dread, isolation, urgency, nausea, absurdity, and vacuum. Existential moods differ from emotions and psychopathology, as they do not have a specific object or meaning, but regard a primary unstructured experience of existence-as-such (Vos et al. 2015a). The existence, prevalence, and distinctive character of these moods have been confirmed in many questionnaire studies (e.g., Ryff 1989; Brandstätter et al. 2012; Van Bruggen et al. 2015; Steger 2012). Despite their shown validity and reliability many questionnaires seem of limited use for screening and outcome measurement in clinical settings due to the lack of norm groups and relevant cut-off scores. Moreover, the questionnaire-scores are difficult to interpret and may not reflect the primary experiences of the individuals, as the study participants may have secondarily interpreted the items, presented a social desirable self-image, and answered differently due to their existential defense mechanisms. Therefore, alternative methods such as implicit laboratory measures and narrative and psychodynamic association/projection tests have been suggested (Vos et al 2015a); for instance subliminal cognitive experiments have examined existential anxiety and rigid worldviews that can be provoked by reminders of our mortality (Greenberg, Koole, and Pyszczynski 2004).

Fourth, many existential-phenomenological therapists assume that individuals are free in every situation to modulate their *inner attitude* towards the situation. For instance, in response to boundary situations in life, we can choose to sink into despair and resignation, or distance ourselves from the situation by taking a leap of faith and transcending the situation in space and time, developing a larger, more authentic, and meaningful perspective on life (Jaspers 1925/2013; Frankl 1980). Although the freedom of will is an unverifiable given-of-life (Lukas 1986/2014, p. 16), many empirical studies have confirmed that individuals are flexible in the way they cope with experiences in life (e.g., Zeidner and Endler 1996). Being flexible in coping styles seems more important than using one particular strategy in dealing with adversity (Kashdan and Rottenberg 2010).

Other empirical studies show how this inner attitude may be reflected in someone's worldview: many individuals live their daily life on the basis of the assumption that "the world is benevolent, the world is meaningful, and the self is worthy," and they expect themselves and the world around them to "remain decent and meaningful under all circumstances" (Janoff-Bulman 1992; Brewin and Holmes 2003). However, these positive assumptions may collide with the reality of life's givens, for instance after a diagnosis of cancer (Park et al. 2008; Park, Chmielewski, and Blank 2010). An individual can determine his inner attitude: accept life's hard givens or continue positive illusions. Thus, individuals are assumed to be free to either authentically accept these existential moods and face these givens ("un-cover reality"), or to inauthentically deny or avoid these ("cover reality"). This is confirmed by many laboratory and field studies showing that many individuals respond with *existential defense mechanisms* such as denial, avoidance, and re-interpretations, in confrontation with the existential experiences such as one's mortality (e.g., Greenberg et al. 2004); however speaking in terms of defense mechanisms seem reductionist labels and existential-phenomenological therapists would not use this terminology, although they do describe self-deception and denial. Research seems to indicate the importance of having positive assumptions for well-being (Janoff-Bulman 1989, 1992), as well as the large negative personal and social consequences of rigid existential defenses (e.g., Pyszcyzynski and Solomon 2003). Thus, self-deception and denial may be beneficial in the short term and in the long term these are bad for psychological and existential well-being. In the long term it is more beneficial for our psychological and existential well-being to face the actual lack of control and predictability in life, and embrace anxiety and uncertainty.

Fifth, in many books and case studies, existential-phenomenological therapists report that clients ask for therapeutic support for many different reasons, for instance about their physical, personal, social, and spiritual ways of being-in-the-world. These *questions and concerns* are often assumed to be the result of their inner attitude and defense mechanisms towards their given life situation. Empirical studies confirm that many individuals report existential questions, particularly when they are confronted with life's givens, such as the majority of individuals ask existential questions after the diagnosis of a chronic or life-threatening disease, or during bereavement over a lost loved one (Park et al. 2010; Henoch and Danielson 2010; Maguire et al. 2014).

Sixth, having existential questions does not necessarily imply problems or psychopathology. Existential-phenomenological therapists avoid pathological labels and try to understand the concerns from the totality of the client's experiences and attitude. Some therapists are also modest about their own role: clients may not require therapy and other sources of support may suffice. However, unattended existential suffering could lead to strong depression, low quality-of-life (Park and Hwang 2012), demoralization, and suicidal ideation (Kissane, Clarke, and Street 2001). Existential therapists have traditionally described these as *crisis* situations. Although many authors do not define and operationalize this term, "crisis" has been used to describe latent or manifest concerns regarding meaning in life (what makes life worth to be lived?), spirituality/religion (where are we called to go in life?), identity (who am I?), existence (what does life demand from me?), psychology (how can I cope with my feelings and thoughts?), and relationships (how can I cope with others?) (Vos 2011).

Seventh, although little research has been conducted, it seems that having existential questions and being-in-crisis leads to individuals asking for professional therapeutic help (e.g., Henoch and Danielson 2010).

Eighth, EPT focuses on the uniqueness of individuals and assumes that all individuals differ from each other in their experiences and inner attitude, which can change over time. These differences may be due to having different *existential skills and life experiences*, as we are continuously emerging, dynamic, unfolding beings. In line with many psychological-developmental studies, some research confirms for instance that individuals can develop existential resilience and hardiness over the years (e.g., Maddi 2014), and that different individuals report different existential concerns in different life stages (Vos 2016b).

Ninth, a debate between existential-phenomenological therapists and other existential therapists is the question of the extent to which individuals experience existential drives, needs, or a will that gives them orientation and motivation in life. For example, meaning-centered therapists have argued that human beings function most effectively when they actualize their human potential and take responsibility for their choices, even in the context of life's limitations and existential moods. Research describes how individuals experience a subjective sense of purpose, values, understanding of self and world, self-worth, action-directed goals, and self-regulation (e.g., MacKenzie and Baumeister 2014 George and Park in Batthyany and Russo-Netzer 2014; Wong in Wong 2012). Hundreds of studies indicate that a large majority of the general population actively search for meaning or experience its presence, and that this presence is moderately or strongly correlated with higher quality-of-life, lower levels of psychological stress such as depression and anxiety, and better physical well-being (e.g., Steger 2012; Brandstätter et al. 2012; Roepke, Jayawickreme, and Riffle 2014; Ryff et al. 2006). Furthermore, meaning-based coping has been found to improve psychological adjustment to stressful life events, as concordant with widely accepted models in medical and health psychology such as the stress-coping model (Park et al. 2010; Vos 2016b). Other research describes how well-being is influenced by the need for certainty and positive world assumptions (Janoff-Bulman 1992).

In summary, many existential-phenomenological therapists mention these nine clinical-etiological assumptions, some of which are unverifiable due to their philosophical nature, but many core assumptions are supported by empirical research. For instance many clients report existential moods and existential concerns, especially in response to life situations when they are confronted with life's given limitations such as suffering, guilt, and death (cf. Lukas 2014). Individuals are able to decide their inner attitude by coping flexibly with the situation, and meaning-based coping seems to improve their well-being. However, better instruments need to be developed to measure existential moods, concerns, and crises, and to examine how these relate to psychopathology in the medical paradigm and with the client's request for help.

Research on therapeutic relationships and processes

Existential-phenomenological therapists often follow Buber's relational philosophy (1947/1966, 1958) which tells that "authentic personhood is found in the in-depth encounter between two human beings," and focus on "establishing an in-depth, authentic therapeutic relationship with clients; along with reflection on, and analysis of, the relational encounter" (Vos et al. 2015a, p. 54; e.g., Boss 1963; Mearns and Cooper 2005; Spinelli 1997). By focusing on the therapeutic relationship, the therapist supports the phenomenological explorations and explication of existential themes.

Correia et al. (2015) found four different types of relational practices amongst existential therapists: adopting a "relational stance" (e.g., being present, caring, authentic encounter), "addressing what is happening in the therapeutic relationship" (e.g., working here-and-now, being aware of one's reactions to the client, self-disclosure), "relational skills" (e.g., therapeutic listening), and "person-centered skills" (e.g., equal power relationship, unconditional positive regard). The beneficial effects of these relational aspects are strongly supported by a substantive body of literature, with the APA Task Force concluding that "the therapy relationship makes substantial and consistent contributions to psychotherapy outcomes independent of the specific type of treatment" (Norcross and Lambert 2011, p. 423). For example, several studies showed small to moderate positive effects for the therapeutic alliance (Hovarth et al. 2011), the therapist's positive regard (Farber and Doolin 2011), congruence and capacity to repair alliance-ruptures (Kolden et al. 2011), self-disclosure (Hill and Knox 2002), the clients' ratings of their therapist's presence (Geller 2013), genuine care (Bedi, Davis, and Williams 2005; Cooper 2008; Knox and Cooper 2010), and the depth of relating between therapist and client (Mearns and Cooper 2005, p. xii; Wiggins, Elliott, and Cooper 2012; Wiggins 2011). Evidence is inconclusive for the value of focusing on the here-and-now (Orlinsky, Grawe, and Parks 1994).

In summary, research indicates that clients benefit from a positive therapeutic relationship and from a focus on the therapeutic process.

Conclusions and future directions

In conclusion, relatively few studies have been conducted on EPT from a positivist perspective, which is understandable as EPT is based on fundamental criticism of positivist paradigms. However, for reasons of reflexivity and pragmatism, researchers have conducted several clinical studies. Preliminary findings from ongoing clinical trials and relatively similar therapeutic approaches are promising regarding overall effectiveness. Many assumptions in EPT are merely based on conceptual reasoning, but several aspects have been validated by qualitative and quantitative research. Most evidence supports a pragmatic phenomenological approach, which focuses on the therapeutic process of unpeeling the experiences of clients, without imposing specific aims or end states on the clients. There is some empirical evidence for the helpfulness of phenomenological therapeutic skills –particularly systematic phenomenological analyses such as van Deurzen's worlds, relational skills, and skills of explicating existential themes.

In line with Heidegger, it is recommended that research and therapeutic practices should not stay in their own "house" by critically and systematically examining the relationships with the wider surroundings. For example, the EPT field may benefit from more multidisciplinary research with a pluralistic perspective, and from clarification and validation of core assumptions in the therapeutic approach. This chapter was based on methodological pluralism (Cooper and McLeod 2011), although for pragmatic reasons most of the cited studies followed a positivist epistemology. Therefore, it is recommended more studies are conducted with other epistemological foundations. The combination of different research perspectives "may bring to light different facets of the diamond that the client's lived experience and the therapeutic relationship is; casting only one light may leave many other facets undiscovered" (Vos et al. 2015b, p. 49; Vos 2013). This review may be regarded as an example of how pluralistic methodologies may synergize to validate, justify, and improve clinical, etiological, and therapeutic foundations. Of course, the general "laws" that the dominantly positivist studies have revealed in this chapter need to be critically assessed and confirmed in therapeutic practices with real life clients: their real 'existence precedes the essence" identified in this chapter. This could for instance be achieved by developing "a culture of systematic feedback, from clinical practice to research and vice versa – for instance, via routine outcome monitoring" (Vos et al. 2015a, p. 53).

Despite these limitations, this research seems to indicate that, overall, EPT may be regarded as bona fide, although differences may exist between different therapists and different clients with different needs at different moments in time (Wampold 2001). The current research evidence suggests practitioners should focus on a positive therapeutic relationship, a pragmatic phenomenological approach, systematic analyses of different worlds/relationships to the surroundings, acceptance of the flow of experiencing and worlding, and fostering a dual attitude. These recommendations are founded in the belief that clinical practitioners and researchers with different epistemological, clinical, etiological, and therapeutic assumptions need each other: "to develop ourselves as a dynamic therapeutic community, and to enable us to offer our clients the most effective, validated type of care. Only in this way are we able to balance like a tightrope walker on the metaphorical Nietzschean rope that stretches from ignorance to development, and that prevents our community from falling into the abyss of internal disputes and external neglect by society and standard mental health care" (Vos et al. 2015b, p. 55.

References

Batthyany, A. and Russo-Netzer, P. (2014). *Meaning in Positive and Existential Psychology*. New York: Springer.

Bedi, R.P., Davis, M.D., and Williams, M. (2005). Critical incidents in the formation of the therapeutic alliance from the client's perspective. *Psychotherapy: Theory, Research, Practice, Training 42* (3): 311–323.

Binswanger, L. (1963). *Being-in-the-World: Selected Papers of Ludwig Binswanger*. New York: Basic Books.

Boss, M. (1963). *Psychoanalysis and Daseinsanalysis*. New York Basic Books.

Brandstätter, M., Baumann, U., Borasio, G.D. et al. (2012). Systematic review of meaning in life assessment instruments. *Psycho-Oncology 21* (10): 1034–1052.

Brewin, C.R. and Holmes, E.A. (2003). Psychological theories of posttraumatic stress disorder. *Clinical Psychology Review 23* (3): 339–376.

Buber, M. (1958). *I and Thou*, 2e (trans. R.G. Smith). Edinburgh: T & T Clark.

Buber, M. (1996). *I and Thou* (trans. W. Kaufmann). New York: Simon & Schuster. (Original work published 1947.)

Classen, C., Butler, L.D., Koopman, C. et al. (2001). Supportive-expressive group therapy and distress in patients with metastatic breast cancer: A randomized clinical intervention trial. *Archives of General Psychiatry 58* (5): 494–501.

Condrau, G. (1994). Phenomenological features of psychosomatic disorders. *International Forum of Psychoanalysis 3* (4): 235–238.

Cooper, M. (2008). *Essential Research Findings in Counselling and Psychotherapy: The Facts are Friendly*. London: Sage.

Cooper, M. (2009). Counselling in UK secondary schools: A comprehensive review of audit and evaluation data. *Counselling and Psychotherapy Research 9* (3): 137–150.

Cooper, M. (2017). *Existential Therapies*. London: Sage.

Cooper, M. and McLeod, J. (2011). Person-centered therapy: A pluralistic perspective. *Person-Centered & Experiential Psychotherapies 10* (3): 210–223.

Cooper, M., Wild, C., van Rijn, B. et al. (2015). Pluralistic therapy for depression: Acceptability, outcomes and helpful aspects in a multisite open-label trial. *Counselling Psychology Review 30* (1): 6–20.

Correia, E.A., Cooper, M., and Berdondini, L. (2015). Existential psychotherapy: An international survey of the key authors and texts influencing practice. In: *Clarifying and Furthering Existential Psychotherapy* (ed. S.E. Schulenberg), 5–17. Cham, Switzerland: Springer.

Craske, M.G., Maidenberg, E., and Bystritsky, A. (1995). Brief cognitive-behavioral versus nondirective therapy for panic disorder. *Journal of Behavior Therapy and Experimental Psychiatry 26* (2): 113–120.

Damasio, A. (1999). *The Feeling of What Happens – Body, Emotion and the Making of Consciousness*. New York: Vintage.

Dilthey, W. (1895). *Gesammelte Schriften* (Collected works). Gottingen: Vandenhoeck & Ruprecht.

Elliott, R. (2002). The effectiveness of humanistic therapies: A meta-analysis. In: *Humanistic Psychotherapies: Handbook of Research and Practice* (ed. D.J. Cain), 57–81. Washington, DC: American Psychological Association.

Farber, B.A. and Doolin, E.M. (2011). Positive regard. In: *Psychotherapy Relationships that Work: Therapist Contributions and Responsiveness to Patients*, 2e (ed. J.C. Norcross), 168–186. New York: Oxford University Press.

Feijoo, A.M.L.C. de. (2012). A clínica psicológica em uma inspiraçao fenomenológica hermenêutica. *Estudos e Pesquisas em Psicologia 12* (3): 973–986.

Frankl, V. (1980). *Man's Search for Ultimate Meaning*. London: Hachette.

Frankl, V. (1998). *Man's Search for Meaning: An Introduction to Logotherapy*. London: Random House. (Original work published 1946.)

Geller, S.M. (2013). Therapeutic presence. In: *The Handbook of Person-Centred Psychotherapy and Counselling*, 2e (ed. M. Cooper, P.F. Schmid, M. O'Hara et al.), 209–236). Basingstoke: Palgrave.

Gendlin, E.T. (1986). *Focusing*. London: Bantam.

Giorgi, A. (2009). *The Descriptive Phenomenological Method in Psychology: A Modified Husserlian Approach*. Pittsburgh, PA: Duquesne University Press.

Goossen, W., Goossen-Baremans, A., and Zel, M. van der (2010). Detailed clinical models: A review. *Health Information Research 16* (4): 201–214.

Goss, S. and Mearns, D. (1997). A call for a pluralist epistemological understanding in the assessment and evaluation of counselling. *British Journal of Guidance and Counselling 25* (2): 189–198.

Greenberg, J., Koole, S.L., and Pyszczynski, T.A. (eds.) (2004). *Handbook of Experimental Existential Psychology*. New York, London: Guilford Press.

Heidegger, M. (1987). *Zollikon Seminars – Protocols – Seminars – Letters* (ed. M. Boss). Evanston, IL: Northwestern University Press.

Heidegger, M. (2001). *Sein und Zeit*. Tubingen: Max Niemeyer Verlag. (Original work published 1927.)

Hendricks, M.N. (2002). What difference does philosophy make? Crossing Gendlin and Rogers. In: *Client-Centered and Experiential Psychotherapy in the Twenty-first Century* (ed. J. Watson, R. Goldman, and M. Warner), 52–63. Ross on Wye, UK: PCCS Books.

Henoch, I. and Danielson, E. (2010). Existential concerns among patients with cancer and interventions to meet them: An integrative literature review. *Psycho-Oncology: Journal of the Psychological, Social and Behavioral Dimensions of Cancer 18* (3): 225–236.

Hill, C.E. and Knox, S. (2002). Self-disclosure. In: *Psychotherapy Relationships that Work: Therapist Contributions and Responsiveness to Patients* (ed. J.C. Norcross), 255–265. New York: Oxford University Press.

Hovarth, A.O., Del Re, A.C., Fluckinger, C. et al. (2011). Alliance in individual psychotherapy. In: *Psychotherapy Relationships that Work: Evidence-Based Responsiveness*, 2e (ed. J.C. Norcross), 25–69. New York: Oxford University Press.

Husserl, E. (1975). *Logische Untersuchungen*. Tubingen: Holenstein. (Original work published 1901.)

Janoff-Bulman, R. (1989). Assumptive worlds and the stress of traumatic events: Applications of the schema construct. *Social Cognition 7* (2): 113–136.

Janoff-Bulman, R. (1992). *Shattered Assumptions: Towards a New Psychology of Trauma*. New York: The Free Press.

Jaspers, K. (2013). *Psychologie der Weltanschauungen*. Berlin: Springer-Verlag. (Original work published 1925.)

Kashdan, T.B. and Rottenberg, J. (2010). Psychological flexibility as a fundamental aspect of health. *Clinical Psychology Review 30* (13): 865–878.

Kazdin, A.E. (2005). Treatment outcomes, common factors, and continued neglect of mechanisms of change. *Clinical Psychology: Science and Practice 12* (2): 184–188.

Kazdin, A.E. (2008). Evidence-based treatment and practice: New opportunities to bridge clinical research and practice, enhance the knowledge base, and improve patient care. *American Psychologist 63* (3): 146–159.

Kissane, D.W., Bloch, S., Smith, G.C. et al. (2003). Cognitive-existential group psychotherapy for women with primary breast cancer: A randomised controlled trial. *Psycho-Oncology 12* (6): 532–546.

Kissane, D.W., Clarke, D.M., and Street, A.F. (2001). Demoralization syndrome – a relevant psychiatric diagnosis for palliative care. *Journal of Palliative Care 17* (1), 12–21.

Knox, R. and Cooper, M. (2010). Relationship qualities that are associated with moments of relational depth: The client's perspective. *Person-Centered & Experiential Psychotherapies 9* (3): 236–256.

Kolden, G.G., Klein, M.H., Wang, C.C. et al. (2011). Congruence/genuineness. *Psychotherapy 48* (1): 65–71.

Längle, A. (2013). *Viktor Frankl: Eine Begegnung*. Vienna: Facultas Verlags and Buchhandels AG.

Loewenthal, D. (2003). *Post-Modernism for Psychotherapists: A Critical Reader*. Hove: Brunner-Routledge.

Lukas, E. (2014). *Meaning in Suffering*. Berkeley: Institute of Logotherapy Press. (Original work published 1986.)

MacKenzie, M.J. and Baumeister, R.F. (2014). Meaning in life: Nature, needs, and myths. In: *Meaning in Positive and Existential Psychology* (ed. A. Batthyany and P. Russo-Netzer), 25–37. New York: Springer.

Maddi, S.R. (2014). Hardiness leads to meaningful growth through what is learned when resolving stressful circumstances. In: *Meaning in Positive and Existential Psychology* (ed. A. Batthyany and P. Russo-Netzer), 291–302. New York: Springer.

Maguire, A., McCann, M., Moritarty, J. et al. (2014). The Grief Study: Using administrative data to understand the mental health impact of bereavement. *European Journal of Public Health 24* (suppl. 2): 266–267.

Mearns, D. and Cooper, M. (2005). *Working at Relational Depth in Counselling and Psychotherapy.* London: Sage.

Mohanty, J.N. (1985). Transcendental philosophy and the hermeneutic critique of consciousness. In: *The Possibility of Transcendental Philosophy* (J.N. Mohanty), 223–246. Springer, Dordrecht.

Neimeyer, R.A. and Raskin, J.D. (2000). *Constructions of Disorder: Meaning-Making Frameworks for Psychotherapy.* Washington, DC: American Psychological Association.

Norcross, J.C. and Lambert, M.J. (2011). Evidence-based therapy relationshps. In: *Psychotherapy Relationships that Work: Evidence-Based Responsiveness*, 2e (ed. J.C. Norcross), 3–21. New York: Oxford University Press.

Orlinsky, D.E., Grawe, K., and Parks, B.K. (1994). *Process and Outcome in Psychotherapy: Noch Einmal.* Oxford: John Wiley.

Orlinsky, D.E., Ronnestad, M.H., and Willutzki, U. (2004). Fifty years of psychotherapy process-outcome research: Continuity and change. In: *Bergin and Garfield's Handbook of Psychotherapy and Behavior Change*, 5e (ed. M.J. lambert), 307–389. New York: John Wiley & Sons.

Park, B.W. and Hwang, S.Y. (2012). Unmet needs of breast cancer patients relative to survival duration. *Yonsei Medical Journal 53* (1): 118–125.

Park, C.L., Chmielewski, J., and Blank, T.O. (2010). Post-traumatic growth: Finding positive meaning in cancer survivorship moderates the impact of intrusive thoughts on adjustment in younger adults. *Psycho-oncology 19* (11): 1139–1147.

Park, C.L., Edmondson, D., Fenster, J.R. et al. (2008). Meaning making and psychological adjustment following cancer: The mediating roles of growth, life meaning, and restored just-world beliefs. *Journal of Consulting and Clinical Psychology 76* (5): 863–875.

Popper, K.R. (1956). Three views concerning human knowledge. *Contemporary British Philosophy 387*: 357–388.

Pyszcyzynski, T. and Solomon, S. (2003). *In the Wake of 9-11: The Psychology of Terror.* New York: American Psychological Association.

Rayner, M. and Vitali, D. (2016). Short-term existential psychotherapy in primary care: A quantitative report. *Journal of Humanistic Psychology 56* (4): 357–372.

Rayner, M. and Vitali, D. (2018). Existential experimentation: Structure and principles for a short-term psychological therapy. *Journal of Humanistic Psychology 58* (2): 194–213.

Roepke, A.M., Jayawickreme, E., and Riffle, O.M. (2014). Meaning and health: A systematic review. *Applied Research in Quality of Life 9* (4): 1055–1079.

Ryff, C.D. (1989). Happiness is everything, or is it: Explorations on the meaning of psychological well-being. *Journal of Personality and Social Psychology 57* (6): 1069–1081.

Ryff, C.D., Love, G.D., Urry, H.L. et al. (2006). Psychological well-being and ill-being: Do they have distinct or mirrored biological correlates? *Psychotherapy and Psychosomatics 75* (2): 85–95.

Sartre, J.P. (1967). *L'être et le néant. Essai d'ontologie phénoménologique.* Paris: Gallimard.

Smith, J. (2009). *Interpretative Phenomenological Analysis.* London: Sage.

Smith, J., Flowers, P., and Larkin, M. (2009). *Interpretative Phenomenological Analysis: Theory, Method and Research.* London: Routledge.

Spiegel, D., Kraemer, H., Bloom, J. et al. (1989). Effect of psychosocial treatment on survival of patients with metastatic breast cancer. *The Lancet 334* (8668): 888–891.

Spinelli, E. (1997). *Tales of Un-Knowing: Therapeutic Encounters from an Existential Perspective.* London: Duckworth.

Spinelli, E. (2005). *The Interpreted World. An Introduction to Phenomenological Psychology.* London: Sage.

Spinelli, E. (2006). The value of relatedness in existential psychotherapy and phenomenological enquiry. *Indo-Pacific Journal of Phenomenology 6* (sup1): 1–8.

Spinelli, E. (2015). Experiencing change: A phenomenological exploration. *Existential Analysis: Journal of the Society for Existential Analysis 26* (1): 4–20.

Steger, M.F. (2012). Experiencing meaning in life. In: *The Human Quest for Meaning: Theories, Research, and Applications* (ed. P. Wong), 165–184. New York: Routledge.

Van Bruggen, V., Vos, J., Westerhof, G. et al. (2015). Systematic review of existential anxiety assessment instruments. *Journal of Humanistic Psychology 55* (2): 173–201.

Van Der Pompe, G., Duivenvoorden, H.J., Antoni, M.H. et al. (1997). Effectiveness of a short-term group psychotherapy program on endocrine and immune function in breast cancer patients: An exploratory study. *Journal of Psychosomatic Research 42* (5): 453–466.

Van Deurzen, E. (2010). *Everyday Mysteries: A Handbook of Existential Psychotherapy.* London: Routledge.

Van Deurzen, E. (2012). *Existential Counselling and Psychotherapy in Practice.* London: Sage.

Van Deurzen, E. and Adams, M. (2011). *Skills in Existential Counselling and Psychotherapy.* London: Sage.

Van Deurzen, E. and Iacovou, S. (eds.) (2013). *Existential Perspectives on Relationship Therapy.* London: Macmillan International Higher Education.

Van Deurzen-Smith, E. (1984). Existential therapy. In: *Individual Therapy in Britain* (ed. W. Dryden), 152–179. Harper & Row: London.

Visser, A., Garssen, B., and Vingerhoets, A. (2010). Spirituality and well-being in cancer patients: A review. *Psycho-Oncology 19* (6): 565–572.

Vos, J. (2005). Migratie als grenssituatie: "niet-meer en nog-niet." Wijsgerig-fenomenologisch onderzoek naar het migrant-zijn, in het voetspoor van Martin Heidegger, Wilhelm Dilthey en Karl Jaspers. PhD thesis. Leiden University.

Vos, J. (2011). *Crises in life: A systematic literature review.* Unpublished report, Vrije Universiteit Amsterdam.

Vos, J. (2013). Quantitative research and existential therapies: Hard science versus hard words? *Hermeneutic Circular 2*: 10–11.

Vos, J. (2014). How to develop and validate conceptual models in psychotherapy research. Paper presented at the Twentieth Annual British Association for Counselling and Psychotherapy (BACP) Research Conference, London.

Vos, J. (2015). The conceptual components model: How to build the conceptual model of your research or thesis. Paper presented at the British Psychology Society, Research Conference, May, London.

Vos, J. (2016a). Working with meaning in life in mental health care: A systematic literature review and meta-analyses of practices and effectiveness. In: *Clinical Perspectives on Meaning* (ed. P. Russo-Netzer, S.E. Schulenberg, and A. Batthyany), 59–88. New York: Springer.

Vos, J. (2016b). Working with meaning in life in chronic or life-threatening disease: A review of its relevance and the effectiveness of meaning-centred therapies. In: *Clinical Perspectives on Meaning* (ed. P. Russo-Netzer, S.E. Schulenberg, and A. Batthyany), 171–200. New York: Springer.

Vos, J. (2018). *Meaning in Life: An Evidence-Based Handbook for Practitioners.* London: Palgrave Macmillan.

Vos, J. (accepted for publication). Developing a world-wide typology of meaning in life and evaluating its effectiveness in psychotherapies: a systematic literature review and meta-analyses.

Vos, J., Cooper, M., Correia, E. et al. (2015a). Existential therapies: A review of their scientific foundations and efficacy. *Existential Analysis: Journal of the Society for Existential Analysis 26* (1): 49–69.

Vos, J., Cooper, M., Correia, E. et al. (2015b). Existential therapies: A review of scientific studies and their underlying philosophies. *International Journal of Psychotherapy 19* (1): 47–57.

Vos, J., Craig, M., and Cooper, M. (2015). Existential therapies: A meta-analysis of their effects on psychological outcomes. *Journal of Consulting and Clinical Psychology 83* (1): 115–128.

Wampold, B.E. (2001). *The Great Psychotherapy Debate: Models, Methods, and Findings.* Mahwah, NJ: Erlbaum.

Wong, P.T. (2012). From logotherapy to meaning-centered counseling and therapy. In: *The Human Quest for Meaning: Theories, Research, and Applications*, 2e (ed. P.T. Wong), 619–647. Abingdon, UK: Routledge.

Wiggins, S. (2011). Relational depth and therapeutic outcome. Paper presented at the Seventeenth Annual British Association for Counselling and Psychotherapy (BACP) Research Conference, Portsmouth.

Wiggins, S., Elliott, R., and Cooper, M. (2012). The prevalence and characteristics of relational depth events in psychotherapy. *Psychotherapy Research 22* (2): 139–158.

Wrathall, M.A. (2010). *Heidegger and Unconcealment: Truth, Language, and History.* Cambridge: Cambridge University Press.

Yalom, I.D. (1980). *Existential Psychotherapy*, New York: Basic Books.

Zeidner, M. and Endler, N.S. (eds.) (1996). *Handbook of Coping: Theory, Research, Applications.* New York: John Wiley & Sons.

38

Conclusions by the Editors

In the previous pages you have been able to see a wide vista of existential perspectives and ways of working, currently spread around the globe. These are supported by a diversity of training schools and established therapy organizations.[1] We hope you have enjoyed reading about the many aspects of existential therapy as much as we enjoyed writing about them.

As you have seen we have carefully interwoven these various modalities and methods of existential therapy to create a colorful tapestry of therapeutic possibilities. You will have noted the contrasting designs and patterns that have gone into this patchwork quilt and hopefully you will have savored and appreciated the matching shades and shapes that we all share. We are fully aware that other authors might have created an entirely different sampler of existential work.

We never thought of this text as exhaustive, complete, or final, and we are very happy to acknowledge that this volume, as with all books and all art, is a mere beginning, an opening statement, an initial sketch of what we hope will become a continuing process of development and collaboration. We took our first step towards the creation of a worldwide, recognized, and growing profession of existential therapy at our first World Congress of Existential Therapy in London and this is our second step, soon to be followed by the second World Congress in Buenos Aires.

Let us never forget that this profession will have to stay true to its nature: which is that of existential freedom. This means that none of us should feel obliged to obey the rules we have formulated. Nobody needs to give in to a particular demand on technical prowess. We do not wish to put any practitioner into an existential straitjacket of measurement and normalization. This is what matters more than anything at the end of our journey through existential therapy: to remember that these are just ideas and personal ways of working. Our words are not meant to stop you. They are meant to

[1] A full list can be found on www.existentialpsychotherapy.net

The Wiley World Handbook of Existential Therapy, First Edition. Edited by Emmy van Deurzen, Erik Craig, Alfried Längle, Kirk J. Schneider, Digby Tantam, and Simon du Plock.

encourage and tempt you. We do not want you to imitate us, but to initiate, explore, and create new ways of working. We hope to have inspired you with a desire to experiment; to listen and reflect with ever greater care and bring out the best of your abilities in making sense of human existence. Our mission was to equip you with some of the knowledge and tools you might use to practice existential therapy and to show you our different ways of working, but not to prescribe what you should do with them.

Having drawn to your attention some of the tensions and challenges, paradoxes and contradictions, possibilities and transformative experiences that human life holds, we hope you feel emboldened to trace some of your own as you watch them unfold.

What we have placed in your hands is a catalogue of what is currently available. This has allowed you to sample various flavors of existential work and hopefully get a taste for it. We are delighted to invite you to create your own new combinations of fragrances, aromas, and savors. We expect that there will be an abundance of new ideas, new practices, and new authors of existential therapy in the years to come, as existential therapy finally comes into its own. (Emmy van Deurzen)

This book has aimed to fulfil the original mandate of existential psychotherapeutic practice – namely, to address human existence squarely. What we work with are people's lives – the suffering in those lives, the demands of those lives, and the depth and poignancy of those lives, no matter where those lives arose or will end. To the extent that this book accomplishes this task, it advances beyond the cultural silos that have thus far characterized the field and hopefully turns them into interconnecting hubs. Hence we now have the hubs of Existential-Analysis, Daseinsanalysis, Existential-Phenomenological therapy, Existential-Humanistic therapy, Existential-Integrative therapy, Zhi-Mian therapy, Logotherapy, and diverse variations beyond. I am deeply appreciative to be a part of these interconnecting networks, this "tapestry," as Emmy van Deurzen eloquently put it, and which decidedly echo the spirit of our World Congresses of Existential Therapy. My hope is that the field of psychotherapy as a whole will follow our lead – that it too will aspire to a comprehensive picture of lives; not only in relation to physiology, family, or even culture, but also in relation to existence itself, and to the breathtaking ranges it unveils. (Kirk J. Schneider)

Although small in size compared with the big clusters of behavioral therapy, depth psychology, systemic therapy, and the other humanistic psychotherapies, we see the existential movement in psychotherapy and counselling not as a mere adjunct but as a pivot in the field. The existential axis focusses the human being not only in the psychic or somatic dimension but comes closer to them by meeting their "spiritual dimension" (Frankl). It does so by making use of the freedom of choice and the possibility to choose oneself (authenticity) and thus living essentially, by focusing on the free responsibility and the inherent search for meaning, this space for free investment and development (especially when it is lost). So, the existential approach to psychotherapy and to the human being is a necessary element in the field of psychotherapy, a guardian for the wholeness of existence and depth of personal being. It represents somehow the roof in psychotherapy, the total view on the human being independently of how they have been treated: by depth psychology, or by modifying their behavior or systems. The existential axis always puts into the center of its work the human capacity and necessity to decide, that is, that which makes us free, what inevitably draws us to select an action, to identify with it or not, to becoming more oneself or foreign to oneself. (Alfried Längle)

Too many psychotherapy originators at the start of this profession relied on intuition and clinical anecdote to inform their approaches. Even so, many of these early forms of therapy took deep root and some are now unassailable because they have become surrounded by enthusiastic disciples. More recently developed approaches to psychotherapy have started from psychology, and sometimes more recently from neuroscience. This has created a huge gap between what scientific studies show in one laboratory and the interpretation of these studies in the complex human enterprise of psychotherapy. Existential psychotherapy, particularly the existential-phenomenological therapy of van Deurzen, has taken philosophy as its starting point to bridge that gap between our human experience and the careful observation of scientific exploration. Philosophy is its own form of research that does not very often make assertions but provides a constant drizzle of often acidic comments to slowly wear away what we think we know, exposing the beliefs and values that we cannot live without. This is exactly the right approach for psychotherapy and counselling, as we are in the business of encouraging self-reflection in our clients – and in ourselves too. We aim to replace the habit of thinking what we think we should think, or choosing what others choose, or doing what we have always done with the thoughts, choices, and actions that make us who each of us is and can become. One of the added benefits of starting with philosophy as our base is that it is a near inexhaustible resource. Not only are there neglected philosophers in our field of existential and phenomenological enquiry (such as Stein, Scheler, de Beauvoir, and Schutz among others) but there is the added exhilarating fact that the re-reading of even familiar philosophers often yields new insights, much like listening to a late Beethoven string quartet provides us with a new and different movement of the spirit even if we have heard it many times previously.

This rich and varied book will hopefully inspire the reader not only to follow the new shoots of innovation in the expanding field of existential therapy but to follow its roots as they tunnel ever deeper and more widely into existential philosophy. (Digby Tantam)

It has been a privilege to play a part in bringing this ambitious project to fruition. Building on the stimulating exchange of knowledge afforded by the first World Congress has provided me, personally, with a wonderful opportunity to connect more deeply over the past three years with colleagues internationally in ways that have already enriched my thinking and practice. It has been interesting to note how much we hold in common. It has also been fascinating to see where we diverge. As is the case in therapeutic practice and in life more generally, it is often the differences of perspective – the respectful challenge of the other – that encourages us to reconsider and perhaps revise our own stance. I feel sure that this experience is one that will be shared by all those who read this book.

In providing the first really comprehensive overview of the varied traditions which, together, comprise existential theory and practice, the World Handbook gives us all an invaluable insight into the past development of our therapeutic orientation. It also offers us a snapshot of contemporary existential theory and practice. Who can say what directions existential therapy will pursue in the future? Human existence is by its nature inevitably changing and precarious, and doubtless our profession, engaging as it does with the fundamental nature of what it means to be human, will be challenged to find ways to assist humanity to live as fully and authentically as possible in response to whatever life brings. My hope for this book is that it will help us to appreciate our existential heritage, and in the process inspire us to continue our existential journey. (Simon du Plock)

One of the great responsibilities and choices in our entire human existence concerns what we want to do with our one and only life. How do we want to spend our time, that most precious of resources? And for what? We "grey haired" ones, here known as editors, made this choice many decades ago and remain here as existential therapists because we found attending to the lives and sufferings of others in such gentle and respectful ways to be the most meaningful and fulfilling way to spend our own time, to *be*, on this good earth. Furthermore, although from different origins and paths, we have wound our way not only toward *doing* psychotherapy but *being* existential psychotherapists who are inexplicably moved by the question, "What does it mean to be a human being?" "What does it mean to be myself?" "What do I want my life to be about or, better, *for*?" Such a privilege this, to spend one's days with other human beings wondering the same things. Such a privilege to wonder like this without ever knowing what will come back to us in reply. This is the life of the existential therapist and, if this volume helps anyone on their way to answering or not answering such ultimate questions it has been worth the many, many hours of solitary and collective effort on our part. For it is the path of the stubborn inquirer that matters, not its destination. Privilege, too, it is to join these particular editors, authors, and, now readers on such a path. That there is variety and vigorous disagreement on so many common concerns is not only stimulating but also our proof and protection against existential dogma. That we hold so dear what we most deeply share in common allows such differences to survive, indeed thrive, compelling a sharpening of thought and clarity of feeling.

So welcome, dear reader, to this remarkable world of existential therapy. And please never forget Nietzsche's wise remark that, "One repays a teacher badly if one always remains a pupil." (Erik Craig)
The Editors

Index

Page numbers in *italics* refer to Figures

The Wiley World Handbook of Existential Therapy, First Edition. Edited by Emmy van Deurzen, Erik Craig, Alfried Längle, Kirk J. Schneider, Digby Tantam, and Simon du Plock.